Lecture Notes in Computer Science

Commenced Publication in 1973
Founding and Former Series Editors:
Gerhard Goos, Juris Hartmanis, and Jan van Leeuwen

Tatyana Yakhno   Erich J. Neuhold (Eds.)

Advances in Information Systems

4th International Conference, ADVIS 2006
Izmir, Turkey, October 18-20, 2006
Proceedings

 Springer

Volume Editors

Tatyana Yakhno
Dokuz Eylul University
Computer Engineering Department
Kaynaklar Campus, Buca
Izmir, Turkey
E-mail: yakhno@cs.deu.edu.tr

Erich J. Neuhold
Darmstadt University of Technology
Fraunhofer IPSI
Dolivostr. 15
64293 Darmstadt, Germany
E-mail: neuhold@ipsi.fhg.de

Library of Congress Control Number: 2006933392

CR Subject Classification (1998): H.2, H.3, H.4, I.2, C.2, H.5

LNCS Sublibrary: SL 3 – Information Systems and Application, incl. Internet/Web and HCI

ISSN   0302-9743
ISBN-10   3-540-46291-0 Springer Berlin Heidelberg New York
ISBN-13   978-3-540-46291-0 Springer Berlin Heidelberg New York

Springer is a part of Springer Science+Business Media

springer.com

© Springer-Verlag Berlin Heidelberg 2006

Typesetting: Camera-ready by author, data conversion by Scientific Publishing Services, Chennai, India
Printed on acid-free paper   SPIN: 11890393   06/3142   5 4 3 2 1 0

Preface

This volume contains the proceedings of the Fourth International Conference on Advances in Information Systems (ADVIS) held in Izmir, Turkey, October, 18-20, 2006. This is the fourth conference dedicated to the memory of Professor Esen Ozkarahan, who was one of the pioneers of database machine research and a founder of database systems in Turkey.

The main goal of the conference is to bring together researchers from all around the world working in different areas of information systems to share new ideas and represent their latest results. This time we received 120 submissions from 27 countries.The Program Committee selected 38 papers for presentation at the conference.

The invited and accepted contributions covered the main research topics related to information systems such as information representation and exchange, databases and datawarehouses, Semantic Web and ontologies, data mining and knowledge discovery, information retrieval and knowledge engineering, architecture of information systems, and distributed and wireless information systems. All these topics were discussed in detail during the conference.

The success of the conference was dependent on the hard work of a large number of people. We gratefully acknowledge the members of the Program Committee, who helped to coordinate the process of refereeing all submitted papers. We also thank all the other specialists and our additional referees, who reviewed the papers.

August 2006

Tatyana Yakhno
Erich Neuhold

Organization

Honorary Chair

Irem Ozkarahan, Dokuz Eylul University, Turkey

Program Committee Chairs

Tatyana Yakhno, Dokuz Eylul University, Turkey
Erich Neuhold, Darmstadt University, Germany

Program Committee

Sibel Adali, USA
Adil Alpkocak, Turkey
Farhad Arbab, Netherlands
Frederic Benhamou, France
Fazli Can, Turkey
Yalcin Cebi, Turkey
Paolo Ciaccia, Italy
Mehmet E. Dalkilic, Turkey
Dursun Delen, USA
Oguz Dikenelli, Turkey
Nadia Erdogan, Turkey
Maria Ganzha, Poland
Fabio Grandi, Italy
Ugur Gudukbay, Turkey
Cuneyt Guzelis, Turkey
Malcolm Heywood, Canada
Alp Kut, Turkey
Brian Mayoh, Denmark
Eric Monfroy, France

Erich Neuhold, Germany
Selmin Nurcan, France
Irem Ozkarahan, Turkey
Gultekin Ozsoyoglu, USA
Marcin Paprzycki, Poland
Dana Petcu, Romania
Ilias Petronias, UK
Malcolm Rigg, UK
Albrecht Schmidt, Denmark
Mike Shepherd, Canada
Ahmad T.Al-Taani, Jordan
Ozgur Ulusoy, Turkey
Olegas Vasilecas, Lithuania
Irina Virbitskaite, Russia
Carolyn Watters, Canada
Adnan Yazici, Turkey
Nur Zincir-Heywood, Canada

Additional Referees

Ismail Sengor Altingovde
Sulieman Bani-Ahmad
Bilge Bilgen
Xavier Bonnaire
Lucas Bordeaux
Pascal Bouvry
Alexander Bystrov

Jean Bzivin
Ozgu Can
Ali Cakmak
Ben Carterette
Carlos Castro
Sylvie Cazalens
Broderick Crawford

Valerie Cross
Halil Ibrahim Cuce
Gokhan Dalkilic
Yigithan Dedeoglu
Engin Demir
Guillaume Fertin
Marc Gelgon
Lidija Gorodnjaja
Ozgur Gumus
Didier Hoareau
Serdar Korukoglu
Geylani Kardes
Mustafa Kirac
Burcin Bostan Korpeoglu
Serge P. Kovalyov
Ibrahim Korpeoglu
Remi Lehn
Malik Magdon-Ismail
Rob van der Mei
Hongyu Liu
Evangelos Milios
Gabriele Monti
Fedor Murzin
Niels Nes
Jacco van Ossenbruggen
Tugba Ozacar

Pinar Mizrak Ozfirat
Ovunc Ozturk
Esther Pacitti
Brice Pajot
Algirdas Pakstas
George A. Papadopoulos
Olivier Perrin
Evgenij Petrov
Gerard Ramstein
Guillaume Raschia
Nattakarn Ratprasartporn
Stefano Rizzi
Uwe Roth
Simonas Saltenis
Latif Salum
Claudio Sartori
Maria Rita Scalas
Hans Schumacher
Aidas Smaizys
Dilek Tapucu
Murat Osman Unalir
Fons J. Verbeek
Chrtien Verhoef
Yakup Yildirim
Yury Zagorulko

Conference Secretary

Emine Ekin

Local Organizing Committee

Ozlem Aktas
Hulusi Baysal
Tolga Berber
Derya Birant
Gokhan Dalkilic

Taner Danisman
Ufuk Demir
Kali Gurkahraman
Giyasettin Ozcan
Serife Sungun

Semih Utku
Zeki Yetgin
Meltem Yildirim

Sponsors

Support from the following institutions is gratefully acknowledged:

- Dokuz Eylul University President's Office, Izmir, Turkey
- The Scientific and Technical Research Council of Turkey (TUBITAK)
- Gonen Bilgi Teknolojileri Danismanlik Ltd., Izmir, Turkey

Table of Contents

Invited Talks

Information Representation and Exchange

Databases and Datawarehouses

Semantic Web and Ontologies

Data Mining and Knowledge Discovery

Information Retrieval and Knowledge Representation

Architecture of Information Systems

Distributed and Wireless Information Systems

Processing Preference Queries
in Standard Database Systems*

Paolo Ciaccia

DEIS, University of Bologna, Italy
pciaccia@deis.unibo.it

Abstract. Locating the "right" piece of information among a wide range of available alternatives is not an easy task, as everyone has experienced at least once during his/her lifetime. In this paper we look at some recent issues arising when a database query is extended so as to include *user preferences*, which ultimately determine whether one alternative is reputed by the user better than another one. In particular, we focus on the case of *qualitative preference* queries, that strictly include well-known skyline queries, and describe how one can take advantage of the sorting machinery of standard database engines to speed-up evaluation both in centralized and distributed scenarios.

1 Introduction

> *But society has now fairly got the better of individuality;*
> *and the danger which threatens human nature is not the excess,*
> *but the deficiency, of personal impulses and preferences.*
> John Stuart Mill

Consider the problem of finding a good hotel where to stay while spending one week in Bologna, and that the available alternatives are:

Name	Price	Stars	Rooms
Jolly	30	2	40
Continental	35	2	30
Excelsior	60	3	50
Rome	60	5	100
Holiday	40	4	20
Capri	50	2	60

Obviously, many other hotel's properties, such as phone number, number of floors, etc., are present in the Hotels relation, but you are only interested in the three ones above, namely Price, Stars, and number of Rooms, to make your choice. Which is the "best" hotel? Is it *Jolly*, which is the cheapest one? Or, perhaps, is the *Rome* hotel, which attains the maximum number of stars? Or, as your wife suggests, is *Holiday*, that is a

---

* Part of this work has been supported by the MIUR PRIN Project WISDOM (Web Intelligent Search based on DOMain ontologies).

T. Yakhno and E. Neuhold (Eds.): ADVIS 2006, LNCS 4243, pp. 1–12, 2006.

4-stars hotel, costs 20 Euros less than *Rome*, and promises to be a very quiet place with only 20 rooms?

The above is a simple, yet realistic, example of how *preferences* can easily enter into the task of extracting from a database the "best" alternative(s) to take and how they can largely influence the result of a query. In this paper we will go through some basic issues concerning how queries with preferences can be formulated and how they can be efficiently evaluated, even on standard SQL databases. We start by considering the specific case of *numerical preferences*, and then we move to the more general scenarios in which preferences are *qualitatively* represented through a preference relation. The paper concludes by addressing the problem of evaluating preference queries over peer-to-peer networks.

2   Numerical Preferences

For everything you have missed, you have gained something else,
and for everything you gain, you lose something else.
Ralph Waldo Emerson

Traditionally, database queries in which the user wants to discriminate between "good" and "bad" solutions have been dealt with by resorting to *numerical scoring functions*. In its essence, the basic idea is simple: if you have a relation r with schema $R(A_1, \ldots, A_n, \ldots)$, and you want to find the best alternatives according to the values of attributes $\mathcal{A} = \{A_1, \ldots, A_n\}$, then define a function $f(\mathcal{A})$ that assigns to each tuple $t \in r$ a numerical value, $f(t.\mathcal{A})$, called the *score*, or the *utility*, of t. For instance, consider the function:

$$f_1(\text{Price}, \text{Rating}, \text{Rooms}) = 40 \times \text{Stars} - 1 \times \text{Price} - 0.5 \times \text{Rooms}$$

where the negative weights for Price and Rooms mean that lower values for such attributes are preferred. Using f_1 one obtains, say, $f_1(Rome) = 40 \times 5 - 1 \times 60 - 0.5 \times 100 = 90$, and $f_1(Holiday) = 40 \times 4 - 1 \times 40 - 0.5 \times 20 = 110$.[1] By the way, no other hotel in our sample relation can do better than *Holiday* (thus, your wife is fine with f_1!). Clearly, changing the weights can lead to different top-ranked results. For instance, lowering the weight of Rooms, thus the relative importance of this attribute, from 0.5 to 0.1, would make *Rome* better than *Holiday*.

A database system can naïvely evaluate a numerical preference query by first sorting data according to descending values of f and then returning only the first, top-k, tuples, where k is either specified by the user or set to a default value by the application. It is now well understood that this strategy can incur a large overhead, since it does not take advantage of the fact that only k tuples need to be produced. How the knowledge of k can be exploited for minimizing sorting costs, exploiting available indexes, and, more in general, determining an effective top-k query evaluation strategy is described in [1].

---

[1] For the sake of conciseness we slightly abuse the notation and write $f(Rome)$ to mean that we are applying f to the tuple whose identifier is *Rome*. Similarly, $f(t)$ is sometimes used as shorthand of $f(t.A_1, \ldots, t.A_n)$.

Specific solutions that require f to be a linear function or to be derivable from a metric distance are presented in [2] and [3], respectively.

The A_0 algorithm by Ronald Fagin [4] was the first one to provide an efficient solution for evaluating numerical preference queries in a *distributed* scenario. A_0 assumes that one has n independent "sub-systems", each managing the tuple identifier and one of the attributes in $\mathcal{A}$. Each sub-system can return its (sub-)tuples ordered according to the preference on that attribute (*sorted access*) and also supports a *random access* interface, by means of which one can obtain the needed attribute value, given the tuple identifier. The key result in [4] is that, if f is *monotone*, then one can stop performing sorted accesses as soon as k complete tuples are obtained through sorted access. This is to say that all sub-systems have returned at least k common tuple identifiers. The final result is obtained by performing random accesses for all the tuples that have been returned by at least one sub-system, and then computing their scores. Using f_1 as defined above, A_0 would determine the top-1 result of the (now vertically partitioned) Hotels relation by fetching 3 tuples from each sub-system, since at that point one hotel (*Holiday*) has been returned by all the three sub-systems.

Name	Price
Jolly	30
Continental	35
Holiday	40
Capri	50
Excelsior	60
Rome	60

Name	Stars
Rome	5
Holiday	4
Excelsior	3
Capri	2
Jolly	2
Continental	2

Name	Rooms
Holiday	20
Continental	30
Jolly	40
Excelsior	50
Capri	60
Rome	100

We note that *Capri* will not be evaluated at all, and that on this instance A_0 will *always* stop after 3 sorted accesses, since its stop condition does not consider the specific form of f_1 at all.

Although numerical preferences have been largely adopted for modelling user preferences, they have an intrinsic limit, in that *not all reasonable preferences can be expressed using a scoring function*. For instance, assume that your preferences on hotels are (P_1): "*I definitely prefer hotels with less than 50 rooms. Then, I want the minimum price and the highest quality*". Any scoring function f respecting these preferences should assign the same score to, say, *Holiday* and *Jolly*, since both have less than 50 rooms, and the first costs more but has also more stars than the second. On the other hand, it should be $f(Jolly) > f(Continental)$, since both hotels have less than 50 rooms and 2 stars, but the first is cheaper. From this one derives that $f(Holiday) > f(Continental)$, which is definitely not a consequence of your preferences (since *Continental* costs less than *Holiday*)!

A further caveat of scoring functions is that they force the user to compromise between different attributes, that is, to choose specific weights for each of them. However, for every possible choice of weights, it is likely that some good alternative remains hidden in the database. Moreover, weights are difficult to set up, and predicting the effects of changing one of them is a hard task, especially when the number of attributes is moderately large.

3   Qualitative Preferences

The basic idea underlying the approach based on *qualitative preferences* is that, in order to rank tuples, it is indeed sufficient to specify a *preference relation* on them.

Definition 1 (Preference Relation). *Let $dom(A_i)$ be the domain of attribute A_i, and $\mathcal{D} = dom(\mathcal{A}) = dom(A_1) \times \ldots \times dom(A_n)$. A preference relation (or simply a preference) over $\mathcal{A}$ is a binary relation $\succ \subseteq \mathcal{D} \times \mathcal{D}$. If $t_1, t_2 \in \mathcal{D}$ and $(t_1, t_2) \in \succ$, also written $t_1 \succ t_2$, this means that t_1 is preferred to t_2 or, equivalently, that t_1 dominates t_2. If neither $t_1 \succ t_2$ nor $t_2 \succ t_1$ hold, then t_1 and t_2 are* indifferent, *written $t_1 \sim t_2$.*

Usually one requires that $\succ$ satisfies some basic properties. In particular, $\succ$ is a *strict partial order* (spo) iff it is irreflexive and transitive and is a *weak order* (wo) if it is an spo for which $\sim$ is transitive. Here, the key result is that a preference $\succ$ is representable by a scoring function only if it is a wo [5]. As exemplified in Section 2, this is indeed a severe limitation, and explains why a high interest has recently emerged towards queries in which preferences are based on the qualitative model. Before looking at algorithmic issues, let us briefly consider how preference relations can be formally specified.

3.1   Formulating Preference Queries

A first approach to specify a preference relation is by means of logical formulas [6]. A binary formula P defines the preference $\succ_P$, that is: $t_1 \succ_P t_2$ iff $P(t_1, t_2)$ is true. For instance, the preference P_1 in Section 2 translates into the formula:

$$(p_1, s_1, r_1) \succ_{P_1} (p_2, s_2, r_2) \Leftrightarrow (r_1 < 50 \wedge r_2 \geq 50) \vee$$
$$(((r_1 < 50 \wedge r_2 < 50) \vee (r_1 \geq 50 \wedge r_2 \geq 50)) \wedge$$
$$((p_1 \leq p_2 \wedge s_1 > s_2) \vee (p_1 < p_2 \wedge s_1 \geq s_2)))$$

Thus, now we have *Jolly* $\succ_{P1}$ *Continental, Continental* $\sim_{P1}$ *Holiday*, and *Jolly* $\sim_{P1}$ *Holiday*. Since $\sim_{P_1}$ is not transitive, no scoring function can represent $\succ_{P_1}$.

A second approach, pioneered by Werner Kießling [7], is based on an algebraic formalism. In this way a preference P is naturally obtained by composing simpler preferences. The specific language we consider here is:

$$P ::= \mathsf{pos}(BE) | \mathsf{min}(NE) | \mathsf{max}(NE) | P \,\&\, P | P \rhd P | (P) \tag{1}$$

where:

- $t_1 \succ_{\mathsf{pos}(BE)} t_2$ iff $BE(t_1) = \texttt{true}$ and $BE(t_2) = \texttt{false}$, where BE is a Boolean expression.
- $t_1 \succ_{\mathsf{min}(NE)} t_2$ iff $NE(t_1) < NE(t_2)$, where NE is a numerical expression. A similar definition holds for $\mathsf{max}(NE)$.
- (Pareto composition) $t_1 \succ_{P_1 \,\&\, P_2} t_2$ iff $[t_1 \succ_{P_1} t_2 \wedge (t_1 \succ_{P_2} t_2 \vee t_1 \cong_{P_2} t_2)] \vee [(t_1 \succ_{P_1} t_2 \vee t_1 \cong_{P_1} t_2) \wedge t_1 \succ_{P_2} t_2]$
- (Prioritized composition) $t_1 \succ_{P_1 \rhd P_2} t_2$ iff $t_1 \succ_{P_1} t_2 \vee [t_1 \cong_{P_1} t_2 \wedge t_1 \succ_{P_2} t_2]$

In order to guarantee that Pareto and prioritized composition operators define an spo, the "≅" symbol appearing in the definitions of such operators should be interpreted as equality of values (=) for the attributes involved by the preference, unless one of the following cases occur, in which the more flexible interpretation of indifference ($\sim$) can be adopted:[2]

- For Pareto composition, when both P_1 and P_2 are wo's
- For prioritized composition, when P_1 is a wo.

Note that pos(), min(), and max() define weak orders, and that weak orders are preserved only by prioritized composition when both P_1 and P_2 are wo's.

The preference P_1 in Section 2 can now be concisely expressed as:

$$P_1 = \text{pos}(\text{Rooms} < 50) \rhd (\text{min}(\text{Price}) \;\&\; \text{max}(\text{Stars}))$$

The preference pos(Rooms < 50) formalizes your priority over hotels with less than 50 rooms. The other two base preferences (min(Price) and max(Stars)) are considered equally important, thus Pareto composition is applied to combine them. As an example, let us see how *Jolly* $\succ_{P1}$ *Continental* can be derived. Since both hotels satisfy pos(Rooms < 50), and this preference defines a wo, it does not matter that the two hotels have a different number of rooms (i.e., the "$\sim$" interpretation is used for the $\rhd$ operator). Then, since *Jolly* $\succ_{\text{min}(\text{Price})\;\&\;\text{max}(\text{Stars})}$ *Continental*, one concludes that *Jolly* is better than *Continental* according to P_1. Figure 1 shows the complete "preference graph" induced by P_1 on our sample Hotels instance. The graph has a node for each tuple $t \in r$ and there is an edge (t_1, t_2) if $t_1 \succ_{P_1} t_2$ and this cannot be obtained by transitivity. Since P_1 is an spo, the graph is acyclic. From the graph it is immediate to see that P_1 does not order the *Jolly* and *Holiday* hotels, which are indeed the best available alternatives.

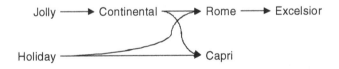

Fig. 1. The preference graph of P_1

4 Evaluating Queries with Qualitative Preferences

I am easily satisfied with the very best.
Winston Churchill

Given a relation r, it is natural to ask for those tuples in r which are the best possible ones according to a preference P. This set of tuples can be formally defined as

---

[2] Actually, there are other cases in which the "$\sim$" interpretation can be safely used. Since they are not relevant here we omit a more detailed description.

$\beta_P(r)$ [8], where the *Best* operator β returns all and only those tuples in r for which no better alternative is available:[3]

$$\beta_P(r) = \{t \in r| \ \not\exists t' \in r : t' \succ_P t\} \qquad (2)$$

Clearly, $\beta_P(r)$ coincides with the set of source nodes in the preference graph of P, i.e., those nodes with no incoming edge.

Now we describe two algorithms for efficiently computing $\beta_P(r)$ in two rather different scenarios. In the first case we assume the availability of a standard relational source, such as a commercial DBMS, and consider that the algorithm runs on the client side. In the second case we consider a distributed scenario in which r is vertically partitioned and present an algorithm that generalizes A_0 (see Section 2).

4.1 The Centralized Scenario

The simplest way in which a client can compute $\beta_P(r)$ is to retrieve from the server all the tuples in r and then perform all possible comparisons between tuples. This is a poor strategy, since it wastes a lot of client resources and generates a high traffic in the network.

The SaLSa algorithm [10] can cleverly exploit the capability of a relational server to sort tuples so as to reduce both the number of comparisons as well as the number of tuples to be fetched by the client. Consider first the specific, yet relevant, case of so-called *skyline queries* [11]. A skyline query over numerical attributes $A_1, \ldots, A_n$ and for which, say, higher values are better, corresponds to the Pareto composition of n max() preferences, i.e.,: $P_{sky} = \text{max}(A_1)$ & $\ldots$ & $\text{max}(A_n)$. Without loss of generality, assume that all attributes have values in the $[0, 1]$ domain. Further, consider that the server is able to sort tuples by decreasing values of a *monotone* function $\mathcal{F}$. For instance, $\mathcal{F}$ could be a function that sums attribute values, i.e., $\text{sum}(t) = t.A_1 + \ldots + t.A_n$. For functions like sum it is easy to prove that if $\mathcal{F}(t_1) \geq \mathcal{F}(t_2)$, then t_2 cannot be better than t_1 according to P_{sky} ($t_2 \not\succ_{P_{sky}} t_1$). Among other things, this implies that as soon as a tuple t is read, and no previously read tuple dominates t, then t can be returned as part of the result. This is also to say that SaLSa can progressively deliver the result without waiting for the algorithm to terminate. Sorting the input has also beneficial effects on the number of comparisons, as it can be experimentally observed [10].

How can SaLSa determine when all the tuples in $\beta_{P_{sky}}(r)$ have been seen? The key idea is to determine a so-called *stop point*, t_{stop}, and to compare t_{stop} with the current *level*, l, of $\mathcal{F}$. Then, SaLSa can stop as soon as the following is true:

$$\mathcal{F}(t) \leq l \Rightarrow t_{stop} \succ_{P_{sky}} t \qquad \forall \, t \in \mathcal{D} \qquad (3)$$

We have the following basic result:

Theorem 1. *Let $\mathcal{F}$ be any symmetric monotone function, and let S be the current set of skyline tuples. For each tuple $t \in S$, let $\underline{t} = \min_j\{t.A_j\}$. The following MaxiMin rule for choosing the stop point is optimal, i.e., no other rule can allow SaLSa to stop earlier:*

$$t_{stop} = \arg\max_{i \in S}\{\underline{t_i}\} \qquad (4)$$

Algorithm 1. SaLSa

1: $S \leftarrow \emptyset$; $Output \leftarrow \emptyset$; $t_{stop} \leftarrow$ undefined; $stop \leftarrow$ `false`
2: Send query q to the server, which sorts tuples using $\mathcal{F}$
3: **while** `not`$(stop) \wedge$ the input stream is not empty **do**
4:     $t_i \leftarrow GetNext(q)$ ▷ fetch next tuple from the server
5:     **if** $\not\exists t \in S : t \succ_{P_{sky}} t_i$ **then** $S \leftarrow S \cup \{t_i\}$; $Output \leftarrow Output \cup \{t_i\}$; Update t_{stop}
6:     **if** t_{stop} dominates all unread tuples in the stream **then** $stop \leftarrow$ `true`

Let us see how SaLSa works on our sample Hotels instance, when the skyline preference is $P_2 = \mathsf{min}(\text{Price})$ & $\mathsf{max}(\text{Stars})$. In the table below we show normalized values for the Price and Stars attributes assuming the domains $dom(\text{Price}) = [20, 100]$ and $dom(\text{Stars}) = [2, 5]$. For instance, since $Holiday$.Price $= 40$, the normalized price is $(100 - 40)/(100 - 20) = 0.75$. Note that this normalization is only for the purpose of sorting tuples and does not influence at all the result.

Hotels marked with an asterisk are those in the skyline. Tuples are sorted using the max function, which equals the maximum of the (normalized) attribute values of a tuple. Values of max are also shown, together with the order in which tuples are read.

Name	Price	Stars	max	order
Jolly(*)	0.88	0.00	0.88	2
Continental	0.81	0.00	0.81	3
Excelsior	0.50	0.33	0.50	6
Rome(*)	0.50	1.00	1.00	1
Holiday(*)	0.75	0.67	0.75	4
Capri	0.63	0.00	0.63	5

After retrieving the third (and last) skyline hotel, namely *Holiday*, this hotel is used as stop point, since its worst value (0.67) is the highest one among skyline tuples (*Jolly* and *Rome* yield 0 and 0.5, respectively). Next step retrieves the *Capri* hotel, which is definitely not part of the result. At this point the level of the max sorting function has dropped to 0.63. This is sufficient to make SaLSa conclude, even without reading *Excelsior*, that the result is complete.

SaLSa can also deal with preferences more complex than skyline ones. As a simple example, consider again $P_1 = \mathsf{pos}(\text{Rooms} < 50) \triangleright P_2$, where P_2 is as above. From Figure 1 we know that $\beta_{P_1}(\text{Hotels}) = \{Jolly, Holiday\}$, since the *Rome* hotel has more than 50 rooms. Using CASE expressions (which are part of the SQL standard), one can assign value "1" to all tuples t for which it is t.Rooms < 50 and value "0" to the others. Sorting first on these values, and then on the combination of Price and Stars attributes, would now allow SaLSa to stop without reading hotels *Capri* and *Excelsior*.

4.2 The Distributed Scenario

Now we turn to consider a distributed scenario, in which data are vertically partitioned. The algorithm we introduce is a generalization of A_0 (as well as of TA [12] and similar others) and applies to any *strictly monotone* preference:

---

[3] This operator is called *winnow* in [9,6] and *preference selection* in [7].

Algorithm 2. iMPO-1

1: $Result \leftarrow \emptyset; Output \leftarrow \emptyset; \underline{t} \leftarrow (\max\{P_1\}, \dots, \max\{P_n\})$
2: **while** $\nexists t \in Result$ such that $t \succ_P \underline{t}$ **do**
3:    **for all** sub-queries q_j $(j = 1, \dots, n)$ **do**
4:      $t_i.A_j \leftarrow GetNext(q_j)$ ▷ sorted access
5:      Complete tuple t_i with random accesses; $Undominated \leftarrow$ true
6:      **while** $Undominated \wedge \exists t \in Result$ not compared with t_i **do**
7:        Compare t_i with t: $\begin{cases} t_i \succ_P t & Result \leftarrow Result \setminus \{t\} \\ t_i \sim_P t & \text{do nothing} \\ t \succ_P t_i & Undominated \leftarrow \text{false} \end{cases}$
8:      **if** $Undominated$ **then** $Result \leftarrow Result \cup \{t_i\}$
9:      Let a_j be the lowest value seen by sorted access on q_j; $\underline{t} \leftarrow (\underline{a_1}, \dots, \underline{a_n})$
10:    $Output \leftarrow Output \cup \{t \in Result \mid \underline{t} \nsucc_P t\}$ ▷ send to output

---

Definition 2 (Strictly Monotone Preferences). *Let P_j be a preference defining a weak order over attribute A_j, $j = 1, \dots, n$. A preference $P = P(P_1, \dots, P_n)$ is* strictly monotone *with respect to $P_1, \dots, P_n$ iff:*

$$\bigwedge_j (t_1 \succ_{P_j} t_2) \Rightarrow t_1 \succ_P t_2 \qquad \forall t_1, t_2 \in \mathcal{D} \tag{5}$$

Intuitively, P is strictly monotone whenever improving on all base preferences P_j also leads to an overall improvement, which indeed is a very natural requirement. Algorithm iMPO-1 [13,14,15][4] exploits the strict monotonicity of P as follows. The algorithm maintains a *threshold point* $\underline{t}$, whose j-th component, a_j, is the last (thus worst) value seen so far for attribute A_j. Since values of A_j are orderly returned, no subsequent value of A_j can be better than a_j with respect to P_j. This is sufficient to conclude that if $\underline{t} \nsucc_P t$, then t is part of the result. When a tuple t dominates $\underline{t}$ no other unseen tuple can be part of the result and the algorithm stops.

How efficient is iMPO-1? In [15] it is proved that no algorithm, on any instance, can improve over iMPO-1 by more than a constant factor, which is to say that iMPO-1 is *instance-optimal* [12].[5]

5   Preferences Queries in P2P Networks

I Still Haven't Found What I'm Looking For.
U2

We conclude by considering the case in which one wants to search for best tuples in *peer-to-peer* (P2P) networks, and sketch how the SaLSa and the iMPO-1 algorithms

---

[4] The "1" in iMPO-1 means that the algorithm only computes the best tuples with respect to P. Generalizing the algorithm to return also good, yet sub-optimal, tuples is described in [13,14].
[5] Technically, halting when $t \succ_P \underline{t}$ also requires P to be *Pareto-consistent*. This means that $(t_1 \succ_P t_2) \wedge (t_2 \succ_{P_{sky}} t_3) \Rightarrow t_1 \succ_P t_3$, where P_{sky} is the skyline preference on $A_1, \dots, A_n$. From a practical point of view, it should be observed that all "reasonable" strictly monotone preferences are also Pareto-consistent and that extending iMPO-1 to work correctly also with non Pareto-consistent preferences is an easy task, as described in [14].

could still be used as key ingredients for evaluating preference queries in such scenario. Part of what follows is being developed within the context of the Italian WISDOM project [16].[6]

To start with, assume that all peers export a same schema R, and that each peer p_k holds an instance, r_k, of R, thus $r = \cup_k r_k$. Further, assume that the query q : $\beta_P(r)$ is issued at a peer p_{init}, and that p_{init} forwards q to (a subset of) its neighbors, which in turn forward q to (a subset of) their neighbors, and so on. The specific policy according to which the execution tree, $T(q)$, of q is determined is not relevant here. How can peers compute the *global* best results according to preferences P? A naïve strategy would be that each peer p_k computes its *local* best results, $L_k = \beta_P(r_k)$, and then sends them to p_{init}. Since $\succ_P$ is an spo, in particular transitive, it is indeed guaranteed that $\beta_P(r)$ can be computed by just looking at the local best results of each peer, i.e., $\beta_P(r) = \beta_P(\cup_k \beta_P(r_k))$. However, depending on how global best results are distributed among peers, this naïve strategy could generate a high network overhead, especially if $|\beta_P(r)| \ll |\cup_k L_k|$. Further, all comparisons among local best results would be performed by p_{init}, thus not exploiting at all the parallelism offered by the network.

It turns out that if P induces a weak order, then there is a simple and provably optimal way of computing the result of q. The LocalBest$_{WO}$ algorithm [17] works in two phases. In the 1st *probe* phase each peer asks its children to return a *single* tuple from their local best results. This request is recursively propagated through $T(q)$, thus each peer p_k will actually return to its parent a tuple which is optimal in its subtree, $T_k(q)$. Since $\succ_P$ is a wo, $\sim_P$ is transitive. Thus, if the tuple t_1 returned from p_1 dominates the tuple t_2 returned from p_2, this is sufficient to conclude that *all* best results coming from p_1 are better than those coming from p_2. It follows that each peer can easily determine which of its children need to stay *active* in the second *collect* phase of the algorithm, during which all best results of active peers are sent to p_{init}. Note that if a peer is not active, none of its children can be active as well.

Algorithm 3. LocalBest$_{WO}$ @ peer p_k

  Probe phase
1: Compute $L_k = \beta_P(r_k)$; $active = \emptyset$
2: Get a tuple $t_j \in T_j(q)$ from each child peer p_j and a tuple from L_k
3: **if** t_j is not dominated **then** $active \leftarrow active \cup \{p_j\}$
4: Return to the parent peer an undominated tuple t ($t \in T_k(q)$) and wait for next invocation
  Collect phase
5: **for all** peers $p_j \in active$ **do** Collect all tuples from p_j and return them to the parent peer

---

When $\succ_P$ is not a wo, above algorithm would not deliver the correct result. In this case one could improve over the naïve strategy by having each peer p_k that sends to its parent only the best results of the subtree rooted at p_k itself. We call this the LocalBest$_{SPO}$ algorithm. LocalBest$_{SPO}$ can indeed reduce the computational overhead at p_{init}, but cannot guarantee that only tuples contributing to the final result are

---

[6] WISDOM stands for *Web Intelligent Search based on DOMain ontologies*, see also
  http://dbgroup.unimo.it/wisdom/index_i.html

transmitted through the network. Can LocalBest$_{SPO}$ be somehow improved? The answer is affirmative, and builds on the ideas on which the SaLSa algorithm is based. Briefly, consider that all peers deliver their results according to a common order (e.g., sum). Then, while peer p_k collects results from its children, it can establish a *local* stop point, $t_{stop,k}$, and with it determine if a children, say p_j, can still contribute tuples that have a chance to enter into the final result. If this is not the case, then all the subtree rooted at p_j can be discarded from the active execution tree and the result still be correctly computed.

As an extension to the above scenario, consider now the case where $r = \cup_k r_k$ and $r_k = r_{k,1} \bowtie \ldots \bowtie r_{k,n_k}$, $k = 1, \ldots, m$. The basic strategy for evaluating $q : \beta_P(r)$ corresponds to the expression:

$$\beta_P[\beta_P(r_1) \cup \ldots \cup \beta_P(r_m)] \tag{6}$$

where, as in the non-join case, one can push the Best operator down the Union and adopt a SaLSa-like evaluation if each peer p_k evaluating $\beta_P(r_k)$ agrees to return results using a same order. However, efficiently evaluating $\beta_P(r_k)$ now is an issue, since r_k is a join of n_k relations ($n_k \geq 1$), each one possibly managed by a different peer $p_{k,j}$. Clearly, having each $p_{k,j}$ that sends to p_k its whole data $r_{k,j}$ would result in a poor execution strategy. The key for a smarter approach is to push some of the preferences in P down the join, and implement this along the lines of the iMPO-1 algorithm described in Section 4.2.

As a simple example, let $n_k = 2$ and $P = \text{pos}(R_{k,1}.A_1 > 20 \wedge R_{k,2}.B_1 < 30) \rhd (\min(R_{k,1}.A_2) \ \& \ \max(R_{k,2}.B_2))$. From P one can derive the two preferences: $P_{k,1} = \text{pos}(R_{k,1}.A_1 > 20) \rhd \min(R_{k,1}.A_2)$ and $P_{k,2} = \text{pos}(R_{k,2}.B_1 < 30) \rhd \max(R_{k,2}.B_2)$, each defining a weak order. Since P is strictly monotone with respect to $P_{k,1}$ and $P_{k,2}$ (see Equation 5), we are in the position to apply the iMPO-1 algorithm. Clearly, suitable modifications (not described here) are needed if the join is not 1-to-1.

6   Conclusions

Preference queries are a fascinating and relatively new subject in the database field. Although at present several important results have been obtained, much remains to be done. What follows is a, necessarily incomplete and somewhat biased, list of relevant issues which will be worth addressing in the future.

- Effective optimization of queries, and preference queries are no exception at all, is only possible when one can reliably estimate the cost of executing operations and the cardinality of results. Both issues have not been adequately addressed until now, and only some preliminary results for the case of skyline queries have been obtained [18].
- Complementary to the above, is the issue of designing effective synopses able to concisely characterize the distribution of best results in a database relation. For instance, this would allow to improve routing policies in P2P networks, by letting the search focus only on the most "promising" paths.

- Still related to the issue of processing preference queries in P2P networks, is the problem of how to set up the most appropriate buffer size for transferring tuples. Indeed, working one-tuple-at-a-time, as we hypothesized in our discussion, will generate far too many messages to get acceptable response times. On the other hand, algorithms like SaLSa and iMPO-1 can be easily made to work one-block of tuples-at-a-time, but this could result in fetching too many unnecessary tuples. Again, a principled approach seems to be possible only if a statistical characterization of peers' contents is available.
- Most of the research on preference queries has been limited to so-called *intrinsic* preferences [9], which guarantee that $t_1 \succ_P t_2$ can be decided by looking only at t_1 and t_2. Although this considerably simplifies the evaluation process, it leaves out many natural and interesting cases. *Aggregate* preference queries are one of such cases (e.g., I prefer hotel chain A to hotel chain B iff the average price of hotels in A is less than the one of hotels in B). A further interesting situation is when the relation r on which preferences are specified is *recursively* defined (e.g., I prefer flight route A to route B iff it is cheaper and has fewer stops).

References

1. Carey, M., Kossmann, D.: On saying "enough already!" in SQL. In: Proceedings of the 1997 ACM SIGMOD International Conference on Management of Data, Tucson, AZ (1997) 219–230
2. Hristidis, V., Koudas, N., Papakonstantinou, Y.: PREFER: A system for the efficient execution of multi-parametric ranked queries. In: Proceedings of the 2001 ACM SIGMOD International Conference on Management of Data, Santa Barbara, CA (2001) 259–270
3. Ciaccia, P., Patella, M.: Searching in metric spaces with user-defined and approximate distances. ACM Transactions on Database Systems 27(4) (2002) 398–437
4. Fagin, R.: Combining fuzzy information from multiple systems. In: Proceedings of the Fifteenth ACM SIGACT-SIGMOD-SIGART Symposium on Principles of Database Systems (PODS'96), Montreal, Canada (1996) 216–226
5. Fishburn, P.C.: Preference structures and their numerical representations. Theoretical Computer Science 217(2) (1999) 359–383
6. Chomicki, J.: Preference formulas in relational queries. ACM Transactions on Database Systems 28(4) (2003) 427–466
7. Kießling, W.: Foundations of preferences in database systems. In: Proceedings of the 28th International Conference on Very Large Data Bases (VLDB 2002), Hong Kong, China (2002) 311–322
8. Torlone, R., Ciaccia, P.: Which are my preferred items? In: AH2002 Workshop on Recommendation and Personalization in eCommerce (RPeC 2002), Malaga, Spain (2002) 1–9
9. Chomicki, J.: Querying with intrinsic preferences. In: Proceedings of the 8th International Conference on Extending Database Technology (EDBT 2002), Prague, Czech Republic (2002) 34–51
10. Bartolini, I., Ciaccia, P., Patella, M.: SaLSa: Computing the Skyline without scanning the whole sky. (To appear)
11. Börzsönyi, S., Kossmann, D., Stocker, K.: The Skyline operator. In: Proceedings of the 17th International Conference on Data Engineering (ICDE 2001), Heidelberg, Germany (2001) 421–430

12. Fagin, R., Lotem, A., Naor, M.: Optimal aggregation algorithms for middleware. In: Proceedings of the Twentieth ACM SIGACT-SIGMOD-SIGART Symposium on Principles of Database Systems (PODS'01), Santa Barbara, CA (2001) 216–226
13. Bartolini, I., Ciaccia, P., Oria, V., Özsu, T.: Integrating the results of multimedia sub-queries using qualitative preferences. In: Proceedings of the 10th International Workshop on Multimedia Information Systems (MIS 2004), College Park, MD (2004)
14. Bartolini, I., Ciaccia, P., Oria, V., Özsu, T.: Flexible integration of multimedia sub-queries with qualitative preferences. (To appear in Multimedia Tools and Applications Journal)
15. Bartolini, I., Ciaccia, P.: Optimal incremental evaluation of preference queries based on ranked sub-queries. In: Proceedings of the 13th Italian Conference on Advanced Database Systems (SEBD 2005), Bressanone, Italy (2005) 308–315
16. Bergamaschi, S., Bouquet, P., Ciaccia, P., Merialdo, P.: Speaking words of WISDOM: Web Intelligent Search based on DOMain ontologies. In: Proceedings of the 2nd Italian Semantic Web Workshop - Semantic Web Applications and Perspectives (SWAP 2005), Trento, Italy (2005)
17. Bartolini, I., Ciaccia, P., Patella, M.: Distributed aggregation strategies for preference queries. In: Proceedings of the 14th Italian Conference on Advanced Database Systems (SEBD 2006), Ancona, Italy (2006) 139–146
18. Chaudhuri, S., Dalvi, N., Kaushik, R.: Robust cardinality and cost estimation for skyline operator. In: Proceedings of the 22nd International Conference on Data Engineering (ICDE 2006), Atlanta, GA (2006)

Turkish Information Retrieval: Past Changes Future

Fazli Can

Bilkent Information Retrieval Group,
Department of Computer Engineering,
Bilkent University, Bilkent, Ankara 06800, Turkey
canf@cs.bilkent.edu.tr

Abstract. One of the most exciting accomplishments of computer science in the lifetime of this generation is the World Wide Web. The Web is a global electronic publishing medium. Its size has been growing with an enormous speed for over a decade. Most of its content is objectionable, but it also contains a huge amount of valuable information. The Web adds a new dimension to the concept of information explosion and tries to solve the very same problem by information retrieval systems known as Web search engines. We briefly review the information explosion problem and information retrieval systems, convey the past and state of the art in Turkish information retrieval research, illustrate some recent developments, and propose some future actions in this research area in Turkey.

1   Introduction

The size of information has been growing with enormous speed. For example, it is estimated that in 2003 for each person on earth 800MB of information is produced. The majority of this information is boring such as supermarket scanner data. (Please also note that data, which is considered as boring by most people, can be interesting for data miners.) It is also estimated that 90% of currently produced information is in a digital form. It is expected that the most useful information will be in digital form within a decade [1].

Abundance of information has been a problem for a long time [2], [3]. Humans in their pursuit of truth, happiness, security, and prosperity have always chased the siblings "data, information, knowledge and wisdom." In the second half of the 20th century regarding the quantity of data, Donald E. Knuth writes "Sometimes we are confronted with more data than we can really use, and it may be wisest to forget and to destroy most of it..." Many of us do this successfully mostly by ignoring the available data or by conscious or unconscious selective attention. At the same time, we try to register and process as much information as possible, and produce a meaningful output, in the form of knowledge and finally wisdom. In this direction Knuth continues "... but at other times it is important to retain and organize the given facts in such a way that fast retrieval is possible" [4]. Herbert Simon indicates that the abundance of information creates poverty of attention: "... information ... consumes the attention of its recipients. Hence

T. Yakhno and E. Neuhold (Eds.): ADVIS 2006, LNCS 4243, pp. 13–22, 2006.

a wealth of information creates a poverty of attention, and a need to allocate that attention efficiently among the overabundance of information resources that might consume it." [5].

The exponential growth of information is referred to as "information explosion" [3], [6], [7]. The abundance of information and the abundance of options provided by it create excessive stress on individuals in the form of information and decision overload [7]. Information retrieval systems, and more recently Web search engines, come to the rescue: these systems stretch our limits by storing and organizing information, and finally retrieving and prioritizing (ranking) relevant information when it is needed.

The goal of this paper is to review the information explosion problem and information retrieval process in general, convey the state of the art in Turkish information retrieval and some recent developments in that area, and propose some pointers for future actions in Turkey.

2   Information Explosion and Information Retrieval Systems

Information explosion is a long-term phenomenon. For example, in 1945, Dr. Vannevar Bush in his frequently cited classic article "As we may think" indicated that society was creating information much faster than it could use. Bush was then headed six thousand scientists in the application of science to warfare in the US [2]. In his article, Bush imagined a mechanized private file and library called "Memex" for personal information management. Memex was imagined as a device in which an individual stores all his books, records, communications, photographs, memos, etc. that can be consulted with "exceeding speed and flexibility." It can be seen as a forerunner of the present day information retrieval systems.

Fig. 1. An example of personal information explosion and brute force solution to problem (boxes on the left mostly contain personal documents)

Today many people experience information explosion first in their personal lives: as individuals we have to deal with many documents related to our family members and ourselves. We have to keep and organize these documents for possible future needs, for example, to prove a payment. Figure 1 illustrates the "information explosion" problem that I experienced and my brute force solution to that problem. In years, we accumulate a good amount of paper documents: tax forms and related papers, insurance policies, health related documents, receipts and statements, cancelled checks, etc. In years, this accumulation can reach to an unnecessarily huge size. The left picture of Figure 1 shows the physical evidence of the problem in my case. In this picture, the boxes mostly contain aforementioned documents. As a solution to this, I went over these boxes, filtered the necessary items - a small amount- and shredded the rest as shown in the right picture. In the second picture, next to the shredder, only one of the many bags is shown and in my case, this process took several days. Paper shredders are a kind of Occam's razor [8]: a device that simplifies our lives by safely eliminating unnecessary documents.

In our daily lives, in addition to paper we have huge amount of digital information: digital pictures and movies, emails, papers in various electronic formats, news articles, etc. Handling them effectively and efficiently is not easy. For keeping our personal data in order, we start to see the emergence of a new technology, a new kind of information retrieval system, called personal information management systems. In the future, such systems may even provide a total recall of our lifetime experiences [9].

The size of the Web provides another example for the "information explosion" phenomenon. Regarding the overall size of the Web, or on the coverage of the Web by search engines, we see continuously increasing numbers. Finding the actual Web size or its coverage by Web search engines is difficult and beyond the scope of this article (a good resource about this is searchenginewatch.com).

Information retrieval systems aim to locate documents that would satisfy a user's information needs. Here we limit our discussion to retrieval from natural language text. Users of such systems usually specify their information needs using a few words. The information retrieval research field was emerged in 1950s as a part of computer science and information science. Calvin Moores, a pioneer of information science, coined the term in 1951; Gerard Salton, a computer scientist, is known as the father of modern information retrieval [6].

Since document collections are very large, IR systems perform retrievals on document representatives. Various models exist for document representation one of which is the vector space model [10]. In the vector space model, a document collection can be represented by an imaginary document by term matrix. In this matrix, each row represents a single document as a collection of terms. Each row element is called an index term. Usually this matrix is stored as an inverted index structure that contains a posting list for each term used in the documents [8]. Each posting list contains a list of documents containing the corresponding term.

During indexing, terms are assigned weights (importance) according to their occurrence patterns in individual documents and collection. The importance of a term in a document is usually proportional to its number of occurrences in that particular document (indicated by *tf* - term frequency). Term importance is inversely proportional to its collection frequency (indicated by *idf* - inverse document frequency), that is, a term that appears in several documents are assigned a lower weight since such terms are not good at discriminating documents from each other during the retrieval process [8] [10]. By using query-document matching functions documents containing more query terms with higher weights are listed first. In ranking, Web search engines may also take advantage of the hypertext link structure available on the Web [11].

3   Research on Turkish Information Retrieval

In this section, we provide a short survey of the research done on Turkish information retrieval. The coverage may be incomplete; however, still a good representative of the published studies. On the Web there are many Turkish Web search engines/directories (after a simple search we were able to identify about thirty of them). Their quality and coverage vary. We keep them out of our concern since they conceal their retrieval techniques [12].

The first component of most IR related research is test collection. IR test collections consist of three parts: a set of documents, a set of user information requests or queries, and the set of relevant documents for each query. Standard test collections facilitate reproducibility of results and easy comparison among the performance of different retrieval techniques. The major concern of IR research is effectiveness. In information retrieval measuring effectiveness involves two concepts: precision and recall. Precision is proportion of retrieved documents that are relevant, and recall is proportion of relevant document retrieved. Other effectiveness measures used in IR are usually the derivatives of these two concepts [13].

The earliest published Turkish IR study, which is done by Köksal, uses 570 documents (title, keywords, section titles, and abstract) on computer science with twelve queries. It measures the effectiveness of various indexing and document-query matching approaches using recall precision graphs and uses a stop list of size 274 that includes frequent words of Turkish (such as "bir, ve") in order to not to use them in the retrieval process. For stemming purposes, Köksal uses the first five characters (5-prefix) of words. This selection is done after experimenting with various prefix sizes [14].

Solak and Can use a collection of 533 news articles and seventy-one queries. For stemming, a morphological parser has been used and the study uses several query-document matching functions. The study shows effectiveness improvement with stemming with respect to no stemming. The reported experiments employ seven different term weighting approaches [15].

Sever and Bitirim describe the implementation of a system based on 2468 law documents and fifteen queries. First, they demonstrate the superior performance of a new stemmer with respect to two earlier stemmers (one of them is the Solak-Can stemmer mentioned above). Then they show that their inflectional and derivational stemmer provides 25% precision improvement with respect to no stemming [16].

Table 1. Turkish IR test collections

Researcher(s), Year	Contents	No. of Documents	No. of Queries
Köksal , 1981	Computer Science	570	12
Solak, Can, 1994	Newspaper articles	533	71
Sever, Bitirim, 2003	Law documents	2468	15
Pembe, Say, 2004	Various topics from Web	615	5

Pembe and Say study the Turkish information retrieval problem by using knowledge of the morphological, lexico-semantical and syntactic levels of Turkish. They consider the effects of stemming with some query enrichment (expansion) techniques. In their experiments, they use 615 Turkish documents about different topics from the Web and five long natural language queries. They use seven different indexing and retrieval combinations and measure their performance effects [17]. For easy reference, Table 1 provides the characteristics of the Turkish IR test collections mentioned above.

If we consider the research done in information retrieval for the English language, we see two distinct periods. These are the pre-TREC and the TREC periods. TREC, Text Retrieval Conference, is co-sponsored by the National Institute of Standards and Technology (NIST), the Information Technology Office of the Defense Advanced Research Projects Agency (DARPA/ITO), and the Department of Defense Advanced Research and Development Activity (ARDA) of the United States. The first TREC conference was held in 1992. TREC workshop series aims: "a) to encourage research in information retrieval based on large test collections; b) to increase communication among industry, academia, and government by creating an open forum for the exchange of research ideas; c) to speed the transfer of technology from research labs into commercial products by demonstrating substantial improvements in retrieval methodologies on real-world problems; and d) to increase the availability of appropriate evaluation techniques for use by industry and academia, including development of new evaluation techniques more applicable to current systems" [18]. The TREC conference had a remarkable effect on the quality and quantity of the IR research.

Before TREC the following (English) test collections were commonly used (name, size in number of documents, number of queries): (ADI, 82, 35), (CACM, 3200, 64), (INSPEC, 12684, 84), (NPL, 11429, 100), and (TIME, 423, 83) [13] [19]. Compared with Turkish collections these are mostly larger and involve significantly more number of queries. The TREC collection sizes change depending on factors such as needs, application and availability of data. Information for "some" of the TREC collections used for ad hoc information retrieval based on a few query words is as follows: (WSJ-Wall Street Journal 1987-1989: 98,732 documents), (FT-Financial Times 1991-1994; 210,158), (FR-Federal Register 1994: 55,630). These TREC collections are used with 50 queries and their sizes respectively are 267, 564, 395MB [13]. A new TREC collection is the GOV2. It contains Web data crawled from the .gov domain. It is 426GB in size and contains approximately twenty-five million documents [18]. Different from ad hoc searches the use of this collection involves meta data in the query (topic) statements. Experimental results obtained by using large test collections like those of TREC would be easier to generalize to real world cases.

4   Turkish Information Retrieval Changes: New Developments

In Turkish information retrieval, we have a new research project undertaken by the Bilkent Information Retrieval Group [20]. It aims to investigate various aspects of Turkish information retrieval in large-scale dynamic environments. One of the goals of the group is to develop a Turkish news portal that would provide information retrieval, information filtering, new event detection and tracking, and output clustering and summarization services [21].

The first step of this effort is creating a TREC-like large standard test collection for Turkish information retrieval and measuring the performance of several retrieval techniques that involve various stemming and query-document matching functions. The test bed, which has been created for this study, contains 95.5 million words including numbers (1.3 million distinct words and 0.1 million distinct numbers), 408,305 documents and has a size of about 800MB. All documents come from the Turkish newspaper *Milliyet* (www.milliyet.com.tr). The collection contains news articles including columns of five complete years, 2001 to 2005. We also have seventy-two Web-like ad hoc queries created by more than thirty participants by spending more than total of three days of query evaluation time. The relevant documents of the queries are determined by using a TREC-like pooling approach [20].

In the experiments we use eight query-document matching functions (MF1 to MF8) based on the vector space model. The first one, MF1, is the well-known cosine function. MF1 involves no *idf* component just computes the cosine of the angle between query and document vectors within a multi dimensional space. The matching functions, MF2 to MF7, are highly recommended in [19]. Finally, MF8 [8] reflects the *idf* effects of collection changes to query term weights and requires no change in document term weights as the collection size changes and therefore especially suitable for dynamic environments.

In the experiments, we use four stemming options: no stemming (NS), first-n characters (Fn) of each word, the successor variety (SV) method [22], and a lemmatizer-based stemmer supported by a morphological analyzer [23] for obtaining more accurate stems [24]. The Successor Variety, SV, algorithm determines the root of a word according to the number of distinct succeeding letters for each prefix of the word in a large corpus. The expectation is that the stem of a word would be the prefix at which the maximum successor variety, i.e., the distinct number of successor letters, is observed. On the other hand, a lemmatizer identifies the "lemma" of a word, i.e., its base form in dictionary. For a given word, a lemmatizer can provide more than one alternative. In such cases, we choose the alternative whose length is closest to the average lemma length (6.58 characters) of word types. If there are multiple candidates we choose the one whose corresponding

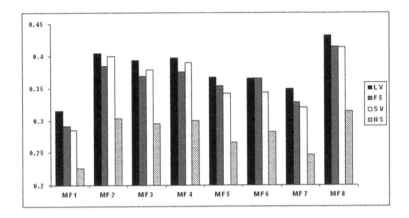

Fig. 2. Retrieval effectiveness (bpref) of matching functions MF1-MF8

part of speech, POS, information is most frequent in Turkish. It is experimentally shown that this approach is more than 90% accurate [24]. In choosing lemmas, we also use the length of 5 characters instead of 6.58 (since retrieval with F5 gives good results). This way, we have two lemmatizer-based stemmer versions: LM5 and LM6. For miss spelled and foreign words, which cannot be analyzed by the lemmatizer (about 40% of all distinct words), in an additional **LM5** version we use the **SV** method for such words, this version is referred to as LV.

The queries are created according to the TREC ad hoc query tradition using binary judgments. The relevant documents are identified by taking the union of the top 100 documents of the twenty-four possible retrieval combinations, "runs," of the eight matching functions and the stemmers NS, F6, and SV. In our experiments for measuring effectiveness, a relatively new measure, bpref, has been used to prevent any possible bias effect on the systems not involved in query pool construction [25]. The bpref is designed especially to handle cases like this and can have a value between 0 and 1, where 1 is the best possible value which indicates that all relevant documents appear at the beginning of the ranked query results. For the final analysis, we have LV, F5, SV and NS. The other cases are not included in the final evaluation process due to their poor or similar performances to these stemmers, NS is our baseline case. Figure 2 shows the results and illustrates that NS (no stemming) is much worse than the others. The most effective one is LV. The SV method and the simple prefix method F5 are also effective, but not as good as LV. The comparisons involve statistical tests as reported in [20].

The experiments show that truncating words at a prefix length of 5 provides an effective retrieval environment in Turkish. However, a lemmatizer-based stemmer provides better effectiveness over a variety of matching functions. Our TREC-sized test collection for Turkish, which we plan to share with other researchers, is one of the main contributions of this project. Currently our group is working on experiments such as query length effects on Turkish information retrieval and the scalability issues.

In addition to our experimental evaluation, we also have an operational system called BIRnews (Bilkent Information Retrieval -Group- News) which is based on our experimental findings . This is the first step towards the multi functional news portal that we plan to implement. By using this system, users can search our *Milliyet* news archive. BIRnews is available on the Web at the following address: `http://bilkent.edu.tr/birnews`. The current advanced users's interface of the system allows users to experiment retrieval with various stemmer and matching function combinations.

5 Conclusions

Information retrieval systems can be used to control how (which, why, when, and where) things are remembered. In other words, these systems can have a bias in terms of what they retrieve and present to their users. They can affect or even control how we perceive, think, and decide. Web search engines can do this simply for advertisement or their bias can be due to their Web crawling and indexing decisions [26]. In addition to these, Web sites can try to embed their own bias to the retrieval process. This is done by techniques known as search engine optimization. Such techniques try to make some Web pages more accessible, i.e., ranked higher in search results.

It may be an old cliché, but it is true that "information is a valuable commodity." Effective information retrieval systems provide better communication between information resources and receivers. Such systems can have a significant impact on improving society and making it more prosperous and better educated. Furthermore, in several applications (one good example is "national security") we would need to have information retrieval systems that could retrieve data not only effectively and efficiently, but also objectively without any bias. Most IR research findings could be language independent and therefore universal. However, when we look at the research done on Turkish information retrieval, although we have some efforts, this research area still looks like an uncharted land. We need to explore and claim this territory. This can be done by

- promoting intra- and inter-institution collaboration among researchers,
- encouraging research and development for applications ranging from personal information management to national digital library development,
- generating communication among different groups by creating an open forum for the exchange of research and development ideas.

In Turkey, we need a TREC-like initiative to promote, and support these important actions. This should be done in an organized manner. For this purpose, governmental institutions and non-governmental organizations can provide support and resources.

Acknowledgements. I am grateful to late Prof. Esen A. Özkarahan; my friend, teacher, Ph.D. advisor, mentor, and colleague; who traveled with me and introduced me to the field of information retrieval. I would like to thank Ismail Sengör

Altingövde for his valuable comments on an earlier version of this paper. This work is partially supported by the Scientific and Technical Research Council of Turkey (TÜBITAK) under the grant number 106E014. Any opinions, findings and conclusions or recommendations expressed in this article belong to the author and do not necessarily reflect those of the sponsor.

References

1. Varian, H. R.: Universal Access to Information. Com. of the ACM **48** (10) (2005) 65-66
2. Bush, V.: As We may Think. The Atlantic Monthly **176** (1) (1945) 101-108
3. de Solla Price, D.: Little Science, Big Science. . . and Beyond. Columbia University Press, New York, 1986 (originally published in 1963)
4. Knuth, D. E.: The Art of Computer Programming, volume 3: Sorting and Searching. Addison-Wesley, Reading, MA (1973)
5. Stefik, M.: The Internet Edge. MIT Press, Cambridge, MA, 1999
6. Saracevic, T.: Information Science. Journal of the American Society for Information Science **50** (12) (1999)1051-1063
7. Toffler, A.: Future Shock. Bantam Books, New York , 1990 (originally published: 1970)
8. Witten, I. H., Moffat, A., Bell T. C.: Managing Gigabytes Compressing and Indexing Documents and Images, 2nd edition. Morgan Kaufmann Publishers, San Francisco (1999)
9. Gemmell, J., Bell, G., Lueder, R.: MyLifeBits: a Personal Database for Everything. Com. of the ACM **49** (1) (2006) 89-95
10. Salton, G..: Automatic Text Processing: the Transformation, Analysis and Retrieval of Information by Computer. Addison Wesley, Reading, MA (1989)
11. Brin, S., Page, L.: The anatomy of a large scale hypertextual Web search engine. Computer Networks and ISDN Systems, **30** (1-7), (1998) 107-117
12. Bitirim, Y., Tonta, Y., Sever, H.: Information Retrieval Effectiveness of Turkish Search Engines. In: Yakhno, T. (ed.): Advances in Information Systems. Lecture Notes in Computer Science, Vol. 2457. Springer-Verlag, Berlin, Heidelberg New York (2002) 93-103)
13. Baeza-Yates, R., Ribeiro-Neto, B.: Modern Information Retrieval. Addison-Wesley, Reading, MA (1999)
14. Köksal, A.: Tümüyle Özdevimli Deneysel Bir Belge Dizinleme ve Erisim Dizgesi: TÜRDER. In the Proceedings of 3. Ulusal Bilisim Kurultayi, Ankara, Turkey. (1981) 37-44
15. Solak, A., Can, F.: Effects of Stemming on Turkish Text Retrieval. Int. Symposium on Computer and Information Sciences (ISCIS), (1994) 49-56
16. Sever H., Bitirim, Y.: FindStem: Analysis and Evaluation of Stemming algorithms for Turkish. In: String Processing and Information Retrieval. Lecture Notes in Computer Science, Vol. 2857. Springer-Verlag, Berlin, Heidelberg New York (2003) 238-251
17. Pembe, F. C., Say, A. C. C.: A Linguistically Motivated Information Retrieval System for Turkish. In: Aykanat, C., Dayar, T., Korpeoglu, I. (eds.): Computer and Information Sciences. Lecture Notes in Computer Science, Vol. 3280. Springer-Verlag, Berlin, Heidelberg New York (2004) 741-750

18. Voorhees, E.: Overview of TREC 2004. `http://trec.nist.gov` (accessed on June 16, 2006)
19. Salton, G., Buckley, C:. Term Weighting Approaches in Automatic Text Retrieval. Information Processing and Management **24** (1988) 513-523.
20. Can, F, Kocberber, S., Balcik, E., Kaynak, C., Ocalan, H. C., Vursavas, O. M: First Large Scale Information Retrieval Experiments on Turkish Texts. (Poster paper) In: Proceedings of the 29th Annual International ACM SIGIR Conference on Research and Development in Information Retrieval, Seattle, Washington, (2006), to appear
21. Radev, D., Otterbacher J., Winkel, A., Blair-Goldensohn, S.: NewsInEssence: Summarizing Online News Topics. Com. of the ACM **48** (10) (2005) 95-98
22. Hafer, M. A., Weiss, S. F.: Word Segmentation by Letter Successor Varieties. Infor. Stor. Retr. **10** (1974) 371-385
23. Oflazer, K.: Two-level Description of Turkish Morphology. Literary and Linguistic Computing, **9** (2) (1994) 137-148
24. Altintas, K., Can, F., Patton, J. M.: Language Change Quantification Using Time-Separated Parallel Translations. Literary and Linguistic Computing (accepted)
25. Buckley, C., Voorhees, E. M.: Retrieval Evaluation with Incomplete Information. In Proceedings of the 27th annual international ACM SIGIR Conference on Research and Development in Information Retrieval. (2004) 25-32
26. Mowshowitz A, Kawaguchi A.: Assessing Bias in Search Engines. Information Processing and Management **38** (1) (2002) 141-156

From On-Campus Project Organised Problem Based Learning to Facilitated Work Based Learning in Industry

Flemming K. Fink

Aalborg University, Fredrik Bajers Vej 7, DK-9220 Aalborg, Denmark
fkf@kom.aau.dk

Abstract. The pedagogical concept of Project Organised Problem Based Learning (POPBL) has been implemented since 1974 at Aalborg University. With take-off in the experiences from this concept we have developed methodologies to integrate productive engineering and engineering education. We all know that the best way to learn and understand a theory is trying to see whether you can apply the theory. Engineering is problem solving – by applying results from engineering research. Therefore it is obvious to try to combine the fundamental learning process and engineering problem solving. Recently we have developed a methodology for continuing education integrated into the daily tasks called *Facilitated Work Based Learning (FWBL)* – mainly based on the same way of thinking. POPBL and FWBL as well as the link between these to methodologies will be presented in this paper.

Keywords: Problem Based Learning, Facilitated Work Based Learning, University-Industry relations, Continuing Professional Development.

1 Fundamentals of Project Organised Problem Based Learning

The main principles of Problem Based Learning can be illustrated as in figure 1. The curriculum is organized in semesters. One semester is a 20 weeks program on-campus. Each semester has its own theme such as *Programming in the Large* (3rd semester SW engineering), *Language Technology* (4th semester SW engineering), *Application Development* (5th semester SW engineering) etc. The project work – approximately 500 hours of workload for each student - must be within the frame of the theme description. A few project-related courses are offered to the students for implementation and application in the project work. In addition, the students must take some mandatory courses such as mathematics, programming paradigms, and complexity and computability. The load for coursework will normally be another 400 hours each semester. This organisation of the curriculum implies that students learn to apply the theoretical courses from the very beginning and on the other hand that fundamental courses are spread over several semesters – in due time before the theories are needed.

Real life problems are not defined in engineering terms. Therefore the problem analysis, definition and formulation in engineering terms are very important before starting with the problem solving. The problem solving part of the project is by far the

T. Yakhno and E. Neuhold (Eds.): ADVIS 2006, LNCS 4243 , pp. 23 – 33, 2006.

most demanding part, but it is also very important that the students learn how to document and communicate the process and the results to other engineers.

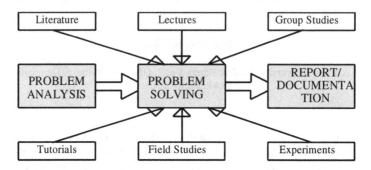

Fig. 1. Principles of project organised problem solving [1]

At the end of each semester the students must pass an oral assessment based on a report of up to 150 pages plus HW and SW documenting their project organised team work. This assessment normally takes up to six hours on team basis. The students will obtain individual marks. In addition to this the students must pass individual assessments in the mandatory courses.

The *Problem Based Learning* concept allows the students to develop excellent analytical skills and they add up with good experiences in coping with and attacking complex engineering problems. In addition to a thorough theoretical insight the students become experienced in applying the theoretical elements from the lecturing in practical engineering problem solving.

A great variety of projects on complex engineering problems at all professional levels are always needed, and co-operation between university (students, researchers) and industry has increased significantly with benefit to all partners. With take-off in the experiences from this concept some further development has made it possible to integrate productive engineering and engineering education.

2 Results from Teamwork in Engineering and Science Education

The pedagogical model centred on problem based, project organised teamwork is evaluated to be an absolute strength of the educational system. In a recent international benchmarking of Danish Computer Science [2] it is stated that the strong emphasis on employability, focus on professional knowledge and competences and substantial co-operation with industry combined with a problem-based learning approach ensures that AAU makes an important contribution to computer science education in Denmark.

The *group based project organised teamwork* is a very important element in the learning process. It increases the students' skills in professional argumentation, presentation of own proposals for solutions, and critical evaluation of proposals from the other students. Preparation of documentation such as reports, scientific papers, and posters together with the oral presentation is exercising the students for future production of written material and preparation and performance of oral presentations.

Because of the size of the projects the students get some insight in combining engineering material with applications, and they get used to seeking and sorting new information/knowledge on their own. They learn how to sort information in what is needed now and what is nice to know later.

Being part of a team the students learn how to co-operate in solving major engineering problems. They learn how to deal with professional discussions in situations like problem definition and argumentation for their choice of solution. Students learn how to argue about and explain in scientific terms what they believe is the right solution – it is not enough to claim you are right; you must be able to convince other group members. *Argumentation is a god way of learning.*

They learn how to organise teamwork, learn that a team does not work if not everybody is doing their part of the job. In this way the students assimilate an attitude to work different from what is possible for students doing traditional university study on their own. In return to this the students will get the feeling of safe social surroundings: "The extensive use of problem-based learning in groups has a very positive effect on the social integration....The student feels responsible to the other group members to stay and do the work, and dropout is therefore less likely" [2].

The teamwork also has the effect that students push each other. Of course the students go for solving the problem - engineering is problem solving, and they define some subtasks for each member of the group. To succeed with your task, you have to read the book, seek out some extra information, read some scientific papers, search the Internet, and do some programming or whatever is needed. And as no students want to end up with a bad solution, they work very hard with their project. The project is the key element in the curriculum; they apply the theoretical courses in problem solving, they can via the project reflect on their professional work. "The group work at AAU also has a positive effect on the graduation time. The individual student feels responsible to the group and is motivated to pass exams and to generally keep pace with the rest of the students" [2].

Each team is assigned a supervisor or facilitator. The facilitator meets with the group approximately once a week to discuss the progress of the project, to guide them back on track if necessary and to read and discuss drafts for their documentation. It is very important that the facilitator is aware of not being a problem solver, but a facilitator. At the end of the semester he is responsible for the final assessment of the project work together with external examiners appointed by the minister of education. Average graduation time for the five year programme is 5.0 years compared to 6.7 – 8.8 at the more course based computer science programmes in Denmark [2].

3 Continuing Professional Development as Cooperative Programmes

Continuing Professional Development (CPD) for engineers within the fields of electronics, information technology and software engineering has become increasingly vital. CPD includes the development of professional theoretical skills in addition to the practical work functions i.e. a combination of continuing engineering education along with productive engineering. The extremely SW-engineering intensive field of mobile communications, subject to very rapid innovation processes in which the development of new products and services accounts for the majority of the costs provides an excellent example of an environment in which software engineering CPD is especially valuable.

Most innovative companies are aware of the importance of improvement of professional competence. However, it is known that [3] even though professional development is identified as vital for the future of the company, the individual engineering staff member often tells that he must find the time for CPD courses himself – they are not integrated in the time-plan for the project. Money for financing the course is normally no problem – but *time* is.

Another parameter that must be considered is the recognition of the course as being part of the personal curriculum – which means that some kind of accreditation is desirable. This means that CPD-programmes must be developed to meet the expectations of both the managers as well as the engineers, programmes that integrate new academic knowledge into the productive daily process.

3.1 Part-Time Master Programmes

At Aalborg University (AAU) we have implemented this in some specific "Master – programmes" as research based PBL – like the ordinary programmes described above but adjusted to the daily situation for lifelong learners. These "Master-programmes" are 1-1½ year programmes on half-time basis, which means that it takes 2-3 years to succeed. The programme consists of courses and project work. As in the ordinary daytime studies the project must cover at least 50% of the time and some of the courses must be applied in the project. The programme is also organised in themes and for the engineers attending the programme it should be possible via the project to integrate his job tasks into his study – or to integrate the application of the courses into his job tasks. In this way the workload from following the study will nominally be reduced. Until now we have only urged the engineer to do this integration of study and work. We have however realised that this is not always easy. Therefore we have developed new ways of more direct cooperation between university and company on management level to define the framework of the educational process. This will be described on sections 5 and 6.

In these master-programmes IT-based distance education is very important [4] [5]. In the courses as well as the dialog between students, the dialog between students and teachers, development in the project work etc. distance education tools are being used. This means for example that even though an engineer for a period is posted to work from another country he can still be an active student. Face-to-face seminars though are still important if possible. We tend to schedule 4-7 two-day seminars a year on-campus. Here the students and teachers can meet, hands-on laboratory exercises can be carried out, etc. This concept for CPD-programmes has been implemented at AAU for several years.

4 Company Commitment to Staff Development

The awareness of the importance of professional development of engineering staff differs from company to company. As more and more consumer products, industrial equipment, etc. includes an increasing amount of advanced functionalities and features the demands for skilled engineering staff increases as well. Different strategies for meeting these requirements can be identified from company to company. Based on several years of dialog with industry concerning engineering staff development these strategies can be divided into different idealised categories.

4.1 Decentralised Strategy

We still find even very large companies with old traditions without any company strategy for engineering competence development. They will normally have a defined strategy for the company products, and the management level will be well prepared to follow this strategy. However the decision about competence development is decentralised to as low a level in the organization as possible. Organising courses for staff members with similar professional profiles across department boarders will normally not take place, and there will probably be no correlation between individual ideas of professional profile development and management decisions on future company development. The individual engineer may risk finding himself on a wrong track of competence development without correlation to decisions made on department or company level.

4.2 Competence Import

Many companies still do not have a strategy for competence development for their engineering staff and for the company as such. So far the individual engineer has managed to improve his skills on individual basis. The manager of the company is quite aware of the limitations in professional capacity in the company, and if new competence is needed for new products he will try to engage a skilled person. Participation in external seminars, courses etc. are only on individual and ad hoc basis. The only way for engineering staff in such a company to improve his academic skills is to follow a course on individual basis in his leisure time or find another job.

4.3 Internal Staff Development

Companies with theoretically well skilled engineering staff, with a thorough knowledge of what is needed for the development tasks in the near future may want to use their capacity as a basis for internal professional development of the engineering staff. This is seen to be the situation in companies with fast innovative processes: They engage continuously new engineering staff, young graduates with fresh theoretical competence from the university. Mixing these new staff with elder colleagues in project teams and in organised seminars the common professional level will improve for both groups. If new knowledge is needed ad hoc courses will be organised or bought. As there is no CPD strategy for each individual engineer, a busy development engineer might be too busy to realise new opportunities, theories or tools.

4.4 Buying Courses

There are a large number of enterprises, schools etc. trying to sell courses on all professional levels for every kind of staff. Courses like intensive 3-5 day seminars with world wide well known experts, video taped courses, streamed web-based courses, self-study courses etc. are available. Buying such courses is an easy way to try to catch up with the fast innovation in new technology – if you can find the course meeting your needs.

4.5 Future Opportunities

The implemented strategy for CPD will in many cases be a mix of the above listed categories. CPD will in the coming years be more and more a parameter in the competition – in two ways: 1) you need to have the best skilled engineering staff in your company to compete your rival firms, 2) young engineers are seeking companies with good opportunities for developing their skills and carrier i.e. the CPD-strategy will influence the possibility to attract new staff members.

5 Facilitated Work Based Learning

In PBL the engineering problem solving is a tool for learning. Learning is the goal. In industrial engineering the goal is to solve the engineering problem, professional skills are the tools. Combining these two ways of thinking is obvious. The challenge is to use a modified PBL concept to combine productive engineering and academic learning, to combine industrial tasks for engineers with their tasks in CPD. Learning objectives will be defined based on the needs for new competences in the company, and the learning and knowledge transfer from university will be facilitated by a university researcher. This is called *Facilitated Work Based Learning (FWBL)* [6].

Facilitated Work Based Learning can be defined as a lifelong learning method based on a partnership between university and enterprise with the purpose of research based knowledge transfer as an integral part of daily business. Together the enterprise, the university and the employees define the competence needs and learning objectives on the basis of the competence strategy for the enterprise, but at the same time the course of learning is tailor-made to the individual employee or to a team of employees. The learning process is supervised or facilitated by scientific staff from the university and the learning process will be based on the learning teams engineering tasks.

Consequently, the aim of the FWBL methodology is:

- To facilitate knowledge transfer to the busy employee in industry without necessarily having to reserve time for participation in traditional taught courses.
- To integrate new knowledge directly and for immediate practical use to the employee in his/her job function
- To plan a learning process matching the competence development strategy of the enterprise
- To tailor-make the learning process to the individual employee
- To schedule the learning process to match the specific project in the enterprise

- To use the experiences from the on-campus project organized problem based learning model
- To optimise the methods and tools related to the individual enterprise, its organization, competence situation and enterprise culture etc.

6 The Definition of Facilitated Work Based Learning

In the previous section the idea of Facilitated Work Based Learning (FWBL) was briefly introduced. In this section the FWBL is discussed in depth and is compared with PBL and WBL to facilitate an understanding of the similarities and differences of the methodologies.

PBL - Problem Based Learning is on-campus studies. The learning objectives are academically defined in the curriculum which is prepared by the university and in some countries approved by the government or an accreditation body. A major part of the curriculum is dedicated to projects in teams, and the learning outcomes will be assessed thoroughly. The student teams will be allocated a university teacher to supervise them in their project work with solving real life engineering problems. The team will be a homogeneous team of students who all have to meet the same learning requirements. The aim for the student is to obtain a degree [7].

WBL – Work Based Learning can be either an individual learning programme or a thematic programme for a group of engineers where competences / knowledge based skills are developed and evidenced through delivery of the work set by the organisation [8]. The learning objectives are the subject of negotiation between the University, the company and the learner. Work Based Learning also relates to Workplace Learning which involves the completion of learning objectives within the curriculum of a degree through the use of the workplace environment and the work programme of the individual [8]. Here the negotiation involves agreement with the organisation and the learner that the work programme is suitable for delivery of the learning objectives set within the academic degree programme.

FWBL - Facilitated Work Based Learning is a learning programme designed for individuals or teams of engineers in a company, a learning programme that will be considered as continuing professional development. Here the learning objectives will not be defined to meet academic goals but be defined to match the strategy for competence development in the company. The learning will be defined based on a combination of individual and company needs. Mainly the learning takes place in the company, integrated into the engineering tasks. A university researcher will be allocated as learning facilitator for the individual learner or the learning team. The team will normally be a very inhomogeneous team consisting of technicians and engineers with different educational background and different obligations in the teamwork and hence different learning objectives, all though the team must hold or acquire some common knowledge. The aim for the learner is to be better qualified for her/his job.

FWBL can be described in different continuing phases. However the content of each phase is not unambiguous for all FWBL programmes as the distinctive mark of FWBL are precisely their individualities. The FWBL programmes are designed not only to meet competence needs of the company but also to match the preferences of the individually engineers - the learners. FWBL can be characterised as a partnership between three partners - the company, the learners and the university as facilitators. This partnership is very important for the success of the FWBL programme. All partners are equally responsible for the programme which means that commitment from all is essential.

6.1 The FWBL Process

The process of FWBL does not follow a rigid scheme such as a standard five day course. This learning process will normally run for more than half a year and often much longer depending on the extent and depth of the learning objectives, the intensity and the time frame of the project in which the FWBL is incorporated. University researchers and educators do normally not have experience with supervising engineers in their attempt to apply new theories or methods. Therefore the knowledge and experiences of PBL as the pedagogical method or at least some experience with supervising major team working is a prerequisite to be involved as facilitators in FWBL. Furthermore it is very important that the companies involved in FWBL are organized in teams or project groups.

The FWBL process can be described in 5 continuous phases:

- Contact phase
- Defining Learning objectives
- Defining Learning contract
- Implementation of FWBL
- Evaluation

6.2 Contact Phase

The contact between company and university is often new for both parts, or at least the situation might involve new persons. To ensure a fruitful collaboration it is very important to ensure everyone involved is in agreement. Therefore, the time used on harmonizing wishes, expectations and request is often very well refunded. The company (strategic leaders) will introduce the overall theme of the learning objectives - professional area, extent and depth, and relate it to the company internal project in which the FWBL programme is needed. But very important is also that the strategic leaders are familiar with the FWBL method and the difference between this method and more traditional methods of CEE. The university will in this phase focus on communicating the FWBL method. The dialog in this phase will be in the nature of a mutual interaction between equal partners [9].

6.3 Defining Learning Objectives

The process of defining the learning objectives is essential to the success of the FWBL programme. The contact phase is the introduction phase - now it is important to be exact. The university researcher will in a dialog with the strategic leaders of the company establish a very precise description of their preferences and requirements for the learning objectives. This precise description will partly be based on what is needed in their engineering project and its time frame and partly on the engineers (learners) involved in the FWBL programme. Based on the definition by the strategic leaders the university researcher will carry out interviews with each individual learner to expose the professional competences of the learners and try to match it to the learning objectives defined by the leaders.

The dialogue in this phase will definitely have a power asymmetry. The university researcher defines the situation, introduces the theoretical subject to be discussed and guides the learning objective definition process by asking predefined questions [9]. However, the university researcher must be aware that the aim is not to meet objectives for academic reasons but for the learner to obtain competences and skills needed to solve engineering problems.

6.4 Defining Learning Contract

The learning contract is prepared according to the outcome of the previous phase. The overall theme is defined by the strategic leaders and the individual competence level of the learners. The learning contract is negotiated and signed by all three partners to create a feeling of ownership and to commit all on an equal basis.

The learning contract will as a minimum consist of:

- Definition of an overall theme for the learning programme.
- Description of learning objectives
- Agreement on learning methods
- Agreement on learning time frame
- Definition of success criteria for the learning process
- Description of process and outcome assessment

6.5 Implementation of FWBL

When the learning contract is signed the FWBL programme is ready to start. This of course is the most important phase in FWBL - now the learning will actually take place. The contents, proportions, professional area and time frame of the FWBL programme will depend on what the three partners agreed within the contract. In an attempt to integrate the learning in the organization, the training will take place in the company. The facilitator (researcher) from the university will give face to face training to the learners and will continuously make sure the learning is in progress and in accordance with the learning contract. It is very important that the facilitator is not presumed to be a consultant with the purpose of helping the learners to solve their problem. The facilitator will always focus on theories and methodologies to help the learners solve their problem and find solutions.

6.6 Assessment

Assessment will have two targets. Firstly to ensure quality of the FWBL programme – the process and secondly to make sure that the learning objectives are accomplished. The FWBL process will be subject to an evaluation through the whole programme. The purpose of this evaluation is primarily to ensure the quality of the programme and if possible and necessary to modify the programme and the contract. The evaluation of the learning objectives will be according to the description of the evaluation in the contract. If the learner is going to earn credits by the learning process, a formal assessment must take place. Otherwise the assessment must give evidence to that the learning objectives as agreed on has been reached. The learner can as part of the assessment give an oral presentation for his colleagues of his learning outcome to establish some knowledge sharing within the company.

7 Conclusion

"AAU has developed programmes with a strong professional orientation, with emphasis on employability, especially through group-work that emulates the way work is conducted in industry" [2].The pedagogical model centred on problem based, project organised teamwork is evaluated to be an absolute strength of the educational system. The problem based part – the *Problem Based Learning (PBL)* concept allows the students to develop excellent analytical skills and they add up with good experiences in coping with and attacking complex engineering problems.

"The problem-based learning approach succeeds in involving and motivating students, as well as creating a sense of responsibility towards fellow group members. This contributes towards student retention and is reflected in low dropout rates and short graduation times, something that could inspire other departments" [2].

Compared to the PBL concept it is identified that there is a strong similarity between projects carried out by students in an ordinary PBL curriculum and projects carried out by learners in a continuing education programme. As the demand for continuing professional development programmes, formal or informal, short or long, is growing and the time for following these programmes are very limited, it is an obvious task to further develop and implement the PBL concept from full time programmes. Such re-engineering of the PBL curriculum can be seen as a way for the modern university to change from being a closed academic world to be an open an integral part of the community.

First of all both companies and universities must be prepared to start the process. University staff is still often asking the question: Why should we be involved in this – we should teach students and focus on our research. Companies on the other hand will often request short courses (courses-on-demand), and they would like to have a number of course offered to choose between, as this is a well-known way of knowledge transfer. A list of courses will also be recognised as a menu of the expertise the university can offer. Traditionally the individual engineer is seeking for relevant courses and his/her superior such as line manager is making the final decision. This means you have a split between the search for new competence and the final decision.

The definition of learning objectives will involve both the learner and his/her superior. This is however a very difficult process – often it is not possible for them to describe by words what they do not know. Often they will request solutions and tools, and not theories and methodologies.

In the implementation phase university teachers and researchers must leave their academic context and enter into an industrial context, which for many will be an unknown world. The knowledge transfer will only be successful if a mutual understanding between facilitator and learner exists, if the facilitator understands the industrial context and the conditions for the learner. The dialog must be open and the process followed according to the learning contract – or the contract must be revised. It is recommended that universities organises some teacher training courses for their staff as a support for this new challenge.

It should be obvious that a mutual agreement as described in the learning contract should be followed. Based on the contract a more detailed agreement will be made between the learner and the facilitator. This will be a schedule of learning sessions such as meetings, academic discussions, reviews of designs, programmes, assignments etc. However, if a conflict between these agreements and some deadlines or new tasks from the management shows up, the learner will normally be forced to cancel the learning session. This must of course be reduced to a minimum if the learning process should be respected and be successful. Commitment to the agreed learning activity from all partners is essential.

We have briefly in this presentation described a new method for facilitating Continuing Engineering Education integrated into engineering practise. This process is not easy.

References

1. Kjersdam, F. and Enemark, S.: The Aalborg Experiment – project innovation in university education. Aalborg University Press (1994)
2. The Danish Evaluation Institute: Computer Science, International Benchmarking of Danish Computer Science. The Danish Evaluation Institute, Copenhagen (2006) http://www. eva.dk/Udgivelser/Rapporter_og_notater/Videregående_uddannelse.aspx?
3. Fink, F. K.: Modelling the Context of Continuing Professional Development. Proceedings Frontiers in Education (FIE'01), Reno (2001)
4. Borch, O., Knudsen, M., Helbo, J.: From Classroom Teaching to Remote Teaching. EURO Education Conference 2000, Aalborg, Denmark (2000)
5. Knudsen, M. et al: Project Work in Networked Distance Education. International Conference on Networked Learning, Lancaster, UK. (2000)
6. Fink, F., K. and Nørgaard, B.: The Methodology of Facilitated Work Based Learning. 10th IACEE World Conference on Continuing Engineering Education, Vienna (2006)
7. Kolmos, A., Fink, F. K. and Krogh, L. (eds): The Aalborg PBL Model – Progress, Diversity and Challenges. Aalborg University Press (2004)
8. Chisholm, C., U.: Negotiated Learning Systems – A Way Forward for Engineering Education. Proceedings of 1st North-East Asia International Conference on Engineering and Technology, Taiwan (2003)
9. Kvale, S.: Interview, An Introduction to qualitative research interview. Sage Publications, London (2005)

Innovative Information and Knowledge Infrastructures – How Do I Find What I Need?

Wolfgang Nejdl

L3S and University of Hannover
30167 Hannover, Germany
nejdl@l3s.de
http://www.l3s.de

Abstract. L3S research focuses on three key enablers for the European Information Society, namely Knowledge, Information and Learning. The first part of the talk will review this project background context and highlight some of these projects in more detail.

The second part focuses on "Personal Information Management" as guiding theme for several of these projects. Personal information management infrastructures provide advanced functionalities for accessing information from institutional repositories / digital libraries as well as personal collections, and facilitate knowledge sharing and exchange in work and learning contexts. Federated and peer-to-peer infrastructures, integrated search on metadata and full-text collections, and advanced personalization and ranking algorithms play an important role in this context.

Background and Projects

L3S research focuses on innovative and cutting-edge methods and technologies for three key enablers for the European Information Society, Knowledge, Information and Learning. LS3 projects focus on digital resources and their technological underpinnings (semantic web, digital libraries, distributed systems, networks and grids), as well as the use of these resources in E-Learning and E-Science contexts.

Technology Enhanced Learning

In these projects we focus on innovative methods and technologies to support new educational approaches and to enable advanced learning scenarios in schools, at universities and in companies. Our work concentrates on personalized search for and provision of learning resources based on advanced annotation and information retrieval technologies and distributed infrastructures, distributed usage of advanced simulations and laboratories, as well as authoring and using audiovisual learning material in synchronous and asynchronous learning arrangements. We address standardized descriptions of, interfaces for and identification and storage of learning resources, building upon results achieved in our projects on

T. Yakhno and E. Neuhold (Eds.): ADVIS 2006, LNCS 4243, pp. 34–37, 2006.

Semantic Web and Digital Library Technologies. Experiments about the learning efficiency of multimedia audiovisual presentations complement these projects by providing insights into the creative-content oriented aspects of multimedia learning resources.

Research projects include the EU/IST funded Network of Excellence in Technology Enhanced Learning PROLEARN, coordinated by L3S, which focuses on facilitating innovative technology enhanced professional learning scenarios. The Integrated Project PROLIX aims to align people and processes in complex and dynamic working situations, integrating business processes and learning environments. PROLIX will develop an open, service oriented reference architecture for process-oriented learning and information exchange based on a central competency/skill matching facility. The Integrated Project TENCompetence focuses on lifelong competence development, and will provide learning infrastructures based on open-source, standards-based, sustainable and extensible technology. The STREP COOPER, coordinated by L3S, will develop and test a model-driven, extensible environment that supports individual and collective competency building in virtual teams, whose members are geographically dispersed, have different backgrounds and competencies, working together in projects to solve complex problems. Two main components are the integration of business process models with data and navigation models in a data-driven web environment, and recommendation and collaboration facilities for teams.

Semantic Web and Digital Libraries

Metadata play a major role in extending Internet and Web with semantic information towards a Semantic Web, providing machine understandable content and enabling personalized and adaptive access to distributed information resource and advanced search and recommendation functionalities. Metadata based access structures enable collaborative and distributed work environments, and enhance traditional libraries with digital content and personalized library services. L3S projects investigate metadata, advanced information retrieval, ranking and search techniques are important ingredients for future information environments, used in ecommerce scenarios, science communities and personal information management.

The L3S projects Edutella, iSearch and PeerTrust focus on peer-to-peer networks and distributed (search) infrastructures. The schema-based peer-to-peer network Edutella connects distributed information sources, including learning resources. The main goal of iSearch is to propose new solutions for personalized search and ranking, and for advanced desktop search exploiting activity-based metadata and social network information. In the PeerTrust project, we investigate trust negotiation in peer-to-peer and grid environments and credential wallets, also to be investigated in the BMBF-funded D-GRID project.

L3S participates as core partner in the two Semantic Web Networks of Excellence KnowledgeWeb and REWERSE, focusing on Semantic Web languages, infrastructures and reasoning. Based on this background, L3S also successfully markets its knowledge in semantic web and digital libraries technologies to various companies and institutions in Germany. As an example we developed a solution for the German publishing house Cornelsen, where the goal was to structure and annotate the large number of learning objects available at this publishing house, based on semantic web technologies.

In the new EU/IST financed STREP ELEONET, we aim to extend the scope of the DOI (Digital Object Identifier) to European E-Learning. In the new Integrated Project NEPOMUK, we focus on a new technical and methodological platform for personal and organizational information management, the Social Semantic Desktop. This platform will provide urgently needed solutions for the personal knowledge lifecycle and personal work-process management, unified information management via cross-application and cross-media linking based on standard semantic web data structures, and knowledge sharing and structured communication within existing and emerging social networks via distributed search, storage and communication. The NEPOMUK consortium consists of 16 partners including HP, IBM and SAP, and is the largest IP funded under the recent 4th EU/IST call in the area of knowledge technologies with a total budget of about 12 Mill. Euro.

Starting in 2007, the new EU/IST Integrated Project PHAROS will focus on building a next generation audiovisual search platform, developed and applied jointly by a consortium consisting of high-profile academic and industrial players with proven track records in innovation and commercial success. PHAROS will advance the state-of-the-art in areas crucial for such a search platform, including intelligent content publishing mechanisms, automated semantic annotation of audiovisual content, advanced query brokering integrating schema-agnostic and content-based search indices, context-awareness and personalization, innovative user interfaces with advanced lateral browsing as well as content protection and spam detection.

Distributed Systems and Networks

Loose coupling of services and usage and integration of distributed services becomes increasingly important in replacing centralized infrastructures. We work on a number of projects dealing with peer-to-peer information systems, ad hoc networks, grid-based environments and service oriented architectures. We focus on self-organisation and sustainability of such networks, and on infrastructure and services necessary for such networks including security, access-control, monitoring, accounting and billing methods especially for virtual grid-based organisations. Based on these projects as well as on projects from our technology enhanced learning area, we are also working in the DFG context on projects which develop new applications for ultrawide- and flexible spectrum technologies in innovative learning scenarios.

Relevant publications highlighting some results from these projects are [1, 2, 3, 4, 5, 6, 7, 8, 9, 10].

References

1. P. Chirita, W. Nejdl, R. Paiu, and C. Kohlschütter. Using ODP metadata to personalize search. In *Proceedings of the 28th ACM Intl. Conference on Research and Development in Information Retrieval (SIGIR)*, Salvador, Brazil, August 2005.
2. Wolf-Tilo Balke, Wolfgang Nejdl, Wolf Siberski, and Uwe Thaden. DL meets P2P - distributed document retrieval based on classification and content. In *Proceedings of the 9th European Conference on Research and Advanced Technology for Digital Libraries*, Vienna, Austria, September 2005. Best Paper Award.
3. P. Chirita, J. Diederich, and W. Nejdl. Mailrank: Using ranking for spam detection. In *Proceedings of the 14th ACM Intl. Conference on Information and Knowledge Management*, Bremen, Germany, November 2005.
4. Stefano Ceri, Peter Dolog, Maristella Matera, and Wolfgang Nejdl. Adding client-side adaptation to the conceptual design of e-learning web applications. *Journal of Web Engineering*, 4(1), March 2005.
5. Stefania Ghita, Wolfgang Nejdl, and Raluca Paiu. Semantically rich recommendations in social networks for sharing, exchanging and ranking semantic context. In *Proceedings of the 4th Intl. Semantic Web Conference*, Galway, Ireland, November 2005.
6. Wolf-Tilo Balke, Wolfgang Nejdl, Wolf Siberski, and Uwe Thaden. Progressive distributed top-k retrieval in peer-to-peer networks. In *Proceedings of the 21st International Conference on Data Engineering (ICDE2005)*, Tokyo, April 2005.
7. Stefano Ceri, Peter Dolog, Maristella Matera, and Wolfgang Nejdl. Model-driven design of web applications with client-side adaptation. In *Proceedings of the 4th International Conference on Web Engineering*, Munich, July 2004. Springer Verlag. Best Paper Award.
8. Wolfgang Nejdl, Martin Wolpers, Wolf Siberski, Christoph Schmitz, Mario Schlosser, Ingo Brunkhorst, and Alexander Lser. Super-peer-based routing strategies for RDF-based peer-to-peer networks. *Web Semantics*, 1(3), 2004. Elsevier.
9. Wolfgang Nejdl, Wolf Siberski, Uwe Thade, and Wolf-Tilo Balke. Top-k query evaluation for schema-based peer-to-peer networks. In *Proceedings of the 3rd International Semantic Web Conference*, Hiroshima, Japan, November 2004.
10. Wolfgang Nejdl, Boris Wolf, Changtao Qu, Stefan Decker, Michael Sintek, Ambjrn Naeve, Mikael Nilsson, Matthias Palmr, and Tore Risch. Edutella: A P2P networking infrastructure based on RDF. In *Proceedings of the 11th International World Wide Web Conference (WWW2002)*, Hawaii, USA, June 2002.

XMask: An Enabled XML Management System

Moad Maghaydah and Mehmet A. Orgun

Department of Computing, Macquarie University, Sydney, NSW 2109, Australia

Abstract. Storing XML documents in relational database systems is still the most affordable and available storage solution. Meanwhile more work is still needed to provide efficient support for dynamic XML data stored in RDBMS. We present an abstract design for an Enabled XML Management System, and also propose a new labeling approach for nodes in XML documents, which we call XMask. XMask is a Dewey based labeling technique where each element is identified by a label consisting of two values (1) node Id (2) and node Mask. XMask can efficiently maintain the document structure and order with a short-length label that can fit in a 32-bit integer. We report the results of experimental evaluation using XML data between our approach and two other approaches, namely Edge and XRel, which use integer values for labeling as well. We show that our approach outperforms the other two approaches for complex queries.

1 Introduction

XML has become the dominant language for Internet applications, and a technology for information representation and exchange. The efforts to store and manage XML data have explored most available technologies from flat file systems to advanced Object-Oriented Database Systems. Other systems have been developed from scratch based on semi-structured models to handle XML data [4, 9]; these systems are called Native XML Management Systems. However, Enabled XML Management Systems [10], that is, RDBMS based systems, are still the most available and affordable solutions because most of these solutions have off-the-shelf RDBMS at the backend.

In Enabled XML Management Systems, an XML document is shredded down and stored into the RDB database tables based on certain mapping rules. YoshiKawa *et al* [15] classify the mapping techniques that are used in Enabled XML solutions into two main approaches: (1) Structure-Mapping where a database schema is defined for each XML document DTD as in [13]; and (2) Model-Mapping where a fixed database schema is used to store the structure of all XML documents [3, 5, 15]. The Model-mapping approach offers advantages over the Structure-mapping approach; first it can be a DTD and XML-Schema independent. Second, it is capable of supporting any sophisticated XML application, be it static or dynamic [5]. In either approach, when an XML document is shredded down and stored in a relational database, the original structure of the document will be lost. To maintain the document order, the nodes and the attributes of XML documents have to be identified and numbered; these numbers are meaningful based on the mapping rule that is used to store the data into RDBMS.

Several approaches to labeling XML documents have been proposed [2, 3, 5, 6, 7, 12, 15]; however we can classify the numbering methods into two main categories; the

T. Yakhno and E. Neuhold (Eds.): ADVIS 2006, LNCS 4243, pp. 38–47, 2006.

intervals approach and the Dewey based approach. In the intervals approach [7, 15, 16], each node is identified by a pair of numerical start and end values (S, E). The S value represents the order when the node is visited for the first time and E represents the node's order after visiting all of its children and sub children. A node X is descended from node Y if and only if: $S_Y \leq S_X$ and $E_Y \geq E_X$. The intervals approach provides a better representation for static XML documents.

The Dewey coding concept for XML trees [12] provides a more semantic labeling scheme which can reduce the cost of relabling in case of dynamic XML data. The authors encoded the order information in UTF-8 strings and used the prefix match functions, as in [6, 12], to evaluate ancestor-descendent relationships. There is the problem of having long path labels with storage and processing-time drawbacks.

In this paper we introduce a new fixed-schema approach which we call XMask, using RDBMS at the backend. the labeling technique that is used in XMask is developed on top of the preliminary labeling approach in [8]. XMask adapts the idea of the IP network addressing technique where each computer can be uniquely identified by two values: an IP address and a network Mask. For our system the analogous values will be (Node ID, Node Mask). XMask can efficiently maintain the document structure and order with a short-length label that can fit in an integer data type. XMask has the ability of numbering large and deeply nested documents effectively. XMask also simplifies the procedure for translating XML queries into SQL queries by reducing the number of joins that is required for complex queries.

The rest of the paper is organized as follows. Section 2 briefly discuses related work. Section 3 presents the XMask approach. Section discusses how the stored XML data would be processed in XMask. In section 5 we present the evaluation test and results. Section 6 concludes this paper.

2   Related Work

Recently there have been quite a few works conducted to support efficient path evaluation and order in XML data stored into RDBMS; since that has been the major problem with Edge [3], which is one of the early fixed schema solutions.

XRel [15], based on the intervals approach, employs a node based labeling scheme with a four-table RDB schema including one table for all possible paths in the document. In XRel, each node is identified by a pair of start and end values and a third field is used for document Id. This solution can handle ancestor-descendent relationships efficiently. To support child-parent relationship, an enhanced intervals approach was proposed in [16], which added another field for the node's level. However all interval based approaches perform poorly with dynamic data insertion and deletion, because they require a complete relabeling of all elements that follow the point of insertion.

Path-based labeling scheme is another approach to maintain document order and structure. This technique assigns a code (binary string) to each element using the prefix-free algorithm [2]. The label of an element is the concatenation of the codes associated with the elements on the path from the root node to the end element. This approach can handle dynamic XML documents but the label length could grow significantly for deeply nested trees. In addition, it does not maintain the document order for siblings.

In [12], the Dewey order scheme for XML trees is considered with paths like 1.4.9.1. The Dewey order provides byte string comparisons via UTF-8 encoding. The major drawback of UTF-8 is its inflexibility since its compression is poor for small ordinals, e.g. the label (1.1.1.1) uses four one-byte components. Also the string-index size can grow significantly for large and deep XML trees. Other approaches have been proposed based on Dewey coding techniques, where most of them label a path as a string obtained by concatenating the codes of elements from the root to the end element on the path. To reduce the size of the label, compressed binary strings have been used and some unused labels have been reserved for future insertion to minimize the need for path relabeling in case of document updates [11]. Although our work uses the similar Dewey concept for node Ids, we process the labeling data as numeric data rather than strings.

3   XMask: An Enabled XML Management System

A complete Enabled XML management system is shown Figure 1. An RDB engine sits at the heart of this system. XML Parsing and Mapping Manager (XPMM) is the most important component in XMask. XPMM works between two different data models; the XML data model and the relational data model, it is built on top of XML SAX Parser and it can shred, map, and store XML documents into the relational database with the absence of the XML meta-data (DTD or XSchema) as well as with the existence of the DTD. Different mapping rules can be passed on to XPMM for different structures of XML documents. The Data Guide is a structure descriptor outside the RDBMS which provides useful information during the translating of XML queries into SQL queries. With the existence of the DTD, the Data Guide can help to validate an XML query during the translation phase into an SQL query. And finally the XML formatter processes the query result to produce the required format, tags, and/or order.

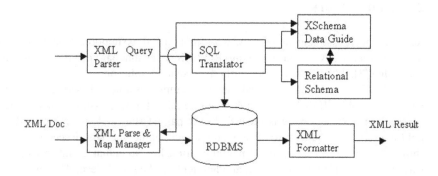

Fig. 1. The structure of an enabled XML management system

3.1   Node ID and Node Mask Approach

The hierarchical structure of an XML document resembles the structure of the Internet, where every computer has a unique identifier (IP address) and a subnet mask. The combination of the IP address and the Subnet Mask uniquely identifies any computer on the net, and both the IP address and subnet mask are numerical values which fit into 32-bit integers. A similar idea can be adapted and modified to identify the nodes of an XML document, with the following features:

1. An XML node can be uniquely labeled using two values: (1) the Node ID which is the Dewey-based component, and (2) the Mask ID is a sequence of zeros and ones with the set bits referring to the positions of node Ids that are concatenated.
2. The pair (ID, Mask) is unique regardless of the starting point of the sequences (ID and Mask) if fixed-width labels are used. In other words, if the length of node ID is L and that implies the length of the Mask, and if value of node ID and Mask are shifted to left by K units (or right padded by a special number; i.e. 0's or 1's) then the new pair (ID1, Mask1) with length L+K is still unique and that will have no impact on the total number of nodes that can be labelled because only one pair can occur in the same document. Note: Based on the implementation, the unit will be a digit in decimal based implementation or a bit in binary based implementation.

Proposal: Let I and M be the node Id and mask for node N and both with fixed length L; where $IN = i_0 i_1 \ldots i_k 0 \ldots 0$ and $MN = m_0 m_1 \ldots m_k 0 \ldots 0$. Then a node Z is said to be descended from node N if and only if:

$$(IN \leq IZ \leq (i_0 i_1 \ldots i_k 1 \ldots 1)) \text{ and } (MN \leq MZ \leq (m_0 m_1 \ldots m_k 1 \ldots 1))$$

One advantage of the above proposal is that we can apply interval calculations to find all nodes that descend from a certain node while it is still a Dewey like labeling method. Also it can be used to implement easier algorithms to verify parent-child and ancestor-descendent relationships.

3.2 Binary Representation

In order to be able to number big documents with deeply nested structures and at the same time keep small node id values (fewer number of digits), we use binary representation for both the node id and node mask. Binary coding will speed up the processing time for node Id and node mask because we can apply binary mathematics (bit wise operations) instead of string matching.

Another advantage of the binary representation is the ability to build a dense index; for example if a parent node N with id (z) has got 5 children nodes (0, 1, 2, 3, and 4) then the possible node ids for the five nodes will be: $(z0, z1, z10, z11, z100)_2$. We can see how values z00, z01 and z000 are missing. From the previous example we can tell that $z0 \neq z00$ and $z1 \neq z01$. That means we can uniquely identify more nodes under the same parent node with a fewer number of digits. If we apply this idea to our example again then we can number the five children nodes as follows: z0, z1, z00, z01, z10.

3.3 Database Schema

In our solution we follow the model-mapping approach where a fixed database schema is used to store the XML document structure. A basic database schema of three tables is proposed as follows: **Path** table stores all possible combinations in an XML document associated with unique path ids. **All_nodes** table contains identification information about all nodes in the document (no attribute nodes). And **Value** table contains the values for text nodes and attributes.

Path (Path_id, PathExp);
All_nodes (ID, Mask, Path_id, Forward_index);
Value (ID, Mask, Path_id, Value);

The tables in (Tables 1, 2, and 3) show how the sample XML document in (Figure 2) would look like in a relational schema. For the path expression values, we used the same technique that was used in XRel [15].

```
<Booklist>
   <Book>
       <Title> XML: the Complete Reference </Title>
       <Year> 2005 </Year>
       <Authors>
           <Author id = Williamson>
               <Name>
                   <firstname> Heather </firstname>
                   <lastname> Williamson </lastname>
               </Name>
               <Address>
                   <City> New York </city>
                   <zip> 99999 </zip>
                   <Contacts>
                       <Email>name@net-address</Email>
                   </Contacts>
               </Address>
           </Author>
       </Authors>
   </Book>
</Booklist>
```

Fig. 2. A sample XML document

4   Query Processing

Due to the mismatch between the relational model and XML data model, We use some user-defined functions to process the data that is stored in the relational database. These functions are based on bitwise operations and binary mathematics. XML queries need to be translated into SQL queries. Using our model, the translated queries would contain join operations on functions.

In the following we show how we can get the parent ids for a particular node if its identification details are known (id, mask). The notation $\oplus$ is XOR, & is AND, and $\overline{M_z}$ is the bitwise complement operation.

Table 1. All nodes table

Node_ID	Node_Mask	Path_id	Forward_index
110000..	1000...	1	1
101000..	1100...	2	1
100100..	11100...	3	1
101100..	11100..	4	1
100010..	11100..	5	1
100001..	111010.	6	1
10000110	1110110.	8	1
100001010	11101110.	9	1
:	:	:	:
111000..	11000...	2	2

Table 2. Path table

Path_id	PathExp
1	#/Booklist
2	#/Booklist #/Book
3	#/Booklist #/Book #/Title
4	#/Booklist #/Book #/Year
5	#/Booklist #/Book #/Authors
6	#/Booklist #/Book#/Authors #/Author
7	#/Booklist #/Book #/Authors #/Author@id
8	#/Booklist #/Book #/Authors #/Author #/Name
9	#/Booklist #/Book#/Authors #/Author#/Name#/Firstname
:	:

Table 3. Value table

ID	Mask	Path_id	Value
100100..	111000..	3	XML: the Complete Reference
101100..	111000..	4	2005
10000010.	1110110.	7	Williamson
100001010	11101110	9	Heather
100001110	11101110	10	Williamson
:	:	:	:

– Function xpm( ): gets the parent's mask for node Z with mask M: $\mathrm{xpm}(M_z) = M_z \oplus (M_z \& (\overline{M_z} + 1))$

– Function xp( ): gets the parents id for node Z with id I and mask M: $\mathrm{xp}(I_z, M_z) = I_z \& (0x80000000 - (M_z \& (\overline{M_z} + 1)))$

Other useful functions are defined as follows:

– xrpm(mask,l): finds the mask for any ancestor node for the context node at level l.
– xrp(id,mask,l): finds the id for any ancestor node for the context node at level l.

- xlo(id,mask): finds the local order for the context node.
- xlv(mask): finds the node's level.

Since our model has a path table, the translation procedure for simple path queries will be similar to that in intervals approach XRel [15]. We use the following example to show how the translated SQL statement would look like for complex queries, that is, queries that contain patterns, in both XRel and XMask.

Example: Based on the sample document in Figure 1, find the book titles where the book's publishing year equals 2005: "/Booklist/Book [Year = 2005]/Title". Since XRel model does not preserve parent-child relationship explicitly, some extra join operations are required to address this query. The nodes Title and Year are contained by node Book. So we need to get node Book involved as follows:

```
SELECT t1.docID, t1.start, t1.end, t1.path_id, t2.path, t1.value
FROM text t1, path t2, text t3, path t4, element t5, path t6
WHERE t2.pathExp LIKE #/Booklist#/Book#/Title
    AND t1.path_id = t2.path_id
    AND t4.pathExp LIKE #/Booklist#/Book#/Year
    AND t3.path_id = t4.path_id AND t3.value = 2005
    AND t6.pathExp LIKE #/Booklist#/Book
    AND t5.path_id = t6.path_id
    AND t5.docID = t3.docID AND t5.docID = t1.docID
    AND t5.start < t3.start AND t5.end > t3.end
    AND t5.start < t1.start AND t5.end > t1.end
```

The XMask approach can reduce the number of joins in the resulting SQL queries. Since the sibling nodes have the same mask value, the mask field can be used to narrow down the number of potential tuples, and then we join on function xp( ) which retrieves the parent id for the context node:

```
SELECT t1.id, t1.mask, t1.path_id, t2.pathExp, t1.value
FROM value t1, path t2, value t3, path t4
WHERE t2.pathExp LIKE #/Booklist#/Book#/Title
    AND t1.path_id = t2.path_id
    AND t4.pathExp LIKE #/Booklist#/Book#/Year
    AND t3.value = 2005 AND t3.path_id = t4.path_id
    AND t3.mask = t1.mask
    AND xp(t3.id,t3.mask) = xp(t1.id,t1.mask)
```

5 Performance Evaluation

We have implemented our approach based on the proposal discussed in this paper and two other approaches, XRel and Edge and compared their performance. We selected XRel and Edge because they also use fixed relational schema mapping technique, and we wanted to do further comprehensive performance test than the preliminary test reported in [8]. The tests were conducted on 2.7MHz Pentium 4 machine with 256MB RAM. We used the Apache XML SAX Parser 2.6-2 for Java with SUN Java standard edition 1.4-2 as XML documents processor. The XML documents were parsed and mapped into three relations. MySQL database server was used as backend database server (InnoDB storage engine was used for all tables).

For performance comparison we also implemented XRel as it was implemented by authors [15]. For the Edge solution, we used the universal mapping method but we also added a second table to store all possible paths, as in XRel [15], as follows:

```
Edge(source, target, path_id, fwd index, value);
Path(path_id, pathExp);
```

Path table helps the Edge model to evaluate the paths for some queries without the need to perform a number of costly self-joins on **Edge** table as in the original approach [3]. The Bosak's collection for Shakespeare plays [1], 37 documents with 8MB approximate size, is used as the experimental data.

We conducted an experimental study using the same data set and the same eight queries that were used in [15]. As shown in Table 4 we extended the test with three further complex XML queries (Q9-Q11). We ran every query 10 times. We excluded the first run; then we calculated the average runtime for each query. Table 5 shows the average elapsed time for the three systems for the 11 queries.

Table 4. The queries that were used for test

Query	Query Expression
Q1	/PLAY/ACT
Q2	/PLAY/ACT/SCENE/SPEECH/LINE/STAGEDIR
Q3	//SCENE/TITLE
Q4	//ACT//TITLE
Q5	/PLAY/ACT[2]
Q6	(/PLAY/ACT)[2]/TITLE
Q7	/PLAY/ACT/SCENE/SPEECH[SPEAKER='CURIO']
Q8	/PLAY/ACT/SCENE[//SPEAKER='Steward']/TITLE
Q9	/PLAY/ACT/SCENE[TITLE='SCENE II. A room of state in the same.']/*
Q10	/PLAY/ACT/SCENE/SPEECH/SPEAKER[text()='CURIO'] /ancestor-self::
Q11	/PLAY/ACT/SCENE/* [4]

We found that our approach outperformed the enhanced Edge approach for almost all complex queries. And it also outperformed XRel approach for some queries and for other queries it performed competitively. Meanwhile we found that the Edge approach, with a second table for paths, became a competitor solution for some type of XML documents. For simple path queries with either short or long paths as in Q1 and Q2 or for queries with double path notation (//) as in Q3 and Q4, the three systems performed at the same level because they all take advantage of the path table.

Q5 is used to find a node at a particular position. The three models maintain the node order within the same parent node for the same type of nodes in a separate column. In this query we found the three systems performed almost similar. Q6 is more complicated where the potential tuples are selected based on the document order. None of the three models can answer this query in a straightforward way and the translated query includes sub queries. We see that Edge performed the best because of the simplicity of joining conditions while XRel was the worst due to the number of θ joins.

Table 5. Average elapsed times(sec) for Q1-Q11

Query	Edge	XRel	XMask
Q1	0.0010	0.0012	0.0011
Q2	0.0028	0.0029	0.0028
Q3	0.0028	0.0035	0.0029
Q4	0.0034	0.0038	0.0031
Q5	0.0015	0.0018	0.0012
Q6	0.0190	1.0600	0.1010
Q7	0.0770	0.0820	0.0080
Q8	———	0.4470	0.0100
Q9	———	0.0280	0.0110
Q10	49.7000	0.0070	0.6600
Q11	32.2200	0.2800	1.0050

In Q7 and Q8, XMask performed the best because the translated queries for XMask contained joins on functions so the query optimiser started with matching tuples from Path table and joined back on All_Nodes and Value tables. We also needed fewer numbers of joins. In Q8, Edge is not a competitor at all.

We also ran additional tests on more complex queries on the XML structure. Q9 tests the ability of retrieving a sub tree based on selection criteria. The approaches based on intervals method can answer this kind of queries best but XMask was faster than XRel, because it did not need another level of joins. Again Edge is not competitive.

Q10 is used to find all the ancestor nodes for a particular node with text matching. The enhanced Edge did poorly while XRel was the fastest because XRel mapping preserves the ancestor-descendent relationship. XMask also performed quite well because the ancestor-descendent information is encoded in the node ID.

Q11 is another query about structure and local order. The XRel performed the best again but XMask performed very well too. For those types of queries XMask has an advantage over XRel which is the simplicity of translated queries. That is again because the local order information is encoded in the node ID. The translated query for XRel would become impractical for queries with big index numbers for the local order.

6   Conclusions

In this paper, we have proposed a new model-mapping approach called XMask, which is able to maintain the structure and order of XML documents using only two encoded integer values (the node ID and node Mask). As we used the Dewey concept for the node ID, we have introduced the Mask concept which makes it possible to label very large deeply nested XML documents using binary sequences. The performance evaluation against two approaches, the enhanced Edge and the intervals (XRel), showed that our solution outperformed the other two approaches for most of the queries in the test and performed competitively for the others.

In XMask, ordering the result would happen outside the database, because our current approach can order the results for some queries inside any RDBMS but not for all kinds of XML queries. This part will be our future work besides further performance evaluation to compare with other more recent proposals [11].

References

1. Bosak, J., Shakespeare 2.00. 1999, http://www.cs.wisc.edu/niagara/data/shakes/shaksper.htm.
2. Cohen, E., H. Kaplan, and T. Milo. Labeling Dynamic XML Trees. in Twenty-first ACM SIGACT-SIGMOD-SIGART Symposium on Principles of Database Systems. 2002. Madison, Wisconsin, USA.
3. Florescu, D. and D. Kossmann, Storing and Querying XML data using an RDBMS. IEEE Data Engineering Bulletin, 1999. 22(3).
4. Jagadish, H., et al., TIMBER: A native XML database. VLDB, 2002. 11: p. 274-291.
5. Jiang, H., et al. Path Materialization Revesited: An Efficient Storage Model For XML Data. in Australasian Database Conference. 2002.
6. Kaplan, H., T. Milo, and R. Shabo. A Comparison of Labeling Schemes for Ancestor Queries. in the Thirteenth Annual ACM-SIAM Symposium on Discrete Algorithms. 2002. San Francisco, CA, USA.
7. Li, Q. and B. Moon. Indexing and Querying XML Data for Regular Path Expressions. in The 27th VLDB Conference. 2001. Roma, Italy.
8. Maghaydah, M. and M. Orgun, Labeling XML Nodes in RDBMS. APWeb Workshops 2006:122-126.
9. McHugh, J., et al., Lore: A Database Management System For SemiStructured Data. SIGMOD, 1997. 26(3): p. 54-66.
10. Nambiar, U., et al., Current Approaches to XML Management. Internet Computing, IEEE, Jul-Aug, 2002. 6(4): p. 43-51.
11. O'Neil, P., et al. ORDPATHs: Insert-Friendly XML Node Labels. in ACM SIGMOD. 2004. Paris, France.
12. Shanmugasundaram, J., et al., Storing and Querying Ordered XML Using a Relational Database System, in ACM SIGMOD. 2002. p. 204-215.
13. Shanmugasundaram, J., et al., Relational Databases for Querying XML Documents: Limitations and Opportunities, in the 25th VLDB Conference. 1999. p. 302-314.
14. XQuery 1.0 and XPath 2.0 Data Model, http://www.w3.org/TR/xpath-datamodel/.
15. YoshiKawa, A., XRel: A path-based approach to Storage and Retrieval of XML Documents using Relational Database. ACM Transactions on Internet Technology, 2001. 1(1).
16. Zhang, C., et al. On Supporting Queries in Relational Database Management Systems. in SIGMOD. 2001. Santa Barbara, California USA.

Validation of XML Documents: From UML Models to XML Schemas and XSLT Stylesheets*

Eladio Domínguez[1], Jorge Lloret[1], Ángel L. Rubio[2], and María A. Zapata[1]

[1] Dpto. de Informática e Ingeniería de Sistemas.
Facultad de Ciencias. Edificio de Matemáticas.
Universidad de Zaragoza. 50009 Zaragoza. Spain
{noesis, jlloret, mazapata}@unizar.es
[2] Dpto. de Matemáticas y Computación. Edificio Vives.
Universidad de La Rioja. 26004 Logroño. Spain
arubio@dmc.unirioja.es

Abstract. The widespread use of XML brings out the need of ensuring the validity of XML data. The use of languages such as XML Schema makes easier the process of verification of XML documents, but the problem is that there are many constraints that can not be expressed by means of XML Schema. Besides, several works in the literature defend the consideration of a conceptual level in order to save XML designers from dealing with low level implementation issues. The approach of this paper is based on the inclusion of such a conceptual level, using UML as a conceptual modeling language. Starting from a UML class diagram annotated with conceptual constraints, our framework automatically generates an XML Schema together with a set of XSLT stylesheets to check those integrity constraints that can not be expressed in XML Schema.

1   Introduction

Nowadays XML [15] is accepted as *de facto* standard format for data interchange and XML Schema [15] is the preferred schema language for XML documents. These widespread uses bring about new software engineering challenges, of which we will emphasize two that are interrelated: first, the critical need of ensuring the validity of XML data, which should be done by imposing various structural and content *constraints*; and second, the desirable integration of design of XML schemas and documents into general development processes, in particular by bringing this kind of design up to a *conceptual level*.

With regard to the need of ensuring the validity of XML data, the problem is that there are many integrity constraints, frequently used in schema definition, that can not be expressed in XML Schema [3]. This fact makes the validation of XML documents difficult since those constraints are either not verified, or

---

* This work has been partially supported by DGI, project TIN2005-05534, by the Government of La Rioja, project ANGI 2005/19, by the Government of Aragon and by the European Social Fund.

T. Yakhno and E. Neuhold (Eds.): ADVIS 2006, LNCS 4243, pp. 48–59, 2006.

implementers have to write their own validating code, therefore exposing the developers to time–consuming, error–prone tasks. Apart from this solution, several authors have presented different ways of augmenting the possibilities of expression of constraints at the XML level. Summarizing, there are two kinds of proposals in this sense: on the one hand, to increment XML Schema by means of other schema languages (Schematron [9], SchemaPath [12]), and, on the other hand, to use XSLT stylesheets [3,15].

One drawback of either of these proposals is that a conceptual level for the specification of constraints is not considered so that designers are exposed to low level implementation issues. For this reason, several authors [1,4,6,10,14] advocate using a conceptual level for XML document design since it allows the designer to work at a higher level of abstraction. The problem is that, in general, the approaches that propose a conceptual modeling language for data design (and the automatic generation of XML structures) either do not deal with the specification of conceptual constraints, or do not give a general solution in order to check constraints that can not be expressed in the chosen schema language.

Therefore, there exist partial solutions for each one of the two issues we have mentioned, but, as far as we are aware, there are very few proposals that tackle both of them. As a step in this direction, in this paper we describe our approach in which the conceptual design is expressed by means of UML class diagrams annotated with OCL conceptual constraints commonly found in semantic modeling. From this model, an XML schema is automatically created and XSLT stylesheets are generated for those conceptual constraints that can not be expressed by means of XML Schema. We have decided to use XSLT in our solution for the reasons pointed out by [3]: XSLT is a core technology, it is a very powerful language and there is expected to be long term support for it.

There are several strengths of our approach that we want to highlight. Firstly, we do not present 'yet another approach' to the mapping of UML class diagrams into XML Schema, but we use, as much as possible, existing solutions to this problem. Secondly, our approach considers different OCL constraints that either are not easy to express or can not be expressed in XML Schema. Lastly, it should be stressed that our approach does not require any new technologies, and it can be implemented by means of XML Schema and XSLT.

The remainder of the paper is organized as follows. In Section 2 we offer an overview of our approach, describing in Section 3 the specification of constraints we have used. Section 4 and 5 are devoted to explaining the algorithms we propose. We finish with related work in Section 6 and conclusions in Section 7.

2   Overview

According to the ideas we have outlined in the introduction, the aim of our approach is twofold: (1) to facilitate the specification of integrity constraints by incorporating a conceptual level and (2) to augment the possibilities of expression of constraints at the XML level using XSLT stylesheets.

In order to make feasible these two goals, we have developed a *transformation algorithm* which takes as input a UML class diagram and generates an XML

Schema together with XSLT stylesheets to check those constraints which can not be expressed inside the XML Schema (see Figure 1, translation process). Once these documents have been generated, an XML document is valid if the following three conditions are met: (1) it has an XML schema associated to it, (2) the document complies with the constraints expressed in it and (3) for every XSLT stylesheet stored in the XSLT processor, the true value is obtained when the stylesheet is applied to the XML document (see Figure 1, validation process).

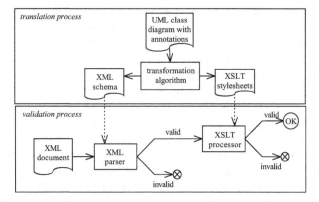

Fig. 1. Schema of our proposed approach

The transformation algorithm that we propose consists of two subalgorithms: the structure generation algorithm and the constraints generation algorithm. The main goal of the *structure generation algorithm* is to generate the corresponding XML schema without any kind of constraint. Since there exist several ways of translating a UML class diagram into an XML schema, we have considered it appropriate to allow the designer to choose among different transformation options. In general, we have tried to make our proposal as automatic as possible, taking default decisions as far as is feasible. When this is not the case, the control is transferred to the designer.

This algorithm, besides the XML schema, also generates additional information that is sent to the next algorithm, the constraints generation algorithm. Specifically, identifiers of the UML elements and transformation constraints are generated. On the one hand, an *identifier* is a set of XML attributes and/or elements which accomplish a similar role to that played by an OID at the UML level. These will be used by the constraint generation algorithm to build the XML constraints and XSLT stylesheets. On the other hand, the *transformation constraints* appear due to the fact that in many cases the conceptual model does not contain all the information necessary to complete the final data, for example constraints about null values not allowed in the XML documents.

Once the structure generation algorithm has finished, the constraints generation algorithm acts. The *constraints generation algorithm* is the main contribution of this paper and offers a solution for the general problem of representing, at the XML level, conceptual constraints that can not be specified inside the XML schema. The input of this algorithm is the conceptual model containing the conceptual constraints together with the information generated by the structure generation algorithm. Its output is the XML schema including XML constraints together with the XSLT stylesheets for checking the conceptual constraints which are not expressible within the XML Schema.

3   Conceptual Constraints Specification

The consideration of a conceptual level allows the designer to focus on domain modeling issues rather than implementation issues [14]. In this respect, UML [13] class diagram is one of the most widely accepted as a standard notation for conceptual modeling. With regard to the conceptual constraints that cannot be expressed in a class diagram, the UML 2.0 recommends using OCL [13] in order to express them.

For example, Figure 2 contains a class diagram representing people, the department in which they work and the products they develop. Apart from the constraints specified in the class diagram, three more conceptual constraints have been specified by means of OCL. For instance, one of these constraints establishes that a person necessarily develops a product or works in a department.

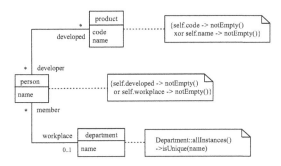

Fig. 2. UML schema and conceptual constraints

In this paper, we restrict our attention to conceptual constraint types commonly found in semantic modeling. In order to determine the types of constraint to be considered, we have reviewed several papers on constraints for conceptual models such as [7,11], and we have selected an extensive and useful number of them. Table 1 contains the types of constraint on which we focus our attention. In order to understand the description of each one of them, a previous explanation must be given.

We propose to use an intermediate representation of the constraints with the aim of facilitating the transformation of the conceptual constraints into constraints at the XML level. This representation is defined considering that a constraint tells us what has to be verified in a set of places (target place) when something is verified in another place (source place). In our approach, a place is an element of a model like, for example, a class or an association. For instance, the constraint associated to the class person in Figure 2 can be seen as the following condition: given a person then either the set containing the products (s)he develops or his/her department are not empty. In this example, the source place is the person class and the target place is formed by the associations developed and workplace. In Table 1 the meaning of each one of the considered types of constraint has been described making use of these source and target notions.

Table 1. Condition types

Type	Meaning
m..n	each instance of the source must participate in at least m and at most n instances of the target
isa	each instance of the source must also be an instance of the target
exists	each instance of the source must have as participant an instance of the target
unique	each instance of the source must be uniquely identified by the set formed by one instance of each component of the target
total	each instance of the source must be related to at least one instance of the components of the target
exclusive	each instance of the source must be related to at most one instance of the components of the target
subset	if an instance of the source is related to one instance of one of the components of the target then it must be related to one instance of each one of the rest of components of the target
coexistence	each instance of the source must be related to an instance of every component of the target or to no instance of any component of the target

All these considerations allow us to translate each conceptual constraint into a tuple containing three elements: (a) type of constraint, (b) source place and (c) target place. In this way the different conceptual constraints of the class diagram depicted in Figure 2 can be specified such as appears in Figure 3.

```
1. (0..*,person,developed)          7. (exists,developer,person)
2. (0..*,product,developer)         8. (exists,developed,product)
3. (0..1,person,workplace)
4. (0..*,department,member)         9. (unique,department,name)
5. (exists,member,person)          10. (total,person,(developed,workplace))
6. (exists,workplace,department)   11. (exclusive,product,(code,name))
```

Fig. 3. Constraints expressed in the UML class diagram (1 to 8) and in OCL (9 to 11)

For each constraint type, we have identified the admitted source and target places, which are attributes, classes or associations. The possible, admitted combinations are shown in Table 2. The source and target inside each constraint category must meet the preconditions shown in the precondition row of Table 2. Their meaning is as follows: (1) the attribute belongs to the class, (2) the class is a participant of the association, (3) both associations have the same participants, (4) there is an isa constraint from each class of the target to the source class, (5) there is a common participant for every association. Moreover, some combinations of type, source and target do not make up a constraint category. In total, we have considered thirty-three constraint categories.

Table 2. Conceptual constraints

source →	class	class	class	assoc	assoc	class	class	class	assoc	assoc
target →	attr	assoc	class	assoc	class	attrs	assocs	classes	assocs	assocs
precondition →	(1)	(2)		(3)	(2)	(1)	(2)	(4)	(3)	(5)
constraint type ↓										
m..n	√	√								
isa			√	√						
exists					√					
unique	√					√				
total	√	√				√	√	√	√	√
exclusive				√	√	√	√	√	√	√
subset						√	√	√	√	√
coexistence						√	√	√	√	√

4   Structure Generation Algorithm

In paper [5] we sketched a translation algorithm within a database evolution context. Moreover, several papers such as [10] propose the generation of XML schemas from UML class diagrams. We have used [5,10] as a starting point for our structure generation algorithm but we do not detail it here for space reasons. It is only worth noting that the algorithm considers the basic structural modeling elements, that is, classes, attributes, associations and generalizations. When it is applied to our running example, the XML schema of Figure 4 is generated. Moreover, the structure generation algorithm produces two further outputs: identifiers and transformation constraints. Let us describe them.

As we have pointed out in Section 2, the identifiers are used for identifying, at the XML level, instances of the UML elements. They depend on the transformation rules applied inside the structure generation algorithm. For example, the identifier of a class is a new attribute added to the XML element into which the class is transformed. The identifier of an association is formed by the identifier of its participants. The identifier of a participant in an association is formed by the attributes and/or elements which represent the participant in the element into which the association is embedded. The identifier of an attribute is the XML element or attribute into which the attribute is transformed. In Table 3, we can see the identifiers of the classes, associations and attributes of our running example according to the transformation rules applied.

Another issue relating to transformation frameworks such as the one we describe is that the conceptual model does not contain all the information necessary to obtain the final result. We distinguish two kinds of information not available at the conceptual level and provided during the structure generation algorithm execution: key constraints and null constraints (these constraints are referred to

```
<xsd:schema                                           <xsd:complexType name="persontype">
 xmlns:xsd="http://www.w3.org/2001/XMLSchema">         <xsd:sequence>
 <xsd:element name="root">                               <xsd:element name="name"/>
  <xsd:complexType>                                    </xsd:sequence>
   <xsd:sequence>                                      <xsd:attribute name="idperson"/>
    <xsd:element name="person"                          <xsd:attribute name="iddepartment"/>
     type="persontype"                                 </xsd:complexType>
     minOccurs="0" maxOccurs="unbounded"/>            <!--here comes producttype spec -->
    <xsd:element name="product"                        <xsd:complexType name="departmenttype">
     type="producttype"                                 <xsd:sequence>
     minOccurs="0" maxOccurs="unbounded"/>               <xsd:element name="name"/>
    <xsd:element name="department"                      </xsd:sequence>
     type="departmenttype"                              <xsd:attribute name="iddepartment"/>
     minOccurs="0" maxOccurs="unbounded"/>            </xsd:complexType>
    <xsd:element name="person_develops_product"      <xsd:complexType
     type="person_develops_product_type"               name="person_develops_product_type">
     minOccurs="0" maxOccurs="unbounded"/>             <xsd:sequence>
   </xsd:sequence>                                       <xsd:element name="idperson"/>
  </xsd:complexType>                                     <xsd:element name="idproduct"/>
 </xsd:element>                                         </xsd:sequence>
                                                      </xsd:complexType>
                                                     </xsd:schema>
```

Fig. 4. XML schema generated by the structure generation algorithm

as *transformation constraints*). With respect to the former, the algorithm adds a key constraint for each UML class. The source and the target of the constraint is the same class. The key constraints for our running example appear in Figure 5 numbered (12), (13) and (14).

The null constraints appear due to the fact that the designer has to specify in the XML schema the information about prohibited null values but this information is not available in the UML schema. XML Schema offers the following three ways of representing null values for an element e: 1) `<e xsi:nil="true"/>`, 2)`<e/>` and 3) the element e is left out. The first one uses the `xsi:nil` attribute of the `XMLSchema-instances` namespace. There are also two ways of representing nulls for an attribute e1: 1) `<e e1="">` and 2) the attribute e1 is left out.

Table 3. Identifiers for our running example

UML element	Identifier
person	idperson attribute of the person element
product	idproduct attribute of the product element
department	iddepartment attribute of the department element
developed	(idperson subelement of the person_develops_product element, idproduct subelement of the person_develops_product element)
workplace	(idperson attribute of the person element, iddepartment attribute of the person element)
code	code subelement of the product element
name	name subelement of the product element
name	name subelement of the department element
name	name subelement of the person element

The structure generation algorithm asks the designer to decide which null values are prohibited for the identifiers of the UML elements. In order to integrate this information in our framework, these constraints are expressed according to our proposed tuples constraint language. Thus, if the `xsi:nil="true"` representation is not allowed, then a constraint of type `not-nillable` must be imposed. If the `<e/>` or `<e e1="">` representations are not allowed, a constraint of type `not-zerolength` must be specified. Finally, if it is not allowed to leave out an attribute or an element, a constraint of type `not-absence` must be imposed. The null constraints are specified for participants in associations and for class attributes. In the first case, the source is the participant class and the target is the role in the association of the other participant. In the second case, the source is the class and the target is the attribute. In Figure 5, we can see an archetypical set of transformation constraints for our running example.

```
12.  (pk,person,person)                18.  (not-absence,product,developer)
13.  (pk,product,product)              19.  (not-nillable,product,developer)
14.  (pk,department,department)        20.  (not-absence,person,developed)
15.  (not-zerolength,department,name)  21.  (not-nillable,person,developed)
16.  (not-absence,department,name)     22.  (not-absence,person,workplace)
17.  (not-nillable,department,name)    23.  (not-zerolength,department,member)
```

Fig. 5. Example of transformation constraints

5   Constraints Generation Algorithm

The constraints generation algorithm embeds constraints in the XML schema and generates XSLT stylesheets to verify constraints which the XML Schema is not able to express. Each stylesheet (see skeleton in Figure 8(a)) includes a condition which evaluates to `true` when the constraint is met. Otherwise, the document will be transformed by the stylesheet into `false`, meaning that the XML document violates the constraint. In Table 4, we can see a sketch of this algorithm which we now describe.

Algorithm description. For each conceptual constraint c, the XML element of the source of c and the identifiers of the components of the target are found. Next, three cases are distinguished.

Case 1. If the constraint c can be expressed as an identity constraint (this happens when the type of the constraint is `unique`, `pk`, `exists` or `isa`) the procedure `writeXMLConstraint` writes the identity constraint by using the skeleton of Figure 6(a) and adds it to the XML schema.

In this skeleton, the type is `unique`, `key` or `keyref`, the name is automatically generated, and the selector is the `sourceelement` previously calculated in the algorithm. There can be several `xsd:field` elements, each one corresponding to one component of the identifier of the target. The `refer` attribute is optional and only appears for keyref constraints. Its value is the name of the primary key referred to by the keyref constraint we are specifying. For example, the constraint (12) of Figure 5 is translated into the identity constraint (b) of Figure 6. The constraints (6) to (9) of Figure 3 and constraints (13) and (14) of Figure 5 are also transformed into identity constraints.

Table 4. Sketch of the constraints generation algorithm

INPUT: XML schema without constraints together with identifiers, and
transformation constraints expressed as tuples
OUTPUT:XML schema with constraints and set of XSLT stylesheets
```
for each conceptual constraint c
```
$sourceelement \leftarrow findElement(c.source)$
$targetidentifier \leftarrow findIdentifier(c.target)$
```
  if c can be expressed as an identity constraint
```
$writeXMLConstraint(c.type, sourceelement, targetidentifier)$
```
  else if c can be expressed as an XML but not identity constraint
```
$complextype \leftarrow findComplexType(c.source)$
$writeXMLConstraint(c.type, complextype, targetidentifier)$
```
  else /*generates XSLT for the constraint*/
```
$sourceidentifier \leftarrow findIdentifier(c.source)$
$condition \leftarrow writeCondition(c.type, sourceidentifier, targetidentifier)$
$writeXSLTTemplate(sourceelement, condition)$
```
  end if
end for
```

Case 2. If c can be expressed as an XML constraint but not as an identity constraint (this happens when the type is `not-nillable` or `not-absence`),
then the complex type associated to the source is found. Next, the procedure
`writeXMLConstraint` writes in the XML schema, by using the attributes `nillable`,
`use`, `minOccurs` or `maxOccurs`, the XML constraint associated to the complex type
previously found. For example, constraints (16) to (22) of Figure 5 are translated
into XML but not identity constraints. The final XML schema for our running
example, once the XML constraints have been added, is shown in Figure 7.

```
<xsd:type name=string refer=keyname>      <xsd:key name="keyperson">
  <xsd:selector xpath=sourceelement />      <xsd:selector xpath="person" />
  <xsd:field xpath=target />                <xsd:field xpath="@idperson" />
</xsd:type>                                 </xsd:key>
                (a)                                        (b)
```

Fig. 6. Template for identity constraints generation and generated constraint

Case 3. If the constraint c can not be expressed as an XML constraint, the
procedure `writeXSLTTemplate` writes the XSLT stylesheet which checks the constraint by using the skeleton of Figure 8(a). In this skeleton, the *sourceelement*
has been previously calculated in the algorithm, the lines 2 to 4 are optional
and their presence depends on the kind of constraint. Basically, they are present
for the `exclusive`, `total`, `subset` and `coexistence` constraints whose source and
target are classes or associations and for `m..n` constraints. Finally, the condition
of the template is determined by the procedure `writeCondition`. This procedure
first determines the elementary conditions for each component of the target and
next substitutes them in the logical formula associated to the type of conceptual constraint (see the types in Table 1). Thus, the logical formula associated

to the total constraint is $c_1 \, or \, c_2 \ldots or \, c_n$ and for the exclusive constraint is $(c_1 \, and \, not c_2 \, and \ldots \, not c_n) \ldots or \, (not \, c_1 \, and \, not \, c_2 \, and \ldots c_n)$. In these formulas, each c_i is an elementary condition.

For example, when applying this procedure to the total constraint of Figure 3, the elementary conditions and the obtained condition can be seen in Figure 8(b). The XSLT stylesheets generated for the total and exclusive constraints of Figure 3 and for the non–zerolength constraint numbered (15) in Figure 5 are shown in Figures 8(b)(c) and (d).

```
<xsd:schema                                    <xsd:complexType name="departmentype">
xmlns:xsd="http://www.w3.org/2001/XMLSchema">    <xsd:sequence>
<!--here comes elements spec. as                   <xsd:element name="name"
   in Figure 4 -->                                  minOccurs="1" maxOccurs="1"
<xsd:key name="keyperson">                           nillable="false"/>
 <xsd:selector xpath="person"/>                  </xsd:sequence>
 <xsd:field xpath="@idperson"/>                  <xsd:attribute name="iddepartment"
</xsd:key>                                         use="required"/>
<!--here comes the rest of identity            </xsd:complexType>
   constraints specification-->                 <xsd:complexType
<xsd:complexType name="persontype">               name="person_develops_product_type">
 <xsd:sequence>                                   <xsd:sequence>
  <xsd:element name="name"                         <xsd:element name="idperson"
 minOccurs="0" maxOccurs="1" nillable="true"/>  minOccurs="1" maxOccurs="1"
 </xsd:sequence>                                     nillable="false"/>
 <xsd:attribute name="idperson"                   <xsd:element name="idproduct"
 use="required"/>                                 minOccurs="1" maxOccurs="1"
 <xsd:attribute name="iddepartment"               nillable="false"/>
 use="required"/>                                 </xsd:sequence>
</xsd:complexType>                              </xsd:complexType>
<!--here comes producttype  spec-->            </xsd:schema>
```

Fig. 7. In bold, some constraints added to the initial XML schema after applying the cases 1 and 2 of the constraints generation algorithm

```
<xsl:template match=sourceelement>     <xsl:template match="root/person">
 <xsl:for-each select=".">              <xsl:for-each select=".">
  <xsl:variable name=v_sourceelement     <xsl:variable name="v_person" select="."/>
    select="."/>                         <xsl:choose>
  <xsl:choose>                            <xsl:when
   <xsl:when test=condition>              test="(/root/person_develops_product/idperson
    true</xsl:when>                           [.=$v_person/@idperson]) or
   <xsl:otherwise>                            ($v_person[@iddepartment!=''])">
    false</xsl:otherwise>                 true</xsl:when>
  </xsl:choose>                          <xsl:otherwise>false</xsl:otherwise>
 </xsl:for-each>                         </xsl:choose>
</xsl:template>     (a)                 </xsl:for-each>
                                        </xsl:template>       (b)

<xsl:template match="root/product">        <xsl:template match="root/department">
 <xsl:choose>                               <xsl:choose>
  <xsl:when test="(code[.!=''] and name[.=''])   <xsl:when test="name[.!='']">
   or (code[.=''] and name[.!=''])">          true</xsl:when>
   true</xsl:when>                            <xsl:otherwise>
  <xsl:otherwise>false</xsl:otherwise>         false</xsl:otherwise>
 </xsl:choose>                                </xsl:choose>
</xsl:template>      (c)                    </xsl:template>    (d)
```

Fig. 8. XSLT template for stylesheets generation and some generated stylesheets

Implementation. We have implemented our approach with Oracle 10g Release 1 and PL/SQL. A PL/SQL procedure generates the XML schema with XML constraints and stylesheets. The XML schema is registered and a new table is created based on this XML schema. When we try to insert a new document into the table or to modify previously existing ones, a trigger is fired which checks the document against the XSLT stylesheets. If the value `false` is returned, the document violates some constraints and the user is informed of the violated constraints. A rollback on the database is done. The DBMS_XMLSCHEMA package has been a handy tool for this task.

6   Related Work

XML Schema does not have enough expressive power to express several constraints frequently used in XML documents. In the literature, several approaches have been proposed in order to overcome this shortcoming. As is pointed out in [3], basically, this issue is addressed in three ways. One option is to increment XML Schema by means of other schema languages. This is the case, for example, with Schematron [9] and SchemaPath [12]. The advantage is that, in general, these languages are relatively simple to learn and use, but the disadvantage is the 'yet another language' problem and that long term support is not guaranteed. Another option is to postpone the verification of the constraints to the final implemented code but the disadvantage is that this choice leads to time–consuming, error–prone tasks so that developers are faced with difficult maintenance issues. The third option is to express additional constraints by means of XSLT stylesheets. In this case, the advantage is that XSLT is a powerful language and that long term support is guaranteed. The disadvantage is that the management is more difficult due to the constraints being specified in separate documents.

Several authors [1,4,10,14] advocate using a conceptual level in order to generate the XML Schema in an automatic way. In this way, the designer is free, to a great extent, of the low-level issues related to the management of the XML-based documents. However, the approaches proposing a conceptual modeling level hardly deal with the specification of conceptual constraints (see for example [4,10,14]). Besides, the approaches that deal with conceptual constraints do not normally give a general solution with regard to the verification of those constraints that cannot be expressed in the chosen schema language (see for example [2]). To our knowledge, [8] is the only one, apart from ours, that proposes a general framework for generating constraints for the XML documents using a conceptual level. The main difference is that in [8] the authors consider it more suitable to increment XML Schema defining a new schema language without suggesting any ways of overcoming the disadvantages that this option entails.

7   Conclusions and Future Work

In the present paper we have described a solution for the validation of XML documents when different integrity constraints must be applied to XML data. This solution is based on the consideration of a conceptual level where the structural and content constraints are specified. In particular, UML and OCL have been used respectively as conceptual modeling language and constraint specification language. Starting from a UML class diagram with OCL annotations, an XML schema is automatically created, and XSLT stylesheets are generated in order to validate those constraints that can not be expressed in XML Schema.

There exist several possibilities for follow–up research. On the one hand, we can explore *extensibility* properties, that is to say, how to include in our approach a mechanism that allows the smooth incorporation of other kinds of integrity constraints. On the other hand, we could investigate the relationships between the evolution of models, in particular the evolution of constraints, and XML. Finally, other more generic implementations, and the possible integration of our approach in existing tools, should be considered.

References

1. M. Bernauer, G. Kappel, G. Kramler, Representing XML Schema in UML - A Comparison of Approaches, in N. Koch, P. Fraternali, M. Wirsing (eds.), ICWE 2004,LNCS 3140, Springer 2004, 440-444.
2. L. Bird, A. Goodchild, T. A. Halpin, Object Role Modelling and XML-Schema, *Conceptual Modeling - ER 2000*, LNCS 1920, 2000, 309–322.
3. R. Costello, Extending XML Schemas, www.xfront.com/ExtendingSchemas.html.
4. R. Conrad, D. Scheffner, J. C. Freytag, XML Conceptual Modeling Using UML, in Alberto H. F. Laender, Stephen W. Liddle, Veda C. Storey (Eds.) *Conceptual Modeling - ER 2000*, LNCS 1920, 2000, 558–571.
5. E. Domínguez, J. Lloret, A. L. Rubio, M. A. Zapata, Elementary translations: the seesaws for achieving traceability between database schemata, in S. Wang et al, (Eds.), *Conceptual modeling for advanced application domains- ER 2004 Workshops*, LNCS 3289, 2004, 377–389.
6. E. Domínguez, J. Lloret, A. L. Rubio, M. A. Zapata, Evolving XML schemas and documents using UML class diagrams, in K. V. Andersen et al, (Eds.), *Database and Expert Systems Applications- DEXA 2005*, LNCS 3588, 343–352
7. J–L Hainaut, J–M Hick, V. Englebert, J. Henrard, D. Roland, Understanding the implementation of ISA relations, in B. Thalheim (ed.), *Conceptual Modeling - ER'96*, LNCS 1157, 42–57
8. J. Hu, L. Tao, An Extensible Constraint Markup Language: Specification, Modeling, and Processing, *XML 2004 Conference*, IDEAlliance 2004.
9. R. Jellife. Schematron, www.ascc.net/xml/resource/schematron/, October 2002.
10. T. Krumbein, T. Kudrass, Rule-Based Generation of XML Schemas from UML Class Diagrams, in Robert Tolksdorf, Rainer Eckstein (Eds.), *Berliner XML Tage 2003*, XML-Clearinghouse 2003, 213–227
11. A. H. F. Laender, M.A. Casanova, A. P. de Carvalho, L. F. G. G. M. Ridolfi, An analysis of sql integrity constraints from an entity-relationship perspective, *Information Systems*, 10:4, 331–358.
12. P. Marinelli, C. S. Coen, F. Vitalli, Schemapath, a minimal extension to xml schema for conditional constraints, in *Proceedings WWW 2004*, 164–174.
13. OMG, *UML 2.0, OCL 2.0 specifications*, available at www.omg.org, 2005.
14. N. Routledge, L. Bird, A. Goodchild, UML and XML schema, in Xiaofang Zhou (Ed.), *Database Technologies 2002, 13th Australasian Database Conference*, 2002.
15. W3C XML Working Group, *Extensible Markup Language (XML) 1.0 (3rd ed), XML Schema Part 1: Structures (2nd ed), XSL Transformations (XSLT) Version 1.0*, available at www.w3.org.

A Novel Clustering-Based Approach to Schema Matching

Jin Pei, Jun Hong, and David Bell

School of Electronics, Electrical Engineering and Computer Science,
Queen's University Belfast, Belfast BT7 1NN, UK
{jpei02, j.hong, da.bell}@qub.ac.uk

Abstract. Schema matching is a critical step in data integration from
multiple heterogeneous data sources. This paper presents a new approach to schema matching, based on two observations. First, it is easier to find attribute correspondences between those schemas that are
contextually similar. Second, the attribute correspondences found between these schemas can be used to help find new attribute correspondences between other schemas. Motivated by these observations, we
propose a novel clustering-based approach to schema matching. First,
we cluster schemas on the basis of their contextual similarity. Second,
we cluster attributes of the schemas that are in the same schema cluster to find attribute correspondences between these schemas. Third, we
cluster attributes across different schema clusters using statistical information gleaned from the existing attribute clusters to find attribute
correspondences between more schemas. We leverage a fast clustering
algorithm, the K-Means algorithm, to the above three clustering tasks.
We have evaluated our approach in the context of integrating information from multiple web interfaces and the results show the effectiveness
of our approach.

1 Introduction

With the dramatic growth of distributed heterogeneous data sources on the Web,
data integration has become a challenging problem. Since databases on the Web
are usually heterogeneous and accessed via Web interfaces only, it is essential to
reconcile heterogeneous semantics among query interfaces before querying data
from the underlying databases. The process of finding attribute correspondences
between schemas are usually called schema matching.

While it has been extensively studied in recent years [1,2,3,4,5,6,7,8], schema
matching remains a difficult problem due to various syntactic representations
of attributes and the diversity of schema structures. Current solutions can be
grouped into two major types: pair-wise matching [1,5,6] and holistic matching
[2,3,4,7,8]. Traditionally, schema matching has been done by finding pair-wise
attribute correspondences between two schemas, which typically uses linguistic information about attributes themselves. Pair-wise matching cannot find attribute correspondences without using auxiliary information such as dictionaries
or thesauri. Holistic matching, on the other hand, matches multiple schemas at

T. Yakhno and E. Neuhold (Eds.): ADVIS 2006, LNCS 4243, pp. 60–69, 2006.

the same time to find attribute correspondences among all the schemas at once. While holistic schema matching benefits from a large quantity of data, it also suffers from noisy data. In this paper, we aim to address this issue.

This paper proposes a novel, holistic approach to schema matching across Web interfaces. Our approach is based on two observations. First, attributes are more likely to be matched if their schemas are contextually similar. Second, the attribute correspondences found between these schemas can be used to help find new attribute correspondences between other schemas. These observations motivate us to develop a novel three-step clustering approach to schema matching. First, we cluster schemas on the basis of their contextual similarity. Second, we cluster attributes in each schema cluster. After these attribute correspondences have been found, some knowledge such as important words can be gleaned and is used to find attribute correspondences across different schema clusters.

Current clustering-based holistic approaches to schema matching [3,7] commonly use the agglomerative clustering algorithm [9]. We propose instead to use a much faster and effective clustering algorithm, the incremental K-Means algorithm [10].

Motivating Example: Suppose there are 3 schemas in the Books domain to be matched:

S_1: {title}, {category}, {author}
S_2: {title name}, {category of book}, {author}
S_3: {title of book}, {keyword}

In the current clustering-based approach [3,7], attributes S_3.{title of book} and S_2.{category of book} will be matched due to their higher linguistic similarity, which is obviously wrong. The main reason for this is that no background knowledge is used to infer which term is more important in a specific domain. In our approach, we first cluster schemas according to their contextual similarity. Schemas S_1, S_2 and S_3 are put into two clusters: {S_1,S_2} ,{S_3}. We then cluster the attributes in each schema cluster. In the first schema cluster {S_1, S_2}, we cluster all the attributes into three attribute clusters which are further abstracted as three candidate concepts C_1, C_2 and C_3:

C_1: {title:2, name:1} = {title, title name}
C_2: {category:2, of:1, book:1} = {category, category of book}
C_3: {author:2} = {author, author}

where we use the expression, term:number (e.g. title:2), to represent the frequency of a term in the attribute cluster. Similarly, in the second schema cluster {S_3}, the attributes are clustered into two attribute clusters and further abstracted as two candidate concepts C_4 and C_5:

C_4: {title:1, of:1, book:1} = {title of book}; C_5: {keyword:1} = {keyword}

As shown above, some knowledge can be gleaned from these candidate concepts (e.g., important terms such as title, category) that will be used in the next step. The next step is concept clustering: We cluster candidate concepts C_1-C_5 into four final concepts:

FC_1: {**title**:3, **name**:1, **of** :1,**book**:1} = {{**title**:2, **name**:1}, {**title**:1, **of**:1, **book**:1}; FC_2: {**category**:2, **of**:1, **book**:1}; FC_3: {**author**:2}; FC_4: {**keyword**:1}.

In FC_1, attribute S_3.{**title of book**} has been matched to the correct attributes S_1.{**title**} and S_2.{**title name**} rather than S_2.{**category of book**}.

The rest of the paper is organized as follows. Section 2 describes our extended incremental K-Means algorithm. Section 3 proposes a stability measure to estimate the best K number of clusters. Section 4 describes our experiments. Section 5 discusses related work, and Section 6 discusses some open issues and concludes the paper.

2   Clustering Algorithms

In this section, we describe the K-Means algorithm and its use in the schema matching problem.

2.1   Preliminary

A clustering-based approach to schema matching can be treated as a special case of document clustering. A document can be seen as a bag of words and represented by a TFIDF [11] weighting vector d:

$$d = \{tf_1 * \log(\frac{N}{df_1}), \dots, tf_n * \log(\frac{N}{df_n})\} \tag{1}$$

where tf_i is the frequency of the ith term in the document, df_i is the frequency of the ith term in the collection of documents and N is the number of documents in the collection. The *inverse document frequency*(IDF) of the term, denoted by $log(\frac{N}{df_i})$ discounts the importance of a term which appears frequently in many documents. Finally, in order to handle documents of different lengths, the vector is normalized as unit length.

While the basic K-means is often considered as a poor-quality clustering approach compared with hierarchical clustering. it has been demonstrated that the incremental K-means algorithm has better quality in document clustering [12]. The incremental K-Means assumes that each cluster can be represented by a center point. A center point is called the centroid which is the mean point of the points in the cluster. In document clustering, a centroid vector C for a set of documents D is defined as follows:

$$C = \frac{1}{|D|} \sum_{d \in D} d \tag{2}$$

where C is the average weights of terms in D and $|D|$ is the number of documents in D. Initially K points are selected as centroids, and each of other points is assigned to a cluster whose centroid is the closest to the point. After a point is assigned to its cluster, the centroids will be computed. This continues until the centroids do not change any more.

2.2   Schema Clustering

Schema clustering is treated as a special case of document clusteirng. Each schema consists of a schema name and a set of attributes. Each attribute has two mandatory properties: *name* and *data type* and an optional property: *text description* (also called label in the Web interface). While a database normally consists of more than one relation, a database on the Web is often represented by a Web interface. Therefore, the schema name of a Web interface is not important. We assume that the schema of a Web interface consists of a set of attributes only. We treat the *names* and *text descriptions* of attributes in a schema as a bag of words and represent the schema using the weighting vector defined in Equation 1), where tf_i is the frequency of the ith term in the schema, df_i is the frequency of the ith term in the collection of schemas and N is the number of schemas. Schema clustering is then done using the incremental K-Means. [10]

2.3   Attribute/Concept Clustering

Attribute clustering can also be treated as a special case of document clustering. Again we use Equation 1) to represent an attribute, where tf_i is the frequency of ith term in the attribute, df_i is the frequency of ith term in the set of attributes in a schema cluster and N is the number of attributes in the schema cluster. Figure 1 shows the attribute clustering algorithm. The following are taken as input: a set of attributes A in a schema cluster, the criterion function I_a and a threshold τ_a. Each attribute is represented by a TFIDF weighting vector plus its data type. Unlike the traditional incremental K-Means algorithm (e.g. the one used for schema clustering in the previous section), the number of attribute clusters K is not fixed in the attribute clustering algorithm. In our approach, we first choose the attributes of a schema that has the largest number of attributes in the schema cluster as the initial seeds of the algorithm.

As shown in Figure 1, before assigning an attribute to a cluster, we compute the similarity between the attribute and each centroid using the criterion function I_a. If no similarity is above threshold τ_a, we create a new cluster for the attribute. Otherwise, we assign the attribute, denoted by a, to the closest cluster c_2. If another attribute b that is in the same schema as attribute a is already in cluster c_2, we assign b to the cluster c_1 which attribute a is previously in.

The criterion function I_a is shown in Figure 2. It takes the following as input: attribute **a**, cluster **c** and a weighting parameter ω_c. In Step 1 the **DataType-Compatible** function is used to check the compatibility of the data types of attribute **a** and cluster **c**. In schema matching, data types are usually considered as constraints on semantics. In our approach, the attributes in the same cluster have the same data type unless the data type of an attribute is **any**. In our current implementation, there are only the following data types: **any, string, date, year, month, day, time, integer**. We assume that two attributes of a

Attribute Clustering(A, I_a, τ_a)
1). Seed Selection: Select attributes from A, whose schema has the largest
   number of attributes in a schema cluster, as centroids.
2). Randomly choose each attribute a from A
   2.1) Compute the similarity between a and each centroid using I_a.
   2.2) If no similarity between a and the centroid is above threshold τ_a
        then
   2.3) create a new cluster and assign attribute a as the centroid of the cluster
        else
   2.4) a).Assign attribute a, where a belongs to cluster c_1, to cluster c_2
             whose centroid has the highest similarity with a.
        b). If attribute $b \in c_2$, where b and a are in the same schema
             then assign b to cluster c_1.
        c). Re-compute the centroids.
3). Repeat Step 2) until attribute clusters do not change any more.
4). return K attribute clusters.

Fig. 1. The Attribute Clustering Algorithm

schema cannot be in the same cluster. When two attributes in the same schema
are in conflict in attribute clustering, the one with the higher similarity prevails.
Steps 2) and 3) show how this assumption is applied. The similarity function is
based on the Cosine [11] function used in information retrieval.

Criterion Function $I_a(a, c, \omega_c)$
1). If $DataTypeCompatible(a, c)$ is false, then return 0;
2). If there exists $b \in c$, where b is in the same schema as a, then
3).   if a has not been assigned to any cluster before,then return 0.
       else if $(cos(b, c) \geq cos(a, c))$, then return 0.
       else return $\omega_c * cos(a, c)$
4). else return $\omega_c * cos(a, c)$.

Fig. 2. Criterion Function I_a

2.4   Concept Clustering

Each attribute cluster C is abstracted as a candidate concept which is represented as follows:

$$c = \{\sum_{a \in C} tf_{a1} * \log(\frac{N}{df_{a1}}), \dots, \sum_{a \in C} tf_{an} * \log(\frac{N}{df_{an}})\} \tag{3}$$

where $\sum_{a \in C} tf_i$ is the sum of the frequency of the ith term in cluster C, N
is the number of attribute clusters in all the schema clusters, and df_i is the
number of attribute clusters in which the ith term appears. We treat candidate
concepts as generalized attributes and schema clusters as generalized schema.
We then make use of the same algorithm for *attribute clustering* (Figure 2) to
cluster candidate concepts. To some extent, the concept vector can show not only

important terms, but also noisy terms. Suppose a candidate concept consists of N attributes. When N becomes larger, the dimension of the concept vector might also become larger due to various noisy data. To solve this problem, we remove those entries in the concept vector whose terms appear infrequently. Suppose x_i is the ith entry of concept C. If the total number of attributes in C is N, and the term frequency of x_i is n, we remove x_i when $\frac{n}{N} < \tau_{filter}$. In our implementation, we set $\tau_{filter} = 0.2$.

3   Cross Validation

In schema clustering, we want schemas in each cluster to have high contextual similarity. On the other hand, if contextual similarity between schemas is too high, schema clusters may become too small, which affects attribute/concept clustering. Since holistic matching uses machine learning techniques, it relies on large data sets to discover useful patterns. Generally speaking, we try to make sure that each cluster has high contextual similarity and contains sufficient data. How to decide the specific number of schema clusters for the data sets of each domain becomes an issue. Currently, cross validation is usually used to validate the clustering results of data analysis [13,14], which we use to estimate the best number of clusters. The assumption is that if the number of clusters is correct, then the cluster structure is stable. In our approach, we use the same mechanism as [14] to estimate the number of schema clusters.

Suppose that there are M schemas that have N attributes in total. A clustering result can be represented in the form of an $N \times N$ matrix, denoted by $A(i,j)(1 \leq i \leq N, 1 \leq j \leq N)$, where $A(i,j)=1$ if attributes i and j are in the same cluster; $A(i,j)=0$ otherwise. In order to evaluate the clustering result of k schema clsuters, we make use of the re-sampling method to randomly select subsets of schemas and use the same clustering approach on each subset of schemas to obtain a $N' \times N'(N' < N)$ matrix. If a high proportion of attribute pairs are in the same cluster in both the whole set of schemas and each subset of schemas, we consider that the clustering result from k schema clusters is highly stable. We use the criterion function below [14] to measure the stability of the clustering result of k schema clusters.

$$M_k(A^{\bar{u}}, A) = \frac{1}{r} \sum_{t=1}^{r} \frac{\sum_{i,j}(1\{A_{i,j}^{u_t} = A_{i,j} = 1, s_i \in S^{u_t}, s_j \in S^{u_t}\})}{\sum_{i,j}(1\{A_{i,j} = 1, s_i \in S^{u_t}, s_j \in S^{u_t}\})} \qquad (4)$$

where S_{u_t} is a subset of schemas in the tth re-sampling. The criterion function M_k measures the average proportion of attribute pairs in each cluster computed on S, which are also in the same cluster on $S_{u_t}(t = 1, 2, r)$ using k schema clusters.

4   Experiments

In this section we describe the experiments that we have carried out to evaluate our clustering-based schema matching. We also show the effectiveness of using weight parameter ω_c in attribute/concept clustering. Finally, we describe the experiments that show the usefulness of cross validation.

We use 4 Web interface domains from the ICQ Query Interface data sets [15]: Airfare, Automobile, Books and Jobs. Each domain contains 20 Web interface schemas. For each Web interface schema, we preprocess its attributes. First, we identify the data type of each attribute by its value. Second, we tokenize the *attribute name* and *text description* of each attribute into a bag of terms. We then do some normailization such as removing stop words, lowercasing each term and stemming terms using the potter algorithm.

The performance of our clustering-based approach to schema matching is evaluated by three common measures: **Precision**, **Recall** and **F-measure** [3,4,1]. **Precision** is the ratio of the number of correct matches to the number of correct and incorrect matches. **Recall** is the ratio of the number of correct matches to the total number of real matches. **F-measure** F is a function of the Precision p and Recall r defined as follows: $F = \frac{2pr}{p+r}$. Note that we treat 1:m mappings as m matches. For example,the matches between {passenger} and {adult, children, infant, senior} count as 4 correspondences.

4.1   Experimental Results

We now describe the experimental results in the above four domains. In each domain, we evaluate two contributions of this paper: the effectiveness of the schema clustering in our approach, and how well cross validation can be used to estimate the best number of schema clusters.

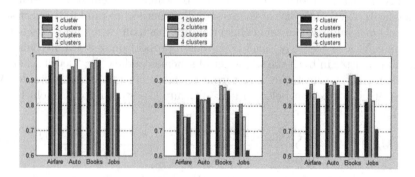

Fig. 3. Precision, Recall and F-Measure in Four Domains

First, the effectiveness of our schema clustering is shown in Figure 3. Since there are only 20 data sets in each domain, in order to make sure that each schema cluster has sufficient data instances, we require that the number of schema clusters k is not higher than 4. When k is 1, no schema clustering takes place. As shown in Figure 3, schema clustering results in better performance. In each domain, 2 clusters or 3 clusters have better F-Measures than 1 cluster (no schema clustering). The relatively poor performance of 4 clusters might be due to lack of enough data sets.

Second, we show how well cross validation can be used to estimate the number of schema clusters. In Table 1, it is shown that the number of schema clusters, which leads to the best clustering result, can be correctly identified using the cross validation techniques in three domains (Airfare, Auto, Jobs). While it fails to find the correct number of schema clusters in the Books domain, the F-Measure that is based on the estimated number of schema clusters is very close to the best F-Measure. Figure 4 shows how stability measure M_k is used for estimating the number of schema clusters. Here we set $f_1=0.8, r=20$.

Table 1. Comparison of Estimated Numbers of Schema Clusters with Correct Number of Schema Clusters

Domain	Correct No. of Schema Clusters	Estimated No. of Schema Clusters
Airfare	2	2
Auto	3	3
Books	3	2
Jobs	2	2

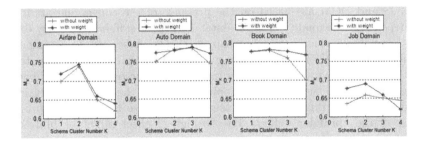

Fig. 4. Relationship between M_k and the Estimated Numbers of Schema Clusters

Finally, we compared our approach (CP_{kmean}) with an existing clustering-based approach (CP_{hac})[3] which uses the same data sets and performance measures (e.g. Precision, Recall and F-Measure). While [3] utilizes domain values to improve clustering results, our approach does not since it is hard to capture data instances in most cases. In our experiment, we assume that domain values

Table 2. The Performance Comparison of Schema Matching

Domain	Airfare			Auto			Books			Jobs		
	Prec	Rec	F	Prec	Rec	F	Prec	Rec	F	Prec	Rec	F
CP_{kmean}	0.99	0.804	0.887	0.983	0.825	0.897	0.971	0.879	0.922	0.945	0.808	0.871
CP_{hac}	0.822	0.834	0.828	0.901	0.888	0.895	0.977	0.868	0.919	0.791	0.747	0.768

are not available. Table 2 shows the comparison of three measures in four domains. The three measures of our approach CP_{kmean} are based on the estimated number of schema clusters which is obtained by cross validation. In Table 2, it is shown that our approach achieves high precision. The precision of CP_{kmean} increases in three domains (Airfare, Auto, Jobs) with the largest increase 19.4% in the Jobs domain. While Recall is lower in the Airfare and Auto domain, the F Measure of CP_{kmean} is still higher than that of CP_{hac}.

5   Related Work

While there has been a lot of work on schema matching, most work so far has been focused on pair-wise schema matching [1,5,6] . Recently, holistic schema matching [2,3,4,7] has received much attention due to its effectiveness in exploring the contextual information and its scalability.

MGS [4] and DCM [2] rely on the distribution of attributes rather than linguistic or domain information. Superior to the other schema matching approaches, these approaches can discover synonyms only by analyzing the distribution of attributes in the given schemas. DCM [2] can even discover m:n complex mappings. However, they work well only when enough evidence can be observed. That is, only those attributes that appear frequently can be matched. Second, both MGS and DCM are based on the presence of the converging attributes which depend on the quality of input data. That is, it suffers from noisy data.

Another holistic schema matching approach [3], makes use of common Information Retrieval (IR) techniques (e.g. Cosine Function [11]) to compute the linguistic similarity between attributes. Similar to some pair-wise matching approaches that re-use the existing mappings, it takes the "bridging" effect by leveraging the clustering algorithm. Nevertheless, there is a common problem with use of the "bridging" effect. The "bridging" effect might be blurred by "noise".

WISE [7] proposes a clustering and weight-based two-step method to find attribute correspondences, which is similar to our approach. However, the performance of WISE mainly relies on the quality of input data (e.g., the percentage of exact attribute names) and manual construction of semantic relationships such as synonymy, hypernymy, meronymy and so on.

Corpus-based schema matching [8] makes use of a corpus of schemas as a training set to improve future matching. Similar to our approach, [8] can learn knowledge from past results to improve schema matching, but it uses the supervised learning algorithm while our approach is based on the unsupervised algorithm.

6   Conclusions

We have presented a novel clustering-based approach to schema matching which achieves high accuracy across different domains. Rather than matching all attributes at once, our approach matches those attributes which are most likely to be matched first and glean some knowledge from these matches for further matching. Our experimental results show the effectiveness of our approach. Furthermore, we leverage a popular clustering algorithm, the K-Means algorithm to schema matching and show its good performance in experiments. K-Means is a linear-time clustering algorithm and much useful for large-scale schema matching.

Despite of its novelty and efficiency, our approach still has some limitations. First, our approach currently focuses on 1:1 mappings only. While our approach can integrate with DCM [2] and [3] to find 1:m mappings, we would like to extend our approach to solve this problem in the future. Our approach only matches flat schemas such as Web interfaces. In future work, we plan to extend our approach to match structured schemas such as XML files.

References

1. Melnik, S., Garcia-Molina, H., Rahm, E.: Similarity flooding: A versatile graph matching algorithm and its application to schema matching. In: ICDE '02, Washington, DC, USA, IEEE Computer Society (2002) 117–128
2. He, B., K.Chang, Han, J.: Discovering complex matchings across web query interfaces: a correlation mining approach. In: KDD'04, ACM Press (2004) 148–157
3. Wu, W., Yu, C., Doan, A., Meng, W.: An interactive clustering-based approach to integrating source query interfaces on the deep web. In: SIGMOD '04, New York, NY, USA, ACM Press (2004) 95–106
4. He, B., Chang, K.: Statistical schema matching across web query interfaces. In: SIGMOD '03:, New York, NY, USA, ACM Press (2003) 217–228
5. Do, H., Rahm, E.: Coma - a system for flexible combination of schema matching approaches. In: VLDB'02, HongKong (2002)
6. Rahm, E., Bernstein, P.A.: A survey of approaches to automatic schema matching. VLDB jounal **10** (2001) 334–350
7. He, H., Meng, W., Yu, C.T., Wu, Z.: Wise-integrator: An automatic integrator of web search interfaces for ecommerce. In: VLDB'03. (2003) 357–268
8. Madhavan, J., Bernstein, P., Doan, A., Halevy, A.: Corpus-based schema matching. In: ICDE'05. (2005)
9. L.Kaufman, P.Rousseeuw: Finding Groups in Data: An Ingroduction to Cluster Analysis. John Wiley & Sons (1990)
10. Larsen, B., Aone, C.: Fast and effective text mining using linear-time document clustering. In: KDD '99, New York, NY, USA, ACM Press (1999) 16–22
11. G.Salton, M.McGill: Introduction to Modern Information Retrieval. McCraw-Hill, New York,USA (1983)
12. Steinbach, M., Karypis, G., Kumar, V.: A comparison of document clustering techniques. In: In KDD Workshop on Text Mining. (2000)
13. T.Lange, Roth, V., Braun, M.L., Buhmann, J.: Stability-based validation of clustering solutions. Neural Computation **16** (2004) 1299–1323
14. Levine, E, E.: Resampling method for unsupervised estimation of cluster validity. Neural Computation **13** (2001) 2573–2593
15. UIUC: (Icq datasets:http://metaquerier.cs.uiuc.edu/repository/datasets/icq/index.html)

BFPkNN: An Efficient k-Nearest-Neighbor Search Algorithm for Historical Moving Object Trajectories

Yunjun Gao, Chun Li, Gencai Chen, Ling Chen,
Xianta Jiang, and Chun Chen

College of Computer Science, Zhejiang University, Hangzhou 310027, P.R. China
{gaoyj, lichun, chengc, lingchen, jxt, chenc}@cs.zju.edu.cn

Abstract. This paper studies k-nearest-neighbor (kNN) search on R-tree-based structures storing historical information about trajectories. We develop BFPkNN, an efficient best-first based algorithm for handling kNN search with arbitrary values of k, which is I/O optimal, i.e., it performs a single access only to those qualifying nodes that may contain the final result. Furthermore, in order to save memory space consumption and reduce CPU overhead further, several effective pruning heuristics are also proposed. Finally, extensive experiments with synthetic and real datasets show that BFPkNN outperforms its competitor significantly in both efficiency and scalability in all cases.

1   Introduction

With the rapid growth of wireless communication, mobile computing, and positioning technologies, it has become possible to model, index and query the trajectories of moving objects in real life. Therein, a useful type of query is the so-called k-Nearest-Neighbor (kNN) search, which retrieves the k moving objects' trajectories in the database that are closest to a given query object q. For instance, *"find the 3 nearest ambulances to the scene of the accident in the time interval of $[t_1, t_2]$ before and after the accident, suppose that the trajectories of the ambulances are known in advance"*. Figure 1 illustrates this case in 3-dimensional space (two dimensions for spatial positions, and one for time). $\{Tr_1, Tr_2, Tr_4\}$ (specified thick line) is the 3 nearest neighbors (NNs) of Q_1.

kNN search is one of the most important operations in spatial and spatio-temporal databases, and has received considerable attention in the database community [2,4,5,7,8,9,10,13,14,15,16,19,20]. However, there is little prior work on kNN queries for moving object trajectories so far. To the best of our knowledge, only one work that has explored algorithms for this topic is done in [5]. The authors of [5] employ a depth-first (DF) retrieval paradigm [13] on dataset indexed by TB-tree [12] that stores historical trajectories of moving objects to deal with kNN retrieval. As known, however, DF traversal induces a backtracking operation which results in reaccessing some nodes that were visited before. Hence, the number of node accesses incurring in the algorithms of [5] is large. This means that the I/O overhead is high, and the CPU cost is also expensive accordingly.

T. Yakhno and E. Neuhold (Eds.): ADVIS 2006, LNCS 4243, pp. 70–79, 2006.

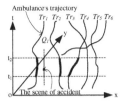

Fig. 1. *k*NN search over moving object trajectories

To address the above problem, in this paper, we investigate *k*NN search on R-tree-based structures storing historical information about moving object trajectories such as 3DR-tree [18], STR-tree [12], TB-tree [12], and SETI [3]. Specifically, using best-first (BF) traversal [7], an algorithm, called BFP*k*NN, is presented for the processing of *k*NN retrieval with arbitrary values of *k*. Notice that the case of 1NN is treated as a special case of *k*NN queries. BFP*k*NN is I/O optimal, i.e., it performs a single access only to those qualifying node entries that may contain the final result. Additionally, since the performance of BF algorithm mainly depends on the size of the priority queue kept by it, we also develop several effective pruning heuristics for discarding the non-qualifying entries in order to save memory space consumption (i.e., gain less queue length) and reduce CPU overhead further (i.e., capture less CPU time). Finally, extensive experimental evaluation with real and synthetic datasets confirms that BFP*k*NN outperforms its competitor significantly in terms of both efficiency and scalability under all cases. In particular, BFP*k*NN accesses fewer nodes and expends less CPU cost than Point*k*NNSearch proposed in [5].

The rest of the paper is organized as follows. Section 2 surveys the related work, focusing on indexing of moving object trajectories and *k*NN search in spatial and spatio-temporal databases. Section 3 presents BFP*k*NN, together with some pruning heuristics and a proof of its I/O optimality. Section 4 experimentally evaluates BFP*k*NN, comparing it with Point*k*NNSearch under a variety of settings. Section 5 concludes the paper with some directions for future work.

2 Related Work

2.1 Indexing of Moving Object Trajectories

One area with related work concerns indexing of moving object trajectories. The trajectory of a moving object is the path taken by it across time. Therefore, trajectories can be considered as two (*x*-*y* plane) or three (*x*-*y*-*z* plane) dimensional time slice data. Towards the existing access methods for moving object trajectories, we are only focus on R-tree-based structures storing historical information about trajectories such as 3DR-tree [18], STR-tree [12], TB-tree [12], and SETI [3]. Although the proposed algorithm in this paper can be used with any above access approach, we assume that the dataset is indexed by a TB-tree due to its high efficiency of trajectory-based queries. Next, we outline this tree structure.

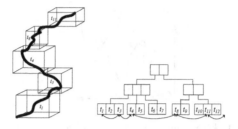

Fig. 2. Example of the TB-tree structure

TB-tree aims for strict moving object trajectories preservation. Thus, each leaf node in the tree only contains segments belonging to the same trajectory, and is of the form $(id, MBB, Orientation)$, where id is the identifier of the 3-dimensional (3D) trajectory segment (handling time as one dimension), MBB denotes the Minimum Bounding Box of the 3D line segment, and $Orientation$ whose value varies between 1 and 4 specifies how the 3D line segment is enclosed inside the MBB. All leaf nodes containing the same trajectory segments are connected by the double linked list. This preserves trajectory evolution and greatly improves the performance of trajectory-based query processing. Figure 2 shows a part of the TB-tree structure and a trajectory illustrating the overall data structure. Note that the trajectory is plotted by a thick line fragmented across five nodes specified t_1, t_3, etc.

2.2 *k*NN Search in Spatial and Spatio-temporal Databases

Another area with related work is that of kNN search in spatial and spatio-temporal databases. In the last decade, a large number of kNN query techniques have been proposed in the database literature [2,4,5,7,8,9,10,13,14,15,16,19,20]. We categorize these methods in three types. The first one involves kNN retrieval over static query and static data objects [4,7,13]. The existing approaches thereinto follow either depth-first [4,13] or best-first [7] traversal paradigm. The second category deals with kNN queries in the settings of moving query and static data objects, referred to as CNN [14,15]. Specifically, the first algorithm for CNN query, proposed in [14], employs a periodical sampling technique to compute the result. Later, [15] presents CNN query processing algorithms using R-trees [1,6] as the underlying data structure that avoid the pitfalls of previous algorithms, namely the false misses and the high query cost. The last classification includes kNN search on moving query and moving data objects [2,8,9,10,16,19,20]. Specifically, [2] develops an algorithm to answer NN retrieval for continuously moving points. [16] proposes a technique, termed *time-parameterized* queries, which can be applied with mobile queries, mobile objects or both, given an appropriate indexing structure. [8] investigates the problem of continuous kNN queries for continuously moving points, suppose that the updates which change the functions describing the motions of the points are allowed. Recently, [9,10,19,20] study the problem of the CNN monitoring in the either centralized [9,19,20] or distributed [10] settings.

3 BFPkNN

3.1 Pruning Heuristics

Unlike the algorithms of [5], BFPkNN uses a BF traversal on the TB-tree [12] structure to process the kNN search over moving object trajectories. As pointed out in [7], BF can incrementally return result, i.e., it reports the NNs of a given query object q in ascending order of their distances from q. Although the I/O overhead (i.e., the number of node accesses) of BF is small, its running time relies on the size of the priority queue (in this paper we use heap H) maintained by BF. In particular, once H becomes very large, both main-memory consumption and CPU cost are high. Intuitively, the less the memory space requires, the more scalable the algorithm is. Based on this observation, it may be helpful to prevent the non-qualifying entries that do not contribute to the final result from being en-heaped. Fortunately, we can achieve this target, using several effective pruning heuristics that are inspired by the analysis of the TB-tree's feature and the BF processing approach. Then, we discuss them in detail.

Recall that TB-tree considers time as one dimension in addition to another two spatial dimensions. Thus, kNN search for moving object trajectories has to take some time interval into account. If the specified query time extent is $[T_{qs}, T_{qe}]$, any entry whose lifetime does not drop into $[T_{qs}, T_{qe}]$, i.e., either smaller than T_{qs} or greater than T_{qe}, should be excluded from H. This also means that only those entries whose lifetime partially or completely overlaps $[T_{qs}, T_{qe}]$ need to be en-heaped there, since they may contain the final outcome. Continuing the example of Figure 1, for instance, trajectory Tr_6 can be removed safely as its lifetime does not across $[t_1, t_2]$. But the remainder including Tr_1 to Tr_5 have to be visited because they may contain result, e.g., $\{Tr_1, Tr_2, Tr_4\}$ is 3 NNs of Q_1. To summarize the above discussion, we present the first pruning heuristic as follows.

Heuristic 1. *Given a query time interval $[T_{qs}, T_{qe}]$, the qualifying entries only if their lifetime partially or fully falls into $[T_{qs}, T_{qe}]$, otherwise, they are unnecessary ones and need not to be inserted into heap.*

By applying heuristic 1 to kNN query processing, the search space can be decreased. However, further pruning can be achieved yet. Again review the feature of TB-tree, each leaf node in TB-tree contains only segments that belong to the same trajectory. This implies that if and only if one identifier of trajectory (represented as id) is enclosed in a leaf node. Furthermore, kNN retrieval on moving object trajectories actually returns k different trajectories' identifiers (specified ids) that are closest to q, together with their distances to q. Based on this observation, during the processing of kNN search, we can pick only the entry Ery with the minimum distance from q in a leaf node E retrieved currently and insert it into H, whereas prune any other entries in E. Heuristic 2 implements this pruning resulting in the less main-memory consumption (i.e., heap size). Although heuristic 2 can discard more unnecessary entries, it also incurs some CPU overhead than heuristic 1, as it requires computing the distance from q to each entry in a leaf node. Hence, it is applied only for entries that satisfy the first heuristic.

Heuristic 2. *Given a query object q and a leaf node E, the entry in E with the smallest distance from q is a qualifying one and requires en-heaping there, but the remaining ones in E can be pruned instantly.*

When a kNN query algorithm encounters an intermediate (i.e., non-leaf) node N, there are two possible operations. The first one is that the algorithm exhaustively scans the child nodes in N. The other one is that it does not access all child nodes of N, as opposed to visiting only the qualifying ones that may contain the final result. For the two cases, the latter over the former is that it avoids accessing nodes, if they cannot contain qualifying nodes. The problem is now how to discriminate the non-qualifying nodes in N. Our solution is to introduce $kPruneDist$ metric to determine and prune those unnecessary nodes, assuming that $kPruneDist$ denotes the current smallest $maxdist$ from q guaranteeing that it covers at least k ids. Specifically, let N_i be any child node in N. Then, N_i is a non-qualifying one if $mindist(N_i, q) > kPruneDist$ holds. In contrast, if $mindist(N_i, q) \leq kPruneDist$ holds, the node N_i is a qualifying one and has to be visited later. Here and now, the problem is transformed to how to compute the value of $kPruneDist$. Let us proceed to explain it below.

Assume that, without loss of generality, we want to find k NNs of q. Let N be a non-leaf node and $\{N_1, N_2, \ldots, N_i\}$ the child nodes in N. $S = \{N'_1, N'_2, \ldots, N'_i\}$, a counterpart of $\{N_1, N_2, \ldots, N_i\}$, is sorted in ascending order of their $maxdist$, i.e., $maxdist(N'_1, q) \leq maxdist(N'_2, q) \leq \ldots \leq maxdist(N'_i, q)$. Then $kPruneDist$ can be defined as:

$$kPruneDist = maxdist(N'_j, q), N'_j \in S \qquad (1)$$

such that $Count(id(N'_1) \bigcup id(N'_2) \bigcup \cdots \bigcup id(N'_{j-1})) < k$, and $Count(id(N'_1) \bigcup id(N'_2) \bigcup \cdots \bigcup id(N'_{j-1}) \bigcup id(N'_j)) \geq k$, where $id(N')$ is a set of ids contained in node N', $count()$ returns the number of different ids. Noted that $mindist$ and $maxdist$ metrics can be computed as [11,13]. Also note that, the heuristic 3 is also applied only for entries that meet the heuristic 1.

Heuristic 3. *Let q be a query object, N an intermediate node, and N_i any child node in N. Then, N_i is a qualifying node if and only if $mindist(N_i, q) \leq kPruneDist$, in which $mindist(N_i, q)$ specifies the minimum distance between the MBB of Ni and q, and $kPruneDist$ is the smallest $maxdist$ from q ensuring that it contains at least k moving object trajectories.*

3.2 Algorithm Description

BFPkNN implements a best-first traversal that follows the entry with the minimum distance among all those visited. To achieve this goal, it keeps a heap containing the candidate entries and their smallest distances from the query object, sorted in ascending order of their $mindist$. At the same time, to avoid suffering from buffer trashing if the heap becomes larger than the available memory, we also enable several effective pruning heuristics (discussed in Section 3.1) to discard the non-qualifying entries.

```
Algorithm BFPkNN (TB-tree R, 2D query point Q, time period Q_per, kNNcount k)
/* Rslt stores the final k NNs of Q; NearestE denotes the entry with the minimal distance from Q in a leaf
node; minhp and maxhp sort all entries in ascending order of their Mindist and Maxdist, respectively. */
1.   Create and initialize heaps hp, maxhp, and minhp
2.   Insert all entries of the root R into hp
3.   Do While hp.count > 0
4.      De-heap top entry E in hp
5.      If E is an actual entry of trajectory segment and its id is not in Rslt then
6.         If Rslt.count < k then
7.            Insert E as a NN of Q into Rslt
8.         Else   // Report the final k NNs of Q
9.            Return Rslt
10.        Endif
11.     ElseIf E is a leaf node
12.        MinimalDist = ∞
13.        For Each entry e in E
14.           If Q_per overlaps (e.t_s, e.t_e) then    // e is partially or fully inside Q_per
15.              ne = Interpolate (e, Max (Q_per, t_s, e.t_s), Min (Q_per.t_e, e.t_e))
16.              Dist = Euclidean_Dist_2D (Q, ne)
17.              If Dist < MinimalDist then
18.                 MinimalDist = Dist
19.                 NearestE = ne
20.              Endif
21.           Endif
22.        Next
23.        Insert NearestE as a qualifying entry into hp
24.     Else   // E is an intermediate (i.e., non-leaf) node
25.        Initialize heaps maxhp and minhp
26.        For Each entry e in E
27.           If Q_per overlaps (e.t_s, e.t_e) then
28.              MaxDistE = Maxdist (Q, e)
29.              MinDistE = Mindist (Q, e)
30.              Insert e into minhp and maxhp, respectively
31.           Endif
32.        Next
33.        Find the minimal kPruneDist in maxhp ensuring that it covers at least k trajectories
34.        Insert all the entries in minhp whose Mindist from Q is not larger than kPruneDist into hp
35.     Endif
36. Loop
37. Return Rslt   // Report the final k NNs of Q
End BFPkNN
```

Fig. 3. The BFPkNN Algorithm

The pseudo-code of BFPkNN algorithm is shown in Figure 3. It takes TB-tree R, 2D query point Q, query time extent Q_{per}, and an integer value k as inputs, and finds the k NNs of Q in R with respect to Q_{per}. BFPkNN starts by inserting the root entries (line 2) in heap hp constructed and initialized in line 1. Then, at each step, it visits the entry in hp with the minimum $mindist$. When the top entry E retrieved in hp is an actual entry of trajectory segment and its id is not contained in $Rslt$ storing the final result, BFPkNN inserts E as a NN of Q into $Rslt$ (line 7) if the number of elements in $Rslt$ is less than k. Otherwise, the algorithm returns $Rslt$ (line 9) since the final k NNs of Q have already been discovered. When E is a node entry, there are two possible cases as follows. The first one is that E is a leaf node, then BFPkNN picks the entry $NearestE$ in E with the smallest distance from Q and inserts it into hp (lines 12-23). This actually achieves the pruning heuristics 1 and 2, resulting in the removals of the vast non-qualifying entries. The other is that E is a non-leaf node, then BFPkNN accesses only the qualifying ones that may contain the final result and en-heaps hp (lines 25-34). This also means that the algorithm applies the pruning heuristics 1 and 3 to filter the unnecessary nodes in E. Note that the counting of $kPruneDist$ exploits the formula 1 (proposed in Section 3.1 of this paper). Also note that, the distance between Q and the entry of trajectory segment e (line 16) is computed as [5].

3.3   Analysis

Based on best-first traversal, BFPkNN gains the least number of node accesses. Furthermore, by applying several effective pruning heuristics to BFPkNN, it also reduces main-memory consumption greatly (i.e., capturing the fewer heap size) and facilitates its execution (i.e., obtaining the less CPU overhead). As demonstrated by the considerable experimental results shown in Section 4.2.

Lemma 1. *If an entry, either an intermediate or a leaf one, is not inserted into heap, then it must be pruned by heuristics 1 to 3.*

Proof. The proof is straightforward because our proposed pruning heuristics discard all non-qualifying entries that cannot contain the answer.   □

Lemma 2. *Entries (satisfying heuristics 1 to 3) are visited in increasing order of their minimum distances to a given query object q.*

Proof. The proof is clear, as BFPkNN follows best-first search paradigm.   □

Theorem 1. *The number of node accesses performed by BFPkNN is optimal.*

Proof. The Theorem 1 trivially holds, since the lemmas 1 and 2 ensure that the heap kept by BFPkNN stores only those qualifying entries that may contain the final result, and they are en-heaped there at most once, by their *mindist*.   □

4   Experiments

In this section, we experimentally verify the efficiency and scalability of BFPkNN by comparing it against Point$k$NNSearch under various settings. We implemented two variants of BFPkNN, called BFPkNN-LO and BFPkNN-IO, respectively. In particular, BFPkNN-LO incorporates pruning heuristics 1 and 2, as well as BFPkNN-IO employs pruning heuristics 1 to 3. All algorithms were coded in Visual Basic. All experiments were performed on a Pentium IV 3.0 GHz PC with 1 GB RAM running Microsoft Windows XP Professional.

4.1   Experimental Settings

Similar to the methodology in [5], we utilized two real datasets[1] involving a fleet of trucks that contains 276 trajectories and a fleet of school buses consisting of 145 trajectories. Additionally, we also used some synthetic datasets generated by the GSTD data generator [17] in order to examine the scalability of the algorithms. Specifically, the synthetic trajectories created by GSTD correspond to 100 through 1600 moving objects with the position of each object sampled approximately 1500 times. Notice that the initial distribution of moving objects was Gaussian while their movement was ruled by a random distribution. Table 1 summarizes the statistics of both real and synthetic datasets. Datasets are indexed by TB-trees [12], using a page size of 4K bytes and a buffer fitting the 10% of the index size with the maximum capacity of 1000 pages. We evaluated several factors, containing k, query time interval, and number of moving objects, which affect the performance of algorithms. Note that, for each experimental instance, the reported results represent the average cost per query for a workload comprising of 100 kNN queries with the same properties.

---

[1] Real datasets can be downloaded from *http://www.rtreeportal.org*

Table 1. Summary of real and synthetic datasets

	Trucks	Buses	GSTD100	GSTD200	GSTD400	GSTD800	GSTD1600
# trajectories	276	145	100	200	400	800	1600
# entries	112203	66096	150052	300101	600203	1200430	2400889
# pages	835	466	1008	2015	4029	8057	16112

4.2 Experimental Results

The first set of experiments studies the effect of k (varied from 1 to 16) with the real and synthetic datasets. The query points exploit random ones in the 2D space, and the time extent (TE) fixes 6% of the temporal dimension. Figures 4 and 5 show the number of node accesses (NA for short), CPU time (ms), and heap size (HS for short) as a function of k. Clearly, for NA, both BFPkNN-LO and BFPkNN-IO are less than Point$k$NNSearch, and the difference increases gradually with the growth of k. Note that the NA of BFPkNN-LO is equal to that of BFPkNN-IO due to the I/O optimality of BFPkNN, which is also demonstrated by the subsequent experiments. Towards CPU time, BFPkNN-LO outperforms BFPkNN-IO. This points out that heuristic 3 expends more CPU overhead than heuristic 2, since the counting of $kPruneDist$ in the heuristic 3 requires some CPU time. However, both algorithms still exceed Point$k$NNSearch, especially for large value of k. In contrast to CPU time, the HS of BFPkNN-IO is fewer than that of BFPkNN-LO, which implies that heuristic 3 can prune more non-qualifying entries than heuristic 2. Also note that, as k increases, the HS of BFPkNN-LO almost invariable, but that of BFPkNN-IO ascends stepwise. This is due to the growth of spatial overlap.

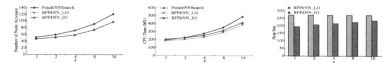

Fig. 4. NA, Query Time (ms), and HS VS. k ($TE = 6\%$, *Trucks*)

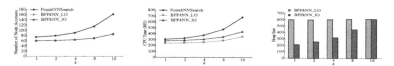

Fig. 5. NA, Query Time (ms), and HS VS. k ($TE = 6\%$, *GSTD400*)

Next, we investigate the influence of query time interval. Towards this, we fix $k = 4$ (which is the median value used in Figures 4-5) and vary TE between 2% and 10% of the temporal dimension. As with the aforementioned experiments, the query points adopt random ones in 2D space. All experimental results are illustrated in Figures 6 to 7, confirming the observations of Figures 4-5. Notice

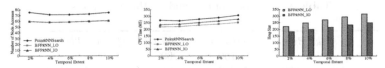

Fig. 6. NA, Query Time (ms), and HS VS. TE ($k = 4$, Trucks)

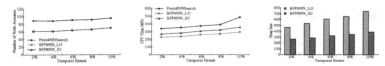

Fig. 7. NA, Query Time (ms), and HS VS. TE ($k = 4$, *GSTD400*)

that the HS of two variants of BFPkNN increases linearly as TE grows, which is caused mainly by the growth of temporal overlap.

Finally, we inspect the impact of the number of moving objects (# MO for short) as well. To achieve this goal, we deploy the GSTD data in the range [100, 1600], and fix $k = 4$. The query points also use random ones in 2D space, and TE sets 6% (which is the midvalue utilized in Figures 6-7) of the temporal dimension. Figure 8 compares NA, CPU time (ms), and HS versus # MO. Obviously, the performance of both BFPkNN-LO and BFPkNN-IO are better than Point$k$NNSearch under all cases. Note that, for CPU time, the efficiency of the algorithms including BFPkNN-LO and BFPkNN-IO are similar when the # MO is small (e.g., 100), and the difference increases gradually as the # MO grows. However, they are still faster than Point$k$NNSearch. Also note that, the HS of BFPkNN-IO is less than that of BFPkNN-LO by factors, and their HS increase (almost) super-linearly with the # MO increases.

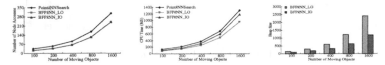

Fig. 8. NA, Query Time (ms), and HS VS. # moving objects ($k = 4$, $TE = 6\%$, *GSTD*)

5   Conclusion

This paper studies a particular subdomain of kNN retrieval, namely kNN search on R-tree-based structures storing historical information about moving object trajectories. We present an efficient best-first based algorithm for the processing of kNN ($k \geq 1$) query, termed BFPkNN, which is I/O optimal, i.e., it performs a single access only to those qualifying entries that may contain the final result. Several effective pruning heuristics are also developed in order to save memory space consumption and reduce CPU overhead further. Finally, considerable experiments with real and synthetic datasets are done to show that BFPkNN outperforms its competitor significantly in both efficiency and scalability. In the future, we will apply our method to other algorithms proposed in [5] such as HcontPoint$k$NNSearch, HcontTrajectory$k$NNSearch, etc. Another interesting direction is to explore other query algorithms (e.g., k-closest pair queries) over moving object trajectories.

Acknowledgement. We would like to thank Elias Frentzos for his useful feedback on the source-code of their proposed algorithms in [5].

References

1. Beckmann, N., Kriegel, H-P, Schneider, R., Seeger, B.: The R*-tree: An Efficient and Robust Access Method for Points and Rectangles. In: SIGMOD (1990) 322-331
2. Benetis, R., Jensen, C.S., Karciauskas, G., Saltenis, S.: Nearest Neighbor and Reverse Nearest Neighbor Queries for Moving Objects. In: IDEAS. (2002) 44-53
3. Chakka, V.P., Everspaugh, A., Patel, J.M.: Indexing Large Trajectory Data Sets With SETI. In: CIDR. (2003)
4. Cheung, K.L., Fu, A.W-C: Enhanced Nearest Neighbour Search on the R-tree. SIGMOD Record 27 (1998) 16-21
5. Frentzos, E., Gratsias, K., Pelekis, N., Theodoridis, Y.: Nearest Neighbor Search on Moving Object Trajectories. In: SSTD. (2005) 328-345
6. Guttman, A.: R-trees: A Dynamic Index Structure for Spatial Searching. In: SIGMOD. (1984) 47-57
7. Hjaltason, G.R., Samet, H.: Distance Browsing in Spatial Databases. ACM TODS **24** (1999) 265-318
8. Iwerks, G.S., Samet, H., Smith, K.: Continuous k-Nearest Neighbor Queries for Con-tinuously Moving Points with Updates. In: VLDB. (2003) 512-523
9. Mouratidis, K., Hadjieleftheriou, M., Papadias, D.: Conceptual Partitioning: An Effi-cient Method for Continuous Nearest Neighbor Monitoring. In: SIGMOD. (2005) 634-645
10. Mouratidis, K., Papadias, D., Bakiras, S., Tao, Y.: A Threshold-based Algorithm for Continuous Monitoring of k Nearest Neighbors. TKDE **17** (2005) 1451-1464
11. Papadopoulos, A., Manolopoulos, Y.: Parallel Processing of Nearest Neighbor Queries in Declustered Spatial Data. In: ACM GIS. (1996) 35-43
12. Pfoser, D., Jensen, C.S., Theodoridis, Y.: Novel Approaches in Query Processing for Moving Object Trajectories. In: VLDB. (2000) 395-406
13. Roussopoulos, N., Kelley, S., Vincent, F.: Nearest neighbor queries. In: SIGMOD. (1995) 71-79
14. Song, Z., Roussopoulos, N.: K-Nearest Neighbor Search for Moving Query Point. In: SSTD. (2001) 79-96
15. Tao, Y., Papadias, D., Shen, Q.: Continuous Nearest Neighbor Search. In: VLDB. (2002) 287-298
16. Tao, Y., Papadias, D.: Time Parameterized Queries in Spatio-Temporal Databases. In: SIGMOD. (2002) 334-345
17. Theodoridis, Y., Silva, J.R.O., Nascimento, M.A.: On the Generation of Spatiotemporal Datasets. In: SSD. (1999) 147-164
18. Theodoridis, Y., Vazirgiannis, M., Sellis, T.K.: Spatio-Temporal Indexing for Large Multimedia Applications. In: ICMCS. (1996) 441-448
19. Xiong, X., Mokbel, M., Aref, W.: SEA-CNN: Scalable Processing of Continuous K-Nearest Neighbor Queries in Spatio-temporal Databases. In: ICDE. (2005) 643-654
20. Yu, X., Pu, K., Koudas, N.: Monitoring k-Nearest Neighbor Queries Over Moving Objects. In: ICDE. (2005) 631-642

Three-Level Object-Oriented Database Architecture Based on Virtual Updateable Views*

Piotr Habela[1], Krzysztof Stencel[2,1], and Kazimierz Subieta[1,3]

[1] Polish-Japanese Institute of Information Technology, Warsaw, Poland
[2] Institute of Informatics, Warsaw University, Warsaw, Poland
[3] Institute of Computer Science PAS, Warsaw, Poland
{habela, subieta}@pjwstk.edu.pl, stencel@mimuw.edu.pl

Abstract. We propose a new architecture for object database access and management. It is based on updateable views which provide universal mappings of stored objects onto virtual ones. The mechanism preserves full transparency of virtual objects either for retrieval and any kind of updating. It provides foundation for three-level database architecture and correspondingly three database development roles: (1) a database programmer defines stored objects, i.e. their state and behavior; (2) a database administrator (DBA) creates views and interfaces which encapsulate stored objects and possibly limit access rights on them; (3) an application programmer or a user receives access and updating grants from DBA in the form of interfaces to views. We present a concrete solution that we are developing as a platform for grid and Web applications. The solution is supported by an intuitive methodology of schema development, determining the perspectives and responsibilities of each participant role.

1 Introduction

The well-know ANSI/SPARC architecture [1] defines three levels which drive the data access and management of a database. These are *internal*, *conceptual* and the *external* levels. The conceptual level is common for all the database environment, while the external level consists of particular views (subschemata) dedicated to particular client applications or particular users. In relational databases the external level is implemented by two kinds of facilities: access privileges to particular resources granted by a database administrator (DBA) to particular users, and SQL views that customize, encapsulate and restrict resources to be accessed. Such an approach has proven to be enough simple and satisfactory for majority of applications of relational databases.

The situation is different for object-oriented and XML-oriented environments, especially in the data/service grid setting (transparent integration of distributed, heterogeneous and redundant data/service resources). Firstly, the database model is much more complex. It includes hierarchies of objects (XML), irregularities in data structures, object-oriented concepts (classes, inheritance, modules, methods, etc.) associations among objects, Web services and other notions. Secondly, the responsibility for the entire environment is more fuzzy than in case of relational systems. Such environments may be

---

* This work is supported by European Commission under the 6th FP project e-Gov Bus, IST-4-026727-ST.

T. Yakhno and E. Neuhold (Eds.): ADVIS 2006, LNCS 4243, pp. 80–89, 2006.

accessed by many kinds of users, supplied with data and services by various local sites and processed by various applications that appear ad hoc during system operation. This requires much more fine and flexible dynamic security, privacy, licensing and non-repudiation control. Thirdly, the encapsulation and customization must be finer than in the case of relational systems. Different businesses supported by the system may require precise customization and access control of data and services according to the needs, preferences and limitations of particular users.

The above external level qualities are hardly to be achieved by SQL views. An SQL view is defined by a single SQL query, thus it is not powerful enough to express all the required mappings (especially in a case of schematic discrepancies between stored and virtual data). Moreover, SQL views are not sufficiently transparent due to the still unsolved view updating problem. Although INSTEAD OF trigger views (implemented in Oracle and MS SQL Server) can map view updates onto updates of stored data, still the problem remains due to the limited power of SQL. Obviously, SQL does not address data structures richer than relational ones (more powerful SQL-99 is still a rough proposal rather than a feasible, complete and consistent solution).

In this paper we propose a new architecture for object database access which has conceptual and technical advantages over the solutions known from relational systems. The central issue considered is the external level of the ANSI/SPARC architecture and its various relationships with the conceptual level. Our research is motivated by the following requirements and expectations with respect to the architecture:

- Customization and conceptual modeling: data and services resources stored in the database are to be shared by various kinds of users. Each group of users can view the resources according to own habits, terminology, organization, etc.
- Encapsulation and information hiding: an application programmer should be constrained to use in the application code only resources that are explicitly granted for the application by the database system programmer and/or (dynamically) by DBA.
- Security, privacy, licensing, non-repudiation and other regulations that the users have to obey w.r.t. the resources. DBA should possess flexible facilities to grant and restrict dynamically the privileges to particular users and particular resources. The privileges may concern not only retrieval, but also any kind of updating.
- Strong typechecking of application codes. Interfaces that are granted to particular application programmers contain the typing information which should be used to typechecking of the written code. In case of semi-structured data (c.f. XML) some semi-strong typechecking system is expected.
- Orchestration/choreography of services: on the external layer data and service resources can be orchestrated (i.e. composed) in order to achieve some defined business goals. On the conceptual layer various applications can be coordinated to obey some business rules (e.g. licensing). Orchestration can be encapsulated, i.e. a composition of services can be externally perceived as a single service.

The last element of the database architectural puzzle is the three-role database application development model. These roles are the *database designer/programmer*, the *database administrator* and the *application programmer* (or database user). The database designer/programmer develops a conceptual database schema and implements classes/methods to be used by applications. DBA defines user privileges on objects and services, defines views and interfaces restricting external access, and determines user privileges concerning the interfaces. Views defined by DBA map stored data/services onto virtual ones, limit the visibility of certain features, customize and encapsulate data/services and/or perform service orchestration. Finally, the application programmer builds the code based on the interfaces to views provided by DBA.

Comparing the above architectural issues with the current state-of-the-art of object-oriented and XML databases, we conclude that significant research and development is still to be done. The most widely known ODMG standard [6] assumes data manipulation through language bindings, very similar to the ones used to implement and access objects in CORBA-based middleware [7] (having roots in programming languages rather than in database architectures). The scope of ODMG standardization is obviously too narrow. The standard assumes the support for monolithic applications based on a single database schema. The external architectural level is not mentioned. Hence the security, privacy, licensing and non-repudiation infrastructure has to be built on top of single interfaces to stored objects. There is even a step back in comparison to Java and COM/DCOM object models, which assume multiple interfaces to objects. Moreover, ODMG defines views (a *define* clause of OQL) as a client-side shortcuts (actually, macro-definitions) rather than as a server-side first-class database entities that can be dynamically handled by DBA. This is a step back in comparison to SQL views. View updating mechanism and interfaces to views are not even mentioned. Hence it was not possible to build our proposal within the framework established by the ODMG specification. However, where possible, we attempt to keep the introduced notions aligned with the terminology of ODMG and UML [8] models.

There are not too many papers on the above topics. In [10] related similar issues are discussed. Although we consider a manual derivation of user schemata, the problems of schema closure and interface positioning discussed in [10] may be important for assuring schema consistency. The main difference of our approach is that we do not follow the ODMG architecture and consider a much wider data and services environment. Eventually, our goal is a kind of enhanced Web services based on a virtual repository integrating distributed, heterogeneous and redundant data and service resources. The discussion and language proposals in this paper are also relevant for more traditional centralized object-oriented client-server architecture.

The proposed architecture allows convenient application development over an object database. It is founded on three concepts: (1) the Stack-Based Approach (SBA) [3] to query/programming languages, (2) updateable views, and (3) the model of three roles in the application development. SBA treats a query language as a kind of programming languages and therefore, queries are evaluated using mechanisms which are common in programming languages. SBA introduces an own query language Stack-Based Query Language (SBQL) based on abstract, compositional syntax and formal operational semantics. SBQL can be equipped with a strong or a semi-strong type system. SBA encompasses also powerful recursive tools [4] which allow defining any computable mapping between stored and virtual data (views).

Our approach to updateable views for SBA is presented e.g. in [5]. The idea is to augment the definition of a view with the information on users' intents with respect to updating operations. The first part of the definition of a view is the mapping of the stored objects onto the virtual objects, while the second part contains redefinitions of updating operations on virtual objects. The definition of a view may also contain definitions of subviews and methods. The mapping and the redefinitions are expressed with

SBQL routines, therefore their power is unlimited. SBQL, including virtual updateable object-oriented views, is implemented in several research prototypes. The most recent of them, named ODRA (Object Database for Rapid Application development), serves as a base for implementing the concepts presented here.

The paper is organized as follows. In Section 2 we describe the overall architecture. Section 3 presents the notion of a module as we use it. Sections 4, 5 and 6 discuss the three roles in the database development (database programmer, DBA, application programmer). Section 7 concludes.

2 Architecture Elements

The principal value of database management systems is that they provide data persistence mechanisms separable from applications. However, the variability of users and applications brings important new requirements concerning the schema management.

Offering DBMS content to various applications makes it necessary to introduce a DBMS-managed "middle layer". The features essential for such a layer are: transparency, ease of management and modification, no conceptual limitations comparing to stored data, more than one transformation step allowed to get the desired form of data. In such architecture, Fig.1, the following user roles and responsibilities are needed.

Database programmer creates internal and conceptual schema of the data upon previously created design, taking into account business goals. His/her task is to implement data classes, their methods, attributes and association, and services. The database programmer can use the implementation inheritance. There may be a number of developers working independently on particular database parts.

Database administrator defines external schemata for particular users with respect to the resources provided by database programmers. The database administrator creates updateable views built over the data store. He/she can create two kinds of views. *Predefined views* preserve the semantics of stored objects but may limit access to certain attributes, methods and generic operations. Such views can be automatically generated by some tool or simply written by the administrator. *Custom views* are created solely by the administrator. Such views can arbitrarily change the semantics of the stored object and introduce a different privilege model than predefined views.

Such views play in fact the role of interfaces restricting and/or refining the access to stored objects. Different views, designed for different users' categories, may be attached to the same object at the same time.

After these views are defined the database administrator grants privileges on them to particular users (application programmers). This views can be reused (views can be built on views) and/or inherited (a view can inherit from a number of classes).

Application programmer (database user) is a programmer, who uses the database, dealing with the user schema assigned. He/she knows the interfaces of views granted by the database administrator. Such an interface (view) serves two purposes. First, it keeps the conceptual model of the database for a particular application programmer. Second, it is used during the static type check of the application code.

From the above we may notice that there are two tasks for the middle layer in our approach. The first one is to transform data schema to the form required by certain usage. The second one is to define access privileges for different groups of users.

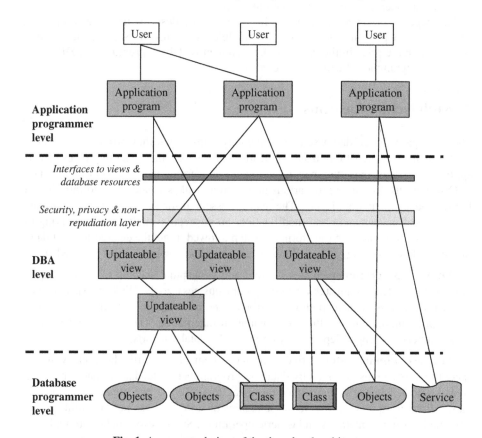

Fig. 1. A conceptual view of the three level architecture

3 Modules: Organizing Schemata and Storage

The data management based on a single, monolithic *database* unit, as assumed by ODMG, we consider problematic for advanced applications. This is confirmed by the fact that commercial ODMG-compliant ODBMSs designed to deal with large data amounts introduce additional levels of storage objects (see e.g. [12]). Thus we have introduced *modules* which partition database contents accordingly to purpose and ownership. This means that the features would be declared for particular modules rather for database as a whole. Since modularization is also useful for the code and related metadata (e.g. classes and interfaces), our modules have two purposes: organizing storage and organizing metadata.

Module declaration results in the creation of a dedicated space for it, both in regular database storage (allows a module to serve as a container of objects) and in the metadata repository (to store module-defined interface definitions). Appropriately, an import clause between modules can serve two purposes. Considering class and interface definitions, it establishes code dependency. At the same time, for stored objects (defined by module's structural features), it specifies side-effects (that is, non-local data dependencies). Depending on particular needs, modules can be purely code-oriented (no features declarations allowing regular object storage) or storage-oriented (no locally defined classes or interfaces). A developer may also decide to mix those responsibilities to reduce the number of modules.

Modules are decentralized in the sense that only interface and feature definitions of each module are located in the common metadata repository. Class implementation including method code and view definitions are located in data store, together with regular objects stored in a given module.

4 Database Programmer

A database programmer creates a database schema. He/she defines collections of objects and their invariants, like the type, default values of attributes, integrity constraints, implementations of methods, and so on. The allowed generic operations (insert, update, delete and retrieve) might also be limited on this level. Here is an example of a module created by a database programmer.

module Studio {

movie [0..*] : Movie   **insert, delete**;
actor [0..*] : Person   **insert, delete**;
director [0..*] : Person   **insert, delete**;

class Person {
 export{
  name : string   **retrieve, update**;
  starsIn [0..*] : **ref** Movie **reverse** stars   **retrieve, insert**;
  directs[0..*] : **ref** Movie **reverse** director   **retrieve, insert**;
  avgPay : double   **retrieve**;
  phoneNo : string   **retrieve, update**;
  setPay (m : Movie) : void;
 }
 name : string;
 virtual starsIn [0..*] : **ref** Person
   { (movie **where** exists (contract **where** contractor=this **and** role="actor") **as** si; }
    retrieve { **return** deref(si); }
    insert newMovie { /* add new contract for this actor to newMovie */ };
 virtual directs [0..*] : **ref** Person
   { (movie **where** exists (contract **where** contractor=this **and** role="director")**as** di; }
    retrieve { **return** deref(di); }
    insert newMovie { /* add new contract for this actor to newMovie */ };

```
 virtual avgPay : double
    { avg((starsIn.Movie.contract where contractor =this).pay) as ap }
    { retrieve { return ap; }  };
 phoneNo : string;
 setPay(m : Movie) : void { /* the implementation code comes here */ }
} // class Person

class Movie {
 export{
   title: string   retrieve, update;
   star[0..*] : ref Person reverse starsIn    retrieve, insert, delete;
   director : ref Person reverse directs   retrieve, update;
   contract[0..*] : struct Contract { contractor : ref Person; pay : double; role:string}
                                                                 retrieve, insert;
 }

   title : string;
   contract[0..*] : struct Contract {contractor : ref Person; pay : double; role:string};

 virtual star [0..*] : ref Person
    { (contract.contractor.Contract where role = "actor") as s; }
      retrieve { return deref(s); }
      insert newActor { /* add new contract with newActor */ }
      delete { /* delete the contract with this actor */ };
 virtual director : ref Person
    { (contract.contractor.Contract where role = "director") as d; }
      retrieve { return deref(d); }
      update newDirector { /* set the director contract with newDirector*/ }

} // class Movie

} // module Studio
```

The module *Studio* defines two classes, including stored and virtual data (attributes). The information on the associations between movies and persons is stored in the (multi-valued) attribute *contract*. This information is further used to establish virtual links *avgPay*, *starsIn*, *directs*, *star* and *director*. Note that the definitions of this virtual attributes are not accessible outside. The *export* clause controls the external access them. Any external entity will perceive these virtual attributes and concrete data in exactly the same way (similarly as in case of methods, whose implementation is invisible outside of a class). This module declares also some stored objects (*director*, *actor* and *movie*). Therefore, *Studio* module serves as both metadata and data storage.

5 Database Administrator

The database administrator defines the data and methods visible for application programmers. He/she uses the modules provided by database programmers and builds appropriate views over these modules. These views are organized into modules which are then granted to application programmers. Here is an example module defined by a database administrator over the module *Studio* (see Section 4). It provides database access for person with low credentials (i.e. they can add a director contract to a movie, but they cannot set the pay).

module CartoonStudio {

  import Studio;

  virtual director[0..*] : Person = Studio.director;
  virtual cartoon : Movie = (Studio.movie **where** count(stars) = 0);

  export Person {
   name : string **retrieve**;
   directs[0..*] : **ref** Movie **reverse** director **retrieve**, **insert**;
  }

  export Movie {
   title: string **retrieve**;
   director : **ref** Person **reverse** directs **update**;
  }

} // module CartoonStudio

Here, the database administrator has limited the movies only to cartoons. Other movies are not visible. Similarly, only the directors (and not stars) are accessible. The interfaces of provided objects are also restricted, i.e. only the attributes *name*, *title* and the associations *directs* and *director* are available. The only update allowed by this module is to change the director of a cartoon. This example uses so called predefined views, offering simplified syntax applicable for access restriction or data selection.

  The following example shows custom views, used here to redefine generic operations to include logging the information on all the changes and retrievals performed.

module PersonalData {

  import Studio;

  virtual person[0..*] { (Studio.actor **union** Studio.director) **as** p; }
  {
    virtual name : string { p.name **as** pfn; }
     retrieve {
       create persistent Log (Username & "retrieved data on" & p);
       return deref(pfn);
     }
     update newName {
       create persistent Log (Username & "changed the name of " & p);
       return pfn := newName;
     };

  } // virtual person

} // module PersonalData

In this module a custom view which provides virtual objects *person* is defined. A single subview *name* is declared. Its generic operations are redefined so as to create a log entry for each update and retrieval. This is an important gain if we compare it to relational databases where triggers fired on retrieval are not available.

6   Application Programmer

The database administrator grants privileges on certain modules to application programmers and/or users. If an application programmer is granted a module, he/she can use all its components (class/export definitions and provided objects). This access is transparent i.e. it does not depend whether an object is virtual or stored. The application programmer simply uses attributes, associations and method of provided objects.

Let us assume that the task of an application programmer is to code a user interface which will display the data on cartoon and directors and allow assigning directors to movies. The user interface could consist of two lists to select names of directors (the list *directorList*) and titles of cartoons (the list *cartoonList*) and a button "Assign" (referenced as *assignButton*). This example shows code of the GUI event handler for event *buttonPress* of this button.

```
module CartoonGUI {

    import CartoonStudio;   import GUI;

    assignButton : GUI.Button {
        proc whenButtonPressed    {
            CartoonStudio.Person p =
                    (CartoonStudio.director where name = directorList.currentSelection;);
            CartoonStudio.Movie m =
                    (CartoonStudio.cartoon where title = cartoonList.currentSelection;);
            m.director := p;            }
    }
}
```

Note that only the features of the module *CartoonStudio* are used here. The full transparency of virtual data has been achieved, as an application programmer needs not be aware of using virtual data (*CartoonStudio.director*, *CartoonStudio.cartoon*, *m.director* are all virtual!).

7   Conclusions

In this paper we have shown, how object interface specifications, class implementations, view definitions and user profiles could be combined to achieve the necessary transparent schema management with no limitations on the generality of the mapping of virtual data and updating operation.

The database design and maintenance architecture outlined distinguishes three main roles of its participants: the database programmer, the database administrator and the application programmer. Their cooperation facilitates the management of user privileges and directs the process of database application development. The proposed architecture clearly separates concerns of those three roles involved. It resembles the model-view-controller design framework with the database programmer as the "model", the database administrator as the "controller" and the application programmer as the "views". Analogously to the MVC, in the proposed architecture the most of coordinative work is in assigned to the database administrator ("controller") who orchestrates the efforts of both kinds of programmers.

The general framework could be similar to ANSI/SPARC in case of relational DBMSs. However, relational views are too limited in terms of virtual data/operation mapping. Moreover, a number of ODBMS-specific issues needs to be addressed. Our main aim was to employ the updateable view mechanism to serve customized user schemata and to prepare them to be a foundation for user privilege management.

Several related issues were not fully addressed here. Although we assume a full administrator's control over the user schema construction, some tool assistance for assuring their consistency and controlling dependencies could be desirable. Also the privilege control issue has only been sketched here. User classification, priorities and metadata updating restrictions require additional research.

Currently in our prototype ODBMS we have implemented the updateable view mechanism. The current work includes interface definitions management and its alignment with views and classes. Next, the user schema management functionality, as outlined here, will be realized. For our future research we plan the integration of the dynamic object role support into the schema and an extension of view mechanism to support parameterized views.

References

1. D.C. Tsichritzis, A. Klug (eds.): The ANSI/X3/SPARC DBMS Framework: Report of the Study Group on Data Base Management Systems, *Information Systems* 3, 1978.
2. C.J.Date, H.Darwen. A Guide to SQL Standard. Addison-Wesley Professional, 1996.
3. K.Subieta, Y.Kambayashi, and J.Leszczyłowski. Procedures in Object-Oriented Query Languages. Proc. VLDB Conf., Morgan Kaufmann, 182-193, 1995.
4. T. Pieciukiewicz, K. Subieta: *Recursive Query Processing in SBQL*, ICS PAS Report 979, November 2004.
5. H. Kozankiewicz, J. Leszczyłowski, K. Subieta: New Approach to View Updates. Proc. of the VLDB Workshop Emerging Database Research in Eastern Europe. Berlin, 2003.
6. R.G.G. Cattell et al: The Object Data Standard: ODMG 3.0. Morgan Kaufmann 2000.
7. Object Management Group: OMG CORBA™/IIOP™ Specifications. http://www.omg.org/technology/documents/corba_spec_catalog.htm, 2002.
8. Object Management Group: Unified Modeling Language (UML), version 1.5, http://www.omg.org/technology/documents/formal/uml.htm, 2003.
9. C.J. Date. Encapsulation Is a Red Herring. Intelligent Enterprise's Database on line, Programming & Design, http://www.dbpd.com/vault/9809date.html, 1998
10. M. Torres, J. Samos: A Language to Define External Schemas in ODMG Databases. in Journal of Object Technology, vol. 3, no. 10, November-December 2004, pp. 181-192.
11. K. Subieta. Theory and Construction of Object-Oriented Query Languages. Polish-Japanese Institute of Information Technology Editors, Warsaw 2004, 522 pages.
12. Objectivity. Objectivity for Java Programmer's Guide. Release 8.0. Objectivity, Inc. 2003.

AEC Algorithm: A Heuristic Approach to Calculating Density-Based Clustering *Eps* Parameter

Marcin Gorawski and Rafal Malczok

Silesian University of Technology,
Institute of Computer Science,
Akademicka 16,
44-100 Gliwice, Poland
{Marcin.Gorawski, Rafal.Malczok}@polsl.pl

Abstract. Spatial information processing is an active research field in database technology. Spatial databases store information about the position of individual objects in space [6]. Our current research is focused on providing an efficient caching structure for a telemetric data warehouse. We perform spatial objects clustering when creating levels of the structure. For this purpose we employ a density-based clustering algorithm. The algorithm requires an user-defined parameter *Eps*. As we cannot get the *Eps* from user for every level of the structure we propose a heuristic approach for calculating the *Eps* parameter. Automatic *Eps* Calculation (AEC) algorithm analyzes pairs of points defining two quantities: distance between the points and density of the stripe between the points. In this paper we describe in detail the algorithm operation and interpretation of the results. The AEC algorithm was implemented in one centralized and two distributed versions. Included test results present the algorithm correctness and efficiency against various datasets.

1 Introduction

Many computer research areas require spatial data processing. Computer systems are used for gathering and analyzing information about traffic in big cities and highways. The systems utilize drivers' cell phones signals to track vehicles. Stored tracking data is then analyzed and used to support the process of making decisions such as building new bypasses, highways and introducing other rationalizations. More and more people are interested in on-line services providing very precise and high-quality maps created from satellite images (an example can be found at [3]). There are more very interesting projects concerning spatial data processing; for details please refer to [1,2].

Another very important branch of spatial systems is telemetry. We work on a telemetric system of integrated meter readings. The system consist of utility meters, collecting nodes and telemetric servers. The meters are located in blocks of flats, housing developments etc. They measure water, natural gas and energy usage and send the readings to the collecting nodes via radio. The collecting nodes

T. Yakhno and E. Neuhold (Eds.): ADVIS 2006, LNCS 4243, pp. 90–99, 2006.

collect the readings and send them to the telemetric servers through the Ethernet network. The data from the telemetric servers are extracted, transformed and then loaded to the database of the data warehouse. Apart from meter readings, the data warehouse database stores information about the meters' geographical location and their attributes.

The remaining part of the paper is organized as follows. In the next subsection we present our motivation and describe the problem we are trying to solve. We then provide all the details of the proposed solution. We also include test results which present the algorithm efficiency and correctness against various datasets. We conclude the paper presenting our future plans.

1.1   Problem Description

The most typical use for the presented telemetric data warehouse is to investigate utilities consumption. Our current research is focused on providing fast and accurate answers to spatial aggregating queries. We are in the process of designing and implementing a hierarchical caching structure dedicated to telemetry-specific data. We named the structure a Clustered Hybrid aR-Tree (CHR-Tree) because we intend to use clustering to create the structure nodes, and, like in the aR-Tree [6], the structure nodes store aggregates.

We already have a solution to a problem of storing and processing the aggregates in the CHR-Tree nodes [5]. Currently we are trying to construct the structure of the CHR-Tree. To create the intermediate level nodes we employ density-based clustering algorithm. We decided to use the DBRS algorithm [7]. Although efficient and scalable, the algorithm requires an user-defined parameter *Eps*. *Eps* is a parameter defining a half of the range query square side. The side length is used by the clustering algorithm to evaluate range queries when searching for neighboring points. To the best of our knowledge, there is no automatic method for calculating the *Eps* parameter for the density-based clustering. Authors of the DBScan algorithm proposed in [4] a simple heuristics to determine the *Eps* parameter. However, the heuristics cannot be considered automatic as it requires user interaction. As we cannot get the *Eps* parameter from the user for every level of the structure, we propose an empirical Automatic *Eps* Calculation (AEC) algorithm. The algorithm is not limited to the telemetry-specific data and can be applied to any set of points located in two-dimensional space.

2   Automatic *Eps* Calculation Algorithm

The AEC algorithm investigates a distribution of the points in a given dataset. The analyzed datasets may be large, hence we have to limit the amount of processed data. We decided to use a random sampling approach because it can give good results in acceptable time. The AEC algorithm uses the following sets of data:

- a set of all points P. The points in the set P are located in some abstract region, in two-dimensional space,

– a set N. The set contains points randomly chosen from the P set. There is a function $createSetN()$ that is used for creating the N set. The function takes one optional parameter r, that defines the region from which the points are being picked. When the r parameter is present during the N set generation, we mark the set with an appropriate subscript: N_r,

– a set H. Like the N set, the H set contains points randomly picked from the P set. In the case of the H set, the function creating the set is named $createSetH()$. Next to the r optional parameter, whose meaning is identical as for the N set, the $createSetH$ function takes another parameter defining the point that is skipped during random points drawing. The H sets are created for points from the N set. The notation H_{r,n_i} means that the H set was created for the point $n_i \in N$; the point n_i was skipped during random points drawing and the points in H are located in a region r.

The cardinalities of N and H sets are the AEC algorithm parameters. Thanks to the parametrization of those values we can easily control the precision and the algorithm operation time. The cardinality of the N set is defined as the percent of the whole P set. The cardinality of the H set is defined directly as the number of points creating the set.

2.1   Algorithm Coefficients

The first step of the AEC algorithm operation is to pick randomly from the P set points creating the set N. In the next step, for each point $n_i \in N$ the algorithm creates set H_{n_i}. Utilizing the created sets, the algorithm evaluates three coefficients.

The first calculated coefficient is the Euclidean distance between the point n_i and point from the related H_{n_i} set. The distances are calculated for all points in the N set and all related H sets.

However, knowing only the distance between points p_i and p_j is not enough to estimate the Eps parameter. Missing is the knowledge about the neighborhood of the analyzed points; actually about the points in the region between the investigated points p_i and p_j. We introduced a coefficient PIS (Points In Stripe). The value of $PIS(p_i, p_j)$ is the number of points located in a *stripe* connecting the points p_i and p_j.

To evaluate the PIS coefficient value for a pair of points we use one spatial query and four straight lines equations. Having the p_i and p_j points coordinates we can easily calculate the parameters a and b of the straight line L equation $y = ax + b$. The line L contains the points p_i and p_j. In the next step we calculate equations of the lines perpendicular to L in points p_i and p_j, respectively L_{p_i} and L_{p_j} (we do not include the equations because of the complicated notation and straightforward calculations). The final step is to calculate two lines parallel to L, the first above line $L - L_a$ and the second below line $L - L_b$. The distance between the parallel lines and the L line (the difference in the b line equation coefficient) is defined as a fraction of the distance between points p_i and p_j. The fraction is the AEC algorithm parameter named *stripeWidth*; $stripeWidth \in (0,1)$. The lines create a *stripe* between the points, and the *stripe* encompasses some number of points.

Having the lines equations we can easily calculate, whether or not an arbitrary point from the set P is located inside the stripe between points p_i and p_j. In order to reduce the number of points being analyzed we evaluate a rectangle encompassing the whole stripe. The rectangle vertexes coordinates are set by calculating the coordinates of the points where the stripe-constructing lines (L_a, L_b, L_{p_i} and L_{p_j}) cross, and then choosing the extreme crossing points coordinates. Using the stripe-encompassing rectangle we execute the range query to choose the points which can possibly be located within the stripe between p_i and p_j. In the next step, only the points chosen by the range query are examined if they are located within the stripe.

After calculation of the PIS coefficient we are equipped with two values, which provide interesting knowledge not only about distance between points p_i and p_j but also about their neighborhood. Basing on the distance between points: $dist(p_i, p_j)$ and the number of points in a stripe between points $PIS(p_i, p_j)$ we can calculate another coefficient, which is a density of the stripe between p_i and p_j: $dens(p_i, p_j) = \frac{PIS(p_i,p_j)}{dist(p_i,p_j)^2 \cdot stripeWidth}$.

Figure 1 presents an example of a stripe between two points. The *stripeWidth* parameter was set to 0.98. In this example we are checking two pairs of points: p_5, p_8 and p_3, p_6. We used a dashed line to indicate the line linking two points. Solid lines depict the parallel and perpendicular lines. Rectangles drawn with spotted lines describe the regions encompassing the stripes. From the picture we see, that there is one point between points p_5, p_8 and there are 3 points between points p_3, p_6.

The distances (in millimeters) between the points p_5, p_8: $dist(5, 8) = 302.1$, and p_3, p_6: $dist(3, 6) = 79.2$. The density of the stripe between p_5 and p_8 is $dens(p_5, p_8) = \frac{1}{302.1^2 \cdot 0.98} = 0.11 \cdot 10^{-4}$ and for p_3, p_6: $dens(p_3, p_6) = \frac{3}{79.2^2 \cdot 0.98} = 4.88 \cdot 10^{-4}$. From the example we see that the density inside the cluster is much greater than outside the cluster. The density coupled with the distance between points brings much more knowledge than the distance itself.   Now we are able to deduce whether two points are relatively close to each other, and whether they are located in a dense neighborhood or, on the other hand, whether the points are relatively distant and there are almost no points in the stripe between them. After analyzing the operation of the density-based algorithms, that is executing a series of range queries, we decided to search not for a distance between points in clusters or for the thinnest cluster diameter, but rather for a minimal distance between clusters. A value based on the minimal distance can be used as the *Eps* parameter in the density-based clustering algorithm. Using a minimal distance between clusters as the *Eps* parameter should result in grouping all the points whose distances to their closest neighbors are shorter than the minimal distance between clusters (they are in one cluster) and not grouping points when the distance between them is greater than the minimal distance between clusters.

2.2 Algorithm Operation

The AEC algorithm operates in iterative mode. In every iteration the algorithm tries to minimize the calculated minimal distance between clusters. Below we present the pseudocode of the algorithm.

```
(1)  CalculateEps(maxIter, maxRptd, distInit, densInit) : Float
(2)    distCur := distInit; densCur := densInit; // initialize variables
(3)    distPrev := distCur;  // stores previously calculated distance
(4)    iter := 0; rptd := 0; // # of iterations and # of repeated results
(5)    WHILE iter < maxIter AND rptd < maxRptd DO
(6)      N := createSetN(); // create set N
(7)      FOR ni IN N DO // for every point ni in N do
(8)        niDist := Float.MAX_VALUE; // initialize results for point ni
(9)        niDens := Float.MAX_VALUE;
(10)       rni := createRect(distCur, ni); // create rectangle for point ni
(11)       rniDens := getAvgDens(rni); // calculate rectangle density
(12)       Hni := createSetH(ni, rni); // create set H for point ni
(13)       FOR hj IN Hni DO
(14)         tDist := calcDist(ni, hj); // calculate distance
(15)         tPIS  := calcPIS(ni, hj);  // calculate # of points in stripe
(16)         tDens := calcDens(tDist, tPIS); // calculate stripe density
(17)         IF tPIS > 0 AND tDist < niDist AND tDens <= rniDens THEN
(18)           niDist := tDist; // set new results for point ni
(19)           niDens := tDens;
(20)         END IF;
(21)       END FOR; // loop for points from Hni set
(22)       IF niDist < distCur AND niDens <= densCur THEN
(23)          distCur := niDist; // update iteration results
(24)          densCur := niDens;
(25)       ELSE
(26)          IF niDist < distCur THEN // check suspected region
(27)             sDist, sDens := checkSuspReg(ni, hj);
(28)             IF sDist < distCur AND sDens <= densCur THEN
(29)                distCur := sDist; // update iteration results
(30)                densCur := sDens;
(31)             END IF;
(32)          END IF; // suspected region condition
(33)       END IF; // updating results condition
(34)       IF distCur = distPrev THEN
(35)          rptd := rptd + 1; // increase number of repeated results
(36)       ELSE
(37)          rptd := 0;
(38)          distPrev := distCur; // store previously calculated value
(39)       END IF; // repeated result condition
(40)       iter := iter + 1; // increase number of performed iterations
(41)     END FOR; // loop for points from N set
(42)   END WHILE; // main loop
(43)   RETURN distCur;
(44) END; // CalculateEps
```

The input parameters are: the maximal number of iterations, the maximal number of repeated results and the initial distance and density. Two first values are used for creating the breaking condition (line 5). The iterations are broken if the number of performed iterations is greater than the maximal number of iterations or the result returned by consecutive iterations was repeated a given number of times. Next two parameters, the initial values, should be set in a way that they reduce the number of iterations to minimum, but do not narrow down the set of possible solutions. We use an average distance between random points, and average density related to the distance as the initial values.

In the iterative section the AEC algorithm first creates the N set (line 6). Then, for every point $n_i \in N$ performs the following:

- creates the r_{n_i} rectangle and calculates its density (lines 10,11). The r_{n_i} rectangle has its center in the n_i point and its sides are $2 \times distCur$ length,
- creates $H_{r_{n_i},n_i}$ set (line 12). Then for every point $h_j \in H_{r_{n_i},n_i}$ the algorithm calculates the distance and the density of the stripe between the n_i and h_j points (lines 14-16).
- from all the results the algorithm chooses the best distance and density pair (lines 17-20) for the n_i point,
- condition in line 22 chooses the best distance and density pair for the whole N set,
- if the results for the n_i point satisfies only the first part of the condition (line 26), the algorithm checks a *suspected region* (see below),
- in line 34 the algorithm checks if the returned result is repeated,
- as the result the function returns the calculated $distCur$ value.

Suspected Region. The case of a *suspected region* is considered for points p_i, p_j when only the distance condition $(dist(p_i, p_j) < dist_{cur}))$ holds, the density condition $(dens(p_i, p_j) <= dens_{cur}))$ does not. Our experiments show that there are two possible scenarios resulting in examining a *suspected region*:

1. the points p_i, p_j are located close to each other inside a cluster. The distance then is short, but the density of the stripe between the points is high (the scenario is marked as rectangle (1) in fig. 2).
2. the points p_i, p_j are located in separate clusters but they are not border points (according to the definition presented in [7]). The situation is presented in fig. 2 as rectangle (2). The density of the stripe between the points is increased by the presence of the border points of both clusters.

Of considerable interest is the second case. The AEC algorithm does not analyze distances with the zero PIS coefficient. There are many cases when the clusters' shapes make it difficult to randomly pick two points so that one of them is a border point of the first cluster and the second is located near the border of the second cluster. The analysis of the *suspected region* is performed as follows:

1. define the *suspected region*. The rectangle r_s for the *suspected region* has its center directly between the points p_i and p_j (fig. 2). In the next step calculate the density $dens_{r_s}$ of the r_s.
2. create a set of points N_{r_s}.
3. for each point $n_i \in N_{r_s}$ create a set H_{n_i,r_s}, then calculate distances and densities of the stripe between points n_i and the related points $h_j \in H_{n_i,r_s}$. As the result choose the minimal distance with the minimal density.

In the event the calculated result density is less than the average density of the r_s region, the *suspected region* analysis results are compared with the results of the analysis in the iterative section of the AEC algorithm. For a pair of points located inside a cluster the *suspected region* analysis does not influence the results because the density condition is not satisfied (the density is high inside a cluster). But for the points located in two different clusters the analysis often gives important results.

The amount of points checked during *suspected regions* analysis depends on the number of points in the r_s rectangle. If the number is less than the N set cardinality, then all the points are checked. But if the number is greater, the cardinality of the N_{r_s} set equals the cardinality of the N set created in the iterative section of the algorithm. The situation is identical for the H sets.

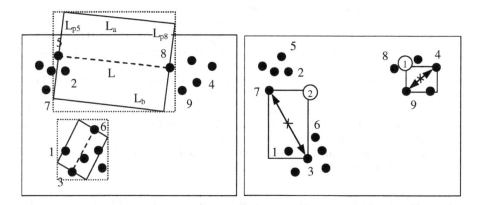

Fig. 1. Hypothetical stripes between two pairs of points

Fig. 2. The *suspected regions* are being analyzed with special attention

2.3   Implementation

In order to improve the efficiency of the AEC algorithm we used distributed processing. The structure of the distributed system consist of a client and a few servers. Each server stores the set of all points P and each server performs the same operations but for different subsets of points. Each server is assigned a set of points from which it creates the N sets. The sets are disjoint for all servers. Thus we minimize the possibility that some servers examine the same pair of points. The H sets are created from the whole P set, with no limitations.

We implemented two different distributed versions of the AEC algorithm. The first version named *at once* (AO) assumes, that client and servers do not communicate during the process of *Eps* evaluation. The servers calculate the minimal distance between clusters with the lowest density and return the results to the client which selects the best result (the shortest distance with the lowest related density). Disadvantage of this approach is that the servers calculations are less precise because they use N sets which cardinalities are only $\frac{1}{K}$ of cardinalities of the sets used in the centralized version (where K is the number of servers). The second version named iterative (IT) assumes that the client requests the servers to perform the ith iteration of the whole process. The servers return results of the ith iteration to the client. The client selects the best result from all the answers. In the next step, the client transfers the chosen result to all the servers. The servers use the result as the initial distance and initial density for the next $i + 1$ iteration. The number of performed iterations and the number of repeated consecutive results are controlled by the client. Operation of the servers is *synchronized* by setting the initial distance and initial density. In this approach client and servers communicate more often, but the obtained results are more precise.

3 Test Results

After the theoretical description of the AEC algorithm we present results of the experiments obtained by means of the described implementations. The main purpose of the experiments was to verify the AEC algorithm correctness and efficiency against various datasets. The AEC algorithm was run with a given set of parameters. The calculated *Eps* parameter was passed to the DBRS algorithm, which was returning the number of created clusters. If the number of clusters declared for a given dataset equaled the number of clusters found by the DBRS, we marked the experiment as a success. If the number of clusters was not equal, we marked the experiment as a failure.

All three implementations (one centralized and two distributed: AO and IT) of the AEC algorithm are written in Java. The experiments were run on machines equipped with Pentium IV 2.8 GHz and 512 MB RAM. The software environment was Windows XP Professional, Java Sun 1.5 and Oracle 10g. The distributed environment consisted of four machines connected with Ethernet 100Mbit network. The communication in distributed implementations was based on Java RMI.

The algorithm was tested on eight various sets of points. The sets were marked from A to H; they vary with cardinality, points distribution and clusters' shapes (fig. 3).

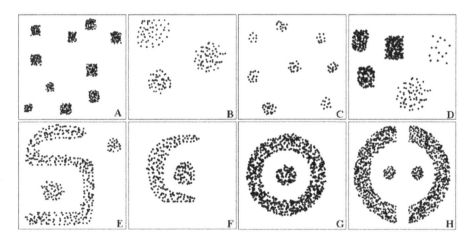

Fig. 3. Sets of points used for testing

The A set contains about 650 points grouped in 10 dense clusters; density of all clusters is very similar. The next set, B, contains about 200 points grouped in three relatively sparse clusters; density of all clusters is similar. The C set contains only about 120 points grouped in eight small clusters. In the D set 400 points are grouped in three dense clusters, one less dense, and one sparse cluster. The E and F sets contain over 400 points. The G and H sets contain respectively 1000 and 1500 points. In all four sets, clusters have similar density but significantly differ in shapes. Small clusters located inside the big ones were intended to disrupt the AEC algorithm when calculating the *PIS* coefficient. For each dataset we performed a set of experiments with the following parameters:

- the cardinality of the N set was 5, 15, 25 and 35% of the input dataset cardinality,
- the cardinality of the H set was 5, 15, 25 and 35 points for each value of the N set cardinality,
- the number of iterations was set to 10, 20 and 30 for each combination of N and H sets cardinality.

A single test set contained $4 \times 4 \times 3 = 48$ tests. In our tests the iterations were broken if the result of the consecutive iterations was repeated more than 5 times. The iteration breaking was always caused by the number of repeated consecutive results. Thus we can treat the tests for identical cardinality of N and H sets as three repeated tests, which is useful in the presence of the random factor.

The graph in figure 4 illustrates the relative number of investigated points for various sets of points. The number of investigated points calculated as $|N| \cdot |P| \cdot |H|$ was related to the cardinality of the set P, hence we can compare the results for sets of different cardinality in a single plot. In figure 5 we present a graph comparing AEC

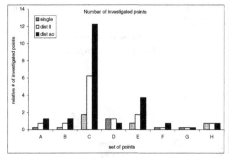
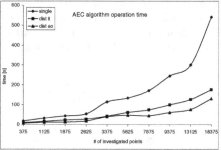

Fig. 4. Relative number of points checked for correct *Eps* calculation

Fig. 5. AEC algorithm operation times as function of investigated points number

algorithm operation times for the three implementation versions. The x axis shows the number of investigated points. The y axis shows AEC algorithm operation times in seconds. We considered only the cases when the algorithm gave the correct results. As expected, the centralized version consumes much more time when compared to the distributed versions. For small cardinalities of investigated points sets (less than 3000) the differences in operation times are not significant. But for greater cardinalities the distributed versions operate much more efficiently. For cardinalities exceeding 10000 points we observe nearly linear speed-up.

Summarizing the tests results we notice that for all tested sets of points the AEC algorithm gives proper results. There are more and less *difficult* sets of points but the algorithm can correctly analyze all of them. The most difficult to analyze are sets of points with a big number of small clusters. The algorithm operation is not disturbed by the differences in densities and/or shapes of the clusters. Also the presence of small clusters inside big ones does not negatively affect the algorithm operation.

The centralized version of the AEC algorithm gives the most accurate results. For all tested sets of points the centralized version always required the smallest N and H sets. This version also needed the smallest number of iterations for obtaining the correct results. The AO distributed version operates most efficiently (is able to examine the biggest number of pairs of points in the shortest time), but on the other hand, the AO version always requires the biggest N and H sets, and the biggest number of iterations. Therefore, the best choice is the iterative distributed version (IT). It is faster than the centralized version and gives better results than the distributed AO version.

4   Conclusions and Future Work

In this paper we addressed the problem of automatic calculation of Eps parameter used in density-based clustering algorithms such as DBRS and DBScan. We proposed a solution called AEC algorithm. The algorithm operates iteratively. In every iteration it chooses randomly a fixed number of sets of points and calculates three coefficients: distance between the points, number of points located in a stripe between the points and density of the stripe. Then the algorithm chooses the best possible result, which is the minimal distance between clusters. The calculated result has an influence on the sets of points created in the next iteration.

The AEC algorithm was implemented in one centralized and two distributed versions. We presented test results for a set of eight different sets of points. With appropriately high number of examined points the algorithm was able to calculate the proper Eps parameter for all tested sets of points. Our future work includes further improving the AEC algorithm efficiency. We want to optimize the most time-intensive fragment of the algorithm which is calculating the value of the PIS coefficient. We are currently searching for conditions allowing us to skip the PIS coefficient calculation.

References

1. Barclay T., Slutz D.R., Gray J.: TerraServer: A Spatial Data Warehouse, Proc. ACM SIGMOD 2000, pp: 307-318, June 2000
2. http://www.lsgi.polyu.edu.hk/sTAFF/ zl.li/vol_2_2/02_chen.pdf
3. http://maps.google.com
4. Ester M., Kriegel H.-P., Sander J., Wimmer M.: A Density-Based Algorithm for Discovering Clusters in Large Spatial Databases with Noise. In proc. of 2nd International Conference on Knowledge Discovery and Data Mining, 1996
5. Gorawski, M., Malczok, R.: On Efficient Storing and Processing of Long Aggregate Lists. DaWaK, Copenhagen, Denmark 2005.
6. Papadias D., Kalnis P., Zhang J., Tao Y.: Effcient OLAP Operations in Spatial Data Warehouses. Spinger Verlag, LNCS 2001
7. Wang X., Hamilton H.J.: DBRS: A Density-Based Spatial Clustering Method with Random Sampling. In proceedings of the 7th PAKDD, Seoul, Korea, 2003

GeoCube, a Multidimensional Model
and Navigation Operators Handling Complex Measures:
Application in Spatial OLAP

Sandro Bimonte, Anne Tchounikine, and Maryvonne Miquel

Laboratoire d'InfoRmatique en Images et Systèmes d'information UMR CNRS 5205
INSA, 7 avenue Capelle, 69621 Villeurbanne Cedex, France
`name.surname@insa-lyon.fr`

Abstract. Data warehouses and OLAP systems help to interactively analyze huge volume of data. Frequently this data contains spatial information which is useful for decision-making process. Spatial OLAP (SOLAP) refers to the integration of spatial data in multidimensional applications at physical, logical and conceptual level. Using spatial measure as a geographical object, i.e. taking in account its geometric and descriptive attributes, raises problems regarding the aggregation operation and the cube navigation in their semantic and implementation aspects. This paper defines an extended multidimensional data model which is able to support complex objects as measures, in order to handle geographical data according with its particular nature in an OLAP context. The model allows the multidimensional navigation process. OLAP operators are described which include this new concept of measure. A prototype of a SOLAP tool that handles geographical object as measures is presented.

1 Introduction

Data warehouses and OLAP (On Line Analytical Processing) systems provide tools to store and analyze huge volume of data loaded from different transactional databases. In multidimensional models, *facts* are analyzed thanks to *measures* or indicators. The *dimensions* represent axis of analysis, their *members* or instances are organized following *hierarchies*. The concept of Spatial OLAP (SOLAP) refers to the integration of this spatial information into multidimensional models at physical, logical and conceptual level. SOLAP technical solutions usually consist in the coupling of OLAP engines used to provide multidimensionality with GIS tools used to store and visualize spatial information [5]. However, SOLAP implies a real rethinking of OLAP concepts: A SOLAP paradigm should define spatial measure with adapted aggregation functions, spatial dimension hierarchies, spatial OLAP algebra extending OLAP operators to topological and spatial operators, suited GUI interface for navigation mixing tabular and cartographic features.

1.1 Spatial Dimensions

Using spatial data in OLAP dimensions brings to the definition of *spatial non geometric* dimension (i.e. text only members), *spatial geometric* dimension (i.e. members with a

T. Yakhno and E. Neuhold (Eds.): ADVIS 2006, LNCS 4243, pp. 100–109, 2006.
© Springer-Verlag Berlin Heidelberg 2006

cartographic representation) or *mixed spatial* dimension (i.e. combine cartographic and textual members) [1]. Numerous works have focused on the definition and usage of spatial dimensions [6], [9]. An example of a SOLAP application with spatial dimension is the supervision of French departments in relation to mortal diseases. The mortality datapack represents the numbers of deaths registered during the studied period for a selected list of causes, location of death, gender and 5 year age-groups. A first possible design model for this application is given in Fig. 1a. It uses an alphanumeric measure (#deaths) and 4 dimensions: time with hierarchy (day, month, year), location with hierarchy (department, region), sexage, that represents the patients' gender and 5 year age-groups, and causes, with hierarchy (disease, classes). location is a spatial dimension, and geometry is a reference to a geometric object stored in a GIS. The aggregation function applied against the measure is SUM.

1.2 Spatial Measures

Spatial measures are used when the studied subject of the decision process is the spatial information itself. In literature, the measure can be represented as a collection of references to spatial objects [11], [10], as objects resulting from topological operations (e.g. union or intersection), or metric operators (e.g. distance) [10], [6], or as measure associated to a spatial dimension [7]. An example of a spatial OLAP application using a spatial measure is shown in Fig. 1b. In this example, the dimension incidence represents ranges of numbers. The spatial measure is the spatial object department. In this kind of model, like in [11], the spatial measure is reduced to its geometric part, and eventually to metric attributes which can be derived directly from the geometry. The aggregation function is restricted to a spatial fusion of the geometries and derived metrics attributes when rolling-up the cube. In Fig. 1b, the lack of thematic attributes associated to the spatial information, as defined in GIS data models, can lead to incomplete or erroneous analysis. For example the population and the number of hospitals can reveal an inadequate medical system, and diseases can sometimes be related to the socio-economic classification (area-class) of the department. The classical solution in order to associate to a spatial measure its thematic attributes is to transfer them into a dimension [4], [11]. Indeed, in the multidimensional paradigm, the dimensions are the only entities that can represent real world complex concepts, whereas measures are restricted to numeric quantitative indicators. This solution raises the problem of formalizing and managing this redundant or distributed representation throughout navigating across the cube. Indeed, in traditional cases, a measure is simple typed, and its semantic is limited to a quantitative description (a quantity, an amount...). On the contrary, in this solution, the spatial measure is linked to an object which is member of a dimension, strongly typed, and constrained. Does the aggregation should be extended to the non geometric part of the measure, how hierarchy and/or semantic relationships are handled between the measure and its dimension representation are pending questions.

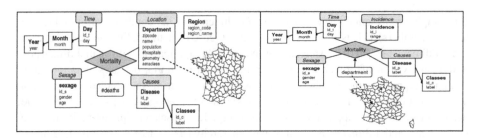

Fig. 1. Mortality DW with a) spatial dimension location, b) with spatial measure Department

1.3 Contributions

The main objective of our work is to provide a multidimensional data model (extending [2]) and an accompanying algebraic query language able to support spatial measures as *geographical* objects i.e. as real world entities described by geometric, metric *and* thematic attributes. Let us reformulate the example of the previous section considering now the spatial measure department as an entity characterized by various descriptive attributes (e.g. zipcode, name, population, number of hospitals and areaclass) and a geometry attribute. In this example, the user can analyze the influence of geographical location of departments in mortality. His analysis is not restricted to a spatial analysis but take into account the descriptive and metric attributes of the department that could reveal important information. The multidimensional model aims satisfy the following requirements. Some of them have been pointed individually in [3] and/or [8], and some are more specific of our context.

- *Support of n to n relationships between facts and dimensions*: This requirement stands because we want measures to be real world objects. Thus different departments can be linked to a same set of date, incidence, sexage and vice versa.
- *Symmetrical treatment of dimensions and measures:* This requirement first stands because we want a measure to be defined as complex as a dimension. A second aspect is that we want to authorize the user to dynamically turn a dimension to a measure and vice-versa, meanwhile changing the semantics of his analysis (for example from application of Fig. 1a to application of Fig. 1b).
- *Measure sets* and *level attributes*: Dimensions and measures, whereas spatial or not, are described by a set of attributes having a meaning as whole.
- *Usage of every kind of spatial and alphanumeric attributes as one single measure.*
  - *Aggregated measures designed differently from detailed ones*: For example, a SOLAP application for controlling car accidents might have as measure the locations of accidents whose geometry is represented by points. A possible spatial aggregation can be the convex hull function which result value is a polygon. In other terms, aggregated attributes could be defined as very different from the detailed one, using for instance different data types, or different classification (i.e. when aggregation is used to generalize data), or having no value, or more values (i.e. the area of the geometry created by the aggregation).

- *Use of ad hoc aggregation functions*: Aggregation should not be restricted to classical SQL operators but should allow spatial and/or ad hoc functions. For example, the aggregated attribute areaclass could be calculated from the areaclass and population of aggregated departments, using a ratio function, the aggregated geometry could be calculated using a spatial union.
- *Support for aggregation semantics*
  - *Correct aggregation*: This requirement is a consequence of the n-n relationship between measure and dimensions and should avoid multiple counting when applying aggregation.
  - *Dependent aggregation functions*: The different aggregation functions performed on the different attributes of a measure are dependant: for example using the convex hull function for the geometry attribute will not imply the same aggregation function for the other attributes than a centroid calculus. These functions must be considered as an indivisible set of aggregation functions.

Although our context is a geographical application, we do no not think these requirements are restricted to our special field. Indeed, all applications requiring a complex measure, i.e. a measure described by a consistent set of attributes, are concerned: as an example, a medical decisional application where the patients are the measures, described by various attributes loaded from their medical record (therapeutic, diagnostic, multimedia data...), with an aggregation process which will consist in calculating a medium profile (medium age, predominant factor, average shape for ECG...).

2   The GeoCube Multidimensional Data Model

We introduce the concepts of entity schema and entity instances which allow modeling indifferently all objects of the analysis universe i.e. members of dimensions and measures. Entity schemas and their instances are organized into hierarchies building a lattice. A base cube is assimilated to a multidimensional space. Instances of entities used to represent the members at the most detailed dimension levels and measures are projected on the axes of this multidimensional space. The concept of aggregation mode is provided to define aggregation for the different attributes of the measure. A cube is a multidimensional space where at least one dimension is not at its most detailed level and the measure schema corresponds to an aggregated schema.

*Definition 1. (**Entity Schema and Entity Instance**). An entity schema S_e is a tuple $\langle a_1, ...,a_n \rangle$ of n attributes a_i defined on a domain $dom(a_i)$. An entity instance t_i of schema S_e is a tuple $t_i = \langle val(a_1), \; val(a_n) \rangle, val(a_i) \in dom(a_i)$. The set of instances is $\mathcal{I}(S_e)$*

*Definition 2. (**Hierarchy Schema and Hierarchy Instance**). A hierarchy schema is a tuple $H_h = \langle \llcorner_h, \swarrow_h, \ulcorner_h, \#_h \rangle$ where $\llcorner_h$ is a set of entity schemas, $\swarrow_h$ and $\ulcorner_h$ are entity schemas, and $\#_h$ is a partial order on $\{ \llcorner_h \cup \swarrow_h \cup \ulcorner_h \}$. The instance of the hierarchy schema H_h is a set of tuples t_i so as if $t_i \in \mathcal{I}(S_i)$ and $S_i \#_h S_j$ then $\exists t_j \in \mathcal{I}(S_j)$ and an order relation $\uparrow_h$ so as $t_i \uparrow_h t_j$*

$\llcorner_h$ is the *bottom* and $\ulcorner_h$ the *top*, entity schemas in a hierarchy are called *levels*. $\ddagger_h$ builds an oriented graph where entity schemas are nodes, $\llcorner_h$ is the root, $\ulcorner_h$ is the top and contains a unique value ('all'). H_i and H_j are *disjoint* if their sets of levels are disjoint.

Definition 3. (Base Cube Schema and Base Cube Instance). *A base cube schema BC_{bc} is a tuple $\langle S_1, \ldots S_m, S_f, \delta \rangle$ where:*

- *$\forall i \in [1,..m,f]$ S_i is an entity schema and a hierarchy schema exists H_i such as S_i is the bottom level and these hierarchies are disjoints*
- *δ is a boolean function defined on $I(S_1) \times .. \times I(S_m) \times I(S_f)$*

  A base cube instance for BC_{bc}, $I(BC_{bc})$, is a set bc_c of tuples such as $bc_c = \{ \langle t_1^j, \ldots, t_n^j, f_m^j \rangle, j=1,..p \}$ where $t_i^j \in I(S_i)$ and $f_m^j \in I(S_f)$ and $\delta(t_1^j, \ldots, t_n^j, f_m^j) = 1$

Example. The Time hierarchy schema of the mortality use case is $H_{time} = \langle \llcorner_{time}, S_{day}, S_{all\_time}, \ddagger_{time} \rangle$ where $\llcorner_{time} = \{ S_{month}, S_{year} \}$ and $(S_{day} \ddagger_{time} S_{month})$, $(S_{month} \ddagger_{time} S_{year})$, $(S_{year} \ddagger_{time} S_{all\_time})$.
The base cube schema for the mortality application is
$BC_{mortality} = \langle S_{day}, S_{sexage}, S_{disease}, S_{incidence}, S_{dept}, \delta \rangle$ (Fig. 2a)
The base cube schema represents a fact table with all dimensions at their bottom level and one will play the role of the measure. The boolean function reveals the presence of data. We can notice that in the definition of the base cube, all bottom levels of dimensions are potential measures.

Definition 4. (Aggregation Mode). An aggregation mode Θ_k is a tuple $\langle S_a, S_b, \Phi \rangle$ where S_a is an entity schema $\langle a_1, \ldots a_m \rangle$, S_b is an entity schema $\langle b_1, \ldots b_p \rangle$, and Φ is a set of p ad-hoc aggregation functions ϕ_l .

The aggregation of n instances $t_1, \ldots, t_n$ of S_a is an instance $t_b = \langle val(b_1), \ldots, val(b_p) \rangle$ of S_b such as: $\forall j \in [1,..p], val(b_j) = \overset{n}{\underset{i=1}{\phi}}(t_i.a_1, \ldots t_i.a_k)$ with $t_i \in I(S_a)$ and $a_r \in A(S_a), r \in [1,..,k]$

We say that S_b is *built-from* S_a and t_b is *built-from* $\{t_1, \ldots, t_n\}$.

The concept of aggregation mode is central to our model and is provided in order to support the measure as a complex entity. The idea is to get one entity representing the detailed measure and another one representing the measure after the aggregation process and to link their instances through aggregation functions for each attribute of the aggregated entity. These functions can be ad-hoc user defined functions.

Example. Let us define $\Theta_1 = \langle S_{dept}, S_{agg\_dept}, \Phi_1 \rangle$. S_{agg_dept} is built-from S_{dept}. S_{agg_dept} = <agg_population, agg_geometry, agg_areaclass, agg_nbHospitals>. Φ_1 (Fig. 2b) is composed of:
ϕ_1 : $dom(S_{dept}.population)^n \rightarrow dom(S_{agg\_dept}.agg\_population)$ // *sum*
ϕ_2 : $dom(S_{dept}.geometry)^n \rightarrow dom(S_{agg\_dept}.agg\_geometry)$ // *fusion*
ϕ_3 : $(dom(S_{dept}.population) \times dom(S_{dept}.areaclass))^n \rightarrow dom(S_{agg\_dept}.agg\_aeraclass)$ // *ratio*
ϕ_4 : $dom(S_{dept}.nbHospitals)^n \rightarrow dom(S_{agg\_dept}.agg\_nbHospitals)$ // *sum*

Definition 5. (Cube Schema and Cube Instance). *A cube schema C_c is a tuple $\langle BC_{bc},$ $\iota, \Theta_f, \gamma \rangle$ where:*

- *$BC_{bc} = \langle S_{b1}, \ldots S_{bm}, S_f, \delta \rangle$ is a base cube schema*
- *ι is a tuple of entity schemas $\langle S_1, \ldots S_m \rangle$ where $\forall i \in [1,..m]$ S_i belongs to H_i and at least one S_i is not the bottom level of H_i*
- *Θ_f is an aggregation mode $\langle S_f, S_{af}, \Phi \rangle$*
- *γ is a boolean function on $\iota(S_1)\times. \times \iota(S_m)\times \iota(S_{af})$*

The instance of the cube schema C_c , $\iota(C_c)$, is a set $c_c = \{ \langle t_1^j,\ldots, t_n^j, f_m^j \rangle, j=1,..p\}$ where $S_i \in \iota$, $t_i^j \in \iota(S_i)$, $f_m^j \in \iota(S_{af})$ and $\gamma(t_1^j,\ldots, t_n^j, f_m^j) = 1$

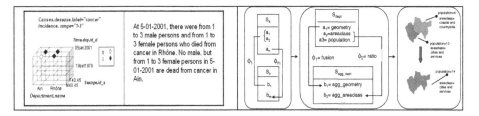

Fig. 2. a) Base Cube of Mortality application, b) Aggregation Mode on Department

3   Operators for Navigation

3.1   The CView Concept for Navigation

Given a list of entities belonging to a hierarchy, we say that they form a *path* on a hierarchy if *(i)* the list is reduced to the bottom level or *(ii)* the first entity in the list is the bottom level and each other is the immediate predecessor of the next one other in the partial order formed by the hierarchy. Moreover we define *leafs*$*(H_h)$ as the set of leafs of the tree formed by $\uparrow_h$. We note *leafs*$(\langle S_1,\ldots S_n, H_h \rangle, t_i)$ the set of leafs of the subtree formed by $\uparrow_h$ having as root t_i and as nodes members of $\{ \iota(S_1) \cup \ldots \cup \iota(S_n)\}$ if t_i is not the 'all' value of H_h, and *leafs*$*(H_h)$ otherwise.

Definition 6.(CView Schema and Instance). *A CView Schema V_V is a tuple$\langle b, C_c, \tau \rangle$:*

- *b is a boolean value*
- *C_c is a cube*
- *τ is a set of m tuples $\{ \langle S_1^1,\ldots, S_{n_1}^1, H_1 \rangle,\ldots, \langle S_1^m,\ldots, S_{n_m}^m, H_m \rangle\}$, $\forall i, j \in [1,\ldots m]$:*
    - *$[S_1^i,\ldots S_{n_i}^i]$ forms a path on H_i*
    - *if b is false then $S_{n_i}^i$ is the ith entity of the base cube (S_{bi}), else $S_{n_i}^i$ is the ith entity of the cube (S_{ci})*

An instance of the CView schema is a set of tuples v_v such as (i) if b is true then $v_v = \iota(C_c)$ (ii) else $v_v = \iota(BC_{bc})$

The CView models the navigation process in the cuboids lattice and associates the appropriate cube to a particular navigation path. At the most detailed levels of hierarchies, the CView contains the base cube instance. τ is a set of tuples representing the paths used for each hierarchy while building the aggregated cube.

3.2 The VRollUp Operator

Let V_v be a CView Schema, and S_t a level of H_t. The *VROLLUP* operator can be applied to V_v, with S_t being the target level. The output is a CView $V'_v = \langle b', C'_c, \tau' \rangle$ where b' is true, τ' is a set of the m tuples of τ excluding the one which has S_t for root. $C'_c = \langle BC_{bc}, \llcorner', \Theta_f, \gamma' \rangle$ represents the new aggregated cube. The levels of C'_c are equal to the levels of C_c minus S_t. C'_c has the same aggregation mode as C_c but a new boolean function γ' calculated considering the paths used to obtain the new cube. For each value $(t_1, ..., t_m, t_{caf})$ of the cartesian product where γ' is defined (denoted $dom(\gamma')$), we consider all values $(t_{b1}, ..., t_{bm}, t_{bfj})$ of the cartesian product where δ_f is defined (denoted $dom(\delta_f)$). If the values $t_{b1}, ..., t_{bm}$ are leafs of $t_1, ..., t_m$ along the paths of τ', and the aggregated measure t_{caf} is built from the $t_{bf1}, ..., t_{bfn}$, then $\gamma'(t_1, ..., t_m, t_{caf})$ is true. An example is shown Table 1 and Table 2.

Table 1. δ_f boolean function of the base cube S_{A0}, S_{B0}

$S_{A0}.a$	$S_{B0}.b$	$S_m.m$	δ_f	
A1	b1	m1	1	t_1
A1	b2	m1	0	
A2	b1	m1	1	t_2
A2	b2	m1	0	
A1	b1	m2	0	
A1	b2	m2	1	t_3
A2	b1	m2	0	
A2	b2	m2	1	t_4

Table 2. γ' boolean function of the cube: S_{A0}, S_{B2} after the VRollUp

$S_{A0}.a$	$S_{B2}.b$	$S_{agg\_m}.am$	γ'	
a1	All-b	m12	1	t_{13a}
a2	All-b	m12	1	t_{24a}

Definition 7. (VROLLUP). *Let $V_v = \langle b, C_c, \tau \rangle$ be a CView, H_t a hierarchy schema of C_c, S_t an entity schema of H_t and $S_{n'_t}' \in pred(H_t, S_t)$ then we define* VROLLUP $(V_v, S_t, H_t) = V'_v = \langle b', C'_c, \tau' \rangle$ *where:*

- *b' is true and τ' is a set of m tuples $\{\langle S_1^{1'}, ..., S_{n_1}^{1'}, H_1' \rangle, \langle S_1^{2'}, ..., S_{n_2}^{2'}, H_2' \rangle, ..., \langle S_1^{m'}, ..., S_{n_m}^{m'}, H_m' \rangle\}$ calculated by the algorithm r1.*
- *$C'_c = \langle BC_{bc}, \llcorner', \Theta_f, \gamma' \rangle$ where:*
  - *$\llcorner' = \langle S'_1, ..., S'_m \rangle$ where $S'_t = S_t$ and $\forall i \in [1.t[\cup]t....m] S'_i = S_{n_i}^i$*
  - *γ' is defined on $\{(S'_1) \times ... \times (S'_m) \times (S_{caf})$ and its instances are calculated by algorithm r2*

Algorithm r1. INPUT: S_t, H_t, τ OUTPUT: τ'	Algorithm r2. INPUT: τ', V_v OUTPUT: γ'
for (i:=1 to m and i $\neq$ t)	**for** ($\langle t_1, ..., t_m, t_{caf} \rangle$ in dom(γ') {
$\{\tau'.H_i' := \tau.H_i$	list := $\varnothing$
	for ($\langle t_{b1}, ..., t_{bm}, t_{bfj} \rangle$ in

```
for (j:=1 to τ.nᵢ)                    dom(Vᵥ.δf) {
{τ'.Sⱼ,¹' := τ.Sⱼⁱ}}                      if (t_{b1} ∈ leafs(τ'.⟨S₁¹',  …
for (j:=1 to τ.n_t-2)                         S_{n₁}¹',  H'₁), t₁)… and t_{bm} ∈
{τ'.Sⱼ,^{t'} :=τ.Sⱼᵗ }                        leafs(τ'.⟨ S₁^{m'},…, S_{nm}^{m'},H'_m),
τ'.S_{n_{t'}-1}^{t'} :=τ.S_{n_t}ᵗ              t_m) and Vᵥ.δf(t_{b1},…,t_{bm},t_{bfj})=1
τ'.S_{n_{t'}}^{t'} :=Sₜ                        and t_{bfj} ∉ list) then
τ'.Hₜ' := Hₜ                                   add t_{bfj} to list }
return (τ')                           if (list != ∅ and t_{caf} is built
                                       from t_{bf1},…,t_{bfn} then
                                      γ'(t₁,…,t_m,t_{caf}):=1
                                       else γ'(t₁,…,t_m,t_{caf}):=0
                                      Return (γ')
```

3.3 The VSlice Operator

Let V_v a be CView, S_t an entity and π a predicate defined on $\iota(S_t)$. The output of the *VSLICE* operator is a $V'_v = \langle b', C'_c, \tau' \rangle$ where $b' = b$, and $\tau' = \tau$. A slice operation simply eliminates some tuples from C_c modifying the boolean functions. Note that the *VSLICE* operator can be applied to the measures as well as to dimensions.

Definition 8. (VSLICE). *Let V_v be a CView Schema $V_v = \langle b, C_c, \tau \rangle$, S_t an entity which is: the root of the t-th path of τ, or the measure if b is false, or the aggregated measure. Let π be a predicate defined on $\iota(S_t)$, VSLICE $(V_v, S_t, \pi) = V'_v \langle b', C'_c, \tau' \rangle$:*

- $b' = b$ *and* $\tau' = \tau$
- (i) *if b is true, then* $C'_c = \langle BC'_{bc}, \llcorner, \Theta_f, \gamma' \rangle$ *where :*
  - $\gamma': \iota(S_{c1}) \times ... \times \iota(S_{cm}) \times \iota(S_{caf})$ *is calculated following s1.*
  - $BC'_{bc} = \langle S_{b1}, ..., S_{bm}, S_{bf}, \delta_f' \rangle$ *where δ_f is calculated following s2.*
- (ii) *if b is false then* $C'_c = \langle BC'_{bc}, \llcorner, \Theta_f, \gamma \rangle$ *where:*
  - $BC'_{bc} = \langle S_{b1}, ..., S_{bm}, S_{bf}, \delta_f' \rangle$ *where δ_f' is calculated following s3.*

```
Algorithm s1. INPUT: π, Vᵥ OUTPUT: γ'        Algorithm s2. INPUT: τ',γ OUTPUT: δ'_f
for each (⟨t₁,…,t_m,t_{caf}⟩ of
dom(Vᵥ.γ) { Let t_t ∈ t₁,…,t_m,t_{caf}       for each (⟨t₁,…, t_m, t_{caf}⟩ of
    if (Vᵥ.γ(t₁,…,t_m,t_{caf})=1 and          dom(γ') {
    π(t_t) is true) then                      Let t_{caf} built from t_{bf1},…,t_{bfn}
    γ'(t₁,…,t_m,t_{caf}):=1 else
    γ'(t₁,…,t_m,t_{caf}):=0 }                   for each(t_{bfj}) {
return(γ')                                       if (t_{b1} ∈ leafs(τ'.⟨S₁¹', … S_{n₁}¹',
                                                 H'₁), t₁) and … and t_{bm} ∈
Algorithm s3. INPUT: π, Vᵥ; OUTPUT: δ'_f        leafs(τ'.⟨S₁^{m'},…, S_{nm}^{m'},H'_m), t_m)
for each(⟨t_{b1},…,t_{bm},t_{bf}⟩ of            and γ'(t₁,…,t_m,t_{caf})=1 and
dom(Vᵥ.δf) {                                     δf(t_{b1},…,t_{bm},t_{bfj})=1)
Let t_t ∈ t_{b1},…,t_{bm},t_{bf}                 then δ'_f(t_{b1},…,t_{bm},t_{bfj}):=1 else
    if(Vᵥ.δf(t_{b1},…,t_{bm},t_{bf})=1 and        δ'_f(t_{b1},…,t_{bm},t_{bfj}):=0}}
    π(t_t) is true) then                      return (δ'_f)
    δ'_f(t_{b1},…,t_{bm},t_{bf}):=1 else
    δ'_f(t_{b1},…,t_{bm},t_{bf}):=0}
return (δ'_f)
```

4 Prototype

We have implemented a prototype based on a 3 tier architecture consisting of a spatial DBMS, an OLAP engine (Mondrian), and a front-end client based on an OLAP web client (JPivot) and a GIS web client. We implement user-defined aggregation functions in the DBMS, and extend Mondrian to support them. Mondrian aggregated tables are used to improve performances. The front-end client creates JSP pages that present the multidimensional data using tabular representation (A) and that visualizes geographical data (B). In Fig. 3 is shown an example of the Mortality application with departments as measures. The applet shows the overlay of 2 maps: a map of all French departments and a map consisting of the geographical object selected in the tabular representation. The applet presents some tools to manage maps and in particular a tool to show the descriptive attributes of the selected measure (C).

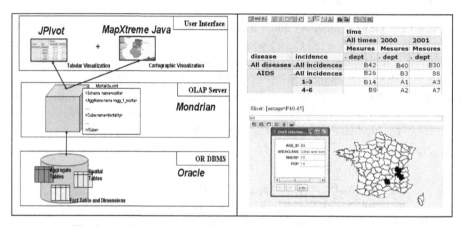

Fig. 3. Architecture and User Interface of the SOLAP tool prototype

5 Conclusions

Our work analyses and reformulates the concept of spatial measure in order to model geographical multidimensional applications. It defines measures and dimension members as complex objects and satisfies requirements to handle spatial measures as geographical object. GeoCube provides the concept of entity to model information involved in the multidimensional application and defines the concepts of hierarchy, base cube, aggregation mode, and cube in order to organize the data into a multidimensional way. The model consents the navigation in the hypercube. Using the concept of CView, used to uniform the cube and base cube concepts, this work defines an algebra consisting of OLAP operators. Our multidimensional model represents a first effort in considering measures not as a set of atomic independent quantitative values but as attributes of complex objects. Possible applications are not limited to geographical application but could be extended to any case where a complex object is needed as measure, for example a medical application using patient as measure. In this work we have presented too a prototype of SOLAP tool able to manage measures as geographical objects. Our future works are the definition of new Spatial OLAP operators in order to introduce spatial analysis in multidimensional applications and the definition of a new visualization paradigm for SOLAP tools.

References

1. Bédard, Y., Merrett, T., Han, J.: Fundaments of Spatial Data Warehousing for Geographic Knowledge Discovery. Geographic Data Mining and Knowledge Discovery. Taylor & Francis, London (2001) 53-73
2. Bimonte, S., Tchounikine, A., Miquel, M.: Towards a Spatial Multidimensional Model. In Proceedings of the 8th International Workshop on Data Warehousing and OLAP (DOLAP 2005). ACM Press, New York, USA (2005) 39-46
3. Blaschka, M., Sapia, C., Hofling, G., Dinter, B.: Finding Your Way through Multidimensional Data Models. In Proceedings of the 9th International Conference on Database and Expert systems Applications. Lecture Notes in Computer Science, Vol. 1490. Springer-Verlag (1998) 198-203
4. Fidalgo, R.N., Times, V.C., Silva, J., Souza, F.F.: GeoDWFrame: A Framework for Guiding the Design of Geographical Dimensional Schemas. In Proceedings of Int. Conf. on Data Warehousing and Knowledge Discovery, Zaragosa, Spain (2004) 26-37
5. Kouba, Z., Matoušek, K., Mikšovský, P.: On Data Warehouse and GIS integration, In Proceedings of the 11th Int. Conf. and Workshop on Database and Expert Systems Applications. LNCS, Vol. 1873. Springer-Verlag, London, UK (2000)
6. Malinowski, E., Zimányi, E.: Representing spatiality in a conceptual multidimensional model, In Proceedings of the 12th annual ACM International workshop on Geographic information systems. ACM Press, New York, USA (2004) 12-22
7. Marchand, P., Brisebois, A., Bédard, Y., Edwards, G.: Implementation and evaluation of a hypercube-based method for spatio-temporal exploration and analysis. Journal of the International Society of Photogrammetry and Remote Sensing , Vol. 59, (2003) 6-20
8. Pedersen, T.,B.: Aspects of data modeling and query processing for complex multidimensional data. Ph.D. Thesis, Aalborg University, Aalborg st, Denmark (1998)
9. Pourabbas, E.: Cooperation with geographic databases. In: Multidimensional Databases: Problems and Solutions. M. Rafanelli, Idea Group Publishing (2003) 393-432
10. Rivest, S., Bédard, Y., Marchand, P.: Toward Better Support for Spatial Decision Making: Defining the Characteristics of Spatial On-Line Analytical Processing (SOLAP). Geomatica, Vol. 55, 4 (2001) 539-555
11. Stefanovic, N., Han, J., Koperski, K.: Object-Based Selective Materialization for Efficient Implementation of Spatial Data Cubes. IEEE TKDE, Vol. 12, 6 (2000) 938-958

Hybrid Index for Spatio-temporal OLAP Operations*

Byeong-Seob You[1], Dong-Wook Lee[1], Sang-Hun Eo[1],
Jae-Dong Lee[2], and Hae-Young Bae[1]

[1] Dept. of Computer Science & Information Engineering, INHA University,
Younghyun-dong, Nam-ku, Inchon, 402-751, Korea
{subi, dwlee, eosanghun}@dblab.inha.ac.kr
hybae@inha.ac.kr
[2] Division of information and computer science, Dankook University,
Hannam-ro, Yongsan-gu, Seoul, 140-714, Korea
letsdoit@dankook.ac.kr

Abstract. According to increase of spatial data, many decision support systems require the fast spatio-temporal analysis. This paper proposes the improved index for efficient OLAP in a spatial data warehouse. The main idea is to use the hybrid index of the extended aggregation R-tree and the sorted hash table. The extended R-tree supports the spatial hierarchy with the level of R-tree. Also, it provides pre-aggregation for fast retrieval of the aggregated value. The sorted hash table is the transformed hash table for supporting the temporal hierarchy. So, it provides pre-aggregation of each temporal unit, year, month and etc. By the proposed hybrid index, an efficient spatio-temporal analysis can be supported since it provides the spatio-temporal hierarchy and the pre-aggregated value.

Keywords: Aggregation R-tree, OLAP, Spatio-Temporal, Spatial Data Warehouse.

1 Introduction

Spatial data warehouse is used in intelligent traffic system by providing spatial OLAP. In intelligent traffic system, traffic supervision requires historical analysis for decision of traffic policy and mobile users require current traffic information [2]. In order to satisfy two cases, it is necessary to integrate analysis of the spatial data and the non-spatial data. And integrated analysis does not need information of each vehicle but summarized information [12]. To solve these requirements in spatial data warehouses, some methods using the extended R-tree have been studied [2], [3], [6]. The aggregation R-tree is extended to store the pre-aggregated values on each entry. The aggregation R-tree provides the fast retrieval of the aggregated value because pre-aggregation values exist already on each entry [2]. However, the aggregation R-tree can not provide historical analysis since it has only total aggregated value on each

---

* This research was supported by the MIC(Ministry of Information and Communication), Korea, under the ITRC(Information Technology Research Center) support program supervised by the IITA(Institute of Information Technology Assessment) .

T. Yakhno and E. Neuhold (Eds.): ADVIS 2006, LNCS 4243, pp. 110–118, 2006.
© Springer-Verlag Berlin Heidelberg 2006

entry. The OLAP-Favored Search composes with the R-tree and the summarized table [3]. The R-tree in the OLAP-Favored Search is extended to store the link to the tuple of the summarized table. The OLAP-Favored Search provides the historical analysis in the summarized table. However, this method must access tremendous data of the summarized table for historical analysis.

In this paper, we propose the hybrid index for providing pre-aggregation with the concept of the spatial hierarchy and the temporal hierarchy in spatial data warehouses. The hybrid index is the efficient index which integrates the sorted hash table into the extended aggregation R-tree. The extended aggregation R-tree has additional information on the basic R-tree. One is currently aggregated value and another is a link to sorted hash table. The sorted hash table is linear hash table of year unit. Each bucket has a sorted year unit and a point of the next year unit. Each year unit has the flexible structure so that other time unit could be stored, such as month, day, hour, and etc. The hybrid index has some advantages as follows. Firstly, the hybrid index provides the spatial hierarchy and total pre-aggregation based on the extended aggregation R-tree. Second is the providing of the temporal hierarchy and the sorted hash table-based pre-aggregation of each temporal unit. And finally, the hybrid index performs efficient and fast decision support.

This paper is organized as follows: Section 2 reviews existing aggregation R-tree and the OLAP-Favored Search. Section 3 proposes the hybrid index which keeps aggregated information and supports the spatial hierarchy and the temporal hierarchy. Section 4 evaluates performance of hybrid index by comparing with existing ap-proaches. The conclusion is Section 5.

2 Related Work

A spatial data warehouse is a subject-oriented, integrated, time-variant, and nonvola-tile collection of spatial and non-spatial data for decision-making process [3], [10]. And, a spatial data warehouse provides data cubes for efficient decision support [5]. The data cube has the conceptual hierarchy for efficient decision support [6]. Since spatial data has various shapes, it is difficult to construct conceptual hierarchy on a dimension of spatial data. Previous works solve this problem by using spatial index trees, such as Quad-tree [9], R-tree [1], R*-tree [7], R+-tree [11], and etc. Among them, the spatial hierarchy on the R-tree is main issue in spatio-temporal OLAP operations.

The aggregation R-tree is an extended R-tree [2]. Thus, each entry has pre-aggregated value for its Minimum Bounding Rectangle (MBR). The pre-aggregated value is total aggregation from past to present. The aggregation R-tree can provide the aggregated value of some region. However, this method can not provide the his-torically aggregated value and does not support temporal hierarchy. Therefore, this method is not able to provide efficient decision support.

The OLAP-Favored Search composes the aggregation R-tree with the summarized table [4]. The aggregation R-tree of this method is just extended for the link to the tuple of the summarized table on each entry. The summarized table stores the pre-aggregated value from past to present [8]. This method can provide the historically aggregated value. However, the execution time of this method is increased as times go on because of increasing size of the summarized table. Therefore, the index for efficient analysis of past to present and the efficient support of the spatial hierarchy and the temporal hierarchy is needed.

3 Efficient Spatial Query Processing Using the Hybrid Index with the Pre-aggregated Value

In this section, we propose the structure of the hybrid index in spatial data warehouses for efficient decision support. The main idea is to integrate the extended aggregation R-tree and the sorted hash table. Each entry of the extended aggregation R-tree has independent sorted hash table. An extended aggregation R-tree stores a link to tuple of the sorted hash table and values of the aggregate function for data within the MBR. The sorted hash table stores aggregated values of temporal unit for each entry of the extended aggregation R-tree. The hybrid index is built on the object of spatial dimension and the time unit of temporal dimension. Therefore the structure of hybrid index has both the spatial hierarchy based on level of the R-tree and the temporal hierarchy based on temporal units.

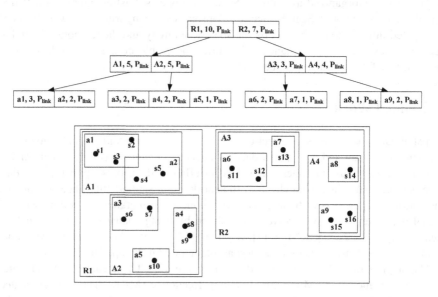

Fig. 1. Extended aggregation R-tree is based on R-tree. Each entry has MBR, aggregated value, and the pointer of sorted Hash Table.

We assumed that every object in some region lies on the arbitrary position and the hybrid index is constructed with those objects. The aggregate function used in the following example of hybrid index is *SUM*.

Fig. 1 logically represents the extended aggregation R-tree of the hybrid index which indexes a set of 9 region segments *r1, r2, ..., r9*, with MBR as *a1, a2, ..., a9* respectively when we assume that the virtual region is in a rectangle. There are 3 objects on the region $r1$, objects of a1 are $s1$, $s2$, $s3$ respectively. And $a1$ has P_{link} which indicates the independent sorted hash table for the temporal hierarchy. There-fore, the total number of objects in $r1$ is 3 and there is an entry $(a1, 3, P_{link})$ in the internal node of the extended aggregation R-tree of the hybrid index. Moving one upper level, MBR $A1$ contains two regions, $r1$, $r2$. The total number of objects in these regions is 5. And $A1$ has P_{link} which indicates the independent sorted hash table. Therefore, there is an entry $(A1, 5, P_{link})$ as a node of level 1 in the extended aggrega-tion R-tree.

The extended aggregation R-tree is not changed in any case since every region is the standard unit for analysis. So, the update of entry has 3 cases according to move-ment of object. First case is that new object enters in some region. In this case, we find region containing the object from the root node to the leaf node. If we find it in the root level, we add measure value of the object to the aggregated value of the entry and we find region contains the object in the next level. Until we find region of leaf node, we continue the same process. Second case is that the object of some region leaves out in the extended aggregation R-tree. In this case, we find region containing the object from root level to leaf level and we subtract the measure value of the object from the aggregated value of the entry found on each level. This case is the same as the operation of first case except that the add operation is changed into the subtract operation. Final case is that one object moves one region to other region. This case is to combine the case which object leaves out of some region and the case which object enters in some region. Therefore, we operate first case and second case in sequence.

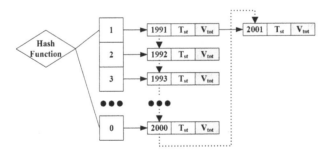

Fig. 2. The sorted Hash Table has ten hash values. Each bucket is composed of unit year, time structure, total value, and the pointer.

Fig. 2 shows the sorted hash table of the hybrid index. Hash function calculates key value of unit year of temporal data. The range of key value is from 0 to 9 and this value is the same as at the most right number of year unit. Each bucket has a linked list of one or more year structures. The year structure has five fields; key value, time structure, totally aggregated value, next bucket pointer, and next year pointer. Key value has year unit and can identify other year unit. Time structure (T_{st}) has aggre-gated values of month and day. In next paragraph, we deal with time structure. Total aggregated value (V_{tot}) is total aggregated value to belong to year unit. For example, if total aggregated value of every month in some year unit is 5, V_{tot} is 60. The next bucket pointer indicates the next year structure on the same bucket and the next year pointer indicates year structure of temporally next year.

Fig. 3 shows the simple structure of the time structure composed with month, day, and hour. Month has twelve slots as from January to December. Each slot has both the identification and total aggregated value of its days. Therefore, there is a slot (M_{id}, V_{tot}). M_{id} means identification of month and it is the same as month number. V_{tot} means the total aggregated value of days in its month. Day and hour have slots of the same form as month slot. The number of day slots is 31 and the number of hour slot is 24. The number of day in each month is different but the number of day slot is fixed. Fixing the number of slots makes structure simple and provides easy processing. If the number of day in some month is smaller than 31, remained slots is masked.

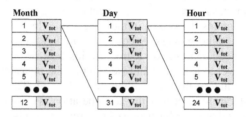

Fig. 3. Time structure is composed of time units under unit year. This shows the composition of time structure composed of three time units: Month, Day, and Hour.

The sorted hash table must maintain historically aggregated values since historical data is important for trend analysis. Therefore, there is only the insert operation in the sorted hash table. We assume that one object enters in an area of the hybrid index and the region containing the object is found on each level of the extended aggregation R-tree. Those entries process the insert operation of each sorted hash table. We calculate key value using the hash function and find the year structure corresponding key value. Next, total aggregated value of the year structure is increased for the measure value of object. The month slot can be found using the month number since the slot number is the same as the month number. After finding the month slot, total aggregated value of that month slot is increased similarly. The day slot and the hour slot can be treated using the same method as the month slot.

Search operation using the hybrid index has two cases. One is to find the currently aggregated value and another is to find the historically aggregated value. Search algorithm using the hybrid index is as follows.

HybridSearch(N, p, T, U)
Input: root node N, search predicate p, temporal range T
wanted time unit U
Output: all slots of both time and aggregated value that satisfies p

SlotList ret = null
IF N is not a leaf THEN
        FOR Each entry E on N
        BEGIN
                IF p.MBR contains E.MBR THEN
                        IF T is current THEN // start time is same to end time

```
                                        add time and the aggregated value to ret
                            ELSE
                                        add HashSearch(E.H, T, U) to ret
                    IF p.MBR is intersected with E.MBR THEN
                            // invoke HybridSearch on the subtree
                            // whose root node is referenced by E.ptr
                            add HybridSearch(E.ptr, p, T) to ret
            END
ELSE    // N is a leaf
            FOR Each entry E on N
            BEGIN
                    IF p.MBR contains E.MBR THEN
                            IF T is current THEN
                                        add time and the aggregated value to ret
                            ELSE
                                        add HashSearch(E.H, T, U) to ret
            END
RETURN ret
```

The hybrid index executes HybridSearch(N, p, T, U) when the query has some given window areas. In the extended aggregation R-tree, it compares query window with MBR of each entry of each node from root node N to leaf node. If query window completely contained by MBR of an entry, it adds the aggregated value of entry to result (ret). In this case, if the wanted temporal range is current, we get the aggregated value of the extended aggregation R-tree. Otherwise, it calls HashSearch function. If query window is intersected with an entry, it invokes HybridSearch function on the subtree.

```
            HashSearch(H, T, U)              // can provide until month unit
Input:      sorted hash table H, temporal range T
            wanted time unit U
Output:     all slots of both time and the aggregated value that is contained T
SlotList ret = null
YearStructure Y = year structure found by hash value of year unit on start time
FOR Y.Year <= Year of end time
BEGIN
            IF U is year unit THEN
                    add total aggregated value of Y to ret
            ELSE IF U is month unit THEN
                    FOR Each month slot M in Y
                    BEGIN
                            IF (M.Month >= month of start time) and
                                    (Y.Year and M.Month is same to end time
                                    or is older than end time)
                                    add total aggregated value of M to ret
                    END
            Y = year structure of next year
END
RETURN ret
```

HashSearch(H, T, U) is executed by HybridSearch function when wanted tempo-ral range is not current. The hash value is calculated by hash function with year value on start time. Using the hash value, the year structure is found. If the wanted time unit is year, it adds total aggregated value of the year structure to result (ret). If the wanted time unit is month, it finds month slots which satisfy temporal condition and it adds total aggregated value of them to result (ret). Until the year value of the year structure reaches it of end time, the same process is continued.

4 Performance Evaluation

In this section, we evaluate the proposed method by simulating a scenario of a traffic system. We use a system which has a CPU (P4 3.0) and a memory (1GB). The base map for experiment is the road of Seoul in KOREA. 5,000 cars exist continuously on the hybrid index and almost 5,000 cars move in the area that hybrid index manages. Also, almost 5,000 of cars move out of management area of the hybrid index. Test data is randomly inserted in the hybrid index.

First performance evaluation compares the accessed number of nodes for search-ing current aggregated information. We survey the accessed number of nodes for processing 100 queries (size of query window is same, but the position of it is dif-fer-ent). And we repeat this evaluation varying the query window area from 0.001% to 20%.

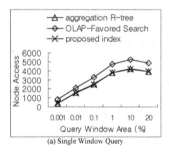
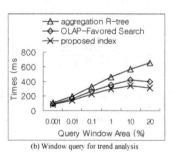

Fig. 4. This shows performance of window query. The performance of the proposed method has similar to aggregation R-tree on single window query. But, in window query for trend analysis, the proposed method is improved more than other methods.

In Fig. 4 (a), performance of both the aggregation R-Tree and the proposed index is almost same because of using similar technique of search operation for the cur-rently aggregated value. But search operation of the OLAP-Favored Search must read the summarized table after searching the aggregation R-tree. Therefore, the OLAP-Favored Search shows the worst performance.

Beyond a threshold size (i.e. 10% of the space) we can observe decreasing the ac-cess number of nodes. At the extreme case that the query window covers the whole space, only one access (to the root node) is required since all data are covered by the entry of root area.

Second performance evaluation compares analysis capability performance with window query for trend analysis. This evaluation conducts under same condition of first evaluation. The period of wanted time is random between the range of 30 ~ 50 days.

Fig. 4 (b) shows that the aggregation R-tree has bad performance since all data of the fact table must be read to find historical data. The OLAP-Favored Search searches the historically aggregated value in the summarized table. This method is better than the aggregation R-tree, but is worse than the proposed index. In case of the proposed index, the aggregated value can be found rapidly because the historically aggregated value is constructed by sorted hash table of year unit containing time structure of temporal units except year.

The proposed method requires more space than other methods. So, we evaluate space size and response time of tendency analysis while period of historical data increases from 1 to 10 year.

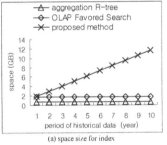 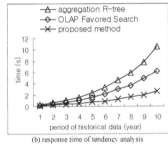

(a) space size for index   (b) response time of tendency analysis

Fig. 5. The proposed method increases the space size for storing historical aggregation value. But this information brings about better performance of tendency analysis.

Fig.5 (a) shows performance evaluation of space size for managing historical data. As period is increased, aggregation R-tree and OLAP Favored Search have a fixed value but the proposed method has an incremental value. Both aggregation R-tree and OLAP Favored Search don't have historical aggregation but the proposed method has historical aggregation. So space size of the proposed method increases in proportion to the number of years. However, the size of storage device is more and more big and its cost is on the decrease. Therefore, space size of the proposed method has no effect on performance.

Fig.5 (b) shows comparison of response time for tendency analysis as period is long. For this evaluation, the size of query window fixed 10%. The proposed method has low incremental ratio since it has sorted Hash Table for tendency analysis. However other methods has higher incremental ratio than the proposed method because those indexes have no historical information. So both should read and aggregate raw data for tendency analysis.

5 Conclusion

In this paper, we focus on design of the hybrid index for spatio-temporal OLAP in spatial data warehouses. The hybrid index structure is composed with the extended aggregation R-tree, And the sorted hash table is established. Each entry of the extended aggregation R-tree has the pre-aggregated value of current data and link for historical data. Year structure of the sorted hash table has five fields; the key value for identification of each year structure, the total aggregated value of year unit, time structure for time units on year, the next bucket pointer linking year structures of the same bucket, and the next year pointer to guarantee serialization of year unit. Therefore, both the window query for current aggregation and trend analysis do not need to access raw data in fact table since the hybrid index provides historical data and spatio-temporal hierarchy.

The single window query and the window query for trend analysis by the proposed hybrid index showed more efficient results without processing aggregation and reduced response time. Our method allows the efficient window query and the temporal oriented range query for decision support in spatial data warehouses.

References

1. A. Guttman, R-trees: a dynamic index structure for spatial searching. ACM SIGMOD, 1984.
2. D. Papadias, P. Kalnis, J. Zhang, and Y. Tao, Efficient OLAP Operations in Spatial Data Warehouses. Technical Report: HKUST-CS01-01, University of Science & Technology, Hon Kong, 2001.
3. ESRI, Spatial Data Warehousing for Hospital Organizations, An ESRI White Paper, 1998. http://www.esri.com/library/whitepapers/pdfs/sdwho.pdf
4. F. Rao, L. Zhang, X. L. Yu, Y. Li, and Y. Chen, Spatial Hierarchy and OLAP-Favored Search in Spatial Data Warehouse. DOLAP, 2003.
5. J. Gray, A. Bosworth, A. Layman, and H. Pirahesh, Data Cube: a Relational Aggregation Operator Generalizing Group-by. ICDE, 1996.
6. L. Zhang, Y. Li, F. Rao, X. Yu, and Y. Chen, An approach to enabling spatial OLAP by aggregating on spatial hierarchy. In Proc. Data Warehousing and Knowledge Discovery, 2003.
7. N. Beckmann, H. P. Kriegel, R. Schneider, and B. Seeger, The R*-tree: an efficient and robust access method for points and rectangles. ACM SIGMOD, 1990.
8. N. Colossi, W. Malloy, and B. Reinwald, Relational extensions for OLAP. IBM SYSTEMS JOURNAL, 2002.
9. R. A. Finkel, and J. L. Bentley, Quad trees: A data structure for retrieval on composite keys. Acta Informatica, 1974.
10. R. Kimball, The Data Warehouse Toolkit. John Wiley, 1996.
11. T. K. Sellis, N. Roussopoulos, and C. Faloutsos, The R+-Tree: A dynamic index for multi-dimensional objects. VLDB, 1987.
12. V. Harinarayan, A. Rajaraman, and J. Ullman, Implementing Data Cubes Efficiently. ACM SIGMOD, 1996.

Managing Evolution of Data Warehouses by Means of Nested Transactions

Bartosz Bebel, Zbyszko Królikowski, and Robert Wrembel

Institute of Computing Science, Poznań University of Technology, Poznań, Poland
{Bartosz.Bebel, Zbyszko.Krolikowski, Robert.Wrembel}@cs.put.poznan.pl

Abstract. In this paper we address problems of managing data warehouses (DWs) that evolve in time and we demonstrate that transactional maintenance of evolving DWs is inevitable. To this end, we propose a nested transaction model. In this model we define 5 types of transactions each of which is responsible for certain tasks. The tasks and properties of these transactions are characterized in the paper.

1 Introduction

A data warehouse (DW) is a centralized repository of data acquired from external data sources. The purpose of building a DW is the integration of data that are further analyzed by the so called On-Line Analytical Processing (OLAP) applications. The results of the analyses are the basis of strategic business decisions.

Typically, external data sources (EDSs) are either autonomous and heterogeneous transactional systems, or various data files, spread sheets, and web pages. EDSs have dynamic nature that is manifested by changes of their content as well as changes to their schema and structures of dimensions. In order to keep the content of a DW up-to-date, the ETL process is run periodically. Typically, DW refreshing with respect to its content is implemented by materialized views [11]. EDS structural changes in practice are difficult to propagate into a DW. Research concepts and commercial systems mostly assume that the structure of a DW remains invariant within its life cycle.

In this paper we propose an approach to handling structural changes of a DW. We analyze typical cases of changes to a DW schema and the structure of dimensions and we show that traditional DW technologies manage these changes inappropriately (cf. Sections 4 and 5). For this reason, we use a multiversion data warehouse as a tool for handling structural changes. In order to manage such a DW, we propose a new transaction model (cf. Section 6).

2 Basic Definitions

Typically, a DW uses the so called *multidimensional data model* [12]. In this model data are organized as n-dimensional cubes. Figure 1 shows an example three-dimensional cube, which represents the sale of sport goods in cities within a given time. It is dimensioned by *Product*, *Location*, and *Time*. Each dimension

T. Yakhno and E. Neuhold (Eds.): ADVIS 2006, LNCS 4243, pp. 119–128, 2006.

is identified by a unique name and it usually has a hierarchical structure that describes the way of aggregating data. An example geographical dimension, called *Location*, is shown in Figure 1. It consists of two levels: base level *City* and its parent level *Region*.

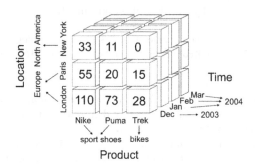

Fig. 1. An example three-dimensional cube

Values in a given dimension level are called *level instances*. In Figure 1, the instances of level *City* include 'New York', 'Paris', and 'London'. Each instance of *City* is connected to an instance of its parent level *Region*, i.e 'New York' has as its parent instance 'North America'. Level instances and the hierarchy they form constitute a *dimension instance*.

A cube stores analyzed data that are called *facts*. Facts are described by numerical values, called *measures*, e.g. the number of items sold, duration time, insurance fee. Measures are stored in cells of a cube.

The multidimensional data model can be implemented either in ROLAP (Relational OLAP) or MOLAP (Multidimensional OLAP) servers. In the MOLAP implementation, data are stored in multidimensional arrays. In the ROLAP implementation, data are stored in relational tables. Some of the tables store facts, and are called *fact tables*, some store values of levels, and are called *dimension level tables*. Typically, fact and dimension level tables are organized either as a star or a snowflake schemas [9].

3   Related Work

Data changes in EDSs are typically handled by means of materialized views [11]. One of the serious problems in this issue concerns the elimination of the so called duplication data anomaly and broken query anomaly. The solutions proposed in the literature use compensation algorithms (e.g. [1,24,26]), distributed processing algorithms (e.g. [21]), and dedicated refreshing transactions (e.g. [7]). Moreover, [19] addressed the problem of the so called view adaptation, i.e. a technique for adjusting a materialized view data after the view definition change. [17,25] proposed a solution to the so called view synchronization problem, i.e. a technique for adjusting a materialized view definition after EDSs schema change.

There are several approaches to handling changes in the structure of dimensions and dimension instances as well as changes in a DW schema. The problem of dimension changes, so called slowly changing dimensions, was initially analyzed in [15]. The author identified three types of changing dimensions and proposed solutions to handle only simple updates to level instances. [4,13,16] proposed to use schema and data evolution mechanism. In these approaches, there is only one DW schema and only one set of data consistent with its schema. As a consequence, it is impossible to manage historical DW states since any change to a schema or dimension instances overwrites a previous DW state. [8,10,22] apply timestamps on dimension instances in order to create temporal versions. These approaches are inappropriate for handling schema changes.

[3,6] propose to apply data and schema versions. [3] uses data model composed of time-stamped structural versions that represent DW evolution. In this approach, only changes to dimension instance structure are taken into consideration.

The multiversion data warehouse (MVDW) proposed in [6] supports the evolution of a DW schema and dimensions. The MVDW is composed of a sequence of versions. A DW version is composed of a *schema version* that stores definitions of all objects (fact and dimension/level tables, attributes and integrity constraints) and an *instance version* that stores data consistent with its schema version. Two types of versions are distinguished, namely real and alternative ones. Real versions reflect a real state of EDSs, whereas alternative versions are used by DW users for simulation/prediction purposes. Each DW version, except an initial real one, is derived from another version, called a *parent version*. A version derivation process consists in the sequence of steps which copy all parent version structures and data to its child version. Versions (real and alternative ones) are physically stored on a disk. User queries can address either a single real or alternative version or can span several consecutive versions.

4   Data Warehouse Dynamics

DW dynamics manifests in two distinct forms: data dynamics as well as schema and dimension structure dynamics.

4.1   Data Dynamics

Data dynamics requires transactional DW refreshing. A software called *monitor* starts a refreshing process after detecting data updates at EDSs (if an EDS is an active system it notifies a DW itself, otherwise a DW is responsible for detecting EDS content changes). The EDS update notification is not sufficient for a refreshing process. The DW needs to read some supplementary data from the EDS. For this purpose, the DW sends to the EDS so called *maintenance queries* [1]. If data read by maintenance queries are concurrently updated locally at the EDS, the results of maintenance queries can be erroneous and may create incorrect data. This case is called a *data duplication anomaly* [1]. Moreover, if the EDS schema has been changed and the DW is not aware of this change, it is not possible either to run a maintenance query or to complete a refreshing process. This case is known as a *broken query anomaly* [1]. The elimination of such anomalies is one of important problems in the area of DW refreshing.

4.2   Dimension Dynamics and Schema Dynamics

One of the basic assumptions concerning traditional DWs states that a DW reflects real world dynamics only with respect to its transactional fact data, while the structures of dimensions remain static [2,14]. Practice shows, however, that this assumption is often too restrictive. As a consequence, the application of traditional DWs is limited to static environments. If a traditional DW is applied to a dynamic environment, it often results in wrong outcomes of analytical queries.

As an example, let us consider a DW that stores information on *Sale* (facts) of *Products* (dimension) in *Shops* (dimension), in *Time* (dimension). In a real business, it is typical that while some shops are being closed down, other shops are being open, and yet others are being split (e.g. a sport shop splits into two shops, one selling bikes and one selling water sport gears). If our example DW is to reflect the real world correctly, its *Shops* dimension should reflect all these changes in dimension instances. If the DW refreshes only transactional fact data while its dimension data remain static, then the DW content will not truly describe the reality, analysis performed by DW users will not be correct, and as a consequence, wrong business decisions may be taken.

The structure of a dimension instance has to follow the real world evolution. We call this process a *dimension instance structure evolution*. In order to support this evolution, we have defined the following operations: (1) adding a new level instance, (2) deleting a level instance, (3) splitting a level instance into n new instances, (4) merging n level instances into a new one, and (5) reclassifying a dimension instance, i.e. changing its parent level instance to another parent level instance (cf. [5]).

Another common assumption for traditional DWs states that a DW schema remains static. We argue that this assumption is also often to restrictive and may limit a DW applicability. In practice, a DW schema requires changing as the result of changes in the structure of EDSs as well as new user requirements that need to analyze new kinds of data, to list the most typical cases.

Returning to our example, let us assume that users want to analyze not only sale of products, but also sale of product categories (e.g. sale of sport clothes). This requirement can be accomplished by changing the DW schema and creating the *Categories* level in the *Products* dimension. Changing the structure of the dimension requires updating dimensions instances, i.e. it is necessary to classify each *Products* instance to one of the *Categories* instances.

We call the process of changing a DW structure a *schema evolution*. In order to support the evolution, we have defined the following operations: (1) creating a new dimension, (2) creating a new dimension level, (3) attaching a level to a dimension hierarchy, (4) detaching a level from a dimension hierarchy, (5) removing a level, (6) removing a dimension, (7) adding a new level attribute, (8) removing a level attribute, (9) altering the domain of a level attribute, (10) creating a new fact table, (11) adding an attribute to a fact table, (12) removing an attribute from a fact table, (13) creating a relationship between a fact table and a dimension, (14) removing a relationship between a fact table and a dimension, and (15) removing a fact table (cf. [5]).

Dynamics of EDSs can not be disregarded [18,23]. Therefore, a proper identification of all potential threats related to a DW schema and dimensions instance evolution is an important issue.

4.3 Schema and Dimension Evolution Problems

In our work we identified four main problems caused by a DW schema and dimensions instance structure evolution, namely: (1) impossible refreshing, (2) data loss, (3) wrong analytical results, (4) query reformulation.

If a DW schema does not follow the changes in EDSs schemas, the difference between a DW schema and the schemas of EDSs will make a DW refreshing process impossible.

Data loss, is caused by an adaptation process that adjusts DW data to a new schema. Let us follow our example and let us assume that shop A was split into shops $A1$ and $A2$. In order to implement this change, two new instances of the *Shops* level have to be created. Since shop A no longer exists, it should be deleted, but there still exist fact instances that describe sale in shop A. Should they also be deleted? If so, users will lose historical information. If the sale instances remain in the DW, than its content will not be consistent with the real world as it will describe sale in the non-existing shop.

The problem of wrong analytical results has its source in changes in the structure of a dimension instance. As an example let us consider our DW where a user periodically executes a query that finds monthly total sale of products per category. At time t_m some products were moved from category $C1$ to $C2$. This change was implemented by the reclassification operation of the instances of level *Products*. After this change, a user executes the query and discovers that sale of products from category $C2$ increased while sale of products from category $C1$ decreased. If a user is not aware of the change in the *Products* dimension instance, then he/she may draw wrong conclusions and come to incorrect business decisions.

Query reformulation is the consequence of schema changes as well as dimension structure changes. An example of a schema change includes replacement of measure *total price* with two measures *item price* and *number of items sold*. Users, who previously were analyzing total prices of products, now have to change their analytical queries and compute total prices by multiplication of the two newly created measures.

Our solution to the aforementioned problems is based on the multiversion data warehouse (MVDW) [6].

5 Activities in the MVDW

User's activities in the MVDW can be categorized as follows: (1) analytical sessions, (2) instance version refreshing, (3) new version derivation, (4) schema evolution, (5) dimension's structure evolution. The concurrently run activities can create various conflicts, as discussed below.

Users analytical sessions can retrieve data from the set of DW versions, real and alternative ones, and therefore their implementation is much more complex than in traditional DWs. A challenging issue is to assure consistent data read in one session, while another session modifies the schema or the instance of a DW version.

In the MVDW only the current real version is being refreshed. The refreshing process has to apply mechanisms which: (1) eliminate the anomalies mentioned in Section 3 and Section 4, (2) isolate the refreshing process from other activities performed concurrently that change a schema and/or an instance version, and (3) assure atomicity of the refreshing process, i.e. instance version changes should be available to other activities only if the refreshing process finishes successfully.

Activities 4 and 5 have similar features. The starting point of both activities can be either EDSs schema or data change detection or a user requesting new kind of functionality offered by a DW. It is necessary to assure that the activities are isolated from effects of other concurrently executed activities and that they are executed atomically. The elimination of the discussed anomalies is also indispensable if a schema version change or dimension change entails DW instance adaptation.

The process of deriving a new DW version during all its activities has to be atomic and it has to see consistent schema and instance of a parent version, i.e. the process is isolated from effects of other activities that may concurrently update the parent version.

6   Transactions in the MVDW

The analysis of various activities in the MVDW and their features leads us to the conclusion that the activities should be implemented as *transactions.* A typical flat transaction used in On-Line Transaction Processing databases is suitable only for short and simple processing, whereas the activities in the MVDW have different characteristics. Firstly, they process large amounts of data that often are distributed among multiple versions. Secondly, the activities last long (hours or even days). Finally, analytical processing is interchanged with operations that manage (create and modify) versions of the MVDW. For these reasons, the *advanced transaction models* seem to be the more suitable for managing MVDW activities. From various advanced transaction models a nested transaction [20] is the most promising.

The most powerful feature of the *nested transaction* is its possibility to split into the set of subtransactions, each of which can be a nested transaction itself. The nested transaction has a hierarchical structure with the main transaction located at the root of the hierarchy. Subtransactions may execute concurrently and their internal components need to be synchronized by internal concurrency control mechanisms, e.g. time-stamping. A subtransaction may succeed and commit, may be replaced by another subtransaction, or may fail and rollback, but the failure of a subtransaction does not invalidate the main transaction.

In this paper we argue that the nested transaction is the most suitable way to implement activities in the MVDW. In our approach, the nested transaction can be of one of the following types: analytic session transaction, version refreshing transaction, version derivation transaction, schema evolution transaction, and dimension evolution transaction. The schematic view on the transactions and their components are shown in Figure 2.

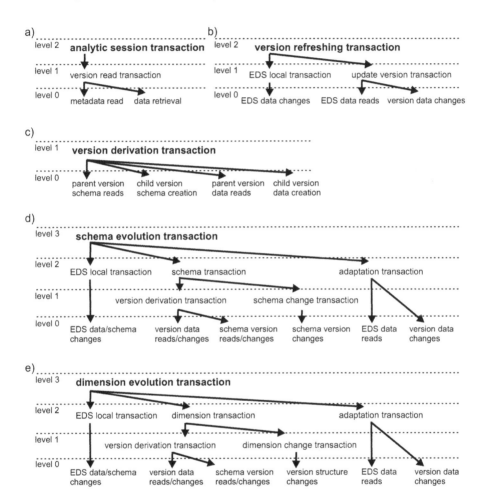

Fig. 2. The schematic view on the nested transactions in the MVDW

The **analytic session transaction** implements a user's analytical session. It consists of the set of subtransactions, each of which retrieves data from one DW version and it is called a *version read transaction*, cf. Figure 2a. A version read transaction addresses one DW version. It consists of elementary operations that include: reading metadata describing a schema version and retrieving data from the addressed version. In order to assure consistent reads, all analytical queries addressing the DW version within a given version read transaction have to retrieve versions of data from the same point in time.

The process of refreshing the content (i.e. data) of the MVDW is similar to refreshing fact and dimension tables in a traditional DW. We assume that only the current real version is refreshed, while other versions remain unchanged. This process is implemented as a nested transaction, called **version refreshing transaction**, cf. Figure 2b. It is composed of two subtransactions, namely a local EDS transaction and an update version transaction. The *local EDS transaction* is applied to changing the content of an EDS. The commit of this transaction triggers the update version transaction. The *update version transaction* is responsible for fetching data from EDSs (cf. *EDS data reads* in Figure 2b) and loading them into the current real version (cf. *version data changes* in Figure 2b). To this end, it sends maintenance queries to EDSs in order to find data necessary for incremental refreshing fact and dimension level tables.

Derivation of a new DW version creates a new version, based on a parent version. This process is represented by a flat transaction, called **version derivation transaction**, cf. Figure 2c. This transaction consists of: (1) reading the schema of a parent DW version, (2) creating the schema of a child version, (3) reading data from the parent version, and (4) creating data in the child version based on its parent version. All steps of the version derivation transaction have to be isolated from other concurrently performed activities. Atomicity of the version derivation transaction has to be assured, i.e. a child version should be accessible for users only if every step in version derivation transaction has completed successfully.

Altering the schema and the structure of dimensions in a given DW version is done by means of a **schema evolution transaction** and a **dimension evolution transaction**, respectively. If the structure of an EDS is changed by local transaction (noted as an *EDS local transaction* in Figures 2d and 2e) then committing the transaction triggers either a schema evolution or dimension evolution transaction. An administrator can also start these transactions manually, e.g. when he/she creates an alternative version for simulation purposes and modifies the schema and structure of dimensions in this version.

A schema evolution transaction as well as a dimension evolution transaction are nested ones. The first subtransaction to start in a **schema evolution transaction** is a *schema transaction*, whose goal is to make changes to a schema version. Changes to a schema version are done by means of a *schema change transaction* (cf. Figure 2d) that includes operations outlined in Section 4 (see also [5]). Changes to a DW schema may require the creation of a new DW version, that is done by a *version derivation transaction*. After altering a schema version, a DW instance version is being adapted to conform to the altered schema. This task is performed by another subtransaction, called an *adaptation transaction*.

A **dimension evolution transaction** consists of two following subtransactions: a dimension transaction and an adaptation transaction. A goal of a *dimension transaction* (cf. Figure 2e) is to make changes to the structure of a dimension instance in a given DW version. The changes are done by means of a *dimension change transaction* (cf. Figure 2e) that includes operations outlined in Section 4 (see also [5]). Changes to the structure of a dimension instance may require the creation of a new DW version, that is done by a *version derivation transaction*. Next, fact data have to be adjusted to the altered dimension instance structure. This task is done by the second subtransaction, called an *adaptation transaction*.

Adaptation transactions executed within the schema evolution transaction and/or dimension evolution transaction perform the same tasks. To adapt an instance version after schema or dimension structure changes, the MVDW often has to send maintenance queries to EDSs in order to retrieve data necessary for adaptation. This process can be disturbed by concurrent local EDSs updates, resulting in incorrect adaptation. To avoid this problem, the adaptation transaction has to apply the same mechanism as a mechanism used to avoid duplication anomaly during fact table refreshing. However, some adaptations can be performed without accessing EDSs data.

7 Summary

In this paper we discussed underexposed issues concerning the evolution of a DW schema and the structures of dimension instances. We have identified the set of evolution operations and we analyzed potential threats related to their implementations in traditional DWs. We analyzed multiple activities in the MVDW and proposed a nested transaction model for managing these activities. In this model we proposed and characterized all types of transactions. Further work will focus on developing and implementing algorithms for scheduling concurrent transactions in the MVDW.

References

1. Agrawal D., El Abbadi A., Singh A., Yurek T.: Efficient View Maintenance at Data Warehouses. Proc. of ACM SIGMOD (1997) 417–427
2. Agrawal R., Gupta A., Sarawagi S.: Modeling Multidimensional Databases. Proc. of ICDE (1997) 232–243
3. Body M., Miquel M., Bédard Y., Tchounikine A.: A Multidimensional and Multiversion Structure for OLAP Applications. Proc. of DOLAP (2002) 1–6
4. Blaschka M., Sapia C., Hofling G.: On Schema Evolution in Multidimensional Databases. Proc. of DaWaK (1999) 153–164
5. Bębel, B.: A Transactional Refreshment of Data Warehouses. Phd thesis, Institute of Computing Science, Poznań University of Technology (2005)
6. Bębel B., Eder J., Koncilia C., Morzy T., Wrembel R.: Creation and Management of Versions in Multiversion Data Warehouse. Proc. of ACM SAC (2004) 717–723
7. Chen J., Chen S., Rundensteiner E.: A Transactional Model for Data Warehouse Maintenance. Proc of ER (2002) 247–262
8. Chamoni P., Stock S.: Temporal Structures in Data Warehousing. Proc. of DaWaK (1999) 353–358

9. Chaudhuri S., Dayal U.: An overview of data warehousing and OLAP technology. SIGMOD Record, 26 (1997) 65–74
10. Eder J., Koncilia C., Morzy T.: The COMET Metamodel for Temporal Data Warehouses. Proc. of CAISE (2002) 83–99
11. Gupta A., Mumick I.S. (eds.): Materialized Views: Techniques, Implementations, and Applications. The MIT Press, ISBN 0-262-57122-6 (1999).
12. Gyssens M., Lakshmanan L.V.S.: A Foundation for Multi-Dimensional Databases. Proc. of VLDB (1997) 106–115
13. Hurtado C., Mendelzon A., Vaisman A.: Maintaining Data Cubes under Dimension Updates. Proc. of ICDE (1999) 346–355
14. Inmon W. H.: Building the Data Warehouse. John Wiley & Sons (1996)
15. Kimball R.: The Data Warehouse Toolkit: Practical Techniques for Building Dimensional Data Warehouses. John Wiley & Sons (1996)
16. Kaas C., Pedersen T.B., Rasmussen B.: Schema Evolution for Stars and Snowflakes. Proc. of ICEIS (2004) 425–433
17. Liu B., Chen S., Rundensteiner E.: A Transactional Approach to Parallel Data Warehouse Maintenance. Proc. of DaWaK (2002) 307–316
18. Marche S.: Measuring the Stability of Data Models. European Journal of Information Systems, 2(1) (1993) 37–47
19. Mohania M., Dong G.: Algorithms for Adapting Materialized Views in Data Warehouses. Proc. of CODAS (1996) 353–354
20. Moss J.E.B.: Nested Transactions: An Approach to Reliable Distributed Computing. M.I.T. Press, Cambridge (1985)
21. Mostefaoui A., Raynal M., Roy M., Agrawal D., El Abbadi A.: The Lord of the Rings: Efficient Maintenance of Views at Data Warehouses. Proc. of DISC (2002) 33–47
22. Mendelzon A., Vaismann A.: Temporal Queries in OLAP. Proc. of VLDB (2000) 242–253
23. Sjøberg D.: Quantifying Schema Evolution. Information and Software Technology, 35(1) (1993) 35–44
24. Zhang X., Rundensteiner E., Ding L.: PVM: Parallel View Maintenance Under Concurrent Data Updates of Distributed Systems. Proc. of DaWaK (2001) 230–239
25. Zhang, X., Rundensteiner, E.: Integrating the maintenance and synchronization of data warehouses using a cooperative framework. Information Systems 27 (2002) 219–243
26. Zhuge, Y., Garcia-Molina, H., Hammer, J., Widom, J.: View Maintenance in Warehousing Environment. Proc. of ACM SIGMOD (1995) 316–327

Optimization of Queries Invoking Views by Query Tail Absorption[1]

Hanna Kozankiewicz[1,3], Krzysztof Stencel[2,3], and Kazimierz Subieta[1,3]

[1] Institute of Computer Sciences of the Polish Academy of Sciences, Warsaw, Poland
[2] Institute of Informatics, Warsaw University, Warsaw, Poland
[3] Polish-Japanese Institute of Information Technology, Warsaw, Poland
{hanka, subieta}@ipipan.waw.pl, stencel@mimuw.edu.pl

Abstract. A widely recognized method to optimize queries invoking virtual views is query modification. The method is based on macro-substitution, where a view invocation is textually unfolded within a query and then optimized together with the query. For complex SBQL views this method is not always applicable because a view can depend on some private server resources (thus it cannot be sent to the client side) or a view is defined by a complex algorithm (thus the view cannot be unfolded within a query). For such cases we propose a reverse technique which assumes absorption of a part of the client query (a query tail) by a view definition and then, optimization of the definition. The technique has the same potential as query modification, but it is less constrained. In the paper we illustrate both techniques on examples and present some architectural peculiarities of the new method.

1 Introduction

A widely recognized method to optimize queries invoking virtual views is query modification [Ston75, SP01, Sub04, Koz05]. Essentially, the method is based on macro-substitution, where a view is treated as a macro-definition. Each view invocation in a query is textually substituted by the view body[2]. Such an expanded version of the query is further rewritten to make it efficient. In the first step the rewriting removes so-called *dead sub-queries* [PS01], i.e. parts of the expanded query that come from the view, but are unnecessary for calculating the final query result. In next steps other optimization methods can be applied, such as factoring out independent subqueries [PK00], pushing selections down query trees, applying indices, etc.

For SQL views query modification can be applied in all cases. This universality, however, is at the cost of the limited power of SQL views. SQL views are defined by single queries, they cannot refer to environments other than a corresponding relational database, they cannot possess an own encapsulated state, they cannot be recursive, etc. The limitations are not much painful for typical applications of relational databases based on a single server. The situation is quite different in a system which has

---

[1] This work is supported by European Commission under the 6th FP project e-Gov Bus, IST-4-026727-ST.
[2] In SQL the method implies some problem caused by renaming in views the original names of columns of stored tables.

T. Yakhno and E. Neuhold (Eds.): ADVIS 2006, LNCS 4243, pp. 129–138, 2006.

to virtually and transparently integrate distributed, heterogeneous and redundant resources according to a predefined global schema, perhaps object-oriented or XML/RDF-oriented. In such applications views may be useful as mediators on the top of local resources, as integrators to fuse local resources into global virtual resources according to the global schema, and as definitions of external schemata for particular users of the integrated system. For such applications SQL views are insufficient. For our recent project e-Gov Bus (devoted to virtual integration of resources being under the control of various European governmental institutions) we have developed and implemented much more powerful views [HKKS05, KLS03, KSS04, Koz05], with the following properties:

- Views are defined in the object-oriented query/programming language SBQL [Sub04, Sub06] that has the power of universal programming languages.

- Views are essentially extended programming functions, possibly recursive, with local objects and a sequence of commands implementing a non-trivial algorithm.

- Views can access the entire computer environment on the side of the server, for instance, local server libraries.

- Views can have its own persistent state (e.g. for security, communication protocols, global transactions, global indexing, etc.); such a state is encapsulated, not seen for the clients.

- Views may call a specific communication protocol (currently Web Services).

- Views support unambiguous updating of virtual objects (i.e. objects generated by a view), with no anomalies.

For such powerful views the query modification method may be inapplicable for a lot of reasons, e.g. for an encapsulated view environment or access to server libraries. If query modification is inapplicable, then a view has to be fully materialized all the times when the view is invoked in a query. The materialization may imply poor performance of the application.

In this paper we propose the solution that works in exactly opposite direction than the query modification and is less constrained than query modification. If the view body cannot be moved to the client query, perhaps it is possible to move the query to the view body. After moving, it would be possible to optimize the body according to all the implemented query optimization methods. Thus the eventual view materialization can be more efficient.

The method is unexplored in the literature. As far as we know, there is no implementation. The only paper dealing with a similar approach to relational views is [LMS94], which proposes a method called *predicate-move-around*. It assumes moving a predicate from a query invoking a view into the view body. Our proposal is more general. Let a client query be of the form $(V\ tail)$, where V is a view invocation, *tail* is a part of the query that follows the invocation, and let the view body be finished by the statement *return(q)*, where q is the final query forming the view output. Roughly our method assumes that the client query is substituted simply by V, and the return statement will take the form *return(q tail)*. After this rewriting the query $(q\ tail)$ is optimized according to all the methods, including removing dead subqueries, pushing selections, indices, etc. Then, the modified V is materialized and the result is sent to the client. The *tail* may include many operators that connect invocation of V with the rest of the client query, in particular, selection, projection/navigation, join, etc. as well as combinations of them.

There are practically no limitations concerning the use of this method. It is sufficient that *tail* has no references to local client resources. This holds for majority of cases and can be checked by a properly designed strong typing mechanism.

A systematic approach to the problem of query optimization requires a strong formal model of a data/object store, precise formal semantics of a query language addressing the store, universality of the language and its full compositionality (allowing easy decomposition of queries). All these qualities are achieved within the Stack-Based Approach (SBA) and its query language SBQL [Sub04, Sub06][3], which allows for designing many decomposition/optimization strategies. The query tail absorption method can be very useful in a distributed environment, because it allows for transferring query tails to sites at which the evaluation of resulting queries will be faster and less resource consuming.

The rest of the paper is organized as follows. In Section 2 we introduce shortly the view mechanism that we have developed and implemented. Section 3 presents the idea of query modification on a simple example. Section 4 discusses basic issues of the query tail absorption method. Section 5 presents basic architectural assumptions concerning implementation of the method. Section 6 concludes.

2   View Mechanism

In SBA/SBQL we take the position that query languages are specific programming languages rather than realizations of database theories such as relational algebras or calculi. In this setting a classical database view (known from SQL) is a programming function returning a bulk output (determined by a query) that can be processed by a query invoking the view. The output can be treated as an l-value in updating statements addressing virtual objects. Such an approach, however, leads to a lot of updating anomalies, well recognized and described in the literature. To avoid anomalies our view definitions are more complex structure than classical programming functions.

A view definition consists of several parts. The first part describes a mapping between stored and virtual data. It has the form of a procedure that returns entities called *seeds* that ambiguously identify virtual objects. Next parts specify actions that are to be performed when a particular operation is performed on a virtual object. These parts are also specified as procedures, with seeds as implicit parameters. The procedures are written by the view definer and their role is to *overload* generic updating operations acting on a virtual object delivered by the view. A view definition can also contain other elements such as definitions of subviews, internal procedures, classes, state objects, etc.

We have identified several such generic operations on virtual objects:

- **Delete** that deletes a given virtual object.
- **Update** that changes the value of the given virtual object. The operation has a parameter that is a new value of the object.
- **Insert** that inserts a new object into the given virtual object. The operation has a parameter that is a reference to an object to be inserted.

---

[3] For space limits in this paper we are unable to present SBA and SBQL. The interested reader can check the cited sources and a lot of other materials devoted to SBA/SBQL.

- **Dereference** that returns the value of the given virtual object.
- **Create** that creates a new virtual object.

For each generic operation the view definer may write overloading procedure. It will be called during run-time when a generic operation on a virtual object is recognized. The names of procedures are fixed and are respectively *on_delete, on_update, on_insert, on_retrieve* and *on_create*. If some procedure is not defined, it means that the corresponding operation on a virtual object is forbidden. The names of parameters of operations *on_update, on_create* and *on_insert* can be freely chosen by a view definer. For view administration purposes in our approach a name of the view definition is different from the name of defined virtual objects. Usually we apply a naming convention where a view definition name is augmented by the suffix *Def* e.g. *worstSellingBookDef*.

In our approach we can nest views. We follow the *relativity principle* which claims for the same syntax, semantics and pragmatics of language constructs for all the nesting levels. Subviews deliver virtual subobjects for given virtual objects.

This approach also supports views with parameters being regular SBQL queries. Various methods of passing parameters (e.g. *call-by-value* and *call-by-reference*) may be adapted. The mechanism of passing parameters to the body of a view is analogical as passing parameters to the body of a procedure (i.e. through the environment stack).

This approach also supports recursive views because views are entities similar to procedures and are executed by the same stack-based mechanism. A view may possess local volatile data for every procedure defined inside a view, and may possess an own persistent state as an additional component of the view module.

Let the database to store many *Book* objects with attributes *title, author, sold, price* and *currency*. The attribute *sold* determines how many copies of the book have been sold. The example view returns virtual objects *worstSellingBook(vtittle, vauthor, vprice)* concerning books having *sold* < 5. Their virtual prices are always in Euro (€), converted from their original currency according to some procedure. Price of the book can be changed – in such a way we can e.g. give discounts for some books.

```
create view worstSellingBookDef {

    virtual objects worstSellingBook {
        return (Book where sold < 5) as b;}

    on_delete do { delete b; }

    create view vtitleDef {
        virtual objects vtitle { return (b.title) as t; }
        on_retrieve do { return deref( t ); }          }

    create view vauthorDef {
        virtual objects vauthor { return (b.author) as a; }
        on_retrieve do { return deref( a ); }          }

    create view vpriceDef {
        virtual objects vprice { return ( b.price ) as p; }
        on_retrieve do { return convertToEuro( b.currency, p ); }
        on_update (newPrice) do {
                            p:= convertFromEuro(b.currency, newPrice);}}}
```

The view *worstSellingBookDef* contains only *on_delete* procedure that removes the corresponding book from the database, e.g. on the request:

delete *worstSellingBook* **where** *vtitle* = "Lotus ABC";

The sub-view *vpriceDef* contains two operations: returning the price in € and updating that is determined in € and converted to the actual currency. The view can be called e.g. in the following client request:

(*worstSellingBook* **where** *vtitle* = "VDM").*vprice* := *vprice* - 10;

The request reduces the price of the VDM book on 10€. This reduction is automatically converted to the actual currency determined for the book. During execution of this query the view mechanism calls *on_retrieve* from *vtitleDef* and *vpriceDef* when comparison "=" and operation "-" are performed on *vtitle* and *vprise*, correspondingly, and operation *on_update* when we set a new value for *vprice*.

We assume that the functions *convertToEuro* and *convertFromEuro* are accessible only on the server side; a client application cannot call them directly. This implies that the query modification technique can be inapplicable in this case.

3   Query Modification by Example

In this section we shortly present what query modification technique is and how it can be used in SBA. Consider the view from the previous section and the request (print the author of a worst seller on VDM having the price over 20€):

print((worstSellingBook **where** *vtitle* = "VDM" **and** *vprice* > 20).*vauthor*);

Because the *print*, = and > operators force dereferencing, the request can be initially rewritten to the form:

print((worstSellingBook **where deref**(*vtitle*) = "VDM" **and**
                          deref(*vprice*) >20). **deref**(*vauthor*));

Execution of this query can be costly. In naive implementation it required materialization of the view *worstSellingBook*, then processing the selection according to the predicate after **where**, and then projection on *vauthor*. The *vprice* subview will be invoked as many times as the number of the worst sellers, and each invocation implies executing the costly *convertToEuro* function (which presumably would require an access to some remote bank Web Service). Providing there is an index established for book titles, it would be desirable to use it according to the predicate *vtitle* = "VDM". Unfortunately, the index cannot be used because the view is executed on the side of the server, which is unable to recognize and utilize the syntax of the client query.

Consider the same query after query modification, which relies in replacing all view invocations occurring in this query (*worstSellingBook*, *vtitle*, *vprice* and *vauthor*) by queries from the bodies of these views and replacing all dereference operators by queries from *on_retrieve* functions (preceded by dot). In the result we obtain:

print((((Book **where** *sold* < 5) **as** *b*) **where** (((*b.title*) **as** *t*).*t*) = "VDM" **and**
      (((*b.price*) **as** *p*).*convertToEuro*(*b.currency, p*))) > 20)).(((*b.author*) **as** *a*).*a*));

Then, the optimization steps could be the following:
1. Removing the auxiliary names *t*, *p* and *a*:

   print((((*Book* **where** *sold* < 5) **as** *b*) **where** *b.title* = "VDM" **and**
   convertToEuro(*b.currency, b.price*) > 20).*b.author*);

2. Removing the auxiliary name *b*:

   print(((*Book* **where** *sold* < 5) **where** *title* = "VDM" **and**
   convertToEuro(*currency, price*) > 20). *author*);

3. Changing **where** into **and**:

   print((*Book* **where** *sold* < 5 **and** *title* = "VDM" **and**
   convertToEuro(*currency, price*) > 20).*author*);

4. Applying the index for *title*. An index is understood as a function that takes a value and returns references to all objects having this value. The subquery *Book* **where** *title* = ""VDM" can be replace by calling the index function *BookTitleIndex*("VDM"):

   print((*BookTitleIndex*("VDM") **where** *sold* < 5 **and**
   convertToEuro(*currency, price*) > 20).*author*);

This process ends up with a well optimized query. The index is applied and the *convertToEuro* function is called at most once.

4 Query Tail Absorption

Unfortunately, this query modification cannot be applied in this case because we have assumed that the function *convertToEuro* is unavailable on the client side. If it is impossible to send a view to the caller, we can still try to send a part of the query from the caller to the view. This is the essence of the query tail absorption method.

In our example the tail of the query is:

where *vtitle* = "VDM" **and** *vprice* > 20).*vauthor*

This tail is send to the server storing the view and then combined with the view definition. To this end we make a copy of the *worstSellingBookDef* view on the side of the server, naming it *worstSellingBook1Def*. The corresponding virtual objects will be named *worstSellingBook1*. The client request will be reduced simply to:

print(*worstSellingBook1*);

The *worstSellingBook1Def* view definition should be altered by sticking the tail with the query that occurs after the return command of the virtual objects procedure. In the result we obtain the following form:

```
virtual objects worstSellingBook1 {
return (((Book where sold < 5) as b) where vtitle = "VDM" and
                                            vprice > 20).vauthor ;}
```

Now we unfold *vtittle*, *vauthor* and *vprice* according to the *virtual objects* and *on_retrieve* procedures of the corresponding subviews:

---

virtual objects *worstSellingBook1* {
return ((((*Book* **where** *sold* < 5) **as** *b*) **where** (((*b.title*) **as** *t*).*t*) = "VDM" **and**
      (((*b.price*) **as** *p*).*convertToEuro*(*b.currency*, *p*)))> 20).((((*b.author*) **as** *a*).*a*);}

We see that the situation is very similar as in the case of query modification. Eventually, we obtain the following optimized form:

---

virtual objects *worstSellingBook1* {
  return (*BookTitleIndex*("VDM") **where** *sold* < 5 **and**
                              convertToEuro(*currency*, *price*) > 20).*author*;}

This time, however, there is no problem with the use of the *convertToEuro* function. After execution of the request *print*(*worstSellingBook1*) the *worstSellingBook1* view definition should be removed.

The tail of a query invoking a view may be arbitrarily complex and can be connected with the view invocation not only by the *where* operator, but also by other non-algebraic operators of SBQL, such as dot, join, quantifiers, etc. For instance, in the same way we can treat the query:

worstSellingBook .(*vtitle*, *vprice*, *vauthor*)

and the query (join each worst seller with full information on its author):

worstSellingBook **join** ((*Author* **as** *x*) **where** *x.name* = *vauthor*)

Although the method looks very simple (at least in the above examples), there are a lot of issues and technical details that must be considered if we would like to implement the method within practical software. Some of these issues will be considered in the next section.

Let us take a look at a slightly more complex example of a view with local variables and complex local processing. We will consider an example of an integrating view for three servers located in Cracow, Warsaw and Radom. Fig. 1 depicts the schema of local databases which is also the schema exported by the integrating view.

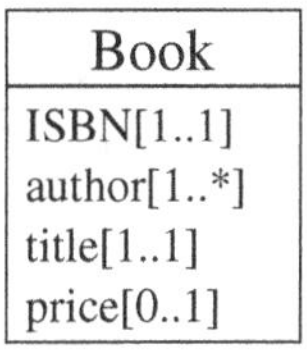

Book
ISBN[1..1]
author[1..*]
title[1..1]
price[0..1]

Fig. 1. Schema of example database

The local server in Cracow is a replica of the server in Warsaw. More precisely, we have the following information:

1. ISBN is a unique identifier of a book.
2. There are no duplicates in databases in Warsaw and Radom.
3. The local servers in Cracow and in Warsaw contain the same information.
4. Data should be retrieved from the server that has shorter access time.

Below we show a fragment of the integrating view definition. Only the procedure generating virtual objects is shown. We assume that the integrating view will return virtual attributes *vISBN*, *vauthor*, *vtitle* and *vprice* (not shown here).

---

create view *myBookDef* {

    virtual objects *myBook* {
        int *timeToWarsaw* := 1000000; **int** *timeToCracow* := 1000000;
        if <u>alive</u>(*Warsaw*) **then** *timeToWarsaw* := <u>checkAccessTime</u>(*Warsaw*);
        if <u>alive</u>(*Cracow*) **then** *timeToCracow* := <u>checkAccessTime</u>(*Cracow*);
        if *min*(**bag**(*timeToWarsaw, timeToCracow*)) > 100 **then** {
                exception(*AccessTimeTooHigh*); **return** $\varnothing$; }
        return ((*Radom . Book* **as** *b*) $\cup$
                if *timeToWarsaw* < *timeToCracow* **then** (*Warsaw . Book* **as** *b*)
                                else (*Cracow . Book* **as** *b*));

    }
    ... definitions of subviews for *vISBN, vauthor, vtitle* and *vprice* ....

}

Functions <u>alive</u> and <u>checkAccessTime</u> are a part of the communication protocol. They are used to determine which of the two local servers (Cracow or Warsaw) is to be used when constructing the seeds of virtual objects.

The procedure which generates virtual objects is complex. It performs many commands and has local variables. Therefore, this view cannot be the subject of the query modification method. If we would like to avoid full materialization of this view, the query tail absorption method is perhaps the only choice. Let us consider the following call to this integrating view:

myBook **where** *vtitle* = "Databases" **and** *vprice* < 1000

All names in the predicate of this selection represent subviews of the integrating view. Thus, the predicate can be absorbed in the view. This means that the last **return** statement in the procedure generating seeds can be evaluated as if it had the following form:

    return ((*Radom . Book* **as** *b*) $\cup$
        if *timeToWarsaw* < *timeToCracow* **then** (*Warsaw . Book* **as** *b*)
                           else (*Cracow . Book* **as** *b*)
) **where** *vtitle* = "Databases" **and** *vprice* < 1000;

As before, virtual attributes *vtitle* and *vprice* can be unfolded according to their definitions.

The query tail absorption method creates the potential for other optimization techniques. We can rewrite the query using the distributiveness of union and the conditional statement. As the result we can push the selection towards subqueries which transfer objects from distant servers (*Radom.Book, Cracow.Book* and *Warsaw.Book*). This way we could limit the amount of transferred data, because the selections could be executed by remote servers (*Radom, Cracow* and *Warsaw*). This also creates the potential for parallel execution of the query on many servers.

5 Architectural Issues

There are many architectural and technical details which should be resolved during implementation of the query tail absorption method. We shortly summarize some of them in the following points:

- In our current implementation queries and views are internally represented as well-formed data structures known as syntax trees. They allow for easy manipulation during optimization, e.g. moving a part of a tree to another tree place. A syntax tree keeps pure abstract syntax of a query; it is free from syntactic sugar and parentheses.
- A syntactic tree is produced by a parser and then modified by a strong type checker. The modification aims several goals, such determining types of literals, resolving ellipses, coercions and automatic dereferences, resolving some binding issues (e.g. the level of the environment stack where a particular name has to be bound) and resolving some environment issues (e.g. determining if a query/subquery does not refer to local objects of an application). This information is crucial for query optimization methods, in particular, the query tail absorption.
- Each persistent entity based on SBQL, such as a view, is kept in two forms: original (non-optimized) and optimized. In the SBQL optimizer we do not assume that the optimization process is performed once and forever. Because different conditions for query execution can change (e.g. the size of the database), the optimization of the same query can be repeated many times. Some of these optimizations can be manually forced by the database administrator. Some other can be called automatically. The query tail absorption method is the optimization case when the optimization process may be repeated automatically, depending on a query invoking a given view.
- In contrast to SQL we assume that a significant part of query optimization has to be done on the client side, thus the server would have smaller workload. This implies that on the server side each public view should be registered in a special register that makes basic properties of available views public to clients. In particular, the information may concern whether a particular view is ready for query modification of not. If it is not ready, the register should record how a query has to modify a view, i.e. which nodes of its syntactic tree are necessary for the method and how they are to be used.
- On the client side there must be implemented a procedure that would efficiently recognize what is actually the tail of a query that has to be absorbed by the view definition. The procedure should recognize as long tail as possible.
- Another register that should be public to clients is the register of indices that are established on the database server. This information can be used by clients to change query trees in the form that makes the use of these indices explicit.

6 Conclusions

We have proposed a new optimization technique for queries invoking views. It concerns views that are too tangled to be the subject of the simple query modification method. It includes a view that has its own persistent state, has local variables, that is recursive, that is defined by a sequence of commands, or that implies an access to features that are private to the server. The proposed optimization technique is the query tail absorption, which consists in shifting the query following the view invocation to the body of the view. The shift means that a part of the query is moved from the client to the server, is stuck with the view definition and then commonly optimized. Moving a part of the query into view definitions opens opportunities for other optimization methods based on query rewriting, on indices and perhaps others.

Because SBQL views are much more powerful than SQL views, the query tail absorption method can be the only imaginable and reasonable method of optimization of queries involving views. In our opinion, every limitation to the power of view definitions will result in some inconvenience or impossibility, especially concerning virtual integration of legacy, distributed, heterogeneous and redundant resources.

The research is done within the e-Gov Bus European project that aims at integrating data and service resources being under control of various EC governmental institutions.

References

[HKKS05]   P.Habela, K.Kaczmarski, H.Kozankiewicz, K.Subieta: Modeling Data Integration with Updatable Object Views. SOFSEM 2005 Conf., Springer LNCS 3381, 2005, pp.188-198

[KLS03]   H.Kozankiewicz, J.Leszczyłowski, K.Subieta. Updateable XML Views. ADBIS 2003 Conf., Springer LNCS 2798, 2003, pp.381-399

[KSS04]   H.Kozankiewicz, K.Stencel, K.Subieta. Integration of Heterogeneous Resources through Updatable Views. Prof of the ETNGRID, 2004, Proc. published by IEEE

[Koz05]   H.Kozankiewicz: Updateable   Object   Views.   PhD   Thesis,   2005, http://www.ipipan.waw.pl/~subieta/ -> Finished PhD-s -> Hanna Kozankiewicz

[LMS94]   A.Y.Levy, I.S.Mumick, Y.Sagiv: Query Optimization by Predicate Move-Around. VLDB 1994: 96-107

[PK00]   J.Płodzień, A.Kraken. Object Query Optimization through Detecting Independent Subqueries. Information Systems 25(8), Pergamon Press, 2000, pp. 467-490

[PS01]   J.Płodzień, K.Subieta. Query Optimization through Removing Dead Subqueries. ADBIS 2001 Conf, Springer LNCS 2151, 2001, pp.27-40

[Sto75]   M.Stonebraker. Implementation of Integrity Constraints and Views by Query Modification, SIGMOD Conf., 1975

[SP01]   K.Subieta, J.Płodzień. Object Views and Query Modification. Databases and Information Systems, Kluwer Academic Publishers, 2001, pp. 3-14

[Sub04]   K.Subieta. Theory and Construction of Object-Oriented Query Languages. Polish-Japanese Institute of Information Technology Editors, Warsaw 2004, 522 pages.

[Sub06]   K.Subieta. Stack-Based Approach (SBA) and Stack-Based Query Language (SBQL). http://www.sbql.pl, 2006

Checking Violation Tolerance of Approaches to Database Integrity

Hendrik Decker[1,*] and Davide Martinenghi[2,**]

[1] Instituto Tecnológico de Informática,
Ciudad Politécnica de la Innovación, E-46071 Valencia, Spain
`hendrik@iti.es`
[2] Free University of Bozen/Bolzano,
Faculty of Computer Science, Piazza Domenicani 3, I-39100 Bolzano, Italy
`martinenghi@inf.unibz.it`

Abstract. A hitherto unquestioned assumption made by all methods for integrity checking has been that the database satisfies its constraints before each update. This consistency assumption has been exploited for improving the efficiency of determining whether integrity is satisfied or violated after the update. Based on a notion of violation tolerance, we present and discuss an abstract property which, for any given approach to integrity checking, is an easy, sufficient condition to check whether the consistency assumption can be abandoned without sacrificing usability and efficiency of the approach. We demonstrate the usefulness of our definitions by showing that the theorem-proving approach to database integrity by Sadri and Kowalski, as well as several other well-known methods, can indeed afford to abandon the consistency assumption without losing their efficiency, while their applicability is vastly increased.

1 Introduction

Virtually all known approaches to integrity checking assume that each constraint be satisfied in the "old state", before the update. At least, this means to require that the union of the database and its integrity constraints be consistent, as, e.g., in [16]. Many other approaches, such as [15,12] and others, even require that each constraint be a theorem, or a logical consequence of the database, which of course entails consistency. Only under this quite strong consistency assumption (which, by the way, is also quite unrealistic, in terms of large, "real-life" databases that typically contain some amount of inconsistent data) are the known approaches for integrity checking guaranteed to correctly indicate integrity satisfaction in the "new state", after the update has been committed.

For the approaches described in [15,4,12,16], this consistency assumption can be significantly relaxed without risking that their integrity invariance guarantees would go astray. Informally speaking, it can be shown that, even if there is any number of cases of integrity violation in the old state, the rest of the database will remain satisfied in the new state if the outcome of the respective approach

---

* supported by Spanish grant TIC2003-09420-C02.
** supported by EU project TONES IST FP6-7603.

T. Yakhno and E. Neuhold (Eds.): ADVIS 2006, LNCS 4243, pp. 139–148, 2006.

indicates that the given update does not violate integrity, i.e., does not introduce new cases of violation.

After some preliminaries in section 2, where we also give an abstract definition of the correctness of integrity checking, we define and discuss the property of violation tolerance in section 3. This property is not obvious in general and has to be analysed individually for each given integrity checking approach. Independently of any approach, however, we develop in section 3 a general condition by which it is possible to check whether a given correct integrity checking approach is violation-tolerant. In subsection 3.2 we apply this condition to the theorem-proving approach to database integrity in [16] and prove that it is indeed violation-tolerant. Then we recapitulate results about the violation tolerance of approaches in [15] [12] and ascertain that also the integrity checking method in [4] is violation-tolerant. After addressing related work in section 4, we conclude in section 5 with an outlook on a broader notion of violation tolerance.

2   Preliminaries

Throughout we assume the usual terminological and notational conventions for relational and deductive databases, as used in the cited writings about database integrity [15,4,12,16].

The following definitions are independent of any concrete method. We only point out that integrity constraints are usually conceived as closed well-formed formulae of first-order predicate calculus in the underlying language of the database. Two standard representations of integrity constraints are in use: either prenex normal form (where all quantifiers are outermost and all negation symbols are innermost) or denial form (datalog clauses without head). Unless explicitly mentioned, we are impartial about these representations, i.e., when speaking of an integrity constraint W, it may be given in any of these two forms.

Different methods to check database integrity employ different notions to define integrity satisfaction and violation, and use different criteria to determine these properties. Such criteria are always meant to be more efficient than to plainly evaluate the integrity status of all integrity constraints upon each update. In fact, each method, say, $\mathcal{M}$ can be identified with its criteria, which in turn can be formalised as a function that takes as input a database (i.e., a set of database facts and rules), a finite set of integrity constraints, and an update (i.e., a bipartite finite set of database clauses to be deleted and inserted, resp.), and outputs upon termination one of the values {*satisfied, violated*}. (In general, a multivalued range is conceivable for also dealing with unknown, under- or over-determined integrity, or graded levels of satisfaction or violation, as, e.g., in [7]; for simplicity, we only deal with two-valued integrity here.)

For a database D and an update U, let, for convenience, D^U denote the updated database. Thus, the correctness of an approach $\mathcal{M}$ can be stated in the following form.

Definition 1 (Correctness of integrity checking). *An integrity checking method $\mathcal{M}$ is correct if, for each database D, each finite set IC of integrity constraints such that D satisfies IC, and each update U, the following holds.*

(*) IC is satisfied in D^U if $\mathcal{M}(D, IC, U) = satisfied$.

For instance, the approach in [15] generates a conjunction $\Gamma(U, IC)$ of simplifications of certain instances of those constraints in IC that are possibly affected by an update U, and asserts that, under the assumption that integrity is satisfied in the old state, integrity remains satisfied in the new state (i.e., $\mathcal{M}(D, IC, U) = satisfied$, in terms of the definition above) if and only if $\Gamma(U, IC)$ evaluates to $true$ in the updated state D^U; otherwise, integrity is violated.

Under the same assumption, the approach in [16] runs an SLDNF-based resolution proof procedure, extended by some forward reasoning steps by which it is possible to delimit the search space to those parts of the union of database and integrity constraints that are actually affected by a given update. The procedure asserts that integrity remains satisfied in D^U if the resulting search space is finitely failed; integrity is violated if the search space contains a refutation indicating inconsistency. In terms of the definition above, the $\mathcal{M}(D, IC, U)$ of [16] is the result of the traversed search space with given input from D, IC, U.

Similarly, the $\mathcal{M}(D, IC, U)$ of the integrity checking method in [12] is determined by the outcome of running SLDNF resolution with essentially the same input as in the approach of [16]. For details of technical and conceptual differences between the latter two approaches, which are not directly relevant to the objectives of this paper, we refer the reader to [16].

3   Violation Tolerance

Next, we formally define the notion of violation tolerance. Rather than using the perhaps more popular term "inconsistency tolerance", we prefer to speak of violation tolerance because (in)consistency is a slightly more general concept than integrity satisfaction (violation, resp.); we also want to avoid terminological interferences with the discussion in [16] of differences between the consistency approach and the theoremhood approach of integrity checking.

As indicated in section 1, the intuition of violation tolerance of an approach $\mathcal{M}$ to integrity checking is that we want to tolerate (or, rather, be able to live with) cases of violated constraints as long as we can ensure that no new cases of integrity violation are introduced, such that the cases of integrity that had been satisfied before the update will remain satisfied afterwards. Thus, we first need to make precise what we mean by "cases".

Definition 2 (Global variable, Case). *Let W be an integrity constraint.*

a) Each variable x in W that is $\forall$-quantified but not dominated by any $\exists$ quantifier (i.e., $\exists$ does not occur left of the quantifier of x in W) in the prenex normal form of W is called a global variable *of W. Let $global(W)$ denote the set of global variables in W.*

b) The formula $W\sigma$ is called a case *of W if σ is a substitution such that $Range(\sigma) \subseteq global(W)$ and $Image(\sigma) \cap global(W) = \emptyset$.*

Clearly, each variable in a constraint W represented by a normal datalog denial is a global variable of W. Note that cases of an integrity constraint need not be ground, and that each constraint W as well as each variant of W is a case of W.

With this, violation tolerance of an approach $\mathcal{M}$ to integrity checking can be defined as follows.

Definition 3 (Violation tolerance). $\mathcal{M}$ *is* violation-tolerant *if, for each database D, each finite set IC integrity constraints, each finite set IC' of cases of constraints in IC such that D satisfies IC', and each update U, the following holds.*

(**) IC' is satisfied in D^U if $\mathcal{M}(D, IC, U) = $ *satisfied.*

Even though there may be an infinity of cases of constraints in IC, the finiteness requirement for IC' entails no loss of generality, since integrity satisfaction is defined compositionally (i.e., a finite set of constraints is satisfied if each of its elements is satisfied). Moreover, $\mathcal{M}(D, IC, U) = $ *satisfied* guarantees satisfaction of any number of cases that have been satisfied in D.

Clearly, for checking integrity with a violation-tolerant method $\mathcal{M}$, (**) suggests to compute the very same function as in the traditional case, where satisfaction of all of IC in D is required. Hence, with this relaxation, no loss at all of efficiency is associated, whereas the gains are immense: with a violation-tolerant method, it will be possible to continue database operations even in the presence of (obvious or hidden, known or unknown) cases of integrity violation (which for better or worse is rather the rule than the exception in practice), while maintaining the integrity of all cases that have complied with the constraints. Whenever $\mathcal{M}$ is employed, no new cases of integrity violation will be introduced, while existing "bad" cases may disappear (by intention or even accidentally) by executing updates that have passed the integrity test of $\mathcal{M}$. So far, with the strict requirement of integrity satisfaction in the old state, not the least bit of integrity violation was tolerable. Hence, the known correctness results of virtually all approaches to database integrity would remain useless for the majority of all practical cases, unless they can be shown to be violation-tolerant.

Of course, the preceding observations, as nice as they may be, would be void if no violation-tolerant method existed. Fortunately, however, all known approaches to database integrity that we have checked so far for violation tolerance do enjoy this property. The following subsection introduces a sufficient condition by which it is fairly easy to check and assert violation tolerance.

3.1   A Sufficient Condition for Violation Tolerance

For a database D, an update U and a finite set IC' of cases of constraints in IC such that IC' is satisfied in D, a straightforward special case of (*) obviously is

(***) IC' is satisfied in D^U if $\mathcal{M}(D, IC', U) = $ *satisfied*

This is already pretty close to (**), which we have identified above as the desirable property of violation tolerance. It is easy to see that, for a given method $\mathcal{M}$, (**) directly follows from (***) if the following condition is satisfied for each database D, each finite set of integrity constraints IC, each finite set IC' of cases of constraints in IC such that IC' is satisfied in D, and each update U.

(#) If $\mathcal{M}(D, IC, U) = satisfied$ then $\mathcal{M}(D, IC', U) = satisfied$

Hence, with regard to definition 3, we immediately have the following result.

Theorem 1. *Let $\mathcal{M}$ be an approach to integrity checking by which the satisfaction and violation of a finite set of constraints can be determined. Then, $\mathcal{M}$ is violation-tolerant if (#) holds.*

Proofs by which (#) is verified for the approaches in [15] and [12] are fairly easy because both generate simplified forms of constraints, such that, roughly speaking, the truth value of the simplified form of any case of a constraint W in IC is implied by the truth value of the simplified form of W itself, from which (#) follows. Violation tolerance of the method in [4] is also easily verified: essentially, it generates all ground facts (which are always finitely many in a range-restricted database without function symbols) that are either false in the old and true in the new state, or vice-versa, corresponding to all facts that are effectively inserted in or deleted from D, respectively. For each such fact, simplified forms of potentially affected constraints are obtained and evaluated that are essentially the same as those in [15], so that the verification of (#) for the approach in [4] can recur on the latter.

In section 3.2, we show that also the approach in [16] is violation-tolerant, and, again, the proof is fairly easy. However, it would be wrong to think that violation tolerance comes for free with any correct approach to integrity whatsoever. The following counter-example shows that this is indeed not the case.

Example 1. We construct here a method for integrity checking $\mathcal{M}$ for which (#) does not hold, i.e., $\mathcal{M}(D, IC, U) = satisfied$ does not entail that $\mathcal{M}(D, IC', U) = satisfied$, where IC' is a set of cases of constraints in IC. Let $\mathcal{M}(D, IC, U)$ be

1. *satisfied* (resp., *violated*) if $\exists x(p(x) \wedge x \neq a)$ is satisfied (resp., violated) in D^U, whenever $IC = \{\leftarrow p(x)\}$ and U precisely consists of inserting $p(a)$.
2. *satisfied* (resp., *violated*) if IC is satisfied (resp., violated) in D^U otherwise.

Clearly, $\mathcal{M}$ is correct in the sense of definition 1, i.e., if $\mathcal{M}(D, IC, U) = satisfied$ then IC is satisfied in D^U (here, actually, the converse holds too). Indeed, whenever IC holds in D and point 1 applies, $\mathcal{M}(D, IC, U) = violated$, which correctly indicates that the update violates integrity; when point 2 applies, the evaluations of IC in D^U and $\mathcal{M}(D, IC, U)$ coincide by definition, so correctness is trivial.

Now, let U and IC be as in point 1 above. Further, let D be a database containing the sole fact $p(b)$, and $W' = \leftarrow p(a)$ be a case of the constraint in IC. Note that W' is satisfied in D but IC is not. Although $\mathcal{M}(D, IC, U) = satisfied$, W' is satisfied in D but not in D^U, i.e., the satisfied case W' is not preserved after the update even though the corresponding checking condition given by M is satisfied for IC. Therefore $\mathcal{M}$ is correct but not violation-tolerant.

3.2   Violation Tolerance of Sadri and Kowalski's Approach

In this subsection, we are going to verify the condition (#) above for the approach to integrity checking in [16].

Before recalling the function $\mathcal{M}(D, IC, U)$ of this approach for verifying (#), it should be interesting to note that none of the proofs of the theorems and corollaries in [16] effectively makes use of the assumption that integrity is satisfied in the old state D_0 except the completeness results following from theorems numbered 4 and 5 in [16].

For inferring from those theorems the completeness of $\mathcal{M}$ with regard to checking integrity violation, it is argued that, "since $\mathrm{Comp}(D_0)$ is consistent with the constraints, any inconsistency after the transaction must involve at least one of the updates." Clearly, this builds on the assumption that integrity is satisfied in the old state. However, rather than completeness of computing violation, what is of interest to us here is the generalisation of correctness results of approaches to check integrity satisfaction.

Related to the fact that proofs in [16] do not make use of the assumption that integrity is satisfied in the old state, a certain form of inconsistency tolerance of the approach $\mathcal{M}$ in [16] with regard to integrity violation can be observed, in the following sense: whenever $\mathcal{M}(D, IC, U) = $ *violated*, then the correctly indicated violation of integrity is independent of the integrity status before the update. However, rather than inconsistency tolerance with regard to integrity violation, what we are after in this paper is violation tolerance with regard to integrity satisfaction, as expressed in (*). The independence of detecting integrity violation by the approach in [16] from the integrity status before the update is fairly trivial, and has been addressed above only in order to be precise about what and what not we are dealing with.

As the main result of this subsection, we are going to prove the following.

Theorem 2. *The approach $\mathcal{M}$ to integrity checking by Sadri & Kowalski is violation-tolerant.*

Proof. First, we recall the function $\mathcal{M}(D, IC, U)$ associated to $\mathcal{M}$, as described at the end of section 2. It determines integrity violation and satisfaction by the existence or, respectively, absence of a refutation in the search space of the theorem-prover defined in [16] with an element from U as top clause. Thus, to show violation tolerance of $\mathcal{M}$, we need to verify

(#) If $\mathcal{M}(D, IC, U) = $ *satisfied* then $\mathcal{M}(D, IC', U) = $ *satisfied*

i.e., that the search space, say, $\mathcal{T}(D, IC', U)$ of $\mathcal{M}$ with top clause from U and input from $D \cup IC'$ is finitely failed if the search space $\mathcal{T}(D, IC, U)$ of $\mathcal{M}$ is finitely failed (in the latter search space, input from IC is considered, instead of IC', as in the former). To see that this holds, assume that $\mathcal{M}(D, IC, U) = $ *satisfied*, i.e., $\mathcal{T}(D, IC, U)$ is finitely failed.

Now, we recall that, in each derivation δ of $\mathcal{M}$, at most one denial is taken as input clause, for resolving a literal selected in the head of a clause in δ. As assumed above, each derivation in $\mathcal{T}(D, IC, U)$ is finitely failed. It remains to be shown that each derivation δ in $\mathcal{T}(D, IC', U)$ from the same root which has IC' instead of IC in the set of candidate input clauses is also finitely failed.

For that, we distinguish the two cases that δ either does or does not use an input clause from IC'. If is does not, then, by definition of the proof procedure in [16], δ necessarily is also a derivation in $\mathcal{T}(D, IC, U)$ (up to a possible permutation of the sequence of used input clauses) and hence is finitely failed. If it does, then, by definition of IC', that input clause is a case I' of some constraint I in IC. Now, to initiate the conclusive *reductio-ad-absurdum* argument of this proof, suppose that δ is not finitely failed, i.e., it terminates in the empty clause. Since I is more general than I', it follows from the definition of $\mathcal{M}$ that a refutation δ^* in $\mathcal{T}(D, IC, U)$ can be constructed which is almost the same as δ except, instead of I', uses I as an input clause and continues, possibly with less instantiated variables and up to a possible permutation of input clauses, in the same manner as δ until the empty clause is reached. This, however, contradicts the assumption that $\mathcal{T}(D, IC, U)$ is finitely failed.   □

In case negation may occur only in literals of denials in IC but not in D, a shorter proof is possible. To see then that that the search space with input from is finitely failed if taking input from IC finitely fails, simply assume that $\mathcal{T}(D, IC', U)$ would contain a refutation. Then, by the lifting lemma [2], there must be a refutation in $\mathcal{T}(D, IC, U)$, which contradicts the assumption.

Below we illustrate violation tolerance of the approach in [16] by an example adapted from [11].

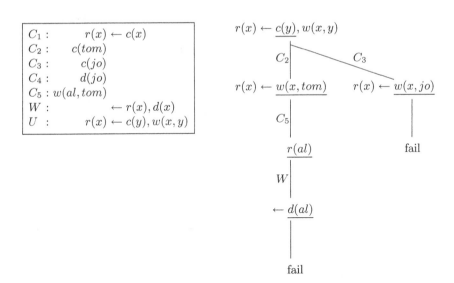

Fig. 1. Clauses and derivation tree of example 2

Example 2. Consider a database D consisting of clauses C_1–C_5 shown in figure 1 for unary relations r (regular residence), c (citizen), d (deported) and binary relation w (works for) and the integrity constraint W, expressing that it is impossible to both have a regular residence status and be registered as a deported person at the same time. The given update U inserts a new rule asserting that people working for a registered citizen also have regular residence status.

Clearly, W is not satisfied in D, since $r(jo)$ is derivable via C_1 and C_3, and $d(jo)$ is a fact (C_4). However, $W' = \leftarrow r(tom), d(tom)$ is a case of W that is satisfied in D since $d(tom)$ does not hold in D.

With U as top clause and $D \cup \{W\}$ as input, the approach of [16] traverses the search space given by the tree shown in figure 1 (selected literals are underlined). Since this tree is finitely failed, we can conclude that U will not introduce new cases of inconsistency: all cases of integrity constraints that were satisfied in D remain satisfied in D^U. In particular, W' is also satisfied in D^U.

4   Related Work

To the best of our knowledge, no other author has ever cared to render moot the putatively fundamental assumption that integrity would need to be satisfied before an update in order to correctly perform a simplified integrity check.

Notwithstanding this, interesting work has been going on in recent years under the banner of "inconsistency tolerance". The majority of work in this area is concerned with query answering in inconsistent databases in connection with repairs of violated integrity (cf., e.g., [1]). Consistent query answering defines answers to be correct if they are logical consequences of each possible repaired state of the database, i.e., in each state which satisfies integrity and differs from the given violated state in some minimal way.

To query constraints or simplified forms thereof for evaluating their integrity status is usual in many approaches. However, using consistent query answering techniques for that is very different from what the results of this paper suggest. Rather than catering for repairs at query time (which often is impossible, e.g., due to untimeliness or because inconsistency is hidden and not even perceived) and determining truth values for all possible repaired states (which may be unfeasibly inefficient), the results of this paper justify that it is possible to simply "live with" inconsistencies as given by integrity violation. Instead of being preoccupied with obtaining perfectly consistent database states in which integrity is a hundred percent satisfied, advantage can be taken of the fact that, in practice, the majority of stored information is consistent and can be queried without further ado. In other words, the use of a violation-tolerant approach to integrity checking allows a straightforward use of standard query evaluation procedures.

Repairing integrity violation by modifications of the database is not dealt with in this paper (cf., e.g., [9,17] for abductive or active database techniques for repairing violation). However, with violation-tolerant integrity checking, the repair of violated cases of integrity can be delayed and dealt with at more convenient points of time (e.g., off business hours or when the system workload is lower). The price to be paid for this convenience, of course, is that querying data causing violated cases of integrity may yield answers that are not in accordance with the intended semantics, as expressed by the constraints.

Related to inconsistency tolerance, also a variety of paraconsistent logic approaches have received some attention (cf., e.g., [8]). Most of them, however, deviate significantly from classical first-order logic as the basis of database logic, which we do not. However, standard resolution-based query answering (which is used for implementing the approach of [16] in [11]) can be characterised as a procedural form of paraconsistent reasoning (as done in [10,5,6]) that merits attention with regard to violation tolerance. It does not take irrelevant database clauses into account for evaluating constraints upon some update, even if such clauses would be involved in some case of integrity violation that has not been caused by the update but by some earlier event. In general, logic-programming-based reasoning in databases does not exhibit any explosive behaviour as predicted by classical logic in the presence of inconsistency, which would render each given answer worthless, but reasons soundly in consistent subsets of relevant clauses. This paraconsistency aspect qualifies logic programming as an ideal conceptual paradigm for violation-tolerant approaches to database integrity.

5   Conclusion

First, we have defined violation tolerance of approaches to database integrity as their capacity of abandoning the assumption that integrity is satisfied before each update, i.e., of admitting cases of integrity violation while preserving the invariance of satisfied cases, without forfeiting efficiency. Based on that, we then have defined a condition by which any method for determining integrity satisfaction or violation upon given updates can be checked for violation tolerance. We have successfully performed this check for some of the most well-known methods. We have traced this check in detail for the approach of Sadri & Kowalski, and have seen that it can indeed abandon the assumption of integrity satisfaction before each update without impairing its efficiency.

In general, by abandoning the assumption of integrity satisfaction, the applicability of approaches successfully checked for violation tolerance not only is not curtailed, but in fact formidably increased. To require that assumption would have the effect of making such approaches useless for many practical applications (e.g., replicated databases and data warehousing, to name just two of the most prominent application areas) where cases of intermittent or undetected integrity violation are rather the rule than the exception. The results of this paper, however, encourage the use of well-established approaches that hitherto have been known to function only in an "academically clean" context with a hundred percent absence of violated integrity constraints.

It could be asked why we have preferred to look at rather "old" methods for integrity checking, given that many more approaches have been presented and discussed in the literature more recently. To defend this preference is easy: most of the methods that have emerged later build, at least partially, on the results and achievements of those we have looked at, and improvements often have been just marginal, or interesting mainly for "advanced" scenarios that yet are hardly usual in practice, although some notable exceptions have been identified in [14]. Moreover, we expect that the task of checking more recent approaches for violation tolerance will become easier when violation tolerance checks of more fundamental methods can be referred to.

Apart from checking other, more recent approaches for violation tolerance, e.g., the one presented in [3], we also intend to investiagte the viability of such approaches for integrity checking in distributed databases using lazy replication, where full satisfaction of integrity is particularly hard, if not impossible to achieve. Moreover, we have in mind to broaden the notion of violation tolerance such that also methods for actively repairing violated constraints, for integrity-preserving view updating and, more generally, for abductive belief revision can be checked to be applicable in scenarios with manifest violations of integrity constraints, without immolating effectiveness and efficiency of these methods.

References

1. L. Bertossi: Consistent Query Answering in Databases. *ACM SIGMOD Record* 35(2):68–77, 2006.
2. C.-L. Chang and R. Lee: Symbolic Logic and Mechanical Theorem Proving. *Computer Science Classics*. Academic Press, 1973.
3. H. Christiansen, D. Martinenghi: On Simplification of Database Integrity Constraints. *Fundamenta Informaticae* 71(4):371–417, A. Pettorossi, M. Proietti (eds.), IOS Press, 2006. See also [13].
4. H. Decker: Integrity Enforcement on Deductive Databases. In L. Kerschberg (ed), *Expert Database Systems*, EDS'86, 381–395. Benjamin/Cummings, 1987.
5. H. Decker: Historical and Computational Aspects of Paraconsistency in View of the Logic Foundation of Databases. In L. Bertossi, G. Katona, K.-D. Schewe, B. Thalheim (eds), *Semantics in Databases*, 63–81. LNCS 2582, Springer, 2003.
6. H. Decker: A Case for Paraconsistent Logic as Foundation of Future Information Systems. *Proc. CAiSE'05 Workshops*, vol. 2, 451–461. FEUP edicoes, 2005.
7. H. Decker: Total Unbiased Multivalued Paraconsistent Semantics of Database Integrity. *DEXA Workshop LAAIC'05*, 813–817. IEEE Computer Society, 2005.
8. H. Decker, J. Villadsen, T. Waragai (eds): *Paraconsistent Computational Logic*. Proc. ICLP Workshop at FLoC'02. Dat. Skrifter vol. 95, Roskilde Univ., 2002.
9. A. Kakas, R. A. Kowalski, F. Toni: Abductive Logic Programming. *J. Logic and Computation* 2(6):719-770, 1992.
10. R. A. Kowalski: *Logic for Problem Solving*. Elsevier, 1979.
11. R. A. Kowalski, F. Sadri, P. Soper: Integrity Checking in Deductive Databases. In *Proc. 13th VLDB*, 61-69. Morgan Kaufmann, 1987.
12. J. W. Lloyd, L. Sonenberg, R. W. Topor: Integrity constraint checking in stratified databases. *Journal of Logic Programming*, 4(4):331–343, 1987.
13. D. Martinenghi: *Advanced Techniques for Efficient Data Integrity Checking*. PhD thesis, Roskilde University, Denmark, in *Datalogiske Skrifter* vol. 105, http://www.ruc.dk/dat/forskning/skrifter/DS105.pdf, 2005.
14. D. Martinenghi, H. Christiansen, H. Decker: Integrity Checking and Maintenance in Relational and Deductive Databases, and beyond. In Z. Ma (ed), *Intelligent Databases: Technologies and Applications*, to appear. Idea Group Publishing, 2006.
15. J.-M. Nicolas: Logic for Improving Integrity Checking in Relational Data Bases. *Acta Informatica*, 18:227–253, 1982.
16. F. Sadri, R. A. Kowalski: A Theorem-Proving Approach to Database Integrity. In J. Minker (ed), *Foundations of Deductive Databases and Logic Programming*, 313–362. Morgan Kaufmann, 1988.
17. J. Widom, S. Ceri: *Active Database Systems*. Morgan Kaufmann, 1996.

A Metadata Repository Model to Integrate Heterogeneous Databases of Hardware Dependent Legacy Systems

Ahmet Tümay, Kıvanç Dinçer, Özgür Yürekten, Müberra Sungur,
Ahmet Dikici, and Yusuf Tambağ

TÜBITAK-UEKAE/G222 Unit, Atatürk Blv. No:211/20
06100 Kavaklıdere, Ankara, Turkey
{ahmet.tumay, kivanc.dincer, ozgur.yurekten, muberra.sungur,
ahmet.dikici, yusuf.tambag}@tubitak.gov.tr

Abstract. In a large modern enterprise, it is almost inevitable that different parts of an organization use different systems to produce, store, and search their critical data. In addition, the maintenance of heterogeneous database systems is becoming an overhead and a big problem for companies. Meanwhile, it is only achieved by combining the information from these various systems so that the enterprise can use the combined value of the data they contain. One way to solve this problem is to replace the legacy applications with a single information system. Introducing the new software is not enough; it is also necessary to migrate the data from the old system to the new one. As data has been collected over many years and contains a lot of information and knowledge, this most important value of a company must be preserved. Here, we present a specific solution based on a metadata repository model that we applied which addresses an organization's operational need to integrate the custom databases of some specific hardware dependent legacy systems.

1 Introduction

If current trends continue, more data will be generated in the next three years than in all of the recorded history [1]. Recent studies indicate that business-relevant information is growing at around 50 percent compound annual growth rate with about one to two exabytes (10^{18}) of information being generated each year [14].

In a large modern enterprise, it is almost inevitable that different parts of the organization use different applications to produce, store, and search their critical data stored on different systems. So it can only be achieved by combining the information from these various systems so that the enterprise can realize the combined value of the data they contain [2].

In many companies it is an urgent problem to remove old legacy applications because they have become inflexible with respect to new requirements or have bad performance [3]. To replace the old application software is not enough; it is also necessary to migrate the data from the databases of the old system to the new one [4]. As data has been collected over many years and contains a lot of information and knowledge, this most important property of the company must be preserved [5].

T. Yakhno and E. Neuhold (Eds.): ADVIS 2006, LNCS 4243, pp. 149–157, 2006.

A major challenge for integrating existing databases is the construction of a global unified schema that represents the integration of local schemas. Several problems arise in schema integration in this environment due to the structural and semantically differences of the schemas that are to be merged [9]: First, existing databases might be representing different data models. This situation requires the use of a common data model to interconnect these diverse data models. Second, many conflicts may arise when integrating different schemas. The identification and resolution of these conflicts are therefore crucial for the problem of integration. These possible conflicts are name and representation conflicts and semantic heterogeneity which respectively refers to the differences in meaning, interpretation, or intended use of the related data [10]. Third, when integrating different schemas, hidden relationships that do not appear in the individual schemas are required to be discovered.

In our case, we address the data integration problem of a number of programmable hardware dependent legacy systems that rely on their custom databases in order to operate. The hardware devices produce new data records continuously during operation and store them in their individual databases. The collected data is analyzed by a special analysis software and the new data needed for programming the hardware device is produced. Our aim is to integrate the databases of several legacy systems in one central data store and do the analysis on all of the data at once. Ease of expandability and low maintenance and new system integration costs of the data store are important for the effectiveness of the solution.

In the next section we present various alternatives for data and information integration and then in later sections we explain our solution in detail.

2 Data and Information Integration

There are many mechanisms proposed for integrating data in the literature. These include application-specific solutions, application-integration frameworks, workflow (or business process integration) frameworks or meta-search-engine integration [15], data warehousing [11], and database federations [2, 6].

Perhaps the most common way of data integration is via special-purpose applications those access the source databases directly and combine the data retrieved from those sources with the application itself [2]. This approach is an expensive alternative since adding a new data source requires new software code. It is also hard to extend because the existent structure is pretty fragile, any changes to the present sources may all break the application too easily.

The second mechanism, a database federation, simultaneously queries the source databases online [7]. The systems are left separately but an integration layer is used to make queries on all data that are collected from either system. The disadvantages of this solution are as follows: First the required maintenance cost of the system is usually much more than the original system. Second, the generated query statements have to use the field labels of the original database. Although the fields contain the same kind of information they are generally labeled in different databases. In order to solve this problem, a second system based on some kind of ontology and necessary data conversion functions have to be developed, which together make this solution an elaborate one.

On the other hand, a data warehouse is built by loading data from one or more data sources into a newly defined schema in a relational database. The data are often cleansed and transformed in the load process [2]. This will make the analysis and reporting easy on all the records in the database and will also reduce the maintenance cost since there is one single common database. The data warehouse architecture can be formally understood as layers of data in which data from one layer is derived from data of the lower layer [8]. Data sources, also called as operational databases, form the lowest layer. The central layer of the architecture is the global data warehouse. It keeps a historical record of data that result from the integration, transformation and aggregation of detailed data found in the data sources. The next layers of views are the local and client warehouses, which contain the highly aggregated data, directly derived from the global warehouse [8].

3   The Proposed Solution

After evaluating the above mentioned alternatives, key aspects of the data warehousing scheme and the ontology system concept commonly used in database federations were adopted to address our problem.

The multi-layer architecture illustrated in Fig.1 addresses the data integration challenge and provides a scalable and expandable solution that keeps the required effort at minimum for adding new legacy systems to the existent data store.

The layers and components of the architecture will be shortly introduced here and will be elaborated in later sections. The bottom layer, called the Data Layer, supports the physical storage and the retrieval of the actual data transferred from the individual databases of the legacy hardware-dependent systems.

Client applications of the data can access the data stored in the Data Layer only by using the data model abstractions defined in the metadata layer. The metadata layer, is designed as a structural organizer for the construction of a dynamic database whose

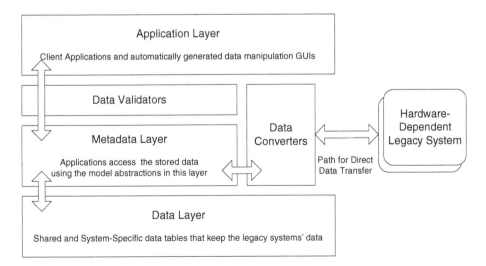

Fig. 1. The layers and main components of the data integration architecture

structure could be easily revised or expanded by its maintainers when necessary; for example in case of future system additions.

And finally the Application Layer provides dynamically generated graphical user interfaces (GUI) that allow users to access and manipulate the data and the services provided by the two layers under it. This layer also embarks other applications that access data via the metadata layer.

The data converters and validators in Fig.1 are for the representation format and content conversions of the data during transfers and for the required data validity checks upon data entry, respectively.

3.1 The Metadata Layer Design

In this section, the details of the metadata layer, which is the hearth of the proposed solution, will be explained. The applications that require access to the actual data in the data store need to determine the database entities and their relationships prior to access or modification of data. This is commonly referred to as *reflection*, which denotes the possibility of dynamic construction and invocation of requests. A key support feature for this task is the presence of the metadata layer. In this layer, the database structure is described and a catalogue of data types and their properties; user defined entities such as tables or classes, and their relationships; and the signatures for the validator and converter methods is included.

The metadata layer design is based on the (legacy) system data model and the system data type model concepts. Each legacy hardware dependent system that collects, analyzes and uses the data is represented as a logically unique entity, called

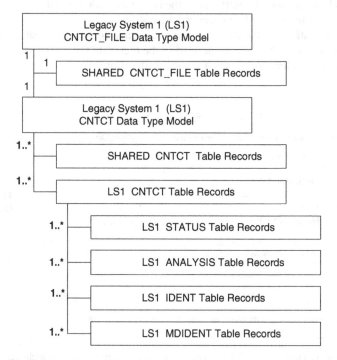

Fig. 2. The representation of the data type model as a tree structure

the *(Legacy) System Data Model*. An application can access all data of a specific system stored in the data store by just referring to the system data model corresponding to that system in the metadata layer.

Domain Data Types are used to define and represent domain specific data types or categories. They are usually represented as multiple tables in the data store and some domain classes correspond to them in the software applications. Each system (so the system data model) may support the whole or a subset of data types defined in the metadata layer.

System data models, which represent each legacy system as a unique entity in the data store are constructed by using system data type models. The *System Data Type Model* represents the domain data types supported in each legacy system, i.e., in system data models. It describes the data types and other tables used in that data model as a tree where a data type model or a table exists at each branch. A representative example of this structure is shown in Fig. 2.

3.2 Data Model Definition Tables

Each legacy system is represented as a unique Data Model in the metadata layer. Table 1 lists and defines the major metadata layer database tables, called Struct tables, used to store data model definitions. Table 2 gives the information need to be kept for each field in the metadata layer. Many of these are useful for automatic GUI generation.

Table 1. Struct tables and their definitions (some details omitted). 1. Each table name starts with the prefix "STRUCT." 2. Captions are used in automatic GUI generation.

Table Name	Description
DMODEL	Keeps information related to each legacy system to be integrated, such as its name, caption, textual description, name of its contact reader class. * Each model is given a unique ID
DTYPE	Keeps the name, caption, textual description, the name of the database sequencer that will generate a unique number for each record, and other info. * Name is used as the primary key.
DTYPEMODEL	Keeps the names of all domain data types supported by a specific system, and other info (such as whether to show it in GUI menus or not)
DMODEL_TABLES	Keeps the database names and captions of all tables related to a data model. * Each table is given a unique ID
DTABLE_FIELDS	Keeps the database field names, captions, and other properties (such as if it is a field to be used in analysis, if it is a sequence field, etc.) of all table fields in database tables. * Each field is given a unique ID
DTYPEMODEL2DTYPEMODEL_RELSHIPS	Keeps the structural relationships (parent, child and other associations) and cardinalities (1:1, 1:n, n:n) of the data type models or tables as shown in Fig.2.
DTABLE2DTABLE_RELSHIPS	* Each relation is given a unique ID
DMODEL2DTABLE_RELSHIPS	Keeps the database names and captions of all tables related to a specific data type model.

Table 2. Database field properties

Property	Description
Field Name	Name
Type	Type (and display format for GUI generation)
Description	Text description
Valid Range	Minimum and maximum values
Sample	Sample records (for helping correct value entry in the GUIs)
Shared / Private	<Schema><Table><Field> Omitted if this parameter will not be stored

3.3 Naming Rules for Tables and Fields

The tables and table fields in the metadata layer are named according to some prede-fined rules. We will mention only a few of them here. The rules were deducted so that the application developers can use Java Reflection API to call corresponding data conversion and validation methods at runtime easily. A sample table naming rule is as follows: <R / "''><Shared / Data Model><Data Type>.

Table 3. Selected Table Naming Rules

Naming Part	Description
Reference Table / Other	If it is a reference table, prefix "R" is added to the table name. Otherwise, no prefix is added to the table name
Data Model Name	The data model name or prefix "SHARED" is added as the next identifier to table name
Data Type	Domain type or category name

The names of the data tables and fields, that are used to store data model records, are kept as close to their original name as possible to keep track of their origins. There are specific rules that help us to differentiate the shared and private data model tables from each other. Some other table naming rules are given in Table 3.

3.4 Shared and Private Data Tables

As the legacy systems under consideration are used for the same purpose, many data items they store will be similar to each other. While designing the data type models, the database structure of each legacy system is analyzed and the tables and data fields that represent the same kind of information in multiple systems are determined. These are identified as the shared data, while the items that belong to only one legacy sys-tem are called as the system-specific (or private) data.

The shared data is stored in a separate schema "SHARED", distinct from the sys-tem-specific schemas of the legacy systems. It is also important to note that the shared schema has to store the data in the most precise way so that we will not loose any precision that will inhibit conversions back to any legacy system representation. The copies of the database tables in the shared schema are also created in the private schemas of each legacy system, but only the fields private to that specific system are put into the tables to prevent the inconsistencies between them. Therefore, there are both shared data tables and system specific data tables for keeping the data of each legacy system, so the data of a specific system is formed as a combination of all those data records. Remember that the relations between these shared and private data tables are defined as data type models in the metadata layer as shown in Fig. 3.

3.5 Ontology System and Data Converters

A type of ontology system that keeps the semantic information of database fields is developed in order to make the data transformations possible between different systems and to improve the focus of the analysis and reporting applications on the data of interest. An ontology is itself a schema integration technology and has tools that can be used to map data from different applications in related domains into a common schema [1,12,13,16].

The ontology tables keep domain-specific data annotations to better understand each system and describe how they are related to other data in various systems. In the ontology tables, parameters shown in Table 4 are kept for all fields in all shared and system-specific schemas.

We also have to define bi-lateral data conversion rules between the shared fields and their system-specific representations. Based on the parameters kept in the ontology tables, conversion rules for all such fields are deducted. These rules include things such as boundary value control rules, unit conversions, calculations and mappings between enumerations.

Table 4. Parameters showing the origin of a shared field

Parameter	Description
Field Name	Field name in shared table
Field Info	Field's type, Field's unit and precision Boundary values determined to preserve the most precise format, Data conversion rules for each legacy system, Whether it is a Primary Key or a Foreign Key Whether it must have a value (i.e., Not Null)
Corresponding Field of Legacy System 1	The field's type, unit, precision and boundary values If this parameter does not exist in this system, this cell is left blank
. . .	. . .
Corresponding Field of Legacy System n	The field's type, unit, precision and boundary values If this parameter does not exist in this system, this cell is left blank

3.6 Procedure for Introducing a New System

The procedure for introducing a new system, that defines a new data model, is given in Table 5. As can be seen, a new system can be added to an existent data store with a reasonable amount of effort. Note that, in order to keep the data consistent for each data model, first the shared fields are put into the shared schema tables, then the relationships between the shared and system-specific data tables are defined in the metadata layer relationship definition tables.

Table 5. Pseudocode for introducing a new data model definition

```
if System Data Model is NOT defined
   Define the System Data Model
if Domain Data Types are NOT defined
   Define Domain Data Types
if Data Type Model is NOT Defined
   Define Data Type Model
if relationships between Data Type Models are NOT defined
   Define relationships between those Data Type Models
if Tables in Data Model are NOT defined
   Define Tables
if Data Fields in Tables in Data Model are NOT defined
   Define Data Fields of Tables
if relationships between Tables in Data Model are NOT defined
   Define relationships between Tables
```

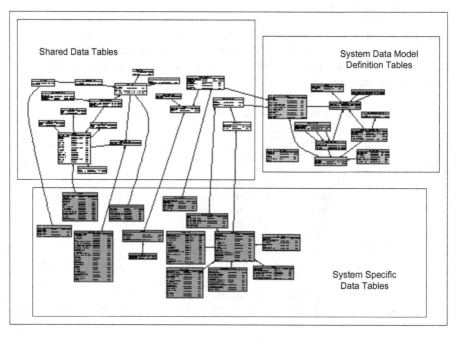

Fig. 3. A general view of the data store table structure – Table and field names are not important here, but the structural relationships are

4 Conclusion

We introduced a specific problem where the databases of the hardware dependent legacy systems must be integrated in a single data store. The proposed solution has been in operational use successfully for a while. One of the important constraints was that while storing similar type of data items coming from multiple legacy systems, the precision of the values should be preserved to allow future system-to-system data transfers and transformations. The system exploits some key aspects in data warehouses, database federations and ontology based integration efforts. The metadata repository model supports dynamic database schema construction for ease of expandability and also helps the automatic generation of data manipulation GUIs by keeping a description of the global schema structure.

References

1. Roth, M.A., Wolfson, D. C., Kleewein, J. C., Nelin, C. J.: Information Integration: A New Generation of Information Technology. IBM Systems Journal, Vol. 41, No 4. (2002).
2. Haas L. M., Lin, E. T., Roth, M. A.: Data Integration Through Database Federation. IBM Systems Journal, Vol. 41, No.4. (2002).
3. Hohenstein, U.: Supporting Data Migration between Relational and Object-Oriented Databases: Using a Federation Approach. IEEE. (2000).
4. Keller, A., Turner, P.: Migrating to Object Data Management. In OOPSLA Workshop on Legacy Systems and Object Technology, Austin, Texas (1995).
5. Brodie, M., Stonebraker, M: Migrating Legacy Systems: Gateways, Interfaces & the Incremental Approach. Morgan Kaufman Publisher. (1995).
6. Radeke, E., Scholl, M.: Framework for Object Migration in Federated Database Systems. In Proc.of Third Int. Conf. on Parallel and Distributed Information Systems (PDIS'94), Austin, Texas. IEEE Computer Science Press (1994)
7. Kohler, J., Lange, M., Hofestadt, R., Schulze-Kremer, S.: Logical and Semantic Database Integration. In Proc. of International Symposium on Bio-Informatics and Biomedical Engineering. (2000) 77-80.
8. Vassiliadis, P., Bouzeghoub, M., Quix, C.: Towards Quality Oriented Data Warehouse Usage and Evolution. Information Systems, Vol.25, No.2. (2000) 89-115.
9. Kamel, M.N., Kamel, N.N.: Federated Database Management System: Requirements, Issues and Solutions, Computer Communications. Vol.15, No.4. (1992) 270-280.
10. Balsters, H., de Brock, E.O., Meersman, R., Tari, Z. (Eds.):Integration of Integrity Constraints in Federated Schemata Based on Tight Constraining, CoopIS/DOA/ODBASE 2004. LNCS Vol. 3290. Springer-Verlag. (2004) 748–767.
11. Bec´arevic, D., Roantree, M.: A Metadata Approach to Multimedia Database Federations. Information and Software Technology, Vol.46. (2004) 195–207.
12. Goble, C.A., Stevens, R., Ng, G., Bechhofer, S., Paton, N. W., Baker, P. G., Peim, M. and Brass, A.: Transparent Access to Multiple Bioinformatics Information Sources. IBM Systems Journal, Vol.40, No.2. (2001) 532–551.
13. Hernandez, M., Miller, R. and Haas, L.: Clio: A Semi-Automatic Tool for Schema Mapping. Proceedings of ACM SIGMOD Conference, Santa Barbara, CA. (2001)
14. Lyman, P., Varian, H., Dunn, A., Strygin, A. and Swearingen, K.: How Much Information? http://www.sims.berkeley.edu/research/projects/how-much-info/.
15. Chawathe, S., Garcia-Molina, H., Hammer, J., Ireland, K., Papakonstantinou, Y., Ullman, J., Widom, J.: The TSIMMIS Project: Integration of Heterogeneous Information Sources. Proc. of IPSJ Conference, Tokyo, Japan. (1994) 7-18.
16. Wache, H., Vogele, T., Visser, U., Stuckenschmidt, H.,Schuster, G., Neumann, H. & Hubner, S.: Ontology-Based Integration of Information - A Survey of Existing Approaches, in Proc. of the IJCAI-01 Workshop: Ontologies and Information Sharing. (2001) 108–117.

Semantic Information Retrieval on the Web

Ebru Sezer[1], Adnan Yazıcı[2], and Ünal Yarımağan[1]

[1] Hacettepe University, Computer Engineering Department, 06532 Beytepe
esezer@cs.hacettepe.edu.tr, unal@hacettepe.edu.tr
[2] Middle East Technical University, Computer Engineering Department
yazici@ceng.metu.edu.tr

Abstract. In this study, a semantic information retrieval system to access web content is proposed. Web pages existing in the web contain not only textual but also visual data. When textual and visual data are combined, the semantics of the information presented in a web page becomes richer. Consequently, types of text body and visual data are queried as one entity in a single query sentence to improve the precision, recall and r_{norm} parameters of a web query. Fuzzy domain ontology to fill the gap between raw content and semantic features is used, and a model namely OAC (Object, Action and Concept) is proposed. The core of our system is the OAC Model used for fuzzy domain ontology derivation. The OAC Model serves both images and texts, equally. Several experiments are carried out on selected real web pages, and good results are obtained.

1 Introduction

Generally, contemporary search engines are mainly based on text. It is argued that using only text to search the web is not always adequate because most of the web pages consist of not only textual part but also some visual information. These two complementary information sources help us to derive semantic features of a web page. For this reason, we argue that using this complementary relationship in queries increases the reliability of the results. Considering this lack of contemporary search engines, it is possible to say that the main target of this study is to develop a search engine using complementary relationship in queries. In the first stage of the study, images from visual data are selected and then, text and images are used together while indexing and querying. Generally, images and texts are included in a web page and complementary relationships among them are clear. In a web page, information in the textual part can be sampled using an image. Consequently, some semantic features of the page are emphasized. In other situation, an image has some information different from its textual part. In this case, some additional semantic features are added to the web page. The basic features of the system suggested in this paper are ability of semantic querying images and texts by the same query sentence at the same time, and the ability of enclosing all semantic levels *(object, action, and concept)* by using fuzzy domain ontology.

There are a number of related studies on ontology development and ontology based retrieval in literature. We briefly overview the most relevant ones to our

T. Yakhno and E. Neuhold (Eds.): ADVIS 2006, LNCS 4243, pp. 158–167, 2006.

study here. Sugumaran et al. [2] proposes a methodology for creating and managing domain ontologies. In this work, architecture for an ontology management system is presented. Lagoze et al. [3] describes the ABC metadata model collaborated with CIMI museums and libraries. Based on this model they are able to build a RDF metadata repository. Reinberger et al. [4] extracts semantic relations from text in an unsupervised way and use outputs as preprocessed material for ontology construction. Bodner et al. [5] explores the possibility of extending traditional information retrieval systems with knowledge-based approaches to automatically expand natural language queries. Elliman et al. [6] describes a method for constructing an ontology which represents the set of web pages on a specifed site. Khan et al. [7] describe a method for the automatic construction of ontologies based on clustering and vector space model. The similarity of images is based on similarity of objects that appear in the images. Vallet et al. [8] propose a model for the exploitation of ontology to improve search over large document repositories. Documents are annotated semi automatically based on ontology and the retrieval model is based on an adaptation of the classic vector-space model. Song et al [9] describe ontology-based information retrieval model for the Semantic Web. By using OWL Lite as standard ontology language, ontology is generated through translating and integrating sub domain ontologies. They obtain the equivalent classes by using description logic reasoner. Parry [10] discusses the ontology fuzzification, by both analysis of a corpus of documents and the use of a relevance feedback mechanism. Chang-Shing et al. [11] present a fuzzy ontology and its application to news summarization. Ontology is constructed in crisp form and uncertainty problem of it is solved by fuzzy inference mechanism. Widyantoro et al. [12] propose automatic construction of fuzzy domain ontology that consists of broader and narrower term relationships by using term frequencies.

The first task performed on raw web pages is to extract their content features. Web pages are divided into two parts such as texts and images. Content features of text are terms and their weights calculated by using Vector Space Model. Content features of images are their region names and spatial relations of each other. This process is implemented semi-automatically while regions are marked and annotated by user and spatial relations are extracted automatically.

The second task is to extract semantic features automatically. A fuzzy domain ontology derived from the OAC Model is used throughout this task. The OAC Model divides domain terms into three main types: object, action and concept. Objects are existential entities of the domain. Actions are the momentarily situation names that can only be described by using objects and spatial relations. Concepts are disjoint from objects and actions. They have extensive meanings and enclose other concepts, actions and objects in their meanings.

In the extraction of text's semantic features, terms of the text and their weights are recalculated by using ontological relationships of terms. In extraction of image's semantic features, after region annotation, actions and concepts implied by the image should be interpreted. Since actions and concepts are not expressed only regions, they are not directly extracted from images by using visual content. In the fuzzy domain ontology, each action and concept has simple rule used for interpretation of them. There are three different process levels for an image, these are: (a) extraction of objects and spatial relations; (b) interpretation of actions by employing first step and, (c) interpretation of concepts by using first and second steps.

The main difference between our study and the studies mentioned above is that we extract semantic features of images and texts separately and combine them to produce web page semantics by using common fuzzy domain ontology. Therefore, we propose a model for ontology derivation that can serve for images and texts. More specifically, the main aspects of the developed system can be stated as follows: semantic features of web pages are produced by combination of semantic features of image and text. In fact, this approach reflects the complementary relationships of images and texts. Additional features such as action and concept names are acquired from domain ontology and they are added to the web page semantics. A model namely OAC Model is proposed here to use domain ontology derivation. Domain ontologies are represented by OWL [1] to supply sharing property. In our system, semantic features of web pages constitute its metadata. All metadata are collected in a repository and represented by RDF [1]. Queries are formed with domain terms and Boolean operators. User's queries are transformed to RDQL [1] sentence and they are executed on the RDF repository.

This paper is organized as follows: Section 2 explains the OAC Model. In Section 3, semantic indexing and querying process are presented and in Section 4, performance experiments are conducted, and experimental results are discussed. Finally, conclusion is included in Section 5.

2   The OAC Model

The fuzzy ontology combines the fuzzy logic with ontological representation of knowledge. Its fundamental logic is based on extensions of a crisp ontology. In fuzzy ontologies, relations between entities have values denoting the degree of relations. The OAC (Object, Action and Concept) Model is a conceptual model for derivation of fuzzy domain ontology. Properties of OAC Model can be summarized as follows: the OAC Model suggests a way to model a selected domain. Modeling a domain manually is a time consuming process. However, building associations of data with ontology is more time consuming depending on the size of data. One concern of OAC Model is to associate web pages as data with domain ontology automatically. Domain dependent ontologies are derived with OAC Model. It divides the domain terms into three meaning levels from narrow to wide. However, in the model, there is no domain specific entity or relation. Because of this strategic decision, model has limited entities and relations, but selected entities are basic requirements for semantic retrieval of web pages. Derived ontologies by using OAC Model can serve both images and text of web pages. OAC Model defines 3 main and 2 complemantary entities as illustrated in Fig. 1:

- *Objects* have the narrowest meaning in the domain and they correspond to existential entities. An object can be a region name in an image.
- *Actions* are momentary situation names in the image. They are described by using objects and spatial relations only. Each action can have several definitions shown in Fig. 1 as "action definition". Using this relation provides an action having different definitions. Each action definition has an "action rule" (Fig. 1) and these rules describe the action with some certainty degree. In other words, each action definition has a fuzzy relation with its action rule and, degree of relation denotes the clarity of description. Action rules are composed of {object, spatial relation, object} triples. These triples show required arrangement of objects to interpret action.
- *Concepts* are meaning of momentarily situations and regions. They have the most widely meanings and they are disjoint from object and actions. Concepts express some special meaning themselves. A concept can enclose object, actions and other concepts having narrower meaning than its meaning. Each concept has a relation with the term that can be placed in its meaning. This relation is fuzzy and degree of it denotes the degree of inclusion.
- *Spatial relations* express the relative region positions between two regions such as above, far, near etc. These relations are used to produce action rules. Available spatial relations are found as predefined in the OAC Model.
- *Events* are occurrences of concepts and actions. In the ontology, description of actions and concepts are abstract. They have no place, time or actor information. If this information occurs, events come up. An event of an action means that the described action occurs in some where, at some time, by some one.

The view of the OAC Model is illustrated in Fig. 1. We handle term's synonyms, part of objects and actions, precedence relations between actions, co-occurrence of objects that can be used in an action rule, different action definitions for one action and inclusion relation between concept and terms.

3   Semantic Indexing and Querying

The system developed herein consists of two modules. The first module called as "ontology management" is responsible from derivation of the fuzzy domain ontology by using OAC Model. Expert user models his domain and represents the ontology with OWL automatically. Second module, "semantic retrieval", implements the semantic indexing by using the domain ontology represented in OWL and raw web pages as inputs. The output of the indexing process is repository of web pages' metadata represented by RDF. Queries are gathered from user as combination of terms and Boolean operators and they are transformed to RDQL statements. In other words, the RDF repository is queried by the RDQL statements. This indexing and querying scheme is compatible with information flow principles of Semantic Web. In Fig. 2, the general view of system is illustrated and four main tasks such as ontology management, extraction of content

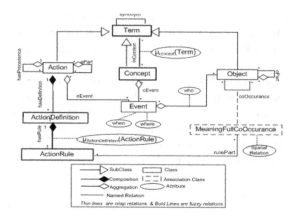

Fig. 1. Schematic representation of the OAC Model entities and relations

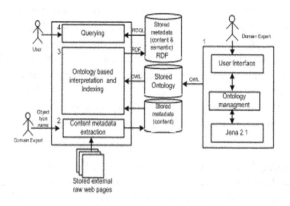

Fig. 2. Illustration of detailed system with all inputs and outputs

features, extraction/interpretation of semantic features (RDF repository construction) and querying are represented.Details of four processes are as follows:

1.Ontology management: Ontology management is performed by using Jena Library Software [14]. It is an ontology management tool developed by HP Labs with Java. The template of OAC Model is supplied to Jena and its facilities are used to derive ontology entities and relations.

2.Extraction of content metadata: It is obvious that images and texts have different content features. Terms and their weights are composed of content features. Weights of terms are calculated taking into consideration the principles of Vector Space Model and finally they are normalized. These weights are called as "raw weights" because they don't reflect the ontological relations. This vector is illustrated in Fig. 3 as the term of "web page matrix".

Content features of images are not only region names but also spatial relations of regions. Regions are marked and labeled by user and then, spatial relations are calculated automatically. Region names must be a type name not a role name. For example, "human" is a valid region name but the system doesn't need the "driver". User should behave like an automatic object recognition module. Content feature of an image is demonstrated as region – region matrix in Fig. 3. In this matrix, each cell contains spatial relations of regions located in corresponding row and column. These relations are expressed in a triple like as {topological, distance, directional} relations.

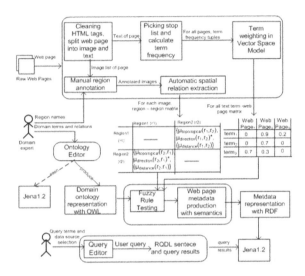

Fig. 3. Detailed system process view

3. Ontology based interpretation and indexing: Semantic interpretations of images and texts are different from each other. In the semantic interpretation of texts, term – web page matrix is tested with term's relations that were defined in the domain ontology. Weights of terms are recalculated by taking into consideration of ontological relations. Propagated weight approach is used and new weights called as "deduced weights" are calculated by equation 1:

$$W_{im} = w_{im} + (\sum_{p=0}^{\#terms} (w_{ip}|m! = p \&\& Ontological Relation(t_m, t_p)! = 0))/\#terms \quad (1)$$

In the equation 1, W_{im} is deducted weight of m. term in i. web page, w_{im} is raw weight of m. term in i. web page, $OntologicalRelation(t_m,t_p)$ is 0 when m. term and p. term have not a relation in the ontology. If p. term and m. term has an ontological relation then raw weight of p. term is used in summation. In this approach, if ontological related terms are used in the same web page, then their weights increase. Although a term has not raw weight, it can have deduced weight. Consequently, expansions are done on the term list of the page. For this reason, query is not required to expand again.

In the semantic interpretation of images, region – region matrix of each image is tested considering rules defined previously in the domain ontology. Each region corresponds to an object. When actions are interpreted, action rules are tested with region- region matrix directly. Definitions in the action rule are based on objects and spatial relations. Spatial relations in the image are extracted as fuzzy. Consequently, a fuzzy testing between matrix and action rules is required. Let denote an image by G that has four regions denoted by a, b, c, d and E is the name of an action with action rule E_{AR}, typical E_{AR} can be sampled as follows: "$E_{AR} : if$(a above b)&&((c below d) || (c left d)) then μ_E (E_{AR}) = $value$." In this example, each {object, spatial relation, object} triple means rule part and each part is connected with Boolean operators. $\mu_E(E_{AR})$ means clarity degree of action definition. Expert user can specify this $value$ while domain ontology derivation. In the fuzzy testing, "&&" operator is handled with fuzzy min and "||" operator is handled with fuzzy max operators and the resulted fuzzy equation is formulated as equation 2. In the equation 2, $\mu_E(G)$ denotes the interpretation degree of action E in the image G. Other membership functions, whose names are placed in the subscript, denote the automatically extracted values of spatial relations from the image G.

$$\mu_E(G) = min(\mu_{above}(a, b), max(\mu_{below}(c, d), \mu_{left}(c, d))) * value \qquad (2)$$

In the interpretation of concepts, concept rules are used. Concept rules based on {term, inclusion degree} couples. Let C, a concept and action E is enclosed by C with some value denoted by $\mu_{CinContext}(E)$. The one rule of C is {E, $\mu_{CinContext}(E)$} couple and the interpretation result of C in image G is evaluated with equation 3. In the equation 3, $\mu_C(G)$ denotes the interpretation degree of C and $\mu_E(G)$ denotes the interpretation degree of action E in the image G.

$$\mu_C(G) = \mu_{CinContext}(E) * \mu_E(G) \qquad (3)$$

4. Querying: The result of ontology based interpretations semantic features of images and text are produced and stored in the metadata of the page. Textual part of the web page is placed into metadata with terms and deduced weights. Images of the web page are placed into metadata with region names, spatial relations of them, interpreted actions and concepts with degrees. All metadata are represented in RDF and stored as RDF file. User constructs his query with domain terms and Boolean operators. Then query is translated into RDQL and run on RDF repository. User can query information which is stored in metadata partially or whole.

4   Experiments

The system is tested using a set of real web pages related to "volleyball" domain. Total 15 web pages are included in the set. Two of them have no image and the other 2 of them have no text. Except these 4 web pages, the rest of web pages have both images and texts. "Fuzzy Volleyball Ontology" was constructed with 20 objects, 14 actions and action rules and 12 concepts and concept rules.

Measurement parameters of retrieval efficiency are precision, recall and r_{norm}. We compare our system with Apache Lucene. Apache Lucene full-featured text search engine library written entirely in Java [14]. Three type of retrieval are implemented with the same queries: text retrieval with Lucene, text retrieval with the system and web page querying (text + image) with the system. Queries are too simple and consist of one term at the different semantic level. Total 6 queries are used. Three of them are actions in the domain (Q1:"spike", Q2:"service", Q3:"block"). The others are concepts in the domain (Q4:"attack", Q5:"defense", Q6:"match"). Performance charts of retrievals are illustrated in Fig. 4.

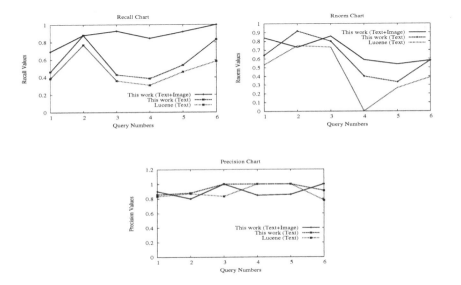

Fig. 4. Recall,R_{norm} and Precision charts of experiments

Based on the experiments, our system considering only text exhibits a better recall performance than the Lucene's system, as shown in Fig.4. This is because the queries developed in our study use not only keywords but also ontological relations. It is also likely that the web pages the Lucene's system do not have query terms in their text bodies. In addition the query terms can be placed in the retrieval output, since the deduced weight of a query term can be a non-zero value. As can be seen in Fig.4, among the systems considered, the recall coefficients of the system considering text and image together are the best for all the queries that we had. The main reason for this good result is the semantic contribution of images on text. In the system exhibiting the highest performance, semantics of images and text are combined and used as web page semantics. In a statistical approach, if a term included by a web page passes through only one time in the page, then it has a weight, e.i., more or less. However, if the term covering meaning of an image is not included by the textual part of a web page, this term is completely ignored by the text retrieval. The system including text and image is able to interpret image meanings, convert them to terms and give some weight values. These are the advantageous of the system including text and image when comparing the other systems employed herein. As a result, the system considering test and image retrieves more relevant pages easily.

R_{norm} values of retrievals are illustrated in Fig.4. R_{norm} is an indicator of the quality of retrieval output sorting. Text retrieval performance of the system developed in this study is better than the Lucene's performance. In fact, the reason of this improvement is similar with the reason of the improvement in the recall. In other words, if the query term passes in the text body of a web page with another term related to it, the deduced weight of the term is greater than its raw weight calculated previously. The increment in the weight provides the web page to be more related to the query. R_{norm} values of the retrievals which were implemented by using text and image together are higher than the others except for query 2. The reason of this improvement is to use combination of text and image semantics. The term which passes throughout text and covers an image meaning in the web page, acquires more weight and effects the sorting of retrieval output. In query 2, during the querying of images, some irrelevant images are matched with query term. In fact, matching degrees of these irrelevant images are very low. Since any threshold is not used, they are not eliminated and irrelevant images cause an increase in semantics wrongly.

Precision values of retrievals are given in Fig.4. These tests are implemented to the closed web page collection. All of them are relevant only with the major topic of "volleyball". Hence, there is no logical reason causing a sharp decrease in precision. Text querying performance of this work is higher than that of Lucene at three points. Retrieval performance of querying by using text and images is better for 2 points, but lower for 3 points than the text retrieval performance of our system and they are close to each other at 1 point. If an explanation is carried out for this reason, it is possible to say that recall values are increased by expanding retrieval outputs. While providing these expansions, some irrelevant pages can also be retrieved, because some erroneous image semantics can be extracted. However, it can be deduced from R_{norm} chart, these irrelevant pages are placed at the end of the retrieval output. It should not be forgotten that a threshold value is not used during determination of image similarity.

5   Conclusions

In this paper, we discuss that complementary relationships of textual and visual information in the web pages help us to derive more semantic features from them. This study is limited to query web pages containing only still images and text. To achieve semantic retrieval purpose,we use the fuzzy domain ontology and propose OAC Model for domain ontology derivation. We implemented several retrievals and results are promising and encourage us about using this work in some real life applications. Although it could not be completely described in this paper (due to the space limitations), we used OAC Model in the domain of volleyball as a case study. As a future work, we have been working on applying our model into other real life applications; one is being a medical sub domain.

References

1. W3C Semantic Web, http://www.w3.org/2001/sw
2. Vijayan Sugmaran and Veda C. Storey. Ontologies for Conceptual Modeling: Their Creation, Use and Management, Data Knowledge Eng., vol. 42, 2002.
3. Carl Lagoze, Jane Hunter, The ABC Ontology Model, Journal of Digital Information, Volume 2 Issue 2, Article No. 77, 2001.
4. Marie-Laure Reinberger, Peter Spyns, A. Johannes Pretorius and Walter Daelamans. Automatic Initiation of an Ontology, Proc. of ODBase'04, Springer-Verlag, 2004.
5. Richaer Bodner and Fei Song. Knowledge-based Approaches to Query Expansion in Information Retrieval, Proc. Of Advances in Artificial Intelligence, pp. 146-158, New York, Springer, 1996.
6. Dave Elliman, J. Rafael and G.Pulido. Automatic Derivation on On-Line Document Ontology, Int. Work. on Mechanisms for Enterprise Integration: From Objects to Ontology (MERIT 2001) 15th Eur. Conf. on Obj. Ori. Prog.,2001.
7. Latifur Khan and Lei Wang. Automatic Ontology Derivation Using Clustering for Image Classification, Multimedia Information Systems, pp 56-65, 2002.
8. David Vallet, Fernandez Miriam and Pablo Castells, An Ontology Based Information Retrieval Model, ESWC05 pp 455-470, 2005.
9. Jun-feng Song, Wei-ming Zhang, Wei-dong Xiao, Guo-hui Li and Zhen-ning Xu, Ontology-Based Information Retrieval Model for the Semantic Web, IEEE Int. Conf. on e-Tech., e-Commmerce and e-Service (IEEE'05) , pp. 152-155, 2005
10. David Parry, A Fuzzy Ontology For Medical Document Retrieval, Proc. of the Second Workshop on Australasian Information Security, Data Mining and Web Intelligence, and Software Internationalization , vol. 32, pp. 121-126, 2004.
11. Lee Chang-Shing, Jian Zhi-Wei, A Fuzzy Ontology and Its Application to News Summarization,IEEE Tran. on Sys., Man and Cybernetics Part B, 35:5, 2005.
12. Dwi H. Widyantoro, John. Yen, A Fuzzy Ontology Based Abstract Search Engine and Its User Studies, IEEE Int. Fuzzy System Conference'01, 2001.
13. The Jena Ontology Management Library, http://jena.sourceforge.net
14. The Apache Software Foundation, http://lucene.apache.org/java/docs

Contextual Ontologies
Motivations, Challenges, and Solutions

Djamal Benslimane[1], Ahmed Arara[1], Gilles Falquet[2],
Zakaria Maamar[3], Philippe Thiran[4], and Faiez Gargouri[5]

[1] LIRIS Laboratory, Lyon 1 University, Villeurbanne, France
{djamal.benslimane, ahmed.arara}@liris.cnrs.fr
[2] University of Geneva, Genva, Switzerland
Gilles.Falquet@cui.unige.ch
[3] Zayed University, Dubai, U.A.E
Zakaria.Maamar@zu.ac.ae
[4] University of namur, Namur, Belgium
pthiran@fundp.ac.be
[5] ISIM, University of Sfax, Sfax, Tunisia
faiez.gargouri@fsegs.rnu.tn

Abstract. Contextual ontologies are ontologies that characterize a concept by a set of properties that vary according to context. Contextual ontologies are now crucial for users who intend to exchange information in a domain. Existing ontology languages are not capable of defining such type of ontologies. The objective of this paper is to formally define a contextual ontology language to support the development of contextual ontologies. In this paper, we use description logics as an ontology language and then we extend it by introducing a new contextual constructor.

Keywords: Context, Description logics, Ontology.

1 Introduction

Known as shared, common, representational vocabularies, ontologies play a key role in many information integration applications. They offer a basis for consistent communication among heterogeneous and autonomous systems [4,6,11]. Ontologies are now so large that users in the same domain with different interests cannot identify concepts relevant to their needs. In fact, existing ontologies [8,12,14] are context-free with respect to their concept representation and definition. Contexts appear in many disciplines as meta-information to characterize the specific situation of an entity, to describe a group of conceptual entities, and to partition a knowledge base into manageable sets or as a logical construct to facilitate reasoning services [10].

Domain ontologies are developed by capturing a set of concepts and their links according to a given context. A context can be seen from different perspectives. For instance it could be about abstraction level, granularity scale, interest of user communities, and perception of ontology developer. Therefore, the same domain can have several ontologies, where each ontology is described in a particular

T. Yakhno and E. Neuhold (Eds.): ADVIS 2006, LNCS 4243, pp. 168–176, 2006.

context. We refer to this as **MonoContext Ontology (MoCO)**. Concepts in a MoCO are defined for one and only one context. The motivation of our research is to see how an ontology can be described according to several contexts at a time. We refer to this as **MultiContext Ontology (MuCO)**. A MuCO characterizes an ontological concept by a variable set of properties in several contexts. As a result, a concept is defined once with several representations while a single representation is available in one context.

Current ontology languages do not permit defining a single MuCO. They do not offer any possibility to hide or filter the ontology content. For example, it is not possible to hide the irrelevant *Road* concept from a user who is only interested in land coverage. Information on green areas and constructed areas are more relevant to him. The objective of this paper is to propose a contextual ontology language to support the development of Multi-Context ontology. We only consider languages that are based on description logics (DLs). DLs are a subset of first order-logic describing knowledge in terms of concepts and roles to automatically derive classification taxonomies, and provide reasoning services. Concepts in DL intentionally specify the properties that individuals must satisfy.

The rest of this paper is organized as follows. Section 2 gives the syntax and semantics of the proposed contextual language and presents some equivalence rules needed during syntax manipulations. Section 3 discusses the subsumption problem in this language. Section 4 surveys some works that are relevant to the issue of multiple viewpoints of ontologies. Finally, Section 5 concludes the paper.

2 Towards an Enhanced Version of Description Logics

For the purpose of our research on multiple context ontologies, we adopt the term contextual ontology to emphasize the importance of context in first, solving the multiple representation problem and second, providing a better visibility and access to ontological information elements (concepts, roles, individuals). The term contextual ontology is used as well to indicate that the ontology we deal with is context dependent. Therefore, a contextual ontology consists of two key words context and ontology. To meet the contextual ontologies' requirements, we propose the notion of contextual concepts. Contextual concepts are basically derived from atomic concepts by using a set of non-contextual and/or contextual constructors. To formally define a contextual concept, we propose adding a new constructor known as projection to the syntax given in Definition 1. This projection constructor is expressed in Definition 3. Definition 4 gives the new contextual interpretation of concepts.

2.1 Contextual Constructors

Definition 1. Syntax of contextual concept terms *Let $s_1, \cdots, s_m$ be a set of context names. Contextual concept terms C can be formed according to the following syntax:*

$$C \longrightarrow (C)[S] \ (contextual \ restriction)$$
$$S \longrightarrow list \ of \ context \ names$$

The definition of non-contextual concepts remains always possible. Such concepts will exist in all contexts with a single representation. The semantics of a non-contextual language is extended with the contextual notion as per Definition 1.

Definition 2. Semantics of contextual concept terms *The semantics of the contextual part of the language is given by a contextual interpretation defined in a context j over S. A contextual interpretation $\mathcal{I} = (\mathcal{I}_0, \mathcal{I}_1, \cdots, \mathcal{I}_j, \cdots, \mathcal{I}_t)$ is a t-tuple indexed by the contexts $\{1, \ldots, t\}$ where each $\mathcal{I}_j$ is a (non-contextual) interpretation $(\Delta^{\mathcal{I}}, \cdot^{\mathcal{I}^j})$, which consists of an interpretation domain $\Delta^{\mathcal{I}}$, and an interpretation function $\cdot^{\mathcal{I}^j}$. The interpretation function $\cdot^{\mathcal{I}^j}$ maps each atomic concept $A \in \mathcal{C}$ onto a subset $A^{\mathcal{I}^j} \subseteq \Delta^{\mathcal{I}}$ and each role name $R \in \mathcal{R}$ onto a subset $R^{\mathcal{I}^j} \subseteq \Delta^{\mathcal{I}} \times \Delta^{\mathcal{I}}$.*

The extension of $\cdot^{\mathcal{I}^j}$ to arbitrary concepts is inductively defined as follows:

$$\bot^{\mathcal{I}^j} = \emptyset$$
$$\top^{\mathcal{I}^j} = \Delta^{\mathcal{I}}$$
$$(C \sqcap D)^{\mathcal{I}^j} = C^{\mathcal{I}^j} \sqcap D^{\mathcal{I}^j}$$
$$(C \sqcup D)^{\mathcal{I}^j} = C^{\mathcal{I}^j} \sqcup D^{\mathcal{I}^j}$$
$$(\exists R.C)^{\mathcal{I}^j} = \{x \in \Delta^{\mathcal{I}} \mid \exists y : (x, y) \in R^{\mathcal{I}^j} \wedge y \in C^{\mathcal{I}^j}\}$$
$$(\forall R.C)^{\mathcal{I}^j} = \{x \in \Delta^{\mathcal{I}} \mid \forall y : (x, y) \in R^{\mathcal{I}^j} \rightarrow y \in C^{\mathcal{I}^j}\}$$
$$(\leq nR)^{\mathcal{I}^j} = \{x \in \Delta^{\mathcal{I}} \mid \ \|\{y \mid (x, y) \in R^{\mathcal{I}^j}\}\| \leq n\}$$
$$(\geq nR)^{\mathcal{I}^j} = \{x \in \Delta^{\mathcal{I}} \mid \ \|\{y \mid (x, y) \in R^{\mathcal{I}^j}\}\| \geq n\}$$
$$((C)[S])^{\mathcal{I}^j} = \begin{cases} C^{\mathcal{I}^j} & \text{if } j \in S \\ \emptyset & \text{otherwise} \end{cases}$$

2.2   Examples

The following suggests some concept definitions in multiple contexts.

Example 1. An employee is defined in context s_1 as anyone who has an employee number and in context s_2 as anyone who works for a company.

$$Employee = (\exists EmployeeNumber.Number)[s_1] \sqcup (\exists WorksFor.Company)[s_2]$$

Example 2. In context s_1 a student is a person who is enrolled in at least one course, while in s_2 a student is a person who has an id-card.

$$Student = Person \sqcap ((\exists EnrolledIn.Course)[s_1] \sqcup (\exists Has.StudentIDCard)[s_2])$$

Example 3. In context s_1 a married man is a man who has exactly one wife, while in s_2 he may have up to 4 wives and in s_3 he may have an unlimited number of wives.

$$MarriedMan = Man \sqcap \exists wife.Woman \sqcap ((\leq 1 wife)[s_1] \sqcup (\leq 4 wife)[s_2] \sqcup (\top)[s_3])$$

The expression $\top[s_3]$ is interpreted as the whole domain $\Delta^{\mathcal{I}}$ in s_3, which expresses the absence of number constraint on *wife* in s_3.

2.3   Algebraic Manipulations

It is straightforward to prove the following equivalences

$$C[s] \sqcup D[s] \equiv (C \sqcup D)[s]$$
$$C[s] \sqcap D[s] \equiv (C \sqcap D)[s]$$
$$\exists R.(C[s]) \equiv (\exists R.C)[s]$$
$$C[s] \equiv C \sqcap \top[s]$$

For negations and universal quantifiers the rules are slightly more complex. In fact we have

$$(\neg C)[s] = \neg C \sqcap \top[s] \equiv \neg(C[s]) \sqcap \top[s]$$
$$\neg(C[s]) \equiv \top[\bar{s}] \sqcup (\neg C)[s]$$
$$(\forall R.C)[s] \equiv (\forall R.C[s]) \sqcap \top[s]$$
$$\forall R.(C[s]) \equiv (\forall R.C)[s] \sqcup \forall R.\bot$$

where $\bar{s}$ is the complement of the set of contexts s.

These equivalences can thus be used to shift the projection operator inside or outside expressions.

3   Subsumption in Multiple Contexts

In a contextual ontology it is necessary to redefine the notion of subsumption to take into account the challenging of managing different contexts.

Definition 3 (Contextual subsumption). *The contextual concept description D subsumes the contextual concept description C (written $C \sqsubseteq D$) iff for all contextual interpretations $\mathcal{I} = (\mathcal{I}_1, \ldots, \mathcal{I}_t)$ $C^{\mathcal{I}^k} \subseteq D^{\mathcal{I}^k}$, $k = 1, \ldots, t$.*

According to this definition, D subsumes C if for each interpretation and for each context, the interpretation of C is a subset of the interpretation of D.

Using the contextual restriction operator in an ontology with contexts $\{1,\ldots,t\}$ the condition $C \sqsubseteq D$ is equivalent to $C[1] \sqsubseteq D[1]$ and $\ldots$ and $C[t] \sqsubseteq D[t]$.

Decidability of Subsumption

It is possible to prove that a contextual subsumption is decidable by adapting and extending the classical tableau algorithm [1] for description logics. Note that this algorithm works only on concept descriptions in negative normal form, i.e. expressions where the negations occur only at the lowest level, just in front of the concept names. Thanks to the transformation rules of Section 2.3, any contextual concept description can be put into a negative normal form.

Let us start by defining the notion of contextual ABox[1].

Definition 4. *Let N_I be a set of individual names. A contextual ABox is a finite set of assertions in the form $C(a) : s$ (contextual concept assertion) or $r(a, b) : s$ (contextual role assertion), where C is a concept description, r a role name, s a context name, and a, b are individual names.*

A contextual interpretation $\mathcal{I}$, which assigns elements $a^{\mathcal{I}} \in \Delta^{\mathcal{I}}$ to the corresponding individual name a of N_I, is a model of an ABox $\mathcal{A}$ iff $a^{\mathcal{I}} \in C^{\mathcal{I}^k}$ holds for all assertions $C(a)/k$ and $(a^{\mathcal{I}}, b^{\mathcal{I}}) \in r^{\mathcal{I}^k}$ holds for all assertion $r(a, b)/k$ in $\mathcal{A}$.

The classical tableau algorithm aims at constructing a model of a concept description C_0. It does achieve this by starting with an initial (singleton) set of ABoxes $\widehat{S} = \{\mathcal{A}_0\}$ where $\mathcal{A}_0 = \{C_0(x_0)\}$ and then exhaustively applying transformation rules. These rules either add new assertions to an ABox or create new ABoxes in $\widehat{S}$. C_0 is satisfiable if and only if the set in $\widehat{S}$ of ABoxes obtained by this process contains at least one consistent ABox (without clash). To test if $C \sqsubseteq D$ amounts to prove that $C \sqcap \neg D$ is unsatisfiable.

In a contextual case, a concept description C_0 is satisfiable if there is at least one context k such that the tableau algorithm applied to $\widehat{S} = \{\{C_0(x_0)/k\}\}$ yields one consistent ABox. The rules to apply are the same as those of [1] plus the following rule that deals with contextual restrictions.

Contextual Restriction-Rule
Condition: The ABox $\mathcal{A}$ contains $(C[s](x)/k$ but neither $(C(x)/k$ nor $\perp(x)$.
Action: if $k \in s$ then $\mathcal{A}' := \mathcal{A} \cup \{C(x)/k\}$ else $\mathcal{A}' := \mathcal{A} \cup \{\perp(x)\}$.

(In the terms of [1] $\perp(x)$ should be expressed as $Q(x) \sqcap \neg Q(x)$, where Q is any arbitrary concept name.)

This rule creates a clash ($P(x)$ and $\neg P(x)$ in the same ABox) when the ABox contains a restriction $C[s](x)/k$ with $k \notin s$, which is clearly unsatisfiable, otherwise the restriction operator is dropped.

4   Related Work and Discussions

This section presents some of the works that are inline with developing multiple and/or contextual ontologies.

4.1   Distributed Description Logics

Distributed description logics (DDLs) are proposed to better present heterogeneous information in distributed systems by modeling the relations between

---

[1] A knowledge base in a description logic system is made up of two components: (1) the *TBox* is a general schema concerning the classes of individuals to be represented, their general properties and mutual relationships; (2) the *ABox* contains a partial description of a particular situation, possibly using the concepts defined in the *TBox*. The *ABox* contains descriptions of (some) individuals of the situation, their properties and their interrelationships.

objects and concepts of heterogeneous information systems [9]. Formal semantics of DDLs is proposed in [2]. Borgida and Serafini argue that there is no single global view of a real world but correspondences between different local conceptualizations should be provided through directed import feature and mapping. They suppose that there are binary relations r_{ij} and r_{ji} that describe the correspondences (at the instance level) between two ontologies O_i and O_j. A bridge rule concept is proposed to constrain these correspondences. A bridge rule from ontology O_i to ontology O_j is expressed in the following two forms:

$$o_i : C \rightarrow^{\sqsubseteq} o_j : D$$
$$o_i : C \rightarrow^{\sqsupseteq} o_j : D$$

These bridge rules allow concepts of an ontology to subsume a concept or to be subsumed by a concept of another ontology. These rules mean that the interpretation of C in O_i, once mapped onto O_j through r_{ij}, must be a subset (resp. a superset) of the interpretation of D in O_j.

Let us consider the example presented in [2] where a concept $Book\_on\_the_s helves$ in ontology O_1 is defined to represent all the books that are not currently on loan in a given library. Assume the existence of the role $locate\_at$ in ontology O_2 which associates a book with a location on the shelves. To combine both ontologies in a distributed way, the following bridge rule can be defined: $O_1 : Book\_on\_shelf \sqsupseteq O_2 : \exists located\_at\_\{"lyon\_library"\}$. This bridge rule formalizes the fact that people know something is located in lyon_library only if it is a book that is not on loan there. DDLs have a solid logical ground and look very attractive to deal with multiple ontologies but coordination through mapping/bridge rules is necessary for any pair of ontologies that need to collaborate.

4.2 Contextualized Ontology ($C - OWL$)

In [3], Bouquet et al. consider that an ontology is built to be shared while a context is built to be kept local. To take advantage of both notions (ontology and context), they propose combining them in a unique framework. Thus, they propose the contextual ontology notion as an ontology with a local interpretation. This means that its contents is not shared with other multiple ontologies.

To cope with the semantic-heterogeneity problem, Bouquet et al. argue that imposing a single schema will always cause a loss of information. Their theoretical framework considers the following: (i) different conceptualizations provide a set of local ontologies that can be autonomously represented and managed, (ii) inter-relationships between contextualized ontologies can be discovered and represented, and (iii) the relationships between contextualized ontologies can be used to give semantic-based services and preserving their local "semantic identity". The OWL language is extended with respect to its syntax and semantics to meet the contextualized ontology's requirements. The new C-OWL language is augmented with rules (or bridge rules) that relate (syntactically and semantically) concepts, roles, and individuals of different ontologies.

4.3   E-Connections

E-connections is proposed in [7] as a formalism (i) to provide an expressive way for combining different heterogeneous logical formalisms such as description, modal, and epistemic logics, and (ii) to ensure the decidability and computational robustness of the combined formalism. The key idea in E-connections is to consider that the domains of the ontologies to combine are completely disjoint. The ontologies are then interconnected by defining new links between individuals belonging to distinct ontologies. For example, assume that O_1 and O_2 are two disjoint ontologies dealing with people and books respectively. The combination of both ontologies can be done by defining new links between individuals of O_1 and individuals of O_2, and creating new concepts from the existing concepts of both ontologies. Hence, the link buy can be defined in O_1 to represent the fact that a person can buy books. In a similar way, the concept $FrequentBuyer$ can be added to O_2 to define persons who buy at least one book is described as follows: $FrequentBuyer = Person \sqcap \exists buy.Book$. A framework is proposed in [5] to combine multiple, disjoint OWL ontologies. It is important to note that $E - connections$ does not allow concepts to be subsumed by concepts of another ontology, which limits the expressivity of the language.

4.4   Modal Logics

Modal logics [13] are a formalism for expressing dynamic aspects of knowledge such as beliefs, judgments, intuitions, obligations, time, actions, etc. In modal logics, the semantics of expressions or formula is defined in terms of things' trustworthiness in different worlds or contexts. This contrasts with the classical description logic, where things are just true or false, and not true in one context and false in another. The syntax of a modal description logics consists of the classical description logic constructs and the modal operators ($\Box_i C, \Diamond_i C$) known as necessity and possibility operators respectively. Modal concept C is defined as follows: $C \longrightarrow \Box_i C \mid \Diamond_i C$. For example, a faithful wife who loves her husband is expressed in classical DLs as: $faithfulWife = wife \sqcap \exists loves.husband$. If we would like to emphasize the fact that a faithful wife necessary loves her husband, which means that she always loves her husband, we need to express the same concept as: $faithfulWife = wife \sqcap \Box_i \exists loves.husband$.

4.5   Discussions

We highlight how our proposed approach is different from the aforementioned approaches. Both $DDLs$'s and $E - connections$'s objective is to preserve the independence of each local ontology. To work with multiple ontologies, they propose either a set of axioms (bridge rules) or $e - connections$ concept in order to establish interconnections between ontologies. Our approach differs from both approaches. Indeed, while DDL and $E - connections$ are concerned with how to work and reason about multiple ontologies, our approach deals with how a single ontology is defined in a way that different perspectives are included. This means that with DDL and $E-connections$, different ontologies are available and represented in a classical way and then a new mechanism is added to link them. In our approach, we aim at creating a single ontology in which the definition of a concept includes the notion of multiple contexts in order to separate concepts from one context to another.

Our approach's objective is rather closed to the ones targeted in the ontology views and modal description logics approaches. Our approach can be different from the ontology views approach by the fact that a view is extracted by querying the ontology content and this assumes that users have to master both a query language and the ontology content. With our approach, users only need to specify the current context to extract a sub-ontology from another one. A modal description logics approach allows modal interpretations of concepts. Our contextual interpretation is a somehow a special case of modalities as well as temporal and spatial description logics. Hence, this work is different from ours in the sense that it does not give us the ability to explicitly designate context names.

5   Conclusion

In this paper, we argued that both ontology and context complement each other to achieve the goal of resolving partially the semantic heterogeneity in the scope of multiple context ontology where the same concept may need to be shared by more than one application. The notion of contextual ontologies approach was presented and formalized based on using the description logic language. Throughout this paper, we advocated the multi-representation rather than mono-representation of real world entities. Our rationale for the need of multi-context definition of concepts is: new requirements and information needs impose that many systems to coordinate, access shared entities of one another, and query autonomous, heterogeneous information sources. As future work, we aim at finalizing and implementing the proposed constructs. Further, we intend to validate and test the proposed language in the domain of urbanism where we expect a wide range of contexts like transportation, land use, urban planing, etc.

References

1. F. Baader and U. Sattler. An overview of tableau algorithms for description logics. *Studia Logica*, 69:5–40, 2001.
2. Alexander Borgida and Luciano Serafini. Distributed description logics: Directed domain correspondences in federated information sources. In Robert Meersman and Zahir Tari, editors, *CoopIS/DOA/ODBASE*, volume 2519 of *Lecture Notes in Computer Science*, pages 36–53. Springer, 2002.
3. P. Pouquet et al. C-owl: Contextualizing ontologies. *In Proceedings of the 2nd International Semantic Web Conference (ISWC2003), 20-23 October 2003, Sundial Resort, Sanibel Island, Florida, USA.*, Oct 2003.
4. A. Gangemi, D.M. Pisanelli, , and G. Steve. An overview of the onion project: Applying ontologies to the integration of medical terminology. *Data and Knowledge Engineering*, 31:183–220, 1999.

5. Bernardo Cuenca Grau, Bijan Parsia, and Evren Sirin. Working with multiple ontologies on the semantic web. In Sheila A. McIlraith, Dimitris Plexousakis, and Frank van Harmelen, editors, *International Semantic Web Conference*, volume 3298 of *Lecture Notes in Computer Science*, pages 620–634. Springer, 2004.

6. J. Martins H.S. Pinto, A. Gomez-Prez. Some issues on ontology integration. In *Proceedings of IJCAI 1999Workshop on Ontologies and Problem Solving Methods: Lessons Learned and Future trends*, pages 7.1–7.2, 1999.

7. O. Kutz, C. Lutz, F. Wolter, and M. Zakharyaschev. E-connections of abstract description systems. *Artificial Intelligence)*, 156(1):1–73, 2004.

8. Douglas B. Lenat. Cyc: A large-scale investment in knowledge infrastructure. *Commun. ACM*, 38(11):32–38, 1995.

9. Yinglong Ma and Jun Wei. A default extension to distributed description logics. In *IEEE/WIC/ACM International Conference on Intelligent Agent Technology (IAT'04)*, pages 38–44, 2004.

10. D. Salber, A. Day, and G. Abowd. The context toolkit: Aiding the development of context-aware applications. In *Proceedings of the SIGCHI conference on Human factors in computing systems*, pages 434 – 441. ACM Press, 1999.

11. Thomas Strang, Claudia Linnhoff-Popien, and Korbinian Frank. Cool: A context ontology language to enable contextual interoperability. In Jean-Bernard Stefani, Isabelle M. Demeure, and Daniel Hagimont, editors, *DAIS*, volume 2893 of *Lecture Notes in Computer Science*, pages 236–247. Springer, 2003.

12. P.C.H. Wariyapola, N.M. Patrikalakis, S.L. Abrams, P. Elisseeff, A.R. Robinson, H. Schmidt, and K. Streitlien. Ontology and metadata creation for the poseidon distributed coastal zone management system. In *IEEE Forum on Research and Technology Advances in Digital Libraries*, pages 180–189, May 1999.

13. F. Wolter and M. Zakharyaschev. Satisfiability problem in description logics with modal operators. In *In Proceedings of the 6th Int. Conf. on Knowledge Representation and Reasonning, KR'98, Trento, Italy, June 1998.*, pages 512–523, 2001.

14. Toshio Yokoi. The edr electronic dictionary. *Commun. ACM 38(11)*, 38(44):42–44, 1995.

Matchmaking of Semantic Web Services Using Semantic-Distance Information

Mehmet Şenvar and Ayşe Bener

Boğaziçi University, Computer Engineering Department, İstanbul, Turkey
msenvar@yahoo.com, bener@boun.edu.tr

Abstract. This paper mainly focuses on proposing efficient and extensible matchmaking architecture. We ran an improved algorithm using the semantic-distance information, based on OWL-S, UDDI and semantic web architectures. Current matchmaking architectures and algorithms lack vision and they are unable to use all available information. However, our proposed architecture uses information such as path-length of the ontological tree nodes and partial results sets for composing required service even no exact match is found. Semantic-distance information may be used as selection criteria and it provides accuracy in service selection. To define concept-similarity rating by ontology managers or local users may provide a way for service selection. We can then gather second level of information other than the pre-defined match levels such as exact, subsume or plug-in. We exploit this fact in our architecture and algorithm by providing a layered and extended architecture. Different filtering layers and different specifications are applied in the matchmaking to give an extendable architecture.

Keywords: Web Services, Semantic Web Service Discovery, OWL-S, UDDI, WSDL, Semantic Web Service Discovery Algorithm, Semantic Distance.

1 Introduction

With the increasing number of available web services, discovery of correct web service for our needs based on the services capabilities is difficult. Semantic web aims to solve this problem by attaching semantic meta-data to web service descriptions some of which are mostly based on OWL-S [1], RDF [2] and so on.

Based on this semantic information, web service discovery architectures are mainly divided into three main categories which are matchmaking, brokerage and P-2-2 architectures. Matchmaker is mainly the simplest and most general kind of architecture. These architectures and solutions have different privileges and are suitable for different kind of web service discovery needs [3]. For example in contrast to a broker agent, a matchmaker does not deal with the task of contacting the relevant providers, transmitting the service request to the service provider and communicating the results to requestor.

To define basically, "Matchmaking is the process of finding an appropriate provider for a requestor through a middle agent and has the following general form: (1) Provider agents advertise their capabilities to middle agents, (2) middle agents store these advertisements, (3) a requestor asks some middle agents whether it knows of providers with

T. Yakhno and E. Neuhold (Eds.): ADVIS 2006, LNCS 4243, pp. 177–186, 2006.
© Springer-Verlag Berlin Heidelberg 2006

desired capabilities, and (4) the middle agent watches the request against the stored a advertisements and returns the result, a subset of the stored advertisements". [3]

Although matchmaking systems seems to have simple and clear definition and functionality, the importance of matchmaking is really high in the development of semantic web [4]. The matchmaking process in total should be extendable, efficient, general and modular to answer different needs of service discovery problem. In this paper we will focus on some important aspects of matchmaking and propose a matching algorithm.

2   Related Work

Currently, there are several algorithms and architectures are proposed for semantic web service matchmaking and discovery [5, 6, 7]. However most of them set strict architectures and limited capabilities. Also they are based on formerly accepted semantic concepts such as DAML-S, which is now extended as OWL-S. Also current approaches mainly focus on only input and output matching. They do not use all the ontological information in matchmaking either.

One of the approaches on matchmaking has been LARKS [5] system proposed by Sycara et al. LARKS tries to offer a flexible architecture in a scalable manner. LARKS is written in a specific concept language called ITL (Information Terminological Language). The LARKS matchmaking process performs both syntactic and semantic matching and in addition allows the specification of concepts (local ontologies) via ITL. The matching process uses five different filters: context matching, profile comparison, similarity matching, signature matching and constraint matching. Different degrees of partial matching can result from utilizing different combinations of these filters. LARKS represent services on the basis of their inputs and outputs.

Another solution proposed for matchmaking is Ian Horrocks and Lei Lui's architecture [6]. Their design and implementation of a service matchmaking prototype is based on DAML-S ontology and a Description Logic reasoner to compare ontology based service descriptions. A sample representation on DAML-S is given and some revisions on service profile are done to cover larger set of queries that can be matched. Also a matching algorithm is proposed here. The degrees of matches defined in this paper are Exact, PlugIn, Subsume, Intersection, and Disjoint. Degrees of the match are organized in a discrete scale. Here also matching is based on inputs and outputs. However, it is not based on OWL-S and it eliminates any mismatches on inputs or outputs. There is no match value defined either. A similar approach is Colucci et al. work [8] where DL based matchmaking is proposed and potential, partial matches are identified. A sorted list is returned to service requestor. However, semantic distance information is not used in this study also.

3   Background Concepts

3.1   Ontologies

Ontologies play a key role in the semantic web by providing vocabularies that can be used by the applications in order to understand the shared information. These ontologies are defined in standardized syntaxes such as RDF.

During the development of the matchmaking algorithm we have assumed that there exists some ontology descriptions and ontology homogeneity in the system. The automatic or semi-automatic merging of ontologies is a difficult problem, which we do not take into consideration in this research. However there may also exist local ontologies. In this case a local-to-global ontology mapping is required.

3.2 UDDI

UDDI [9] is a cross-industry effort and it aims to create a global, platform-independent, open framework to enable businesses to discover each other, define how they interact over the Internet and share information in a global registry that will more rapidly accelerate the global adaptation. However, UDDI does not represent service capabilities [10], only tModels may be used to provide a tagging mechanism and search on them is performed by string matching on some fields defined. Thus, locating services on the basis of a semantic specification of their functionality is not possible.

3.3 OWL-S

"OWL-S is an OWL-based Web service ontology, which supplies web service providers with a core set of markup language, constructs for describing the properties and capabilities of their Web services in unambiguous, computer-interpretable form." [1]. The aim of OWL-S is to semantically describe web services for discovery and invocation. OWL-S [1] is characterized by three modules: Service Profile, Process Model and Grounding. Three properties of the service class are:

Presents: The Service Profile provides detailed description of the service and its provider in a human readable way. Inputs, outputs, preconditions and post conditions of services are defined in service profile.

Describedby: The Service Model describes what the service does, how it works and what functionality it provides as a process.

Supportedby: The Service Grounding provides information about service access specifications, such as; communication and transportation protocols.

4 Definitions and Functionalities

4.1 Query Types

Matchmaker should be able to answer two types of querying. For *Volatile Query*, the seeker submits a query to the matchmaker, the matched advertisements are immediately returned and then this query is discarded by the matchmaker. The *Persistent Query* is a query that will remain valid for a length of time defined by the requestor itself. The matchmaker returns the available web services immediately and when a new web service is advertised it will be tried to be matched with the persistent set of look ups.

4.2 Matching on Inputs/Outputs

Based on inputs and outputs separately there is a matching level and matching value calculated. These matching levels are calculated for each input and output, and based on this evaluation final values of inputs and outputs are calculated. Based on the subsumption relation of the ontological tree there are 4 types of match levels:

- **Exact:** the searched criteria is same as the services definition.
- **Plug-in:** the provided criterion by the web service is a more general concept than the searched criteria.
- **Subsume:** the provided criteria is a smaller concept than the searched criteria; it is a subclass of the searched criteria.
- **Fail:** if criteria is not related with the definition of the web service on related concepts it will be set as fail.

The matching order of input/output types is: *exact > plug-in > subsume > fail*

Fig. 1. Concept Matching-level Definitions

Based on this strength we assume to assign the following values for the match types as: Exact =1, Plug-in = 0.8, Subsume = 0.5; Fail =0. These values will be used in the calculation of match-value. Although they may be changed, their effect should be in the order defined.

The level of the match will be the minimum of the set of matches for input and outputs. For example, when two output match levels are plug-in and subsume, it will have a final match-degree of subsume for outputs. The minimum match-level value for inputs and outputs will be the level of matching for all input and outputs. Output and input levels and match values will be evaluated separately and outputs are given priority according to the inputs. The reason for this is that the important point for web service discovery is finding web services that satisfy our need. Satisfaction is highly dependent on output. Match number is calculated as an aggregate of all level matches and used specially in ordering of same kind of matched level services.

4.3 General Rules of Concept Similarity

A general concept similarity weight assignment is done on the ontological representation by the ontology managers. Based on the usage of global or global&local ontologies, there may be two cases.

Case I: Assignment is done on the global ontology. All users and agents use this ontology and similarity weight assignment.

Case II: Agents and users define their local ontology and assignment is done on this representation by local ontology managers.

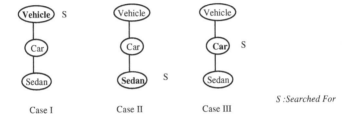

Fig. 2. Sample Ontology for Concept Similarity

Axiom I: Strongest match is where target concept match with itself directly. This is the natural criteria, as in Case III, that we match with the input/output that exactly the one searched for.

Axiom II: For the search result concepts under the target concept, the one that is upper in the ontological representation is preferred. As Case I, while searching for a web service with parameter output Vehicle, Car is chosen instead of Sedan since it is located at the upper level in the hierarchy of the ontology.

Axiom III: For the concepts over the target concept, the one that is closer to the searched concept which is in the lower part of the ontological representation is chosen. As in Case II, while we are searching for a web service with output Sedan, Car is chosen instead of Vehicle, since it is semantically closer.

4.4 Semantic-Distance Weight Assignment

We define the semantic-distance as the similarity of concepts, which may be the rate of coverage of sub-concepts for each concept in relation to subClassOf. For each tuple having a subClassOf relation a weight is assigned in the range [0-1]. The total weight of all subclasses of a parent concept should be 1.

This similarity weight assignment may be done by sub-ontology managers. These people define and assign these weights during the first development of ontologies. However sometimes there may not be such a similarity rating. Even in this situation the properties defined is valid and a homogenous rate assignment may be assigned. For a concept having 3 subclass relations each may be assigned 0.33 (1/3) rating with the parent concept. This homogeneity will be assumed all over the ontological representation.

The semantic distance information can be held as a tuple relation.

$$SD = (parent\_concept, subclass\_concept, similarity) \qquad (1)$$

SD1 = (Vehicle, Car, 0.8)
SD2 = (Vehicle, Truck, 0.2)
SD3 = (Car, Sedan, 0.4)

This similarity info will be used during the matching process in rating the input and output matching. Rather than just classifying as exact, subsume match etc., at the second level we use this similarity values to order the matching.

5   Algorithm

Algorithms in literature are mainly based on matching of inputs and outputs and any mismatches are also eliminated directly. Also only a match level scale is defined without a match number value so sorting of similar services is not clearly specified. Steps described below are applied in order in the matchmaking. In each step, the web services that are filtered pass to the next step and others are eliminated.

5.1   Concept/Domain Matching

The web services will be categorized on high level web service definition ontology and searches will be limited to the specified ontologies. Some examples may be Buy-BookService, SellComputerBook service etc. This level of filtering is especially important for specifying the range of searches directly and efficiently. For example when searching for book buying services, health services will be eliminated directly.

5.2   Input/Output Matching

The most important matching criteria of semantic web services will be matching of the inputs and outputs. Especially outputs are more important because the main reason of using of some web service is getting the required output. The algorithm uses the subsumption relation of inputs/outputs similar to the approaches in [7], [11] and [12]. However, here the path-length from reached output to the requested output on the ontology tree representation information is used in the calculation of match value. We define this information as semantic-similarity rating.

For further explanation the ontology in Figure 3 will be assumed. This ontology is mainly composed by the RDF subClassOf relation. The semantic-distance weight assignments to nodes are done homogeneously.

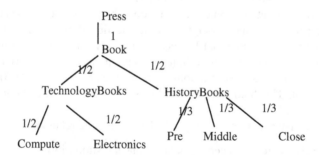

Fig. 3. Sample Ontology for Input/Output Matching

5.3   Pre/Post Condition Matching

Pre and post condition matching is based on a rule defined setting. In this matching elimination is done on the constraints of inputs and outputs. For example web services having output of age, value greater than 18 may be defined as pre condition. Also to discharge my credit card account may be defined as a post condition of Book-SellingService. The matching should be done using some DL-based rule. SWRL

(Semantic Web Rule Language) is currently used for this kind of matching. Although pre/post condition matching is not done in detail through implementation theoretically it may be added to the implementation.

5.4 Add-Value Matching

This step of matching tries to match the service according to specified add-value of the use of the services that would be gained by the user when the service is used. For example when a web service for hotel reservation, say webServiceHotelReservA, is used with a web service buying bus ticket together, say webServiceBusTicketBuyA, user will get a %10 discount. This matching is also based on semantic-rule languages used by the pre/post condition matching.

5.5 Level of Filtering Applied

At this step of matchmaking if service requestor defines a level of matching, meaning a threshold value, only the services specified over this threshold level will be returned to the requestor. These levels are defined as strict, medium, none. For *Strict*; only exactly matching web services are returned. For *Medium*, failed web services are eliminated and highly ranked %70 percent of remaining matching services is returned. *None*: no level is defined so all results are returned.

5.6 Maximum Result Size

If this criterion is specified by the user, only the specified number of web services, matched with highest level and value will be returned to the user. This step is required when a large number of web services are returned from the matchmaker.

   The result of matchmaking returned to the service requestor will be (Service_information, match_level, match_value) set. The results will be an ordered set restricted to the predefined and specified criteria. Another set named as PartialResult Set will be returned. This set will be the set of services that fail on some inputs or outputs but provide some subset of inputs/outputs. This result set is especially important for composing the required web service by the requestor if no matched service is found. When no service is found matching the requirements, it may be composed from the ones in the partial set. As an example assume a web service request that "Given Price, return list of Electronics and Pre(Histroy) books". And two web services that is defined as (WS1: Input: Price Output: ComputerBooks,PreHistory) and (WS2: Input:Price OutPut: ComputerBooks, ElectronicBooks). None of the two provide all requirements but partially they do.

6 Simulation and Results

We implemented the algorithm by using Java. The OWL-S descriptions of web services are simply defined in OWL-S structure. For parsing owls documents OWL-S API [14] developed by MINDSWAP laboratory is used.

   On the assumed ontological representation each path is assigned a weight based on the number of child nodes from the parent. For example under the Book there are 2 child nodes so each path is assigned 1/2. For History books there are 3 child nodes which are Pre, Middle and Close; so the path weight of each is 1/3. To calculate the combined path weight, for example from Books to Middle (History) books we find the path weights as: $1/2 * 1/3 = 1/6$

$$total\_weight = match\_degree\_value * path\_length\_value \qquad (2)$$

The idea behind this multiplication and taking 1/n value is to decrease the similarity value as the nodes get far from each other and as more sub branches are added to the tree. Because the similarity of concepts decrease as they get far from each other. Although numbers might be modified or predefined semantic-similarity weights may be used, the result will remain valid because it is based o decrease relative to path length and path count.

Scenario I: Assume a service requestor searches for a web service with input Price and output ComputerBooks, mainly based on input and output criteria:

WS1: Input: Price   Output: Book
WS2: Input: Money   Output: ComputerBooks
WS3: Input: Output: HistoryBooks

Table 1. Scenario I Output Table

	WS-I	WS-II	WS-I
Inputs	Exact, 1.0	Subsume, (1/2*0.5)	None
Outputs	Plug-in((1/2*1/2)*0.8)	Exact, 1.0	Fail

Sorted list (O2 > O1, I1 > I2) outputs given precedence

1. WS-2
2. WS-1

WS-3 fails (but inserted into partial Result set because it returns history books which match with certain attributes at some level)

Scenario II: Given Price, return list of Electronics and Pre(Histroy) books

WS1: Input: Price   Output: ComputerBooks, PreHistory
WS2: Input: Price   OutPut: ComputerBooks, ElectronicBooks

None of the web services directly satisfy or are directly related with all the input and output criteria. Only half of the output set is returned for the request.

Table 2. Scenario II Output Table

	Partial List
WS-I	weight = 1/4
WS-II	weight = 1/6

Both of WS1 and WS2 satisfies part of the output sets. Weight of each is calculated according to the path length of the parent-child nodes of the ontologic tree on assigned values.

Scenario III
Assume there are 100 web services registered in the matchmaker and 10 of them are related with the context of BuyBookService and others are unrelated. They may be health services, financial services etc. As a service requestor, specify the search context as BuyBookService on the highest level, set matching degree to strict, maximum result set size to 5 without further given any other constraints or specification, and specify inputs and outputs. In context level matching, 90 of the 100 web services will be eliminated directly since they do not share the same context of search. After input/output/pre/post condition match, only web services that match on these values strictly (having matching level as strict) will remain. Assume 8 web services strictly match the requirements. As the last step, we have restricted the size of maximum result set as 5, so top 5 services will be returned to the user as a result.

7 Conclusion

In this research, we proposed an extendable and efficient matchmaking algorithm and architecture. Our main concern was to fill the missing points in the systems that are already proposed. By increasing the information using semantic-distance information we tried to get more accurate matchmaking results and a better ordered result set.

The main contribution of this research is the use of information on the ontological representation of parent-child relations with path-length values which we define as semantic-distance information. A new PartialResult set is defined and discovered for the services that only satisfy some subset of input/output parameters. Rather than eliminating them directly, this set is proposed for composition architectures. A layered algorithm and architecture is designed to be efficient and extendable. Add-value definition is added for search criteria to match different web services and to assist the benefits of users on behalf.

References

1. *OWL-S Submission*, http://www.w3.org/Submission/OWL-S, 2006.
2. Resource Description Framework, W3C, http://www.w3.org/RDF/, 2006.
3. Sycara, K., K. Decker and M. Williamson, "Middle-Agents for the Internet" *Proceedings of the 15th Int. Joint Conference on Artificial Intelligence (IJCAI-97)*, Nagoya, Japan, 1997.
4. *Semantic Web, W3C*, http://www.w3.org/2001/sw/, 2006.
5. Sycara, K., S. Widoff, M. Klusch and J. Lu, "LARKS: Dynamic Matchmaking Among Heterogeneous Software Agents in Cyberspace", *Autonomous Agents and Multi-Agent Systems*, Vol. 5, pp. 173-203, 2002.
6. Li, L. and I. Horrocks, "A Software Framework for Matchmaking Based on Semantic Web Technology", *Proc. of the Twelfth International (WWW 2003)*, pp 331-339, Budapest, 2003.
7. Paolucci, M., T. Kawamura, T. Payne and K. Sycara, "Semantic Matching of Web Services Capabilities", *Proceedings of the First International Semantic Web Conference (ISWC)*, Sardinia, Italy, pp. 333 - 347, 2002.

8. Colucci, S., T. Di Noia, E. Di Sciascio, F.M. Donini, M. Mongiello, G. Piscitelli, G. Rossi. "An Agency for Semantic-Based Automatic Discovery of Web-Services", In Proc. of Artificial Intelligence Applications and Innovations Conference IFIP (WCC2004-AIAI 2004), Kluwer, pp. 315-328, August 2004.

9. UDDI, Universal Discovery Description and Integration Protocol, http://www.uddi.org.

10. Paolucci, M., T. Kawamura, T. R., Payne and K. Sycara, "Importing the Semantic Web in UDDI", *Proceedings of Web Services, E-business and Semantic Web Workshop*, Toronto, Canada, pp. 225-236, 2002.

11. Srinivasan, N., M. Paolucci and K. Sycara, "An Efficient Algorithm for OWL-S Based Semantic Search in UDDI", *First International Workshop on Semantic Web Services and Web Process Composition (SWSWPC)*, Vol. 3387 of LNCS., 96-110, 2004.

12. Trastour, D., C. Bartolini and J. Gonzalez-Castillo, "A Semantic Web Approach to Service Description for Matchmaking of Services", *HP Labs white paper*, 2001.

13. Martin, D., M. Paolucci, S. McIraith, M. Burstein, D. McDermott, D. McGuiness, B. Parsia, T. Payne, M. Sabou, M. Solanki, N. Srinivasan, K. Sycara, "Bringing Semantics to Web Services: The OWL-S Approach", *Proc. of the First International Workshop on Semantic Web Services and Web Process Composition (SWSWPC 2004)*, July 6-9, 2004.

14. OWL-S API, http://www.mindswap.org/2004/owl-s/api/, 2006.

Ontology-Based Information Systems Development: The Problem of Automation of Information Processing Rules

Olegas Vasilecas and Diana Bugaite

Department of Information Systems, Vilnius Gediminas Technical University,
Sauletekio al. 11, LT-10223, Lithuania
Olegas.Vasilecas@fm.vtu.lt, diana@isl.vtu.lt

Abstract. The business rule approach is used in information systems to represent domain knowledge and to maintain rules systems efficiently in volatile business environment. A number of methods were proposed to develop rule models, but only few deal with reuse of knowledge acquired in the analysis of some particular domain and automatic implementation of rules. In this paper, a method for representing knowledge by ontology transformation into the rule model is described. The method is based on ontology transformation of axioms presented in a formal way into (semi-)formal information processing rules in the form of executable rules, like active DBMS triggers. The method is implemented into the developed prototype, which is described in the case study section.

Keywords: Ontology, ECA rule, SQL trigger, axiom.

1 Introduction

In the research of information systems development, the business rules approach has achieved a lot of attention and already has a strong motivation behind its application ([1,2,3]). A business rule is a directive, intended to govern, guide or influence business behavior, in support of business policy that has been formulated in response to an opportunity, threat, strength, or weakness [4]. Business rules are used in information systems to represent domain knowledge and to maintain rule systems efficiently in volatile business environment. A number of methods were proposed to develop rule models, but only few deal with reuse of knowledge acquired in the analysis of some particular domain and automatic implementation of rules. In computer science, ontologies are used to represent real-world domain knowledge. Therefore, knowledge represented by ontology can be used for generating rules. Moreover, ontology expressed in a formal way [5] can be transformed into rule model automatically.

In this paper, a method for representing knowledge by ontology transformation into the rule model is described. The method is based on transforming ontology axioms presented in a formal way into (semi-)formal information processing rules in the form of executable rules, like active DBMS triggers. The method is implemented into the developed prototype, which is described in the case study section.

T. Yakhno and E. Neuhold (Eds.): ADVIS 2006, LNCS 4243, pp. 187–196, 2006.

2 Related Work

A definition of a business rule (BR) depends on the context in which it is used. From the business system perspective, a BR is a statement that defines or constrains some aspects of a particular business. At the business system level, BRs are expressed in a declarative manner [6]. For example: *A customer could not buy more than credit limit permits.*

From the perspective of information systems (IS), a BR is a statement, which defines the major rules of information processing using a rule-based language [7]. Expressions of information-processing rules are very precise, e.g. terms used in expressions are taken from the particular data model. For example: *'Total Value' of an ORDER could not be greater than the 'Credit Limit' of a CUSTOMER* [8].

At the execution level (or software systems level), rules are statements that are transferred to the executable rules, like active DBMS triggers.

The more fundamental question in defining 'BR' can arise: 'What rules are BRs?' BRs are rules that are under business jurisdiction, e.g., the business can enact, revise and discontinue BRs as it sees fit [9].

Information-processing rules are used in ISs to process the required information correctly. These information-processing rules are derived from BRs, which are taken from the business system level. In practice, information-processing rules are implemented by executable rules. Information-processing rules should be expressed as ECA (*event-condition-action*) rules to be implemented by executable rules, like active DBMS SQL triggers.

Therefore it is necessary to determine and elicit rules from the application domain and develop ECA rules.

One of the possible ways to solve the defined problems is the use of the domain ontology.

The term 'ontology' is borrowed from philosophy, where Ontology means a systematic account of Existence. In computer science, the definition of ontology is rather confusing. By [10] all definitions of the term 'ontology' attempt to explain what an ontology is from three different aspects: the content of an ontology, the form of an ontology and the purpose of an ontology.

Gruber's definition of ontology, as a specification of a conceptualisation [11], is rather confusing. It explains the content of ontology, but does not explain what a conceptualisation is. According to Genesereth, a conceptualisation includes the objects and their relations which an agent presumes to exist in the world. The process of a conceptualisation is the process of mapping an object or a relation in the world to a representation in our mind [10].

Ontology defines the basic terms and their relationships comprising the vocabulary of an application domain and the axioms for constraining the relationships among terms [6]. This definition explains what an ontology looks like [10].

In the simplest case, an ontology describes a hierarchy of concepts related by particular relationships (like, is-a, part-of, etc.). In more sophisticated cases, constraints are added to restrict the value space of concepts and relationships. They, for example, express cardinality, possible length (like, maxLength, minLength) In most sophisticated cases, suitable axioms are added in order to express complex relationships between concepts and to constrain their intended interpretation [5].

Ontologies are being built today for many reasons. The reason of creating an ontology depends on a research field and an application area where it is going to be used. In this paper, ontology is used for its transformation into the rule model.

3 Transformation of Ontology Axioms into Business Rules

In the application domain or ontology, to which the BRs belong, they are not always expressed in terms of ECA rules. Some of these BRs have explicit or implicit condition and action parts. The missing condition can always be substituted with a default condition state as TRUE. Some BRs may have no explicit action since they can state what kind of transition from one data state to another is not admissible [12]. But the majority of these BRs do not define explicitly or implicitly the event. There are three possible ways to trigger rules:

- automatically trigger all rules every time when any related event occurs,
- trigger rules manually when somebody decides it is necessary,
- specify necessary events and link them to actual rules.

In this research, the third way was used for rules triggering, since the specification of the events and their linking to actual rules enable the system automatically react to the defined events and perform the defined operations, e.g. trigger rules automatically. Moreover, it is not necessary to execute all rules when some event occurs. Only related rules are executed.

Obviously, it is confusing to form information-processing rules of ECA form and consequently implement them by executable rules.

3.1 Formal Foundation of Ontology for Business Rules Elicitation

The mathematical models of ontology and business rules were analysed to determine the relationship between ontology and BRs.

From [13,14,15,16,17] it was determined that ontology could be expressed in the following way:

$$\Psi = \langle \{\Psi_i | i = 1, \ldots, k\}, A \rangle, \tag{1}$$

where Ψ_i is the ontology element which can be expressed by triplet:

$$\langle \nu_i, R'_I, I_i \rangle \quad \text{with } \nu_i \in V \wedge R'_i \in R' \wedge I_i \in I, \tag{2}$$

where $V = \{\nu_0, \nu_1, \ldots, \nu_n\}$ is a universal set of atomic terms, $R = \{r_0, r_1, \ldots, r_m\}$ is a universal set of relationships (e.g. is-a, synonym, related-to, part-of, etc.) between the terms and $I = \{I_i | i = 1, \ldots, n\}$ is a set of term definitions. A stands for the axioms expressing other relationships between terms and limiting their intended interpretation.

An axiom is a statement which is assumed to be true without proof [18]. Axioms define the state in which the domain should be. From the perspective of the ECA rule, axioms can have a clearly defined action and, sometimes, a condition under which the specific actions can be taken. When the state is changed, it is necessary to take an action. Events are not defined in axioms.

BRs-structural assertions [12] can be expressed as follows:

$$\langle \nu_i, \nu_j, c_i \rangle \quad \text{with } \nu_i, \nu_j \in V \wedge c_i \in C, \tag{3}$$

where ν_i and ν_j are terms used in structural assertions and c_i is a relationship-constraint, such as prerequisite (for example, *an order must have an order-data*), temporal (for example, *reservation precedes tour*), mutually-inclusive (for example, *to travel to a foreign country a VISA is required, based upon citizenship*), mutually-exclusive (for example, *a cruise cannot be listed as being sold out and have availability at the same time*) etc.

The analysis of formulas (1–3) allows us to state that terms and relationships expressing constraints which are used in structural assertions are adopted from sets of ontology terms and relationships. Therefore, we can assume that structural assertions are part of ontology.

The other part of rules is more complex. They consist of more than two terms and relationships between them. For example: *A customer must not place more than three rush orders charged to its credit account.*

These BRs are captured and fixed in the domain ontology by axioms (A).

Since BRs are captured in ontology by axioms and constraints of relationships among terms [6], ontology axioms (and ontology as a whole) represented in a formal way can be transformed into BRs (and into conceptual schema) automatically. Moreover, it facilitates BRs transformation into consequent information-processing and executable rules.

The general schema of axioms transformation into BRs is presented in Fig. 1. It is independent of implementation.

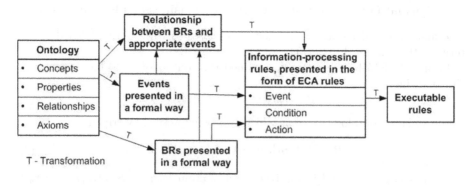

Fig. 1. Transformation of ontology axioms into ECA rules and consequent executable rules

Axioms do not stand alone in ontology. Since axioms define constraints on terms, terms are used to specify axioms. Therefore, these terms and their relationships should be transformed into (conceptual) schema in parallel with transformation of axioms into BRs. For the sake of simplicity, the schema of ontology axioms transformation into BRs is presented only in Fig. 1.

According to the examples (see [19,20,21,22,23]), there are two ways to define events in ontology. They are – to define necessary events by creating event ontology, which is related to other particular ontology/(-ies), or to define necessary events as a part of some other ontology. For the sake of simplicity, the second way for events definition was used, since in both cases, events are defined by terms used in ontology vocabulary.

Terms are used to link axioms with appropriate events, since ontology axioms and events are defined by terms used in ontology vocabulary (see Fig. 2).

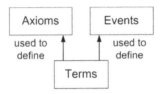

Fig. 2. Linking of ontology axioms and events

4 A Case Study of Ontology Axioms Transformation into Rule Model

The ontology for a particular business enterprise was created using Protégé-2000 ontology development tool to support the statement of the authors that ontology axioms and events can be transformed into information-processing rules and consequent executable rules. We chose Protégé-2000 to develop the ontology because it allows the open source software to be installed locally. A free version of the software provides all features and capabilities required for the present research as well as being user-friendly [24].

The axioms are implemented in Protégé-2000 ontology by the Protg Axiom Language (PAL) constraints. PAL is a superset of the first-order logic which is used for writing strong logical constraints [25].

The EZPal Tab plug-in is used to facilitate acquisition of PAL constraints without having to understand the language itself. Using a library of templates based on reusable patterns of previously encoded axioms, the interface allows users to compose constraints using a "fill-in-the-blanks" approach [26].

The definitions of the following axioms using the EZPal Tab are shown in Fig. 3 and Fig. 4.

Since PAL constraints are expressed in a formal way, it is reasonable to use this feature for their transformation into ADBMS SQL triggers.

*The discount of a contract product depends on quantity of units of a contract
product customer buys per time.
If quantity is greater then 19, discount is 3 %.*

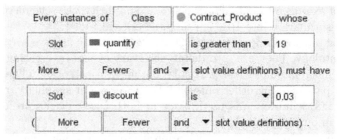

Fig. 3. An example of axiom creation using the EZPal templates

Every Contract must have a Contract_product.

Fig. 4. An example of axiom creation using the EZPal templates

PAL constraints and SQL triggers were analysed in detail to automate constraints transformation into SQL triggers. The schema of automatic transformation is presented in Fig. 5.

The more detailed schema of PAL constraints transformation into SQL triggers is presented in Fig. 6. The main parts of PAL constraints (denoted by grey clouds) are transformed into the main parts of SQL triggers (denoted by grey clouds). 'PAL-documentation', 'PAL-name' and 'PAL-range' are transformed into SQL 'Comment', 'trigger_name', 'table | view' without significant changes. But 'if statement or condition' and 'action or possible state' should be properly processed and then transformed into 'sql_statement'.

Some fields of SQL trigger stay blank, since necessary information is lacking and cannot be taken from PAL constraints or Protégé-2000 ontology. For example, the time when trigger should be fired (FOR | AFTER | INSTEAD OF) should be specified manually.

The table or view on which the trigger is executed should be specified manually when more then one range in 'PAL-range' are defined. In other words, the trigger table or view should be chosen from the list of possible values manually. Specifying the owner name of the table or view is optional.

An event of a trigger (DELETE, INSERT, UPDATE) should be taken from events defined in ontology.

The relationships between axioms and events are determined by classes, used to define particular axioms and events. An example of the event is shown in Fig. 7.

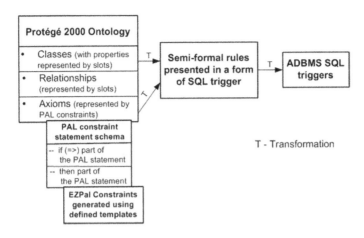

Fig. 5. The schema of automatic transformation of PAL constraints into SQL triggers

PAL constraint	SQL trigger
([*ID*] of {%3A | EZ}Pal-CONSTRAINT	/* Comment */
(%3APAL-DESCRIPTION "*{PAL-documentation}*")	CREATE TRIGGER *trigger_name*
(%3APAL-NAME "*{PAL-name}*")	ON { *table* | *view* }
(%3APAL-RANGE "*{PAL-range}*")	{{ { FOR | AFTER | INSTEAD OF } { [DELETE] [,] [INSERT] [,] [UPDATE] }
(%3APAL-STATEMENT	[NOT FOR REPLICATION]
"([forall | exists] {*variable*}	AS
([=> [(*if statement or condition*)]	[IF *sql_statement* [...*n*] }]
{ (*action or possible state*) }	*sql_statement* [...*n*]
))""))	}}

Fig. 6. The detailed schema of automatic transformation of ontology axioms into SQL triggers

For example, the event 'Making contract' (Fig. 7) and the axiom 'contract-must-have-contract-product' (Fig. 4) use the same class 'Contract' in their definitions. Moreover, the axiom 'contract-must-have-contract-product' is directly related with the axiom 'discount-3-percent' (Fig. 3), e.g., 'Contract_Product' is used in definitions of both axioms. Therefore, the following ECA rules can be generated:

> When *'Making contract'*, then *'Contract_product' should be defined.*
> When *'Making contract'*, if *'quantity' of a 'Contract_product'*
> *'is greater than 19',*
> then *'discount' of a 'Contract_product' 'is 3 %'.*

The prototype of necessary plug-in 'AxiomTransformation' was developed to carry out the experiment of ontology PAL constraints automatic transformation into semi-formal rules presented in the form of SQL trigger (see Fig. 8).

Fig. 7. An example of the event 'Making contract'

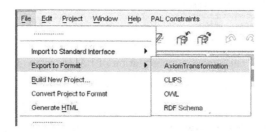

Fig. 8. The plug-in for Protégé-2000 ontology axioms transformation into semi-formal rules presented in a form of SQL trigger

It is necessary to specify a file, where only semi-formal rules will be saved. All axioms will be transformed into semi-formal rules automatically.

An example of the semi-formal rule presented in a form of SQL trigger is as follows:

```
/* Documentation */
/* The discount of a product depends on quantity of product units',
customer buys per time. If quantity is 10-19, discount is 3
   CREATE TRIGGER discount-3-percent
   ON
   Contract_Product
   {FOR | AFTER | INSTEAD OF}}
   [DELETE] [,] [INSERT] [,] [UPDATE]
   AS
   (=> (> ('quantity' ?Contract_Product) 19)
   (= ('discount' ?Contract_Product) 0.03)))
```

As mentioned above, some corrections are necessary for semi-formal rule to implement it by SQL trigger. User should also link the generated SQL triggers with particular DB, since some names of columns or tables can vary for some reasons. PAL-STATEMENT can be transformed into sql_statement only manually at the moment.

The next step of the research is extending the developed prototype, e.g., automation of PAL-STATEMENT transformation into sql_statement and events defined in ontology transformation into keywords (or events of the trigger) (DELETE, INSERT, UPDATE) that specify which data modification attempted against the table or view activate the trigger.

A full case study employing the proposed concepts and ideas of the proposed method is under development.

5   Conclusions and Future Work

The analysis of the related works on knowledge-based information system development using the domain ontology shows that the business rules are part of knowledge represented by ontology. Business rules are captured in ontology by axioms.

The method for ontology transformation into business rules, which are implemented by information-processing rules, was offered. We argue that the ontology axioms can be used to create a set of information-processing rules. They can be transformed into ECA rules and then to active DBMS triggers. Such transformation is possible, since ontology axioms can be mapped into active DBMS SQL triggers.

The prototype was developed and the experiment of ontology axioms automatic transformation into SQL triggers was carried out. The experiment shows that the suggested approach can be used to transform ontology axioms described in a formal way into SQL triggers. For this transformation, a suitable tool – Protégé-2000 – was chosen.

The next step in our research should be the refinement of the suggested method and the developed prototype. A full case study employing the proposed concepts and ideas is under development.

References

1. Business Rules Group: Defining Business Rules – What are they Really? Business Rules Group, 3rd Ed. (2000)
2. Morgan, T. Business Rules and Information Systems: Aligning IT with Business Goals, Addison-Wesley (2002)
3. Von Halle, B. Business Rules Applied: Building Better Systems Using the Business Rules Approach. John Wiley & Sons (2002)
4. Business Rules Group: The Business Motivation Model. Business Governance in a Volatile World, Business Rules Group (www.BusinessRulesGroup.org) (2005)
5. Guarino, N.: Formal Ontology and Information Systems. In Proc. of FOIS'98, Trento, Italy, 6–8 June, 1998. Amsterdam, IOS Press (1998) 3–15
6. Bugaite, D., Vasilecas, O.: Ontology-Based Elicitation of Business Rules. In A. G. Nilsson et all (eds.): Advances in Information Systems Development: Proc. of the ISD'2005. Springer, Sweden (2006) 795–806
7. Lebedys, E., Vasilecas, O.: Analysis of business rules modelling languages. In Proc. of the IT'2004, Lithuania, Technologija (2004) 487–494

8. Hay, D. C.: Requirement Analysis. From Business Views to Architecture. Prentice Hall PTR, New Jersey (2003)
9. Semantics of Business Vocabulary and Business Rules (SBVR). OMG (2005). (March, 2006): http://www.omg.org/docs/bei/05-08-01.pdf
10. Yang, X.: Ontologies and How to Build Them (2001). (March, 2006): http://www.ics.uci.edu/ xwy/publications/area-exam.ps
11. Gruber, T.: What is an Ontology? (March, 2004): http://www-ksl.stanford.edu/kst/what-is-an-ontology.html
12. Valatkaite, I., Vasilecas, O.: On Business Rules Approach to the Information Systems Development. In H. Linger et all (eds.): Proc. of ISD'2003. Australia, Kluwer Academic/Plenum Publishers (2004) 199–208
13. Zacharias, V.: Kaon – towards a large scale semantic web. In Proc. of EC-Web 2002, LNCS, Springer (2002) 304–313
14. Goncalves, M. A., Watson, L. T., Fox, E. A.: Towards a Digital Library Theory: A Formal Digital Library Ontology. Virginia Polytechnic Institute and State University. (December, 2005): http://www.dcs.vein.hu/CIR/cikkek/MFIR_DLOntology4.pdf.
15. Culmone, R., Rossi, G., Merelli, E.: An Ontology Similarity algorithm for BioAgent in NETTAB Workshop on Agents and Bioinformatics, Bologna (2002). (December, 2005): http://www.bioagent.net/WWWPublications/Download/NETTAB02P1.pdf.
16. Hu, Z., Kruse, E., Draws, L.: Intelligent Binding in the Engineering of Automation Systems Using Ontology and Web Services. IEEE Transactions on Systems, Man, and Cybernetics – Part C: Applications and Reviews, Vol. 33, No.3 (2003) 403–412
17. Lin, S., Miller, L. L., Tsai, H.-J., Xu, J.: Integrating a Heterogeneous Distributed Data Environment with a Database Specific Ontology. The International Conference on Parallel and Distributed Systems (2001). (December, 2005): http://dg.statlab.iastate.edu/dg/papers_presentations/pdfs/lin_miller_et_al_2001_pdcs.pdf.
18. IMAGES. Glossary of Geometric and Mathematical Terms: Axiom (2004) (March, 2006): http://images.rbs.org/appendices/d_glossary_geometric.shtml.
19. Cilia, M., Bornhovd, C., Buchmann, A. P.: Event Handling for the Universal Enterprise. Information Technology and Management – Special Issue on Universal Enterprise Integration, Vol. 5, No.1 (2005) 123–148
20. Chen, H., Perich, F., Finin, T., Joshi, A.: SOUPA: Standard Ontology for Ubiquitous and Pervasive Applications. In Proc. of the First Annual International Conference on Mobile and Ubiquitous Systems: Networking and Services 2004, Boston (2004) (March, 2006): http://ebiquity.umbc.edu/get/a/publication/105.pdf
21. Event Ontology. KendraBase – server 3. (March, 2006): http://base4.kendra.org.uk/event_ontology
22. Ubiquity Event Ontology :: Classes and Properties. SchenaWeb (March, 2006): http://www.schemaweb.info/schema/SchemaInfo.aspx?id=114
23. Chen, H.: SOUPA Ontology 2004-06. semantic web in ubicomp (March, 2006): http://pervasive.semanticweb.org/soupa-2004-06.html
24. Jakkilinki, R., Sharda, N., Georgievski, M.: Developing an Ontology for Teaching Multimedia Design and Planning (September, 2005): http://sci.vu.edu.au/~nalin/MUDPYOntologyPreprintV2.pdf
25. Grosso, W.: The Protg Axiom Language and Toolset ("PAL") (2002) (September, 2005): http://protege.stanford.edu/plugins/paltabs/pal-documentation/index.html
26. Hou, J.: EZPal Tab. Stanford University (2005) (March, 2006): http://protege.stanford.edu/plugins/ezpal/

Data Mining with Parallel Support Vector Machines for Classification

Tatjana Eitrich[1] and Bruno Lang[2]

[1] Central Institute for Applied Mathematics, Research Centre Juelich, Germany
`t.eitrich@fz-juelich.de`
[2] Applied Computer Science and Scientific Computing Group,
Department of Mathematics, University of Wuppertal, Germany
`lang@math.uni-wuppertal.de`

Abstract. The increasing amount of data used for classification, as well as the demand for complex models with a large number of well tuned parameters, naturally lead to the search for efficient approaches making use of massively parallel systems. We describe the parallelization of support vector machine learning for shared memory systems. The support vector machine is a powerful and reliable data mining method. Our learning algorithm relies on a decomposition scheme, which in turn uses a special variable projection method, for solving the quadratic program associated with support vector machine learning. By using hybrid parallel programming, our parallelization approach can be combined with the parallelism of a distributed cross validation routine and parallel parameter optimization methods.

Keywords: Data Mining, Classification, Support Vector Machine, Parallelization.

1 Introduction

Support vector machines (SVMs) are important and well-known state-of-the-art machine learning methods for classification and regression. Classification is one of the most important tasks of data mining in our days. Given a training set with attributes the goal is to learn a model that later on can be used to classify unseen data in a reliable way. Much work has been done to apply support vector learning to challenging classification problems in pharmaceutical research, text mining, and many other application areas [1,2,3].

While the SVM theory is widely accepted, there still seems to be some gap between the theoretical framework given by learning theory, and the real world data to be classified [4]. Most current SVM models suffer from large, noisy and unbalanced data, and therefore the development of more robust algorithms remains an important topic for research. In addition, the data sets are becoming increasingly large, and therefore parallel processing is essential to provide the performance required by large-scale data mining tasks. The latter issue is addressed in this paper.

T. Yakhno and E. Neuhold (Eds.): ADVIS 2006, LNCS 4243, pp. 197–206, 2006.

Work on parallel data mining for distributed memory systems has been done during the last years [5]. Currently more and more machines are becoming available with either global shared memory or with multi-processor shared memory nodes that are connected with some network. In [6] and [7] the authors present parallelization techniques for data mining algorithms on shared memory systems. Methods like decision trees, nearest neighbors and artificial neural networks have been analyzed and parallelized. Our intention is to broaden this work by the development of a parallel support vector machine for multi-processor shared memory (SMP) clusters.

The remainder of the paper is organized as follows. In Sections 2 and 3 we briefly review the basic concepts of support vector learning and our hierarchical SVM training method. Section 4 gives a run time analysis for the serial case, which motivates our shared memory parallelization scheme presented thereafter. Experimental results are given in Section 5. Section 6 contains a summary and points to directions for future work.

2   Support Vector Learning

Support vector learning means to determine functions that can be used to classify data points. Here, we discuss binary classification, but the SVM learning framework also works for multi-class and regression problems [8]. The supervised SVM learning method is based on so-called reference data of given input–output pairs (training data)

$$(\boldsymbol{x}^i, y_i) \in \mathbb{R}^n \times \{-1, 1\}, \quad i = 1, \ldots, l,$$

that are taken to find an optimal separating hyperplane [9]

$$f_l(\boldsymbol{x}) = \boldsymbol{w}^T \boldsymbol{x} + b = 0.$$

Using assumptions of statistical learning theory the desired classifier is then defined as

$$h(\boldsymbol{x}) = \begin{cases} +1, & \text{if } f_l(\boldsymbol{x}) \geq 0, \\ -1, & \text{if } f_l(\boldsymbol{x}) < 0, \end{cases}$$

with the linear decision function f_l. If the two classes are not linearly separable then f_l is replaced with a nonlinear decision function [10]

$$f_{nl}(\boldsymbol{x}) = \sum_{i=1}^{l} y_i \alpha_i K(\boldsymbol{x}^i, \boldsymbol{x}) + b,$$

where $K : \mathbb{R}^n \times \mathbb{R}^n \to \mathbb{R}$ is a (nonlinear) kernel function [11]. The classification parameters α_i can be obtained as the unique global solution of a suitable (dual) quadratic optimization problem [10]

$$\min_{\boldsymbol{\alpha} \in \mathbb{R}^l} \quad g(\boldsymbol{\alpha}) := \frac{1}{2} \boldsymbol{\alpha}^T H \boldsymbol{\alpha} - \sum_{i=1}^{l} \alpha_i \tag{1}$$

with $H \in \mathbb{R}^{l \times l}$, $H_{ij} = y_i K(\boldsymbol{x}^i, \boldsymbol{x}^j) y_j$ $(1 \leq i, j \leq l)$, constrained to

$$\boldsymbol{\alpha}^T \boldsymbol{y} = 0, \quad 0 \leq \alpha_i \leq C.$$

The Hessian H is usually dense, and therefore the complexity of evaluating the objective function g in (1) scales quadratically with the number l of training pairs, leading to very time-consuming computations. The parameter C controls the trade-off between the width of the classifier's margin and the number of weak and wrong classifications on the training set. This parameter has to be chosen by the user. Due to space limitations we omit a detailed introduction to the SVM theory. For readers who are not familiar with this topic we refer to the tutorial [12].

3   A Hierarchical Approach for Support Vector Machine Training

Support vector machine training corresponds to solving (1), which is a quadratic problem (qp) with simple constraints. A well-known method for the solution of such problems is the decomposition algorithm [13], where each iteration consists of four steps:

1. Select a working set of $\tilde{l}$ "active" variables from the l free variables α_i.
2. Solve the quadratic subproblem of size $\tilde{l}$ that results from restricting the optimization in (1) to the active variables and fixing the remaining variables.
3. Update the global solution vector $\boldsymbol{\alpha}$.
4. Check a stopping criterion.

The second step leads to the computational complexity of the training. In our implementation we rely on the usual working set selection scheme that uses a method of feasible directions originally described in [14]. In contrast to other implementations our convergence criterion is not based on the fulfillment of the Karush–Kuhn–Tucker conditions but on the number of pairs given by the working set selection method [15]. The size $\tilde{l} \leq l$ of the subproblems may be chosen by the user and is limited to the available memory of the system. The overall SVM training time depends heavily on the efficiency of the qp solver for the subproblems. We use an own implementation of the generalized variable projection method introduced in [16]. This method again defines subproblems (with diagonal matrices) and solves them iteratively with a very fast inner solver [17]. Figure 1 summarizes the resulting hierarchical algorithm for the SVM training. The decomposition routine includes two updates of kernel matrices, the so-called active kernel matrix $H_{\text{active}} \in \mathbb{R}^{\tilde{l} \times \tilde{l}}$ that defines the quadratic subproblem to be solved and the mixed kernel matrix $H_{\text{mixed}} \in \mathbb{R}^{\tilde{l} \times (l - \tilde{l})}$ that is necessary for the gradient update. For the tests in this paper we use the well known Gaussian kernel

$$K(\boldsymbol{x}^i, \boldsymbol{x}^j) = \exp\left(-\frac{\|\boldsymbol{x}^i - \boldsymbol{x}^j\|^2}{2\sigma^2}\right) . \tag{2}$$

$\sigma > 0$ is the width of the kernel and needs to be chosen by the user.

input: training data initialization of working set $\alpha = \mathbf{0}$ optimality$_{\text{global}} = 0$	
while optimality$_{\text{global}} \neq 1$	decomposition
compute active kernel matrix H_{active} compute mixed kernel matrix H_{mixed} initial projection optimality$_{\text{active}} = 0$	
while optimality$_{\text{active}} \neq 1$	variable projection
projection step with inner solver line search procedure for update of solution α_{active} compute new step length	
update gradient and solution α select new working set check optimality$_{\text{global}}$	

Fig. 1. Structure chart (slightly simplified) for the hierarchical SVM training with the decomposition scheme (main loop) and the projection based qp solver (inner loop)

4   Shared Memory Parallelization of the SVM Training

There are three ways to insert parallelism into SVM methods: parallelizing the training of a single SVM, training several SVMs in parallel, and using a parallel algorithm for optimizing the learning parameters, such as C and the kernel parameter. The second of these options has been addressed with mostly straightforward approaches, for example, parallel mixture of SVMs [18], parallel training of binary SVMs for multiclass problems [19], parallel training of SVMs on splitted data [20] and parallel cross validation models [21]. Parallel parameter optimization has been discussed in [22] and [23]. All these methods do not reduce the bottleneck of a single training on large data. Concerning the first option, a promising technique for parallelizing the SVM training on distributed memory systems has been described in [24] and is under development. It uses standard C and MPI communication routines. In this paper our focus is on speeding up the learning step of support vector machines on shared memory systems to by-pass the bottleneck of SVM training.

We introduce a new shared memory parallelization of SVM training which is well suited for speeding up the learning stage. Most of today's high-end machines are built from "fat nodes," each of which contains multiple processors with access to a rather large shared memory. Thus, while it is possible to use all processors of such machines under the message passing paradigm, a hybrid distributed/shared memory parallelization is natural, relying on message passing for very coarse-grained parallelism (training of several SVMs in parallel, parameter optimization), and running the training of each single SVM with its finer grained parallelism on a few processors within a shared memory node. Thus, the shared memory parallelization needs not scale to high numbers of processors. Note that shared memory multi-processors are becoming increasingly popular even in workstations and PCs, in particular in the form of multi-core processors offering functionality of multiple CPUs on a single chip.

We have used several data sets from pharmaceutical industry for our tests. All data sets include a classification task which is aimed at QSAR (quantitative structure activity relationship) modeling; see [1] for a description of the pharmaceutical background and the data. In this paper we present results for two data sets with 10 and 50 features and 20000 instances each. Our numerical experiments were made on the Juelich Multi Processor (JUMP) at Research Centre Juelich [25]. JUMP is a distributed shared memory parallel computer consisting of 41 frames (nodes). Each node contains 32 IBM Power4+ processors running at 1.7 GHz, and 128 GB shared main memory. All in all the 1312 processors have an aggregate peak performance of 8.9 TFlop/s.

4.1   Performance Characteristics of Serial SVM Training

In order to obtain a highly efficient parallel SMV training routine, the serial version must be optimized as well. That is, in addition to using adequate algorithms, the computations must be performed at maximum speed. This can be achieved in a portable way by relying on the Level–1 and 2 Basic Linear Algebra Subroutines (BLAS) [26,27], which comprise routines for computing norms ($DNORM$) or linear combinations of vectors ($DAXPY$), matrix–vector products ($DGEMV$), and others. While the calling sequences for the BLAS routines are standardized, most vendors provide optimized implementations for their machines, so that optimum performance can be obtained by simply linking with an appropriate library. In the case of IBM, their Engineering Scientific Subroutine Library ($ESSL$) includes Power4-tuned versions of the BLAS and of many other basic mathematical operations. We have also made use of the latter, where appropriate (for example, $DYAX$, $DVEA$, $DVES$).

The GNU profiler *gprof* is a commonly-available tool for profiling the execution of jobs. It gives detailed timing information for identifying bottlenecks in the program, which can then be addressed by parallelization. We used *gprof* to determine the main computational bottlenecks during a single SVM training. In Table 1 the individual costs are given for the decomposition routine (A), the

Table 1. Run time analysis for a serial SVM training (20000 instances, 10 features)

overall time (in seconds)	319.38
time for decomposition (A)	21.03
time for kernel evaluations (B)	107.90
time for projection (C)	0.03
time for inner solver (D)	6.33
sum of times for $ESSL$ routines (E)	184.09

evaluations of the multi-parameter kernel function (B), the variable projection method (C), the inner solver (D), and all calls to *ESSL* routines (E). Please note that these times comprise only the computations carried out *within* the respective routines and thus do not include calls to lower-level routines. This is important since (E) is called from (A), (C) and (D), (D) is called from (C), (C) and (B) are called from (A). The timings were obtained for a data set with $l = 20000$ instances and $n = 10$ features with a working set size of 5000. We have also tested other values for $\tilde{l}$ (between 100 and 5000), but they always led to worse training times. For small working sets each subproblem can be solved fast, but the number of decomposition steps increases heavily. Due to the available memory in our tests we limited $\tilde{l}$ to 5000. Depending on the dimensions of the data and on the working set sizes the relative contributions of (A) through (E) to the overall time may vary, but for complex models on large data the vast majority of time is always consumed by

- the kernel function evaluations in the decomposition routine and
- the matrix–vector multiplications called from the qp solver.

By contrast, the decomposition and projection steps themselves (not counting their calls to *ESSL* routines) and the inner solver do not consume a significant amount of time.

4.2 Mixed Library/Loop Parallelization

We now present the shared memory parallelization of a single SVM training which we have implemented incrementally, addressing the performance hot spots one-by-one. The parallelization is based on the training algorithm introduced in Sect. 3. The performance analysis in Sect. 4.1 marks the *ESSL* operations as interesting targets for an incremental shared memory parallelization. *ESSL* routines are called in the decomposition routine, the variable projection method and the inner solver. IBM provides a shared memory parallel version of the *ESSL*, called *ESSLSMP*. It is possible to achieve multi-processor execution for these routines by linking to another version of the library.

Usage of parallel *ESSL* routines will not lead to satisfactory speedups of the SVM training, see Table 1. The remaining parallelization was done using OpenMP [28]. OpenMP is a standardized API defining a set of Fortran compiler directives (or C pragmas), library routines, and environment variables that can be used to describe and exploit shared memory parallelism. The directives allow the programmer to mark areas of the code, the so-called "parallel regions", that are suitable for parallel processing. On entering a parallel region, additional threads are created (or available active threads are bound to the "master thread"), and they are freed again when the parallel region is left. The statements within the parallel region are executed by all threads, except for those statements occurring in so-called work-sharing constructs, such as parallel loops, etc. Only these constructs lead to true parallelism. For example, the passes of parallel loops are distributed *at run-time* to all available threads. The scheduling mechanism and the number of threads can be controlled via environment variables. Since all threads originating from a single process share the latter's memory space, OpenMP also provides directives for defining which variables should be accessible to all threads and for which variables each thread should have a private copy in order to avoid write conflicts. The directives are written as a special kind of comment, and thus the same program can easily be run in serial or parallel mode on a given computer, or even on a computer that does not have an OpenMP-aware compiler at all.

The most important parallel OpenMP loops in our decomposition scheme compute the active kernel matrix $H_{\text{active}} \in \mathbb{R}^{\tilde{l} \times \tilde{l}}$ and the mixed kernel matrix $H_{\text{mixed}} \in \mathbb{R}^{\tilde{l} \times (l-\tilde{l})}$ in the decomposition scheme by assigning a set of columns of the matrix to each thread. We also parallelized the working set selection and the gradient update in the decomposition routine. All in all, in our mixed approach the parallelism is provided alternatingly by work-sharing constructs within parallel OpenMP regions and by the shared memory parallelized ESSL routines, implying frequent re-binding of the active threads. Some parts of the code have not been parallelized, such as parts of the variable projection method and the inner solver. However, as our analysis in Sect. 4.1 showed, these parts show minor contributions to the overall training time.

5   Experimental Evaluation

We have tested the parallel SVM training method for the two data sets mentioned in Sect. 4. Again, we used a working set size of 5000 points for the inner subproblems ($l = 20000$, $\tilde{l} = 5000$). The corresponding SVM parameters were $\sigma = 2$ and $C = 10$ for both data sets. Table 5 summarizes the results for the data sets with 10 features and Table 5 summarizes the results for the data sets

Table 2. Training times (in seconds) and speedup values for the small data set

setting	training time	speedup
serial	319.4	–
2 threads	161.0	2.0
3 threads	117.1	2.7
4 threads	99.2	3.2
5 threads	80.3	4.0
6 threads	69.8	4.6
7 threads	62.7	5.1
8 threads	55.5	5.8

with 50 features. The speedup s is computed via

$$s(t) := \frac{\text{serial time}}{\text{time with } t \text{ threads}} .$$

The speedups are satisfactory for all numbers of threads. The tests have been run several times, and the times reported in the table are the average values of

Table 3. Training times (in seconds) and speedup values for the large data set

setting	training time	speedup
serial	980.9	–
2 threads	546.2	1.8
3 threads	371.6	2.6
4 threads	279.9	3.5
5 threads	229.5	4.3
6 threads	195.8	5.0
7 threads	169.0	5.8
8 threads	151.9	6.5

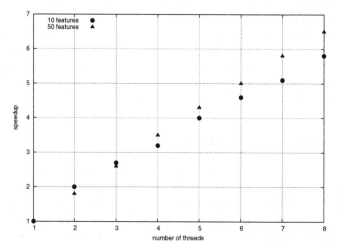

Fig. 2. Comparison of speedup values for the two data sets

all runs. In Fig. 2 we show the speedup values for both data sets. Obviously, the attainable speedups are better for the data set with 50 features. We analyzed this effect. For data sets with a large number of features the computations of the Gaussian kernel values take longer than for a small number of features, see (2) and thus the updates of the kernel matrices make the major contributions to the training time. For the data set with 50 features this is 80%, whereas for 10 features the kernel computations made up only 34% of the overall time, see Table 1. Since we parallelized a large number of routines and loops, our parallel training method works well for data sets with either a large number of instances or a large number of attributes, or both. With this flexible parallel training method a large amount of time can be saved.

6   Conclusions and Future Directions

We have discussed a mixed library/loop-based shared memory parallelization for SVM training. Numerical experiments show that our approach can yield rather satisfactory speedups for moderate numbers of processors, as available, for example, in high-performance workstations and PCs. Tests on other data sets have shown similar behavior. On high-end machines with an SMP cluster architecture our shared memory parallelization can be complemented with message passing-based approaches to increase the level of parallelism in, for example, the training of multiple SVMs or the optimization of learning parameters. The potential of such hybrid strategies has to be investigated in the future.

Our implementation still includes some serial parts that limit the attainable speedup. If good speedups are desired for larger numbers of processors then the serial sections of the code have to be reduced further. In addition it is important to study the influence of the working set size on the behavior of the parallel ESSL routines.

References

1. Kless, A., Eitrich, T.: Cytochrome p450 classification of drugs with support vector machines implementing the nearest point algorithm. In López, J.A., Benfenati, E., Dubitzky, W., eds.: Knowledge Exploration in Life Science Informatics, International Symposium, KELSI 2004, Milan, Italy. Volume 3303 of Lecture Notes in Computer Science., Springer (2004) 191–205
2. Han, H., Giles, C.L., Manavoglu, E., Zha, H., Zhang, Z., Fox, E.A.: Automatic document metadata extraction using support vector machines. In: JCDL '03: Proceedings of the 3rd ACM/IEEE-CS joint conference on Digital libraries, Washington, DC, USA, IEEE Computer Society (2003) 37–48
3. Yu, H., Yang, J., Wang, W., Han, J.: Discovering compact and highly discriminative features or feature combinations of drug activities using support vector machines. In: 2nd IEEE Computer Society Bioinformatics Conference (CSB 2003), 11-14 August 2003, Stanford, CA, USA, IEEE Computer Society (2003) 220–228
4. Hettich, S., Blake, C.L., Merz, C.J.: UCI repository of machine learning databases. (1998) http://www.ics.uci.edu/~mlearn/MLRepository.html.
5. Dhillon, I.S., Modha, D.S.: A data-clustering algorithm on distributed memory multiprocessors. In: Large-Scale Parallel Data Mining, Lecture Notes in Artificial Intelligence. (2000) 245–260
6. Jin, R., Yang, G., Agrawal, G.: Shared memory parallelization of data mining algorithms: techniques, programming interface, and performance. IEEE Transactions on Knowledge and Data Engineering **17** (2005) 71–89
7. Zaki, M.J., Ho, C.T., Agrawal, R.: Parallel classification for data mining on shared-memory multiprocessors. In: ICDE. (1999) 198–205
8. Hsu, C., Lin, C.: A comparison of methods for multi-class support vector machines. IEEE Transactions on Neural Networks **13** (2002) 415–425
9. Cristianini, N., Shawe-Taylor, J.: An introduction to support vector machines and other kernel-based learning methods. Cambridge University Press, Cambridge, UK (2000)
10. Schölkopf, B., Smola, A.J.: Learning with kernels. MIT Press, Cambridge, MA (2002)
11. Schölkopf, B.: The kernel trick for distances. In: NIPS. (2000) 301–307
12. Burges, C.J.C.: A tutorial on support vector machines for pattern recognition. Data Mining and Knowledge Discovery **2** (1998) 121–167

13. Hsu, C.W., Lin, C.J.: A simple decomposition method for support vector machines. Machine Learning **46** (2002) 291–314
14. Zoutendijk, G.: Methods of feasible directions: a study in linear and non-linear programming. Elsevier (1960)
15. Eitrich, T., Lang, B.: Efficient optimization of support vector machine learning parameters for unbalanced datasets. Journal of Computational and Applied Mathematics (2005) in press.
16. Serafini, T., Zanghirati, G., Zanni, L.: Gradient projection methods for quadratic programs and applications in training support vector machines. Optimization Methods and Software **20** (2005) 353–378
17. Pardalos, P.M., Kovoor, N.: An algorithm for a singly constrained class of quadratic programs subject to upper and lower bounds. Mathematical Programming **46** (1990) 321–328
18. Collobert, R., Bengio, S., Bengio, Y.: A parallel mixture of SVMs for very large scale problems. Neural Computation **14** (2002) 1105–1114
19. Selikoff, S.: The SVM-tree algorithm (2003) http://scott.selikoff.net/papers/CS678_-_Final_Report.pdf.
20. Graf, H.P., Cosatto, E., Bottou, L., Dourdanovic, I., Vapnik, V.: Parallel support vector machines: the cascade SVM. In Saul, L.K., Weiss, Y., Bottou, L., eds.: Advances in Neural Information Processing Systems 17. MIT Press, Cambridge, MA (2005) 521–528
21. Celis, S., Musicant, D.R.: Weka-parallel: machine learning in parallel. Computer Science Technical Report 2002b, Carleton College (2002)
22. Runarsson, T.P., Sigurdsson, S.: Asynchronous parallel evolutionary model selection for support vector machines. Neural Information Processing - Letters and Reviews **3** (2004) 59–67
23. Eitrich, T., Lang, B.: Parallel tuning of support vector machine learning parameters for large and unbalanced data sets. In Berthold, M.R., Glen, R., Diederichs, K., Kohlbacher, O., Fischer, I., eds.: Computational Life Sciences, First International Symposium, CompLife 2005, Konstanz, Germany. Volume 3695 of Lecture Notes in Computer Science., Springer (2005) 253–264
24. Serafini, T., Zanghirati, G., Zanni, L.: Parallel decomposition approaches for training support vector machines. In: Proceedings of the International Conference ParCo2003, Dresden, Germany, Elsevier (2004) 259–266
25. Detert, U.: Introduction to the JUMP architecture. (2004)
26. Lawson, C.L., Hanson, R.J., Kincaid, D.R., Krogh, F.T.: Basic linear algebra subprograms for FORTRAN usage. ACM Trans. Math. Softw. **5** (1979) 308–323
27. Dongarra, J.J., Croz, J.D., Hammarling, S., Hanson, R.J.: An extended set of FORTRAN basic linear algebra subprograms. ACM Trans. Math. Softw. **14** (1988) 1–17
28. OpenMP architecture review board: OpenMP Fortran application program interface, version 2.0 (1999)

Association-Rules Mining Based Broadcasting Approach for XML Data

Cameron Chenier[1], J. James Jun[1], Jason Zhang[1],
Tansel Özyer[1,3], and Reda Alhajj[1,2]

[1] Dept. of Computer Science, University of Calgary, Calgary, Alberta, Canada
[2] Dept. of Computer Science, Global University, Beirut, Lebanon
[3] Dept. of Comp. Eng., TOBB Economics & Technology University, Ankara, Turkey

Abstract. Mobile databases are becoming more available and thus are drawing more attention from both research and industrial communities. They are currently being widely used in devices such as cell phones, handheld devices, and notebook computers, among others. Broadcasting is a scalable way to send data from a server to multiple clients. Broadcasting algorithms must be constructed in a way that minimizes the average waiting time for clients. XML is a new standard for representing data in a hierarchical structure, and has many advantages over relational representations due to its portability, flexibility, readability, and customizability. XML has recently been deployed onto many mobile devices; thus a new kind of broadcasting algorithm should be constructed to address the unique characteristics of the way XML databases are queried and accessed. In this paper, we presented a new kind of broadcasting algorithm (BA) by utilizing association-rules in clients' request trends. We implemented three BAs: namely, Exhaustive, Recursive, and Greedy. We tested and compared our BAs with the conventional BAs: namely Sequential and Popularity. The experimental results show that our BAs utilizing association rules perform better than the conventional BAs in both skewed-request situations and requests with association-rules.

Keywords: Data mining, mobile database, XML, broadcasting algorithms, association rules.

1 Introduction

The use of mobile devices is increasing at a tremendous rate. These devices include cell phones, PDAs, and notebook computers, among others. Most of these devices can be used to access documents and web content from a database server through an access point. This type of content is well suited to be represented in XML because of its document-centric nature. XML is a new specification for the representation of hierarchical data. The structure of XML documents will consequently affect the way the data is accessed by clients.

There are usually two accepted ways to disseminate information: pull-based and push-based. Pull-based dissemination is connection-oriented, while push-based dissemination is broadcasting. If database servers use connection-oriented

T. Yakhno and E. Neuhold (Eds.): ADVIS 2006, LNCS 4243, pp. 207–216, 2006.
© Springer-Verlag Berlin Heidelberg 2006

channels to deliver the data to each mobile device, it would be unable to scale to the demands of the increasing number of clients that require connections. The better solution would be to use a connectionless broadcast channel to send data to the mobile clients and retain the connection-oriented channel for clients to make queries. This way, the servers are able to send large amounts of data to an unlimited number of clients simultaneously by sequentially scheduling the entire database to the broadcast stream. Unfortunately, as the database size increases, sending an entire database across the broadcast stream is either very slow or impossible. We need a broadcast scheduler that will allow us to send only specific data items in an order that will minimize response time for clients requesting the data.

In this paper, we present two algorithms based on popularity [8] and associations [2] that will decrease the average waiting time for client requests. The reason why these algorithms work is because database access is not purely random and that certain items are accessed more frequently than others. These items should be broadcasted more often, and closer to the beginning of the stream. Another reason is that there are also patterns in the way people access a database. These patterns will be captured and utilized by the association-rules based broadcasting algorithm. Finally, we tested and compared our broadcasting algorithms with the conventional broadcasting algorithms. The experimental results show that our broadcasting algorithms utilizing association rules perform better than the conventional broadcasting algorithms in both skewed-request situations and requests with association-rules.

The rest of the paper is organized as follows. Section 2 reviews the related work and the necessary background. Section 3 describes the broadcasting algorithms. Section 4 presents the implementation details. Section 5 reported experimental results. Section 6 is summary and conclusions.

2   Related Work and Background

There are several algorithms proposed for the optimization of the broadcasting process, e.g., [3,4,5,6,7,8]. Most of them seem to be of the popularity based variety, e.g., [1,8]. Popularity based algorithms take into account the frequency a data item is accessed for the scheduling of the broadcast. Items that are more frequently requested are broadcasted more frequently and earlier in the broadcast stream. In this paper, we attempt to take this idea a little farther by taking advantage of associations among data requests.

An association rule is a correlation of the form $A \rightarrow B$; it is interpreted as the likeliness of itemset B given itemset A [2]. Associations are based on two criteria, called support and confidence. Support is defined as the ratio of the occurrences of A and B together in the whole considered set. Confidence is the ratio of all occurrences of A and B together versus all occurrences of item A.

By attempting to combine the two ideas of Popularity and Associations, we further improve upon the response time on specific datasets by ordering the broadcast stream so that associations are broadcasted in order.

XML (Extensible Markup Language) is one of the most popular mediums for exchanging data and documents. The flexibility of XML gives the user the ability to format their data to their own specifications. Much like HTML, XML uses tags to keep track of its data, but also allows custom tags and custom rules for each tag. This makes XML much more extensible than HTML.

XML is stored in a hierarchical view. This means that there may be repeating sub-tags. XML is an ideal coding standard for document-centric data; and this is one of the main reasons for its popularity on web sites. For now, note that when the city tag is requested in a citizenship database, the address tag and client tag will also be requested. This will be further discussed later.

When a mobile device requires information, it must get its data from an external source. These sources are usually fixed location access points that the mobile device communicates in wireless media . Broadcasting is the concept of sending data to many clients simultaneously. We consider it as connectionless, which means that the server does know what clients are receiving the data.

There are two main ways of data dissemination; pull-based and push-based. Pull-based dissemination is connection oriented where clients connect to the server for a request. The server then serves the request to the client before the connection is closed. This style of dissemination is similar to the way most web servers communicate. On a wireless network where bandwidth is very limited, the pull-based approach lacks scalability when there are an excessive number of clients, each requiring specific personalized views of the data. Push-based dissemination is broadcasting where the server itself decides what data will be broadcasted. The broadcast channel is considered high bandwidth and clients can tune in to the broadcasting channel to receive data. This works very well if the database is very small and the amount of data that needs to be transmitted is small, but becomes problematic when the database becomes larger. Fortunately, not all data is accessed equally on a database and not all data requires transmission on each broadcast cycle.

There are many different methods for deciding what gets sent out on the broadcast stream. One such method is based on popularity by using several broadcast disks [1]. A broadcast disk is a circular buffer that has a specific number of buckets to store data. The content of the broadcast disk are transmitted on each broadcast cycle. By interleaving broadcast disks of different speeds and by putting more frequently accessed data on the faster disks, a popularity based broadcasting schedule is achieved. It is up to the server to decide what data should be on which disk.

Client requests for data can be categorized based on the personalization of the request. Requests with low personalization are the requests that are highly popular and are often requested by clients frequently. These likely include root nodes on an XML document such as the home page of web sites. Requests with high personalization are the requests that are very specific and are infrequently requested. Popularity-based broadcasting algorithms attempt to decrease average waiting times by decreasing response time for requests that have low personalization.

3 Design of Broadcasting Algorithms Using Association Rules

Sequential Broadcasting Algorithm: The most basic strategy for a broadcasting algorithm is to simply broadcast the entire database sequentially in a predetermined order. Unfortunately, this approach does not scale well as the size of the database increases. Clients will have an average waiting time of $t/2$, where t is the time taken to broadcast the entire database.

Popularity Based Algorithm: To solve the waiting time problem of the Sequential Broadcasting Algorithm, we can use a popularity-based algorithm that takes into account the likeliness of an item to be requested based on the number of times it had been accessed in the past. We expect this approach to work because data access is not random. There are usually items in a database that are accessed much more frequently than others. By using a popularity-based algorithm, popular items would be densely distributed onto the broadcast disk while less popular items are either sparsely distributed or not distributed at all. We expect this to have the effect of decreasing the waiting time for popular items and increasing the waiting time of less popular items, which will ultimately decrease the average waiting time of every client.

Association Based Algorithm: Since XML databases have a hierarchical structure, the Popularity Based Algorithm will almost always rank leaf node items last. This may give undesirable waiting times for popular leaf nodes data items. The Popularity Based Algorithm can be further improved by taking associations into consideration. An association is simply a localized version of popularity. The idea is simple, given a request A, how likely is the following request going to be B. This is called the confidence of the association $A \rightarrow B$. By applying this idea to the Association Based Algorithm, we can position high confidence data items in the proper sequence on the broadcast stream so that clients will have access to the data immediately if their request turns out to fit the association. We expect this to further decrease the average access time of clients on data sets that contain a large amount of associations.

4 Implementation of the Broadcasting Algorithms

We implemented three types of Broadcasting Algorithms by utilizing association-rules. The first approach attempts to find the optimal broadcasting disk by brute-force, and is called *Exhaustive*. The second approach utilizes a graph and a recursive algorithm to traverse the edges, and is called *Recursive*. The third approach uses a greedy algorithm, and is called *Greedy*. Next, we present how each algorithm is implemented and its pseudo-code.

4.1 Exhaustive Broadcasting Algorithm

The exhaustive broadcasting algorithm organizes the broadcasting disk in a brute-force manner. Given the maximum number of possible queries, this algorithm generates and evaluates every possible sequence of queries to generate

> *Input:* {1,1,2,3}
>
> *Output:* (1,1,2,3), (1,2,1,3), (1,2,3,1), (2,1,1,3), (2,1,3,1), (2,3,1,1),
>
> (1,1,3,2), (1,3,1,2), (1,3,2,1), (3,1,1,2), (3,1,2,1), (3,2,1,1)

Fig. 1. Typical Broadcasting Network

a broadcast disk that best satisfies the detected associations. It first determines the number of slots for each query on the broadcast disk by multiplying popularity of each query by the size of the broadcast disk. After determining the number of slots each query occupies on the broadcast disk, it rearranges the positions of queries by calling permutation generator. It then evaluates the generated broadcast to determine how successful it addressed the association rule. Evaluation is done by counting the number of associations contained in the stream that matches the associations coming from client requests. The most important part of the exhaustive broadcasting algorithm is the sequence generation. The exhaustive algorithm has run time of $O(n!)$; it is only studied to understand the nature of an optimal broadcast disk. Figure 1 contains test input and output, and Algorithm 1 contains the pseudo-code.

Algorithm 1. *Pseudo-code of Exhaustive Broadcasting Algorithm*

Input: support, confidence
Output: broadcast string
Function repeating_permutation(I[]) returns Sequence[]
OriginalSize = I.length
n = count how many unique symbols are in the array I
O[] = new Array[n]
i = 0
for each unique symbols
    O[i] = number of occurrences for each symbol
    i=i+1
Sequence[] = new Arrray[OriginalSize]
/*fill in the blank spots in the Sequence array which contains
  permutation of the received array.*/
CurrSize¡-OriginalSize
i¡-0
for each unique symbols
    P[] = new Array[O[i]]
    P[] = nCr(CurrSize, P.length)
    CurrSize = CurrSize-P.length
    Fill_In_Blank(Sequence[], P[])
    i=i+1
/* return then sequence array. Next time it's called, it will return
  different permutation until all nCr exhaust all of its combinations*/

4.2   Recursive Broadcasting Algorithm

Support takes popularity into account on a global basis, and Confidence takes popularity into account on a local basis. The idea of this algorithm is to calculate a general popularity value P based on support and confidence using the formula:

$$P = support \times confidence$$

This way, support and confidence are equally weighted and if any one of support or confidence is low, the association is given a low probability. After calculating P for every set of associations, we can generate the broadcast disk by doing a graph traversal. In this graph, each data item is represented as a node, and each P is the weight of an edge connecting two nodes. The algorithm traverses the graph, outputting each node it traverses, until each edge is traversed at least once. The pseudo code is given in Algorithm 2.

Algorithm 2. *Pseudo-code for Recursive Broadcasting Algorithm*

Input: support, confidence
Output: broadcast string
Function RecursiveAlgorithm(support, confidence)
for each pair of nodes x and y
    generate edges[x][y] with
    P[x][y] = support[x][y] × confidence[x][y]
for all nodes[x]
    traverse starting from nodes[x] until no more edges are left

4.3   Greedy Broadcasting Algorithm

The basis for the greedy algorithm is to select and organize the broadcast disk in a way that satisfies the association rule. It also takes into consideration the most popular item. The algorithm starts out with two tables of collected data: Table A tracks the number of requests for each XML tag; and Table B tracks the tag request order (e.g., tag 10 requested, then tag 12 requested, etc)

It starts out by selecting the most frequently requested tag from Table A. This tag will be placed into the first available spot on the broadcast disk. From there, it will decide what was the most popular tag requested directly after the first tag from Table B. This is then placed into the broadcast disk. The last two steps are repeated until the broadcast disk is full.

Algorithm 3. *Pseudo-code of Greedy BA*

Input: Table A, Table B **Output:** *broadcast string*
Function GreedyAlgorithm(support, confidence)
x ← pick most popular in Table A
put x in circular broadcast disk
dec x in Table A

loop:
$y \leftarrow$ *pick most popular follower from Table A with respect to* x
put y*in circular broadcast disk*
dec y *in Table A, dec (x,y) in Table B*
$x \leftarrow y$
End loops(while there is still elements to follow in Table B)

This can be run in O(n) time, which is considerably faster than sequential. This is required to keep up with a fast broadcast stream. The algorithm neglects unpopular items, but heavily reduces response time on popular ones.

5   Experimental Setup and Results

We performed two types of experiments: skewed popularity test and association-rule test. Skewed popularity tests are done on each of our working algorithms to ensure that our broadcasting algorithms are effective when clients' requests are skewed. The tests are repeated on Sequential and Popularity broadcasting algorithms [1] to show how our algorithms perform relative to them. The association-rule test is then performed on all of the algorithms to show how our algorithms outperform the Sequential and Popularity broadcasting algorithms. Since the exhaustive algorithm runs very slow (complexity of O(n!)), it will not be tested.

5.1   Skewed Popularity Testing

In reality, some queries are requested more often than other queries. To simulate this real life behavior of how queries are requested, we setup clients so that they request certain queries more often than other queries based on an input file. Even though popularity of each query is predetermined, the order of queries being requested is random. Average waiting time of clients is calculated by the following formula:

$$Average\ Waiting\ Time\ of\ all\ clients = \sum_{i=1}^{n} P_i\ x\ T_i$$

where T_i is the average waiting time of the ith query and P_i is the probability of the ith query being called.

Effect of Varying Degree of Skew-ness in Queries on Average Waiting Time of Clients. Experimental setup:We generated a set of input files for the client that contains how likely a query is going to be requested. The likelihood of a query to be requested is expressed as a probability. If the probably of each query is all equal, there is no skewness in the dataset, but if the probability of each query varies, it is considered to be skewed. To generate varying degrees of skewness, we used half of the normal curve with a varying degree of standard deviation. To generate higher skewness in our dataset, we used a smaller standard deviation because with a smaller standard deviation, the distribution curve is more peaked around the mean. Similarly, to generate lower skewness in our dataset, we used high value of standard deviation because the distribution flattens.

We tested 4 algorithms: Sequential, Popularity, Recursive, and Greedy. The number of queries is fixed to 60, and skewness (standard deviation of normal distribution) is chosen from this set {20, 10, 4, 2, 0.5}.

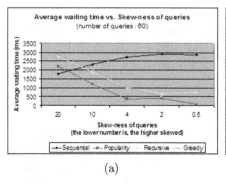
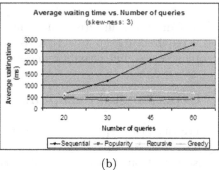

(a)   (b)

Fig. 2. a) Average waiting time vs. skew-ness of queries; b) Average waiting time vs. skew-ness of queries

The experiments clearly show that our broadcasting algorithms perform better than the Sequential broadcasting algorithm as the requests become more skewed. The popularity broadcasting algorithm however slightly outperforms our algorithms. This is expected since our algorithms take associations into consideration and have slightly more overhead than the popularity based algorithm.

Effect of Number of Total Queries on Average Waiting Time of Clients.
Experimental setup: We varied the number of queries in order to test the scalability of our algorithms. We set the number of queries to 15, 30, 45, and 60.

As shown in Figure 2, our broadcasting algorithms perform better than the sequential broadcasting algorithm. As the number of queries increase, the average waiting time of clients for sequential broadcasting algorithm increases proportionally. This result is expected since the size of the broadcast increase as the number of queries increases; thus, it takes more time to broadcast the same query again. All of our broadcasting algorithms perform better than the Sequential broadcasting algorithm. The number of queries does not affect average waiting time of clients for our algorithms, which proves that our broadcasting algorithms are scalable with respect to increasing number of queries. Finally, our broadcasting algorithms perform about the same as the Popularity broadcasting algorithm.

5.2   Association-Rule Testing

Effect of Varying Number of Associations in Queries Versus Average Waiting Time of Clients. Experimental setup: We made five input files for the client side to introduce association-rule pattern in clients' requests. We varied

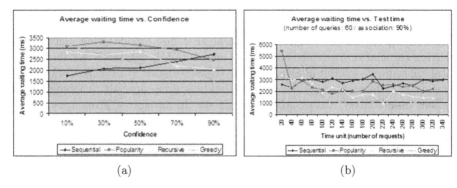

Fig. 3. a) Average waiting time vs. Confidence; b) Average waiting time vs. Test time

the confidence between queries from 10% to 90%. The higher confidence, the stronger is the association between two consecutive queries.

The experiment shows that as the confidence become stronger, our broadcasting algorithms perform better. The average waiting time of clients increased for the Sequential broadcasting algorithm. Our broadcasting algorithms' average waiting time decreased as was intended. It also performs slightly better than the popularity based algorithm.

Average Waiting Time vs. Testing Time. Experimental setup: We fixed association to 90%, number of queries to 60, and watched how the average waiting time changes over time. We want to show the "adaptiveness" of our broadcasting algorithm, which means that as our broadcasting algorithm listens to the request longer, it learns the association-rule as time progresses.

The experiment results plotted in Figure 3 show that as time progresses, our broadcasting algorithms actually adapt to association-rules in clients' requests. We can observe the decreasing trends on average waiting time, which clearly proves that our algorithm is adaptive to client's requests. The sequential broadcasting algorithm performs relatively constant as time progresses, since it simply repeats all the queries as it broadcasts. The Popularity broadcasting algorithm also decreases average waiting time, but it does not decrease anymore below 2000ms because it does not take associations into consideration.

6   Summary and Conclusions

In this paper, we presented a new kind of broadcasting algorithm by utilizing association-rules in clients' request trends. We implemented three broadcasting algorithms: Exhaustive, Recursive, and Greedy. We tested and compared our broadcasting algorithms with the conventional Sequential, and Popularity broadcasting algorithms. The experimental results show that our broadcasting algorithms utilizing association rules perform better than the conventional broadcasting algorithms in both skewed-request situations and requests with association-rules.

According to our test results, it is clear that our broadcasting algorithm's utilizing association rules are effective to mobile XML databases because XML database requests exhibit association-rule characteristics. For future work and to possibly see even better results, clients should utilize client side caching where a client immediately caches adjacent data on the broadcast stream so that if the client's request matches the guessed association, the data will be available immediately. Our tests in this paper do not utilize client side caching, but we expect average waiting time to decrease dramatically as the data contains more associations. We hope that more broadcasting algorithms utilizing association-rules will appear in the future and eventually hope to see practical applications of it in the industrial communities.

References

1. Swarup Acharya, Rafael Alonso, Michael J. Franklin, and Stanley B. Zdonik. Broadcast disks: Data management for asymmetric communications environments. In *SIGMOD Conference*, pages 199–210, 1995.
2. Daniele Braga, Alessandro Campi, Stefano Ceri, Mika Klemettinen, and Pier Luca Lanzi. A tool for extracting xml association rules. In *ICTAI*, pages 57–, 2002.
3. A. Ganesh, A. Kermarrec, and L. Massoulie. Peer-to-peer membership management for gossip-based protocols, 2003.
4. Meng-Jang Lin, Keith Marzullo, and Stefano Masini. Gossip versus deterministic flooding: Low message overhead and high reliability for broadcasting on small networks. Technical Report CS1999-0637, 18, 1999.
5. Yücel Saygin and Özgür Ulusoy. Exploiting data mining techniques for broadcasting data in mobile computing environments. *IEEE Transactions on Knowledge and Data Engineering*, 14(6):1387–1399, 2002.
6. Ping Xuan, Subhabrata Sen, Oscar González, Jesus Fernandez, and Krithi Ramamritham. Broadcast on demand: Efficient and timely dissemination of data in mobile environments. In *IEEE Real Time Technology and Applications Symposium*, pages 38–48, 1997.
7. Xu Yang. Adaptive data access in broadcast-based wireless environments. *IEEE Transactions on Knowledge and Data Engineering*, 17(3):326–338, 2005.
8. Wai Gen Yee, Shamkant B. Navathe, Edward Omiecinski, and Chris Jermaine. Bridging the gap between response time and energy-efficiency in broadcast schedule design. In *EDBT '02: Proceedings of the 8th International Conference on Extending Database Technology*, pages 572–589, London, UK, 2002. Springer-Verlag.

CSDTM
A Cost Sensitive Decision Tree Based Method

Walid Erray and Hakim Hacid

Lyon 2 University
ERIC Laboratory- 5, avenue Pierre Mendès-France
69600 Bron cedex - France
{werray, hhacid}@eric.univ-lyon2.fr

Abstract. Making a decision has often many results and repercussions. These results don't have the same importance according to the considered phenomenon. This situation can be described by the introduction of the cost concept in the learning process. In this article, we propose a method able to integrate the costs in the automatic learning process. We focus our work on the misclassification cost and we use decision trees as a supervised learning technique. Promising results are obtained using the proposed method.

1 Introduction

Making a decision has aftereffects. These aftereffects can be more or less serious according to the considered decision. For example, in the medical field, classifying positive diagnostic as a negative one has more serious aftereffects than making the opposite. Unfortunately, in the traditional learning methods, all the decisions are considered to have the same importance. To take into account this kind of situation, the cost sensitive learning was introduced. That is, for a learning, we can associate several types of cost. Turney [14] has identified ten, quote for example, the misclassification cost [2], and the test cost.

In this article, we are interested in the cost sensitive learning and we deal especially with the misclassification cost. So, we propose a method, based on decision trees, able to integrate the real cost. For that, we intervene on the various levels of the decision tree construction process. Throughout this article we will use the term "cost" to indicate the "real misclassification cost".

The rest of this article is organized as follows: the following section introduces the notations used throughout this paper. Next, in Section 2, a brief description of the related work is presented. After that, we introduce the basic version of our decision tree based learning method in Section 3. In Section 4, we give the improved version of our learning method for considering the costs. Section 5 presents the experiments performed in order to check the validity of our method. Finally, we conclude and give future directions in Section 6.

T. Yakhno and E. Neuhold (Eds.): ADVIS 2006, LNCS 4243, pp. 217–226, 2006.
© Springer-Verlag Berlin Heidelberg 2006

2   Notations and Related Work

Consider a set of data Ω composed by n items $I_1, I_2, \ldots, I_n$ described by p features $V_1, V_2, \ldots, V_p$. In this article we focus exclusively on the two classes problems. We note these two classes C_1 and C_2. The total misclassification cost Θ of a prediction model Φ obtained using a given learning method, is calculated starting from the confusion matrix M_f (Table 1) obtained after validation (either traditional or cross validation), and the costs matrix M_c (Table 2).

Table 1. Confusion Matrix (M_f)

	C_1'	C_2'
C_1	n_{11}	n_{12}
C_2	n_{21}	$n_2 2$

Table 2. Costs Matrix (M_c)

	C_1	C_2
C_1	0	c_{12}
C_2	c_{21}	0

C_1' and C_2' represent the predicted classes. The number of objects, actually belonging to class $C_i, i = 1, 2$ and whose model predicts their membership in the class $C_j', j = 1, 2$ is n_{ij}.

The costs matrix represents the misclassification costs c_{ij} which is the cost related to the fact of predicting, for an object actually belonging to class i, as an object belonging to the class j. The total misclassification cost is given by $\Theta = c_{12} \times n_{12} + c_{21} \times n_{21}$. The quality of the prediction model increases as Θ decreases.

Several work, allowing to take into account the real misclassification cost were proposed. We can classify these methods into three main categories: the consideration of the cost before the learning process (handling the learning set for example), the consideration of the cost during the learning process (the use of specific measures, post-pruning, etc.), and finally, the consideration of the cost after the learning process (handling of the decision rules for example).

In the case of the costs consideration before the learning process, If Ω is a balanced data set (50% of the objects belong to the class C_1, and 50% of the objects belong to the class C_2), then the prediction probability of the class C_1 will be about 0.5 as well as the one of predicting the class C_2. If the misclassification cost of C_1 (c_{12}) is more significant than the misclassification cost of C_2 (c_{21}), it will be necessary to increase the probability of predicting the class C_1 in order to reduce the total cost. An intuitive and simple solution is to increase the number of objects belonging to the class C_1 in the learning set [15]. So, to have a probability p^* of predicting the class C_1, it is necessary to multiply its initial objects count by the term $\frac{p^*}{(1-p^*)}$ [2]. In the same category we can quote Metacost [3].

In the case of the decision trees based methods, the goal is to build a succession of partitions which lead to a good model. In order to measure the quality of each partition, one can use an information measurement like the Shannon's entropy [12]. In order to take into account the cost, certain authors propose other measures sensitive to the costs like the proposal in [4]. A cost sensitive pruning [1] can also give very interesting results by combining it with a classical learning or with a cost sensitive learning. Other methods make it possible to take into account the cost after the learning process. The goal is to handle the obtained prediction model in order to reduce the total cost [9] [6] [7].

3   Basic Decision Tree Method (BDTM)

The general principle of our method is rather similar to that of the other decision trees methods. Starting from the main partition P_0, representing the root S_0 of the tree and containing all the objects of Ω using the features $V_1, V_2, \ldots, V_p$ to build, in an iterative way, a succession of increasingly detailed partitions of Ω.

3.1   Association and Selection

In order to produce a decision tree with a little complexity and having a good quality, we adopt an already used principle in $ChAid$[8] and $CART$ [2]. This principle consists in gathering the values of the predictive features, having the same behavior with respect to the predictive class, during the splitting of a tree node S_k.

The association principle, $FaUR$, used in our method is described in [5]. So, We start from the finest partition, we seek in each iteration, the two best candidates columns to the fusion. These two columns are those whose fusion maximizes the total value ts of $Tschuprow$ measure [13] based on $Chi2$ measure (Pearson,1904). The algorithm stops when no fusion can increase the value of ts. The $FaUR$ algorithm [5], given in Algorithm 2.hereafter, describes the stages of our association method. The optimized version of $FaUR$ [5] makes it possible to perform associations with a complexity of $O(l \log l)$. This association method is applied to the contingency tables of all the features. As a finality, we select the variable V_j miximizing the ts value of its contingency table.

3.2   Stopping Criteria

The tree construction is stopped if one of the following conditions is checked:

- *minimum objects count in a node*: We admit that a rule obtained from a sheet is considered valid only if it is checked by a minimum number of objects (*effmin*). In other words, a sheet whose minimum object count, of the dominant class, is lower than *effmin* will not be able to produce a valid rule. From there, any node wish do not respect this constraint will not be developed. This is the pre-pruning process.
- *Node homogeneity*: a node S_k is considered to be homogeneous if it contains only objects belonging to the same class C_i. In this case, any node obtained from the splitting of S_k will, automatically, have the same conclusion as S_k, i.e. C_i. Thus, it is useless to continue the splitting of such a node.

Algorithm 1. Algorithm FaUR

$Stop = false$
while $(Stop = false)$ **do**
    $min = t_0 = t(T_K) : T_K$ = contingency table of V_K
    for all (v_{ki}, v_{kj}) **do**
        Calculate $t_{i,j} : t(T_k)$ after association of v_{ki} and v_{kj}
        if $(ts_{ij} > ts_{min})$ **then**
            $ts_{min} = tij$; $z_1 = i, z_2 = j$
        end if
    end for
    if $(t_{min} > t_0)$ **then**
        Associate column z_1 and column z_2
    else
        $Stop = true$
    end if
end while

3.3 Basic Decision Tree Method Algorithm

Algorithm 2. summarizes the operations performed in the proposed method.

Obtaining the rules starting from a decision tree is made on the sheets level. Let us recall that a rule is composed of a conjunction of conditions and a conclusion. The conditions are obtained by traversing the tree from the root to the sheets, each traversed node bring a condition.

A conclusion generated by a sheet of the tree is considered as valid if the minimum object count constraint is satisfied (the object count of the dominant class is higher than the predefined minimum objects count). In the opposite, the conclusion is determined by the parent node.

The application of the above described stages produces a decision tree having a rather similar aspect to the classical decision trees. In the following, we'll introduce our contribution for the consideration and the integration of the costs in the learning process by extending the above described method.

4   A Cost Sensitive Decision Tree Based Method

The final goal of our work is to propose a learning algorithm sensitive to the real misclassification costs. This can be carried out on three levels: before the learning process, during the learning process, and after the learning process. In what concern us, we do not intervene before the learning, i.e. no data handling. Indeed, we consider that the data sets are balanced.

Using the decision trees as a learning method, our contribution is at the construction level of the tree, the post-pruning level, and the generation of the rules level. More concretely, the idea is to intervene, first, locally, on the node level, and this during the processing of the contingency tables, during the selection of the splitting features, and during the pre-pruning task. After that, we act in a

Algorithm 2. BDTM Algorithm

L : set of free nodes
$A = V_1, \ldots, V_p$: set of features
$Div(k, j)$: features obtained after splitting S_k with V_j ;
$L = S_0$
while $(L \neq \emptyset)$ **do**
   Let $S_k \in L$
   if $((S_k \neq homogne)$ **and** $(S_k \neq effmin))$ **then**
     $ts_{max} = -1; best = -1;$
     for $i = 1$ **to** p **do**
       $Get(T_i), T_i$: the contingency table of V_i);
       $FaUR(T_i)$; $ts_i = ts(T_i)$
       if $(ts_i > ts_{max})$ **then**
         $best = i$; $ts_{max} = ts_i;$
       end if
     end for
     Split S_k with V_{best} ; $L = L + Div(k, best)$
   end if
   $L = L - S_k$
end while

global level, and this, during the pruning (post-pruning) and during the decision rules generation.

4.1 Local Level

A New Measure for Contingency Table Association and Splitting Feature Selection: The association of the modalities of the features in the contingency table as well as the choice of a splitting feature depend on the value of the *Tschuprow* measure. These two operations aim to maximize the value of this measure. However, the problem related to this measure is that it considers the costs of the classes equivalent and are equal to 1. In other words, it does not take into account the assigned costs to the classes.

In order to consider the costs, we propose a new quality measure, *tcost*, based on the *Tschuprow* measure and introduce a new element representing the cost. The measure is illustrated by the formula hereafter.

$$tcost = Chi2 - E \tag{1}$$

where:

$$E = \begin{cases} if\ n_{1j} = n_{2j} \begin{cases} if\ C_{12} < C_{21}\ Then\ E_1 \\ else\ E_2 \end{cases} \\ else\ E_3 \end{cases} \tag{2}$$

$$E_1 = C_{12} \times n_{1j}; E_2 = C_{21} \times n_{2j}; E_3 = \sum_{j=1}^{l} (E_{31} + E_{32}) \tag{3}$$

$$E_{31} = C_{12} \times Min\,(Max_i\ n_{ij} - n_{1j};\ 1) \times n_{1j},$$

$$E_{32} = C_{21} \times Min\,(Max_i\ n_{ij} - n_{2j};\ 1) \times n_{2j} \qquad (4)$$

Pre-pruning: This task is ensured by the introduction of the minimum objects count concept. We already introduced a first idea of minimum objects count concept in the previous sections. This concept introduces the conditions of the decision-making at a given node. The principle is that a conclusion on a class C_1 at a node S_k must be checked by a preset minimum object count and this, by disregarding the costs.

Let us consider the two classes C_1 and C_2. If c_{12} is higher than c_{21}, this means that a bad decision on C_2 (classify an object belonging to C_1 in C_2) has more gravity than a bad decision on C_1 (classify an object belonging to C_2 in C_1). We translate this by a stronger penalization of the decision-making on C_2. The penalization translates the fact that the necessary minimum objects count for a conclusion on C_2 must be higher than that for the class C_1.

In order to integrate this concept in our method, we introduce an additional minimum objects count (*effmin2*). This concept corresponds to the minimum objects count that a rule concluding on C_2 must satisfy to be considered as valid. To penalize the class C_2, we allot its own minimum objects count (*effmin2*). Intuitively, the minimum objects count assigned to each class is inversely proportional to its cost.

We illustrate this concept on the example of figure 1 where we consider *effmin*(C_1) = 10 and *effmin2*(C_2) = 25.

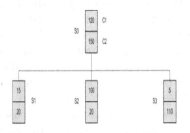

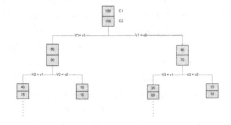

Fig. 1. Illustration of the pre-pruning principle in our method

Fig. 2. Illustration of the rules generation principle in our method

Splitting the node S_1 will continue since we have the possibility to obtain nodes that will conclude on C_1 and respecting *effmin* although S_1 does not respect *effmin2*. In the node S_2, the number of objects belonging to the class C_2 is lower than *effmin2*. Split this node cannot produce any more nodes concluding on C_2 while respecting the *effmin2* constraint. For that, the splitting is not useful any more, it is then stopped. With regard to the node S_3, the class C_1 violates the minimum objects count constraint what prevents the continuation of the splitting task.

4.2 Global Level

Post-pruning: The post-pruning is a significant operation and is necessary to obtain a tree with a rather good quality and to prevent a high complexity of the tree. Indeed, some sheets of the tree can sometimes be useless (too specialized tree). In such a situation, a post-pruning is applied.

At this level, we consider the real cost $\Theta test$, calculated on a test data set, combined with the complexity of the tree π ($\pi = \alpha \times sheetscount$, α: predefined by the user) to perform the pruning. The goal is to minimize the total cost, $\Theta tot = \Theta test + \pi$.

Generation of the Rules. Consider the decision tree illustrated in Figure 2 with the following misclassification costs: $c_{12} = 5$ and $c_{21} = 1$.

Classically, if the minimum objects count constraint is *effmin*= 15 objects, then among the rules we can obtain:

- R_1 : IF $(V_1 = v_1)$ AND $(V_2 = v_2)$ THEN $Class = C_2$
- R_2 : IF $(V_1 = v_2)$ AND $(V_3 = v_2)$ THEN $Class = C_1$

In the standard case, we notice that the two conclusions were taken with the same number of objects (15 objects in this case). This means that we have the same probability to do an error in both cases. However, by taking into account the costs, the consequences of the rule R_1 are more important than the consequences of the rule R_2. In this case, it is necessary that the rules concluding on C_2 have less probability of being mistaken on the class C_1.

By considering the preceding example, if one sets the minimum objects count related to C_2, *effmin2*= 30 objects while leaving objects count related to C_1 (*effmin*= 15), then the conclusion of the rule R_1 will be not valid. In this case, we consider that the conclusion of the rule R_1 inherits from the conclusion of the parent node. Thus, We will have the two following rules:

- R_1 : IF $(V_1 = v_1)$ AND $(V_2 = v_2)$ THEN $Class = C_1$
- R_2 : IF $(V_1 = v_2)$ AND $(V_3 = v_2)$ THEN $Class = C_1$

So, in order to introduce the costs for the decision-making in a node, we use two different minimum objects count: The first one is used to make a decision on C_1, and the second one is used to make a decision on C_2.

By taking into account the presented elements in this paper, we integrated the cost concept in the decision trees construction process. The suggested method makes it possible to support a class having a high cost, and also makes it possible to keep a good quality of the tree in order to prevent the loss of the decision on the other class. The following section introduces some experiments that we performed in order to validate our method. We start with the presentation of the estimation of the evolution of the various parameters of the method then we present our effective evaluation tests.

5 Experiments

5.1 Parameters Evolution

Setting up the initial values of the parameters is often problematic for the user. In our case, the choice of the second minimum objects count (*effmin2*) can appear difficult. In order to give an idea on the possible value to set for this parameter, we will give the evolution and the possible relation between the different parameters.

To perform these experiments, we used breast-cancer data set described in [11]. We balanced this data set in order to have the same decision probability at the beginning of the evaluation. The general principle of the tests is as follows: for each cost, we make correspond it various values of minimum objects count (*effmin2*). For the two test series, we set the cost c_{12} of the class C_1 at 1. We vary the c_{21} cost of the second class C_2 using the values from 5 up to 150. Also, at each cost of the class C_2, we vary *effmin2* from 5 up to 150. *effmin* as for it is defined to 5 for all the experiments. We recover at each iteration, the obtained gain. To show the interest of the method, we made the tests in the first case by supporting class 1 ($C_1 = 1$, $C_2 = 2$) and in the second case by supporting the class 2 ($C_1 = 2$, $C_2 = 1$). Curves of figures 3 and 4 show, the obtained results.

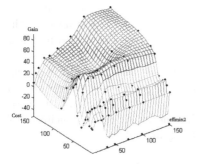 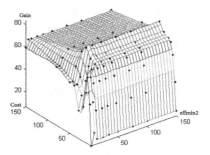

Fig. 3. Evolution of the gain according to the cost and the minimum objects count for the class $C_2 = 1$

Fig. 4. Evolution of the gain according to the cost and the minimum objects count for the class $C_2 = 2$

We can notice that the curves have approximately the same behavior for the two tests series (for the two classes). Globally, one can say that the minimum objects count depends on the cost associated to a class. Indeed, We notice that the obtained gain, at a given cost, increases by increasing *effmin2*. However, from a certain value of *effmin2*, the gain does not increase any more and can even be deteriorated (Figure 4).

5.2   Tests and Results

For the effective evaluation, we took datasets from the UCI Irvine repository [11], and we use the following ones: *Australian-credit, Breast-Cancer, Heart and White-House-Votes-84*. These data sets are two classes problems. We balanced the data sets by taking the totality of the objects of the class having the less objects count. So, We performed three tests series on each data set and on each class. The three tests series correspond respectively to costs 5, 10 and 15. Also, we used three methods: *C4.5* [10], *BDTM*, and *CSDTM*. For *CSDTM*, we use *effmin2* with the values 5, 10 and 15. Table 5.2 summarizes the obtained results in term of real misclassification cost.

Table 3. The obtained results using different data sets

Cost	Dataset	C2	C4.5	BDTM	CSDTM effmin2=5	effmin2=5	effmin2=5
	Australian	1	331	298	217	192	194
	Australian	0	311	314	276	279	266
	Breast	2	62	80	87	76	76
5	Breast	1	70	88	50	49	56
	Heart	1	223	114	170	158	156
	Heart	2	251	162	143	133	140
	House	REPUBLICAN	64	35	35	35	35
	House	DEMOCRAT	80	55	55	55	55
	Australian	1	611	543	453	404	326
	Australian	0	566	579	479	380	315
	Breast	2	112	145	155	115	115
10	Breast	1	130	163	55	56	66
	Heart	1	403	199	268	202	195
	Heart	2	466	307	255	227	230
	House	REPUBLICAN	114	60	60	60	60
	House	DEMOCRAT	150	105	105	105	105
	Australian	1	891	788	631	559	470
	Australian	0	821	844	585	412	284
	Breast	2	162	210	180	180	188
15	Breast	1	190	238	90	62	71
	Heart	1	583	284	358	265	248
	Heart	2	681	452	382	318	320
	House	REPUBLICAN	164	85	110	100	100
	House	DEMOCRAT	220	155	155	155	155

Initially, we can affirm that our initial method offers better results compared to *C4.5*, for these data sets. In addition, the *CSDTM* method makes it possible, in the majority of the cases, to reduce the total cost. Certainly, the cost does not decrease for all the *effmin2*' values (heart, $c_{21} = 15$, $C_2 = 1$, *effmin2*= 15), but there is, at least, a value of *effmin2* for which the cost decreases.

6   Conclusion and Future Work

The cost sensitive learning is a very significant problem. Several work was devoted to this subject. In this work, we were interested in the misclassification cost by using the decision trees like learning method. We proposed a method able to take into account the misclassification cost in the various steps of the decision tree construction process while keeping a good quality of the tree. The major contribution of this work is, certainly, the intervention on the various levels of the learning process. The performed tests show very interesting results.

As future work, we think about an automated manner for initializing the *effmin2* parameter. Also, the method seems to us very simple to generalize to the case of the multi classes data.

References

1. J. P. Bradford, C. Kunz, R. Kohavi, C. Brunk, and C. E. Brodley. Pruning decision trees with misclassification costs. In *Proceedings of the 10th European Conference on Machine Learning*, pages 131–136, London, UK, 1998. Springer-Verlag.
2. L. Breiman, J. Friedman, R. Olshen, and C. Stone. *Classification and Regression Trees*. Wadsworth, 1984.
3. P. Domingos. Metacost: A general method for making classifiers cost-sensitive., 1999.
4. C. Dummond and R. C. Holte. Exploiting the cost (in)sensitivity of decision tree splitting criteria. In M. Kaufmann, editor, *In Machine Learning : Proceedings of the Seventeeth International Conference*, pages 239–246, San Francisco, CA, 2000. Morgan Kaufmann.
5. W. Erray. Faur : Méthode de réduction unidimensionnelle d'un tableau de contingence. In *12ème rencontres de la Société Francophone de Classification*, Montreal, Canada, May 2005.
6. Y. Freund and R. E. Schapire. Experiments with a new boosting algorithm. In *International Conference on Machine Learning*, pages 148–156, 1996.
7. J. Friedman, T. Hastie, and R. Tibshirani. Additive logistic regression: a statistical view of boosting, 1998.
8. G. Kass. An exploratory technique for investigating large quantities of categorical data. *j-APPL-STAT*, 29(2):119–127, 1980.
9. J. Platt. Probabilistic outputs for support vector machines and comparison to regularize likelihood methods. In B. S. D. S. A.J. Smola, P. Bartlett, editor, *Advances in Large Margin Classifiers*, pages 61–74, 2000.
10. J. R. Quinlan. *C4.5: Programs for Machine Learning*. Morgan Kaufmann, 1993.
11. C. B. S. Hettich and C. Merz. UCI repository of machine learning databases, 1998.
12. C. Shannon and W. Weaver. *The Mathematical Theory of Communication*. The University of Illinois Press, 1949.
13. A. Tschuprow. On the mathematical expectation of moments of frequency distribution. *Biometrika*, pages 185–210, 1921.
14. P. D. Turney. Types of cost in inductive concept learning. cs.LG/0212034, 2002.
15. B. Zadrozny and C. Elkan. Learning and making decisions when costs and probabilities are both unknown. In *Proceedings of the seventh ACM SIGKDD international conference on Knowledge discovery and data mining*, pages 204–213, 2001.

Comparative Analysis
of Classification Methods
for Protein Interaction Verification System

Min Su Lee and Seung Soo Park

Department of Computer Science and Engineering,
Ewha Womans University, Seoul, Korea
ssue@ewhain.net,
sspark@ewha.ac.kr

Abstract. A comparative study for assessing the reliability of protein-protein interactions in a high-throughput dataset is presented. We use various state-of-the-art classification algorithms to distinguish true interacting protein pairs from noisy data using the empirical knowledge about interacting proteins. Then we compare the performance of classifiers with various criteria. Experimental results show that classification algorithms provide very powerful tools in distinguishing true interacting protein pairs from noisy protein-protein interaction dataset. Furthermore, in the data setting with lots of missing values like protein-protein interaction dataset, K-Nearest Neighborhood and Decision Tree algorithms show best performance among other methods.

1 Introduction

Protein-protein interaction (PPI) is any relation between proteins in a cell which is the fundamental basis of the cellular operation. PPI knowledge is useful in predicting unknown functions of proteins [1] and in clarifying signal transduction pathways [2]. PPIs have been studied individually in terms of physical and chemical properties of proteins. Recently, large amounts of PPI data have been collected through the evolution of high-throughput experiments. They include genome-scale Yeast Two-Hybrid assays (Y2H) [3, 4] and protein complex identification methods through mass spectrometry [5, 6].

Vast amount of data produced by high-throughput experiments allow for efficient identifications of various PPI information. However, they are prone to higher false positive rates than small-scale studies [7, 8]. Note that the false positive data indicate non-interacting protein pairs yet classified as interacting pairs in experimental results. Von Mering *et al.* estimate that approximately half the interactions obtained from high-throughput data may be false positives [7]. Containing false positive data requires additional tasks to validate the reliability of each candidate PPI pair.

In this paper, we present a verification system for PPI dataset that can distinguish true interacting protein pairs from noisy dataset. The system applies a classification algorithm using the following three characteristics of interacting proteins.

T. Yakhno and E. Neuhold (Eds.): ADVIS 2006, LNCS 4243, pp. 227–236, 2006.
© Springer-Verlag Berlin Heidelberg 2006

1. Frequency of co-localization: interacting proteins are located in close proximity to each other, at least transiently.
2. Similarity of protein functional category: interacting proteins share similar functional categories.
3. Topological properties within the protein interaction network: an interacting protein pair is highly and tightly linked with other proteins in the protein interaction network.

The system first learns from a set of reliable positive data from PPI database and negative data which is randomly generated based on the frequency of co-localization characteristic. The classifier is made at this training phase. Then, the system performs the assessment of input PPI pairs using the similarity of protein functional category and the topological properties within the protein interaction network on the classifier.

Combining a classification algorithm and this heuristic knowledge turns out to be very effective in verifying the reliability of PPI from high-throughput experiments [9]. However, there are many different types of classification methods, and their performances depend heavily upon data characteristics. In this paper, we test the performances of various classification algorithms when they are combined into our PPI verification system.

2 Related Works

To validate the reliability of noisy PPI data, both selection of relevant properties about PPI and the adoption of efficient computational methodologies are important.

The intersection of multiple high-throughput PPI datasets can be effective in obtaining more reliable PPIs. If an interaction is detected by two distinct experiments, the interaction becomes more reliable. However, different high-throughput experimental methods often generate different types of PPIs. Moreover, PPI data produced at different research groups are substantially different even though same technologies are used [3, 4]. Because of these limitations of the high-throughput technologies, the coverage of intersection is very small in the huge amount of PPI dataset [7, 10].

Some studies have been made on the assumption that interacting proteins whose transcripts being co-expressed are more likely to be credible [11, 12]. However, recent research shows that interactions in genome-wide datasets have only a weak relationship with gene expression owing to different degradation rates [13-15].

If two proteins interact in one species, the homologous proteins also interact each other. Many interactions can be predicted by using this nature, but this method is necessarily restricted to proteins which homolog proteins are defined. This approach has been used to enhance the confidence of PPI data. [16, 17]

Most of these methods need whole genome-scale PPI dataset to assess the reliability of each PPI pair. Moreover, it is not clear for biologists to define the proper cutoff value of confidence score to classify between true positives and false positives. To solve this problem, we proposed a verification system which reflects some of heuristic knowledge of biologists using Neural Network algorithm [9].

3   Classification System for PPI Dataset

To separate true positives and false positives from putative PPI dataset, we have developed a classification system based on various state-of-the-art classification algorithms (Fig. 1). Our classification system consists of a MIPS PPI database, an PPI annotation database, a computation module of biological features for each PPI pair, several classification algorithms for filtering false positives, and a PPI classifier generated by the algorithm. The attributes of the PPI database includes protein name, subcellular location information within a cell, protein functional category, and topological information within the interaction network.

Our system first trains from a collection of protein pairs and their attributes. The training dataset consists of the positive PPI dataset of Yeast from MIPS [16] and the negative PPI dataset.

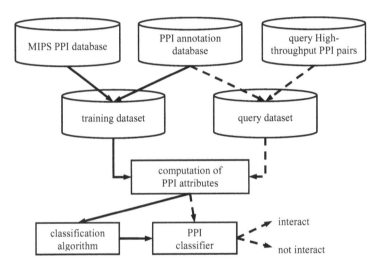

Fig. 1. System architecture for classification of high-throughput protein interaction pairs. Solid arrows indicate the training process to construct classifier, and the dotted arrows show classifying process of query high-throughput protein interaction data.

3.1   Yeast High-Throughput Data Sets

Positive dataset is derived from yeast MIPS PPI dataset which are manually filtered. The positive dataset consists of not only all physical interactions from MIPS but also small-scale yeast-two hybrid experimental data.

Unlike the positive dataset, the negative protein-protein interaction dataset is not fluently defined. However, because interacting protein pairs are closely located, the negative dataset can be derived from the frequency of co-localization data in yeast cells. Huh *et al.* determined the subcellular localizations of each interacting protein pair and the fraction of total number of interactions occurring for each localization pair [18]. The negative PPI dataset is generated by subtracting PPIs whose frequency of co-localization is zero from randomly generated PPI dataset using proteins appears in the MIPS PPI dataset.

3.2 Computation of PPI Attributes

The "computation of PPI attributes" module calculates two attribute values for the training PPI database, namely, similarity of functional category and topological properties within the interaction network structure.

Similarity of Functional Category. Since most proteins function within complexes, interacting proteins share similar functional category. The similarity of functional category between interacting proteins is calculated based on the functional category (FunCat) of MIPS database [16, 19]. The FunCat is described with a hierarchical tree structure (Fig. 2a). It consists of 28 main functional categories with up to six levels of increasing specificity. A unique two-digit number is assigned to each category hierarchy. The levels of categories are separated by dots (eg. 01.02.05.02.01.02). The similarity of the functional categories i and j is determined by the level of the Lowest Common Ancestor (LCA) $Level_{LCA}(i, j)$ of the two categories. For example, the LCA of '01.01' and '01.02.05.02.01.02' is '01', and the level of LCA is 1 (Fig. 2a). Higher level of LCA implies more similar functional category. Since a majority of proteins are included in more than one functional category, we compute all LCAs from combinations of functional categories in each PPI pair. Then, the LCA with the maximum level is selected as the similarity value for the functional category between the pair. Let F be a set of functional categories in FunCat, and F_1 and F_2 be subsets of F associated with interacting proteins p_1 and p_2 respectively. Then, the similarity weight $w_F(p_1, p_2)$ for the functional category of p_1 and p_2 is calculated as follows.

$$w_F(p_1, p_2) = \underset{\forall i \in F_1, \forall j \in F_2}{MAX} [2^{Level_{LCA}(i,j)}] \tag{1}$$

The similarity weight of the functional categories ranges from 1 to 64. The coverage of the similarity weight in the training dataset is 99.97%.

Topological properties within the interaction network. False positive interaction pairs may result sticky proteins which tend to interact with unrelated proteins in vitro. The scale-free nature of biological networks suggests that highly connected proteins are a real feature of protein interaction networks and more likely to be lethal [20, 21]. Hence the reliable interacting protein pair should not only be highly and tightly connected within interaction network, but also have further interactions with many other interacting partners. Saito et al. proposed interaction generality measure (IG2) using five groups of topology of the protein interaction network around the target interacting pair [22]. For each interacting pair, IG2 weight is calculated with the number of common proteins which interact target PPI pair, and specific types of alternative pathways between the target interacting proteins by applying principal component analysis. (Fig. 2b). The IG2 value is distributed from -6.35 to 53. The lower IG2 value implies more tightly connected pairs in the interaction networks. Note that this is different from functional category and co-localization cases. IG2 value covers only 38.72% of our training PPI set.

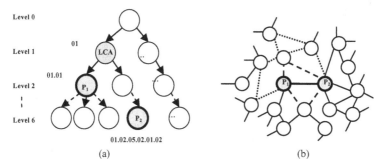

Fig. 2. Calculating three attribute values for interacting proteins. (a) Tree structure for functional categories, (b) Classification of interaction topology in the interaction networks.

3.3 Classification Algorithms

We applied various state-of-the-art classification algorithms for our classification system, and compare their performance. We use five algorithms: Decision Tree (DT), Support Vector Machine (SVM), Naïve Bayes (NB), K-Nearest Neighborhood (KNN), and Neural Network (NN). In our system, the classifying attributes are similarity value of functional category and IG2 value. The target classes are 'interact' and 'not interact'.

Decision Tree. A decision tree algorithm is useful to predict categorical class labels. The decision tree algorithm is a greedy algorithm that constructs decision trees in a top-down recursive divide-and-conquer manner. The tree starts as a single node representing the training instances. The algorithm basically chooses the attribute that provides the maximum degree of discrimination between target classes locally. The information gain is used to measure how well a given attribute separates the training instances according to their target classification. The attribute with the highest information gain (or greatest entropy reduction) is chosen as the test attribute for the current node, and the instances are partitioned accordingly. A post-pruning process is carried out to prevent overfitting. In our experiments, we use the C4.5 version of the decision tree algorithm [23].

Support Vector Machine. Support vector machines have exhibited superb performance in binary classification tasks. Intuitively, SVM aims at searching for a hyperplane that separates the two classes of data with largest margin between the hyperplane and the point closest to it. We use sequential minimal optimization algorithm with logistic regression model and RBF kernel for training a support vector classifier [24].

Naïve Bayes. Naive Bayes is one of the most successful learning algorithms for text categorization. Naive Bayes is based on the Bayes rule assuming conditional independence between classes. Based on the rule, using the joint probabilities of sample observations and classes, the algorithm attempts to estimate the conditional probabilities of classes given an observation [25].

K-Nearest Neighborhood. KNN is a non-parametric classifier. KNN has been applied to various information retrieval problems. KNN uses an integer parameter, K. Given an input x, the algorithms finds the K closest training data points to x, and predicts the label of x based on the label of the K points. In this paper, the parameter for KNN is set to 3. It has been proven that the error of KNN is asymptotically at most two times the Bayesian error [26].

Neural Network. Neural Network is an information processing paradigm that is inspired by the way biological nervous systems, such as the brain, process information. The key element of this paradigm is the novel structure of the information processing system. It is composed of a large number of highly interconnected processing elements (neurones) working in unison to solve specific problems. NNs, like people, learn by example. A NN is configured for a specific application, such as pattern recognition or data classification, through a learning process. We use Neural Network algorithm with backpropagation to train [27].

4 Experimental Results and Discussion

Our implementation of the various classifiers is based on the Weka environment [27]. First of all, we construct five classifiers using aforementioned classification algorithms with a dataset including 7,274 PPI pairs which are labeled with target class. Then, we compare the performance of these classifiers with 10 fold cross-validation. 10 fold cross-validation means that the available examples are partitioned into 10 disjoint subsets. The cross-validation procedure is then run 10 times, each time using one of the 10 subsets as the test set and the others for training sets.

We used various performance criteria to evaluate the capability of our system. Those are calculated based on true positive (TP), true negative (TN), false positive (FP), and false negative (FN) (Table 1). The TP and TN are correct classifications. A FP is when the outcome is incorrectly predicted as interacting protein pairs, when it is in fact non-interacting pairs. A FN is when the outcome is incorrectly predicted as non-interacting protein pairs, when it is in fact interacting pairs.

The performance criteria that we used are as follows.

$$accuracy = (TN + TP) \cdot 100 \ / \ (TP + FP + FN + TN) \tag{2}$$

$$TP\text{-}rate = (TP) \cdot 100 \ / \ (TP + FN) \tag{3}$$

$$FP\text{-}rate = (FP) \cdot 100 \ / \ (FP + FN) \tag{4}$$

$$Precision = (TP) \cdot 100 \ / \ (TP + FP) \tag{5}$$

$$\begin{aligned} F\text{-}measure &= 2 \cdot Precision \cdot Recall \ / \ (Precision + Recall) \\ &= (2TP) \cdot 100 \ / \ (2TP + FP + FN) \end{aligned} \tag{6}$$

The accuracy is the proportion of correctly classified examples among total examples. The true positive rate (TP-rate) is the proportion of examples which were classified as class x, among all examples which truly have class x, i.e. how much part of the class was captured. It is equivalent to Recall. The false positive rate (FP-rate) is the proportion of examples which were classified as class x, but belong to a different class, among all examples which are not of class x. The precision of the proportion of the examples which truly have class x among all those which were classified as class x. F-measure is a single measure that characterizes true positive rate and precision.

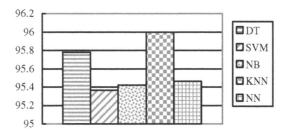

Fig. 3. The accuracies of Decision Tree, Support Vector Machine, Naïve Bayes, K-Nearest Neighborhood, and Neural Network

The accuracies of five classifiers are presented in Figure 3. The accuracies range from 95.36% to 96.0%. KNN whose accuracy is 96.0% is shown to the best classifier for assessing PPI reliability. In general, SVM performs very well in binary classification problems. However, in our experimental results, SVM is shown the worst classifier for assessing PPI reliability. Since all kinds of the biological annotations of a protein are not always available, known information of each protein are varied and some attributes may have many missing values. The implementation of SVM globally replaces all missing values and transforms nominal attributes into binary ones. Since the weakness for treatment of missing values, if attributes have many missing values, the accuracy of SVM classifier becomes lower.

Decision Tree achieves good performance. It outperforms SVM, Naïve Bayes, and Neural Network. Decision Tree algorithm is good at handling missing values. Moreover, Decision Tree classifier generates descriptive rules about some properties of interacting proteins. For example, although IG2 value is missing, if the similarity of functional category is more than 32 (i.e. the level of LCA is more than five), the interacting protein pair must be true positive. To take another example, if a protein pair is very tightly connected within the interaction network (IG2 < 4.8), the interacting protein pair must be true positive. Like this, Decision Tree classifier helps for biologists to understand the biological conditions of interacting proteins.

Table 1. Detailed accuracy by class

Algorithm	Class	TP rate	FP rate	Precision	F-Measure
DT	Interact	92.8	1.8	97.5	95.1
	Not interact	98.2	7.2	94.5	96.3
SVM	Interact	90.3	0.6	99.2	94.5
	Not interact	99.4	9.7	92.8	96
NB	Interact	92.2	2	97.3	94.7
	Not interact	98	7.8	94	96
KNN	Interact	93.2	1.8	97.6	95.4
	Not interact	98.2	6.8	94.8	96.5
NN	Interact	93.6	3.1	96	94.8
	Not interact	96.9	6.4	95	96

Table 1 shows detailed accuracy by target class. All classifiers more correctly classify non-interacting protein pairs than interacting protein pairs. Because of the relatively more false negatives than false positives, the true positive rate of 'interact' class is lower than that of 'not interact' class. However, the false positive rate and precision of 'interact' class are better than those of 'not interact' class. There is a trade-off between true positive rate and precision. The F-measure values which are combined measure for precision and recall indicate that KNN and Decision Tree outperform in classifying true interacting pairs and false interacting pairs.

5   Conclusion

This paper proposes a new classification system to assess protein interaction reliability, and provides comparative analyses on various classification algorithms for the system. We used three biological attributes related to PPIs, namely, frequency of co-localization, similarity of functional category, and topological properties within the interaction network.

The results show that applying classification algorithm supplemented with biological domain knowledge provides good performance overall in distinguishing true interacting protein pairs from noisy PPI dataset. The study suggests that the ability for handling missing values is important in assessment of protein interaction reliability. The good performance of KNN and DT over SVM stems from this property of data setting. Especially, DT algorithm was very attractive in not only their classification performance but also descriptive verification model. Thanks to verification model based on DT, detail characteristics about real protein interaction pairs are grasped.

To improve accuracy of classification, it is needed to reduce the ratio of missing values in topological properties. Ensemble methods, such as bagging or boosting, may help to construct more robust classifier.

Studies about biological networks should be started with reliable interaction data. Assessing protein interaction reliability using classification algorithms may be very useful for this purpose.

Acknowledgements

This work was supported by a grant from Brain Korea 21 Project, Ministry of Education & Human Resources Development, Republic of Korea.

References

1. A. Vazquez, A. Flammini, A. Maritan, and A. Vespignani.: Global protein function prediction from protein-protein interaction networks. Nat Biotechnol. 21, 697-700. 2003.
2. M. Steffen, A. Petti, J. Aach, P. D'haeseleer and G. Church.: Automated modelling of signal transduction networks. BMC Bioinformatics 3, 34-44. 2002.
3. P. Uetz, L. Giot, G. Cagney, T. A. Mansfield, et al. A comprehensive analysis of protein-protein interactions in Saccharomyces cerevisiae. Nature 403, 623–627. 2000.

4. T. Ito, T. Chiba, R. Ozawa, M. Yoshida, *et al.*: A comprehensive two-hybrid analysis to explore the yeast protein interactome. PNAS 98, 4569–4574. 2001.

5. A. C. Gavin, M. Bosche, R. Krause, *et al.*: Functional organization of the yeast proteome by systematic analysis of protein complexes. Nature 415, 141–147. 2002.

6. Y. Ho, A. Gruhler, A. Heilbut, *et al.*: Systematic identification of protein complexes in Saccharomyces cerevisiae by mass spectrometry. Nature 415, 180–183. 2002.

7. C. von Mering, R. Krause, B. Snel, M. Cornell, *et al.*: Comparative assessment of large-scale data sets of protein-protein interactions. Nature 417, 399-403. 2002.

8. E. Sprinzak, S. Sattath and H. J. Margalit.: How reliable are experimental protein-protein interaction data?. Mol Biol. 327, 919-923. 2003.

9. M. S. Lee, S. S. Park, and M. K. Kim.: A Protein verification system based on a neural network algorithm", IEEE Computational Systems Bioinformatics, 151-154, Aug. 2005.

10. L. R. Mattews, P. Vaglio, J. Reboul, H. Ge, *et al.*: Identification of Potential Interaction Networks Using Sequence-Based Searches for Conserved Protein-Protein Interactions or "Interologs". Genome Res. 11, 2120-2126. 2001.

11. H. Ge, Z. Liu, G. M. Church and M. Vidal.: Correlation between transcriptome and inter-actome mapping data from Saccharomyces cerevisiae. Nat Genet. 29, 482-486. 2001.

12. P. Kemmeren, N. van Berkum, J. Vilo, T. Bijma, *et al.*: Protein interaction verification and functional annotation by integrated analysis of genome-scale data. Mol Cell 9, 1133-1143. 2002.

13. S. Gygi, Y. Rochon, B. R. Franza and R. Aebersold.: Correlation between protein and mRNA abundance in yeast, MCB 19, 1720-1730. 1999.

14. R. Jasen, D. Greenbaum and M. Gerstein.: Relating whole-genome expression data with protein-protein interaction. Genome Res. 12, 37-46. 2002.

15. N. Bhardwaj and H. Lu.: Correlation between gene expression profiles and protein-protein interactions within and across genomes. Bioinformatics 21, 2730-2738. 2005.

16. H. W. Mewes, D. Frishman, U. Guldener, G. Mannhaupt, *et al.*: MIPS: a database for ge-nomes and protein sequences. Nucleic Acids Res. 30, 31-34. 2002.

17. T. Sato, Y. Yamanishi, M. Kanehisa and H. Toh.: The inference of protein-protein interac-tions by co-evolutionary analysis is improved by excluding the information about the phy-logenetic relationships. Bioinformatics 21, 3482-3489. 2005.

18. A., Ruepp, A. Zollner, D. Maier, K. Albermann, *et al.*: The FunCat, a functional annota-tion scheme for systematic classification of proteins from whole genomes. Nucleic Acids Res. 32, 5539-5545. 2004.

19. W. K. Huh, J. V. Falvo, L. C. Gerke, *et al.*: Global analysis of protein localization in bud-ding yeast. Nature 425, 686-691. 2003.

20. H. Jeong, S. P. Mason, A. L. Barabasi, Z. N. Oltvai.: Lethality and centrality in protein networks. Nature 411, 41-42. 2001.

21. E. Ravasz, A. L. Somera, D. A. Mongru, A. N. Oltvai, A. L. Barabasi.: Hierarchical or-ganization of modularity in metabolic networks. Science 297, 1551-1555. 2002.

22. R. Saito, H. Suzuki and Y. Hayashizaki.: Construction of reliable protein-protein interac-tion networks with a new interaction generality measure. Bioinformatics 19, 756-763. 2003.

23. R. Quinlan.: C4.5: Programs for machine learning. Morgan Kaufmann Publishers, San Mateo, CA. 1993.

24. J. Platt.: Fast training of support vector machines using sequential minimal optimization. Advances in kernel methods - support vector learning, B. Schoelkopf, C. Burges, and A. Smola, eds., MIT Press. 1998.

25. G. H. John and P. Langley.: Estimating continuous distributions in bayesian classifiers. Proc. of the 11th Conf. on Uncertainty in Artificial Intelligence. 338-345. Morgan Kaufmann, San Mateo. 1995.
26. D. Aha and D. Kibler.: Instance-based learning algorithms. Machine Learning 6, 37-66. 1991.
27. I. J. Witten and E. Frank.: Data mining: practical machine learning tools with java implementations. Morgan Kaufmann, San Francisco, CA. 2000.

Distributed Architecture for Association Rule Mining

Marko Banek[1], Damir Jurić[1], Ivo Pejaković[2], and Zoran Skočir[1]

[1] FER - University of Zagreb, Unska 3, HR-10000 Zagreb, Croatia
{marko.banek, damir.juric, zoran.skocir}@fer.hr
[2] Metronet, Ulica grada Vukovara 269d, HR-10000 Zagreb, Croatia
ivo.pejakovic@metronet.hr

Abstract. Organizations have adopted various data mining techniques to support their decision-making and business processes. However, the mining analysis is not performed and supervised by the final user, the management of the organization, since the knowledge of mathematical models as well as expert database administration skills is required. This paper describes a distributed architecture for association rule mining analysis in the retail area, designed to be used directly by the management of an organization and implemented as a Java web application. The rule discovery algorithm is executed at the database server that hosts the source data warehouse, while the only used client tool is a web browser. The user interactively initiates the rule discovery process through a simple user interface, which is used later to browse, sort and compare the discovered rules.

1 Introduction

Data mining is exploration and analysis of large quantities of data in order to discover meaningful patterns and rules [3]. It typically deals with data that has already been collected for some purpose other than data mining analysis. For this reason, data mining is often referred to as secondary data analysis [9].

Data mining analysis is based on different principles of mathematics, statistics, computer science and artificial intelligence. Various mining techniques (neural networks, decision trees, nearest neighbor approaches, clustering, genetic algorithm approaches etc.) are based on complex mathematical or statistical models. As most techniques require many iteration steps, the mining tasks are expensive in terms of processing costs, both of time and disk memory space. While in some approaches the analysis can be performed automatically, others first require training data to be chosen by humans, which later has a significant impact on the final result.

Many organizations have built their data warehousing systems during the last two decades. Principal decision makers (department executive officers and managers), as well as department analysts, have been trained to use report and OLAP (On-line Analytical Processing) tools. Though the data warehouse is the primary data source for mining analysis as well, mining is not performed by

T. Yakhno and E. Neuhold (Eds.): ADVIS 2006, LNCS 4243, pp. 237–246, 2006.

the decision-makers themselves, but educated domain experts. The reasons are twofold: first, the knowledge of mathematical models and algorithms is required; second, the task of preparing the warehouse data for the mining process (i.e. creating database structures suitable for mining algorithms) needs the skills in database administration.

This paper describes the development of a distributed, robust and scalable framework for market basket analysis in the largest food production and retail company in Croatia. Market basket analysis [1, 3] supports the decision making process in the retail area by telling us which products tend to be purchased together. Typical merchandizing decisions include how to organize promotions, how to design coupons and how to place goods on shelves in order to maximize profit. Generation of association rules is a mining technique most closely allied with sales analysis and has been used for more than a decade. Since no training data are needed, the process can be performed automatically, after choosing the appropriate dataset.

Our framework enables decision makers and knowledge workers (managers and analysts), who are neither data mining nor database administration experts, to create market basket association rules and interpret them. The existing commercial or open-source mining tools (like Weka [12], which we used in our previous work [11]) first transfer data to the user's client machine, where the analysis is performed locally. On the contrary, we propose a distributed, three-tier architecture which does not require any client program except a ubiquitously present web browser. All mining tasks are performed at the database that stores the sales data and thus no data transfer is needed. The framework is implemented as a web application in Java.

A simple user interface enables the user to choose the target data and start the mining analysis with several mouse clicks. Next, the process of data cleansing and rule discovery is performed. The discovered rules can be browsed and sorted in the user interface according to different criteria of interestingness.

The paper is structured as follows. Section 2 gives an overview of the related work. In Section 3 association rules are outlined and various criteria of interestingness are described. Section 4 explains the implementation of the framework as a web application in Java. Finally, in Section 5 the conclusions are drawn.

2   Related Work

The problem of association rules was introduced in [1] and the so-called AIS algorithm proposed to perform the rule discovery process. The intensive research in the association rule mining area has produced two different algorithm strategies: BFS (Breadth-First Search algorithm) and DFS (Depth-First Search algorithm). The most commonly used algorithm is the Apriori [2], which follows the BFS strategy. Many papers have been published subsequently considering various improvements of the basic Apriori algorithm, like DIC (Dynamic Itemset Counting) [4]. On the other hand, the Eclat [8] and FP-growth [10] algorithms use the DFS strategy.

There are many existing commercial and non-commercial systems that support a visual approach to analyzing the discovered knowledge. For instance, the JWAVE software [18] offers a web interface to analyze and interpret large datasets. However, it cannot perform association rule mining, but can only be used as a tool for analyzing the already discovered rules. A noncommercial framework for association rule interpretation, DS-WEB [7], adopts the web-based client/server architecture. The large number of discovered rules is first summarized and then interpreted using dynamically generated web pages. Again, this tool cannot initiate or perform the mining process.

3   Association Rules

Association rules are formally defined as follows [1]. Let $I=\{i_1, i_2, ..., i_m\}$ be a set of literals ([2], in the initial paper [1] the term binary attribute is used instead) called items. Let D be a set of transactions, where each transaction t is a set of items such that $\forall t \in D : t \subseteq I$. The transaction t supports an itemset X if it supports every element $x \in X$. In our case, I is the set of all products sold by the retail company, and a transaction t is a single invoice, with its list X of line items. The support of an itemset X is the ratio of the number of transactions containing the itemset (the number of invoices containing all members of X as line items) and the total number of transactions.

According to [1], an association rule is an implication of the form $X \rightarrow i_k$, where $X \subset I$, $i_k \in I$ and $i_k \notin X$, where X is a set of some items in I and is also called the antecedent, while i_k is a single item, which is not included in X and is also called consequent. The rule $X \rightarrow i_k$ has support s in the set of transactions D if s% of transactions in D contain $X \cup i_k$. The rule $X \rightarrow i_k$ holds confidence c in the transaction set D if c% of transactions that contain X also contain i_k. Actually, the value of confidence c corresponds to the probability $P(X|i_k)= P(X \cup i_k)/P(X)$. Thus, the rule $\{\text{milk}, \text{butter}\} \rightarrow \{\text{sugar}\}$, $c = 60\%$, $s = 2\%$ means that those three products appear together in 2% of all invoices and in 60% of invoices that contain line items milk and butter, the sugar line item appears as well.

There is an extended definition of association rules [2], which allows a multi-part consequent, $X \rightarrow Y$, where $X \subset I$, $Y \subset I$ and $X \cap Y = \emptyset$. However, in our case the order of items in a rule is considered unimportant from the users' point of view, i.e. rules $\{a, b\} \rightarrow \{c\}$, $\{a, c\} \rightarrow \{b\}$ and $\{a\} \rightarrow \{b, c\}$ are considered "equal". Therefore we only display rules with a single-part antecedent.

A standard association rules mining task is to find all association rules within a dataset whose confidence and/or support are equal or greater than certain threshold values.

3.1   Criteria of Interestingness

High support and confidence, though always important, cannot be the only criteria for interpreting the discovered rules. Rules with both the highest confidence and highest support, e.g. $\{\text{bread}\} \rightarrow \{\text{milk}\}$, generally imply something already known. There are several more measures (also called *criteria of interestingness*) that either describe the relevance of a rule or of the items it contains.

Lift [3] describes the predictive power of a rule. It is given by the following equation:

$$lift(X \rightarrow i_k) = \frac{P(X \bigcup i_k)}{P(X) \cdot P(i_k)}$$

The numerator gives the frequency of the transactions that contain both the antecedent and the consequent. The denominator gives the frequencies of the antecedent and the consequent, regarded as independent variables. Thus, when lift is greater than 1, then the resulting rule is better at predicting the result than guessing whether the resultant item is present, based on individual item frequencies. The higher lift of a rule, the bigger is its predictive power.

J-measure, $J(X \rightarrow i_k)$ (the entire formula is given in [9]), can be viewed as the cross-entropy between the binary variables defined by i_k with and without conditioning on the event X. J-measure is useful when we search for the rules with unexpected combinations of items.

Lift and J-measure are both statistical, domain-independent parameters that can be applied any time association rules are calculated. For our system, which analyzes market basket transactions in the retail sector, we introduce a domain-dependent heuristic measure called *price score*. This measure, which takes into account the prices of products within baskets, is defined as: $ps = J(X \rightarrow i_k) \cdot C$.

The parameter C is the sum of unit prices of all products that form the rule (both the antecedent and the consequent). It prefers rules that contain products with higher unit price. The reason why the *ps* measure does not consider the quantity of items contained in the transaction is explained in Section 4.4.

4   Software System Implementation

4.1   Requirements and Design

There are two basic requirements for designing a software architecture to implement our association rule mining framework using the Apriori algorithm. First, we want to enable organization managers to perform the analysis. Therefore, the user interface must be simple and intuitive and any data cleansing or filtering must be performed automatically. Second, the mining process is not performed locally, at the user's machine. The user is not required to install any client program, except the web browser. This leads to a distributed client-server architecture.

The software is implemented exclusively in Java (using J2EE platform [14]) as a three-tier web-application (Fig. 1).

The analysis must be performed in a reasonably short time. An average dataset consists of about one million transactions, containing a few million line items. There are about 200.000 products being sold. The process execution time of several hours is a long, but reasonable waiting period, still bearable for a decision maker and possible only if a powerful workstation with Random Access Memory capacity of several GB is available.

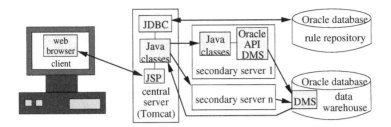

Fig. 1. Three-Tier software architecture for association rule mining

The rule discovering algorithm is performed within the Oracle 10g database that contains the target dataset, using its built-in data mining facility (DMS) [13] which can be accessed via Java API. In this way, we remove the possible bottleneck that appears every time the mining tool and the database are located on different machines (as in case of heavyweight commercial client tools).

The presentation and a part of the application logic are located on a middleware web server called *central server* (in our case, the Apache Tomcat [17]). Another, time-consuming part of the application logic can be performed parallelly on several *secondary* middleware *servers*. The Oracle database is situated on a separate data management server (Fig. 1). The user accesses the application using the internal web of the company. The request is transferred to the middleware server using HTTP. Thus, a web browser is the only program she/he needs to work with to reach the full functionally of the application.

Java Servlet [15] and JavaServer Pages [16] are used to implement the presentation logic. The application logic is implemented within a set of Java classes, using Java Database Connectivity (JDBC) to read the already discovered rules from the database.

4.2 Apriori Algorithm

The *Apriori* algorithm [2] is the most commonly used algorithm for discovering association rules. After the support and confidence thresholds have been determined, the algorithm first creates one-member itemsets. When generating two-member itemsets (and later n-member itemsets), we combine only those one-member (and later $(n\text{-}1)$-member) itemsets whose support exceeds the threshold value.

Oracle 10g data mining facility (DMS) also uses the Apriori algorithm for automatic discovery of association rules. The database is hosted at a Linux server with 2 Intel Xeon 2.4 GHz processors and 2GB of RAM.

4.3 Data Preparation

The source data is collected at POS (point of service) terminals of the retail company and then transferred to the data warehouse of the company. A data warehouse is a database specialized for historical analysis (OLAP and data mining), which contains nonvolatile data. The standard implementation of a data warehouse in relational databases consists of a fact table, which contains different measures and numerical data, and several dimensions, which contain description data used for selecting and filtering the data from the fact table [5]. The company warehouse stores all POS transactions that occurred during last few years.

Each row of the fact table is a separate line item of a transaction (Table 1), with information about the transaction ID, product quantity and income, as well as references to the three warehouse dimensions: time, product and store.

Table 1. Fact table with market basket line items

DATE	TRANSACTION ID	ITEM ID	STORE ID	QUANTITY	TOT INC
1.9.2005.	310904069	01593562	0123	0,63	27,54
1.9.2005.	**310904069**	**02824532**	**0123**	**1**	**13,56**
1.9.2005.	**310904069**	**02824532**	**0123**	**-1**	**-13,56**

The Apriori algorithm requires the input dataset to be given as set of < *transactionID*, *itemID*> pairs, with each line item in a separate row. This exactly corresponds to the structure of the warehouse fact table. However, the fact table contains all transaction records collected at POS terminals, which also includes the canceled transactions or parts of transactions.

An item may be canceled when an operator (cashier) at a POS terminal makes a mistake and registers a wrong product instead of the one being bought. Furthermore, cancelation must also be done if a customer, standing at the cash desk, suddenly changes her/his mind and decides not to buy a product. A canceled line item is registered with a negative value of *quantity* (the third row in Table 1, which cancels the second row).

Unless the canceled line items are removed from the mining dataset before the analysis starts, the results would falsely describe the consumers' behavior, habits and intentions. The dataset must contain only valid transactions. Therefore, we cannot mine the rules directly within the fact table (as in [6], where the richness of information in the dimensions of the warehouse is fully exploited), but need to create a secondary database structure (a view) that will only contain valid line items.

Each line item with a negative quantity value must have its positive value counterpart referencing the same item within the same transaction. For each distinct item in a transaction quantities are summed up. If the sum is positive, either no cancellations have been made, or the customer finally decided to buy a smaller quantity of the product (e.g. she/he took initially 4 packages, and later decided to take only 2). The sum zero indicates that the customer actually did not buy the item and all line items in the transaction referencing that item are excluded from the mining target dataset.

4.4   Algorithm Execution

Running the application in a web browser, the user is first asked to determine the dataset for the analysis. She/he can either define a new dataset by making a restriction on the time and the store dimension, or use an existing dataset. When a new dataset is defined, a view in the database with structure $<transactionID, itemID>$ is created automatically and data cleansing is performed: the view only contains data that describe valid transactions.

The Apriori algorithm has three input parameters: (1) minimum support, $minSupp$, and (2) minimum confidence, $minConf$, of the resulting rules, as well as (3) the maximum number of items in the rules. We always set the last parameter to five. There is a finite number of association rules in a dataset (each single transaction is actually a rule), but the algorithm returns only those whose support and confidence are higher than $minSupp$, and $minConf$, respectively.

We call the rules that result from performing the Apriori algorithm against a specific dataset a *model*. Many models can be created over the same dataset and they may share some of the rules, depending on the values of $minSupp$, and $minConf$ thresholds. Table 2 shows some of the rules that exist in a dataset, while Table 3 shows three models created over the dataset, their threshold parameters and which rules from Table 2 they contain. Obviously, if both threshold parameters of model B have higher values than the threshold parameters of model A $(minSupp_B > minSupp_A$ and $minConf_B > minConf_A)$, the rules contained in model B are a subset of rules contained in model A. Thus, if model A already exists and we want to create model B, we can copy the existing rules without executing the algorithm, which shortens the model creation process about 10-15 times. On the other hand, if only model B exists and we want to create model A, the algorithm must be executed. Models A and C $(minSupp_A > minSupp_C$ and $minConf_A < minConf_C)$ share a common intersect, but none of them is a subset of another.

Table 2. Rules existing in a dataset

Rule id	Support	Confidence	(Items)
1	0.0027	0.64	....
2	0.0032	0.42	....
3	0.0014	0.76	....
4	0.0021	0.52	....

Before executing the Apriori algorithm in the database, the application logic must create some mining-specific Java objects (called function settings), which may take even more than half an hour. The object creation is thus performed parallelly in case there are several mining tasks (Fig. 1).

After the algorithm execution, the rules are stored in the database as a set of metadata. The discovered rules can be retrieved from the database server (i.e. DMS) using a recursive algorithm, which may last, depending on the number of rules and items they contain, even for several minutes. Once a model has been generated, the user would find it very annoying to wait for several minutes each time she/he wants to view the model. Therefore, we created a secondary repository of the rule metadata, which can be accessed momentarily. The rules are transferred to the secondary repository as soon as the Apriori algorithm execution is over. Rules considered "equal" from the users' point of view (e.g. $\{a, b\} \rightarrow \{c\}$ and $\{a, c\} \rightarrow \{b\}$) are merged into one, displaying the rule with the highest value of confidence (their supports are always equal). The algorithm execution generally lasts about 15 or 20 times longer than the rule transfer.

Table 3. Different models produced by analyzing the same dataset

Model ID	MinSupp	MinConf	Rule set
A	0.0020	0.4	1,2,4
B	0.0024	0.5	1
C	0.0012	0.6	1,3

It would be possible to distinguish between the rules that contain different quantities of an item (e.g. {2 kg apples}→{2 kg pears} and {3 kg apples}→{1 kg pears}, i.e. to define an item as a combination of *productID* and *quantity*. However, our experiments on real data show that in this case too many rules would be produced, each of them having an extremely low support. We note the appearance of an item in the basket (i.e. transaction), not the quantity. This is the reason why the quantity of a product in the transaction is ignored when calculating the *price score*.

4.5   Product Taxonomy

The generic three-level taxonomy in the product dimension reflects the retailer's organizational perspective. The three levels are product (e.g. 1 L of milk, with 3% fat, in a plastic bottle, produced by company A), subcategory (e.g. milk products) and category (e.g. food). One subcategory contains many different products and one category contains many subgroups. The opportunity to perform the mining analysis at all taxonomy levels has been specified as a basic user request. When performing the data cleansing, we create a basic database view for the product level (Section 4.3.), but also two additional aggregated views for the subcategory and category level. Obviously, a model created at the subcategory or category level will contain a smaller number of rules with a higher (and much more significant) support value, as the total number of items is much smaller (Table 4). These results are, in general, more useful than those at the product level because the management is more interested in customers' habits concerning a subcategory or category than some particular products.

Table 4. Parameters considering different levels of the product taxonomy

Taxonomy level	**PRODUCT**	**SUBCATEGORY**	**CATEGORY**
Allowed minSupp value	0.0001-0.0010	0.0010-0.0100	≥0.01
Average alg. execution time	40 minutes-5 hours	10-30 minutes	several minutes

The algorithm execution time will also be significantly shorter (values in Table 4 are given for real datasets described at the beginning of Section 4).

4.6 Rule Presentation

Fig. 2 shows a snapshot of the user interface, presenting the rules of an analysis that was performed at the individual product level. The rules can be sorted by the 5 parameters mentioned in Section 3.1 (support, confidence, lift, J-measure, price score) in the ascending or descending order. For each rule the RuleID, the antecedent (in our interface noted as "IF"), the consequent ("THEN"), support (in Croatian: "Značaj"), confidence ("Pouzdanost"), "Lift", "JMeasure" and "Price Score" are displayed.

The application reads the rules from the secondary repository (Section 4.5), using the JDBC interface.

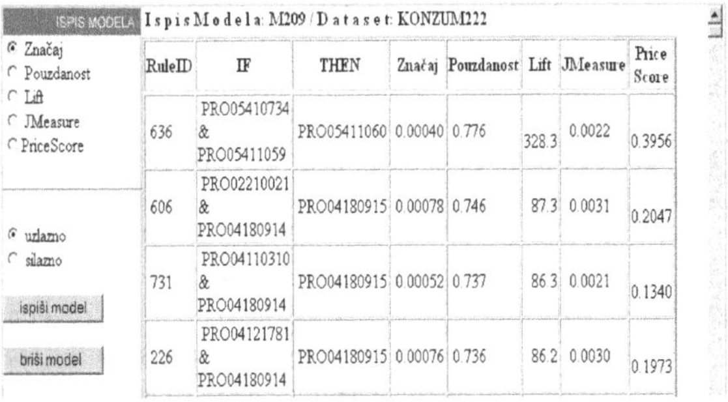
ISPIS MODELA
Ispis Modela: M209 / Dataset: KONZUM222
Značaj
Pouzdanost
Lift
JMeasure
PriceScore
uzlazno
silazno
ispiši model
briši model
RuleID
IF
THEN
Značaj
Pouzdanost
Lift
JMeasure
Price Score
636
PRO05410734 & PRO05411059
PRO05411060
0.00040
0.776
328.3
0.0022
0.3956
606
PRO02210021 & PRO04180914
PRO04180915
0.00078
0.746
87.3
0.0031
0.2047
731
PRO04110310 & PRO04180914
PRO04180915
0.00052
0.737
86.3
0.0021
0.1340
226
PRO04121781 & PRO04180914
PRO04180915
0.00076
0.736
86.2
0.0030
0.1973

Fig. 2. Rules of a model presented in a web browser

5 Conclusion

This paper presents a three-tier architecture for discovering market basket association rules, designed to be used by the decision makers and business analysts, and not only the data mining experts. The architecture is implemented as a Java web application.

The user initiates and manages a mining process by interactively using the web browser interface. The target dataset is extracted from the data warehouse fact table at the user's request, after which the data cleansing is performed automatically. It is possible to analyze data at three levels of product taxonomy: single product, product subcategory and product category. The discovered rules can be sorted by four standard domain-independent, statistical parameters. Additionally, we introduce a domain-dependent parameter called price score, which takes into account the market value of the basket.

The Apriori algorithm, used for rule discovery, is executed within the source database, while the only client tool is a web browser. In this way, no data transfer to the client is needed and we avoid the standard bottleneck that is present when the commercial heavyweight client programs are used.

References

1. Agrawal, R., Imielinski, T., Swami, A.: Mining Association Rules between Sets of Items in Large Databases. In: Proc. 1993 ACM SIGMOD. ACM Press, New York (1993) 207-216.
2. Agrawal, R., Srikant, R.: Fast Algorithms for Mining Association Rules. In: Proc. VLDB Conf. (VLDB'94). Morgan Kaufmann, S. Francisco (1994) 487-499
3. Berry, M.J.A., Linoff G.S.: Data Mining Techniques for Marketing, Sales, and Customer Relationship Management. 2nd edn. Wiley Publishing Inc., Indianapolis (2004)
4. Brin, S., Motwani, R., Ullman, J.D., Tsur, S.: Dynamic Itemset Counting and Implication Rules for Market Basket Data. In: Proc. ACM SIGMOD Int. Conf. on Management of Data. SIGMOD Record, Vol. 26 (2), ACM Press, New York (1997) 255-264
5. Kimball, R., Ross, M.: The Data Warehouse Toolkit, The Complete Guide to Dimensional Modeling. 2nd edn. John Wiley & Sons, New York (2002)
6. Nestorov, S., Jukic, N.: Ad-Hoc Association-Rule Mining within the Data Warehouse. In: Abstract Proc. Hawaii Int. Conf. on System Sciences (HICSS'03), IEEE Computer Society Press (2003) 232, http://people.cs.uchicago.edu/~evtimov/pubs/hicss03.pdf
7. Ma, Y., Liu, B., Wong, C.K.: Web for Data Mining: Organizing and Interpreting the Discovered Rules Using the Web. SIGKDD Explorations, Vol. 2 (1). ACM Press, New York (2000) 16-23
8. Zaky, M.J., Parthasarathy, S., Ogihara, M., Li, W.: New Algorithm for Fast Discovery of Association Rules. Technical Report No. 261, University of Rochester (1997), http://cs.aue.aau.dk/contribution/projects/datamining/papers/tr651.pdf
9. Hand, D., Manilla, H., Smyth,P.: Principles of Data Mining, MIT Press, Cambridge-London (2001)
10. Han, J., Pei, J., Yin, Y.: Mining frequent patterns without candidate generation. In: Proc. ACM-SIGMOD Int. Conf. on Management of Data. ACM Press, New York (2000) 1-12
11. Pejaković, I., Skočir, Z., Medved, D.: Descriptive Data Mining Modeling in Telecom Systems. In: Proc. Int. Conf. on Software, Telecommunicatins and Computer Networks (SoftCom 2004), University of Split, Split (2004) 199-203
12. Weka 3. Data Mining Software in Java. Version 3.4. University of Waikato (2003) http://www.cs.waikato.ac.nz/ml/weka/
13. Oracle Data Mining Concepts 10g Release 1 (10.1). Oracle Corporation (2003) http://oraclelon1.oracle.com/docs/pdf/B10698_ 01.pdf
14. Java 2 Platform, Enterprise Edition, http://java.sun.com/j2ee/
15. Java Servlet Specification, version 2.4. Sun Microsystems (2003) http://java.sun.com/products/servlet/download.html
16. JavaServer Pages Specification, version 2.0. Sun Microsystems (2003) http://java.sun.com/products/jsp/reference/api/index.html
17. Apache Tomcat Servlet/JSP Container, version 5.5, The Apache Software Foundation (2005) http://tomcat.apache.org/
18. JWAWE. http://www.vni.com/products/wave/jwave/index.html

Automatic Lung Nodule Detection Using Template Matching

Serhat Ozekes[1] and A. Yilmaz Camurcu[2]

[1] Istanbul Commerce University, Ragip Gumuspala Cad. No: 84 Eminonu 34378
Istanbul, Turkey
`serhat@iticu.edu.tr`
[2] Marmara University, Goztepe, 81040, Istanbul, TURKEY
`camurcu@marmara.edu.tr`

Abstract. We have developed a computer-aided detection system for detecting lung nodules, which generally appear as circular areas of high opacity on serial-section CT images. Our method detected the regions of interest (ROIs) using the density values of pixels in CT images and scanning the pixels in 8 directions by using various thresholds. Then to reduce the number of ROIs the amounts of change in their locations based on the upper and the lower slices were examined, and finally a nodule template based algorithm was employed to categorize the ROIs according to their morphologies. To test the system's efficiency, we applied it to 276 normal and abnormal CT images of 12 patients with 153 nodules. The experimental results showed that using three templates with diameters 8, 14 and 20 pixels, the system achieved 91%, 94% and 95% sensitivities with 0.7, 0.98 and 1.17 false positives per image respectively.

1 Introduction

The mortality rate for lung cancer is higher than that for other kinds of cancers around the world [1], [2]. At the same time, it appears that the rate has been steadily increasing. Of all the types of cancer, lung cancer is the most common cause of death and accounts for about 28% of all cancer deaths. At the same time, it appears that the rate has been steadily increasing. No smoking is considered the most effective way to reduce the incidence of lung cancer in most countries, while detection of suspicious lesions in the early stages of cancer can be considered the most effective way to improve survival.

Several template-based CAD methods have been proposed to detect abnormalities in medical images. Ozekes *et al.* [3] developed an automated mass detection algorithm using mass templates. ROIs were scanned with templates to find the shapes similar to the templates. The similarity was controlled using two thresholds. The results of this experiment showed that using the templates with diameters 10, 20 and 30 pixels achieved sensitivities of 93%, 90% and 81% with 1.3, 0.7 and 0.33 false positives per image respectively. Betke *et al.* [4] proposed a system to detect anatomical landmarks, in particular, the trachea, sternum and spine, using an attenuation-based template matching approach.

T. Yakhno and E. Neuhold (Eds.): ADVIS 2006, LNCS 4243, pp. 247–253, 2006.

The surface transformation was applied to align nodules in the initial CT scan with nodules in the follow-up scan. For 56 out of 58 nodules in the initial CT scans of 10 patients, nodule correspondences in the follow-up scans were established correctly. Lee et al. [5] proposed a novel template-matching technique based on a genetic algorithm (GA) template matching (GATM) for detecting nodules existing within the lung area. The GA was used to determine the target position in the observed image efficiently and to select an adequate template image from several reference patterns for quick template matching. 71 nodules out of 98 were correctly detected with the number of false positives at approximately 1.1/sectional image. Farag et al. [6] proposed an algorithm for nodule detection using deformable 3D and 2D templates describing typical geometry and gray level distribution within the nodules of the same type. The detection combines normalized cross-correlation template matching by genetic optimization and Bayesian post-classification. The final number of the TPNs became 107 out of 130 giving the overall correct detection rate of 82.3% with the FPN rate of 9.2%.

In this study, we designed a CAD system for lung nodule detection in CT images. Using the density values of pixels in slices and scanning these pixels in 8 directions with distance thresholds, ROIs were found. In order to classify the ROIs, a location change thresholding was used followed by a template matching based algorithm. Hence, the true lung nodules were detected successfully.

2 Materials and Methods

The primary challenge for radiologists and CAD systems alike for lung tumor detection is that, in serial sectional images, there are many objects that have the same appearance and pixel intensity as tumor nodules. In a serial-section slice, a cylindrical vessel can appear circular, and many vessels in the lung have a similar diameter to the lesions of interest. A primary failing point of all the CAD systems referenced above is that they depend upon a first-pass detection of candidates based on 2D image features, producing hundreds of first-pass candidates.

The approach described herein was motivated by the observation that experienced radiologists screen for lung lesions not by considering individual image slices independently, but by paging through the image stack looking for 3D appearance characteristics that distinguish tumors from vessels. On consecutive images, vessels maintain a similar cross-sectional size and their in-plane circular appearance appears to drift across the viewing screen from one slice to the next, following the tortuous anatomy of the vessel. True lung nodules, in contrast, appear seemingly out of nowhere as circular objects that remain at approximately the same on-screen location from slice to slice. Their size quickly increases and then just as rapidly decreases and the tumor disappears after a few slices.

For the development and evaluation of the proposed system we used the Lung Image Database Consortium (LIDC) database [7]. When the data set is examined, it is determined that density values of the nodules are between "*minimum density threshold*" and "*maximum density threshold*" values.

2.1   Regions of Interest Specification Methods

Pixels, which form the candidate lung nodule region, must be members of a set of adjacent neighbour pixels with densities between *"minimum density threshold"* and *"maximum density threshold"* values. It has been observed that diameters of lung nodules are between upper and lower boundaries. So, to understand whether a pixel is in the center region of the shape, first, diameter of the shape (assuming the pixel in question is the center) should be considered. In this stage, we introduce two thresholds which form the boundaries. As seen in Figure 1, one is the *"minimum distance threshold"* representing the lower boundary and the other is the *"maximum distance threshold"* representing the upper boundary.

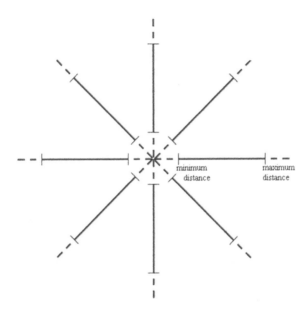

Fig. 1. Minimum and maximum distance thresholds in 8 directions

If a pixel has adjacent neighbours that are less than *"minimum distance threshold"* or more than *"maximum distance threshold"* in 8 directions, it could be concluded that this pixel couldn't be a part of candidate lung nodule. Otherwise, it could be a part of candidate lung nodule. The values of minimum and maximum distance thresholds are dealt with the resolution of the CT image. These thresholds are used to avoid very big or very small structures such as parts of chest bones or heart and vertical vessels. Thus the black and white image of ROIs was obtained showing ROIs in black.

2.2   First Classification Using the Location Change Measurement

On serial images, vessels maintain a similar cross-sectional size and their in-plane circular appearance changes its location. But the true lung nodules, remain at approximately the same on-screen location from slice to slice. In this step, to classify the ROIs the proposed CAD system measured the amount of location changes of ROIs in serial sections. To specify the locations, ROIs of the serial sections were labeled using connected component labeling. For a ROI which was under investigation, its eucledian distances to the ROIs in the upper and the lower slices were calculated. The minimums of these distances ($Ed_{minupper}$ and $Ed_{minlower}$) were compared with the "location change threshold" and each of the candidates was classified according to the following decision rule.

IF $Ed_{minupper} > T_{lc}$ OR $Ed_{minlower} > T_{lc}$ THEN
    normal
ELSE
    nodule candidate

where $Ed_{minupper}$ and $Ed_{minlower}$ are the amounts of location change of the ROI based on the upper slice and the lower slice respectively. T_{lc} is a threshold value. If the ROI was classified as a normal structure then it was removed. Thus the new image of ROIs was obtained with reduced number of ROIs.

2.3 Second Classification Using the Template Matching Based Algorithm

To distinguish true lung nodules from normal structures by using their morphologies lung nodule templates was used. Each pixel of CT images was scanned with nodule templates and was looked for whether there was a shape similar to the nodule in the template, so too small, too thin and too long shapes were removed. If a similar one was detected then appropriate pixels of the shape were recorded as a part of a true lung nodule. This template is formed of black and white pixels. While black pixels represent a lung nodule, white pixels represent pixels having density values outside of the interval from "minimum density threshold" to "maximum density threshold" values. The similarity was controlled using two thresholds.

The slice under investigation was scanned pixel by pixel starting from top left. During this scan, we identified each pixel with the top left pixel of the nodule template. In this identification we compared each and every pixel of the image of ROIs with the pixels of the template and looked for the similarity. Figure 2c demonstrates the use of a template with dimensions 8 X 8 pixels (see figure 2a) to detect a true lung nodule (see figure 2b). In this comparison two kinds of error was occured. One is called the error of white pixels ($E_{whitepixels}$) that is the number of white pixels in the template which are actually black in image of ROIs (see dark grey pixels in figure 2c) and the other one is called the error of black pixels ($E_{blackpixels}$) that is the number of black pixels in the template which are actually white in image of ROIs (see grey pixels in figure 2c). For each pixel of image of ROIs by using these errors, we looked for shapes similar to the nodule in the template. The similarity was considered using two thresholds which were white error threshold ($T_{whiteerror}$) and black error threshold ($T_{blackerror}$).

We defined the following rules and chose the threshold values to avoid small, thin and long shapes.

IF $E_{whitepixels} > T_{whiteerror}$ AND $E_{blackpixels} < T_{blackerror}$ THEN
    nodule
ELSE
    normal

If a similar shape was detected then the coordinates of the black pixels of the shape which were also black in the template were recorded. These coordinates formed a part of a true lung nodule. After searching the image of ROIs pixel by pixel with the template and recording the coordinates of nodule patterns, the true lung nodules were detected.

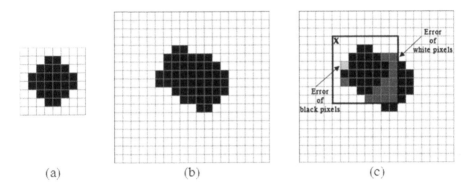

(a)   (b)   (c)

Fig. 2. (a) Nodule template, (b) true lung nodule, (c) detecting a part of a nodule using the template

3   Results

For the evaluation of the proposed system we used the LIDC database [7]. To test the system's efficiency, we applied it to 123 normal and 153 abnormal images of 12 clinical cases with 153 nodules. At first, 4896 ROIs were specified by the ROI specification methods. By the first classification using the location change measurement the numbers of ROIs were reduced to 1254. And finally the second classification was performed using three different templates whose diameters were 8, 14 and 20 pixels.

Scanning the ROIs with these templates, different false positive rates were achieved, which are shown in figure 3. Figure 4 shows the free-response receiver operating characteristic (FROC) curve which is a plot of operating points showing the tradeoff between the true positive rates versus the average number of false positives per image.

Using the template with dimensions 8 X 8 pixels, 91% sensitivity achieved with an average of 0.7 false positives per image. With the template whose diameter

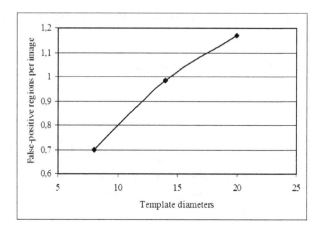

Fig. 3. Curve of the false-positive regions per image versus the template diameters

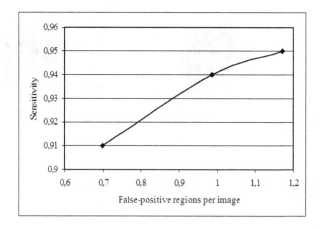

Fig. 4. FROC curve showing the performance of the nodule detection task

was 14 pixels, 94% sensitivity achieved with an average of 0.98 false positives per image. Using the template with dimensions 20 X 20 pixels, 95% sensitivity achieved with an average of 1.17 false positives per image. An example of the ROI classified as nodule is shown in figure 5a, and the detected nodule in the original CT image is shown in figure 5b.

Consequently, the experimental results showed that as template size increases, the false positive rate and the sensitivity increase. With its high sensitivity the present system has the potential to improve doctors' diagnostic performances.

4   Conclusion

A new scheme has been proposed to automatically detect lung nodules in CT images. Morphological analysis of nodules was facilitated by computerized techniques.

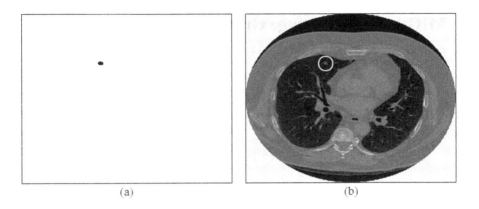

(a)   (b)

Fig. 5. (a) The classified ROI as lung nodule, (b) the detected lung nodule

We presented the effectiveness of our system by applying it to patient's data and comparing the results with the second look reviews of 6 expert lung radiologists. The results showed that the proposed CAD system was an effective assistant for human experts to detect nodule patterns and provide a valuable "second opinion" to the human observer.

References

1. Greenlee, R. T., Nurray, T., Bolden, S., Wingo, P. A.: Cancer statistics 2000, CA Cancer J. Clin., 50 (2000) 7-33
2. Health and Welfare Statistics Association, J. Health Welfare Stat., 46 (1999) 50-51
3. Ozekes, S., Osman, O., Camurcu, A.Y.: Mammographic Mass Detection Using A Mass Template, Korean J Radiol, 6 (2005) 221-228
4. Betke, M., Hong, H., Thomas, D., Prince C., Ko, JP.: Landmark detection in the chest and registration of lung surfaces with an application to nodule registration, Med Image Anal., 7 (2003) 265-281
5. Lee, Y., Hara, T., Fujita, H., Itoh, S., Ishigaki, T.: Automated detection of pulmonary nodules in helical CT images based on an improved template-matching technique, IEEE Trans Med Imaging, 20 (2001) 595-604
6. Farag, A.A., El-Baz, A., Gimel'farb, G., Falk R.: Detection and recognition of lung abnormalities using deformable templates, Proceedings of the 17th International Conference on Pattern Recognition, 3 (2004) 738 - 741
7. Samuel, G., Armato, III., Geoffrey, M., Michael, F., Charles, R., David, Y., et al.: Lung image database consortium -Developing a resource for the medical imaging research community, Radiology, (2004) 739-748

MIGP: Medical Image Grid Platform Based on HL7 Grid Middleware*

Hai Jin, Aobing Sun, Qin Zhang, Ran Zheng, and Ruhan He

Cluster and Grid Computing Lab
Huazhong University of Science and Technology, Wuhan, 430074, China
hjin@hust.edu.cn

Abstract. MIGP (*Medical Image Grid Platform*) realizes information retrieval and integration in extensive distributed medical information systems, which adapts to the essential requirement for the development of healthcare information infrastructure. But the existing MIGPs, which are constructed mostly based on database middleware, are very difficult to guarantee local hospital data security and remote accessing legality. In this paper, a MIGP based on the WSRF-compliant HL7 (*Health Level 7*) grid middleware is proposed, which aims to combine the existing HL7 protocol and grid technology to realize medical data and image retrieval through the communications and interoperations with different hospital information systems. We also design the architecture and bring forward a metadata-based scheduling mechanism for our grid platforms. At last, experimental MIGPs are constructed to evaluate the performance of our method.

1 Introduction

With the development of information technology, there are many different medical information systems, such as HIS (*Hospital Information System*) serving as a whole, and lower level systems like PACS (*Picture Archiving and Communications System*), CIS (*Clinic Information System*) and RIS (*Radiology Information System*). They support each other to share medical information in one hospital efficiently [1]. As the medical researches depend heavily on abundant and extensive patient records and medical cases, new technology or platform should imminently be brought forward to realize medical information retrieval and integration among different information systems. But various hospital information systems, which have no uniform transport standard, data format and message type, hamper the researches and make the task impossible.

HL7 protocol, which was brought out in 1987 and is ANSI-accredited standards, has been widely accepted by healthcare industries to provide a comprehensive framework and related references for the retrieval, integration, and exchange of electronic health information within one hospital or between hospitals [2]. Unfortunately, the medical application environment is very complicated and heterogeneous. Most hospital

---

* This paper is supported by China Next Generation Internet (CNGI) project under grant No.CNGI-04-15-7A.

T. Yakhno and E. Neuhold (Eds.): ADVIS 2006, LNCS 4243 , pp. 254–263, 2006.

information systems have no interfaces to support HL7 or stick on the old HL7 version. In this paper, we propose a MIGP based on HL7 grid middleware, which extents the HL7 protocol and also support DICOM (*Digital Image Communication in Medicine*) protocol, to realize medical information exchange and sharing among different hospitals' information systems widely.

The rest of this paper is organized as follows: the next section introduces the related works. Section 3 presents our HL7 grid middleware. The framework, topology and scheduling mechanism of the MIGP are presented in section 4. Simple experimental MIGP based on different middleware is described in section 5. Finally, we draw the conclusions and give out the future works in section 6.

2 Related Works

MIGP aims to make full use of grid superiorities and realize medical researches, collaborations and services widely [3]. There are some successful applications of MIGP. For example, eDiaMoND[4] addresses linking the medical databases of different BCUs (*Breast Care Units*) all over UK to support the census of breast cancer based on OGSA-DAI, shown in Fig1.a. OGSA-DAI is a middleware which supports the exposure of data resources, such as relational or XML databases, over grids [5]. MammoGrid tries to develop an European-wide database of mammograms belonged to different institutes and hospitals, which provides a virtual file catalogue to allow transparent access among distributed databases [6]. But all of them can not deal with information exchange among numerous hospital information systems at different places to build an extensive healthcare information infrastructure. We focus on constructing our MIGP, which adopts the HL7 protocol as the standard to communicate with information systems in different hospitals, to realize information retrieval and avoid the direct database operations.

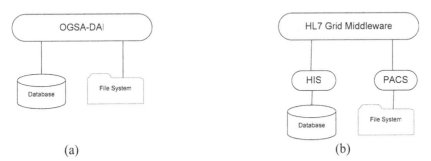

(a)   (b)

Fig. 1. Database and File System Access Modes in MIGP Based on Different Middleware (a) OGSA-DAI Based. (b) HL7 Grid Middleware Based.

3 HL7 Grid Middleware

HL7 v.3.0 adopts HDF (*HL7 Development Framework*) and RIM (*Reference Information Model*), which define a flexible structure for the standard to be applied or extended. Furthermore, it adds an encoding definition for the protocol by using *Extensible Markup Language* (XML) to describe the grammar or syntax of the healthcare language [7].

3.1 HL7 Grid Message

The intercommunication among grid nodes is realized through HL7 grid message. The HL7 grid message format consists of a payload, the medical data, along with several wrappers shown in Fig.2. The transmission wrapper contains the construction for message identification, addressing and reliability, which duplicates some features in the WS-stack Message [8]. The medical data are wrapped in SOAP/XML message, which can be transported over secure HTTP within the grid. HL7 grid message does not contain any message formats, just a toolbox for making message formats, so we have to provide a localized HL7 format definition with the actual XML schema to be used. The medical image data can also be encapsulated in a SOAP message together with medical data of other types. It replaces the separated transfer means (such as GridFTP) based on RPC (*Remote Procedure Call*) and makes the medical information exchange and monitoring more efficiently.

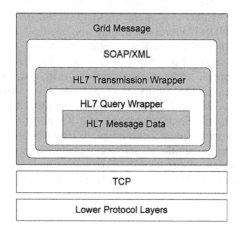

Fig. 2. HL7 Grid Message Layered Structure

3.2 HL7 Grid Middleware Modules

In order to support hospital information systems (e.g. HIS or PACS) which have no HL7 interface or stick on HL7 old version, the existing HL7 v.3.0 protocol must be extended to realize data format and message version transformation, and able to choose different protocols to communicate with. Based on HL7 v.3.0 tools [9] and other developing toolkits such as chameleon [10], we realize the basic modules of the middleware, shown in Fig.3. Their specifications are listed as follows:

Interface Module. It realizes the format translation between user data format and HL7 XML, or parses users request to HL7 message, to make the communication complied with HL7 standard among different HL7 nodes.

Data Validation Module. It checks the medical data to be sent within the MIGP, and guarantees its format complied with HL7 standard. The module can also check the content of a message to insure its layer structure is correct.

Control Module. It supports all kinds of messages and trigger events of HL7 such as doctor's advice checkup, user query and user modification, and can process different

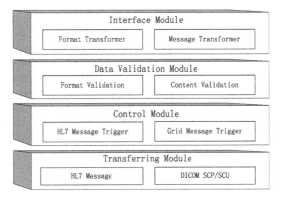

Fig. 3. HL7 Grid Middleware Modules

type messages with user defined or system functions. We also extend the message and trigger event sets of HL7 to support grid environment. It can form different message queues for the incoming and outgoing messages of a hospital, and assign different priorities to the message queues needed to be responded.

Transferring Module. It supports TCP/IP and SOAP protocol, and can send HL7 message to other HL7 nodes with the HL7 Grid Middleware installed, or receive messages from them. But the transferring message format must comply with the HL7 grid message format. It also supports the DICOM protocol and can retrieve DICOM files from PACS of different hospitals.

4 MIGP Based on HL7 Grid Middleware

4.1 MIGP Framework Based on HL7 Grid Middleware

Our MIGP is built on existing WS (*Web Service*) technology. The framework of the MIGP is shown in Fig.4. All kinds of grid resources such as hospital information

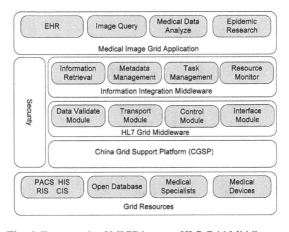

Fig. 4. Framework of MIGP base on HL7 Grid Middleware

systems (as HIS, PACS, RIS and CIS), open medical databases, medical specialists and devices lie in the lowest layer. The various gird resources are administrated by CGSP (*ChinaGrid Support Platform* [11]) which is the base of our MIGP to provide generic interface. Our *HL7 Grid Middleware* realizes the communication among different grid nodes. Above is our information integration middleware, which is another middleware we develop for MIGP and responsible for task administration or scheduling, available resources monitoring and metadata management. The layer on top of Fig.4 consists of our MIGP applications include EHR (*Electronic Health Record*), medical image query, medical data mining and epidemic research.

4.2 MIGP Topology Based on HL7 Grid Middleware

With the supports of our MIGP, we can connect the information systems belonged to different hospitals together to constitute a large-scale grid. Any certificated hospital can register their local information service as WS in the grid and users can utilize the platform to find the proper resource he needs. The topology of one domain of the grid is shown in Fig. 5. Every domain of the grid has a *MIGP Domain Center* (MIGP DC) to serve and manage the whole domain. The other parts of the domain include numerous hospitals as information sources. The main components in one domain are shown as follows:

Portal Server. It works as the gate of the MIGP to provide WS list (i.e. hospital list) for users, accept their requests and deliver the processing result to them at last through JSP web pages.

Central Server. Supported by the *HL7 Grid Middleware* and *Information Integration Middleware*, it works as the administrator of one domain, and also the executants or scheduler of user requests. When computing or storage ability of one central server is

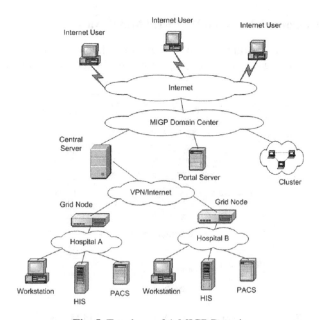

Fig. 5. Topology of A MIGP Domain

not enough for processing users' demand, it can utilize the resources of the cluster connected with the MIGP DC.

Grid Node. Every hospital uses one node as a grid node. The grid node works as information provider of the grid, and also as an agent to access the HIS or PACS to retrieve the medical information with the support of the *HL7 Grid Middleware*. The grid node can be regarded as a user of hospital information systems. Different grid users from Internet or inside of the current hospital have different authorization to access information systems. The hospital can control data security level through software configuration on the grid node.

HL7 Grid Middleware realizes communication between different grid nodes with message transferring mechanism shown in Fig. 6. How the MIGP works can be demonstrated with an information retrieval example as following steps:

Step 1. Internet users acquire WS list through the portal server to access the central server. Hospital workstation users can acquire it from the central server directly.

Step 2. Users select WS (i.e. hospitals) needed to be queried from the list, and submit information requests to the central server. Supported by HL7 grid middleware, the central server then generates a task for the user request, which divides the task into subtasks and assigns them to different grid nodes of selected hospitals through HL7 grid message.

Step 3. The *HL7 Grid Middleware* on the hospital grid node responds the HL7 message. If local HIS does not support HL7 interface, it transforms the request from HL7 message to local data format to be parsed by local HIS, and submits the translation result to it; else it transfers the HL7 message to local HIS directly.

Step 4. Local HIS processes the user request and acquires the results from its database, then returns them to the grid node. The *HL7 Grid Middleware* on the grid node transforms the result format to HL7 XML if needed and parses it to find whether the results include image link (e.g. a DICOM ID). If medical images are requested, DICOM ID is submitted to PACS and medical image files are retrieved.

Step 5. The hospital grid nodes return the results including medical images through HL7 message to the central server. The central server then integrates the data and images from different hospitals, and returns them to the user through the portal server or to the hospital workstation directly.

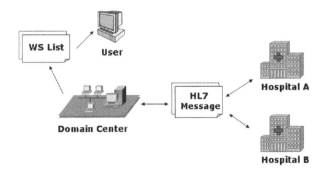

Fig. 6. Information Retrieval Based on HL7 Message Transferring

4.3 Metadata-Based Scheduling Mechanism

We design a metadata-based scheduling mechanism. The metadata includes two kinds of tables to assist task scheduling, and the structure of the tables recording the information about tasks and their subtasks are shown in Fig.7.

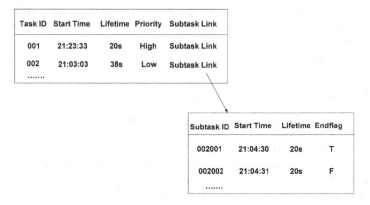

Fig. 7. Metadata Tables Recording Information about Tasks and Their Subtasks

Task Table. After one task is taken out of the task queue and performed on MIGP. The platform creates an item in the metadata task table for it, which records its initial information. After the task is finished or forced to exit due to exhaust its lifetime, its item on the table needs to be deleted.

Subtask Table. Once central server subdivides one task into subtasks and assigns them to different grid nodes, a subtask table is created and the task table's subtask link to point the subtask table is modified. Before a task item is deleted from the task table, its subtask table also needs to be erased.

There are three kinds of WS programs shown in Fig.8 to fulfill task scheduling on the central server of MIGP:

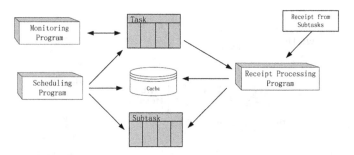

Fig. 8. The Metadata-based Scheduling Mechanism

Scheduling Program. After the user request is parsed, the scheduling program registers the task in metadata task table. It searches the cache to find useable information without beong queried again and checks metadata to locate the usable WS resources. Then it subdivides the task to subtasks which are necessary to be submitted to the hospital grid nodes, and update metadata task table and subtask table. After these works are finished, it exits directly.

Receipt Processing Program. When one of the hospital grid nodes finishes its subtask, it sends out a receipt to the central server to call the receipt processing program: (1) the program checks the metadata task table to find whether the task which assigned the subtask exists. If the task is still running then the program starts to accept the result from the grid node; otherwise the program reckons an error has happened during the task executing, so it gives up the results from the grid node and exit directly. (2) After the central server accepts the data and images from the grid node, it updates the cache which can accelerate the later queries. (3) If the subtask is confirmed as the last one of all subtasks to be finished after checking up subtasks table, the program then integrates all results from different hospitals, returns them to the user and deletes the task item on metadata task table to finish the whole task; otherwise it can update the end flag of itself on the subtask table and exit to release the resources that it occupies.

Monitoring Program. The platform can maintain a monitoring program running constantly which can monitor all the tasks and force the tasks exit whose lifetimes are exhausted to avoid the failed tasks can not exit automatically.

The metadata-based scheduling mechanism avoids maintaining a special program for every request, and takes system error into account adequately. So it can save the resource cost, schedule tasks more efficiently and serve more users simultaneously.

5   Experimental Platforms of the MIGP

We construct a MIGP based on HL7 grid middleware to evaluate the performance of our method. The grid owns two domains and every domain has 2 hospitals, and grid

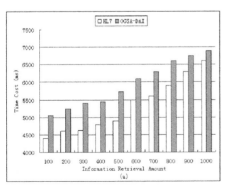
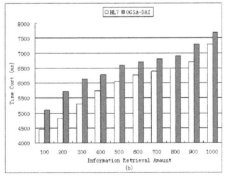

Fig. 9. MIGPs Performances Contrast Based on Different Grid Middleware (a) Information Retrieval in One Domain (b) Information Retrieval in Two Domains

nodes can intercommunicate with its local HIS and PACS produced by different companies (GE or HP), to simulate an actual application environment. The experiments results show that our MIGP based on the HL7 grid middleware can realize medical image and data retrieval successfully through interoperations and communications with different hospital information systems.

Another experimental MIGP is also constructed to achieve medical information retrieval in the same conditions as above but based on the middleware OGSA-DAI, which can access medical database directly [11]. The performances of the two grids processing the same tasks are shown in Fig.9. Due to the occurrence of random bandwidth conflict when several subtasks return results simultaneously, the histogram on Fig.9 all have no apparent linear trend. But contrasted with OGSA-DAI based MIGP, our MIGP costs less time for the same tasks and needs not to reprogram for the functions that have been realized in HIS and PACS.

6   Conclusions and Future Work

The MIGP based on HL7 grid middleware, which avoid the direct medical database accessing, guarantees the information security by HL7 protocol and grid security mechanism together, and makes full use of existing hospital information systems, has more chances to be used widely. The combination of our realization means with semantic grid technology in the future will increase the efficiency of resource locating and verification remarkably, which is also our research goal of next step. With the popularization of HL7 protocol, more and more hospital information systems will comply with the standard, and the MIGP will have more sources to provide all kinds of medical information for patients and doctors. Furthermore, with the deployment of other medical application middleware such as telemedicine and medical collaboration diagnosis, the MIGP will become the entrance of medical information and services to serve the whole society. Certainly, the successes of MIGP will change the lives and work styles of people.

References

1. V. Breton, P. Clarysse, Y. Gaudeau, and T. Glatard, "Grid-enabling medical image analysis", *Journal of Clinical Monitoring and Computing*, pp.339-349, Oct. 2005.
2. C. H. Yang, H. S. Chen, S. J. Chen, and J. S. Lai, "Application of HL7 in a collaborative healthcare information system", *Proceedings of 26th Annual International Conference of the IEEE Engineering in Medicine and Biology Society*, pp.3354-3357, 2004.
3. M. Rahman, W. Mahmudur, D. Tongyuan, and C. Bipin, "Medical image retrieval and registration: Towards computer assisted diagnostic approach", *Proceedings of IDEAS Workshop On Medical Information Systems: The Digital Hospital (IDEAS'04-DH)*, pp.78-89, 2004.
4. M. Jirotka, R. Procter, and M. Hartswood, "Collaboration and trust in health- care innovation: The eDiaMoND case study", *Computer Supported Cooperative Work: an International Journal*, Vol.14, pp.369-398, Aug.2005.
5. M. Antonioletti and M. Atkinson, "Introduction to OGSA-DAI services", *Lecture Notes in Computer Science*, Vol.3458, pp.1-12, 2004.

6. S. R. Amendolia, F. Estrella, and T. Hauer, "Grid databases for shared image analysis in the mammoGrid project", *Proceedings of the International Database Engineering and Applications Symposium*, pp.302-311, 2004.
7. HL7 XML Batch File Protocol for Ireland, http://www.hl7.org/
8. Implementing Web Services for Healthcare, http://wiki.usefulinc.com/
9. HL7 Tools, Utilities and Resources, http:// www.hl7.org.au/HL7-Tools.htm
10. HL7 Messaging Toolkit, http://www.interfaceware.com/chameleon.html
11. ChinaGrid Support Platform, http://www.chinagrid.edu.cn/cgsp/

Structural and Event Based Multimodal Video Data Modeling

Hakan Öztarak[1] and Adnan Yazıcı[2]

[1] Aselsan Inc, P.O. Box 101, Yenimahalle, 06172, Ankara, Turkey
hoztarak@aselsan.com.tr
[2] Department of Computer Engineering, METU, 06531, Ankara, Turkey
yazici@ceng.metu.edu.tr

Abstract. In this paper, a structural and event based multimodal video data model (SEBM) is proposed. SEBM supports three different modalities that are visual, auditory and textual modalities for video database systems and it can dissolve these three modalities within a single structure. This dissolving procedure is a mimic of human interpretation regarding video data. The SEBM video data model is used to answer content-based, spatio-temporal and fuzzy queries about video data. A SEBM prototype system is developed to evaluate the practical usage of the SEBM video data model when storing and querying the video data.

1 Introduction

Multimodality of the video data is one of the important research topics for the database community. Videos consist of visual, auditory and textual channels, [1]. These channels bring the concept of multimodality. Modeling and storing multimodal data of a video is a problem, because users want to query these channels from stored data in a video database system (VDBS) efficiently and effectively. In this paper, we propose a structural, event based and multimodal (SEBM) video data model for VDBSs, as a solution to this problem. The SEBM video data model supports three different modalities that are visual, auditory and textual modalities and we dissolve these three modalities within a single SEBM video data model.

Definition of the multimodality, is given by Snoek et. al. as the capacity of an author of the video document to express a predefined semantic idea, by combining a layout with a specific content, using at least two information channels. Like in [2] and [1], we use three kinds of modalities:

- *Visual modality*: contains everything, either naturally or artificially created, that can be seen in the video document;
- *Auditory modality*: contains the speech, music, and environmental sounds that can be heard in the video document;
- *Textual modality*: contains textual resources that can be used to describe the content of the video document.

T. Yakhno and E. Neuhold (Eds.): ADVIS 2006, LNCS 4243, pp. 264–273, 2006.

The visual part of the video is used to represent something happening in the video. Most probably, one or more entities in the video are acting. The audial part of the video is used to represent things heard in the video. Most probably, some sound is created by some entities either saying or making some sound. The textual part of the video is used to represent something either written on the screen or on some entity in video. All of these visual, audial and textual modalities should be considered in a multimodal video data model.

Nowadays researches are concentrating on efficient and effective ways of querying the multimodal data, which is integrated with temporal and spatial relationships. Modeling is as important as querying, because it is an intermediate step between data extraction and consumption. In general, researchers propose their querying algorithms with their data models. Snoek et. al. give the definition of multimodality and focus on similarities and differences between modalities in [1]. They work on multimodal queries in [18]. They propose a framework for multimodal video data storage, but only the semantic queries and some simple temporal queries are supported. They define collaborations between streams when extracting the semantics from video. Oomoto et. al. don't work on multimodality but investigates the video object concept which is a base for spatio-temporal works [7]. Day et. al. extend the spatio-temporal semantic of video objects [17]. Ekin et. al. introduce object characteristics and actors in visual events [4]. Köprülü et. al. propose a model that defines spatio-temporal relationships of the objects in visual domain which includes fuzziness, [3]. In [2], Durak extends the model proposed in [3]. She introduces a multimodal extension of the model and gives two different structures for visual, auditory and textual modalities. BilVideo is an example for a VDBS, which considers spatio-temporal querying concepts, [8]. Main contributions of our work can be summarized as follows:

1. In this study, we introduce a new multimodal video data model, SEBM, to handle three different modalities, visual, auditory and textual. The proposed multimodal video data model is structural and event-based and it is based on human interpretation of these three modalities. This interpretation is like telling what is happening in videos. In this study we think of videos as reflections of the real world in digital world. So, if one can express information in digital world as human does in real world, then we think that all of the queries coming from a user can be handled more accurately and effectively. Hence, we can bypass the problem of handling the models in different data structures as in [2].

2. In this study, we introduce actor entities in video events in multimodal domains which are only defined for visual domains [4]. These entities give us the ability to express the structure of events. Moreover, we introduce object characteristics that involve a particular feature of an object or the relation of an object with other objects in multimodal domains different than [7].

3. We follow divide and conquer approach in query processing to answer complex, very long, nested and conjunctive spatial, temporal, content-based and possibly fuzzy video queries. This approach gives us the ability to deal with much more complex queries different than ones in [2] and [3].

4. We implement a prototype system based on our model. This system uses automatization while segmenting the video temporally and has the ability to work on multimodal data.

The rest of the paper is organized as follows: Section 2 presents how the SEBM video data model, models the video data. Video segmentation, video entities and video actions are explored in that part too. In Section 3, query processing on SEBM is investigated. The implementation of the model is presented in Section 4. The last section provides conclusion with some future extensions of our model.

2 Modeling the SEBM Video Data Model

Single video is composed of sequential frames, which are individual images. Each frame has individual image properties like color or shape. Every image can contain objects, positioned on the image. However, when we arrange these images sequentially, we can see that these objects are part of some events. These objects may move or may stop even though this stopping event is not considered as an action. As a result, every object can be told to do something. We have developed our SEBM video data model by considering this fact and position the video events at the core part of the SEBM. The SEBM model is based on telling about what is going on in the video. We are interested in the structure of what is happening. This approach is also supported by the idea that human interprets the real world like that. In order to find the answer for the question of how the human interprets the video data, we use the following example: If we want someone to sit down and watch a particular video and then while watching, ask her/him what s/he sees on the screen or what is happening in the video; s/he may describe it for us by some statements such as:

– There is a party happening in the house. (information about the semantic of the video)
– In the party there is a dinner. (information about the subject of a particular video part)
– There is a melody playing in the background. (information about auditory part of the video)
– John is sitting at upper left corner of the dinner table. (information about spatiality of video objects)
– Kylie is standing near John. (information about spatial relationships of the video objects)
– I understand that John is the Kylie's brother.(information about semantic relationships between video objects)
– John is saying "Bon appetite" to Kylie. (information about events and gives clues about event structure)
– John is wearing an orange T-shirt. (information about a color feature of a video object T-Shirt)
– There is happy birthday writing on the screen. (information about textual channel of the video)

As it can be seen, there are some patterns while telling what is going on in a specific video. These patterns give us some clues about what s/he might query. S/he is interested in about parts, entities, actions and relations between them in the video. Moreover, s/he uses patterns that show us the structure of what is happening like telling who is doing what. By considering these interpretations, we introduce the SEBM video data model, which is mainly a combination of five different sub-models. SEBM is a translation of human sentences which s/he uses while interpreting the video data to the video database model. Fig.2 shows the hierarchical structure of these five sub-models that we use while constructing SEBM:

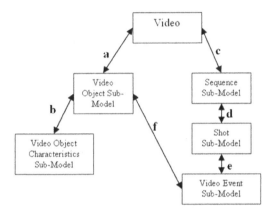

Fig. 1. Hierarchical Structure of Video Sub-Models

1. Video Sequence Sub-Model (segments the video according to the meaning as shown with the link-c in Fig.2)
2. Video Shot Sub-Model (segments the sequences according to low-level features of the video as shown with link-d in Fig.2)
3. Video Object Sub-Model (stores the objects globally and links the spatio-temporal information of the objects through events, as shown with the link-a and f in Fig.2)
4. Video Object Characteristics Sub-Model (stores the objects features and their relationships, as shown with the link-b in Fig.2)
5. Video Event Sub-Model (stores the events under corresponding video segment with spatio-temporal information and links them to the corresponding video objects, as shown with the link-e and f in Fig.2)

2.1   Video Segmentation (Video Sequence Sub-Model and Video Shot Sub-Model)

In [19], it is proposed that successful content-based video data management systems depend on three most important components: key-segments extraction, content descriptions and video retrieval. In our model, we firstly segment the whole video into meaningful intervals temporally according to the semantic; for example "party", "in house conversation" or "escape from prison". We call each of these meaningfully different segments as "scene" or "sequence". Zhang et. al. define video shot as a video sequence that consists of continuous video frames for one camera action and explain how camera changing or motions and special edit effects cause shot boundaries, [9]. By using this definition, we further temporally divide the sequences into smaller segments called "shots" according to the physical changing in parts, like color. These segments are called shots and expressed in video shot sub-model. Then, these shots are grouped into sequences according to their semantics and expressed in video sequence sub-model. From shots, sequences are created. Every shot is a member of exactly one sequence. At the end of grouping, if the video has N number of shots and M number of sequence, N*M sequence-shot pairs are created. Video is a set of sequence-shot pairs. Video is segmented according to the scene changes, where every scene has meaningful differences. Seq=(ID, N, STime, ETime, SL) where Seq=Sequence.

1. ID=Unique Seq ID (positive integer number)
2. N= Name of the Seq (string)
3. STime= Start time of the Seq in the video (positive double number)
4. ETime= End time of the Seq in the video (positive double number bigger than STime)
5. SL (Shot List) = The list of shots that belong to the sequence. STime of the Seq is equal to the STime of the first shot according to the time in the list and ETime of the Seq is equal to the ETime of the last shot in the list.

Every sequence is further divided according to the camera or background changes that consist of the same kind of one or more events related to the same subject. Shot=(ID, N, STime, ETime, EL)

1. ID = Unique Shot ID (positive integer number)
2. N (Name) = Unique name in the same sequence (string)
3. STime = Start time of the shot in the video (positive double number)
4. ETime = End Time of the shot in the video (positive double number bigger than STime; both STime and Etime are in [STime, ETime] of the sequence that shot belongs to)
5. EL (Event List) = The list of events that belongs to the shot. No same event belongs to more than one shot.

2.2 Video Entities (Video Object Sub-Model and Video Object Characteristics Sub-Model)

Specific entities that are visible or tangible are called Video objects. Ekin et. al. call them as action units or interaction units, [4]. If we see or touch the entity in real world, we can declare it as a video object. For example; John, Kylie, t-shirt, hamburger etc. are video objects and expressed in video object sub-model. In

SEBM, every video object has a list of roller event list which one can access the spatio-temporal information of the object directly through the object itself. This list is created automatically while creating the events. While objects are used to structure a particular event, the ID of the event is added to the roller event list of that object. The object is sequentially searched through the present objects and found in O(n) time. Since only the created objects can be added to the events, there is no possibility of not finding the object in present video objects. A video object refers to a semantically meaningful spatio-temporal entity in SEBM. Formally, a video object is described in our model as VO=(ID, N, CL, RL) where VO=Video Object.

1. ID = Unique ObjectID (positive integer number)
2. N = Name of the VO (string)
3. RL (Roller Event List) = The list of Event IDs where VO has a role. By using this list, one can access the spatio-temporal information of the VO directly through object itself.
4. CL (Characteristics List) = The list of characteristics. A particular video object may have a characteristic or not. If it has characteristics, these characteristics are expressed in Video Object Characteristics Sub-Model and inserted in CL. Since objects are stored directly under video, all of the objects can be used to create a relation.

Objects may have features like "John is 25 years old", "Kylie has blue eyes" or may have relationships with other objects like "Kylie is the sister of John", "John is a pilot of the plane". These relationships and features are expressed in video object characteristics sub-model in SEBM. Characteristic is a feature of the Video object or a relation with other video objects. Since video objects are stored directly under the video in hierarchy (Fig.1), all of the objects can be used to create a relation independent than their spatio-temporal information. For example, object *John* may have a relation *brotherof* with *Kylie*. So a video object named John will have a relation VOC={brotherof, Kylie}in SEBM. If *ball* has a *color blue*, then the object named *ball* will have a feature VOC={color, blue}. Video Object Characteristics Sub-Model is formally defined in our model as VOC=(A, o2) where

1. o2 = The subject of characteristic (Object Name or Feature, string)
2. A = Association between object that belongs to characteristic or the subject of characteristic, o2. (string)

2.3   Video Actions (Video Event Sub-Model)

Beside visual, audial and textual modalities, video has spatial and temporal aspects. In our sub-models these aspects are also considered. Spatial aspect is about position of an entity in a specific frame through the video. Spatial position in a specific frame can be given by two-dimensional coordinates. Temporal aspect is about time of a specific frame through the video. Hence a video element can be identified in a video with its frame position(s), X coordinate in frame(s), Y coordinate in frame(s). Specific events that occur in a certain place during a particular interval of time are called video events. Video events occur in a particular shot of the video. As a result, particularly, every event belongs to directly to some specific shot and indirectly to some specific sequence. This situation can be seen in hierarchy of the sub-models, in Fig.1. Video events are formally defined in our model as follows: VE = {ID, N, STime, ETime, ES, K, V, A, TSRL} where

1. ID= Unique Event ID in temporal segmentation (positive integer number)
2. N= Name of the event. It's most probably a verb, like *drive*, *eat*, *walk* etc. (string)
3. STime= Start time of the event. (positive double number)
4. ETime= End Time of the event. (positive double number bigger than Stime; both Stime and Etime are in [STime, ETime] of the shot to which event belongs)
5. ES (Event Structure) = The list of objects that shows the actors and their roles in the event. {Who, Where, What, Whom, With}
   (a) Who= Object who does the event or subject of the event. Such as John, Kylie, cat, dog, plane or tower.
   (b) Where= The semantic place where event occurs. Such as Park, School, House, Table.
   (c) What= A thing, person, or matter to which thought or action is directed, object of the event or an object of investigation. For example, *Hamburger* in a sentence "John gave Kylie a Hamburger".
   (d) Whom= Indirect object of the event, For example, *Kylie* in "John gave Kylie a Hamburger".
   (e) With= Accompanied object or instrument of the event. For example, *Knife* in a sentence "John kills Kylie with knife".
6. K= Keywords of the events, such as extra information about the event or the words that can be heard in the auditory event. Keywords are free texts. If some audio event such as "John said Hello" must be declared, the word "Hello" must be put in the keywords.
7. V (Visuality) = The flag of visuality. If the event has a visual aspect or if the event has some visual scenes, it is set to true. If this is true, we understand that we will realize the event in the visual part of the video.
8. A (Auditorility) = The flag of auditorility. If the event has an audial aspect or if the event has some hearable things, it is set to true. If this is true, we understand that we will realize the event in the auditory part. If visual and auditory parts of the event are both true, this means that, event has both aspects and while watching the video, we should look at the screen and listen the sound.
9. TSRL = Temporal and spatial region list. The members of the list are regions labelled by a specific time in a video. These regions are Minimum Bounding Rectangles defined in [15]. All the objects that belong to the ES must be seen in those rectangles.

Textual information in the video is embedded into the model as making a new event named "isWritten" and put the written text into the K field of the Video Event Sub-Model. The spatial and temporal information of the text is also included in the TSRL of the event.

3   Querying the SEBM Video Data Model

Semi-automatically extracted information from video(s) is stored in a video database and then queried and accessed, [6]. Since there is no standard querying language or query models that can be used in video databases, querying the video database is a challenging problem. One possible solution is to develop a video data model that fits into the area of interest. We introduce SEBM, in which we can put the structural information about events or objects. So, we can answer the queries like; what is going on in the video with their spatio-temporal information, who are the people in the videos, what are the relations between them and what is happening when and where. In our developed prototype system, the database can be queried on visual, auditory and textual contents. Temporal and spatial relations between events and objects can also be queried. Moreover, hierarchical and conjunctive queries can be answered. Besides these, we handle structural queries about objects and events. SEBM prototype system shows the success of SEBM on compound querying rather than other systems like [14, 15 and 16]. These query types can be put into three different groups: 1) Content based queries which include structural queries, 2) Spatial queries which include the queries related to regional and trajectory queries and 3) Temporal queries which include the queries that are related to the timestamps of video entities. The algorithms and the query structure on SEBM are given in [5, 6].

4   Implementation of the Sub-Models

The SEBM prototype system is implemented for evaluating the usage of SEBM. XML (extended mark-up Language) is used to design the SEBM Sub-Models. Since sub-models form a hierarchic tree structure, as shown in Fig.1, XML is very suitable for expressing these sub-models. In Fig.3, the architecture of the system implementation is given. The video is annotated with a semi-automatic fashion. For each video, one SEBM model is constructed and stored. Video is segmented with the help of IBM MPEG-7 Annotation Tool. The output of this tool is consumed by SEBM prototype system. Other sub-models are created manually. All models are embedded in a single structural, event based and multimodal video data model. The model is stored in Berkeley XML DBMS (BDB XML) which is an embedded database specifically designed for the storage and retrieval of XML-formatted documents, [11]. Users query the video data via a query interface. For a particular event, an XML file containing the extracted information is stored in BDB XML. BDB XML supports XQuery which is designed for the examination and retrieval of portions of XML documents, [12]. The application is implemented by using Java programming language.

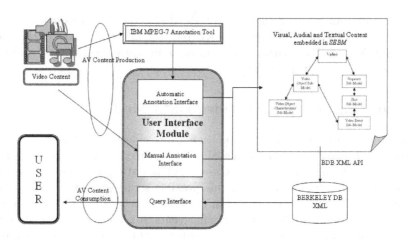

Fig. 2. System Architecture

5   Conclusions

The SEBM video data model, which we propose in this study, makes it easy and effective to store the structural semantic information in a video database and then query the database. This video data model can be adapted to various domains, because it is based on understanding of human about a particular video. Visual, auditory, and textual information in video are all considered in our model. Challenges on modeling the structure of the video are altered by using several sub-models. Very tightly coupled relations among these models result in much more information embedded into the model than treating each independently. Content based, fuzzy, spatial and temporal queries are all supported. In our implementation, XML and Java are used to model information in video and BDB XML is used to store and retrieve video information. Automatization in annotation of video is part of our implementation. IBM MPEG-7 Annotation Tool is used for this purpose. For querying, XQuery facility of Berkeley XML DBMS is utilized.

We plan to improve the SEBM data model to have an implicit inference mechanism. The model will then implicitly be able to make inferences about object characteristics from video events or other video objects characteristics by using their properties like symmetry and transivity or using ontology.

References

[1] C. Snoek, M. Worring, "Multimodal Video Indexing: A review of the State of Art", Multimedia Tools and Applications, 25, pp: 5-35, 2005.

[2] N. Durak, "Semantic Video Modeling And Retrieval With Visual, Auditory, Textual Sources", Ms Thesis, METU, 2004.

[3] M. Köprülü, N.K. Çiçekli, A.Yazıcı, "Spatio-temporal querying in video databases". *Inf. Sci. 160(1-4),* pp.131-152, 2004.

[4] A. Ekin, M. Tekalp, and R. Mehrotra, "Integrated Semantic–Syntactic Video Modeling for Search and Browsing" in IEEE Transactions on Multimedia, VOL. 6, NO. 6, Dec. 2004.

[5] H. Öztarak, "Structural and Event Based Multimodal Video Data Modelling", Ms Thesis, METU, 2005.

[6] H. Öztarak and A.Yazıcı, "Flexible Querying using Structural and Event Based Multimodal Video Data Model", FQAS 2006, LNCS 4027, pp. 75-86, June 2006

[7] E. Oomoto and K. Tanaka, "OVID: Design and implementation of a video-object database system," IEEE Trans. Knowledge Data Eng.,vol.5, pp.629–643, Aug. 1993.

[8] Ö. Ulusoy, U. Güdükbay, M. Dönderler, . Ediz and C. Alper, "BilVideo Database Management System", Proceedings of the 30th VLDB Conference, Toronto, Canada, 2004.

[9] C. Zhang, S. Chen, M. Shyu, "PixSO: A System for Video Shot Detection", Proceedings of the Fourth IEEE Pacific-Rim Conference On Multimedia, pp. 1-5, Dec. 15-18, 2003, Singapore.

[10] IBM MPEG-7 Annotation Tool Web site, www.alphaworks.com/tech/videoannex, Last date accessed: Sept., 2005.

[11] Berkeley DB XML Web Site, www.sleepycat.com Last date accessed: Sept., 2005.

[12] XQuery Web Site, www.w3.org/XML/Query, Last date accessed: Sept., 2005.

[13] S. Pradhan , K. Tajima , K. Tanaka , "A Query Model to Synthesize Answer Intervals from Indexed Video Units", IEEE Trans. on Knowledge and Data Eng. Vol.13, No.5, pp. 824-838, Sept./Oct. 2001.

[14] S. Hammiche, S. Benbernou, M. Hacid, A. Vakali, "Semantic Retrieval of Multimedia Data", MMDB'04, Nov. 13, 2004, Washington, DC, USA.

[15] M.Lyu, E. Yau, S. Sze, "A Multilingual, Multimodal Digital Video Library System", JCDL'02, July 13-17, 2002, Portland, Oregon, USA.

[16] T. Kuo and A. Chen, "Content-Based Query Processing for Video Databases", IEEE Trans. on Multimedia. Vol.2, No.1, Mar. 2000.

[17] Y. Day, S. Data, M. Iino, A. Khokhar, A. Ghafoor, "Object Oriented Conceptual Modeling of Video Data", Proc. Data Eng. (DE '95), pp. 401-408, 1995.

[18] C.G.M. Snoek, M. Worring, "Multimedia event based video indexing using time intervals" Technical Report 2003-01, Intelligent Sensory Information Systems Group, University of Amsterdam, Aug. 2003.

[19] D.Tjondronegoro, P. Chen, "Content-Based Indexing and Retrieval Using MPEG-7 and X-Query in Video Data Management Systems", World Wide Web: Internet and Web Information Systems, 5, 207–227, 2002.

Chat Mining for Gender Prediction

Tayfun Kucukyilmaz, B. Barla Cambazoglu,
Cevdet Aykanat, and Fazli Can

Bilkent University, Department of Computer Engineering,
06800 Bilkent, Ankara, Turkey
{ktayfun, berkant, aykanat, canf}@cs.bilkent.edu.tr

Abstract. The aim of this paper is to investigate the feasibility of predicting the gender of a text document's author using linguistic evidence. For this purpose, term- and style-based classification techniques are evaluated over a large collection of chat messages. Prediction accuracies up to 84.2% are achieved, illustrating the applicability of these techniques to gender prediction. Moreover, the reverse problem is exploited, and the effect of gender on the writing style is discussed.

1 Introduction

Authorship characterization is a problem long studied in literature [1]. In general terms, authorship characterization can be defined as the problem of predicting the attributes (e.g., biological properties and socio-cultural status) of the author of a textual document. The outcome of such studies are primarily used for financial forensics, law enforcement, threat analysis, and prevention of terrorist activities. Consequently, in several studies [2,3], efforts have been spent to increase the prediction accuracies in authorship characterization.

In this paper, we investigate the problem of predicting the gender of a text document's author. In particular, we focus on the text-based communications over the Internet. This type of communications are observed in online services such as MSN messenger, ICQ, and media supporting written discourse such as email, newsgroups, discussion forums, IRCs, and chat servers. We first formulate the problem as a text classification problem, in which the words in a document are used to attribute a gender to the author of the document. Second, we investigate the effect of stylistic features (e.g., word lengths, the use of punctuation marks, and smileys) on predicting the gender. Finally, we exploit the reverse problem and discuss the effect of gender on the writing style.

The rest of the paper is organized as follows. In Section 2, we provide a short literature survey of the studies on authorship analysis. In Section 3, we present the dataset used in this work and define the gender prediction problem. The techniques we employed to solve the problem are presented in Section 4. Section 5 provides the results of a number of experiments conducted to evaluate the feasibility of gender prediction. We finalize the paper in Section 6 with a concluding discussion on the effect of gender on the writing style.

T. Yakhno and E. Neuhold (Eds.): ADVIS 2006, LNCS 4243, pp. 274–283, 2006.

2   Related Work

The authorship studies in literature can be divided into three categories [2]: authorship attribution, similarity detection, and authorship characterization. The authorship attribution is the task of finding or validating the author of a document. Some well-known examples of authorship attribution are the examination of Shakespeare's works [4,5] and the identification of the authors of the disputed Federalist papers [6,7,8]. Similarity detection aims to find the variation between the writings of an author [9] or to differentiate between the text segments written by different authors [10], mostly for the purpose of detecting plagiarism.

Authorship characterization can be defined as the task of assigning the writings of an author into a set of categories according to his sociolinguistic profile. Some attributes previously analyzed in literature are gender, educational level, language origin, and cultural background. In [11], gender and language origin of authors are examined using machine learning techniques. In [12], English text documents are classified according to the author's gender and document's genre. In [13], a set of documents are classified according to their genre under legal, fictional, scientific, and editorial categories.

Authorship studies took more attention with the widespread use of computers, which led to an explosion in the amount of digital text documents (e.g., emails, program codes, chat messages, posts on the forums). In literature, several studies addressed the analysis of these documents based on the writing styles of the authors. In [14], identities of programmers are questioned using several stylistic features such as the use of comments, selection of variable names, and use of programming constructs. In [2,11], a collection of email documents are examined for predicting the identity and gender of the author. The typical features used are message tags, signatures, and the vocabulary richness.

3   Dataset and Problem Definition

The chat dataset used in this paper is collected from a chat server (Heaven BBS), where users have peer-to-peer communication via textual messages. The dataset consists of a collection of message logs storing the users' outgoing messages (typed in Turkish). The messages are logged for a one-month period without the notice of the users, but respecting the anonymity of the users and messages. There are around 1500 users, each with a subscription information including personal details such as gender, age, and occupation. The vocabulary of the dataset contains about 50,000 distinct words, consisting of only ASCII characters. There are around 250,000 chat messages, which are usually very short (6.2 words per message on the average).

In this paper, our aim is to find a classification of users according to their gender by using both term-based and style-based classification techniques and investigate the effect of gender on the writing style. For this purpose, a user document is generated for each user by concatenating all outgoing messages of the user. Each user document forms a classification instance whose features are defined by the information within the user document. Two different techniques are investigated for classifying the users (i.e., their documents) according to the gender: term-based classification and style-based classification. In the first approach, the set of features is taken as the set of distinct words in the user document. In the second approach, the stylistic properties of a user document are incorporated as its features. For this purpose, various stylistic features, including some well-known features used in literature [15] as well as some newly proposed features, are extracted from the message logs and used with the hope of improving the classification accuracies.

Although the chat dataset used in this work is completely textual, the style of chat messages is quite different than that of any other textual data used in literature. First, the use of punctuation marks varies widely for each user. Some users omit punctuation marks in their messages while some overuse them. Second, since conversations occur in real-time and there is no medium for communication other than text, computer-mediated communication has its own means for transferring emotions. Smileys and emoticons are the commonly known and widely used means of representing feelings within text. Smileys (e.g., ":-)", ":-(") are the sequences of punctuation marks that represent feelings such as happiness, enthusiasm, anger, and depression. Emoticons (e.g., "Awesomeeee!") are consciously done misspellings that put a greater emphasis on an expression. Since the use of these emotion-carriers are closely related to the writing style of an individual, they provide valuable information about their author. However, the existence of emotion-carriers makes standard methods (e.g., stemming and part-of-speech tagging) used for authorship analysis impractical for chat datasets. In our case, the messages contain only ASCII characters since all non-ASCII Turkish characters are replaced with their ASCII counterparts. Hence, the use of natural language processing techniques is even more restricted. Another difference of chat datasets from other textual material is that the messages have limited length. According to Rudman [15], in order to gather sound information on the writing style of an author, the documents should contain at least 1000 words on a specific subject. Finally, in most of the work in literature, the documents in question are selected over a restricted topic. In chat datasets, each message may have a different topic, resulting in user documents with multiple topics. Using a dataset without a restricted content may bias the classification with respect to the topic of the message instead of the authors' gender.

4   Gender Prediction

4.1   Term-Based Classification

We formulate the gender prediction problem as a text classification problem as follows. In our case, each user document is composed of the words typed by a user. The vocabulary of the documents forms the feature set, and the users (i.e., their documents) correspond to the instances to be classified. There are two class values for an instance: male or female.

Given these, the gender prediction problem can be considered as a single-label, binary text classification problem [16]. A supervised learning solution to this problem is to generate a prediction function, which will map each user document onto one of the male or female classes. In the rest of the paper, we may use the words "term" and "feature" as well as "user document" and "instance", interchangeably.

The above-mentioned prediction function can be learned by any of the existing supervised classification algorithms via training over a representative set of documents whose authors' genders are known. In order to compute this function, we employ four well-known algorithms (*k*-NN, naive Bayesian, covering rules, and back propagation), which are widely used in machine learning literature. For an excellent survey about the use of machine learning techniques in text classification, the interested reader may refer to [16].

4.2   Style-Based Classification

Although term-based classification is widely used in literature [3], the results of this approach are biased by the topics of the documents. Another method for representing the author is to employ linguistic preferences of an author. Finding writing habits of an author is known as stylometry. The problem in stylometric studies can be summarized as finding similarities between documents using statistics and deriving conclusions from the stylistic fingerprints of an author [3]. A detailed overview of the stylometric studies can be found in [17]. According to Rudman [15], there are more than 1000 stylistic features that may be used to discriminate an author. However, there is no consensus on the set of best features that represents the style of a document.

In this study, several stylistic features are extracted from the chat dataset and examined in order to find the best representation for the messages written by a user. Word lengths, sentence lengths, and function word usage are well-known and widely applied stylistic features [3]. Word lengths and sentence lengths provide statistical information about the author's documents, and function words describe the sentence organization of an author. In our work, a stopword list of pronouns, prepositions, and conjunctions are used as function words. Analysis

Table 1. The stylistic features used in the experiments

Feature	Description	Possible feature values
message length	average message length	low, medium, high
word length	average word length	low, medium, high
stopword usage	frequency of stopwords	low, medium, high
stopwords	a list of 78 stopwords	exists, not exists
smiley usage	frequency of smileys	low, medium, high
smileys	a list of 79 smileys	exists, not exists
punctuation usage	frequency of punctuation marks	low, medium, high
punctuation marks	a list of 37 punctuation marks	exists, not exists
vocabulary richness	number of distinct words	poor, average, rich
character usage	frequency of each character	low, medium, high

of vocabulary richness is also considered as an important stylistic characteristic of an author. The frequency of distinct words within a document is used to represent the vocabulary richness of an author.

In addition to the traditional stylistic features, this study includes several other stylistic features that may describe authors' stylistic fingerprints in written discourse. Since the messages in question are unedited, punctuation usage can be a discriminating factor between different authors. As a computer-mediated text, the chat messages contain emotion-carriers called smileys and emoticons. In this work, an extensive list containing 79 different smileys is used. The overuse of alphabet characters are traced within each message in order to detect the use of emoticons. A summary of the stylistic features used in this study is given in Table 1.

5 Experiments

5.1 Preprocessing

The imbalance in a dataset may form a crucial problem for text classification [18]. The chat dataset used in the experiments is imbalanced due to the following two reasons. First, the number of male and female users is not equal. To alleviate this problem, undersampling [19] is used to balance the number of male and female instances. Each instance is scored with respect to the total number of words he/she uses, and equal number of instances with highest word count are selected as the best representatives of their respective classes. Second, the total number of distinct words used by each user varies. This variance is alleviated by applying a windowing mechanism for each instance. A fixed number of consecutive words are selected from each user document, and the remaining words are discarded.

The high dimensionality of our chat dataset is another factor which badly affects the applicability of machine learning algorithms. Feature selection [20] is a widely used preprocessing step for reducing the dimensionality. In this work, χ^2 (CHI square) statistic is used to calculate the discriminative power of each feature. Experiments are performed using a selected set of the most discriminating features.

5.2 Experimental Setup

A selection of classifiers from the Harbinger machine learning toolkit [21] is used in the experiments. The selected classifiers are k-NN, naive Bayesian, covering rules and back propagation. 10-fold cross-validation is used in all experiments. Each experiment is repeated five times and average accuracy results are reported. The accuracy is defined as the number of instances whose gender is correctly predicted divided by the total number of predictions.

In each experiment, 90% of the most discriminative features are used as representative features. For the text classification tests, a window of 3000 words is selected as the document sample of a user. For the k-NN algorithm, cosine similarity metric is used as the distance metric, and the number of nearest neighbors (k) is set to 10.

Table 2. Accuracies achieved by four different classifiers in predicting the gender of a chat user

	k-NN		Naive Bayesian	
Number of instances	Term-based	Style-based	Term-based	Style-based
25 male–25 female	72.4	56.8	76.0	72.0
50 male–50 female	73.4	63.2	80.0	71.8
100 male–100 female	74.5	60.7	81.5	81.9
200 male–200 female	72.2	62.4	78.2	81.7

	Covering rules		Back propagation	
Number of instances	Term-based	Style-based	Term-based	Style-based
25 male–25 female	49.2	50.4	54.0	71.6
50 male–50 female	53.4	51.2	50.0	75.4
100 male–100 female	58.3	64.2	54.0	80.8
200 male–200 female	56.4	64.9	58.0	79.6

5.3   Results

In this study, it is proposed that the gender of a chat user is distinguishable using the information derived from the messages written by that particular user. In order to test this claim a variety of experiments are done. The experiments are conducted on 100, 200, and 400 users selected from the chat dataset. Table 2 summarizes the accuracy results obtained from the experiments. In term-based classification, naive Bayesian classifier achieves the best results with an accuracy of 81.5%. In general, as the number of instances increases, the use of stylistic features performs better than term-based classification. In style-based classification, naive Bayesian and back propagation perform well with similar accuracies of 81.9% and 80.8%, respectively.

Table 3 shows the effect of feature selection on classification accuracy. The tests are done using the naive Bayesian classifier over a set of 200 users. In order to emphasize the effect of feature selection, a shorter window size of 800 words is used as the document for each user. As the feature space in the style-based classification tests is much smaller than that of the term-based classification

Table 3. Effect of feature selection on classification accuracies

Feature selection	Term-based	Style-based
1%	70.5	60.2
5%	73.4	65.2
25%	76.2	72.6
50%	74.6	77.2
60%	73.8	78.6
70%	75.2	78.8
80%	75.7	78.9
90%	74.7	81.8

Table 4. Effect of discarding a stylistic feature on classification accuracy

Discarded feature	k-NN	Naive Bayesian	Covering rules	Back propagation
none	62.5	81.2	63.7	79.5
message length	60.7	80.7	62.2	80.8
word length	61.6	80.6	63.9	79.4
stopwords	64.6	83.3	67.8	81.9
smileys	59.2	80.2	60.8	80.2
punctuation marks	63.4	75.6	62.4	76.5
vocabulary richness	61.8	81.8	60.7	79.5
character usage	61.8	81.2	62.5	79.6
best feature set	64.6	84.2	68.2	82.4

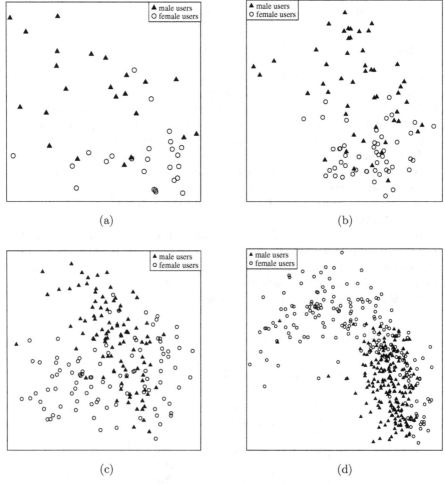

(a)   (b)

(c)   (d)

Fig. 1. Distribution of gender according to the principal component analysis for (a) 50, (b) 100, (c) 200, and (d) 400 users, where each case contains an equal number of males and females

Table 5. The list of the most discriminating words and their respective χ^2 values for male and female users

Male		Female	
Word	χ^2	Word	χ^2
abi (brother)	121.3	ayy (boy!)	9.6
olm (buddy)	94.2	kocam (my husband)	7.6
lazim (required)	80.9	okulum (my school)	7.6
tane (amount)	80.3	sevgilimin (my lover's)	7.1
kac (how many)	78.5	suanda (at the moment)	6.6
olmaz (no way)	74.5	iyilik (fine)	6.6
var (exists)	72.0	mersi (thanks)	6.4
baba (fellow)	70.9	byeeee (byeeee)	6.4
IP (IP)	66.5	beeen (I)	6.1
biri (someone)	65.9	kocama (to my husband)	6.1

tests, discarding a percent of least important features from the instances badly affects the style-based classification relatively more. This is mostly because, as the feature space becomes smaller, instances also become similar to each other, and hence classifiers do not function well.

The effectiveness of stylistic features are also questioned in this study. As there is no consensus in literature on the set of the best stylistic features to be used, experiments are conducted in order to evaluate which stylistic features are useful for discriminating the gender of an author. For this purpose, in each experiment, one of the stylistic features is left out, and the accuracy of the classifier is re-evaluated. Table 4 displays the results of the experiments conducted on a selection of 200 users. According to Table 4, the k-NN classifier works best when the stopwords are left out; the back propagation classifier works best when average message lengths, stopwords, the use of smileys, vocabulary richness, and over-used character frequencies are left out; the covering rules classifier achieves its best results using a feature set without stopwords and word lengths. Among the four classifiers, the naive Bayesian classifier achieves the best accuracy (84.2%) using a feature set without stopwords and vocabulary richness measures.

In order to visualize the predictability of gender, principle component analysis (PCA) is used. In this technique, each user document is represented with a vector generated using the distinct words in the user document, and the dimensionality of this vector is reduced using PCA. Figure 1 shows the PCA results for datasets of varying size. It is important to note that the values on the data points are not displayed since they are not indicative of anything. Only the relative proximities of the data points are important. The results clearly show that the use of words in chat messages can be used to discriminate the gender of a user.

6   Concluding Discussion

In this paper, the predictability of the genders of the users involved in computer-mediated conversations is questioned. The word selection and message organization of many chat users are examined. Experiments are conducted in order to predict the gender over a large, real-life chat dataset. The experimental results led to the finding that both word usage and writing habits of users of different sex vary significantly. Table 5 shows a sample set of discriminative words along with their χ^2 values. It is apparent that males tend to produce more decisive and dominating words that can be considered as slang. On the other hand, female conversations involve more possessive and content-dependent words. Also, the use of emoticons and smileys are distinguishing characteristics of the female writing style.

The stylometric analysis also provides interesting results. In general, female users tend to prefer to use longer and content-bearing words. They also prefer to organize shorter sentences than male users and omit stopwords and punctuation marks. The use of smileys and emotion-carrier words is more common in female users than male users. Long chat messages and the use of short words are the most discriminating stylistic features of male users. Also, the use of stopwords and punctuation marks widely varies for male users. They use punctuation marks and stopwords either heavily or very lightly.

References

1. Love, H.: Attributing Authorship: An Introduction. Cambridge University Press (2002)
2. Corney, M.W.: Analysing E-mail Text Authorship for Forensic Purposes. M.S. Thesis. Queensland University of Technology (2003)
3. Holmes, D.I.: Analysis of Literary Style - A Review. Journal of the Royal Statistical Society **148**(4) (1985) 328–341
4. Elliot, W.E.Y., Valenza, R.J.: Was the Earl of Oxford the True Shakespeare? A Computer Aided Analysis. Notes and Queries **236** (1991) 501–506
5. Merriam, T., Matthews, R.: Neural Computation in Stylometry II: An Application to the Works of Shakespeare and Marlowe. Literary and Linguistic Computing. **9** (1994) 1–6
6. Mosteller, F., Wallace, D.L.: Inference and Disputed Authorship: The Federalist. Addison-Wesley (1964)
7. Holmes, I., Forstyh, R.: The Federalist Revisited: New Directions in Authorship Attribution. Literary and Linguistic Computing **10**(2) (1995) 111–127
8. Tweedie, F.J., Singh, S., Holmes, D.I.: Neural Network Applications in Stylometry: The Federalist Papers. Computers and the Humanities **30**(1) (1996) 1–10
9. Patton, J. M., Can, F.: A Stylometric Analysis of Yasar Kemal's Ince Memed Tetralogy. Computers and the Humanities **38**(4) (2004) 457–467
10. Graham, N., Hirst, G., Marthi, B.: Segmenting Documents by Stylistic Character. Natural Language Engineering **11**(4) (2005) 397–415
11. Vel, O. de, Corney, M., Anderson, A., Mohay, G.: Language and Gender Author Cohort Analysis of E-mail for Computer Forensics. In: Second Digital Forensics Research Workshop. (2002)
12. Koppel, M., Argamon, S., Shimoni, A.R.: Automatically Categorizing Written Texts by Author Gender. Literary & Linguistic Computing **17**(4) (2002) 401–412
13. Kessler, B., Nunberg, G., Schutze, H.: Automatic Detection of Text Genre. In: Proceedings of the 35th Annual Meeting on Association for Computational Linguistics. (1997) 32–38

14. Spafford, E.H., Weeber, S.A.: Software Forensics: Can We Track Code to Its Authors? Computers and Security **12** (1993) 585–595
15. Rudman J.: The State of Authorship Attribution Studies: Some Problems and Solutions. Computers and the Humanities **31**(4) (1998) 351–365
16. Sebastiani, F.: Machine Learning in Automated Text Categorization. ACM Computing Surveys **34**(1) (2002) 1–47
17. Holmes, D.I.: Authorship Attribution. Computers and the Humanities **28**(2) (1994) 87–106
18. Liu, A.Y.C.: The Effect of Oversampling and Undersampling on Classifying Imbalanced Text Datasets. M.S. Thesis. University of Texas at Austin (2004)
19. Kubat, M., Matwin, S.: Addressing the Curse of Imbalanced Data Sets: One-sided Sampling. In: Proceedings of the Fourteenth International Conference on Machine Learning. (1997) 179–186
20. Yang., Y, Pedersen, J.O.: A Comparative Study on Feature Selection in Text Categorization. In: Proceedings of the Fourteenth International Conference on Machine Learning. (1997) 412–420
21. Cambazoglu, B.B., Aykanat, C.: Harbinger Machine Learning Toolkit Manual. Technical Report BU-CE-0503, Bilkent University, Computer Engineering Department, Ankara (2005)

Integrated Expert Management Knowledge on OSI Network Management Objects

Antonio Martín, Carlos León, and Félix Biscarri

Escuela Superior de Ingeniería Informática, Universidad de Sevilla,
Avda. Reina Mercedes, 41012 Sevilla, Spain
{toni, cleon, fbiscarri}@us.es
http://www.dte.us.es

Abstract. The management of modern telecommunications networks must satisfy ever-increasing operational demands. We propose a study for the improvement of intelligent administration techniques in telecommunications networks. This task is achieved by integrating knowledge base of expert system within the management information used to manage a network. For this purpose, an extension of OSI management framework specifications language has been added and investigated. For this goal, we shall use the language Guidelines for the Definition of Managed Objects (GDMO) and a new property named RULE which gathers important aspects of the facts and the knowledge base of the embedded expert system. Networks can be managed easily by using this proposed integration.

1   Introduction

Current communications networks support a large demand of services for which the traditional model of network management is inadequate. It is thus necessary to develop new models, which offer more possibilities. These models are called *Integrated Management Expert Systems*.

We propose a new technique which integrates the Expert System completely within the Management Information Base (MIB) [1]. The expert rules that make up the Knowledge Base are joined to the management objects definitions that belong to the network. These definitions integrate the specifications of management objects representing the network resource and the management expert rules which allow for the intelligent control and administration of the resources represented. In this document we explain the main aspects of this proposal. To achieve this we have used the OSI network management model and the Guidelines for the Definition of Managed Objects, GDMO (ISO/IEC 10165-4 (ITU X.722)) [2].

We present an extension of the standard GDMO, to accommodate the intelligent management requirements. We describe how to achieve this goal using a new extension called GDMO+. This extension presents a new element RULE, which defines the knowledge base of the management expert system.

T. Yakhno and E. Neuhold (Eds.): ADVIS 2006, LNCS 4243 , pp. 284–293, 2006.
© Springer-Verlag Berlin Heidelberg 2006

2 GDMO and Expert Management

Information architecture is based on an object-oriented approach and the agent/ manager concepts that are of paramount importance in the open system inter-connection (OSI) systems management [3]. The denominated Managed Objects have an important role in the normalization. A managed object is the OSI abstract view of a logical or physical system resource to be managed. These special elements provide the necessary operations for the administration, monitoring and control of the telecommunications network. The managed objects are defined according to the International Standardization Organization (ISO) Guidelines for the Definition of Managed Objects (GDMO), which defines how network objects and their behavior are to be specified, including the syntax and semantics [4].

Within the OSI (Open Systems Interconnection) management framework [5], the specification language GDMO (Guidelines for the Definition of Managed Objects) has been established as a means to describe logical or physical resources from a management point of view. GDMO has been standardized by ITU (International Telecommunication Union) in ITU-T X.722 and is now widely used to specify interfaces between different components of the TMN (Telecommunication Management Network) architecture [6].

Basically, a GDMO specification defines a management information model by specifying a set of so called managed object classes that describe all different kinds of network resources. For each managed object class, one has to specify the properties that characterize the objects of this class, i.e. their attributes and their operations as well as their relationships to other objects. Such a managed object class description is meant to supply all the information that is needed to enable a managing system to effectively control the network resource represented by a managed object, and to trigger suitable management operations, if necessary. In this context, it is important that a GDMO specification clearly prescribes the capabilities of managed systems that have to be implemented as well as the meaning of all messages that can be exchanged between the managing system and the managed system. To this purpose, it is essential the knowledge base that the expert systems supply.

GDMO is organized into templates, which are standard formats used in the definition of a particular aspect of the object. A complete object definition is a combination of interrelated templates. There are nine of these templates: class of managed objects, package, attribute, group of attributes, action, notification, parameter, connection of name and behavior [7].

3 Extension of the GDMO Standard

The elements that at the moment form the GDMO standard do not make a reference to the knowledge base of an expert system. To answer these questions, it will be necessary to make changes on the template of the GDMO standard. Specifically, by means of a new item named RULE. This template groups the knowledge base supplied by an expert in a specific management dominion. It allows the storage of the management knowledge in the definition of the resources that form the system to be managed [8].

The standard we propose contains the singular template RULE and its relations to other templates. Two relationships are essential for the inclusion of knowledge in the component definition of the network: Managed Object Class and Package Template. In the standard we propose, both templates have the new property RULES. Let us study both relationships.

3.1 Template for Management of Object Classes

This template is used to define the different kinds of objects that exist in the system. The definition of a managed Object Class is made uniformly in the standard template, eliminating the confusion that may result when different persons define objects of different forms. This way we ensure that the classes and the management expert rules defined in system A can be easily interpreted in system B.

<class-label> MANAGED OBJECT CLASS
    [DERIVED FROM <class-label> [,<class-label>]*;]
    [CHARACTERIZED BY <package-label> [,<package-label]*;]
    [CONDITIONAL PACKAGES   (1)
         <package-label> PRESENT IF condition;
      ,<package-label>] PRESENT IF condition]*;]
    REGISTERED AS object-identifier;

DERIVED FROM plays a very important role, when determining the relations of inheritance which makes it possible to reutilize specific characteristics in other classes of managed objects. In addition, a great advantage is the reusability of the object classes and therefore of the expert rules which are defined.

This also template can contain packages and conditional packages, including the clauses CHARACTERIZED BY and CONDITIONAL PACKAGES.

3.2 Package Template

This template is used to define a package that contains a combination of many characteristics of a managed object class: behaviours, attributes, groups of attributes, operations, notifications, parameters, attributes, groups of attributes, actions, behaviour and notifications. In addition to the properties indicated above, we suggest the incorporation of a new property called RULES, which contains all the specifications of the knowledge base for the expert system [9].

All the properties that we define in the package will be included later in the Managed Object Class Template, where the package is incorporated. A same package can be referenced by more than one class of managed objects.

Next definition shows the elements of a package template, in which it is possible to observe the new property RULES.

```
<package-label> PACKAGE
    [BEHAVIOUR <behaviour-label> [,<behaviour-label>]*;]
    [ATTRIBUTES <attribute-label> propertylist [,<parameter-label>]*
        [,<attribute-label> propertylist [,<parameter-label>]*]*;]
    [ATTRIBUTE GROUPS   <group-label> [<attribute-label>]*
            [<group-label> [<attribute-label>]*]* ;]
    [ACTIONS <action-label> [<parameter-label>]*
            [<action-label> [<parameter-label>]*]* ;
    [NOTIFICATIONS <notification-label> [<parameter-label>]*
        [<notification-label> [<parameter-label>]*]* ;]
    [RULES    <rule-label>   [,<rule-label>]*;]
REGISTERED AS object-identifier;
```

(2)

The property RULES allows a treatment similar to the other properties, including the possibility of inheritance of rules between classes. Like the rest of the other properties defined in a package, the property RULES need a corresponding associated template.

4 Expert Rule Template

This template permits the normalised definition of the specifications of the expert rule to which it is related. This template allows a particular managed object class to have properties that provide a normalised knowledge of a management dominion. The structure of the RULE template is shown here:

```
<rule-label> RULE
    [PRIORITY      <priority> ;]
    [BEHAVIOUR   <behaviour-label> [,<behaviour-label>]*;]
    [IF         occurred-event-pattern [,occurred-event-pattern]*]
    [THEN    sentence [, sentence]* ;]
REGISTERED AS object-identifier;
```

(3)

The first element in a template definition is headed. It consists of two sections:
- <rule-label>: This is the name of the management expert rule. Rule definitions must have a unique characterizing name.
- RULE: A key word indicates the type of template, in our case a definition template and the specifications for the management expert rule.

After the head, the following elements compose a normalised definition of a expert rule.
- BEHAVIOUR: This construct is used to extend the semantics of previously defined templates. It describes the behaviour of the rule. This element is common to the others templates of the GDMO standard.
- PRIORITY: This represents the priority of the rule, that is, the order in which competing rules will be executed.
- IF: It contains all the events that must be true to activate a rule. Those events must be defined in the Notification template. The occurrence of these events is necessary

for the activation of the rule and the execution of their associated actions. We can add a logical condition that will be applied on the events occurred or their parameters.

- THEN: This gives details of the operations performed when the rule is executed. Those operations must be previously defined in the Action template. These are actions and diagnoses that the management platform makes as an answer to network events occurred.

- REGISTERED AS is an object-identifier: A clause identifies the location of the expert rule on the ISO Registration Tree. The identifier is compulsory.

5 Application of the GDMO+ Standard System Network Management

The traditional expert management uses management knowledge and management information separately. Integrating both elements is the main purpose of our work.

This section present a tool based on the proposed GDMO+ standard, which helps administrators in expert network management. Our tool understands transceivers and multiplex equipment. We will describe the basic structure and concepts of our software, especially the knowledge base.

ISO classifies the systems management activities into five functional areas: fault management, accounting management, configuration management, performance management and, security management [10]. We can categorize the expert systems within these five groups. The expert system that we have built would be included in the area of work: fault management. Related work is briefly discussed in the next section.

5.1 Related Work

We present a rule-based expert system applied to error diagnosis in the communications system of SEVILLANA-ENDESA (a major Spanish power utility). Part of

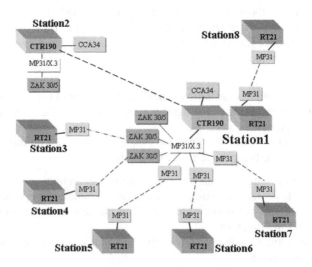

Fig. 1. Power Company Network

SEVILLANA-ENDESA's long-distance traffic is controlled by a wireless System distributed throughout the Endesa network. Expert systems are part of the system dedicated to the management of a power utility's communications system, which we call NOMOS [11]. NOMOS is implemented in Brightware's ART*Enterprise. ART*Enterprise is a set of programming paradigms and tools that are focused on the development of efficient, flexible, and commercially deployable knowledge-based systems. NOMOS+ is an extension for intelligent decision-making and diagnostic reasoning controlled by its own integrated expert system. NOMOS+ is the first production software written and integrated in GDMO+, Fig.1.

The knowledge base is included within the specifications of the managed resources, following the proposed prescriptions in standard GDMO+. These new specifications contain management information of managed resources and include also the set of expert rules that provides the knowledge base of the expert system.

5.2 The System Features

NOMOS+ operation, uses a supervision system called SSC (Communication Supervisory System). This system can monitor, in real time, the network's main parameters, making use of the information supplied by a Supervisory Control and Data Acquisition (SCADA), formed by a Control Center (placed on the main CSE building), and Remote Terminal Units (RTUs) installed into different stations. The use of a SCADA system is due to the management limitations of network communication equipment, Fig.2.

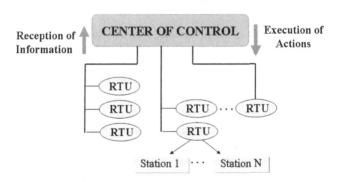

Fig. 2. NOMOS+ System Features

The SSC allows the operator to acquire information, alarms or digital and analogical parameters of measure, registered on each RTU. Starting from the supplied information, the operator is able to undertake actions through the SSC in order to solve the failures that could appear or to send a technician to repair the stations equipment.

5.3 The System Architecture

Our tool has three major components: a knowledge base, an inference engine and a user interface [12], Fig.3.

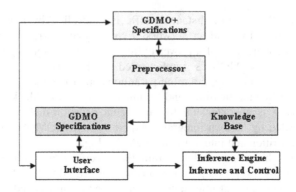

Fig. 3. Elements of the prototype NOMOS+

This structure is typical of expert systems. Those elements are briefly discussed in the following:

The knowledge base: The core of the system, this is a collection of facts and if-then production rules that represent stored knowledge about the problem domain. The knowledge base of our system is a collection of expert rules and facts expressed in the ARTScript programming language ART*Enterprise.

The knowledge base contains both static and dynamic information and knowledge about diferent network resources and common failures. The knowledge base of our system can be extended by adding new higher level rules and facts. To this purpose we can employ user interface.

The inference engine: This is the processing unit that solves any given problems by making logical inferences on the given facts and rules stored in the knowledge base. In our tool we used the ART*Enterprise. By using an existing general purpose tool we were able to build a standard and extensible platform with proven performance and quality.

The user interface: This controls the inference engine and manages system input and output. The user interface of our tool contains a preprocessor for parsing GDMO+ specification files, a set of input and output handling routines, and a simple command prompt interface for managing the system. Also, the user interface components allow administrators to inspect the definitions of management object classes interactively, this allows to modify or include new experts management rules in the managed objects definition.

The prototype has a preprocessor module. A previous phase to the inference is realized by a unit processor-translator, which processes the file that contains the GDMO+ specifications and extracts the normalized knowledge from the expert system. Two exits are obtained: a file with management expert rules and another file with GDMO definitions of the managed object classes. The preprocessor also translates the expert rules into a valid syntax for the programming language of inference engine. Procedures are coded in ART*Enterprise's ARTScript language, a dynamic interpreted language similar in syntax to LISP.

6   Example of a Management Expert Rule

This section shows a complete example of an expert rule integration in the GDMO+ proposed standard; it defines the managed object of a CTR 190-type radio transceiver. This device belongs to a private network that gives service to a power utility.

In the next example a Class of Managed Object is radioTransceiver, which defines the properties corresponding to the radio transceiver. This class includes the compulsory transceiverPackage which contains all the specifications corresponding to the device. The most important properties that we can indicate are the two expert rules that have been associated with the defined class by means of the RULES clause. The two rules are defined by using the RULE template.

```
radioTrasnceiver MANAGED OBJECT CLASS
   DERIVED FROM "rec.X721": top;
   CHARACTERIZED BY transceiverPackage;
REGISTERED AS {nm-MobjectClass 1};

transceiverPackage PACKAGE
 ATTRIBUTES
    receptionPower      GET,
    statusTransmission GET, speedTransmission  GET, ...
 NOTIFICATIONS
    damageFeeding, inferiorLimit, repairAction;
 RULE powerError, transmissionError;
REGISTERED AS {nm-package 1};

powerError RULE
 PRIORITY 3;
 BEHAVIOUR powerErrorBehaviour;
 IF (?date ? ?local 7_F_ALIM_2 ?remote ALARM)
   (NOT (?date ? ?local CCA?34_AIS_DE_BB ?remote ALARM))
 THEN ("Severity:" PRIORITY),
 ("Diagnostic: It damages in the electric feeding of the
            station" ?local),
 ("Recommendation:To   revise   the   electric   connection",
?local);
REGISTERED AS {nm-rule 1};

transmissionError RULE
   PRIORITY 4;
   BEHAVIOUR transmissionErrorBehaviour;
   IF (?date ?time1 ?local 7_TX_C2 ?remote ALARM)
      (?date ?time2 ?local 7_TX_C2 ?remote ALARM
            & : (<(ABS(? ?time1 ?time2)) 1.00))
 THEN ("Severity:" PRIORITY),
   ("Diagnostic:
    "It damages in the modulate transmission", ?local),
   ("Recommendation "Revision transceiver");
REGISTERED AS {nm-rule 2};
```

Both rules detect anomalies or defects of operations produced in the transceiver and suggest the necessary measures for solving the problem. The first rule powerError, is in charge of detecting failures in the power supply of the device; the second rule transmissionError, is devoted to the detection of errors in the data transmission module. Both rules give recommendations on how to solve the failures.

6.1 Final Prototype Verification

The purpose is to achieve a functionally correct prototype. To verify the system we feed it with an alarms arbitrary amount. The results of this proof are included in Table 1. From these results we can establish the following conclusions:

– Filtration process effectiveness is very high: almost 90% of the whole. This has the advantage of a decreasing percentage in the amount of indications presented to the operator.
– The speed of the system improves diminishing the number of alarms on which the rest of rules act.

Table1. Prototype Testing Results

Alarms Initial Number	Number After Filtration	Filtered Alarms	Fired Rules	Preceding time	Rules/Sec.	Indications to the Operator
100	1	99	51	0,118 Sec.	432,2034	1
200	10	95	102	0,412 Sec.	247,5728	6
300	31	89,6	155	1,250 Sec.	124,0000	20
400	31	92,25	201	1,438 Sec.	139,7775	16
500	32	93,6	254	2,975 Sec.	85,3782	19
600	38	93,66	293	5,249 Sec.	55,8202	16
700	44	93,71	346	17,982 Sec.	19,2415	18
800	55	93,125	394	26,938 Sec.	14,6262	23

The expert system, with over 150 operation rules, has produced excellent results which, after extensive field-testing, proved to be capable of filtering 93% of produced alarms with a precision of 95% in locating them.

7 Conclusions

Current networks are very complex and demand ever-increasing levels of quality, making their management a very important aspect to take into account. The traditional model of network administration has certain deficiencies that we have tried to overcome by using a model of intelligent integrated management. To improve the techniques of expert management in a communications network, we propose the possibility of integrating and normalising the expert rules of management within the actual definition of the managed objects. Through the integration of the knowledge within the new extension of the GDMO standard, we can simultaneously define the management information and knowledge.

Thus, the management platform is more easily integrated and allows a better adaptation for the network management. We conclude pointing out an important aspect of the obtained integration: by using only and exclusively the extended GDMO specification, the administration platform will be able to obtain the management necessary information with respect to the managed objects as well as the expert rules of management that make up the knowledge base of the expert system.

References

1. Morris, Stephen B.: Network Management, MIBs and MPLS: Principles, Design and Implementation By Publisher: Addison Wesley (2003).
2. CCITT X. 722 / ISO 10165-4 ISO, Structure of management   information. Part 1: Guidelines for the definition of managed objects.
3. ISO/IEC and ITU-T, "Open Systems Interconnection - Systems Management Overview," Standard 10040-2, Recommendation X.701. 1992.
4. Hebrawi, B.: GDMO, Object modeling and definition for network management. Technology appraisals (1995)
5. ITU-T Recommendation X.700, Management Framework for Open Systems Interconnection (OSI). CCITT Applications (1992).
6. ITU-T Rec. M.3010, Principles for a Telecommunications Management Network (TMN). Study Group IV (1996).
7. Black, U.D.: Network Management Standards. McGraw Hill (1995).
8. Stallings, William.: SNMP, SNMPv2, and CMIP: the practical guide to network. Publication Reading, Mass. [etc.] Addison-Wesley, (2000).
9. Garcia, R.C.; Cannady, J.: Boundary expansion of expert systems: incorporating evolutionary computation with intrusion detection solutions. SoutheastCon 2001. Proceedings. IEEE, (2001) 96-99.
10. ITU-T Recommendation M.3400, TMN Management Functions, 1997
11. Leon, Carlos. Mejias, Manuel. Luque, Joaquin. Gonzalo, Fernando.: Expert System for the Integrated Management of a Power Utility's Communication System.   IEEE Trans on Power Delivery, Vol. 14, No. 4, Octubre, (1999), pp 1208-1212
12. Joseph C. Giarratano, Gary D. Riley.: Expert Systems: Principles and Programming. Book, Brooks/Cole Publishing Co. (2005).

Knowledge Integration in Information Systems Education Through an (Inter)active Platform of Analysis and Modelling Case Studies

Birger Weynants, Jan Vanthienen, and Joke Tisaun

K.U.Leuven, Leuven Institute for Research in Information Systems (LIRIS),
Naamsestraat 69, BE-3000 Leuven, Belgium
{birger.weynants, jan.vanthienen, joke.tisaun}@econ.kuleuven.be

Abstract. In this paper we discuss how knowledge integration through-out system analysis, modelling and development courses can be stimulated by giving an overview of our MIRO-project at K.U.Leuven. This includes offering an online knowledge base of all-embracing case studies, structured according to the Zachman framework. Supported by collaborative group-ware, students not only get the opportunity to consult and compare so-lutions for the case studies, but also actively discuss and contribute to alternative solutions. In this Problem Based Learning (PBL)-context, stu-dents are able to influence and understand the development of a certain process through interactive computerized animations and demos.

Keywords: Cooperative information systems, information systems ed-ucation, implementing collaborative groupware, digital libraries, knowl-edge integration.

1 Introduction

1.1 Knowledge Fragmentation Problem

Students in business informatics are exposed to the concepts of analyzing, de-signing, modelling, developing, implementing, evaluating and optimizing infor-mation systems in organizations. Unfortunately, not everything can be studied within one single course, due to the scope and complexity of a complete phased system-development path.

Therefore, this material is spread out over separate individual courses. Each course deals with a certain phase of the development path and illustrates that phase with its own case studies. The dissimilarity in case studies between sepa-rate courses results in severe knowledge fragmentation. Consequently, students experience serious difficulties in acquiring insight in the overall system develop-ment path.

1.2 Unfavorable Aspects of Isolated Courses

- In most of the courses students only analyze a part or a certain phase of the whole development path in depth.

T. Yakhno and E. Neuhold (Eds.): ADVIS 2006, LNCS 4243, pp. 294–303, 2006.

- The different courses illustrate the phases by means of different case studies; sometimes even with seemingly contradictory solutions.
- The comparison of alternative approaches is limited because the different courses are not well adjusted to each other. Due to the use of different cases, the comparison of solutions becomes difficult.
- Both students and teachers are putting two times as much effort in the completion of their tasks. Students have to study several cases and teachers have to write several cases, whereas focusing on global cases which are part of several courses would be more effective and efficient.

The figure below presents a summary of the knowledge fragmentation problem described above. A single arrow points at a consequence while a double arrow indicates a contrast:

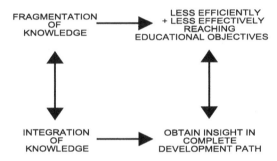

Fig. 1. Knowledge fragmentation problem

1.3   Ways to Stimulate Knowledge Integration

How can this problem of knowledge fragmentation be solved? The solution we had in mind was to make cases covering and integrating the study material of several courses, accessible to students. Those cases can be presented during the contact moments of these courses. Thereby, the offering of cases is possible either with or without support of information and communication technology.

This is where the fundamental nature of the MIRO-project jumps in: giving students the opportunity to quickly compare alternative solutions to certain case-related problems and influence and understand the development of a certain process through interactive computerized animations and demos. Thanks to the computer support that will be organized during the project, students and teachers are offered the possibility to reach their educational objectives more effectively and efficiently.

2   MIRO Solutions and Expected Results

2.1   Main Objective

The major goal of the project is to stimulate the integration of knowledge by offering an interactive online platform with case studies that exceed the fragmental image of the individual courses. This project runs between 2005 and 2007.

2.2   Subgoals in Order to Realize This Main Objective

– Structure the study material in a clearly defined and understandable way.
– Present a navigational framework that gives the opportunity to obtain more and more detailed information as students navigate deeper and deeper into the global picture.
– Stimulate and involve students actively in their process of knowledge integration by offering interactive animations and demos.

2.3   Expected Results

While positioning the project against the core educational purposes of an institution like a university, it shows an added value towards teachers, students and the institution itself.

From the teachers' point of view the project joins the competence and specialization of the separate individual teachers thanks to the exchange of knowledge. Large economies of scale are present because of two reasons. First there is the need for computer aides, demonstrations, simulations and packages according to which computer support offers a clear added value with regard to the knowledge-exchange in a paper version. Second, building such tools and examples is very labor intensive, but by offering them on a common platform, the whole institutional community can take advantage of it.

The project does not offer advantages only for the experienced teachers, but also for new teachers since the adjustment to other related courses is strongly promoted by an educational site.

From the students' point of view it is valuable to consult several examples of packages or solutions to one and the same problem. The opportunity to analyze the same problem from different angles (e.g. the data model in the database course, the object model in the analysis course or programme examples in the software development course) but covered in the same case study stimulates the integration of knowledge originating from related courses. A click-into-detail possibility on the framework's visual representation is also an important stimulator of knowledge integration.

Moreover, it is not only about consulting in a passive way: also interactive animations of several algorithms will be recorded so that students are able to influence and understand the development of a certain process.

On top of that, students are not restricted to consulting alternative solutions. Also the comparison of solutions and the integration of these comparisons during course discussions contribute to an actual educational improvement. Besides, students actively contribute to the project by elaborating solutions themselves in a PBL-context during seminars and course projects and adding them to collaborative software. Their dynamic learning process can be stimulated by giving them opportunities to participate in online-community discussions and actively further build and complete the content by elaborating solutions with the support of collaborative software.

By giving an overview of the students' contributions, the collaborative software can offer students a possibility to self-reflexion on their learning activities. Thereby students can get a clear sight on the level of understanding they have achieved during and after the learning process. Additionally, practical experience suggests that people learn in a more motivated way when they not only learn for themselves but are also able to share the yield of their learning process with others on collaborative groupware [1]. These results can in turn be used as subject matter for other students in the group based learning environment.

From the institutional point of view, the project fits perfectly into the educational concept of "guided self-study" in which guidance by teachers and more active contributions of students is expected, which will be both driven by the project. A learning management system (LMS) is already available but does not cross the boundaries of single courses. Moreover extra attention will be given to specific themes like the development of course-exceeding capabilities like handling a lot of information, reporting results, communication and presentation skills, participating in a virtual community and the completion of study material by students.

3   Identification of the Target Group

Courses are often part of different educational programs with different educational objectives which can be viewed on three levels (Fig. 2):

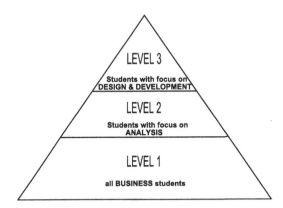

Fig. 2. Levels of educational programs in business informatics

– Level 1: all business students
  • Objective: obtain insight in an organization and its underlying processes by recognizing the role and evaluating the impact of information systems.
– Level 2: students with a focus on analysis of information systems
  • Objective: previous objective + analyze and optimize those organizational processes.

– Level 3: students with a focus on design and development of information
  systems
  • Objective: previous objectives + design and develop the organizational
    systems technically.

The information systems that are subject of discussion are the same, but
the angle from which they are studied varies from recognizing, evaluating and
analyzing to designing and developing the system. As a consequence, the role
and contribution of students is different for each target group.

4   Actual Realization of the Integration Project

4.1   Create Structure with the Zachman Framework

The framework that will support students in structuring their acquired knowledge is the Zachman framework for Information Systems Architecture which
has been further developed in cooperation with J. Sowa. [2], [3]. This Zachman
framework offers the opportunity to structure system architectures on the basis
of 6 questions (What?, How?, Where?, Who?, When?, Why?) and 6 interest
groups (the planner, the owner, the designer, the builder, the programmer and
the end user). That reasoning scheme has specially been designed to aide getting
an overview of complex subjects like an enterprise. In addition, students can focus on one subcomponent at a time without losing sight on the system's global
context.

4.2   Cover the Different Courses with Extensive Case Studies

A number of problem descriptions will be offered in the form of real life case
studies. Thereby students can brainstorm about what actions they would take
under realistic conditions to solve the problems described in the case. As a consequence, students do not remain passive observers, but are forced and trained
in a learning-by-doing context to take concrete decisions and actions in order to
obtain a reasonable outcome to the problem and analyze their results [4].

These case studies include problem descriptions of a complete development
path of an organizational system and vary from the organization of a classical
order entry system or library-system to a more complex insurance process [5], [6].
Dependent of the technique, language or method used, several solutions will be
obtainable for the different phases of one and the same case-study. The solutions
will be structured into the earlier-mentioned framework.

Several questions related to the lifecycle of case studies emerge, for example:
how long will it take to produce a complete case study, what is the optimal
number of authors to contribute to the case study, how many students will use
the case study and what about the evolution of case studies? Out of the average
number of students participating in the courses involved, we know that the total
number of students that can use the case studies for reaching their educational
objectives, will be in the order of 600-700 students. This average total number

of students is spread over the different business informatics courses: on average, there are 500 business students, roughly 150 analysis students and about 30 students with a focus on design and development. As illustrated in Fig. 2, the more upwards the pyramid, the narrower the group.

For the moment we cannot give an exact answer to the other questions however, since the project is still in an experimental phase and will be implemented next academic year (starting October 2006).

4.3   Different Roles for Different Groups

As mentioned above, the role and contribution of students is different for each target group and depends on the profiling of the educational program and the specific goals of the courses involved:

Business Students approach the organizational systems from the point of view of the upper rows in the Zachman framework (solid circles in Fig.3). They take a look at the contextual scope of the information system and the conceptual model of the enterprise in order to get insight in the organization and its underlying processes.

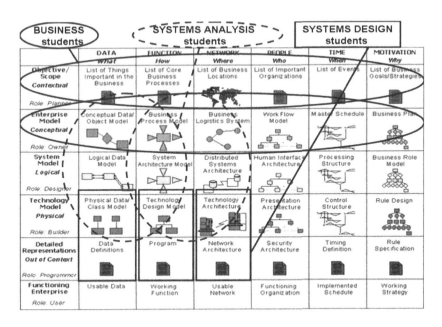

Fig. 3. Zachman framework - Points of view

Besides, these students are also able to obtain additional information about for example more technical cells in the framework that are not part of the top layers, by clicking on that cell (Fig.4). In that way, students can focus on certain parts of the case study and have a look at demos and implementations, without loosing sight on the position of that part in the overall picture.

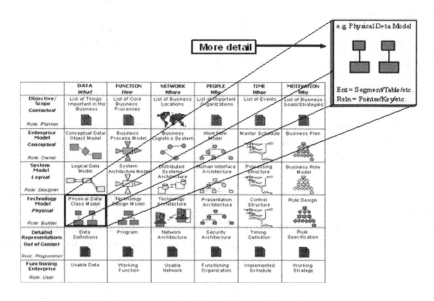

Fig. 4. Zachman framework - Detailed view

Systems Analysis Students following a program focused on analysis, have another approach towards the framework: they analyse the business models, data and processes (e.g. MDA, UML) and try to find and describe a more optimal model of the information system (dotted circles in Fig.3). Thereby, they integrate the data view with the process view, which are often taught in separate courses.

Systems Design Students whose educational program is focused on design and development have a more chronological progress approach towards the framework. They take a look at the total evolution of an information system starting from the model, going through model transformation and ending with the implementation, with a clear focus on technical aspects (solid rectangles in Fig.3).

These students are able to view and compare additional implications involved when adjusting the technical implementation to the business model specifications. They can thereby develop different technical solutions to the same (business) problem.

4.4   Stimulate the Active Learning Process with wiki-Technology

Last but not least, the case studies will be collected and offered on a wiki. The database behind the wiki is not just a collection of material however, but an integrated crosspoint bank of (alternative) solutions to well chosen case studies. During the courses involved in the project, the common cases will be used to facilitate students studying the same problem via different approaches; for example the data model in the database course, the object model in the analysis course or the programming examples in the software development course.

Teachers will be able to refer to the case studies on the wiki where students can use the wiki in different stages (Table 1).

Table 1. Different stages in the use of the wiki

Passive	Interactive	Active
Analyze problems in case studies	Execute simulations to understand the practical working of solutions	Elaborate (alternative) solutions themselves
Consult solutions to problems and compare alternative solutions	Experiment with interactive demos (e.g.SQL-query processor)	Add solutions to the wiki in the context of class projects
Combine and integrate knowledge from different courses	Discuss solutions and the way of reasoning with colleagues	Add comment to solutions of colleagues

Because of active online participation, the contact time during lessons can be experienced as more productive. The advantage of working with collaborative groupware like a wiki is that it encourages active participation of its users (students and teachers) [7]. For that reason, the maintainability of the wiki will be guaranteed in the long term. Thanks to the online-discussions and the results that follow, students of following years do also profit in this group based learning-process. Up-to-date research topics can be easily added and discussed on the wiki in order to close the teacher-research gap [8].

The Learning Management System that is used today [9], offers merely a limited possibility for cooperation and input of students only by discussion groups-functionality [10]. In contrast, a wiki invites every user to take the opportunity in contributing to the content itself. The combination of the present Learning Management System with an open, collaborative platform can be an interesting path of growth in the context of group based learning.

4.5 Criteria for Evaluating the Project

The evaluation criteria that can be used in order to measure the level of success of the project are divided into quantitative and qualitative criteria:

- **Quantitative criteria:**
    - Content:
        * The number of case studies available on the wiki.
        * The completeness of the case studies in terms of the number of cells elaborated in the Zachman framework.

* The average number of alternative solutions for each cell in the Zachman framework per case study.
- Effective use of the wiki:
  * The number of persons visiting the site (measured through the wiki-software).
  * The number and extent of contributions by teachers and students (measured through webstatistics e.g. IBM history flow software [11]).
- **Qualitative criteria:**
  - Evaluation by students:
    * Online survey investigating the level of student satisfaction in using the wiki.
  - Evaluation by teachers:
    * Examining the level of integration of the wiki-project into the involved courses.

5   Conclusion

When different phases of an information system's complex development path are taught in separate courses, a problem of knowledge fragmentation often occurs. This paper gave an outline of the MIRO-project at K.U.Leuven which proposes a knowledge integration solution.

The integration of knowledge is achieved by first putting forward the Zachman framework as a reasoning scheme in which students can position the knowledge they acquired in one course relatively to the knowledge acquired in other courses. Second, real life case studies are at hand that cover the whole system development path and integrate the knowledge of the different courses in order to prevent students from losing the thread. Last but not least, the cases and the supporting framework are presented on a wiki. In this way, students are encouraged to actively analyze, compare, discuss with their colleagues, experiment with interactive demos and add alternative solutions to the wiki.

Thanks to the active stimulation by computer support, business students, systems analysis students, system design students and teachers are offered the possibility to reach their educational objectives more effectively and efficiently.

References

1. Goldberg, A., Russell, M., Cook, A.: The effects of computers on student writing: A meta-analysis of studies from 1992 to 2002. The Journal of Technology, Learning and Assessment **2** (2003)
2. Zachman, J.: A framework for information systems architecture. IBM Systems Journal **26** (1987)
3. Zachman, J., Sowa, J.: Extending and formalizing the framework for information systems architecture. IBM Systems Journal **31** (1992) 590–616
4. Hudson, J., Buckley, P.: An evaluation of case-based teaching: Evidence for continuing benefit and realization of aims. Advances in Physiological Education **28** (2004) 15–22

5. Solutionmatrix: (Examples of case studies on http://www.solutionmatrix.com/business-case-studies.html)

6. Prenhall: (Examples of case studies on http://www.prenhall.com/divisions/bp/app/alter/student/useful.html)

7. Augar, N., Raitman, R., Zhou, W.: Teaching and learning online with wikis. Beyond the comfort zone: Proceedings of the 21st ASCILITE Conference (2004) 95–104

8. Bajaj, A., Batra, D., Hevner, A., Parsons, J., Siau, K.: Systems analysis and design: Should we be researching what we teach? Communications of AIS **15** (2005) 478–493

9. Blackboard: (Blackboard learning management system on http://www.blackboard.com/us/index.aspx)

10. Tisaun, J., Vanthienen, J.: Best practices: support for a virtual learning environment on decentralized level. World Conference on Educational Multimedia, Hypermedia and Telecommunications (ED-MEDIA 2005) (2005) 381–386

11. IBM: (History flow software on http://www.alphaworks.ibm.com/tech/historyflow)

Knowledge Management in Different Software Development Approaches

Broderick Crawford[1,2], Carlos Castro[2], and Eric Monfroy[2,3,*]

[1] Pontificia Universidad Católica de Valparaíso, PUCV, Chile
FirstName.Name@ucv.cl
[2] Universidad Técnica Federico Santa María, Valparaíso, Chile
FirstName.Name@inf.utfsm.cl
[3] LINA, Université de Nantes, France
FirstName.Name@univ-nantes.fr

Abstract. In this paper we present some ideas, concepts and experiences related with our work of implementing solvers to combinatorial optimization problems. We have been designing, implementing and using solvers for important kind of problems, and painfully, the process of developing them is not optimal at all. The most used practice, which is based on trial and error, often incurs an enormous amount of resources. Clearly, this is a Software Engineering problem, then to find better ways of developing optimization algorithms, solvers and metaheuristics is our interest too. The software development community has a wide spectrum of methodologies when it decides to implement a software project. From the more traditional Tayloristic practices to Agile methods. Software development is a knowledge intensive activity and the knowledge creation and sharing are crucial parts of the software development processes. This paper presents a comparative analysis between knowledge sharing approaches of Agile and Tayloristic software development teams sprinkled with concerns about the development of Metaheuristics.

Keywords: Knowledge Management, Agile Development, Optimization Algorithms, Metaheuristics, Reusability, Knowledge Sharing.

1 Introduction

In the last time Metaheuristics have grown to be an important paradigm in solving large scale combinatorial optimization problems and rapid prototyping of Metaheuristics is an important topic of research today. Clearly, this is a Software Engineering problem, then a vision of the methodologies that improve productivity and quality of software is absolutely necessary to find better ways of developing solvers and metaheuristics, our main research topic. Software engineering is a knowledge intensive process that includes some aspects of Knowledge Management (KM) in all phases: eliciting requirements, design,

---

* The authors have been partially supported by the project INRIA-CONICYT VANANAA. The first author has also been partially supported by the project PUCV 209.473/2006. The third author has also been partially supported by the Chilean National Science Fund through the project FONDECYT 1060373.

T. Yakhno and E. Neuhold (Eds.): ADVIS 2006, LNCS 4243, pp. 304–313, 2006.
© Springer-Verlag Berlin Heidelberg 2006

construction, testing, implementation, maintenance, and project management. No worker of a development project possess all the knowledge required for fulfilling all activities. This underlies the need for knowledge sharing support to share domain expertise between the customer and the development team [5]. The traditional approaches (often referred to as plan-driven, task-based or Tayloristic), like the waterfall model and its variances, facilitate knowledge sharing primarily through documentation. They also promote usage of role based teams and detailed plans of the entire software development life-cycle. It shifts the focus from individuals and their creative abilities to the processes themselves. In contrary, agile methods emphasise and value individuals and interactions over processes. Tayloristic methods heavily and rigorously use documentation for capturing knowledge gained in the activities of a software project life-cycle [4]. In contrast, agile methods suggest that most of the written documentation can be replaced by enhanced informal communications among team members internally and between the team and the customers with a stronger emphasis on tacit knowledge rather than explicit knowledge [2].

The development life cycle of Optimization Algorithms and Metaheuristics assumes the same connotations it assumes in the field of Software Engineering. Then, the software development life cycle of them might be quite diverse and different life cycle models can be appropriate. In recent years Component Based Software Engineering has become an established approach. There are several strong arguments in favor of reusable software components for metaheuristics and software tools for rapid prototyping of algorithms would save considerable resources.

We believe that in Optmization Algorithms development projects, a better understanding of knowledge sharing and transfer, from a Knowledge Management perspective, offers important insights about the use of Software Engineering methodologies and Reusability.

This paper is organised as follows: Section 2 is dedicated to the presentation of Knowledge Management in Software Engineering. We include a short overview of basic concepts from the area of Knowledge Management in Section 3, presenting the two approaches to KM: Product and Process. A Background on Agile Development Approaches is given in section 4. Section 5 presents some important issues about the development of Optimization Algorithms: Reusability and Agility. Section 6 briefly shows Software Reuse from KM perspective. In Section 7 we compare how knowledge sharing is handled by both Agile and Tayloristic methods in some relevant topics and activities in software development projects. Finally, in Section 8 we conclude the paper and give some perspectives for future research.

2   Knowledge Management in Software Engineering

The main argument to Knowledge Management in software engineering is that it is a human and knowledge intensive activity. Software development is a process where every person involved has to make a large number of decisions and individual knowledge has to be shared and leveraged at a project and organization level, and this is exactly what KM proposes. People in such groups must collaborate, communicate, and coordinate their work, which makes knowledge management a necessity. In software development one can identify two types of knowledge: Knowledge embedded in the products or artifacts, since they are the result of highly creative activities and Meta-knowledge, that is knowledge about the products and processes. Some of the sources of knowledge (artifacts, objects, components, patterns, templates and containers) are stored in electronic form. However, the majority of knowledge is tacit, residing in the brains of the employees. A way to address this problem can be to develop a knowledge sharing culture, as well as technology support for knowledge management. There are several reasons to believe that knowledge management for software engineering would be easier to implement than in other organizations: technology is not be intimidating to software engineers and they believe the tools will help them do a better job; all artifacts are already in electronic form and can easily be distributed and shared; and the fact that knowledge sharing between software engineers already does occur to a large degree in many successful software collaborative projects [16].

3   A Framework for Knowledge Management

Knowledge Management focuses on corporate knowledge as a crucial asset of the enterprise and aims at the optimal use and development of this asset, now and in the future. Knowledge Management has been the subject of much discussion over the past decade and different KM life-cycles and strategies have been proposed. One of the most widely accepted approaches to classifying knowledge from a KM perspective is the *Knowledge Matrix* of Nonaka and Takeuchi [15]. This matrix classifies knowledge as either explicit or tacit, and either individual or collective. Nonaka and Takeuchi also proposes corresponding knowledge processes that transform knowledge from one form to another: socialisation (from tacit to tacit, whereby an individual acquires tacit knowledge directly from others through shared experience, observation, imitation and so on); externalisation (from tacit to explicit, through articulation of tacit knowledge into explicit concepts); combination (from explicit to explicit, through a systematisation of concepts drawing on different bodies of explicit knowledge); and internalisation (from explicit to tacit, through a process of learning by doing and through a verbalisation and documentation of experiences). Nonaka and Takeuchi model the process of organisational knowledge creation as a spiral in which knowledge is amplified through these four modes of knowledge conversion. It is also considered that the knowledge becomes crystallized within the organisation at higher levels moving from the individual through the group to organisational and even inter-organisational levels [3].

3.1   Two Approaches to KM: Product and Process

Traditional methods of software development use a great amount of documentation for capturing knowledge gained in the activities of a project life-cycle.

In contrast, the agile methods suggest that most of the written documentation can be replaced by enhanced informal communications among team members and customers with a stronger emphasis on tacit knowledge rather than explicit knowledge. In the KM market a similar situation exists and two approaches to KM have been mainly employed; we will refer to them as the *Product* and the *Process* approaches. These approaches adopt different perspectives in relation to documentation and interactions between the stakeholders [12].

Knowledge as a product. The product approach implies that knowledge can be located and manipulated as an independent object. Proponents of this approach claim that it is possible to capture, distribute, measure and manage knowledge. This approach mainly focuses on products and artefacts containing and representing knowledge.

Knowledge as a process. The process approach puts emphasis on ways to promote, motivate, encourage, nurture or guide the process of learning, and abolishes the idea of trying to capture and distribute knowledge. This view mainly understands KM as a social communication process, which can be improved by collaboration and cooperation support tools. In this approach, knowledge is closely tied to the person who developed it and is shared mainly through person-to-person contacts. This approach has also been referred to as the *Collaboration* or *Personalisation* approach. Choosing one approach or other will be in relation to the characteristics of the organization, the project and the people involved in each case [1].

4   Agile Methods

A new group of software development methodologies has appeared over the last few years. For a while these were known as lightweight methodologies, but now the accepted term is Agile methodologies. The most common of them are: eXtreme Programming, the Crystal Family, Agile Modeling, Adaptive Software Development, Scrum, Feature Driven Development, Dynamic System Development Method [9]. There exist many variations, but all of them share the common principles and core values specified in the Agile Manifesto [4]. Through this work they have come to value individuals and interactions over processes and tools. Working software over comprehensive documentation. Customer collaboration over contract negotiation. Responding to change over following a plan. These new methods attempt a useful compromise between no process and too much process, providing just enough process to gain a reasonable payoff. The result of all of this is that agile methods have some significant differences with the former engineering methods [9]:

Agile methods are adaptive rather than predictive. Engineering methods tend to try to plan out a large part of the software process in great detail for a long span of time, this works well until things change. So their nature is to resist change. Agile methods, however, welcome change. They are processes that try to adapt and thrive on change, even to the point of changing themselves.

Agile methods are people oriented rather than process oriented. The goal of engineering methods is to define a process that will work well whoever happens to be using it. Agile methods assert that no process will ever make up the skill of the development team, so the role of a process is to support the development team in their work.

5   Software Engineering and Optimization Algorithms

In [18], it is argued that given the intangible nature of optimization algorithms, its life cycle assumes here the same connotations it assumes in the field of Software Engineering. They implicitly consider a simple linear life cycle model in which the algorithm undergoes a design/tuning phase and is then employed in production. Beside being the simplest life cycle model, the linear model is also the building block composing more complex models: Iterative, Hybrid (such as the Spiral) and Agile. Spiral, in this context, can be described as a sequence of interleaved design/tuning phases and production phases: At the end of each production phase, sufficient information is gathered which can be employed in the following design/tuning phase for improving the algorithm. Agile methods attempt to minimize risk by developing software in short iterations, each iteration is like a miniature software project of its own, and includes all of the tasks necessary to release the mini-increment of new functionality: planning, requirements analysis, design, coding, testing, and documentation. That is, some agile teams use the waterfall model on a small scale, repeating the entire waterfall cycle in every iteration. Other teams, most notably eXtreme Programming teams, work on activities simultaneously. From this basic description of the development models, it is apparent that the principles and conclusion drawn in [18] referring to the linear model is immediately extend to the general case. Then, the software development life cycle of optimization algorithms might be quite diverse and different life cycle models can be appropriate. In recent years Component Based Software Engineering has become an established approach. It is an entire life-cycle of component-based products has been focused on technologies related to design and implementation of software components and systems built from them. But in many cases, the process of building components can follow an arbitrary development process model.

5.1   Reusable Metaheuristic Software Components

A component is built to be reused; reusability is a popular software engineering practice. Software reuse is using existing software artifacts during the construction of a new software system, in order to reduce development time and costs and benefiting the overall quality of the software. *But, before you can reuse software you need software to reuse.* The types of artifacts that can be reused are not limited to source code fragments, for example, design Patterns and Frameworks enable large scale reuse of software architectures and detailed design respectively. Patterns support reuse of software architecture and design, capturing the static and dynamic structures and collaborations of successful solutions to problems that arise when building applications in a particular domain. Patterns explicitly capture expert knowledge and design trade-offs, and make this expertise more widely available. Patterns help improve developer communication: you can share patterns within a project, within a company, or across many companies. The limitations of a pattern are determined by the pattern design and the intent of the pattern author. Many patterns are currently documented in software publications and on the Internet. Frameworks support reuse of detailed design and code. A framework is an integrated set of components that collaborate to provide a reusable architecture for a family of related applications. Together, design patterns and frameworks help to improve software quality: reusability, extensibility, modularity, performance and reducing the development time.

There are several strong arguments in favor of reusable software components for metaheuristics. First of all, mature scientific knowledge that is aimed to solve practical problems must also be viewed from the technology transformation point of view, it means that we need in practice usable applications that incorporate the results of basic research. Therefore, we also have to deal with the issue of efficiently building such systems to bridge the gap between research and practice. Since algorithms are generally applied in the form of software, adaptable metaheuristic software components are the natural means to incorporate respective scientific knowledge. From a research point of view, software reuse may also provide a way for a fair comparison of different heuristics within controlled and unbiased experiments [8].

In the literature, some implementation frameworks for local search based metaheuristics have been introduced [14,17]. Furthermore, there are some approaches to design domain specific (modeling) languages for local search algorithm, which are partly based on Constraint Programming [13].

Metaheuristics essentially are trial-and-error algorithms design tailored to optimization problems and in many cases they are heavy time consuming in its development and use. For this reason, software tools for rapid prototyping of algorithms would save considerable resources. These tools share the same aims: time saving in code implementation and systematic algorithmic research and experimentation. Furthermore, to an easy creation of hybrids, the tools should introduce genericity through promoting reuse of existing techniques and implementations, and yet have the robustness to incorporate implementation of new techniques.

The idea of a generic and extensible optimization environment is not new. Especially in the area of Evolutionary Computation there are numerous more or less mature libraries (a comprehensive list can be found on the EvoWeb homepage [1].

5.2   Agile Reuse

It would be desirable to employ Agile principles to produce simple clear software which is easily adaptable to changing requirements while also employing

---

[1] Available at http://evonet.lri.fr/evoweb/resources/software

reuse techniques to improve the software quality and reduce development effort, time and cost. In [11] was introduced the term Agile Reuse to describe such an approach. They argue that in practice several inherent difficulties arise when considering the compatibility of Agile and reuse techniques due to differences, often contradictory, in their fundamental principles. For example Agile software tends to be simple and domain specific accompanied with minimal support documentation. Reuse relies on support documentation and favors more generalised components. Others factors vary from technical difficulties such as support environments to more pragmatic issues such as managerial and developer attitudes. As reusability becomes more accepted in software industry, systems and tools that aid and support reuse become key aspects in achieving successful reuse of artifacts. The benefits of reuse-based software development are obvious, nevertheless it is unclear how reusability can be working with Agile development. Meanwhile, keeping with Agile principles, reusability is considered exclusively in relation to source code.

6   Knowledge Management and Software Reuse

It has been said that Knowledge Management implementations in Software Engineering can extract knowledge from its sources of knowledge: documentation, artifacts, objects, components, patterns, templates and code repositories, exploiting this knowledge in future software developments. But, software reuse is not a technology problem, nor is it a management problem. Reuse is fundamentally a Knowledge Management problem. In [10] Jim Highsmith explains how over the last ten or so years, by packaging objects into components and components into templates, we have made the problem bigger, not smaller. Objects, patterns, templates, and components are packaged (explicit) knowledge the larger the package, the greater the encapsulated knowledge. The greater the encapsulated knowledge, the harder it is to transfer. Additionally, the essence of problem solving, innovation, creativity, intuitive design, good analysis, and effective project management involves more tacit knowledge, the harder it is to transfer. By putting tacit knowledge in a principal role and cultivating tacit knowledge environments, KM can play an important role in application development, and particularly in reuse. A second aspect of the explicit knowledge problem, observed by Highsmith, is the fallacy that documentation (explicit knowledge) equals understanding. When, in order to successfully reuse a component, we seek understanding in the documentation, the larger and more complex the component, the harder it is to gain the required understanding from documentation alone. Understanding, in this context at least, is a combination of documentation and conversation about the component and the context in which that component operates. No writer of documentation can anticipate all the questions a component user may have.

An understanding of knowledge sharing and transfer issues offers important insights about Reusability and Software Engineering.

7   Knowledge Sharing Support in Agile and Tayloristic Methods

About knowledge sharing in plan-driven and agile development approaches the main different strategies are in the following dimensions [5]:

Eliciting Requirements and Documentation. Common to all software development processes is the need to capture and share knowledge about the requirements and design of the product, the development process, the business domain and the project status. In Tayloristic development approaches this knowledge is externalised in documents and artifacts to ensure all possible requirements, design, development, and management issues are addressed and captured. One advantage to this emphasis on knowledge externalisation is that it reduces the probability of knowledge loss as a result of knowledge holders leaving the organisation. Agile methods advocate lean and mean documentation. Compared to Tayloristic methods, there is significantly less documentation in agile methods. As less effort is needed to maintain fewer documents, this improves the probability that the documents can be kept up to date. To compensate for the reduction in documentation and other explicit knowledge, agile methods strongly encourage direct and frequent communication and collaboration.

Training. With regards to disseminating process and technical knowledge from experienced team members to novices in the team, Tayloristic and agile methods use different training mechanisms as well. While it is not stated, formal training sessions are commonly used in Tayloristic organizations to achieve the above objective. Agile methods, on the other hand, recommend informal practices, for example, pair programming and pair rotation in case of eXtreme Programming.

Trust and Freedom. As software development is a very social process, it is important to develop organisational and individual trust in the teams and also between the teams and the customer. Trusting other people facilitates reusability and leads to more efficient knowledge generation and knowledge sharing. Through collective code ownership, stand-up meetings, on site customer, and in case of XP, pair programming, agile methods promote and encourage mutual trust, respect and care among developers themselves and to the customer as well. The key of knowledge sharing here are the interactions among members of the teams which happen voluntarily, and not by an order from the headquarters [7,6].

Team Work and Roles. In Tayloristic teams different roles are grouped together as a number of role-based teams each of which contains members who share the same role. In contrast, agile teams use cross functional teams. Such a team draws together individuals performing all defined roles. In knowledge intensive software development that demands information flow from different functional sub-teams, role based teams tend to lead to islands of knowledge and difficulties in its sharing among all the teams emerge. Learning, or the internalisation of explicit knowledge, is a social process. One does not learn alone but learns mainly through tacit knowledge gained from interactions with others. Furthermore, tacit knowledge is often difficult to be externalised into a document or repository. A repository by itself does not support communication or collaboration among people either. Due to the high complexity of the software process in general, it is hard to create and even more difficult to effectively maintain the experience repository [16].

8 Conclusions and Future Directions

In our main research topic of interest we are trying to find better ways of developing Optimization Algorithms. Because it is a Software Engineering problem, some ideas, concepts and open issues about it are important in supporting of our work too.

In Software Engineering many development approaches work repeating the basic linear model in every iteration, then in a lot of cases an iterative development approach is used to provide rapid feedback and continuous learning in the development team. To facilitate learning among developers, Agile methods use daily or weekly stand up meetings, pair programming and collective ownership. Agile methods emphasis on people, communities of practice, communication, and collaboration in facilitating the practice of sharing tacit knowledge at a team level. They also foster a team culture of knowledge sharing, mutual trust and care. Agile development is not defined by a small set of practices and techniques. Agile development defines a strategic capability, a capability to create and respond to change, a capability to balance flexibility and structure, a capability to draw creativity and innovation out of a development team, and a capability to lead organizations through turbulence and uncertainty. They rough out blueprints (models), but they concentrate on creating working software. They focus on individuals and their skills and on the intense interaction of development team members among themselves and with customers and management.

Because Metaheuristics essentially are trial-and-error algorithms design tailored to optimization problems and in many cases they are heavy time consuming in its development and use, software tools for rapid prototyping of algorithms would save considerable resources. It would be desirable to employ Agile principles and Reusability to produce software which is easily adaptable to changing requirements while also improving the quality and reduce development efforts.

Since software development is a knowledge intensive activity, an understanding from a Knowledge Management perspective offers important insights about Reusability and Software Engineering methods for designing and implementing Optimization Algorithms and Metaheuristics.

References

1. D. Apostolou and G. Mentzas. Experiences from knowledge management implementations in companies of the software sector. *Business Process Management Journal*, 9(3), 2003.
2. K. Beck, M. Beedle, A. V. Bennekum, A. Cockburn, W. Cunningham, M. Fowler, J. Grenning, J. Highsmith, A. Hunt, R. Jeffries, J. Kern, B. Marick, R. C. Martin, S. Mellor, K. Schwaber, J. Sutherland, and D. Thomas. Manifesto for agile software development, 2001. Available at http://agilemanifesto.org.

3. E. Bueno. Knowledge management in the emerging strategic business process. *Journal of knowledge Management*, 7(3):1–25, 2003.
4. T. Chau and F. Maurer. Knowledge sharing in agile software teams. In W. Lenski, editor, *Logic versus Approximation: Essays Dedicated to Michael M. Richter on the Occasion of his 65th Birthday*, volume 3075 of *Lecture Notes in Artificial Intelligence*, pages 173–183. Springer, January 2004.
5. T. Chau, F. Maurer, and G. Melnik. Knowledge sharing: Agile methods vs tayloristic methods. In *Twelfth International Workshop on Enabling Technologies: Infrastructure for Collaborative Enterprises, WETICE*, pages 302–307, Los Alamitos, CA, USA, May 2003. IEEE Computer Society.
6. A. Cockburn and J. Highsmith. Agile software development: The people factor. *IEEE Computer*, 34(11):131–133, 2001.
7. B. Crawford, J. Bozo, and K. Rojas. Marco teórico para la proposición fundamentada de una herramienta computacional para la gestión de competencias. In *XI Encuentro Chileno de Computación*, Chillán, Chile, 2003.
8. A. Fink and S. Voss. Reusable metaheuristic software components and their application via software generators. In J. de Sousa, editor, *Proceedings of the 4th Metaheuristics International Conference*, pages 637–642, 2001. Available at http://citeseer.ist.psu.edu/fink01reusable.html.
9. M. Fowler. The new methodology, 2001. Available at http://www.martinfowler.com/articles/newMethodology.html.
10. J. Highsmith. Reuse as a knowledge management problem. Available at http://www.awprofessional.com/articles/article.asp?p=31478.
11. F. McCarey, M. O. Cinnéide, and N. Kushmerick. An eclipse plugin to support agile reuse. In *Proceedings of the 6th International Conference on eXtreme Programming and Agile Processes in Software Engineering*, Sheffield, UK, June 2005.
12. G. Mentzas. The two faces of knowledge management. *International Consultant's Guide*, pages 10–11, May 2000. Available at http//imu.iccs.ntua.gr/Papers/O37-icg.pdf.
13. L. Michel and P. V. Hentenryck. Localizer++: An open library for local search. Technical report, Brown University, Providence, RI, USA, 2001.
14. M. Milano and A. Roli. Magma: A multiagent architecture for metaheuristics. *IEEE Trans. on Systems, Man and Cybernetics Part B*, 34(2), April 2004.
15. I. Nonaka and H. Takeuchi. *The Knowledge Creating Company*. Oxford University Press, 1995.
16. I. Rus and M. Lindvall. Knowledge management in software engineering. *IEEE Software*, 19(3):26–38, 2002. Available at http://fc-md.umd.edu/mikli/RusLindvallKMSE.pdf.
17. S. Wagner and M. Affenzeller. Heuristiclab: A generic and extensible optimization environment. In R. et al., editor, *Proc of The Seventh International Conference on Adaptive and Natural Computing Algorithms, ICCANGA 2005*, Springer Computer Science, pages 538–541, Coimbra, Portugal, March 2005. Springer.
18. M. Zlochin, M. Birattari, and M. Dorigo. Towards a theory of practice in metaheuristics design. A machine learning perspective. Technical Report Technical Report MCS04-01, Computer Science and Applied Mathematics, The Weizmann Institute of Science, Rehovot, Israel, 2004.

PMAP: Framework to Predicting Method Access Patterns for Materialized Methods

Mariusz Masewicz, Robert Wrembel, Michal Stabno, and Rafal Staniszewski

Poznań University of Technology, Institute of Computing Science
Poznań, Poland
{Mariusz.Masewicz, Robert.Wrembel}@cs.put.poznan.pl

Abstract. In this paper we propose a framework for predicting access patterns for materialized methods. To this end, we analyze past access patterns and compute frequencies of method calls. Based on these frequencies, the system automatically decides when to recompute materialized methods. The framework was implemented and experimentally evaluated. The results are reported in this paper.

1 Introduction

Optimizing access to data returned by methods is an important research and technological issue in various object-oriented or object-relational systems, object-relational or multimedia data warehouses, as well as in distributed object environments. Since methods are expressed in an object-oriented language the optimization of their executions challenging. A promising technique applied in this area is called a *method materialization*. The materialization of method m_i consists in computing the result of the method and storing it persistently on a disk. Then, every subsequent invocation of m_i can be handled by reading the already materialized value. A drawback of this technique is that the value of materialized method m_i becomes invalid when its base object, say o_i, used for computing the value of m_i changes. As a consequence, the materialized result has to be invalidated and recomputed. This recomputation

- can either immediately follow the update of o_i; this technique is further called an *immediate recomputation*;
- or can be delayed until the next invocation of m_i; this technique is further called a *deferred recomputation*.

On the one hand, the immediate recomputation reduces response time for a user application. On the other hand, this recomputation technique may introduce additional time overhead spent by a system for unnecessary recomputations. This may happen if two or more consecutive updates of base object o_i happen. In this case, a system recomputes the value of m_i that is never used, i.e. it is invalidated by the forthcoming update of o_i. The deferred recomputation reduces a system time overhead and it introduces a user time overhead. In this mechanism an invalidated method is recomputed only when needed, but a user will wait for its result longer than in the immediate recomputation.

T. Yakhno and E. Neuhold (Eds.): ADVIS 2006, LNCS 4243, pp. 314–323, 2006.

For these reasons, a challenging task is to find such a recomputation technique that will offer acceptable response times for user applications and will incur negligible system time overhead.

1.1 Related Work

Several approaches to method materialization have been proposed in the literature. They can be characterized as persistent approaches, e.g. [1,7,8,9,12] and temporal approaches, e.g. [2,14].

The work presented in [7] analytically estimates costs of caching complex objects accessed procedurally. In this approach, the maintenance of cached (materialized) values was not taken into consideration. In the approach presented in [1], results of materialized methods are stored in a B-tree based method-index. This technique is limited to methods that do not have input arguments, compute values based on only atomic types, and do not modify values of objects. Otherwise, a method is not materialized. The concept presented in [8,9] allows to materialize methods that use input arguments. Materialized results are persistently stored in a dedicated data structure. For the purpose of method invalidations, the system maintains information about attributes whose values are used for the materialization. Moreover, every object has appended the set of method identifiers that used the object. In this approach, a system designer has to explicitly define in advance (during a system design phase) data structures for storing materialized results for all methods, even if the materialization may not be used at all. A common limitation of these three approaches is that they do not take into account dependencies between methods, where one method calls others.

In [12] the authors proposed to decompose complex methods into the graph of component methods. The semantics of complex and component methods is then analyzed in order to figure out which results to cache. The approach requires huge secondary storage as method results are cached extensively. Moreover, the maintenance of cached results is not supported.

In the temporal approaches presented in [2,14] method results are cached in main memory. When a program or a query that uses a cached results ends, then the result is removed from memory. In [14] only methods with constant input values are cached.

Two loosely related concepts to method materialization concern a cost model for method executions [3] and indexing methods along an inheritance hierarchy [11]. The cost model developed in [3] includes the number of O/I operations and CPU time, but it does not consider method materialization. In [11], the authors proposed and evaluated R-tree based indexes for the optimization of searching methods. This approach focuses on indexing metadata on methods, rather than method values.

1.2 Our Approach and Paper Contribution

The work presented in this paper naturally continues and substantially extends our previous achievements on: (1) method materialization techniques, where we developed the hierarchical materialization [4,5], and (2) techniques for selecting methods for materialization [13]. Our technique of method materialization differs from the discussed related approaches since it supports the following functionality:

- the materialization and maintenance of intermediate method results, i.e. results obtained from methods called from other methods;
- automatic selection of methods for materialization;
- the immediate and the deferred method recomputation techniques;
- the prediction of method execution patterns for the purpose of choosing the best recomputation technique.

In this paper we propose a framework for predicting method access pattern. This technique analyzes past access patterns, divides them into time periods of similar usage characteristic, and then, in each of the periods, the technique computes the frequency of a certain event, i.e. method selection or its base object update. Based on the frequency, the system automatically decides which recomputation technique to use. The prediction framework was implemented in our prototype system and it was experimentally evaluated. The experimental results are discussed in this paper. As they show, our framework allows to minimize user response time and system response time for random method access patterns. To the best of our knowledge, this is the first approach to predicting method access patterns.

The reminder of this paper is organized as follows. Section 2 overviews method materialization technique that we use. Sections 3 and 4 present our framework for method access patterns prediction and its experimental evaluation, respectively. Finally, Section 5 concludes the paper.

2   Our Approach to Method Materialization

While applying method materialization one has to address three following issues, namely (1) how to materialize methods, (2) which methods to materialize, and (3) how to maintain/rematerialize method results that became invalid. In our approach, the first issue is solved by applying the *hierarchical materialization*. The second issue is solved by applying the *dynamic materialization*. Finally, the third issue is solved by the *prediction method access patterns* (PMAP).

Hierarchical Materialization
Typically, if method m_i is materialized, then the result of the first invocation of m_i for a given base object o_i and with a given set of input argument values is materialized. Having materialized the value, each subsequent invocation of m_i for the same object o_i and with the same set of input argument values uses the already materialized value.

When the *hierarchical materialization* is applied to method m_i, then not only the result of m_i is stored persistently (materialized), but also intermediate results, i.e. the results of other methods called from m_i, are materialized. When object o_i, used for the materialization of method m_i, is updated or deleted, then the value of m_i has to be invalidated and recomputed. This recomputation can use unaffected intermediate materialized results, thus reducing the recomputation time overhead, cf. [4,5].

Dynamic Materialization

Finding the right set of methods for materialization is difficult as for each method m_i one has to take into account: (1) its execution/response time, (2) the number of reads of materialized m_i, and (3) the number of invalidations of m_i, i.e. the number of updates of its base objects.

In our approach, finding appropriate methods for materialization is supported by the *dynamic materialization* [13]. In the *dynamic materialization*, only these methods are materialized whose computation is costly and whose materialized results can be maintained at low costs. To this end, method execution statistics are collected by the system. The statistics include CPU time and the number of disk accesses for: (1) method executions, (2) method invalidations and recomputations, and (3) reads of materialized values. The statistics also include counters of base objects updates. Based on the statistics, the system automatically selects appropriate methods for materialization. When the number of updates invalidating a materialized result increases beyond a threshold, the system automatically dematerializes a given method.

3   PMAP: Predicting Method Access Patterns

In our PMAP framework we assume that for every materialized method m_i the system logs the history of m_i reads (further noted as R) and its base object o_i updates (further noted as U). For simplicity reasons, we assume that m_i has only one base object. In practice, the described framework works well also for multiple base objects.

The first U operation on o_i invalidates the materialized result of m_i. Depending on the recomputation strategy, m_i can be either computed immediately following U or just before next R. For the performance efficiency it is crucial to know whether the next operation in will be R or U. In the PMAP framework we predict the future operation patterns.

Operations on m_i and o_i are represented as the so called workloads. A *workload* is the set of R and U operations executed within a given time period, e.g. a daily workload, an hourly workload. A workload is noted as [xUxRx], where x denote any number of R or any number of U. Workloads are ordered by time. The interleaved sequences of R and U within a workload form the so called *workload pattern*.

The workload pattern may change in time. For this reason, we combine multiple workloads having similar patterns into the so called *workload sets*. In order to create a workload set, in each workload we compute the percent of U. Consecutive workloads having the same percent value or whose percent value differs less than a threshold are included into the same workload set. The number of operations in a workload set is further called a *workload set length* and it is noted as ϑ.

The access pattern prediction is based on a workload set. It works as follows. Firstly, the longest [UU...U] sequence in the workload set is found. A *sequence length* is defined as the number of consecutive U operations. Let λ denote the maximum sequence length.

Secondly, the system computes the frequency of a sequence of length l in the workload set. This frequency is computed for sequences of length 1 to λ. Let N_U^i is the number of [U...] sequences of length i, where $i = \{1, 2, \ldots, \lambda\}$. The *frequency* ρ_U^i of [U...] sequences of length i in a workload set is expressed by Formula 1. In this formula, $\sum_{n=i}^{\ell} N_U^n$ represents the number of U sequences of length greater than or equal to i; $\sum_{n=1}^{\ell} N_U^n$ represents the total number of U sequences.

$$\rho_u^i = \frac{\sum_{n=i}^{\lambda} N_U^n}{\vartheta + \sum_{n=1}^{\lambda} N_U^n} \tag{1}$$

Next, the system checks if the frequency is grater than a given (parameterized) value. If so, m_i is left as invalidated since it is likely that the next operation in the current workload is U. Otherwise m_i is recomputed immediately since it is likely that the next operation in the current workload is R.

Example. Let us consider past daily workloads from four days, as shown below.

[URUUURRRUR   UUUUURUUUR   UURRRRURUU   URURRUUURU]
<- day1 ->   <- day2 ->   <- day3 ->   <- day4 ->

For each of these four daily workloads independently we compute coefficients representing the percent of U operations. In our example, the coefficients are as follows: 5/10 for $day1$; 8/10 for $day2$; 5/10 for $day3$; and 6/10 for $day4$. Let us assume that all consecutive workloads whose coefficients differ by less than or equal to 10% are included into the same workload set. In our example, this condition is fulfiled by workloads from $day3$ and $day4$ that are included in workload set W. The other two workloads are left separated. Further analysis is performed for W whose workload set lenght $\vartheta = 20$. In W, we search for the longest U sequence. In our example it is [UUU], i.e. $\lambda = 3$. Next, we count the number of occurences of sequence [UUU] in W. Such a sequence appears twice, which we note as $N_U^3 = 2$. Next we count the number of sequences shorter by 1, i.e. [UU], i.e. $N_U^2 = 1$. Finally, we compute the number of [U] sequences, i.e. $N_U^1 = 3$.

For every detected sequence of [U...] we compute its frequency ρ_U^i, according to Formula 1. Thus $\rho_U^3 = N_U^3/(\vartheta + (N_U^3 + N_U^2 + N_U^1))$; $\rho_U^3 = 2/(20 + (2 + 1 + 3))$; $\rho_U^3 = 1/13$. In a similar way we compute $\rho_U^2 = (N_U^3 + N_U^2)/(\vartheta + (N_U^3 + N_U^2 + N_U^1))$ ($\rho_U^2 = 3/26$) and $\rho_U^1 = 3/13$. The acceptable value of ρ is parameterized in our prototype system. If ρ is greater or equal to the given value then the test condition returns true and m_i is recomputed.

Let us now assume that a new workload arrives with the first operation U. It invalidates the value of m_i. Now we have to decide whether the next operation in the new workload is [U] (we do not need to recompute m_i) or [R] (we have to recompute m_i). Based on the past workload we compute the frequency that the next operation is U, i.e. there will be a sequence of [UU]. In our example the frequency $\rho_U^2 = 3/26$ and and if it is greater than the parameterized value then m_i is recomputed immediately.

4   Performance Evaluation

The PMAP was implemented in our prototype system [6] and evaluated by experiments on a PC AMD Athlon 2GHz with 512 MB of RAM, under WindowsXP. Data were stored in object-oriented database FastObjects t7 9.0. The size of our test data equaled to 2GB.

In each of the experiments we measured a system response time and a user response time for:

- executing a non-materialized method (noted in charts as *'no materialization'*);
- deferred recomputation (noted as *'deferred remat.'*);
- immediate recomputation (noted as *'immediate remat.'*);
- executing and recomputing a method after applying our PMAP technique (noted as *PMAP*).

The system response time included all the activities done by the prototype system in order to provide a user the value of a requested method. The user response time was defined as a time a user has to wait since calling a method until getting its result.

The experiments were conducted for workloads of different lengths (ϑ) ranging from 10 to 5000 interleaved operations of R and U. The number of base object updates in every workload was parameterized. We tested the performance for three scenarios with 25% of updates (75% of reads), 50% of updates (50% of reads), and 75% of updates (25% of reads). In every test a workload pattern was randomly generated.

Figure 1 presents overall system response times for a randomly generated workload with 75% of base object updates. As we can observe from the chart, the maintenance of a on-materialized method does not introduce any time overhead that is quite obvious as the system simply executes a method without any additional maintenance. However, such execution is substantially costly, cf. the *'no materialization'* curve in Figure 2 and it disqualifies such a strategy.

For materialized methods, from a system point of view, the deferred recomputation offers the best performance, cf. the *'deferred remat.'* curve in Figure 1, whereas the immediate recomputation offers the worst performance, cf. the *'immediate remat.'* curve. The worst performance of the immediate recomputation is caused by unnecessary recomputation of a method whose base objects are updated before the method is read. It happens when there are at least two consecutive base object updates in a workload. The performance characteristics.

The performance of the PMAP technique is much better than the immediate recomputation and slightly worse than the deferred recomputation. It results from: (1) the maintenance costs of statistics describing method access patterns, (2) time overhead introduced by the access pattern prediction procedure that

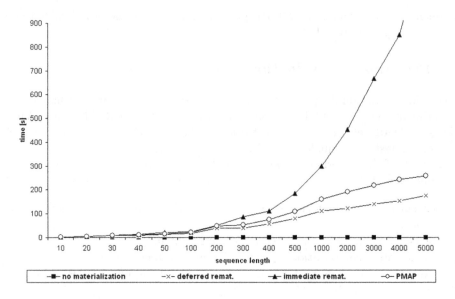

Fig. 1. System response times (75% of U in the workload; ϑ ranges from 10 to 5000)

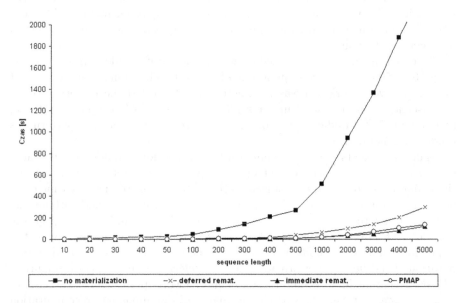

Fig. 2. User response time (75% of U in the workload; ϑ ranges from 10 to 5000)

computes frequencies, and (3) wrongly predicted access pattern causing unnecessary method recomputations. It is worth to note that our prediction procedure some time fails and results in wrong predictions.

On the contrary, if we analyze the chart shown in Figure 2 we observe that for materialized methods, from a user perspective, the deferred recomputation

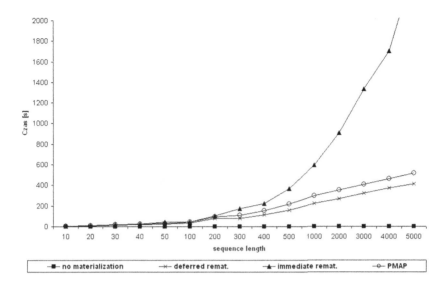

Fig. 3. System response times (50% of U in the workload; ϑ ranges from 10 to 5000)

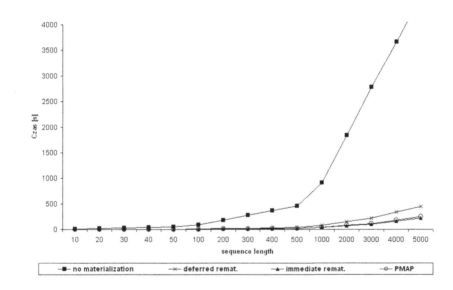

Fig. 4. User response times (of U in the workload; ϑ ranges from 10 to 5000)

offers worse performance than the immediate one. It is because a method is rematerialized at the moment it is needed and a user has to wait for a result until it is computed. The best performance is offered by the immediate recomputation as a method result is ready before it is requested. The performance of the PMAP is as good as the performance of the immediate recomputation and better than the deferred recomputation.

Figures 3 and 4 show the system response time and the user response time, respectively. These results are measured for randomly generated workloads including 50% of base object updates. These performance characteristics are similar to the characteristics discussed above. We also measured performance characteristics for workloads including 25% of base object updates (not shown here due to space limits). Those characteristics are also similar to the characteristics discussed in this paper.

As we can observe from the discussed performance characteristics, the immediate recomputation offers the best performance from a user perspective but it incurs a substantial time overhead from a system perspective. The deferred recomputation has opposite performance characteristics. The PMAP technique offers the most balanced performance characteristics. Notice that the 'PMAP' curves on Figures 1, 2, 3, and 4 are always located between the 'immediate remat.' and the 'deferred remat.'.

We can conclude that the PMAP technique is slightly worse than the best recomputation technique, i.e. the deferred one, from a system perspective. The deferred recomputation is worse than the PMAP from a user perspective. At the same time the PMAP is as good as the best recomputation technique, i.e. the immediate one, from a user perspective. The performance of the PMAP can be further improved by further development of the prediction mechanism.

5   Conclusions and Future Work

In this paper we presented a framework for predicting access patterns to materialized methods. It allows to choose the best recomputation technique and, as a consequence, improve a system's performance.

As our experiments show, even a simple technique of predicting method access patterns based on operation frequencies can substantially improve the performance of a system from a user's point of view, offering at the same time an acceptable performance from a system's point of view.

We think that the developed framework can also be applied to: (1) dynamic partitioning algorithms in distributed databases; (2) scheduling refreshing of replicas in distributed databases as well as materialized views in data warehouses; (3) scheduling data clustering (e.g. the 'database cracking' technique in the Monet/DB system [10]).

Future work will focus on further development and experimental evaluation of prediction techniques. As the next step we plan to apply the Hidden Markov Models to predict method access patterns.

References

1. Bertino E.: Method precomputation in object-oriented databases. SIGOS Bulletin, 12 (2, 3), 1991
2. Eder J., Frank H., Liebhart W.: Optimization of Object-Oriented Queries by Inverse Methods. Proc. of East/West Database Workshop, 1994

3. Gardarin G., Sha F., Tang Z. H.: Calibrating the Query Optimizer Cost Model of IRO-DB, an Object-Oriented Federated Database System. Proc. of VLDB, 1996
4. Jezierski J., Masewicz M., Wrembel R., Czejdo B.: Designing Storage Structures for Management of Materialised Methods in Object-Oriented Databases. Proc. of OOIS, 2003, LNCS 2817
5. Jezierski J., Masewicz M., Wrembel R.: On Optimising Data Access via Materialised Methods in Object-Oriented Systems. Proc. of ADVIS, 2004, LNCS 3261
6. Jezierski J., Masewicz M., Wrembel R.: Prototype System for Method Materialisation and Maintenance in Object-Oriented Databases. Proc. of the ACM SAC, 2004
7. Jhingran A.: Precomputation in a Complex Object Environment. Proc. of ICDE, 1991
8. Kemper A., Kilger C., Moerkotte G.: Function Materialization in Object Bases: Design, Realization, and Evaluation. IEEE Transactions on Knowledge and Data Engineering, Vol. 6, No. 4, 1994
9. Kemper A., Moerkotte G.: Object-Oriented Database Management: Applications in Engineering and Computer Science. Prentice Hall, 2004, ISBN 0-13-104092-8
10. Kersten M.L: Database Architecture Fertilizers: Just-in-Time, Just-Enough, and Autonomous Growth (invited lecture). Proc. of EDBT, 2006
11. Kratky M., Stolfa S., Snasel V., Vondrak I.: Efficient Searching in Large Inheritance Hierarchies. Proc. of DEXA, 2005, LNCS 3588
12. Liu Y. A., Stoller S. D., Teitelbaum T.: Static Caching for Incremental Computation. ACM Trans. on Programing Languages and Systems. Vol. 20, No. 3, 1998
13. Masewicz M., Wrembel R., Jezierski J.: Optimising Performance of Object-Oriented and Object-Relational Systems by Dynamic Method Materialisation. Proc. of ADBIS (short papers), 2005
14. Pugh W., Teitelbaum T.: Incremental Computation via Function Caching. Proc. of Principles of Programming Languages, 1989

An Architecture Design Process Using a Supportable Meta-architecture and Roundtrip Engineering

Halûk Gümüşkaya

Department of Computer Engineering, Fatih University
34500 Büyükçekmece, İstanbul, Turkey
haluk@fatih.edu.tr

Abstract. In this paper a software architecture design process based on a supportable meta-architecture (SMA) and roundtrip engineering is proposed for large software projects. Our process is applied after the requirements elicitation and analysis phases of a software project. The process begins with designing a SMA aimed at minimizing and managing software complexity. The meta-architecture should be highly supportable, i.e. understandable, maintainable, scalable, and portable and based on software engineering principles particularly object oriented design techniques, design patterns and frameworks. Roundtrip engineering embraces various supportability metrics to ensure that the implementation conforms to the meta-architecture and that the resulting system at the end of each development iteration period is supportable. Two project case studies using this design process are also presented in the paper.

1   Introduction

Today many large software projects first start the development process choosing a reference software platform, like J2EE or .NET. Selecting a reference software platform as the starting point for a product or product line has strategic and cost implications. There are many architectural choices, frameworks and open source alternatives that can be used for enterprise application development on that chosen reference platform.

The right combination of technologies, software engineering and object oriented design principles are increasingly getting important in software development especially for large projects. Although project management techniques, software development methodologies, design patterns, development, testing and architectural modeling techniques and tools have developed in the last decade [1], [2]; many software projects still fail and the percentage of successful projects completed on-time and on-budget is still very low. The Standish Group's "Chaos Report" in 1994 [3] reported that only 16.2% of software projects were completed on-time and on-budget. In 2004, 29% of projects completed on-time and on-budget, with required features and functions. Although the improvement is significant, it is dismal when compared with traditional engineering disciplines, such as architecture or electrical engineering.

In this paper a software architecture design process based on a supportable meta-architecture (SMA) and roundtrip engineering is proposed. The process begins after the software requirements are specified with a definition or selection of a SMA aimed

T. Yakhno and E. Neuhold (Eds.): ADVIS 2006, LNCS 4243 , pp. 324 – 333, 2006.

at minimizing and managing software complexity. The meta-architecture should be highly supportable, i.e. understandable, maintainable, scalable, and portable and based on software engineering principles particularly object oriented design techniques. The architecture is mainly based on frameworks, basic and enterprise design patterns and few patterns specific to problem domains. Roundtrip engineering embraces various supportability metrics to ensure that the implementation conforms to the meta-architecture and that the resulting system at the end of each development iteration period is supportable. Two project case studies using the process given in this paper are also presented.

This paper is structured as follows. The next section 2 describes the concepts of software quality and process centered architecture from our meta-architecture's point of view. In section 3, the principles and design guidelines in our architecture design process are presented. Then two project case studies using our process model are given in section 4, and finally in section 5, some of our findings are summarized.

2 Supportability and Process Centered Software Architecture

Software quality is a nonfunctional characteristic of a software component or system and can be defined for different contexts. According to IEEE 1061 [4] it represents the degree to which a software product has a desired combination of defined quality attributes. Another standard, ISO/IEC 9126-1 [5], defines a software quality model. According to this definition, there are six categories of characteristics (functionality, reliability, usability, efficiency, maintainability, and portability), which are divided into subcharacteristics. Other simpler, widely accepted quality metrics for software systems are *understandability*, *maintainability*, *scalability*, and *portability* [6]. We call these four properties the system's *supportability* features and use these quality metrics as the basic quality criteria for selecting or designing our meta-architecture.

Supportability brings layering to a project. Layering is a very useful approach for enterprise projects but it may cause some performance reduction for some applications. There are certain types of applications, like some real time applications, that can not resist this kind of a performance limitation. High supportability in enterprise application projects developed by a large number of programmers and business people is more important than runtime efficiency.

The quality of a software product can be predicted from its *higher-level design description*. This was first introduced by Parnas [7] in 1972. He described the use of *modularization* and *information hiding* as a means of high level system decomposition to improve flexibility and comprehensibility. In 1974, Stevens et al. [8] introduced the notions of module *cohesion* and *coupling* to evaluate alternatives for program decomposition. A software module is stable if cohesion (intra-module communication) is strong and coupling (inter-module interaction) is low. Good software architecture tries to maximize cohesion and minimize coupling.

One of the major tasks in building software applications is to design good *software architecture*. The software architecture of a system is defined as "the structure or structures of the system, which comprise software components, the externally visible properties of those components, and the relationships among them" [9]. This definition focuses only on the *internal aspects* of a system and most of the software analysis methods and tools are based on it. Another definition establishes software architecture as "the structure of components in a program or system, their interrelationships, and the *principles and design guidelines* that control the design and evolution in time". This *process-centered definition* takes into account the presence of principles and guidelines in the architecture description. This second definition is more comprehensive and defines better our architectural approach which has principles and guidelines in its roundtrip architectural modeling activities.

3   Principles of the Architecture Design Process

Software development phases of a typical process based project are shown in Fig 1 [10]. A software product is first carefully defined and designed and then functionality is delivered in successive iterations. Our architecture design process is applied after the requirements elicitation and analysis phases of a software project.

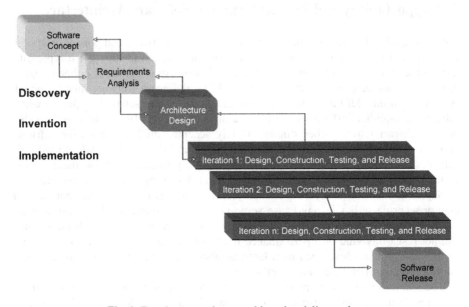

Fig. 1. Development phases and iterative delivery plan

In the following subsections the important aspects of our architecture design process, roundtrip architectural modeling and designing a supportable meta-architecture are explained.

3.1   Roundtrip Architectural Modeling

The architecture development of an application in our process model embraces a *roundtrip architectural modeling* lifecycle. The lifecycle begins with the selection of a reference software platform, such as J2EE or .NET. We chose J2EE as our reference software platform. Then a *meta-architecture* aimed at minimizing and managing software complexity is designed or selected.

The SMA design and conformance verification are performed with proactive and reactive approaches. Architectural design takes a proactive approach to managing dependencies. This is a forward-engineering approach – from design to implementation. The aim is to deliver a software design that minimizes dependencies by imposing an architectural solution on programmers. Proactive approach is supported by the reactive approach that aims at measuring dependencies in the implemented software. This is a reverse-engineering approach –from implementation to design. The implementation may or may not conform to the desired architectural design. The purpose is to show in numbers how much the implemented system is worse than a good SMA solution or another dependency-minimizing architecture. It then embraces various supportability metrics to ensure that the implementation conforms to the architectural design and that the resulting system is supportable. During the reverse engineering phase, the audits, metrics and architecture analysis results produced by modeling and analysis tools are used for conformance to the architecture.

3.2 Designing a Supportable Meta-architecture

The *meta-architecture* can be defined as "a set of high-level decisions that will strongly influence the integrity and structure of the system, but is not itself the structure of the system" [11]. It has an architectural vision, principles, styles, key concepts and mechanisms. The focus in the design of a meta-architecture is to determine high-level decisions that will strongly influence the structure of the system. It rules certain structural choices out, and guides selection decisions and tradeoffs among others.

Our SMA *layered* meta-architecture is comparable to PCMEF [2], [6] and the web framework presented in [12]. A layered architecture is a system containing multiple, strongly separated layers, with minimal dependencies between the layers. Such a system has good separation of concerns, meaning that we can deal with different areas of the application code in isolation, with minimal or no side effects in different layers. By separating the system's different pieces, we make the software supportable, adaptable so that we can easily change and enhance it as requirements change. The layers we are concerned with here include Presentation, Control, Mediator, Entity, and Foundation. With reference to the MVC (Model View Controller) framework, Presentation corresponds to MVC View, Control to Controller, and Entity to Model. Mediator and Foundation do not have MVC counterparts.

Presentation has classes that handle the user interface and assist in human-computer interactions. Control has program logic classes like searching for information in entity objects, asking the Mediator layer to bring entity objects to memory. Entity manages business objects currently in memory. Mediator mediates between Entity and Foundation subsystems to ensure that control gets access to business objects. It manages the memory cache and synchronizes the states of business objects between memory and the database. Foundation has classes that know how to talk to the database and produces SQL to read and modify the database.

The SMA is based on basic and enterprise design patterns and on few patterns specific to problem domains. The main sources of patterns for our architecture are GoF (Gang of Four) patterns [13], enterprise patterns [14] and J2EE patterns [15].

An object oriented software system has a set of collaborating objects. The allowed object communication paths, defined either statically (compile-time) or dynamically (run-time), determine the possible set of object dependencies. A necessary condition to understand a system behavior is to identify and measure all object dependencies. Dependencies can be on classes, messages, events, and inheritance. The idea is to uncover all object dependencies in a system and make them explicit. The associations are established on all directly collaborating classes in compile-time data structures. The dynamic links formed at run-time and uncontrolled polymorphic behaviors are very difficult to control and create maintenance hassle. Because of this, the SMA legitimizes run-time object communication using compile-time data structures and forbids muddy programming solutions utilizing run-time programming structures.

Another principle in the SMA architecture is to break circular dependencies between software components. Circular dependencies can be between layers, between packages and between classes within packages. All cycles must be broken to increase maintainability of the system. Cycles should be resolved by creating a new package specifically to eliminate the cycle, or by forcing one of the communication paths in the cycle to communicate via interface.

The main dependency structure in SMA is top-down. Objects in higher layers depend on objects in lower layers. Consequently, lower layers are more stable than higher layers. Upward dependencies are realized through loose coupling facilitated by interfaces, event processing, an acquaintance package and similar techniques. Dependencies are only permitted between neighboring layers.

The upward notification principle in SMA promotes low coupling in bottom-up communication between layers. This is achieved by using asynchronous communication based on event processing. Objects in higher layers act as subscribers (observers) to state changes in lower layers. When an object (publisher) in a lower layer changes its state, it sends notifications to its subscribers. In response, subscribers can communicate with the publisher (now in the downward direction) so that their states are synchronized with the state of the publisher.

4   Case Projects Based on SMA and Roundtrip Engineering

In the following subsections two project case studies based on SMA and roundtrip engineering are presented. The first one is an enterprise web application using JSF, Spring and Hibernate frameworks [16]. The second project is an indoor location determination and tracking system based on a wireless LAN infrastructure [17].

4.1   An Enterprise Web Application Based on JSF, Spring and Hibernate

A product management system as an enterprise web application was designed and implemented using the principles presented in this paper [16]. The top level view seen from the highest level of the subsystem hierarchy and their dependencies are given in Fig. 2. The acquaintance and exception packages are not in the subsystem hierarchy. The acquaintance package keeps the layers loosely coupled with interfaces. Direct usage and instantiations of classes between layers are prevented by using these interfaces.

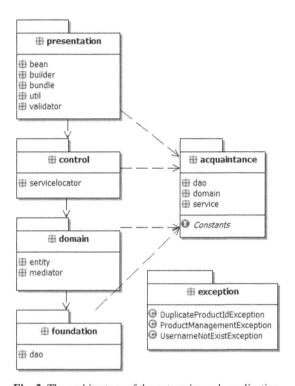

Fig. 2. The architecture of the enterprise web application

For the presentation layer, we had several web application frameworks to choose from, e.g., Struts, WebWork, and JSF (JavaServer Faces) [18], and our choice were JSF. Spring [19] organizes middle layer objects and handles transactions management. The foundation layer handles the data persistence with a relational database. An O/R (object-relational) mapping framework was used to implement the foundation layer. An object-centric approach to implementing data persistence is easy to develop and highly portable. Several frameworks exist under this domain—JDO (Java Data Objects), Hibernate, TopLink, and CocoBase are a few examples. We used Hibernate [20] to map the business objects to the relational database.

A Test Bed for Roundtrip Engineering. In order to evaluate the SMA and design principles, we developed an enterprise web application test bed as shown in Fig 3. We used Eclipse 3.0 [21] as a Java web application development and analysis platform. Borland Together for Eclipse 7.0 [22] was used as a modeling and analysis tool and IBM Structural Analysis for Java (SA4J) [23] was used for analysis, verification and validation purposes. The analysis results of these tools were used in the reverse engineering phase, and several refactoring techniques [24] were applied to improve the existing

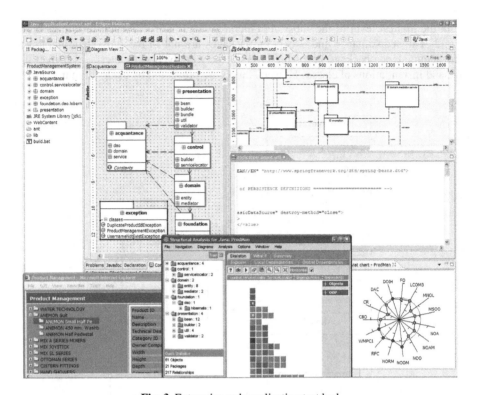

Fig. 3. Enterprise web application test bed

code. At the end of each development period, the resulting application code is analyzed to monitor the overall progress and architectural deviations. To find the architectural deviations in the testing application, SA4J was used as a dependency analysis tool and Together for Eclipse 7.0 was used for monitoring SMA basic design metrics. We used the analysis results of these programs when comparing the implemented architecture with our reference SMA. The skeleton analysis results of the system under test are given in the middle part in Fig. 3. SA4J produces a triangle-like shape for well engineered systems. For poorly engineered systems that allow direct usage of classes between layers, SA4J draws horizontal extensions at the upper levels of the shape. SA4J has many useful dependency analysis features. "What If" scenario allows presenting the future effect of a possible change in one class on the overall system. However, Together is good at calculation of a wide range of audits and metrics and visualization of the results.

The audits and metrics feature of Together was used mainly for our basic metrics analysis. For basic design principles, like layering, coupling and cohesion, the important metrics include: lack of cohesion of methods (LCOM3), coupling between objects (CBO) and weighted methods per class (WMPC1) which is a measure of maintenance costs. Halstead effect together with WMPC1 gives an accurate vision of maintainability. All mentioned metrics for our testing system were found to be in the acceptable boundaries (dots in the red circle) as seen in the diagram given in right bottom corner in Fig. 3. For situations for which metrics and analysis results don't satisfy the expectations, structural refactoring techniques are applied to the deviated subsystems (i.e. packages, classes) at the next software development iteration phase.

4.2   A Real Time Indoor WLAN Positioning System

Wireless positioning using IEEE 802.11 WLAN technologies has been a hot topic in recent years [17], [25]. We worked on the design, implementation and performance evaluation of an indoor positioning system, WiPoD, (Wireless Position Detector). WiPoD was developed in the Computer Engineering Department at Fatih University. The system locates and tracks the user having an IEEE 802.11 supported device across the coverage area of a WLAN. We investigated the possible implementations of WLAN positioning using different algorithms and if the implementation could be achieved at a level of acceptable accuracy to be used in real-life cases. Our experimental results are quite encouraging. With high probability, WiPoD is able to estimate a user's location to within a few meters of his/her actual location [16].

The WiPoD software architecture based on the SMA and roundtrip engineering is shown in Fig. 4. Each layer communicates with only lower and upper layers. The highest layer Presentation is the package that includes the user interface classes and it assists in the human-computer interactions. Control layer is responsible for functionalities such as determining the location, creating the radio map, retrieving the data

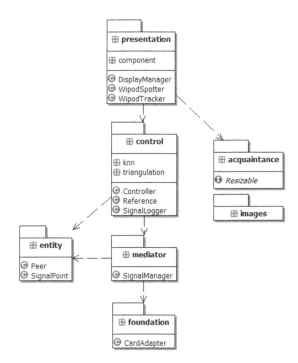

Fig. 4. WiPoD software architecture, subsystems and dependencies

from Mediator and passing this data to the Presentation layer. Two location determination algorithms, K-Nearest Neighbor (KNN) and Triangulation, were implemented in this layer. Mediator is the key point in the system as it mediates between hardware layer classes and high-level application layer classes. While Entity manages the wireless data objects currently in the memory, Mediator ensures that Control subsystem gets access to these data objects.

Foundation provides a communication link between a WLAN interface card and Mediator. Data is retrieved from and sent to the hardware via classes that know how to talk to the wireless adapter. As other subsystems were implemented only in Java, this package was written in both C and Java. In order to communicate with the network adapter, we used RawEther [26] which is a framework for development of Windows products that directly access NDIS (Network Driver Interface Specification) [27] network interface drivers from Win32 applications. The JNI (Java Native Interface) [28] was used to access the native DLL code produced by RawEther. By writing programs using the JNI, we ensure that our code is portable across platforms. The system can be easily ported to different devices having Java and NDIS supports.

5 Summary

In this paper a software architecture design process based on SMA and roundtrip engineering was presented. The designed meta-architecture is supportable and based on design patterns and frameworks. Roundtrip engineering uses supportability metrics to ensure that the implementation conforms to the meta-architecture and that the resulting system is supportable. We successfully applied the architecture design process in two projects having different characteristics.

We first showed how to integrate different web technologies, JSF, Spring and Hibernate, using the well defined SMA to build a real-world Web application. By partitioning the whole Web application into layers and programming using interfaces, the technology used for each application layer can be replaced. For example, Struts can take the place of JSF for the presentation layer, and JDO or Toplink can replace Hibernate in the foundation layer.

Although the second project WiPoD was a real time application, the layered architecture gave also a good acceptable run-time performance. The well defined and separated tasks distributed to the packages and layered architecture made the WiPoD software architecture *understandable* and *maintainable* for developers having different skills in areas of programming, wireless networking and positioning algorithms. The developer having only a high level Java and GUI background can only work in the Presentation layer and uses the Control layer classes. The developers having background in Java, wireless networking and positioning algorithms work on the problems in the Control layer. The C and NDIS low level programmer having some wireless knowledge works in the Foundation layer. It is easy to add new modules, like classes and new packages to the WiPoD architecture. The places, layers and packages, of new modules are clear. Scalability also does not cause any performance problem.

References

1. Bruegge, B., Dutoit, A. H.: Object-Oriented Software Engineering: Conquering Complex and Changing Systems, Using UML, Patterns, and Java. Prentice-Hall (2004)
2. Maciaszek, L. A., Liong, B. L.: Practical Software Engineering. Addison-Wesley (2005)

3. The CHAOS Reports. Available at http://www.standishgroup.com
4. IEEE Standard 1061-1992, Standard for Software Quality Metrics Methodology (1992)
5. ISO/IEC 9126-1, Software Engineering - Product Quality - Part 1: Quality Model (2001)
6. Maciaszek, A., Liong, B., L.: Designing Measurably-Supportable Systems. Advanced Information Technologies for Management. Research Papers No 986. (2003) 120–149
7. Parnas, D.: On the Criteria to be Used in Decomposing Systems into Modules. Communications of ACM, Vol. 15. No. 12 (1972) 1053–1058
8. Stevens, W. P., Myers, G. J., Constantine, L.L.: Structured Design. IBM Systems Journal, Vol. 13. No. 2 (1974) 115–139
9. Bass, L., Clements, P., Kazman, R.: Software Architecture in Practice. 2nd Edition. Addison-Wesley (2003)
10. Gümüşkaya, H.: Core Issues Affecting Software Architecture in Enterprise Projects. Proceedings of the Enformatika, Vol. 9 (2005) 32–37
11. Malan, R., Bredemeyer, D.: Visual Architecting Process. http://www.bredemeyer.com/
12. Knight, A., Dai, N.: Objects and the Web. IEEE Software. March/April (2002) 51–59
13. Gamma, E., Helm, R., Johnson, R., Vlissides, J., Design Patterns, Elements of Reusable Object-Oriented Software. Addison-Wesley (1995)
14. Fowler, M.: Patterns of Enterprise Application Architecture. Addison-Wesley (2003)
15. Alur, D., Crupi, J., Malks, D.: Core J2EE Patterns. Prentice Hall (2003)
16. Bilgi, M., Gümüşkaya, H.: Design Issues for Supportable Enterprise Web Architecture using Frameworks. Turkish Software Architecture Design Workshop, Sep. 24 (2005)
17. Gümüşkaya, H., Hakkoymaz, H.: WiPoD Wireless Positioning System Based on 802.11 WLAN Infrastructure. Proceedings of the Enformatika, Vol. 9 (2005) 126–130
18. Official JavaServer Faces site: http://java.sun.com/j2ee/javaserverfaces/index.jsp
19. Official Spring site: http://www.springframework.org/
20. Official Hibernate site: http://www.hibernate.org/
21. Eclipse program development platform web site: http://www.eclipse.org
22. Borland Together UML modeling tool web site: http://www.borland.com/together
23. IBM Structural Analysis for Java tool web site: http://www.alphaworks.ibm.com/tech/sa4j
24. Fowler, M.: Refactoring, Improving the Design of Existing Code. Addison-Wesley (1999)
25. Bahl, P., Padmanabhan, V. N.: RADAR: An In-Building RF-Based User Location and Tracing System. Proceedings of IEEE Infocom, Tel Aviv, Israel, March (2000)
26. RawEther for Windows web site: http://www.rawether.net/
27. NDIS Developer's Reference web site: http://www.ndis.com/
28. JNI tutorial web site: http://java.sun.com/docs/books/tutorial/native1.1/

Knowledge-Based Enterprise Modelling Framework

Saulius Gudas[1,2] and Rasa Brundzaite[1]

[1] Vilnius University, Kaunas Faculty of Humanities,
Muitines 8, LT-44280 Kaunas, Lithuania
{gudas, rasa.brundzaite}@vukhf.lt
[2] Kaunas University of Technology, Information Systems Department,
Studentu 50, LT-51368 Kaunas, Lithuania
gudas@soften.ktu.lt

Abstract. The Knowledge-Based Enterprise Modelling framework is based on the redefined concept of the knowledge-based enterprise. The Strategic Alignment Framework by Henderson and Venkatraman is modified and used for description of Knowledge-based Enterprise structure. The Enterprise Knowledge Base together with explicitly defined knowledge management activity is treated as the major component of the knowledge-based enterprise. Four domains of the knowledge-based enterprise are abstracted from the enterprise architecture point of view. The process-oriented Knowledge-based Enterprise Model is presented by modifying the Porter's Value Chain Model (VCM). The Knowledge management layer is identified within the modified VCM. Two types of control loops are identified between layers of the Knowledge-Based Enterprise Model.

1 Introduction

The knowledge-based theory of the firm considers knowledge as the most strategically significant resource of the firm [1, 2]. Information technologies (IT) play an important role in the knowledge-based firm in sense that information systems can be used to synthesize, enhance, and expedite large-scale intra-and inter-firm knowledge management [3]. However firms face challenges when implementing IT systems to support of knowledge management. In spite of variety of knowledge management (KM) models [4] and tools, there is a gap between these conceptual models and the practical implementation of knowledge management in organizations based on IT. Organizations require more systematic and formalized methods for the knowledge management implementation and support of KM activities by IT.

The article presents the Knowledge-based Enterprise Modelling framework which can be considered as the formalized knowledge management structure for the implementation of the knowledge management systems. The framework will enable to solve a problem of the knowledge-based business and IT alignment as well as the development and management of the enterprise information systems.

The next chapter deals with the structure and scope of the knowledge-based enterprise in order to identify main constructs for the enterprise knowledge modelling. First, the concept of the knowledge-based enterprise is clarified and illustrated using

T. Yakhno and E. Neuhold (Eds.): ADVIS 2006, LNCS 4243 , pp. 334 – 343, 2006.

Strategic Alignment Model by Henderson and Venkatraman. On the basis of the research four knowledge domains of the knowledge-based enterprise are abstracted.

Structural method for the enterprise knowledge modelling is selected and used for the knowledge-based enterprise model (KBEM) in the chapter three.

2 Aspects of Knowledge Related Enterprise Modelling

Y.Malhotra [5] have analyzed the application of KM technologies in organizational business processes for enabling real time enterprise (RTE) business models and concluded that there are increasing failures of KM technology implementations, which result from the critical gaps between technology inputs, knowledge processes, and business performance outcomes. From the theoretical point of view this gap could emerge because of misunderstanding regarding definition of the knowledge-based enterprise as well as insufficient formality of definition of the enterprise knowledge. From the practical point of view the gap comes from the lack of appropriate methods and tools for the consistent and effective transformation of business into knowledge-based business, based on information technology. Therefore first of all it is necessary to specify the concept of the "knowledge-based enterprise".

In the literature there are a lot of definitions of the knowledge management (analysed in detail by R.Maier in [6]) as well as the definitions, related to the knowledge-based enterprise. In the broadest sense, knowledge management can be considered as a strategic process of an enterprise which is intended to solve critical enterprise adaptability and competitiveness problems in the rapidly changing environment. The main goal of the knowledge management in enterprises is to establish an organizational context for the effective creation, store, dissemination and use of organizational knowledge, which are essential for securing enterprise competitiveness against changing business environment and for setting environment towards a desirable direction. Few concepts related to the knowledge-based enterprise were found in the literature: knowledge-intensive business, knowledge-centric business, knowledge-driven enterprise or business and knowledge-based business. All these concepts in various sources had different semantic, therefore it should be useful to clarify the semantics of these concepts.

Appropriate name for any enterprise, which is based on knowledge intensive work or knowledge intensive products, is a *knowledge-intensive organization* or firm. Proposed definition of the knowledge-intensive enterprise is not in touch with the maturity level of knowledge management in the enterprise. According to the Knowledge management maturity culture and adoption in a company model, presented by KMPG [7] knowledge-intensive enterprise can be at some maturity level: Knowledge chaotic, Knowledge aware, Knowledge enabled, Knowledge managed or Knowledge centric. The presented definitions of the knowledge-centric and knowledge-based enterprise are viewed as different levels of the knowledge management maturity of the organization.

2.1 Knowledge-Centric Enterprise Structure

The knowledge-centric organization, regardless of whether its products are tangible or not, here is defined according to the concept of knowledge-based organization, presented by M.H.Zack [8] and is based on the resource-based view of the firm [1,2];

namely, knowledge-centric organization: a) recognizes knowledge as a key strategic resource, b) rethinks their business processes in the knowledge-oriented sense (i.e. "it takes knowledge into account in every aspect of its operation and treats every activity as a potentially knowledge-enhancing act." [8]), c) aligns its knowledge management activity with its strategy.

Even if the definition of the knowledge-centric enterprise do not emphasizes the use of the information technologies (IT) in the enterprise, it should be noted, that research presented here is concerned with the contemporary enterprise, which uses IT extensively for the support of the management of its business processes. The newest vision of the Real Time Enterprise (RTE) as the most adaptive and responsive enterprise is expressed by Gartner Group [10]. Y. Malhotra [11] have analyzed the knowledge gaps which arise when implementing knowledge management in Real Time Enterprises and pointed out two main KM models: strategy-pull and technology-push model, thus indicating two interrelated RTE domains: business (strategy) domain and technology domain. Henderson and Venkatraman [9] also have analysed business-IT alignment problem and proposed a seminal Strategic Alignment Model (SAM) for business–IT alignment; the model was aimed to support the integration of information technology (IT) into business strategy by advocating alignment between and within four domains. In the SAM two interrelated aspects of computerized enterprise are defined: 1) business domain and 2) IT domain, into two levels of detail: 1) infrastructure and processes level, 2) strategic level. As a result of such decomposition four different domains were identified: Business strategy domain, Business infrastructure and processes domain, IT strategy domain and IT infrastructure and processes domain. It can be concluded, that the model of Henderson and Venkatraman allows modelling various interactions between business and IT domain, which can be expressed as various pull/push models according Y.Malhotra. Contemporary organizations use the integrated data repositories which have to be identified within the model either (the *Data Base* component in figure 1).

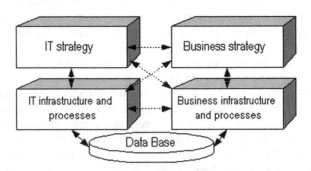

Fig. 1. Business and IT alignment framework according Henderson and Venkatraman [9]

The SAM defines the range of strategic choices facing managers. The authors argue that the potential strategic impact of IT requires "a process of continuous adaptation and change". So cross-domain alignment activity (shown as dotted arrows in figure 1) is continuous decision making process, which is a central element of organizational transformation and thus requires for adequate knowledge. Dotted arrows here is used to highlight, that this decision making process normally is not well defined and potentially there may exist knowledge flow bottlenecks.

For the illustrating the conception of the contemporary enterprise, which is RTE and knowledge-centric enterprise, the Henderson and Venkatraman model have to be complemented by additional components. According to the knowledge-centric organization definition, it rethinks its processes in the knowledge-oriented sense and aligns its knowledge management activity with its strategy. Consequently, in the knowledge-centric enterprise there exist some infrastructure for the knowledge management; thus SAM model is complemented with additional structural element - knowledge management component (see fig. 2).

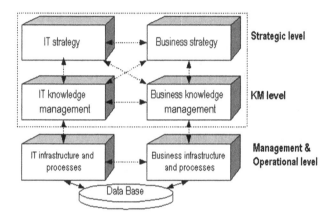

Fig. 2. The knowledge-centric enterprise structure

Summing up, business and IT domains can be analysed into three levels of detail: Strategy, KM and Business processes and infrastructure levels.

Even if knowledge-centric enterprise structures and manages its knowledge management activities, there is a possibility for the knowledge flow bottlenecks left (dotted arrows in figure 2), because the valuable knowledge required for the management solutions about two interrelated enterprise domains typically resides in the heads of the managers and employees, in the unstructured documents etc. As the business-IT alignment is continuous decision making process, it should be supported with reliable information and knowledge accessible across the enterprise.

2.2 Knowledge-Based Enterprise Structure

The scope and structure of the organizational knowledge in the knowledge management literature is investigated. This structure has the name of *organizational memory* or *corporate memory*. The organizational memory is concerned with the organizational learning processes. Organizational memory comprises all the possible forms of organizational knowledge: tacit, explicit, computerized, not-computerized etc. [6].

There are a lot of possible facets for characterising knowledge [6], although it is important in this situation to analyse knowledge in the sense of its "objective" and "subjective" characteristics. According J.M. Firestone [12], there are two kinds of knowledge:

1. "Knowledg`e viewed as belief... Such knowledge is "subjective" in the sense that it is agent-specific, whether the agent is an individual, group, team, or organization".
2. "Knowledge viewed as validated models, theories, arguments, descriptions, problem statements etc. ...This kind of knowledge, further, is "objective." It is objective in the sense that it is not agent specific and is shared among agents. Finally, it is objective because, since it is sharable, we can sensibly talk about community validation of this kind of knowledge."

Business-IT alignment is continuous decision making process and it should be supported with reliable information and knowledge. As it was noted in the beginning of the article, enterprise knowledge based is intended to be used as the source of knowledge about the problem domain (i.e.) also for IS engineering tasks in the IS requirements development stage. Resuming it should be stated that enterprise knowledge base has to be shared, computerised and it have to store the enterprise knowledge in the form of validated Enterprise Knowledge Models. According Knowledge-based IS engineering paradigm [13, 14] enterprise knowledge models have to be validated according formalized enterprise model thus ensuring reliability of the acquired knowledge about problem domain.

Therefore Strategic Alignment Model is complemented by one more additional structural element – Enterprise *Knowledge Base Element* (see fig.3), which supports enterprise knowledge management activities and allows continuous cross-domain alignment process also helps eliminate knowledge flow bottleneck across enterprise (solid arrows lines in the figure 3).

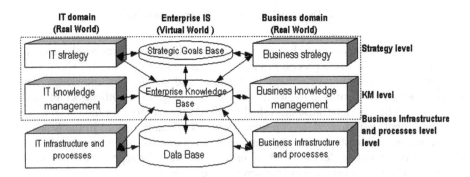

Fig. 3. Knowledge-based enterprise structure

Consequently *knowledge-based enterprise* here is defined as knowledge-centric enterprise (as defined above), which uses EKB as obligatory enterprise management and information system development component.

In the figure 3 the structural element *Strategic Goals Base* is abstracted, which could be as the part of the EKB too.

Contemporary enterprise modelling methods are conceptual methods in the sense how the models are created and what knowledge they represents [13]; they allow to acquire empirical knowledge about the problem domain (i.e. enterprise), which can be hardly validated. *Enterprise Knowledge Base* (EKB) here is considered as the computerised Enterprise Knowledge Model, which consist of integrated set of enterprise knowledge sub models and is validated against the formalized enterprise knowledge model. Thus EKB is the reliable knowledge source for a support of business management decision making, business and IT alignment as well as for support of knowledge management and information systems development processes.

2.3 Four Domains of the Knowledge-Based Enterprise

In Strategic Alignment Model [9] two interrelated aspects of the enterprise are defined: 1) Business domain and 2) IT domain. According to the definition of the knowledge-based enterprise (see section 2.2) another two important aspects of the enterprise are identified: Knowledge domain and Data domain. All these four aspects forms four interrelated domains (see figure 4), which have to be taken into account when transforming business into knowledge-based business.

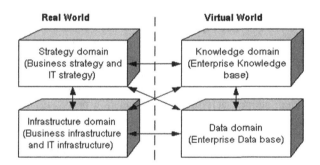

Fig. 4. Four domains of the knowledge-based enterprise

The scheme presented in the Figure 4 sums up findings made in the chapter 2. This four-domain model represents typical way of thinking used in the Enterprise Modelling and Enterprise Information Architecture research fields. The peculiarity of this abstraction is that it clearly separates the Knowledge domain from Data domain, in contrast to other conceptual enterprise models (e.g. presented in [15] or [16]). Well-known ISA framework by J.Zachman [17] do not concerns knowledge domain at all. Though comparing ISA model with the presented abstraction of the knowledge-based enterprise domains it should be noted different purposes and tasks of the ISA and Enterprise Knowledge Modelling framework.

Concept of the knowledge base is also used in the sense of computerized meta-data repository when implementing large-scale data management and business intelligence systems in the contemporary organizations. Meta-data repository helps to provide business data as well as data about data for business and for IT people and to make adequate decisions regarding data management in organizations. Contemporary organizations need to manage not only data, but the whole data-information-knowledge continuum; this is why the role and structure of the enterprise repository or enterprise knowledge base have to change adequately too. The concept of computerized knowledge base become important with the emergence of such intensively computer-based organizational forms as supply chains, virtual organizations etc. Organizations requires for having in virtual environment not only shared data bases, but also knowledge about those data, as well as about the data structure and semantics; knowledge about its infrastructure and processes; process management up to strategic intentions.

The solid lines in the figure four represent the knowledge management activities which are used to assure integration of the enterprise knowledge base into overall enterprise management and development framework as well as support of inter-domain alignment tasks. Knowledge management activity has to be managed and explicitly modelled either.

3 Knowledge-Based Enterprise Model

In the KM field the process-oriented view is recognized as a success factor [18]. Therefore for Porter's VCM was selected as a structural background for enterprise knowledge modelling. The Porter's Value Chain Model is process-oriented and is applied for business systems analysis, based on the separation between primary and support activities. The Porter's VCM here is used as a basis for the enterprise knowledge modelling. VCM represents a process-oriented view to business. In the organizational management practice the Porter's Value Chain Model (VCM) [19] is widely recognized.

S. Gudas, A. Lopata, T. Skersys [14, 20] focused on the informational interactions between primary and support activities. The different nature of these two kinds of activities is revelaed: support activities are information processing activities and are referred to as *Business Process Management Functions*; primary activities typically are material processing (technological) and are named *Processes*. The similar insights are represented in the organizational control systems modelling (OCSM) framework developed by Kampfner [21]. The interrelated elements *Function* and *Process* form the construct *Business Process* (B). The interaction of the elements *Process* and *Function* is formally assumed as a *Control Process* with the *Feedback Loop*, i.e. *Elementary Management Cycle* (*EMCp*). As the *Function* and *Process* interaction is discussed already in detail by Gudas, Skersys and Lopata [20], lets concentrate on enterprise model constructs, which are related to the knowledge management.

According to the knowledge-based enterprise definition and structure (see figure 3), there is another type of business activities – knowledge management activity, which is also identified within VCM. On the basis of these findings the modified value chain model is developed (see figure 5). Whereas the modified Value Chain Model is focused on the enterprise knowledge management activities and components, it is named *Knowledge-based Enterprise Model* (*KBEM*).

Additionally, for the completeness of the enterprise analysis, the component *Resources* (*R*) is included in the KBEM.

The Knowledge-based enterprise model (KBEM) is constructed from the following main components: *Business process* (*B*), *Knowledge management function* (*K*) component, *Elementary Process Management Cycle* (*EMCp*), *Elementary Knowledge Management Cycle* (*EMCz*), *IT* (*T*) component and the *Resource* component (*R*).

The semantics of the knowledge-based enterprise model is described more detail in [22]. The peculiarity of the developed model comparing with the VCM is that the developed model distinguishes between qualitatively different business activities (*F, P* and *K* constructs) and allows formally represent interactions between these activities by using two types of the control processes (*EMCz* and *EMCp* with different semantics).

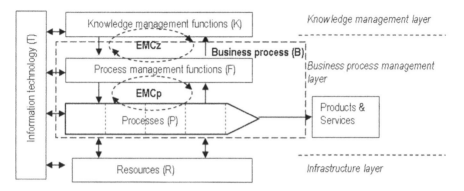

Fig. 5. Knowledge-based Enterprise model

The KBEM is process-oriented model and it refines two different layers (figure 5) of enterprise management hierarchy:

− the component *Knowledge management functions (K)* is aimed to control activities of the component *Process management functions (F)* on *the layer of knowledge management;*
− the component *Process management functions (F)* is aimed to control activities of the component *Processes (P)* on *the layer of business process management.*

The interaction of the different layers of the KBEM is considered as control loop (informational feedback) formally described in [14, 20] as *EMC (Elementary Management Cycle)*. The semantics of identified management transactions *EMCp* and *EMCz* are different, and are defined as follows:

− *Process management cycle EMCp* − implements a set of *Process* management functions. *EMCp* is responsible for control of the component *Processes (P)* − primary activities of enterprise (development of products and services in the proper way (Quality, Time schedule, etc));
− *Knowledge management cycle EMCz* − is the higher level EMC, its component *Knowledge management functions* is responsible for the adequate activities of the *KBEM* component *Process management functions (F)*. The *EMCz* is focused on the alignment of *Business process (B)* with the Enterprise strategic goals.

As the Process management cycle *EMCp* is extensively discussed in [14], next the particularities of the Knowledge management cycle *EMCz* are described in brief.

By definition [14] an elementary management cycle *EMC* consists of the predefined sequence of mandatory steps of information transformation (*Interpretation, Information Processing, Realization*); these steps compose a management cycle (a feedback loop). The content of information and semantics of transformation of these mandatory steps of *EMC* depends on the subject area (domain of the enterprise). For instance, the subject area of the *Knowledge management cycle EMCz* is a definite set of *Processes management functions*. It is evident that this subject area of *EMCz* (i.e. information and semantics of transformation of *EMCz*) is totally different from that of *Process management cycle EMCp*. The *EMCz* deals with the information about the characteristics of management functions (quality, effectiveness, etc.), meanwhile the Process management cycle *EMCp* controls a characteristics of products, services and state of a *Process* (i.e. technological process).

So, the content (semantics) of information processed in these two management cycles (*EMCz* and *EMCp*) is unlike, different. The mandatory steps (*Interpretation, Information Processing, Realization*) of the *Elementary Knowledge Management Cycle (EMCz)* are defined as an information transferring processes focused on the control of the content and set of management functions *F*.

4 Conclusions

Few theoretical findings concerning knowledge management in the enterprise were made thus making prerequisites for the development of the practical methods for the implementation of the knowledge management systems in the enterprises.

The Knowledge-Based Enterprise Modelling (KBEM) framework is based on the redefined Strategic Alignment Framework by Henderson and Venkatraman. Four domains of Knowledge-based Enterprise are abstracted from enterprise architecture point of view thus providing qualitatively new viewpoint to the abstraction of the enterprise.

The Enterprise Knowledge Base (EKB) is concerned as the mandatory construct of the knowledge based-enterprise. In the article it was concluded, that EKB contains validated enterprise knowledge models about the knowledge-based enterprise domain.

The process-oriented Knowledge-based Enterprise Model (KBEM) is presented by modifying the Porter's Value Chain Model (VCM). The peculiarity of this KBEM is Knowledge management layer and business process layer identified within the modified VCM. The interactions between layers of KBEM are formally described as two semantically different control loops: Process Management Cycle (*EMCp*) and Knowledge Management Cycle (*EMCz*).

The presented framework of the Knowledge-based Enterprise is the basis for the development of the practical methods for the knowledge-based enterprise modelling and implementation.

References

1. Grant, R. M. Toward a Knowledge-Based Theory of the Firm: In: Strategic Management J. 17 (1996) 109–122
2. Conner, K. R.: A Historical Comparison of Resource-Based Theory and Five Schools of Thought Within Industrial Organization Economics: Do we have a new theory of the firm? In: J. Management 17(1) (1991)121–154
3. Alavi, M., Leidner, D.E.: Review: Knowledge Management and Knowledge Management Systems, MIS Quarterly (25:1), March (2001) 107-136

4. Holsapple, C. W., Joshi, K. D.: Description and Analysis of Existing Knowledge Management Frameworks. In: Proceedings oh the 32nd Hawaii International Conference on System Sciences, vol. 1 (1999) 1072-1087
5. Malhotra, Y.: Why Knowledge Management Systems Fail. Enablers and Constraints of Knowledge Management in Human Enterprises. Information Today Inc., Medford, NJ, (2004) 87-112, available at: www.brint.org/WhyKMSFail.htm.
6. Maier, R.: Knowledge Management Systems: Information and Communication Technologies for Knowledge Management. Springer; 2nd ed. (2004)
7. KPMG Knowledge Management Research Report (2000), available at: www.kpmg.co.uk
8. Zack, M. H.: Rethinking the Knowledge-Based Organization. In: Sloan management review, vol. 44, no. 4, summer (2003) 67-71, available at: http://web.cba.neu.edu/~mzack/articles/kbo/kbo.htm
9. Henderson, J., Venkatraman, N.: Strategic Alignment: A Model for Organization Transformation via Information Technology. Massachusetts Institute of Technology, Working Paper 3223-90 (1990)
10. Now is the Time for Real-Time Enterprise. Gartner Group (2002) available at: http://www.gartner.com/pages/story.php.id.2632.s.8.jsp
11. Malhotra, Y.: Integrating Knowledge Management Technologies in Organizational Business Processes: Getting Real Time Enterprises to Deliver Real Business Performance. In: Journal of Knowledge Management, vol. 9, No 1 (2005) 7-28
12. Firestone, J. M.: Knowledge Management: A Framework for Analysis and Measurement. In: DsStar, vol.5, No 1 (2001) available at: http://www.taborcommunications.com/dsstar/01/0102/102505.html
13. Gudas, S.: Žiniomis grindžiamos IS inžinerijos metodų principai [The principles of the Knowledge-based IS Engineering methods]. In: IT'2005 (2005), 713-717
14. Gudas, S., Lopata, A., Skersys, T.: Approach to Enterprise Modelling for Information Systems Engineering. In: Informatica, vol. 16 (2005) 175-192
15. Iyer, B., Gottlieb, R.: The Four-Domain Architecture: An approach to Support Enterprise Architecture Design (2004) available at: www.research.ibm.com/journal/sj/433/iyer.pdf
16. Maes, Rik, Rijsenbrij, Daan, Truijens, Onno et al.: Redefining Business – IT Alignment Through a Unified Framework (2000) available at: imwww.fee.uva.nl/ ~maestro/PDF/2000-19.pdf
17. Zachman, J. A., Sowa, J. F.: Extending and Formalizing the Framework for Information Systems Architecture. In: IBM Systems Journal, vol. 31, no. 3 (1992)
18. Maier, R., Remus, U.: Towards a Framework for Knowledge Management Strategies: Process Orientation as Strategic Starting Point. In: Proceedings of the 34th Hawaii International Conference on System Sciences, (2001) available at: http://csdl.computer.org/comp/proceedings/hicss/2001/0981/04/09814023.pdf
19. Porter, M. E.: Competitive Strategy: Creating and Sustaining Superior Performance. New York: The Free Press (1985)
20. Gudas, S., Skersys, T., Lopata, A.: Framework for knowledge-based IS engineering. In: Advances in Information Systems ADVIS'2004, T. Yakhno, Ed., Berlin: Springer-Verlag, (2004) 512-522
21. Kampfner, Roberto R.: Modeling the Information-Processing Aspect of Organizational Functions. IEEE (1999)
22. Gudas S, Brundzaite R.: Decomposition of the Enterprise Knowledge Management Layer. In: Proceedings of the 2006 Seventh International Baltic Conference on Databases and Information Systems (Baltic DB&IS 2006) July-3-6. Vilnius: Technika (2006) 41-47

A Network-Based Indexing Method for Trajectories of Moving Objects

Kyoung-Sook Kim[1], Mario A. Lopez[2], Scott Leutenegger[2], and Ki-Joune Li[1]

[1] Department of Computer Science and Engineering
Pusan National University, Pusan 609-735, South Korea
{ksookim, lik}@pnu.edu
[2] Department of Computer Science
University of Denver, 2360 S. Gaylord St., Denver, CO 80208-0183, U.S.A
{mlopez, leut}@cs.du.edu

Abstract. Recently many researchers have focused on management of historical trajectories of moving objects due to numerous size of accumulated data over time. However, most of them are concentrated in Euclidean spaces with (x, y, t). In real world, moving objects like vehicles on transportation networks have constraints on their movements, and some of applications need to manage and query them. Previous work based on Euclidean is inefficient to process trajectories on road networks. In this paper, we propose a indexing method for trajectories of moving objects on road networks. While some work has been done for indexing the trajectory in spatial networks, little indexing method support the network-based spatiotemporal range query processing. Our method consists of multiple R-trees and graph structures to process the network-based spatiotemporal range query defined by the network distance instead of Euclidean distance. Consequently, we show that our method takes about 30% less in node accesses for the network-based range query processing than other methods based on the Euclidean distance by experiments.

1 Introduction

As a development of wireless communications and position-based technologies, the geographical location information of moving objects such as human or vehicles becomes applied broadly. Moving objects can be divided into two categories depending on the domain where they move: one is Euclidean spaces, and the other is the space with some constraints such as transportation networks or terrain data. Although many researchers have focused on the management of moving objects in Euclidean spaces, the moving objects in the constraint space are more important on the specific application area, especially telematics. Telematics manages the geographical location of vehicles on transportation networks and renders various information about traffic, accident, routes, and so on. In order to improve the qualities and provide manifold services for this kind of applications, we need not only to track the continuous locations of vehicles on

T. Yakhno and E. Neuhold (Eds.): ADVIS 2006, LNCS 4243, pp. 344–353, 2006.

road networks, but also to store and to retrieve them in databases efficiently. However, most of methods that have been developed for indexing and query processing deal with moving objects in Euclidean spaces. Therefore, they have some problems to handle moving objects on road networks.

The network space has three differences comparing to Euclidean:(1) the representation of coordinates; (2) the distance between two objects; (3) the dimensionality of domains. In this paper, we propose a new indexing method for trajectories of moving objects on transportation networks. First, we represent the trajectories using the information of road network instead of 3D Euclidean space with (x, y, t), and introduce the network-based spatiotemporal range query. Second, we involve the network connectivity information in indexing structures to process the network-based spatiotemporal queries. Our method is based on multiple R-trees for trajectories and on a graph structure for connectivity relationship of road networks. For the network-based spatiotemporal query processing, we use the network distance instead of Euclidean distance. Using the network distance leads to a good performance because of reducing the unnecessary searching space in road networks.

The rest of this paper is organized as follows. Section 2 introduces the related works, Section 3 defines the problems in the network spaces, and Section 4 describes our data structures and associated algorithms. Section 5 evaluates the proposed method with some experiments. We conclude our paper in Section 6.

2   Related Work

Many researchers have investigated indexing methods for moving objects to improve the performance of updating data and query processing. Generally, there are two groups of the indexing method for moving objects. The first group of the indexing method tries to both handle current positions continuously changed over time and anticipate their positions in near future. This kind of methods focuses on reducing the cost of query processing as well as the cost of frequent updating for the real-time location-aware services. The other group deals with the historical trajectories of moving objects from past to present. Because of the massive size of trajectory data, we have high retrieval cost in the database into which we store their past positions. Therefore, this kind of indexing methods aims to improve the spatiotemporal query performance.

In this paper, we focus on processing trajectories of moving objects on road networks. Many spatiotemporal access methods are based on R-tree[1]. For example, 3D R-tree[2], HR-tree[3], and MV3R-tree[6] are spatiotemporal access methods to be able to process temporal predicates such as timestamp(or time slice) and time interval queries; but, they have some problems to access to part or whole trajectory for trajectory-based queries or navigational queries due to the absence of the location information of itself. For them, Pfoser et al. have suggested spatiotemporal R-tree(STR-tree) and Trajectory-Bundle tree(TB-tree) in [4]. Besides, some indexing methods like SETI and SEB-tree[10], which have been proposed by Prasad Chakka et al. and Song and Roussopoulos respectively, are for the efficient insertion of trajectory segments using the space partition mechanism. These access methods deal with trajectories of moving objects in (x, y, and t) Euclidean space. However, they overlook moving objects whose movement has some constraints; for instance, a vehicle or a train respectively stays a road or a rail, a human just moves a predefined area. In particular, as increasing the interest of the applications like telematic, many researchers have exploited road networks for data modelling and query processing of moving objects[8,11,12,16]. Furthermore, the access methods for trajectory on road networks have been proposed in [13,14,15]. Pfoser and Jensen use two 2D R-trees in [13]: one is for indexing road segments and the other is for accessing trajectory segments whose coordinates are transformed from 3 dimensional (x, y, t) space to 2 dimensional (x, t) space by Hilbert-Mapping. Also, FNR-tree[14] and MON-tree[15] use a 2D R-trees to index the spatial road segments, and have respectively several 1D R-trees and 2D R-trees to index trajectories on specific road segments. Namely, these three methods retrieve trajectories after finding road segments where are satisfied with a spatial condition using Euclidean distance in 2D R-tree. However, according to the literature [8,9,12], the network distance between two objects on road networks is different from Euclidean one and it may lead to different results for query processing. In order to compute the network distance, we need network connectivity information. Therefore, we consider the connectivity of networks in indexing structures to be able to process the queries based on the network distance.

3   Problem Definition on Networks

In this section, under the assumption that all objects move along the road networks, we present trajectories of moving objects and redefine spatiotemporal range query regarding network spaces. The road network domain has differences from Euclidean domains according to several properties. First, positions of a moving object on the network space can be expressed by the specific road information such as a road identifier and its relative position instead of the coordinates formatted (x, y) in two dimensional Euclidean space. Second, while Euclidean space is represented by generally two or three dimensional space, the network space lies on between one and two dimensional space [13,15]. Further, the distance between two moving objects p and q on road networks is computed by the length of the shortest path from p to q unlike the straight line length in 2D Euclidean space because moving objects can only travel along connected roads. This different distance measure brings out different results of the query processing. For instance, suppose that we process a query of the form "*find all objects which are contained within the radius r from object A on the road*" in figure 1. If we use the Euclidean distance, object B, C, and D are the results of the range query Q; nevertheless, the real result that we want to get is only object B under the constrained movement in road networks. Therefore, we should take into account network properties for the trajectory representation and query processing.

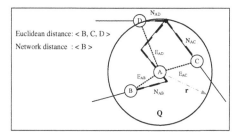

Fig. 1. The difference between Euclidean distance and Network distance

First of all, in this paper a position of a moving object is expressed as a form (rid, d) given in figure 2, where rid is an identifier of a road, d is a displacement, and l is the length of road rid. The displacement is expressed by a relative distance from start position of the road where a objects is located. Therefore, a trajectory of a moving object in road network space is defined as

$$Trajectory = \{(rid, d, t) * | rid \in int, d \in real(0 \leq d \leq l), t \in time\}$$

In other words, the trajectory, denoted T, is represented as a sequence of positions (rid_i, d_i, t_i), (r_1, d_1, t_1),...,(r_n, d_n, t_n). However, in indexing aspect preserving whole trajectory is inefficient due to large amount of dead space. The dead space declines the performance of query processing in the index structure based on R-tree. Therefore, we divide a trajectory into several trajectory segments, whose information is used for constructing our indexing method. Let a trajectory segment denote TS, each trajectory segment, a form $[rid_i, (d_i,t_i), (d_{i+1},t_{i+1})](t_i < t_{i+1})$, is defined with respect to each road segment.

Second, we redefine the spatiotemporal range query that has both spatial conditions in the network spaces and temporal conditions. In this paper, the spatiotemporal range query is retrieving trajectory segments within some distance from a given point on road networks at some time during a given time interval. In addition, when we process the query, we use the network distance instead of the Euclidean distance. For definition of network-based spatiotemporal range query, let TS be a trajectory segment set and q be a range query given by

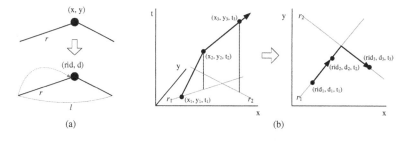

Fig. 2. The network-based trajectories representation

its position (rid, d) and some radius r with a time interval $ti = [t_s, t_e](t_s \leq t_e$, in the timestamp case, $t_s = t_e)$. The network-based spatiotemporal range query retrieves all trajectory segments which satisfy following condition:

$$TS(q) = \{ts | \exists t \in T_I = [(q.ti \cap ts.ti) \neq \emptyset] \wedge ND_{q,ts}(t) \leq q.r\}$$
$$\text{for } ts \in TS = \{ts_1, ts_2, ..., ts_m\}$$

where ts is a trajectory segment in TS, T_I is the temporal intersection interval between the query and a trajectory segment, and $ND_{q,ts}(t)$ is the network distance, the length of the shortest path from the query position to the position of trajectory segment at intersection timestamp t with linear interpolation. If trajectory segment has no temporal intersection with the query time interval, we regard ND as the infinitive real number(∞) to discard it.

4   Network-Based Indexing Method

This section explore the data structures based on R-tree, a graph structure, and a hashtable for our method. Furthermore, we propose algorithms for the network-based range query processing through them. The connectivity relationship and the network distance play important roles in query processing to reduce the searching network space.

4.1   Data Structures

Roughly, our network-based indexing method consists of a hashtable, a B+-tree, and multiple 2D R-trees(see Figure 4). The road networks can be represented by a graph $G=(V, E)$, with a node set V and a edge set E. In this paper, we regard intersections and road line-segments in road networks, respectively, as nodes and edges. To process the network-based rage query, a hashtable HT for edges is created by road segment-id, and each element in HT contains two bounded(start, end) node-ids, the displacement of start node, and a pointer of a R-tree RT with the 2D MBRs $([d_l, d_h], [t_l, t_h])$ of trajectory segments. We use 2D R-tree for adapting both the spatial and the temporal range. This pointer allows to find trajectory segments which passed through this road segment. Also, we use B+-tree based on the node-id values for accessing the connectivity relationship of each node. A node in the data block of B+-tree has its id value, coordinate and adjacency list of following entry: $< adjNode, adjEdge, weight >$, where $adjNode$ is the connected node-id, $adjEdge$ corresponds to the edge which is incident on these two nodes. $|weight|$ indicates the length of $adjEdge$. Nodes are sorted via Hilbert value and stored on node blocks in sequence

4.2   Insertion Trajectory Segments

As above mentioned, we have R-trees as many as a number of road segments and each trajectory segment is inserted into corresponding R-tree. However, it is inefficient both for storage utilization and the query processing. Therefore,

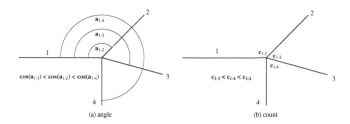

Fig. 3. The case of merging road segment in networks

we try to merge several adjacent road segments to a polyline in order to manage a reasonable number of R-trees. In this paper, we consider two heuristical information: one is an angle between two adjacent road segment, and the other is moving frequency of trajectories. For example, figure 3 shows a road segment is connected with three other segments. If we use the angle between two segment, we select a segment to make straight line along segments because of the observation that vehicles pass straightly when it meets intersection in common case. In the case using the frequency, we merge the segment whose data count is larger than other adjacency list. As a result, segment 1 in figure 3 (a) and (b) will be combined with segment 3 and segment 2, respectively. After merging, hashtable entries contained in the polyline have are assigned by the same R-tree pointer.

Then, we insert a trajectory segment into R-tree via following steps. First, we get the corresponding entries from the hashtable with two rids of successive sampling positions (rid_1, d_1, t_1), (rid_2, d_2, t_2). If two entries is the same, a root of R-tree is loaded with the pointer in the entry, and the 2D MBR $([d_l,d_h],[t_l,t_h])$ where d_l, d_h, t_l, and t_h are the minimum and maximum value of displacements and timestamps of two positions, is inserted into R-tree. Otherwise we find the shortest path from start position to end position. After finding the edge list of the path, a new trajectory segment consists of several trajectory segments of each edge considering that the object moves along this path with same speed for a sampling time interval. Each decomposed trajectory segment is inserted to R-trees by above steps.

4.3   Network-Based Query Processing

Now, we introduce how to process the range query based on the network distance from a query point to a moving object. Generally, our algorithm for query processing consists of two parts: pruning the search space with the network distance, and accessing 2D(displacement and time) R-trees for trajectories.

Figure 4 shows the examples of a range query "find all trajectories which are contained within the radius 6.0 miles from the query position $(r_5, 3.48)$ during the given time interval $ti = [1P.M., 3P.M.]$." For processing the range query, first, we get the entry of hashtable for edges with a given rid r_5 like insertion algorithm, and we add edge r_5 into the edge list for accessing R-trees. Next, its two nodes n_4 and n_6 with remaining query radius are enqueued. Namely,

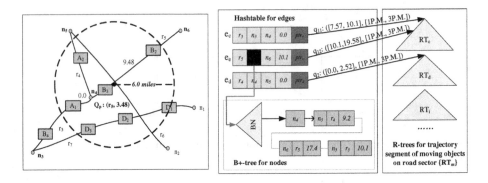

Fig. 4. The example of the range query on road networks

$< n_4, 2.52 >$ and $< n_6, -7.92 >$ are inserted into the priority query. The queue is arranged in an descending order of radius. The node which the radius is larger than others is visited to expanding the search area. Then, node n_4 is dequeued. As the remaining query radius is more than 0, its adjacent edge, r_3 and r_4, are inserted into the edge list, and node n_3 and n_5, the adjacency nodes of n_4, are enqueued in the priority query with the radius -6.68 and -7.58, respectively. This procedure repeats until the priority query becomes empty. If the remaining radius of a node is less than 0, the node is discarded because it does not need to expand the search area. After that, we compute the query set for each R-tree of road segments in order to avoid duplication of accessing the same R-tree shared by several road segments. We retrieve each R-tree with the query set.

5   Experimental Results

We performed experiments to evaluate the performance of the proposed method using synthetic moving objects on real road networks. For the test, we used two kinds of road network datasets: one is synthetic networks like mesh networks, and the other is real networks showed in figure 5. Then we prepared moving objects with the network-based generator developed by Brinkhoff[5] because massive real moving object trajectories are rarely spread wide. About 2M number of trajectory segments are generated during 500 time units using the network-based generator. The location (x, y, t) of generated moving objects is transformed into a network-based location formed (rid, d, t) on each road networks for our method.

In the experiments, we compared the average number of node accesses of R-trees for trajectories of our method and two other index structures for moving objects on road networks showed by literatures [15,13]. We indicated each other index structures to MON-tree[15], Hibert-Mapping[13], and our method is called by NB-tree in the experiments. The page size for nodes was 4096 bytes, which could store at most 102 entries, and the fillfactor was 70%. 5000 queries were randomly generated with a range of 0.01%, 0.1%, 1%, 5%, 10%, 20%, 30%, and 40% in spatial area of whole networks, and a constant range of 25% in temporal domain.

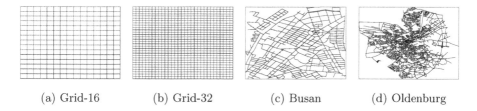

(a) Grid-16   (b) Grid-32   (c) Busan   (d) Oldenburg

Fig. 5. The road networks

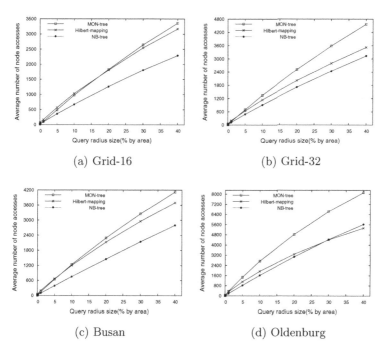

(a) Grid-16

(b) Grid-32

(c) Busan

(d) Oldenburg

Fig. 6. The average number of node accesses for range queries between the network-based distance and Euclidean distance

Figure 6 shows the average number of node accesses for the range queries between the network-based distance and Euclidean distance. Each indexing methods are created by the road segments. the indexing method using multiple R-trees, MON-tree and NB-tree, provide a good performance for smaller query size, while for larger query size MON-tree increases the node accesses more than Hilbert-Mapping, which uses one R-tree for trajectories. These indicate the large number of R-trees has a bad influence on the performance. However, we observe that NB-tree based on the query processing with the network distance reduce the search cost about 40% less than others. Namely, computing the distance using connectivity relationship of road networks restricts the searching space for the range queries comparing Euclidean distance.

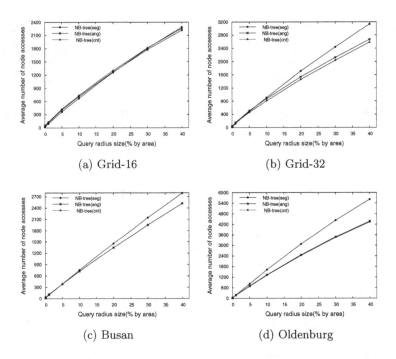

Fig. 7. The comparison of each merge mechanism for network-based range query processing on networks

As we have already mentioned the large number of R-trees for road segments affects the performance of the network-based query processing. Therefore, in this paper, we introduced two heuristical merge mechanisms with statistical information. Figure 7 depicts the performance comparison of these merge mechanism. Although we could not improve the performance by merging in small network data set, in large network data set the performance of the range query was improved at most 25%.

6   Conclusion

Although many indexing methods of trajectories have been proposed, they have dealt with the movement in Euclidean spaces. In this paper, we focused on the constraint movement of moving objects, especially like vehicles on the transportation networks. The idea was to represent trajectories and the spatial range queries in the road network space and to propose the indexing structure for handling them. Our network-based indexing method included the connectivity relationship of road networks to allow the network-based spatiotemporal range query. Moreover, we considered the merging way to share the R-trees for several road segments. The experiments showed lots of R-trees caused a performance degradation for query processing. In the future, we will try to apply other query types like k-nearest neighbor, and evolve analytical cost model for the performance of the network-based query processing.

Acknowledgment. This work was supported by the Korea Research Foundation Grant Funded by the Korea Government(MOEHRD)(KRF-2006-209-D00008), by IRC(Internet Information Retrieval Research Center) in Hankuk Aviation University. IRC is a Regional Research Center of Kyounggi Province, designated by ITEP and Ministry of Commerce, Industry and Energy.

References

1. A Guttman, R-trees a dynamic mdex structure for spatial searching, in Proc ACM SIGMOD Int Conf on Management of Data,pp. 47–57, 1984.
2. Y. Theodoridis, M. Vazirgiannis, and T. Sellis, Spatio-Temporal Indexing for Large Multi- media Applications, in Proc. IEEE Conf. On Multimedia Computing and System, pp. 441–448, 1996.
3. M. Nascimento and J. Silva, Towards historical R-trees, in Proc. ACM-SAC, pp. 235–240, 1998.
4. D. Pfoser, C. S. Jensen, and Y. Theodoridis, Novel Approaches in Query Processing for Moving Object Trajectories, in Proc. VLDB, pp. 395–406, 2000.
5. T. Brinkhoff, Generating Network-Based Moving Objects, in Proc. SSDBM, pp. 253–255, 2000.
6. Y. Tao and D. Papadias, MV3R-Tree: A Spatio-Temporal Access Method for Timestamp and Interval Queries, in Proc. VLDB, pp. 431–440, 2001.
7. M. Vazirgiannis and O. Wolfson, A Spatiotemporal Model and Language for Moving Objects on Road Networks, in Proc. SSTD, pp. 25–35, 2001.
8. C. Shahabi, M. R. Kolahdouzan, and M. Sharifzadeh, A Road Network Embedding Technique for K-Nearest Neighbor Search in Moving Object Databases, in Proc. ACM GIS, pp. 94–100, 2002.
9. D. Papadias, J. Zhang, N. Mamoulis, and Y. Tao, Query Processing in Spatial Network Databases, in Proc. VLDB, pp. 802–813, 2003.
10. Z. Song and N. Roussopoulos, SEB-tree: An approach to Index continuously moving ob- jects, in Proc. IEEE Conf. MDM, pp. 340–344, 2003.
11. L. Speicys, C. S. Jensen, and A. Kligys, Computational Data Modeling for Network-Constrained Moving Objects, in Proc. ACM-GIS, pp. 118–125, 2003.
12. C. S. Jensen, J. Kolar, T. B. Pedersen, and I. Timko, Nearest Neighbor Queries in Road Networks, in Proc. ACM GIS, pp. 1–8, 2003.
13. D. Pfoser and C. S. Jensen, Indexing of Network-Constrained Moving Objects, in Proc. ACM-GIS, pp. 25–32, 2003.
14. E. Frentzos, Indexing objects moving on Fixed networks, in Proc. SSTD, pp. 289–305, 2003.
15. V. de Almeida and R. Guting, Indexing the Trajectories of Moving Objects in Networks, in Proc. SSDBM, pp. 115–118, 2004.
16. R. H. Guting, V. T. de Almeida, and Z. Ding, Modeling and Querying Moving Objects in Networks, Tech. Rep. Informatik-Report 308, Fernuniversitat Hagen, April 2004.

Adaptive Enumeration Strategies and Metabacktracks for Constraint Solving

Eric Monfroy[1,2], Carlos Castro[1], and Broderick Crawford[1,3,*]

[1] Universidad Técnica Federico Santa María, Valparaíso, Chile
FirstName.Name@inf.utfsm.cl
[2] LINA, Université de Nantes, France
FirstName.Name@univ-nantes.fr
[3] Pontificia Universidad Católica de Valparaíso, Chile
FirstName.Name@ucv.cl

Abstract. In Constraint Programming, enumeration strategies are crucial for resolution performances. The effect of strategies is generally unpredictable. In a previous work, we proposed to dynamically change strategies showing bad performances, and to use metabacktrack to restore better states when bad decisions were made. In this paper, we design and evaluate strategies to improve resolution performances of a set of problems. Experimental results show the effectiveness of our approach.

1 Introduction

A Constraint Satisfaction Problem (CSP) is defined by a set of variables, a set of values for each variable, and a set of constraints. A solution is an instantiation of variables satisfying all constraints. These problems are widely studied mainly because a lot of real-life problems can de modeled as CSPs.

Complete solving techniques carry out a depth-first search by interleaving constraint propagation and enumeration. Constraint propagation prunes the search tree by eliminating values that cannot be in any solution. Enumeration creates a branch by instantiating a variable (e.g., $x = v$) and another one (e.g., $x \neq v$) for backtracking when the first branch is proved unsatisfiable. All enumeration strategies preserving solutions are valid, but they have a huge impact on resolution efficiency. Moreover, no strategy is (one of) the best for all problems.

Numerous studies have been conducted about enumeration strategies. Some works focused on determining specific enumeration strategies for given classes of problems (e.g., [5]). For a given problem, some studies also try to determine the best strategy based on some static criteria (e.g., [1] for variable ordering, [7] for the "best" heuristic, [8] for the "best" solver). However, since their effects are rather unpredictable, an a priori decision concerning a good enumeration strategy is very hard (and almost impossible in the general case). Information

---

* The first author has been partially supported by the Chilean National Science Fund through the project FONDECYT 1060373. The authors have been partially supported by the project INRIA-CONICYT VANANAA.

T. Yakhno and E. Neuhold (Eds.): ADVIS 2006, LNCS 4243, pp. 354–363, 2006.

about the solving process can also be used to determine a strategy (see e.g., [4] for algorithm control). The following works are closer to our approach. In [2], adaptive constraint satisfaction is based on a sequence of algorithms: bad algorithms are detected and dynamically replaced by the next candidate. In [9,10] randomisation is introduced for tie-breaking several choices ranked equally by the fixed enumeration strategy. A restart policy jumps to the root of the search tree to try another branch when a given number of backtracks is reached.

In [6], we proposed a framework for adaptive strategies and metabacktracks (an extension of restart to save and capitalise work) to find solutions more quickly and with less variance in solution time, i.e., trying to avoid very long runs when other strategies (or sequences of strategies) can lead quickly to a solution. This framework aims at dynamically detecting bad decisions made by enumeration strategies: instead of predicting the effect of a strategy, we evaluate the efficiency of running strategies, and we replace the ones showing bad results. When this is not sufficient we also perform metabacktracks (several levels of backtracks) to quickly undo several "bad" enumerations and restore a "better" context.

In this paper, using our framework, we design some dynamic enumeration strategies and metabacktracks and we evaluate them. The dynamic strategies are based on packs of static and basic strategies of different natures: based on the size of variable domains, on the number of occurrences of the variables in the CSP, or on random selection of variables. We know that the pack based on the domain size is performant and well-suited for the problems we consider, whereas the two other packs show bad performances. Our goal is the following: as an end-user, we forget which are the good and bad strategies; and we design some dynamic strategies based on the static ones in order to significantly improve resolution compared to bad strategies, without degrading (or only slightly degrading) performances obtained with the good ones. We don't focus on improving the resolution of a single problem, but we are interested in quickly finding solutions on average for a set of problems. The experimental results are more than promising and show some good performances of our dynamic enumeration strategies and backtracks.

We present an overview of our framework (Section 2) and some dynamic enumeration strategies and metabacktrack techniques (Section 3). Some experimental results of our strategies are discussed in Section 4. We conclude in Section 5.

2   The Dynamic Strategy Framework: An Overview

We recall the main principles of our framework. A complete description can be found in [6]. Our framework for dynamic strategies (see Figure 1) is based on 4 components that exchange information. The first component runs resolution, the second one observes resolution and takes snapshots, the third one analyses snapshots and draws some indicators about strategy quality, and the fourth one makes decisions and updates strategy priorities or requests some metabacktrack. This approach is based on two key features: change of enumeration strategy when a strategy behaves badly and when we guess another one could work better, and metabacktracks when changing strategy is not enough because we guess no strategy will be able to repair previously made wrong choices.

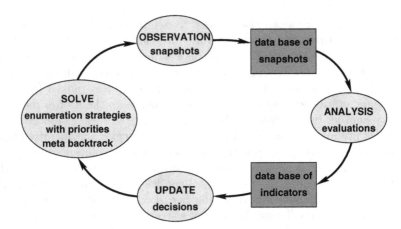

Fig. 1. The dynamic strategy framework

The **SOLVE** component runs a generic CSP solving algorithm performing a depth-first search by alternating constraint propagation with enumeration phases. SOLVE has a set of basic enumeration strategies, each one characterised by a priority that evolves during computation: the other components evaluate strategies and update their priorities. For each enumeration, the dynamic enumeration strategy selects the basic strategy to be used based on the attached priorities. SOLVE is also able to perform metabacktracks (jump back of a sequence of several enumerations and propagation phases) in order to repair a "desperate" state of resolution, i.e., when changing strategies is not sufficient due to several very bad previous choices. The **OBSERVATION** component aims at observing and recording some information about the current search tree, i.e., it spies the resolution process in the SOLVE component. These observations (called **snapshots**) are not performed continuously, and they can be seen as an abstraction of the resolution state at a time t. Taking a snapshot consists in extracting (since search trees are too large) and recording some information from a resolution state. The **ANALYSIS** component analyses the snapshots taken by the OBSERVATION: it evaluates the different strategies, and provides **indicators** to the UPDATE component. Indicators can be extracted, computed, or deduced from one or several snapshots from the database of snapshots. The **UPDATE** component makes decisions using the indicators. It interprets the indicators, and then updates the enumeration strategies priorities and requests some metabacktracks in the SOLVE component.

3   Dynamic Strategies

We consider 12 **basic/static enumeration strategies** (i.e., strategies that are usually fixed for the whole solving process but that we use as part of our dynamic strategies) based on 3 variable selection criteria:

- min selects the variable with the smallest domain (the first one in the order of appearance of variables in the problem for tie-breaking).
- $Mcon$ is the most constrained selection, i.e., selection of the (first) variable that appears the most often in the constraints.
- ran randomly selects a variable which is not yet instantiated.

Variable selection criteria are combined with value selection criteria: Min (resp. Mid, Max, and Ran) selects the smallest (resp. the middle, the largest, a random) value of the domain of the selected variable.

By combining variable selections and value selections, we obtain 12 enumeration strategies that we named $Var_{selection}Val_{selection}$. Hence, $MinRan$ is the enumeration strategy that selects randomly a value in the variable with the smallest domain. We will talk about the min enumeration strategies when referring to the 4 strategies based on the min variable selection.

The **snapshots** we consider focus on the search tree to draw some indicators on the resolution progress. At each snapshot we store:

- $Maxd$: the maximum depth reached in the search tree,
- d: the depth of the current node,
- s: the size of the current search space,
- f, f': the percentage of variables fixed by enumeration (respectively by enumeration or propagation),
- v, vf, vfe: the number of variables, the number of fixed variables, the number of variables fixed by enumeration.

The **indicators** we consider reflect the resolution progress. The indicators we compute in the ANALYSE component are the following, where F is the last taken snapshot, and F^- the previous one:

- $\delta n_1 = Maxd_F - Maxd_{F-}$ represents a variation of the maximum depth,
- $\delta n_2 = d_F - d_{F-}$: if positive, the current node is deeper than the one explored at the previous snapshot,
- $\delta n_3 = 100 * (s_{F-} - s_F)/s_{F-}$: a percentage of reduction since F^-; if positive, the current search space is smaller than the one at snapshot F^-,
- $\delta n_4 = f'_F - f'_{F-}$ (respectively $\delta n_5 = f_F - f_{F-}$): if positive, reflects an improvement in the degree of resolution (resp. resolution made by enumeration),
- $\delta n_6 = d_{F-} - vfe'_{F-}$: an indicator of thrashing, i.e., the solving process alternates enumerations and backtracks on a few number of variables without succeeding in having a strong orientation (going deeper in the search or performing a phase of significant backtracks).

Each strategy has a priority of 1 at the beginning. Then, the priority p of the last running strategy is **updated** as follows based on 5 of the indicators (The reward is less than the penalty to quickly replace a bad strategy):

$$reward : \quad if \quad \sum_{i=1}^{5} \delta n_i \geq 10 \quad then \quad p = p + 1$$
$$penalty : \quad if \quad \sum_{i=1}^{5} \delta n_i \leq 0 \quad then \quad p = p - 3$$

The **dynamic strategies** are based on a set of static enumeration strategies and the rules for decision shown above. We consider two types of strategies.

The first type uses a set of strategies and it always applies the strategy of highest priority (we randomly choose one of the highest when we need tie-breaking, and also the first static strategy is randomly chosen). We consider the following dynamic strategies: $Dynmin$, $DynMcon$, $DynRan$, and $DynAll$ that apply this selection process on the set of strategies min, $Mcon$, and Ran, and all the 12 strategies respectively.

The second type of dynamic strategies uses a partitioning of the basic strategies into subsets. When a strategy s must be changed, the strategy of highest priority from a different subset than the one containing s will be selected. Hence, we may not use the strategy of highest priority w.r.t. all the strategies, but we hope to diversify enumeration by selecting a strategy of different nature. The strategy $DynAllPack$ partitions the 12 strategies into 3 subsets, i.e., the group of min strategies, the one of $Mcon$, and the one of Ran. For example, consider $minMin$ was used and must be changed. $DynAllPPack$ will select the strategy of highest priority among the 8 strategies of the two groups $Mcon$ and Ran.

The **metabacktrack** will be triggered when the thrashing is too important:

$$meta: \quad if \quad \delta n_6 > 4 \quad then \quad meta - backtrack$$

We consider 2 techniques of metabacktracks. The first technique ($mb10$) performs n steps of backtracks, i.e., $mb10$ goes up of n nodes in the search tree undoing n enumerations. n is computed as 10% of the total number of variables of the problem. The second technique (rs) is a restart, i.e., the metabacktrack jumps to the root of the search tree. Whereas $mb10$ tries to capitalize and save some part of the search, rs prefers to restart the search (see [9,10]).

Similarly to the dynamic strategies, the metabacktracks will change the enumeration. The strategy that was used at this node is given the smallest priority (-1) in order not to re-use it before the others. Again we have 2 techniques. The first one selects the enumeration strategy of highest priority inside a set of strategies. We obtain strategies of metabacktrack such as $mb10Min$ (resp. $mb10Mcon$, $mb10Ran$, and $mb10All$) which uses only min (resp. $Mcon$, Ran, and all) static strategies. We also have the same type of metabacktrack based on restart: $rsMin$ (resp. $rsMcon$, $rsRan$, and $rsAll$). The other technique is based on partitioning of the set of strategies: the enumeration strategy of highest priority from another subset is selected: metabacktracks $rsAllPack$ and $mb10AllPack$.

When combined with a dynamic strategy, the metabacktrack has some effect on the enumeration strategy since the priority of the strategy that was used becomes the smallest one. But when combined with a static enumeration strategy, a different strategy is only used to diversify enumeration when backtracking; the next enumerations are performed by the same static strategy.

In order to obtain a **complete solver** (not loosing solutions), after trying all of the strategies at a given node, we do not change it anymore, both for dynamic strategy changing and metabacktracks.

Table 1. min enumeration strategies vs. dynamic strategies over min

	R150	R250	M10	M11	L20	L25	Ps
$minMin$	0	0	100	100	0	0	33
$minMax$	0	0	100	100	0	0	33
$minMid$	0	0	100	100	0	0	33
$minRan$	0	0	0	0	0	0	0
$minAVG$	0	0	75	75	0	0	25
$Dynmin$	3	4	73	63	0	0	24

4   Experimental Results

We are interested in finding the first solution in less than 10 min., time that we call **timeout**. Our prototype implementation in Oz [1] fixes the **constraint propagation** process: arc-consistency [12] computation (with dedicated algorithms for global constraints) with a look ahead strategy [11]. Strategies of enumeration and metabacktracks are the ones described above. The snapshots are taken every 80ms. Tests were run on an Athlon XP 2000 with 256 MB of RAM.

We consider classical problems: 150-queens ($Q150$), 250-queens ($Q250$), magic squares of size 10 ($M10$) and 11 ($M11$), and latin squares of size 20 ($L20$) and 25 ($L25$). Since most of the strategies (both enumeration and metabacktrack) have a random aspect, we performed 100 runs for each resolution of each problem.

All tables are presented as follows. The first six columns represent problems, rows represent strategies: a cell is the percentage of timeouts over 100 runs (i.e., how many times a strategy was not able to find a solution in 10 min.). The last column (Ps) represents the average performance of strategies on the set of problems: it is thus the average number of timeouts (in percentage) obtained by a strategy on 600 runs (100 per problem). A row $xxxAVG$ is the average of some strategies on a problem, e.g., $minAVG$ (resp. $AllAVG$) is the average number of timeouts obtained by the min strategies (resp. by all the 12 static strategies). A cell in a $xxxAVG$ row and a Ps column is thus the average number (in percentage) of timeouts of a set of strategies over the set of problems.

4.1   Dynamic Enumeration Strategies Alone

Now we only consider dynamic enumeration strategies based on the min variable selection without activating the metabacktrack. We call it $Dynmin$ and we compare it with the min enumeration strategies (Table 1). The min enumeration strategies are efficient over our problems except the magic square problems which need random value selection to be solved before the timeout. $Dynmin$ improves the difficult problems (more especially $M11$). Some cases of timeouts happened for the queen problems due to the overhead generated by our system.

For $R150$, $L20$, and $L25$ the best run of $Dynmin$ is the same (in terms of enumerations and backtracks) as the best runs of min strategies. The best run for $R150$ and $L20$ is obtained with $minMid$: 152 backtracks, 7 enumerations,

---
[1] http://www.mozart-oz.org

Table 2. $Mcon$ enumeration strategies vs. dynamic strategies over $Mcon$

	R150	R250	M10	M11	L20	L25	Ps
$MconMin$	100	100	100	100	100	100	100
$MconMax$	100	100	100	100	100	100	100
$MconMid$	100	100	100	100	100	100	100
$MconRan$	0	10	80	100	0	0	32
$MconAVG$	75	78	95	100	75	75	83
$DynMcon$	78	81	90	98	22	57	71

and 339 enumerations, 28 backtracks, respectively; for $L25$ the best run is with $minMid$: 505 enumerations, 8 backtracks. For $R250$, $minRan$ does better than $Dynmin$: surprisingly, a run of $minRan$ find solution in 241 enumerations and 0 backtrack, whereas the best run of $Dynmin$ required 246 enumerations and 1 backtrack. The best improvements in terms of best run are for $M10$ and $M11$: the best run of static strategies was in 13392 enumerations for $M10$ and 406 for $M11$ whereas $Dynmin$ found solutions in only 883 and 173 enumerations.

Now we consider dynamic strategies based on the $Mcon$ variable selection without activating the metabacktrack. We call it $DynMcon$ and we compare it with the $Mcon$ strategies (see Table 2). Three of the four $Mcon$ strategies are rather bad. $DynMcon$ improves the average: results are equivalent for n-queens and magic square problems, but $DynMcon$ significantly improves runs for latin problems: from 75% of timeout to 22% for $L20$, and from 75% to 57% for $L25$. None of the static strategies (even $MconRan$ with randomisation) was able to find a solution for $M11$ before the time out. $DynMcon$ could find one in 2% of the runs. $DynMcon$ improved the best runs of $MconRan$ for the queens and magic square problems, and also the worst run (leading to a solution) for $R250$.

The Ran pack of strategies contains only bad strategies w.r.t. the selected problems. But (see Table 3), sequencing them dynamically $DynRan$ significantly reduced the average number of timeouts (from 90% to 72%) on the set of problems, and from 75% to 6% on $L20$. For each problem, $DynRan$ was also able to improve the best run obtained by the Ran strategies.

Table 4 compares the average of the 12 static strategies with 2 dynamic strategies: $DynAll$ and $DynAllPack$. On the set of problems, $DynAll$ improves the resolution (from 64% of timeouts to 50%). In 4 cases, the best runs of $DynAll$ correspond to the best run of the best static strategies. In one case, there is a slight degradation of the best run, and for $M11$, the best run of $DynAll$ is far better than the best run of the static strategies. Although we though $DynAllPack$ could help by diversifying the choices (enforcing a change of pack), surprisingly, it behaved poorly and worsten the results. After observing the trace, we see that if a good strategy from the min is badly evaluated, we replace it by a strategy from the $Mcon$ or Ran packs, and we apply an even worse strategy.

4.2   Metabacktracks Alone

Now we only consider metabacktracks using a set of strategies to change enumeration when backtracking. The static enumeration strategy is randomly chosen

Table 3. *Ran* enumeration strategies vs. dynamic strategies over *Ran*

	R150	R250	M10	M11	L20	L25	Ps
RanMin	100	100	100	100	100	100	100
RanMax	100	100	100	100	100	100	100
RanMid	100	100	100	100	100	100	100
RanRan	10	30	80	100	0	20	40
RanAVG	78	83	95	100	75	80	85
DynRan	65	77	96	100	6	88	72

Table 4. Enumeration strategies vs. dynamic strategies over all

	R150	R250	M10	M11	L20	L25	Ps
AllAVG	51	54	88	92	50	52	64
DynAll	71	51	59	66	24	31	50
DynAllPacks	79	91	69	70	28	71	68

in the same set of strategies and then it is not changed during the resolution process. As detailed before, $mb10$ executes n steps of backtracks (n being 10% of the number of variables) and rs jumps to the root of the tree when requested. On Table 5, we only keep the average runs of the static strategies. Details for each strategy can be found in Tables 1, 2, 3, and 4.

Table 5. Static enumeration strategies vs. metabacktracks

	R150	R250	M10	M11	L20	L25	Ps
minAVG	0	0	75	75	0	0	25
mb10min	9	0	0	12	0	0	4
rsmin	6	3	3	9	0	0	4
MconAVG	75	78	95	100	75	75	83
mb10Mcon	78	90	34	84	18	50	59
rsMcon	78	75	28	87	9	68	58
RanAVG	78	83	95	100	75	80	85
mb10Ran	81	78	81	93	18	90	74
rsRan	75	84	78	93	12	90	72
AllAVG	51	54	88	92	50	52	64
mb10All	65	63	0	10	28	40	34
mb10AllPack	76	92	0	2	32	62	44
rsAll	72	68	0	11	30	32	36
rsAllPack	71	89	0	4	23	67	42

In Table 5, $mb10$ and rs metabacktracks are rather equivalents, whatever the pack of static strategies they use. This means that for these problems, saving part of the resolution was not really worth. We also note that in all cases they improve the average percentage of timeouts on the set of problems (e.g., from 25% of timeouts to 4% with $mb10min$ and 4% with $rsmin$). When looking at problems separately, metabacktracks improve the average on most cases; some cases are even spectacular, such as $M11$ with the min strategies (from 75% of timeouts to 12% with $mb10min$ and 9% with $rsmin$) or $L20$ with the $Mcon$ strategies (from 75% of timeouts to 18% with $mb10min$ and 9% with $rsmin$) or $M10$ with all the strategies (from 88% of timeouts to 0% whatever the metabacktrack).

On the set of all strategies, all metabacktracks we tried significantly improved results (from 75% of timeouts for *AllAVG* to a percentage between 34% and 44% depending on the metabacktrack). Note that again, enforcing to apply a strategy from another pack is worse than selecting a strategy from the complete set.

4.3   Metabacktracks and Dynamic Strategies

Now we combine metabacktracks and dynamic strategies. As in Table 5, in Table 6 we only keep the average run of the static strategies to ease lecture and synthesise results. Combining metabacktracks and dynamic strategies improve the number of timeouts compared to static strategies. Compared to metabacktracks alone (Table 5), the benefit of adding dynamic strategies varies: *Dynmin* and *DynRan* degrades a bit the performance of *mb10min* (resp. *rsmin*) and *mb10Ran* (resp. *rsRan*); this is due to the overhead of executing the 2 techniques together; *DynAllPack* also slightly degrades *mb10AllPack* and *rsAllPack*. However, combining *DynMcon* with metabacktracks improves the average results (from 59% for *mb10Mcon* and 58% for *rsMcon* to 54% for *DynMcon + mb10Mcon* and 52% for *DynMcon + rsMcon*) in spite of the overhead. *DynAll* also improves *mb10All* and *rsAll*. Moreover, the combination *DynAll + rsAll* defines the best strategy on the average of the solving of the set of problems (29% of timeouts compared to 64% for the average of the static strategies).

Table 6. Static strategies vs. dynamic enumeration strategies and metabacktracks

	R150	R250	M10	M11	L20	L25	Ps
minAVG	0	0	75	75	0	0	25
Dynmin + mb10min	18	2	2	21	0	0	7
Dynmin + rsmin	13	2	0	21	0	0	6
MconAVG	75	78	95	100	75	75	83
DynMcon + mb10Mcon	72	78	24	91	16	43	54
DynMcon + rsMcon	76	76	34	81	7	37	52
RanAVG	78	83	95	100	75	80	85
DynRan + mb10Ran	89	89	75	100	18	91	77
DynRan + rsRan	81	83	68	94	24	82	72
AllAVG	51	54	88	92	50	52	64
DynAll + mb10All	63	65	0	1	29	37	33
DynAllPack + mb10AllPack	78	95	1	7	22	76	47
DynAll + rsAll	56	55	0	8	18	34	29
DynAllPack + rsAllPack	76	87	0	8	23	74	45

5   Conclusion, Discussion, and Future Work

We have presented some dynamic enumeration strategies and metabacktrack based on running strategy performances. Our dynamic approach is able to detect bad cases to repair strategies and states. The experimental results prove that on average, on a set of problems, our dynamic strategies and metabacktracks significantly improve the solving process.

Compared to [9,10] our randomisation concerns the tie breaking when selecting strategies. Moreover, we don't have a fixed but a dynamic strategy. In [2] the meta-strategy consists in changing a "bad" solver by the next one in a sequence. Using priorities, our strategy selection is finer. In both [9] and [2], only complete restarts are considered (either with the same solver [9] or a different one [2]), whereas we try to save and capitalise the work already done (first changing strategies, then, performing metabacktracks).

In the future, we plan to integrate learning to detect relevant "parameters" of our framework (observations, indicators, decisions, ...) and to tune them automatically. It could also be interesting to combine our method with prediction of strategies and notions of intelligent backtracking for our metabacktrack [3].

References

1. J. C. Beck, P. Prosser, and R. Wallace. Variable Ordering Heuristics Show Promise. In *Proc. of CP'2004*, volume 3258 of *LNCS*, pages 711–715, 2004.
2. J. E. Borrett, E. P. K. Tsang, and N. R. Walsh. Adaptive constraint satisfaction: The quickest first principle. In *Proc. of ECAI'1996*. John Wiley and Sons, 1996.
3. M. Bruynooghe. Intelligent Backtracking Revisited. In J.-L. Lassez and G. Plotkin, editors, *Computational Logic, Essays in Honor of Alan Robinson*. MIT Press, 1991.
4. T. Carchrae and J. C. Beck. Low-Knowledge Algorithm Control. In *Proc. of AAAI 2004*, pages 49–54, 2004.
5. Y. Caseau and F. Laburthe. Improved clp scheduling with task intervals. In *Proc. of ICLP'1994*, pages 369–383. MIT Press, 1994.
6. C. Castro, E. Monfroy, C. Figueroa, and R. Meneses. An approach for dynamic split strategies in constraint solving. In *Proc. of MICAI'05*, volume 3789 of *LNCS*, pages 162–174. Springer, 2005.
7. P. Flener, B. Hnich, and Z. Kiziltan. A meta-heuristic for subset problems. In *Proc. of PADL'2001*, volume 1990 of *LNCS*, pages 274–287. Springer, 2001.
8. C. Gebruers, A. Guerri, B. Hnich, and M. Milano. Making choices using structure at the instance level within a case based reasoning framework. In *Proc. of CPAIOR'2004*, volume 3011 of *LNCS*, pages 380–386. Springer, 2004.
9. C. Gomes, B. Selman, and H. Kautz. Boosting combinatorial search through randomization. In *Proc. of AAAI'98*, pages 431–437, Madison, Wisconsin, 1998.
10. H. Kautz, E. Horvitz, Y. Ruan, C. Gomes, and B. Selman. Boosting combinatorial search through randomization. In *Proc. of AAAI'2002*, pages 674–682, 2002.
11. V. Kumar. Algorithms for Constraint-Satisfaction Problems: A Survey. *A.I. Magazine*, 13(1):32–44, Spring 1992.
12. A. K. Mackworth. Consistency in Networks of Relations. *AI*, 8:99–118, 1977.

FORBAC: A Flexible Organisation and Role-Based Access Control Model for Secure Information Systems

Oumaima Saidani[1] and Selmin Nurcan[1,2]

[1] Université Paris 1 - Panthéon - Sorbonne Centre de Recherche en Informatique 90, rue de Tolbiac 75634 Paris cedex 13 France
[2] IAE de Paris - Sorbonne Graduate Business School - Université Paris 1 - Panthéon - Sorbonne 21, rue Broca 75005 Paris France
Tel.: 33 - 1 53 55 27 13; Fax: 33 - 1 53 55 27 01
Oumaima.Saidani@malix.univ-paris1.fr,
nurcan@univ-paris1.fr

Abstract. Security of information systems is an increasingly critical issue. Access control is a crucial technique ensuring security. It should be based on an effective model. Even if some approaches have already been proposed, a comprehensive model, flexible enough to cope with real organizations, is still missing. This paper proposes a new access control model, FORBAC, which deals with the following issues: The first one is the adaptability to various kinds of organization. The second one concerns increasing flexibility and reducing errors and management cost, this is done by introducing a set of components which allow fine-grained and multi-level permission assignment. The paper introduces a framework for evaluating the proposed approach with respect to other related research through views, facets and criteria.

1 Introduction

The security of an information system or a network consists of its protection against unauthorized access or abusive authorized use. It is assumed by three well-known techniques : authentication [25], access control [23] and audit [10]. In this paper we focus our discussion on access control which consists in managing access rights according to the rules specified in the security policies. In a given organization, it can be formally expressed by instantiating an access control model - often a formal language - in order to represent the security policies in a clear and non ambiguous way. Research on access control started in the 1960s with *Mandatory Access Control (MAC)* [6], [4] and *Discretionary Access Control (DAC)* [13] approaches. *RBAC (Role Based Access Control)* [8] appeared with multi-user systems in 1970s and were considered as an alternative to *DAC* and *MAC* [23]. In fact, *MAC* is rigid and imposes strong organizational constraints. *DAC* is vulnerable to information leak. In *RBAC* : instead of permissions being assigned directly to users, they are assigned to roles, and then roles are assigned

T. Yakhno and E. Neuhold (Eds.): ADVIS 2006, LNCS 4243, pp. 364–376, 2006.

to users. *RBAC* was promoted by the National Institute of Standards and Technology and was recognized as an American standard in 2004 [9]. *RBAC* models are "policy-neutral" and can express a wide range of security policies including discretionary and mandatory, as well as user-defined or organizational specific policies [9]. A role-based approach for modelling access control is a natural way to reflect organizational structures and to highlight responsibilities assigned to users. Adopting this approach is useful, particularly if it can meet the flexibility and adaptability requirements of new, complex, evolutionary organizations and widely distributed systems, especially organizational, functional and operational requirements. Nevertheless, approaches dealing with role modelling seem insufficient to meet these requirements.

The purpose of this paper is to improve this kind of approach in order to support flexibility and adaptability requirements. In this paper we illustrate the importance of the flexibility and the adaptability requirements when modelling access control and propose a comprehensive access control model aiming to meet the following requirements related to flexibility:

From the administration point of view:
- R1. Great expressive power allowing to express both simple and complex access control policies
- R2. Reducing cost and risks of errors in administration.
From the usage point of view:
- R3. Adaptability to organizational, functional and operational changes
- R4. Adaptability to various modes of human organizational structures such as functional hierarchies, project teams and knowledge networks.
From the system point of view:
- R5. Suitability to distributed systems and collaborative work.
- R6. Increasing safety

To deal with the requirement R1, we propose modelling access control using a basic model which can be improved with a number of permission assignment sub-models. To meet the requirements R2 and R3, we introduce, on the one hand, the concepts of *function* and *cluster of objects*, and on the other hand, we propose to exploit these concepts for *multi-level* and *fine-grained permission assignment*. To deal with the requirement R4 and R5, we introduce the concept of *organizational unit*. Reducing risks of errors in administration (R2) gives confidence to adopt distributed systems and collaborative work (R5), on the one hand, and to increase safety (R6), on the other hand.

We use these requirements to build a reference framework that is composed of facets or views, each of them is characterised by a set of criteria. This reference framework can be used to evaluate or compare access control models. In this work, we use it to evaluate our approach with respect to the related work.

The paper is structured as follows: Section 2 discusses the requirements cited above and introduces our approach for modelling access control. In Section 3, we propose a reference framework in order to evaluate our approach with respect to the related work. The conclusion of the paper is given in Section 4.

2   The FORBAC Meta-model

2.1   The Basic Model

In this section we introduce our meta-model for access control. It includes the following concepts: *User, Role, Session, Permission, Object, Organizational-unit, Function, Goal* and *Object cluster*. The first fifth concepts have been adapted from *NIST* model [9]. We are going to discuss them in depth.

An organization can be considered as a set of organizational structures which include relevant users that perform functions in order to achieve particular goals. An organization can adopt various kinds of organization structures, for instance (i) Functional hierarchies (tree structures), which are based on the concepts of user authorities and responsibilities and also division and specialization of work; (ii) Project teams, that can be defined as a social structure composed of a head and members with various competencies, collaborating to perform an action or a project for a time duration and (iii) knowledge networks which can be defined as communities of practice [21] inter connected, under the same "governorship", sharing common frameworks, methods and tools (for example, experts or mediators that suggest strategies). A user can be assigned to many organizational structures having different kinds. An access control model have to be able to represent all kinds of organizational structures.

For modelling functional hierarchies, we use the concepts of role hierarchies of RBAC. In our approach, we define a role as a set of responsibilities allowing a user to perform functions affected to him (c.f. Appendix.1) *Role hierarchies* has been often mentioned [8, 22]. We identify two different semantics related to hierarchies: specialization/generalization (*RSH*) and organizational (functional) (*ORH*).

For modelling, teams and communities of practice, we introduce the concept of *organizational unit* which can be considered as a structure gathering users such as teams, communities of practice, departments independently of roles and role hierarchies(c.f. Appendix.2). Organizational units can be organized, using a tree structure in hierarchical organizations, or be structured as a network in team-based organizations. Thus, we identify two kinds of relations between organizational units:
- *include*(ou_2, ou_1) : means that the organizational unit ou_2 includes the organisational unit ou_1, e.g. *include(Financial Services, Financial Management Reporting)*
- *collaborate*(ou_1, ou_2) : means that ou_1 collaborate with ou_2. e.g. *collaborate (Audit department, Knowledge and information management service)*

Fig.2 presents some departments of a bank[1] : *Audit; Corporate Services* including the sections: *Human Resources, Knowledge and Information Management,* and *Security Services*; and *Financial Services* including three teams : *Accounting and Internal Control, Contracts Management and Procurement,* and *Financial Management Reporting.*

---

[1] http://www.bankofcanada.ca/en/hr/departements.html

The concept of role does not allow to express many access control rules, because users that are assigned to the same role have the same authorizations. We have integrated a new level between roles and permissions, following the approach of [12]. Instead of assigning permissions to roles, we assign them to functions and functions to roles(c.f. Appendix.3).

In order to highlight our motivation behind the use of the concept of function, let us consider the following situations: S1: a new organization is set up and it proves to be necessary to distribute the responsibilities of each actor differently; S2 : a responsibility has to evolve. To deal with S1 and S2, current approaches require checking all permission-to-role assignments and modifying them if necessary. This task is time consuming and has risk of error. However, competitive environments require quick reactions to changes and do not tolerate inaccuracies. In FORBAC, to deal with S1, we have to modify some function-to-role assignments, while users keep their roles, with new assigned responsibilities; And to deal with S2, we have to modify some permission-to-function assignments while roles keep their functions, with new assigned permissions. Thus, our approach allows adaptation with organizational, functional and operational changes easily, rapidly with less error (requirements R2 and R3).

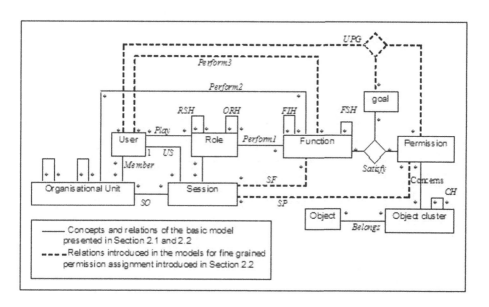

Fig. 1. Illustration of the FORBAC Meta-model using a class diagram

We structure functions in hierarchies. The type of semantics of these hierarchies is either *generalization / specialization* or *inclusion*. Hierarchies of the first type allow specifying most general and abstract functions which are specialized according to particular contexts. For instance, the *financial management reporting* team (c.f. Fig. 2) can be associated with the function *"consulting the financial reporting*" which can be specialized into "*consulting the reporting on screen*" and "*printing the reporting*". We introduce the predicate *specialized_function*(f_1, f_2) which means that the function f_1 is a *specialized-function* of the function f_2. Hierarchies of type *inclusion* allow to isolate functions which will be used on several occasions by other functions. For Example, "*managing planning and budgeting*"f_1 includes "*managing planning*"f_2 and "*managing budgeting*"f_3. So, in order to achieve the goal of f_1, we need to achieve f_2 and f_3.

In order to perform functions, users should have permissions to access to resources. We model resources with the concept of *object*. In addition, we introduce the concept of *object cluster* for gathering similar objects by semantic meaning based on different features (user-specified features or attributes) (c.f. Appendix.4). For instance, customers handled by a given adviser. We structure object clusters into hierarchies *(CH)* in order to take advantage of the generalization (up) /specialization (down) properties inherent in the *CH* structure. The mechanism of construction of clusters and cluster hierarchies is out of the scope of this paper. This can be performed using data mining techniques. An object can belong to one or more clusters. This feature allows more coarse grained access control decisions and then helps to meet requirements R1 and R2.

We define a permission as an approval of a particular access mode to particular object clusters. It confers to the holder of the permission the ability to perform some tasks using these object clusters which can be accessed for various reasons. Permissions allowed for commercial goal are different from those allowed for statistic goals.For this reason we introduce the concept of *goal*.

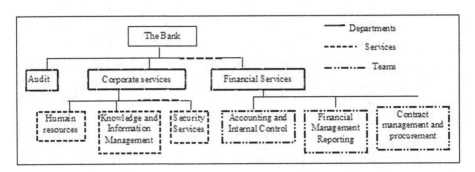

Fig. 2. Example of a hierarchy of organizational units

2.2   Permission Assignment Sub-models

Access control rules depends on particular characteristics of the organization. Indeed, some rules may be crucial for sophisticated organizations and/or inappropriate for simple ones. A perfect access control model has to be rule-independent and reusable to satisfy needs of a variety of organizations. Although their relevance and benefits, RBAC [9] and its different variants are complex for some organizations and/or incomplete for others. Using a composite model including a basic one and a number of assigment sub-models could resolve this problem;

Thus, access control policies can be modelled using a selected set of sub-models which includes only the relevant permission assignment possibilities which are specific to a given organization, rather than using always all the possibilities. A related work in this topic is the NIST RBAC model, which adopts this principle by allowing to integrate only up to four components, nevertheless it is incomplete and imprecise. Further, it does not guide for selecting the most adapted model. That is why we have proposed firstly in Section 2.1 a basic model which can be augmented with a set of assignment sub-models which we are going to discuss in the following.

Basic Model for Permission Assignment. In this paper we focus only on positive permissions, i.e. the right to execute an operation or task. Prohibition, obligation and administrative rights, i.e. the right to manage users, permissions, roles and so on, are not discussed. Permission-to-function assignment relation is formulated using the predicate *Assigned_Permissions* (c.f. Appendix.5).

A user can open many sessions simultaneously. The mapping of a user u onto a set of of sessions is formulated as follows: $User\_Sessions(u : USERS) \rightarrow 2^{SESSIONS}$. He has to select a subset of roles and organizational units assigned to him. According to this selection, a particular set of permissions is granted. The permissions available to the user are the union of permissions from all roles and organizational units in this session. Each session is a mapping of one user to a subset of roles and organizational units. (c.f. Appendix.6).

We define inheritance between roles as follows: For the specialization / generalization hierarchies, we introduce the predicate $Specialized\_role(r_1, r_2)$ which means that r_1 specializes r_2, it is a partial order on $ROLES$, written as $\geq$, where $r_1 \geq r_2$ only if all permissions of r_2 are also permissions of r_1, and all users of r_1 are also users of r_2. (c.f. Appendix.7).

For the organizational hierarchies of roles. We introduce the predicate $Junior\_role(r_1, r_2)$ which means that r_1 is hierarchically inferior to r_2. It is a partial order on $ROLES$, written as $\geq$, where $r_1 \geq r_2$ does not always signify that all permissions of r_2 are also permissions of r_1, nor all users of r_1 are also users of r_2. For example (c.f. Fig.2): *the director of the corporate services does not inherit all permissions of an employee in security services.* (c.f. Appendix.8).

The inheritance through the inclusion hierarchies of organizational units is represented in the following rule: $Include \subseteq ORG\_UNITS \times ORG\_UNITS$ is a partial order on ORG_UNITS, written as $\geq$, where $ou_1 \geq ou_2$ does not always signify that all permissions of ou_2 are also permissions of ou_1, nor all users of ou_1 are also users of ou_2. (c.f. Appendix.9).

The relation of inheritance through hierarchies of functions is a partial order on $FUNCTIONS$ written as $\geq$, where $f_1 \geq f_2$ only if all permissions of f_2 are also permissions of f_1, and all users of f_1 are also users of f_2. The inheritance of the permissions associated with this hierarchy is defined using the predicate Specialiozed_function (c.f. Appendix.10).

We introduce the predicate $Included\_function(f_1, f_2)$ which means that f_1 is used by f_2. This relation is also a partial order on $FUNCTIONS$ written as $\geq$, where $f_2 \geq f_1$ only if all permissions of f_1 are also permissions of f_2, and all users of f_2 are also users of f_1. The inheritance of the permissions associated with this relation is formulated in Appendix.11.

We introduce the predicate $Junior\_Cluster(c_1, c_2)$ which means that c_1 is junior to c_2. $Junior\_Cluster$ a partial order on $CLUSTERS$ written as $\geq$.where $c_2 \geq c_1$ only if all permissions on c_2 are also permissions on c_1, and all users allowed to access to c2 are also allowed to access to c_1. The inheritance of permissions is formulated in Appendix.12.

Models for Fine Grained Permission Assignment

Function-to-User Assignment. A user can be directly assigned to particular functions and select a subset of them in a given session. According to this selection, a particular set of permissions is granted. So, each session is a mapping of one user to a subset functions which can be activated and desactivated at the user's discretion. (c.f. Appendix.13).

Permission - to - User Assignment. In a session, a user can select a subset of permissions which are directly assigned to him.According to this selection, a particular set of permissions is granted. In a session, permissions, can be activated and desactivated at the user's discretion. Each session is a mapping to a set of permissions. (c.f. Appendix.14).

Function_to_User and Permission_to_User assignments allow fine grained assignements offering greater flexibility in handling permissions such as handling exceptions.

Composed Permission Assignment Model. According to the access control roles, we can use an integrated model to model muti-level and fine-grained permission assignments. The integrated model can be composed of the basic model for permission assignment improved with a number of assignment models presented above. In a session, a user can select a subset of roles, organizational units, functions and/or permissions. According to this selection, a particular set of permissions is granted. The permissions available to him are the union of permissions from all roles, organizational units, functions and/or permissions activated in that session and granted directly or indirectly to him. Each session is a mapping of one user to a subset of roles, functions, org-units and/or permissions. Roles, organizational units, functions and permissions, in a session, can be activated and desactivated at the user's discretion.

3   Evaluation of FORBAC with Respect to Related Work Using a Reference Framework

In order to characterize our model with respect to the related work, we developed a reference framework relying on [16]. This framework, initially proposed for system engineering [14], proved its effectiveness in the comprehension improvement of many disciplines of engineering, such as IS [14] and requirement engineering [15]. The approach "by facets" was first proposed in [21]. It was also used in the process engineering domain [24] to compare organizational change management approaches [3, 19]. A facet includes a set of attributes allowing to specify the characteristics of the studied approaches and to build then a comparative state of the art. We identified three views (Administration, Usage and System). Each view is characterized by a set of facets facilitating the understanding and the classification of the studied access control models. The facets identified are: *environment* and *safety* (System view); *type of administration, expressiveness, complexity* and *Cost* (Administration view); *adaptability to changes*, and *adaptability to organizational structures* (Usage view). Some facets include a set of attributes allowing to specify the characteristics of the studied models and to build then a comparative state of the art. For example, the facet complexity in the administration view has an attribute named *level*. Figure 3 represents our framework, its facets, the attributes of some facets, and the set of possible values of attributes. Figure 3 characterizes also our model with respect to the framework. The underlined values, describe the facets characterizing our model.

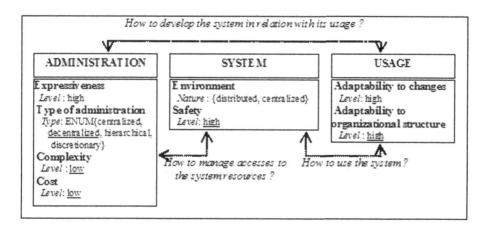

Fig. 3. The Reference Framework used to characterize the proposed model

3.1   System View

Environment. Our model satisfies widely distributed system needs. It is adaptable to various organization types, thanks to the concept of organizational unit. Classifying resources into clusters helps to easily decentralize them.

Safety. Introducing the concepts of function and object cluster allows to precisely specify permissions and then to reduce error risks when managing access control, sequentially. In consequence, safety is better assured.

3.2   Usage View

Adaptability to organizational structure and to changes. Hierarchies are suitable to organize roles and to reflect skills and duties into organizations. Nevertheless, this concept is ambiguous in *RBAC* and the majority of its variants

[5, 8, 11, 17, 9, 22]. The permissions inheritance is sometimes incorrect. For example, based on Figure 2, a user, playing the role of *director of the corporate services*, r_1, is hierarchically superior to a user playing the role of *employee in security services*, r_2, however, r_1 should not inherit all r_2's permissions. In our approach, we use the concept of role hierarchies to structure roles, but we distinguish two distinct semantics for roles hierarchies : the specialization/generalization hierarchies and the functional or organizational hierarchies. Current models do not distinguish between these two hierarchy semantics. What is more, they do not support issues related to adaptability to various organizations and to changes.

3.3   Administration View

Expressiveness. As discussed in Section 2.2, our approach allows managing permissions at different levels of granularity. This feature increases flexibility and allows to express a broad range of security requirements from simple to complex. The concept of goal and the user-to-function and user-to-permission assignment relations give to the model the ability to create more flexible instances (the latter will describe the access control policies of real organizations in a changing environments). *RBAC* is somewhat non flexible for granting specific rights, since it only permits granting rights by defining an appropriate role and assigning users the right to use it. It is appropriate only to organizations whose users are assigned to roles with well defined access rules [9]. *TMAC* [11] introduces the concept of *team*. *C-TMAC* [11] provides explicitly activation permission rules according to the context. *ORBAC* [18] focuses on the concept of organization. *TRBAC* [5] introduces the concepts of periodic role enabling and *temporal dependencies* between roles. *GTRBAC* [17] allows specifying temporal constraints on role enabling and temporal restrictions on the user-to-role and role-to-permission assignments. *TBAC* [26] extends *RBAC* with the concepts of *task, authorization step* and *authorization step life cycle* concepts allowing subjects to dynamically obtain permissions while performing tasks. Most of the existing models are restricted to permissions. *ORBAC* [18] distinguishes three types of privileges: permissions, prohibitions and obligations. This mixed policy can lead to problems related to the management of conflict and redundant rules. Related works cited are less expressive than our approach since they do not allow adaptability with changes and various types of organizations.

Complexity. Permissions can be modified either by explicit authorizations of a user to a role, by changing the set of functions of a role or the set of permissions of a function. Our model is less *complex* to administrate than the others thanks to the operations provided for role handling; Roles, organizational units and functions hierarchies allow us to partially automate user-to-role, role-to-function and function-to-permission assignments. *FORBAC* has multiple advantages compared to *RBAC* (and to quote the other models). Indeed, permission-to-function assignments and function-to-role assignments reduce considerably the total number of permission-to-role assignments as follows : For each function, let R be the number of roles exercing a function and P the number of permissions required for a function: $(R + P) < (R \bullet P), R, P > 2 \Rightarrow (R + P) < (R \bullet P)$. For all job positions, $\sum_{i}^{n_{jp}}(R_i + P_i) < \sum_{i}^{n_{jp}}(R_i \bullet P_i)$.

The concepts of function and object cluster allow to reduce management cost, in fact, fine-grained and multi-level permission assignment allow to suit actual organization requirements. As opposed to assignment at the role level in the *RBAC* model.

Type of administration. There are several kinds of administration: it is discretionary in *DAC*, centralized in *MAC* and decentralized in *RBAC* and *ORBAC*. *ARBAC* and *AdOBAC* [7] are designed to manage respectively *RBAC* and *ORBAC*. As far as we know, there are no administrative models proper to *TMAC*, *C-TMAC*, *TBAC*, *TRBAC* and *GTRBAC*. However, being based on *RBAC*, they can be managed by *ARBAC*.

4   Conclusion and Future Work

We have proposed a new approach for modelling access control, named *FORBAC*, aiming at overcome some weaknesses of the current ones and to meet flexibility requirements in evolutionary environments. We have formally defined the approach's basic concepts and the way permissions can be inherited. We have evaluated our approach with respect to the studied models; that's why we have proposed a reference framework that we have used as basis for evaluating access control models. Based on the reference framework we introduced, our model is more expressive, sufficiently flexible and adaptable to suit to evolutionary requirements of the organizations. Indeed, it allows a great expressive power thanks to the use of a basic model which can be augmented with additional permission assignment sub-models; Thus, *FORBAC* allows several levels for assigning permissions to users. Furthermore, *FORBAC* use the concept of *organizational unit* in order to suit to various types of organization structure and to disributed systems and collaborative work. In addition, we have introduced the concepts of *function* and *object cluster*, and their use for multi-level and fine grained permision assignment help to adapt easilly to organizationa, functional and operational changes with reducing the risk of errors in administration which increase safety.

Several issues have not been discussed here but they will be presented in our future work:

- The translation of users from one organizational unit to another, logically they don't have to keep all rights related to the previous tasks.
- The application to a workflow, that means the change of permissions based on the state of an object.
- Other types of relations between functions need to be discussed, like "*decomposition*".

Modelling this type of decomposition is an important issue in several applications, particularly for business process applications. For example, a function f1 can be decomposed into f_2 followed by f_3. If a given role r has the permission to perform f_1, then it should also have permissions to perform f_2 and f_3. However, it should have the permission to perform f_3 only after having performed f_2.

- It seems necessary to develop an administrative model for *FORBAC*. Such a model has been proposed with *ARBAC* [20] for administrating *RBAC*.
- We also try to define a mechanism allowing to guide the administrator to use the appropriate model in order to meet better with security organization requirements. Such a model has to include just the adequate access control model components and has to be able to manage the security policy changes following organizational, operational and functional changes. This will lead to improve safety and reduce administration cost.

References

[1] G. J. Ahn et R. Sandhu. Role-based Authorization Constraints Specification. *ACM Trans. Inf. and Sys. Sec.*, 3(4), 2000.

[2] E. Barka et R. Sandhu. A role-based delegation model and some extensions. *NISSC*, 2000. *ACM Trans. Inf. and Sys. Sec.*, 4(3):191-233, 2001.

[3] Barrios, J.: Une méthode pour la définition de l'impact organizationnel du changement, Thèse de Doctorat de l'Université Paris1 (2001)

[4] D. E. Bell et L. J. LaPadula. Secure computer systems: Unified exposition and multics interpretation. Technical Report ESD-TR-73-306, The MITRE Corporation, 1976.

[5] E. Bertino, P.A. Bonatti et E. Ferrari. TRBAC:A Temporal Role-Based Access Control Model .

[6] K. J. Biba. Integrity for secure computer systems. Technical report MTR-3153, The MITRE Corporation. *ACM Trans. Inf. and Sys. Sec.*, 4(3):191-233, 2001.

[7] F. Cuppens et A. Miège. Administration model for Or-bac. International Federated Conferences (OTM'03), Workshop on Metadata for Security. Italy, Nov. 3(7): 754-768, 2003.

[8] D. Ferraiolo et R. Kuhn. Role-Based Access Control. Proceedings of 15th NIST-NCSC National Computer Security Conference, 554-563, Baltimore, MD, 1992.

[9] D. F. Ferraiolo, R. Sandhu, S. Gavrila, D.R. Kuhn et R. Chandramouli. Proposed NIST Standard for Role-Based Access Control. ACM Trans. Inf. and Sys. Sec., 4(3):222-274, 2001.

[10] Frederick, G., Daniel, M., Sandra, S., Carol, G.: Information Technology Control and Audit. Auerbach publications (2004)

[11] C. K. Georgiadis, I. Mavridis, G. Pangalos et R. K. Thomas. Flexible Team-based Access Control Using Contexts. ACM RBAC Workshop, Chantilly, VA USA 2001.

[12] Goncalves, G., Hémery, F.: Des cas d'utilisation en UML la gestion de rôles dans un système d'information. Actes du Congrès INFORSID, France (2000).

[13] Harisson, M.A., Ruzzo, W.L., Ullman, J.D.: Protection in Operating Systems. Communication of the ACM, 19:8 (1976) 461-471

[14] M. Jarke, J. Mylopoulos, J.W. Smith et Y. Vassilio. DAIDA - An environment for evolving information systems. ACM Trans. on Inf. Sys., 10(1). 1992.

[15] Jarke, M., Pohl. K.: Requirement engineering : an integrated view of representation, process and domain. Proc. of the 4th European Soft. Conf., Springer, 1993.

[16] M. Jarke, C. Rolland, A. Sutcliffe, R. Dömges, The NATURE Requirements Engineering, Shaker Verlag, Aachen, ISBN 3-8265-6174-0. 1999.

[17] J. B.D. Joshi, E. Bertino, U. Latif, et A. Ghafoor. A Generalized Temporal Role-Based Access Control Model. IEEE Transactions on Knowledge and Data Engineering, 17(1), 2005.

[18] A. E. Kalam, R. E. Baida, P. Balbiani, S. Benferhat, F. Cuppens, Y. Deswarte, A. Miège, C. Saurel et G. Trouessin. Organization Based Access Control. POL-ICY'2003. Italie, 2003.

[19] Nurcan, S., Barrios, J., Rolland C.: Une méthode pour la définition de l'impact organisationnel du changement. ISI, N spécial, INFORSID (2002)

[20] S. Oh et R. Sandhu. A Model for Role administration using Organization Structure. In Proc. of the 7th ACM SACMAT, California, 155-162, 2002.

[21] Prieto-Diaz, R., Freeman, F.: Classifying software reusability. IEEE Software (1987)

[22] R. Sandhu. Future Directions in Role-Based Access Control Models. MMM-ACNS 2001.

[23] Sandhu, R., Coyne, E., Feinstein, H., Youman, C. E.: Role Based Access Control Models. IEEE Computer, 29:2 (1996) 38-47

[24] Si-Said Cherfi, S.: Proposition pour la modélisation et le guidage des processus d'analyse des systèmes d'information. Thèse de Doctorat Université Paris 1 (1999)

[25] Smith, R. E.: Authentication From Passwords to Public Keys. Addison Wesley, 2002.

[26] R. Thomas et R. Sandhu. Task-based Authorization Controls (TBAC): A Family of Models for Active and Enterprise-oriented Authorization Management. 11th IFIP Working Conference on Database Security, Lake Tahoe, USA, 1997.

A   Appendix

We are going to express basic concepts and permissions-assignment of FORBAC in a formal functional specification based on first-order logic

1. $Play \subseteq USERS \times ROLES$, $play(u,r), u \in USERS, r \in ROLES$, means that u can play r.
   $Assigned\_Users1(r : ROLES) \rightarrow 2^{USER}$ (adapted from the RBAC model, maps a role r onto a set of users)
   $Assigned\_Users1(r) = \{u \in USER/(u,r) \in Play\}$

2. $Member \subseteq USERS \times ORG\_UNITS, member(u, ou), u \in USERS$,
   $ou \in ORG\_UNITS$, means that the user u is a member of the org-unit ou.
   $Assigned\_Users2(ou : ORG\_UNITS) \rightarrow 2^{USER}$ maps an org-unit ou onto a set of users.
   $Assigned\_Users2(ou) = \{u \in USER/(u, ou) \in Member\}$

3. $Satisfies \subseteq PERMISSIONS \times FUNCTIONS \times GOALS$
   $Satisfies(p, f, g), p \in PERMISSIONS, f \in FUNCTIONS, g \in GOALS$
   means that f is authorized to p in order to achieve g.
   $Assigned\_Function(r : ROLE) \rightarrow 2^{FUNCTION}$, is a mapping of a role r onto a set of functions.
   $Assigned\_Function(r) = \{f \in FUNCTION/(f, r) \in Perform1\}$

4. $Belongs \subseteq OBJECTS \times CLUSTERS$, an object-to-cluster assignment.
   $Objects\_of\_cluster(c : CLUSTER) \rightarrow 2^{OBJECT}$ the mapping of cluster c onto a set of objects
   $Object\_of\_cluster(c) = \{o \in OBJECT/(o, c) \in OC\}$.

5. $Assigned\_Permissions(f: FUNCTION, g \in GOAL) \rightarrow 2^{PERMISSION}$
$Assigned\_Permissions(f, g) =$
$\{p \in PERMISSION, g \in GOAL)/(p, g, f) \in Satisfies\}$

6. $Sessions\_Role(s: SESSIONS) \rightarrow 2^{ROLES}$
$Session\_Roles(S_i) \subseteq \{r \in ROLES/(User_{session}(S_i, ou) \in Play\}$
$Sessions\_Org\_units(s: SESSIONS) \rightarrow 2^{ORG\_UNITS}$
$Session\_Roles\_units(S_i) \subseteq$
$\{ou \in Org_u nits/(User\_Session(S_i), ou) \in Member\}$

7. $\forall r_1, r_2 \in ROLES, p \in PERMISSIONS, u \in USERS, g \in GOALS$
$Specialized\_role(r_1, r_2) \wedge Authorized(r_2, p, g) \rightarrow Authorized(r_1, p, g)$
$Specialized\_role(r_1, r_2) \wedge Play(r_1, r_2) \rightarrow Play(r_1, r_2)$

8. $\exists r_1, r_2 \in ROLES, u \in USERS, p \in PERMISSIONS, g \in GOALS$
$Junior\_role(r_1, r_2) \wedge Authorized(r_2, p, g) \wedge \neg Authorized(r_1, p, g)$
$Junior\_role(r_1, r_2) \wedge Play(u, r_1) \wedge \neg Play(u, r_2)$

9. $\exists ou_1, ou_2 \in UNIT\_ORG, u \in USERS, p \in PERMISSIONS, g \in GOALS$
$Include(r_1, r_2) \wedge Authorized(ou_2, p, g) \wedge \neg Authorized(ou_1, p, g)$
$Include(ou_1, ou_2) \wedge Member(u, ou_1) \wedge \neg Member(u, ou_2)$

10. $\forall f_1, f_2 \in FUNCTIONS, p \in PERMISSIONS, g \in GOALS$
$Specialized\_function(f_1, f_2) \wedge Authorized(f_2, p, g) \rightarrow Authorized(f_1, p, g)$

11. $\forall f_1, f_2 \in FUNCTIONS, p \in PERMISSIONS, g \in GOALS$
$Included\_function(f_1, f_2) \wedge Satisfies(f_2, p, g) \rightarrow Satisfies(f_1, p, g)$

12. $\forall c_1, c_2 \in CLUSTERS, p \in PERMISSIONS$
$Authorized(c_2, p) \wedge Junior\_Cluster(c_1, c_2) \rightarrow Authorized(c_1, p)$

13. $Sessions\_Functions(s: SESSIONS) \rightarrow 2^{FUNCTIONS}$
$Session\_Functions(S_i) \subseteq$
$\{f \in FUNCTION/(User\_Session(S_i), f) \in Perform\}$

14. $Sessions\_Permissions(s: SESSIONS) \rightarrow 2^{PERMISSIONS}$
$Session\_Permissions(S_i) \subseteq$
$\{p \in PERMISSIONS/(User\_Session(S_i), p) \in UPG\}$

An Anycasting Protocol for Anonymous Access to a Group of Contents-Equivalent Servers in a Distributed System

Alexander E. Kostin

Department of Computer Engineering, Eastern Mediterranean University,
Famagusta, North Cyprus, via Mersin 10, Turkey
Alexander.kostin@emu.edu.tr

Abstract. A novel anycasting protocol for timed asynchronous distributed multiserver systems is proposed. It is based on an anonymous multicast communication in a network of servers. In contrast with known approaches, the task of selection of a server in the given group is shifted from clients and the network to the servers that make a selection decision themselves as a result of a negotiation. The protocol was investigated with the use of a detailed simulation model using a class of the extended Petri nets. The results of simulation study of the proposed protocol are compared to the behavior of an ideal, centralized multiserver queuing system.

Keywords: Distributed systems, anycasting messaging, protocols.

1 Introduction

Anycast service, defined in the latest IP protocol IPv6 for the Internet [1], can be considered as a form of communication in distributed client-server systems in which clients (or *anycast initiators*) are served by a group of replicated or contents-equivalent servers (or *anycast responders*) in such a way that each clients request is initially addressed anonymously to the service provided by each of the servers in the group, but eventually only one of them is selected to actually handle the request. The importance of unicast communication stems from a desire to improve scalability of Internet services with the use of their replication and to increase reliability in providing a service.

In RFC 1546 [3], anycasting is formally defined as a service which provides a *stateless* best effort delivery of an anycast datagram to at least one host, and preferably only to one host, which serves the anycast address. And while the definition permits delivery to multiple hosts, it makes clear that the goal is delivery to just one host. It is important also to note that, since anycasting is a stateless service, according to [3] a network has no obligation to deliver two successive packets, or requests, sent to the same anycast address, to the same host.

In general, anycast service includes two activities which are selecting a server from a group and routing, i.e. determining a client-server path in the underlying network to satisfy the client requirements. Unfortunately, RFC 1546 and IPv6 do

T. Yakhno and E. Neuhold (Eds.): ADVIS 2006, LNCS 4243, pp. 377–386, 2006.

not specify how to select a server from the desired group and how to determine a path from the client to the selected server. This is the most important problem in any attempt to practically implement anycasting in a computer network. As soon as a server is selected from a group, the subsequent communication with it can be done with the use of conventional unicast mode, connection-less (with the use of UDP) or connection-oriented (with TCP).

Since the time when anycast service has been defined in RFC 1546, a number of approaches were proposed to organize and implement this service in the Internet. All these approaches belong to one of two groups. The first group includes the application-layer, or *client-centric* schemes [4], [5], [6]. In these schemes, the address of a destination anycast server is determined at the client machine where the request for an anycast service is generated. The main disadvantage of these schemes is that the client machine needs to collect and maintain a large volume of information about the underlying network and anycast servers, such as network topology, list of servers, load of servers, transmission and propagation times etc. What is important and difficult to achieve, this information must be updated by each client dynamically along with the changes that take place in the network and among the servers.

The second group consists of the network-layer, or *network-centric* schemes [2], [7], [8], [9], [10]. The main feature of the network-centric schemes is that, given an anycast address, the selection of a server and the necessary routing of a packet to the selected server is done by *anycast-aware* network routers. As a result, these schemes do not involve the client in the server selection process, but they require the use of routers with anycast capabilities in the network. These capabilities can become available only in future, after the deployment of IPv6 in the Internet, with the necessary support in routers.

In this paper, we propose an anycast service scheme that can be implemented with the currently available Internet technology, without the need to have anycast-aware routers or to use any form of application-layer anycast. The proposed approach to anycasting is a generalization of a distributed load-balancing scheme described in our paper [11]. In contrast to application-layer (client-centric) and network-layer (network-centric) schemes that dominate currently all known proposals to implement anycasting in the Internet, our scheme is *server-centric*. In this scheme, an anycast client sends its request to a group of servers in the *multicasting mode*. In addition to IP multicast, with a number of working solutions [12], [13], [14], recently proposed end-system multicast has relatively simple deployment schemes in the Internet, without the necessity to make any changes in routers [15], [16]. When servers in the group receive a multicast request, they start a *negotiation* to decide which of the servers should handle the request. The inter-server negotiation has a form of a competition, in which only *idle* servers participate. The server that wins the competition will handle the received request. As a by-product, the proposed scheme will provide also load balancing among servers since, in the competition between servers, no preferences are taken into account, so that each participating server can become a winner with equal chance.

2   System Architecture and Assumptions

At an abstract level, the distributed system with the proposed protocol can be considered as a *timed asynchronous* distributed system. In such a system, communication delays and scheduling delays are *unbounded* although most messages arrive at their destination within a known delay and most actual scheduling delays at processing nodes are shorter that some known constant [17].

Functionally, this system can be viewed also as a distributed *multiserver queuing system* consisting of a group of n autonomous server nodes connected to a network. This group receives a random flow of requests from clients to be serviced according to the anycasting scheme. In addition to its specific function, each server maintains a *copy* of the common waiting FIFO queue of requests, and runs a protocol that supports anycasting and provides consistency of its copy of the common queue. The grain of work for servers is a client request. It is assumed that requests are not related in any way which is consistent with the definition of anycast in [3]. It is assumed also that, if the server starts handling a request, it will do this to the end unless the server crashes during processing of the started request.

To be able to compare the behavior of the distributed multiserver system to that of the multiserver queuing system with an ideal, centralized scheduler, it is assumed that requests from clients constitute a Poisson process, with a specified parameter. It is also assumed that each server serves requests during random time corresponding to the exponential probability distribution, with the same mean value for each server. If the time needed for the transmission of a request or a protocol message by the underlying network is small, compared to the time needed to service the request, then the idealized model of the distributed system to run the proposed protocol is a multiserver queuing system of type $M/M/n$, where n is the number of functionally identical servers [18].

It should be stressed that the assumptions for servers to be identical and to have exponential probability distributions for the interarrival time of requests and of servicing time are done to solely simplify the validation of simulation model. In its work, the protocol does not rely on these assumptions.

For communication, only *multicast* messages are used. This means, in particular, that communication between a client and servers and between servers is *anonymous*, so that each sender needs to know only the group address of servers. It is assumed that multicasting is *reliable*. It means here that a message, multicast by a sender, is eventually delivered to all members of the multicasting group. It is important to note that the proposed anycasting scheme does not require *bounded delays* to deliver multicast messages. That is, according to the definition of a timed asynchronous distributed system [17], some messages can be delivered to a destination after any specified time-out.

We assume next that, in our multiserver queuing system, there is only one *virtual* common queue used to store all incoming client requests for a service. However, physically this virtual queue is represented by n private *replicated* copies, one copy per each of n servers in the system. Maintenance of the consistency of all private replicated copies is a relatively simple task, since each client request is multicast to all servers. Such a scheme provides an easy possibility for load balancing of servers in the group and solves the unreliability problem of any centralized solution [11].

It is assumed further, that each server knows at least the *approximate* size of the group to which it belongs. This information is used by servers to calculate the *persistency* probability of attempting to service the received request. The difference between the actual size of the group and the size known to a server will affect only the performance of the protocol but will not preclude its correct operation. As is customary for timed asynchronous distributed systems, the protocol uses a few time-outs and delays. A significant part of the architecture of our distributed system is a failure model. According to this model, the proposed protocol takes into account possible server crashes. Servers crash by *halting* failures, and crashed servers may recover later. When a server crashes or leaves the group, it loses all information on its state existing at the moment of the crash or leave. If the server crashes during servicing a request, then some other server in the group will repeat the task of servicing this request. The crash of the server during processing of a request is detected by alive servers on base of an estimated time to perform the request. The details of this part of the protocol are omitted due to space limitation.

3   The Distributed Anycasting Inter-server Protocol

The proposed protocol is intended to control the negotiation of individual servers in the network in an attempt to select a server among the participants to handle a received multicast request. The protocol must satisfy the following requirements: 1. Each client request must be executed according to the FIFO rule. This requirement may be violated only if a server, that handles some request, crashes. 2. Each request must be serviced once, *preferably* by only one server, according to [3]. 3. Time overhead of the protocol should be small compared to the time required to service a request.

According to the protocol, servers compete for requests which are multicast by clients to all servers. Therefore, *conflicts* between servers are possible. A conflict is a normal situation when two or more servers choose the same request R from their private queue and assign this request for a possible handling. The assignment of request R by a server S is a local action, being a preliminary step before servicing of R. After the assignment of request R, server S multicasts an *assignment message* to inform all other servers in the group about its *desire* to handle R. At the same moment of time, to detect possible conflicts with other servers that might assign the same request R, server S starts its interruptible time-out interval T_1.

If server S, which sent an assignment message with the identifier of a request R, receives an assignment message from at least one other server with the identifier of the same request R, before the interval T_1 expires, it understands that there is a *local conflict* related to request R. In this case, each server, involved in the conflict, de-assigns request R in its own queue and enters a random delay, or *back-off interval* T_3, after which it can again compete for requests in its queue.

If, during time-out T_1, no assignment messages arrive with the identifier of the assigned request R, server S deduces that no other server desires to service the request R, and starts servicing it. After servicing of request R, server S removes it from its own queue and sends a notifying multicast message to ask all other servers to remove R from their private queue.

On the other hand, each server, that receives an assignment message with the identifier of request R but does not intend to service this request, starts its non-interruptible time-out interval T_2 related to R. During this interval, it may receive more assignment messages with R from other servers. If only one assignment message with R arrives during T_2, then this non-involved server deduces that request R is assigned for handling by only one remote server, and marks request R in its queue as is being remotely serviced. On the other hand, if two or more assignment messages with the same request R arrive during T_2, then the non-involved server understands that there is a *remote conflict* related to request R, and it does not change the status of this request in its queue. If the non-involved server becomes idle before T_2 elapses, it may not assign request R which it knows has been assigned already. This prevents its involvement in a conflict during T_2 because of request R. However, this server is free to compete for the next free request in its private queue.

For each request R, the protocol uses four types of multicast messages - $A(R)$, $E(R)$, $F(R)$, and $N(R)$. A message of type $A(R)$ is an assignment message which is sent by a server to inform all other servers in the anycast group about its desire to handle request R. A message of type $E(R)$ is sent by a server S if, during servicing of request R, this server receives a message $A(R)$, with the same request identifier R, from some other server S_i. Such a situation can arise, for example, when server S_i decides that server S has crashed. In this situation, server S_i may attempt to assign request R for servicing. A message of type $F(R)$ is sent by server S to notify all other servers in the group that request R has been serviced by S. Finally, a message of type $N(R)$ represents a new request R received from some client by this and all other servers in the anycast group.

The proposed protocol handles possible crashes of servers at any of their operational state. An important feature of the protocol is the use of a p-persistence scheme to limit the number of competing servers and, as a result, to achieve *scalability* with respect to communication traffic. Due to space limitation, these aspects of the protocol are not pursued further. Note only that, in the p-persistence scheme, each server assigns a clients request for servicing with dynamically varied probability

$$p = 1 - \exp(-k(l/n)),$$

where n is the number of servers in the system, l is the current length of requests in the waiting queue of the server, and k is a nonnegative configuration coefficient.

4   Simulation Performance Study of the Protocol

To investigate the proposed anycast protocol, its detailed simulation model was developed and studied in a series of simulation experiments. As a modeling formalism, a class of *extended* Petri nets was used [19].

Multicast messages, transmitted by servers in the underlying network, are represented in the model by tokens having numeric attributes. The most important attributes are the type of message (A, F, or E) and the estimated upper bound time to process the chosen request by the sending server (for messages of types A and E). All requests are generated and multicast as messages of type N (i.e. new messages) by one client source, with a mean interarrival time $1/\lambda$ that could be varied to specify different server loads.

The model of each process has a number of constants and variables, with values assigned at start-up time of simulation. For a simulation run, constants are server identifier, duration of time-out T_1, number of servers in the group, n, coefficient k in expression (3), duration of time-out interval T_2, limits $(T_3)_{\min}$ and $(T_3)_{\max}$ for delay T_3, mean time of processing a request by each server fixed at $1/\lambda = 2000$ ms in all our simulation experiments.

As performance measures of the protocol, the average relative time in system, the average number of assignment messages (of type A) sent by a server per processed request, and the relative load unbalance of servers are used.

The *average relative time in system* is important to compare the behavior of the distributed system under study with its ideal centralized queuing system $M/M/n$. For the corresponding centralized queuing system, the expected time in system is well known [18]. The relative time in system is defined here as the ratio (Average time in system for the protocol)/(Mean time in system for the corresponding $M/M/n$ queuing system), with the same values of λ and μ in the protocol and the queuing system. Since, in a centralized $M/M/n$ queuing system, there is no time overhead for message passing and conflict resolution, the relative time in system for the protocol will be not less than 1. Therefore, this performance metric includes the time complexity of the protocol.

The *average number of assignment messages* reflects the *variable* part of the overall communication complexity of the protocol. It is the number of messages of type A per request. This number generally depends on the number of servers in the group, the load of servers, time-outs and delays T_1, T_2, and T_3, and coefficient k in expression (3) used to calculate persistence probability.

Finally, the *relative load unbalance* of servers is used to estimate quantitatively how the protocol is fair in loading servers by incoming requests. We will express the load balancing of a multiserver queuing system in terms of dispersion of servers load according to the scheme proposed in [11]. Let $r_1,\ldots,r_n$ be average loads of n servers for given request traffic, and $r_{\min}$ and $r_{\max}$ are the minimal and maximal loads among these values. Then, as a measure of *relative load unbalance* of the protocol, the value $u = (r_{\max} - r_{\min})/r^*$ is used, where r^* is the overall average of $r_1,\ldots,r_n$. Obviously, with the identical servers, the ideal unbalance $u = 0$.

The majority of simulation experiments have been carried out for three loads of servers: low (0.1), medium (0.5), and high (0.9). With fixed mean time of processing a request by each server, $1/\mu$, and a given number of servers n in an $M/M/n$queuing system, the load of a server is estimated as $\lambda/(\mu n)$.

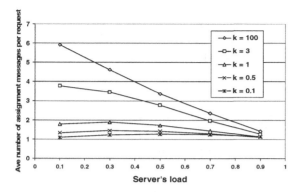

Fig. 1. Average number of assignment messages per request for a service vs. servers load, for a group of five servers and different values of coefficient k in expression (3)

For each load, the number of servers in the model was varied as 5, 10, 15, 25. The maximal number of servers 25 is in line with the majority of known experiments with anycasting [5]. For each of the three server loads, and given number of servers, the following values of coefficient k in expression (3) were used: 100, 3, 1, 0.5, and 0.1. The value $k = 100$ in expression (3) was chosen to make persistence probability close to one. Thus, the value $k = 100$ actually corresponds to 1-persistence scheme. The values 3, 1, 0.5, and 0.1 of coefficient k correspond to a p-persistence scheme, with the decreasing persistence probability.

In the simulation experiments, the following values of time-outs and random delays were used: $T_1 = 25$ ms, $T_2 = 20$ ms, and $(T_3)_{min} = T_1$. Finally, the maximal value $(T_3)_{max}$ for T_3 was fixed at 100 ms, to keep the probability of repeated conflicts between servers at a reasonable level. To eliminate the effect of the transient state, each simulation run was done long enough to ensure that each server handles not less than 2000 client requests.

Figs. 1 and 2 show graphs of the performance metrics, versus servers load, for five servers, with different values of coefficient k in expression (3). Fig. 3 shows the behavior of the average number of assignment messages per request multicast by a server when the number of servers varies from 5 to 25.

From the simulation results, one can make the following observations.

1. The simulation experiments demonstrate a clear dependence of communication complexity, represented by the average number of assignment messages (messages of type A) per processed request, on the number of servers in the system, server's load, and the value of coefficient k in expression (3). As Fig. 1 shows, this dependence is the highest when servers assign requests with 1-persistency, which corresponds to $k = 100$ in the figure.

2. The amount of communication in the underlying network dramatically decreases if servers assign requests for processing with p-persistency, since this helps reduce the competition between servers. As Fig. 1 clearly shows, the average number of assignment messages per request can be made almost constant in all range of server's load, by the appropriate choice of coefficient k in expression

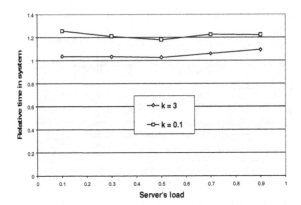

Fig. 2. Relative time spent by a request in a system of five servers vs. servers load

(3). As Fig. 2 indicates for five servers, relative time spent by a request in system is almost constant in all range of servers load. However, this time depends on coefficient k in (3). When this coefficient is large, the relative time spent by a request in system is quite close to one, so that the systems behavior is close to the behavior of the corresponding $M/M/n$ queuing system with respect to this performance metric. On the other hand, according to (3), a small value of coefficient k results in small persistence probability and, correspondingly, in large probability that all idle servers will delay in their attempt to compete for a given request. This will result in the additional time spent by the request in the system.

3. When the number of servers increases, the average number of assignment messages also increases, approximately linearly, as Fig. 3 demonstrates. However, with the five-fold increase in the number of servers, the average number of assignment messages per request increases less than two times for high servers load and even less for low load. It was observed that, with the increase of the number of servers, the relative time in system per request slightly decreases for low servers load and increases, approximately linearly, for high servers load. Thus, with the proper choice of coefficient k in (3), the protocol has a potential for *scalability* with respect to the number of servers in the group, at least in the range up to a few dozens of replicated servers which is appropriate for many applications.

4. Relative load unbalance among servers was quite small for different numbers of servers, with low and high servers load. In particular, for high load of servers, with $k = 0.1$ in (3), the relative load unbalance was in the range (0.0092, 0.0112) when the number of servers was varied from 5 to 25. Thus, the protocol provides quite satisfactory load balancing among servers.

5. It was observed, in sensitivity analysis of simulation experiments, that the protocol is quite robust to variation of values of time-out T_1 and delay T_3. In particular, the change of values of T_1 and $(T_3)_{max}$ of T_3 by a factor of more than two times does not result in noticeable difference in the average number of assignment messages per request. It was observed that other performance

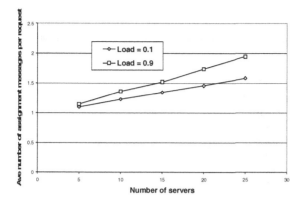

Fig. 3. Average number of assignment messages per request multicast by a server vs. the number of servers in the system, with coefficient $k = 0.1$ in (3)

measures also were not affected noticeably by the change of values of time-out T_1 and delay T_3.

5   Concluding Remarks

In this paper, a server-centric anycasting protocol for timed asynchronous distributed multiserver systems is presented. The protocol is based on a free competition between servers and the randomization in resolving conflicts between servers. Simulation experiments with the detailed simulation model show quite satisfactory behavior of the protocol. In particular, these experiments indicate that the communication complexity of the protocol can be drastically reduced with a p-persistence scheme.

To the best of our knowledge, there are no studies in which the implementation of an anycast service was considered from a server-centric point of view. The protocol can be of interest to designers of replicated servers in distributed systems and of new schemes for their accessing. The protocol can be especially appropriate for accessing *server farms*, which are usually deployed in the same physical network or in the same network domain and for which an end-system multicast technique can be implemented quite easily.

References

1. Deering, S., Hinden, R.: Internet Protocol Version 6 (IPv6) Specification, RFC 2460, Dec. (1998)
2. Hao, F., Zegura, E.W., Ammar, M.H.: QoS Routing for Anycast Communications: Motivation and an Architecture for DiffServ Networks, IEEE Communications Magazine, June (2002) 48-56
3. Partridge, C., Mendez, T., Milliken, W.: Host Anycasting Service, RFC 1546, November (1993)

386   A.E. Kostin

4. Zegura, E.W., Ammar, M.H., Fei, Z., Bhattacharjee, S.: Application-Layer Anycasting: A Server Selection Architecture and Use in a Replicated Web Service, IEEE/ACM Trans. on Networking, vol. 8, no. 4, August, (2000) 455-466
5. Hanna, K.M., Natarajan, N., Levine, B.N.: Evaluation of a Novel Two-Step Server Selection Metric, Proc. of the Ninth Intl. Conf. on Network Protocols, 11-14 November, (2001) 290-300
6. Yu, S. , Zhou, W., Wu, Y.: Research on Network Anycast, Proc. of the Fifth Intl. Conf. on Algorithms and Architectures for Parallel Processing (ICA3PP02), October 23-25, (2002) 154-161
7. Selvakumar, S., Brahmadesam, M.M.: Secure Dynamic Anycasting for Best Server Selection Using Active Networks, Computer Communications, vol. 24, no. 18, (2001) 1819-1827
8. Low, C.P., Tan, C.L.: On Anycast Routing with Bandwidth Constraint, Computer Communications, vol. 26, no. 14, (2003) 1541-1550
9. Lin, C.-Y., Lo, J.-H., Kuo, S.-Y.: Load-Balanced Anycast Routing, Proc. of the Tenth Intl. Conf. on Parallel and Distributed Systems (ICPADS04), 7-9 July, (2004) 701-708
10. Weber, S., Cheng, L.: A Survey of Anycast in IPv6 Networks, IEEE Communications Magazine, January (2004) 127-132
11. Kostin, A., Aybay, I., Oz, G.: A Randomized Contention-Based Load-Balancing Protocol for a Distributed Multiserver Queuing System, IEEE Transactions on Parallel and Distributed Systems, vol. 11, no. 12, December (2000) 1252-1273
12. Almeroth, K.C.: The Evolution of Multicast: From the MBone to Interdomain Multicast to Internet2 Deployment, IEEE Network, vol. 14, no. 1, January/February (2000) 10-20
13. Hamad, A.M., Kamal, A.E.: A survey of Multicasting Protocols for Broadcast-and-Select Single-Hop Networks, IEEE Network, vol. 16, no. 4, July/August (2002) 36-48
14. Maxemchuk, N. F.: Reliable Multicast with Delay Guarantees, IEEE Communications Magazine, September (2002) 96-102
15. Popescu, G, Liu, Z.: Stateless Application-Level Multicast for Dynamic Group Communication, Proc. of the Eight Int'l Symposium on Distributed Simulation and Real-Time Applications (2004)
16. Lao, L., Cui, J.-H., Gerla, M.: TOMA: A Viable Solution for Large-Scale Multicast Service Support, LNCS, vol.3462 (2005) 906-915
17. Cristian, F.: Synchronous and Asynchronous Group Communication, Communications of the ACM, vol. 39, no. 4, April (1996) 88-97
18. Banks, J., Carson, J.S., Nelson, B.L., Nicol, D.M.: Discrete-Event System Simulation, 3rd ed., Prentice-Hall (2001)
19. Kostin, A., Ilushechkina, L.: Winsim: A Tool for Performance Evaluation of Parallel and Distributed Systems, Lecture Notes in Computer Science, vol. 3261, (2004) 312-321

A Wireless Broadcast Generation Scheme Considering Data Access Frequencies

Yon Dohn Chung[1,*] and Chang-Sup Park[2]

[1] Dept. of Computer Science and Engineering, Korea University, Korea
ydchung@korea.ac.kr
[2] Dept. of Internet Information Engineering, The University of Suwon, Korea
park@suwon.ac.kr

Abstract. This paper[1] presents a scheduling scheme for wireless broadcast data which considers data access frequencies. Whereas the previous approaches consider either data replication or index replication, the proposed scheme considers both of them. Through analysis and experiments, it is shown that the new approach has better performance (with respect to the access time and tuning time) than the previous approaches.

1 Introduction

Wireless information systems are currently realized as the wireless technologies are rapidly gaining popularity [1-7]. In the wireless information systems, mobile clients carry small, battery powered hand-held devices such as PDA's and mobile phones with limited data processing capabilities. In wireless environments, data broadcasting is widely used due to the bandwidth restriction of wireless communication [1, 4, 6, 7]. The server disseminates data through a broadcast channel, and mobile clients listen on the channel and retrieve information of their interests without sending requests to the server.

In wireless data broadcasting, indexing and replication approaches are widely used for energy and latency efficiency reasons. The index information, which is broadcast on the air intermixed with data, is a kind of directory information - commonly represented as a set of <data ID, address> tuples. By reading the index information, mobile clients can be informed of the address of their target data. So, they can access the data directly without scanning the full wireless data stream. Also, by replicating hot data items more frequently than cold ones, the overall access time performance can be improved.

In the literature, some indexing approaches for wireless data broadcasting have been proposed for tuning time efficiency, e.g., Tune_opt, Access_opt, (1, M), and Distributed Indexing methods. Although some of these methods replicate index information for better energy-efficiency, they do not consider the access frequencies of data. There were also some data replication methods (e.g., Broadcast Disks) that replicate hot data items based on their access frequencies.

---

* Corresponding author.
[1] This work was supported by a Korea University Grant.

T. Yakhno and E. Neuhold (Eds.): ADVIS 2006, LNCS 4243, pp. 387–397, 2006.

However, they do not consider the tuning time performance but the access time performance.

The main contribution of this research is to propose a broadcast schedule generation scheme for wireless dissemination of information, where both of the index and data are replicated based on access frequencies of data items. Also, the paper considers both the access time and tuning time performance. The proposed scheme is evaluated through analysis and experiments.

The rest of the paper is organized as follows. We first discuss some background information and related work in Section 2. In Section 3, some new scheduling methods are proposed and analyzed. We evaluate the effectiveness of the proposed methods through experiments in Section 4 and draw a conclusion in Section 5.

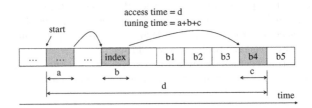

Fig. 1. Access time and Tuning time of wireless data access

2   Background and Related Work

Data broadcasting has many applications in wireless information systems due to its beneficial characteristics such as bandwidth-efficiency (i.e., the broadcast channel is shared by many clients), energy-efficiency (i.e., listening on the broadcast channel requires no energy for sending request messages to the server, where the amount of energy required for sending data is tens of hundreds of that for receiving data), and scalability (i.e., the number of clients listening on a broadcast channel is not limited) [6].

In the wireless data broadcasting, people consider two performance measures for data access: access time and tuning time [4-6]. The former is the duration from the time of query submission (i.e., start to listen on the broadcast channel) to the time of complete download of target information. The latter is the duration when a mobile device remains in the active mode during the access time, which directly relates to the amount of energy consumption of the mobile device. Fig. 1 illustrates the access time and tuning time of wireless data access. When a mobile client tunes into a data stream on the air, it moves[2] to the next nearest index area. By reading the index, the mobile client can be informed of the target address and thus can move to the target address and download the data. In the figure, the access time is 'd', whereas the tuning time is the sum of selective

---

[2] It means that the mobile client waits in the energy-saving mode until the target time (i.e., address) and then returns to the active mode in order to listen the target bucket.

tuning periods of 'a,' 'b,' and 'c.' In the case where there is no index, the whole data stream should be scanned for mobile clients to find the target data, which requires a large tuning time. (The tuning time is the same as the access time.)

There have been some studies for improving the access time performance via effective scheduling of broadcast data [1, 5] and reducing the tuning time via indexing methods which place some index information intermixed with the data on the broadcast stream [1, 2, 6].

Access_opt [6] This method uses no index for the wireless data broadcasting. Since the index information itself is an overhead with respect to the access time performance, this method shows the best access time performance. However, this approach has the worst tuning time performance.

Tune_opt [6] This method places the global index information in front of a broadcast stream. Therefore, it has the best tuning time performance, but the worst access time performance due to the overhead from a large index.

(1, M) index [6] This method replicates the index information m-times equi-distantly over a broadcast stream. By controlling the value m, it controls the preference of the access time vs. tuning time efficiency.

Distributed index [6] This method divides the index into small units and distributes small indices all over the broadcast stream. Since a small index is placed in front of relevant data items, the access time overhead is minimized while the tuning time efficiency is maximized. In this method, some index information is replicated over the stream. All the above methods assume that all data items are equally accessed i.e., no distinction between hot and cold data. Whereas, the methods in the below consider different access frequencies of data.

Broadcast Disks [1] This method replicates hot data items more frequently than cold ones when generating a broadcast stream. Therefore, the aver-age access time performance can be improved with the sacrifice of the cold data. This method considers only scheduling of wireless data and no index structure is used.

CF/VF [2] This method replicates index information according to the access frequencies of data such that the index information for highly accessed data items is replicated more frequently. However, data items are not replicated in this approach.

Although the above two methods consider data access frequencies, they use replication policies for either data or index, not both. This paper proposes a scheduling scheme in which both of the index and data are partly replicated.

3   The Proposed Broadcast Generation Scheme

This paper focuses on the replication of index and data for the wireless broadcast (*bcast*) generation under the consideration of different data access frequencies. The previous broadcast generation methods consider specific index structures or scheduling policies within a single broadcast. This paper deals with the inter-broadcast scheduling, where one broadcast is global one consisting of a global index and the whole data and the other is replicated one.

In the real world, the access frequencies for data items tend to vary. However in this paper, for the sake of simplicity, we classify the data into two groups: hot data group and cold data group. The top 20 % of the data items according to the access frequency are included in the hot data group. The remaining 80 % data items comprise the cold data group. Also, we use the Pareto's rule, that is, 80 % of access requests are concentrated on the 20 % of data (i.e., the hot data group).

According to replication types of index and data, 4 combinations are possible: non-replication, data-replication, index-replication, and index-and-data-replication. In the paper, they are denoted by (I, D), (I, HD, CD), (I, CD, HI, HD), and (I, D, HI, HD), respectively, where 'I' is the global index, 'D' is the entire data set, 'HI' is the index for the hot data, and 'HD' and 'CD' represent the hot and cold data.

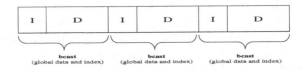

Fig. 2. The non-replication method - (I, D)

3.1   Non-replication - (I, D)

The basic broadcast generation method replicates none of index or data. It places one global index 'I' before each broadcast of data, as illustrated in Fig. 2. The index fragment contains the addresses for all data items. Thus, successive bcasts are homogeneous. It is similar to the Tune_opt method proposed in [6].

In the broadcast structure like this method, the access procedures for all data items, irrespective of whether they are hot data items or not, are the same. That is, the mobile client probes to the start of the next index area after reading the first tuned bucket. Arriving at the index area, the mobile client searches the index entries and finds the target data address. (In a special case where the first tuned bucket happens to be the starting bucket of an index area, the mobile client can directly start to search the index entries.) After finding the target data address, the mobile client waits until the target data arrives on the air and then downloads the data.

Therefore, the average time which is required for a mobile client to access a data item from the broadcast stream is computed as follows. Here, $|I|$ and $|D|$ are the size (i.e., the number of buckets) of the index and data on the stream, respectively.

$$AT = \frac{|I| + |D|}{2} + |I| + \frac{|D|}{2} = \frac{1}{2}(2|D| + 3|I|)$$

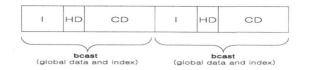

Fig. 3. The data replication method (re-arrangement) - (I, HD, CD)

On the other hand, the tuning time is the sum of '1 bucket for initial bucket tuning', 'the number of buckets for searching index entries' and '1 bucket where the target data is stored.' (Here, we assume for convenience one data item is not bigger than one bucket.) Since the number of buckets required for index searching is half of the index size on average, the average tuning time can be computed as follows: $TT = 2 + \frac{|I|}{2}$

3.2   Data Replication (Rearrangement) for Hot Data - (I, HD, CD)

The second combination is to replicate only the hot data, say (I, D, HD). In this broadcast structure, however, the HD is of no use because all the hot data items included in D are transmitted earlier than those in HD and thus they will not be accessed from the index I. Therefore, we modify the pure structure (I, D, HD) into the following data rearrangement structure.

We divide the data into two parts i.e., hot data and cold data, based on their access frequencies and place the hot data items HD ahead of the cold ones CD in a bcast. A global index for the whole data is created and broadcasted before the data as in the previous (I, D) method. Fig. 3 shows this (I, HD, CD) bcast generation method.

In the stream generated by this method, the hot data items are transmitted earlier than the cold ones right after the global index, so the average access time for the hot data can be improved on the (I, D) method. Suppose that α is the access frequency ratio of the hot data to the whole data and β is the size ratio of the hot data to that of the whole data, which are respectively defined by

$$\alpha = \frac{\sum_{d' \in HD} freq(d')}{\sum_{d \in D} freq(d)} \quad and \quad \beta = \frac{|HD|}{|D|}$$

Then, the average access time for the whole data is represented by

$$AT = \frac{|I| + |D|}{2} + |I| + \alpha \cdot \frac{|HD|}{2} + (1 - \alpha) \cdot (|HD| + \frac{|CD|}{2})$$
$$= \frac{1}{2}((2 - \alpha)|D| + 3|I| + |HD|)$$
$$= \frac{1}{2}((2 - \alpha + \beta)|D| + 3|I|)$$

Here, $|HD|$ denotes the size (i.e., the number of buckets) of the hot data. If we assume that $\alpha > \beta$, which can be considered true in general, the analytical result shows that this method can improve access time performance on the previous non-replication method. On the other hand, the average tuning time of this method is the same as that of the (I, D) method.

3.3 Index Replication for Hot Data - (I, CD, HI, HD)

The third combination is the index-replication i.e, (I, HI, D). However, the HI in this structure is also of no use, since any hot index entry in HI will not be accessed. (On the contrary, they will increase the access time.) So, we modify the (I, HI, D) structure into (I, CD, HI, HD).

In this structure we place the cold data ahead of the hot ones in a bcast and insert an index for only the hot data between the cold and hot data items as shown in Fig. 4. By exploiting the hot index which is relatively small, the hot data items can be accessed from mobile clients more efficiently while the tuning times for the cold data may increase due to unnecessary search against the hot index HI. On the other hand, the access time performance for the cold data can be improved on the previous (I, HD, CD) method because the cold data items are scheduled right after the global index.

As shown in Fig. 4, a bcast can be divided into two sub-bcasts, i.e., the first one consisting of the global index and cold data, and the second one consisting of the hot index and hot data. In this broadcast structure, the access time and tuning time vary according to the sub-bcast in which the start position (i.e., the initial tuning position) of a query is located.

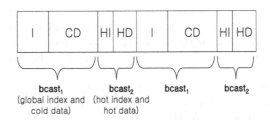

Fig. 4. The index replication method - (I, CD, HI, HD)

If we denote the ratio of the size of the first sub-bcast to the size of a bcast by λ_1, i.e., $\lambda_1 = \frac{|I|+|CD|}{|I|+|D|+|HI|}$, the average access times for the hot and cold data can be expressed as follows:

$$AT_{hot} = \lambda_1\left(\frac{|I| + |CD|}{2} + |HI| + \frac{|HD|}{2}\right)$$
$$+(1 - \lambda_1)\left(\frac{|HI| + |HD|}{2} + |I| + |CD| + |HI| + \frac{|HD|}{2}\right)$$
$$AT_{cold} = \lambda_1\left(\frac{|I| + |CD|}{2} + |HI| + |HD| + |I| + \frac{|CD|}{2}\right)$$
$$+(1 - \lambda_1)\left(\frac{|HI| + |HD|}{2} + |I| + \frac{|CD|}{2}\right)$$

Thus, if we assume that the size of the hot index is proportional to the size of the hot data, i.e., $|HD| = \beta|D|$, the average access time for any data item is described as follows: (Here α and β are defined as in Section 3.2. Note that the result is independent of the value of the parameter λ_1.)

$$AT = \alpha \cdot AT_{hot} + (1 - \alpha) \cdot AT_{cold}$$
$$= \frac{1}{2}\{(1 + \alpha + (1 - 2\alpha)(1 - \beta))|D| + (3 - 2\alpha + \beta)|I|)\}$$

The average tuning time can be described in a similar way to the average access time:

$$TT = \alpha \cdot TT_{hot} + (1 - \alpha) \cdot TT_{cold}$$
$$= \alpha\{\lambda_1(2 + \frac{|HI|}{2}) + (1 - \lambda_1)(2 + \frac{|I|}{2})\}$$
$$+ (1 - \alpha)\{\lambda_1(2 + \frac{|HI| + |I|}{2}) + (1 - \lambda_1)(2 + \frac{|I|}{2})\}$$
$$= 2 + \frac{1}{2}(1 + (\beta - \alpha)\lambda_1)|I|$$

3.4   Index and Data Replication for Hot Data - (I, D, HI, HD)

The last combination is to replicate both the index and data. As depicted in Fig. 5, the first sub-bcast consists of the global index and the whole data while the second one contains only the hot index and hot data. Denoting the ratio of the size of the first sub-bcast to the size of a bcast by λ_2, which is defined as $\lambda_2 = \frac{|I| + |D|}{|I| + |D| + |HI| + |HD|}$, the average access time of a stream generated by this method can be described as follows:

$$AT_{hot} = \lambda_2(\frac{|I| + |D|}{2} + |HI| + \frac{|HD|}{2}) + (1 - \lambda_2)(\frac{|HI| + |HD|}{2} + |I| + \frac{|D|}{2})$$
$$AT_{cold} = \lambda_2(\frac{|I| + |D|}{2} + |HI| + |HD| + |I| + \frac{|D|}{2}) + (1 - \lambda_2)(\frac{|HI| + |HD|}{2} + |I| + \frac{|D|}{2})$$
$$AT = \alpha \cdot AT_{hot} + (1 - \alpha) \cdot AT_{cold} = \frac{1}{2}\{(2 + \beta - \alpha)|D| + (3 + \beta - \frac{2\alpha}{\beta + 1})|I|\}$$

where α and β are defined as in Section 3.2 and the size of the hot index and that of the cold one are assumed to be proportional to the size of the hot data and cold data, respectively, i.e., $|HD| = \beta|D|$ and $|HI| = \beta|I|$.

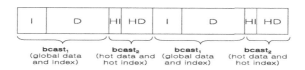

Fig. 5. The index and data replication method - (I, D, HI, HD)

The average tuning time of this method is expressed in the same way as that of the index replication method (I, CD, HI, HD) using λ_2 instead of λ_1. Since $\lambda_2 > \lambda_1$, we analytically observe that the average tuning time of this method is smaller than that of the (I, CD, HI, HD) method supposing that $\alpha > \beta$.

4   Performance Evaluation

In this section, we evaluate the effectiveness of the proposed broadcast generation methods by experiments. We constructed a simulation environment for generating and accessing broadcast data streams on a Linux server and implemented the bcast generation methods presented in Section 4. In the experiments, 4 different types of broadcast streams which contain 32,768 record-structured data items and sequential index information were produced synthetically. 10,000 data searches were performed by the client over each of the given broadcast streams, in which the access time and tuning time were measured by the number of buckets. The same key values were used to search data over the different types of broadcast streams to compare the performance of the proposed methods.

Fig. 6 shows a result of the first experiment, in which the size of a data item is 512 bytes and that of an index entry is 8 bytes. We assumed that the data and indices were transmitted and accessed in the unit of a bucket whose size is 16KB. In the experiment, 20% of the records were randomly selected as hot data and the others were considered cold ones. We made 80 % of the access requests concentrated on the hot data, employing the Pareto's rule.

The result indicates that two index replication methods for hot data i.e., (I, CD, HI, HD) and (I, D, HI, HD), have very similar tuning time performance patterns, which are better than those of the other two methods in accessing the hot data as well as any kinds of data on average. Specifically, their average tuning times for the hot data and for the whole data are about 51 % and 64 % of that of the non-replication or data re-arrangement method, respectively. The average access times for the hot data are similar in all the proposed methods except the non-replication method (I, D); they are about 61 % of that of the latter method. As for the average access time for the cold data, however, those of the (I, HD, CD) and (I, D, HI, HD) methods are about 10 % longer than that of the non-replication method while the average access time for the cold data in the index replication method (I, CD, HI, HD) is about 9 % shorter than that of the non-replication method. As a result, the (I, CD, HI, HD) method has the best access time performance for the whole data, which is improved about 34 % on the (I, D) method. Other experiments with different configurations produced similar results.

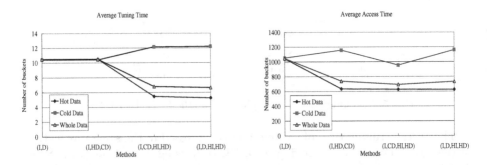

Fig. 6. Tuning time and access time performance of the proposed methods

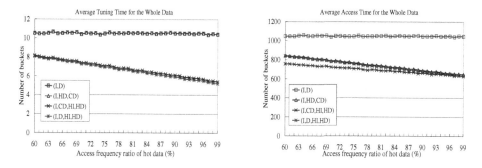

Fig. 7. Tuning/Access times for different access frequency ratios of hot data

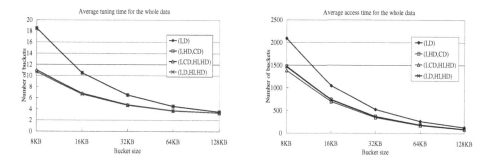

Fig. 8. Tuning time and access time performance for different bucket sizes

Fig. 7 compares the average tuning time and access time of the proposed methods as the access frequency ratio α of the hot data to the whole data, which was defined in Section 3.2, varies from 0.60 to 0.99. The result shows that as the access frequency ratio of the hot data increases, the average tuning time of two index replication methods and the average access time of three data/index replication methods proportionally decreases. Specifically, the average tuning times of two index replication methods (I, CD, HI, HD) and (I, D, HI, HD), which are very close to each other throughout the whole range of the access frequency ratios considered in the experiment, decreased from about 78 % to 53 % of that of the non-replication or data re-arrangement method. The average access time of the proposed methods except the non-replication method decreased from about 80 % to 60 % of that of the non-replication method in a linear fashion. Note that the smaller the access frequency ratio of the hot data is, the more efficient the access time performance of the index replication method (I, CD, HI, HD) is than the (I, HD, CD) and (I, D, HI, HD) methods. Specifically, when the access frequency ratio is 0.60, the access time performance of the former is about 10 % higher than those of the latter two methods. This is due to the fact that, as shown in Fig. 6, the (I, CD, HI, HD) method has a shorter access time for the cold data than the other methods on average.

Fig. 8 shows an experimental result for the broadcast streams with different bucket sizes. The parameters except the bucket size are the same as used in the experiment in Fig. 6. We observe that increasing the bucket size can enhance both of the tuning time and access time performances in all the proposed bcast generation methods. This is because streaming data are accessed in the unit of buckets and the data items in the same bucket are assumed to be processed at the same time. The result shows that three data/index replication methods achieved a similar degree of improvement in access time performance on the non-replication method (I, D), regardless of the bucket size. However, the average tuning time of two index replication methods (I, CD, HI, HD) and (I, D, HI, HD) reduced from about 95 % to 58 % of that of the non-replication method as the bucket size decreased from 128KB to 8KB. Since the bucket size can be reduced as the bandwidth of the wireless network enlarges, the proposed index replication methods can be used for generating broadcast streams which can be accessed more energy-efficiently in a future wireless communication environment.

Finally, Fig. 9 presents the result of an experiment varying the size of a data item in broadcast streams. The configuration except the data item size is the same as in the experiment in Fig. 6. The result shows that access time grows in proportional to the size of data items in all the proposed methods. We omitted the result for tuning time performance since it was shown to be hardly affected by the data item size.

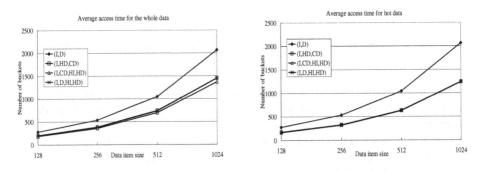

Fig. 9. Access times for the hot/whole data with different data item sizes

5   Conclusions

In this paper, we have proposed a new data broadcasting scheme for wireless computing environments. We exploited different access frequencies of broadcast data and investigated possible ways of inter-broadcast replication of hot data and/or index information for them. We performed analytical and experimental evaluations on the performance of the proposed broadcast generation methods. Experimental results show that the (I, CD, HI, HD) index replication method can improve both the access time and tuning time performance of key-based data access on the broadcast streams and is robust in various wireless broadcasting environments.

References

1. S. Acharya et al., Broadcast Disks: Data Management for Asymmetric Communication Environments, In Proc. of ACM SIGMOD Conf. pp.199-210, 1995.
2. M. S. Chen, et al., Optimizing Index Allocation for Sequential Data Broadcasting in Wireless Mobile Computing, IEEE Trans. on Knowledge and Data Eng., 15(1), pp.161-173, 2003.
3. Y. D. Chung and M. H. Kim, A Wireless Data Clustering Method for Multipoint Queries,Decision Support Systems, 30(4), pp.469-482, 2001.
4. Y. D. Chung and M. H. Kim, An Index Replication Scheme for Wireless Data Broadcasting, Journal of Systems and Software, 51(3), pp.191-199, 2000.
5. Y. D. Chung and M. H. Kim, Effective Data Placement for Wireless Broadcast, Distributed and Parallel Databases, 9, pp.133-150, 2001.
6. T. Imielinski, et al., Data on Air: Organization and Access. IEEE Trans. on Knowledge and Data Eng., 9(3), 1997. 4.
7. J. Y. Lee, Y. D. Chung, Y. J. Lee and M. H. Kim, Gray Code Clustering of Wireless Data for Partial Match Queries, Journal of Systems Architecture, 47(5), pp. 445-458, May, 2001.

Spreading Activation Model for Connectivity Based Clustering

QingYuan Huang, JinShu Su, YingZhi Zeng, and YongJun Wang

School of Computer, National University of Defense Technology,
410073 ChangSha Hunan, China
walker_hqy@yahoo.com.cn

Abstract. Connectivity based clustering has wide application in many networks like ad hoc networks, sensor networks and so on. But traditional research on this aspect is mainly based on graph theory, which needs global knowledge of the whole network. In this paper, we propose a intelligent approach called spreading activation models for connectivity based clustering (SAMCC) scheme that only local information is needed for clustering. The main feature of SAMCC scheme is applying the idea of spreading activation, which is an organization method for human long-term memory, to clustering and the whole network can be clustered in a decentralized automatic and parallel manner. The SAMCC scheme can be scaled to different networks and different level clustering. Experiment evaluations show the efficiency of our SAMCC scheme in clustering accuracy.

1 Introduction

In large distributed network computing environment, it is difficult to manage all participated nodes in a centralized manner, so getting global knowledge of the whole network is not practical. But making all nodes working together in a complete unorganized manner will decrease efficiency. It is necessary to group nodes that exhibit similar attributes for special purpose for collaboration. Connectivity based node clustering is a very important network structure that can be utilized for such decentralized computing scenario. A connectivity based clustering will partition nodes in the network into many different groups based on the connectivity between them.

Much work has been done on connectivity based clustering due to its wide application. The first effort in connectivity based clustering was made by Matula [1]. His approach splits the whole network graph into many sub-graph using cohesiveness function. Cohesiveness between any two vertices in the same subgraph is greater than a constant value k. One of the main drawbacks in this approach is that different real clusters may have different cohesiveness. Wu and Leahy [2] proposed minimum cut algorithm for graph clustering, assuming that the number of clusters is known in their algorithm. The most popular schemes are k-path and MCL algorithm proposed by S. van Dongen [3]. All these methods

T. Yakhno and E. Neuhold (Eds.): ADVIS 2006, LNCS 4243, pp. 398–407, 2006.

are based on graph theoretic techniques, assuming that the entire graph knowledge can be pre-acquired from a central location. So it is necessary to design an efficient connectivity based clustering scheme that can partition nodes of a network into many clusters in a distributed manner. In this paper, we will propose a novel approach for local nodes clustering. In contrast with other clustering methods, inspired by graph theory, our solution for clustering is motivated by spreading activation model and only requires local information of neighboring nodes in a network. [4] has done a similar job to our work. But his scheme is empirical and can not be scaled very well. The approach proposed in this paper provides a uniform method for diverse kinds of distributed clustering and our scheme can be scaled to different level clustering.

The remainder of this paper is organized as follows: Section 2 gives the definition of the problem that we will state. Our SAMCC scheme is proposed in section 3. The evaluation of proposed SAMCC scheme is presented in section 4. Section 5 gives some conclusions about our work in this paper.

2   Problem Definition

Connectivity structure of nodes in a network can be represented by an undirected weighted graph, nodes in a network forming the vertices of the graph and connections between them being the edges of the graph.

We model the network by an undirected weighted graph $G = (V, E)$, in which $V = (v_1, v_2, ...v_n),| V |= n$, is the set of vertices and $E = (e_1, e_2, e_m),| E |= m$, is the set of edges in the graph. There is an edge $(v_i, v_j) \in E$ if and only if v_i and v_j are directly connected. In this case we say that v_i and v_j are neighboring vertices in the graph G. Edges are assigned continuous weights through $W : E \to [0, 1]$. Every vertex v in the graph is assigned a unique identifier (ID). For simplicity, we identify each vertex with its ID and both of them are represented as v. Vertices are also assigned initial weights, which we call initial energy of vertices, through $U : V \to [0, \infty]$. Two vertices v_i and v_j are said to be connected if there is a series of consecutive edges $\{e_{k_1}, e_{k_2}, ... e_{k_l}\}$ such that e_{k_1} is incident on v_i, e_{k_1} is incident on v_j. The series of consecutive edges $\{e_{k_1}, e_{k_2}, ... e_{k_l}\}$ is called a path form v_i to v_j. The number of edges is called the length of the path. Clustering a network means partitioning its nodes into many different clusters. A clustering C of a graph $G = (V, E)$ is a set of clusters $\{c_1, c_2, ..., c_p\}$, each cluster with a clusterhead and possibly some ordinary vertices. The following graph clustering properties are satisfied: 1) each cluster is non-empty set of vertices and .2) any two vertices in the same cluster are connected. 3) the connectivity between two vertices belonging to two different clusters is very low.

3   Spreading Activation Clustering

Spreading activation model for connectivity based clustering (SAMCC) is the main contribution of this paper. It is a novel approach for connectivity based clustering. In contrast with other central clustering schemes based on graph theory, the intuition of our work is based on spreading activation model assuming that each node only has limited view of the whole network.

3.1   Basic Idea of SAMCC

Spreading activation model is an organization structure of long-term memory in human brain. It has first been proposed by Collin and Loftus in 1975 [6] in order to simulate human comprehension through semantic memory. They assumed that spatial and temporal independent aspects of human long-term memory are organized in a semantic network. Cognitive processes that access a node of the semantic network activate all connected nodes in parallel. The term spreading activation refers to a recursive propagation of initial stimuli [7,8].

The spreading phase consists on a number of passages of activation weaves from one node to all other nodes connected to it. First in this phase is the computation of node input using formula:

$$I_{v_j} = \sum_i O_{v_i} \times NW_{ij} \tag{1}$$

where I_{v_j} is the total input energy of node v_j, O_{v_i} is the total output energy of node v_i, NW_{ij} , which is the normalization weight of the edge connecting node v_i and v_j, can be represented by:

$$NW_{ij} = \frac{W_{ij}}{\sum_k W_{ik}} \tag{2}$$

where W_{ij} is the edge weight between neighboring nodes v_i and v_j. After a node has computed its input energy, its output energy must be determined. This is usually computed as a function of the input energy. There are many different functions that can be used to compute the output energy. The most popular is spreading all the input energy that exceeds threshold T. Then the output energy of node v_j can be defined by:

$$O_{v_j} = \{ \begin{matrix} I_{v_j} & I_{v_j} \geq T \\ 0 & I_{v_j} < T \end{matrix} \tag{3}$$

After some rounds, the energy activated by source node spreads over the network reaching nodes that are far from the initially activated ones. To avoid endless propagation, some termination conditions should be checked. If the conditions are verified, then spreading activation process stops, otherwise it goes on for another series of pulses. The pseudo-code for spreading process can be described by algorithm 1 [9].

An example of semantic network of human long-term memory, which is very similar to the ones of real world networks like P2P networks, ad hoc networks, sensor networks e.g, is shown in figure 1. It is naturally organized in clusters. In a network graph model which is identical in structure to the one presented in section 2, edges $(v_i, v_j) \in E \rightarrow V \times V$ connect nodes $v_i, v_j \in V$. Edges are

Algorithm 1. Recursive energy propagation

```
Procedure spreading(u ∈ R, vₛ ∈ V) {
U(vₛ) ← U(vₛ) + u;
u' ← u × NWₛⱼ;
if u' > T then
    ∀(vₛ, vⱼ) ∈ E : spreading(u', vⱼ)
end
}
```

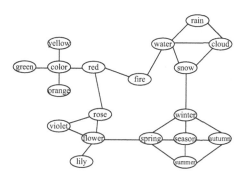

Fig. 1. A simple example for semantic network of human long-term memory

assigned continuous weights $W(v_i, v_j)$. Each node in the networks has direct connections with a few neighboring nodes. Nodes can only communicate with their immediate neighboring nodes. The nodes, from which related concepts are fast to be reflected, are called prime nodes. Such nodes are more likely to be clusterheads than other ordinary nodes. Assuming that prime node v_p, is activated through an injection of initial energy $U(v_p)$, which is then propagated to other nodes along edges according to some set of simple rules: all energy is fully divided among neighboring nodes with respect to their local normalized edge weight $NW(v_i, v_j)$, the higher the local normalized weight of an edge $(v_i, v_j) \in E$, the higher the portion of energy that flows along latter edge[10]. Nodes that receive more energy from vp than from any other prime nodes will be more inclined to join cluster c_{v_p} , where v_p is the head of this cluster. To eliminate endless spreading, energy streaming into node v_x must exceed threshold T.

The concept stated above is our central idea for connectivity based clustering algorithm. Prime nodes are clusterheads. Ordinary nodes acquire energy from prime nodes and decide to join the cluster from which they receive maximum energy. In the next section, we will show how to implement this idea.

3.2   Election of Clusterhead

The spreading process for cluster formation is similar to the procedure in algorithm 1. But some adaptations are necessary in order to tailor algorithm 1 to spreading activation clustering. For instance, the parameter of the procedure in algorithm 1 should be changed to distinguish different initial activated nodes.

Energy initially propagated by a node has following properties:

1. Initial activated node identifier (IANID): this field is a unique identifier of initial activated node. It is used to distinguish energy initiated by different activated node.
2. Timestamp (TS): this field represents the time that initial source node is activated. It is used to distinguish energy initiated by the same activated node.
3. Cost: this field is an indication of that how much initial activated node is ready to pay in propagation path. It is one of the termination conditions for spreading. If cost remained is less than zero, spreading process will end.
4. Energy amount (EA): amount carried by this energy.
5. Path identifier (PathID): this field records the nodes in energy spreading path. It is used to distinguish energy coming from different path.

The value of the first two properties are initialized by initial activated nodes and do not be changed in spreading process. The property of timestamp is used to avoid retention of activation from previous pulses. IANID is enabling to control both activation of single nodes and the overall activation of the network. The value of the last three properties will be changed in spreading. Cost implements a form of "loss of interest" in nodes that are not continually activated. It controls propagation depth of the energy and counterchecks endless propagation. If connectivity between two nodes is very low, propagation will stop. For example, although nodes v_i and v_j are neighboring nodes, if $W(v_i, v_j) = 0.01, cost(v_i, v_j) = 1/W(v_i, v_j) = 100$, while energy.cost $= 80$, propagation initiated by node v_i will end at node v_j.

The election of clusterhead is very important to the performance of clustering scheme. Prime nodes are the nodes from which related concepts are fast reflected. Following properties should be satisfied:

1. The association between two prime nodes is very weak;
2. Prime nodes are highly connected to other nodes in a range;
3. Initial energy $U(p_s)$ of the prime node ps should be large enough.

Property 1 and 2 ensure that the whole network is cut by clusters according to the connectivity between nodes. And prime nodes are scattered over the network graph. The assumption that no two clusterheads are neighbors in many clustering schemes is not proper, as can be illustrated in figure 2. In the scenario shown in figure 2, although node i and j are neighboring nodes, they both will be elected as clusterhead intuitively for the connection between them is negligible. Property 3 ensures the capacity of prime nodes to be clusterhead in network graph.

From the properties stated above, we can conclude that clusterhead is the most powerful and highly connected node in a range. Now the problem is how to exploit an algorithm to find nodes that satisfy these criterions.

We use the concept of "reflection energy" to measure whether a node satisfies those properties. Reflection energy is the energy that originates from a node and propagates back to itself. A node with high reflection energy means that it will

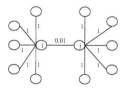

Fig. 2. A simple example for connectivity between nodes

be fast associated by other nodes. In spreading procedure, each node receives energy from other nodes. Then it calculates total energy received from other nodes including from itself for energy is fully divided among a node's neighbors including the predecessor node where it receives the energy. If a node is highly connected and its initial energy is large enough, much energy originated from itself will propagate back to it as there are many paths from intermediate nodes to it.

There are two steps in clusterhead election: *overall activation* and *propagationMax*. At the very beginning, overall network is activated. Each node initializes its energy and spreads the activation. The pseudo-code for initialization process is illustrated in algorithm 2. The initially activated nodes compute the

Algorithm 2. Initial overall network nodes activation

```
Procedure initial_activation(p_s ∈ V) {
energy.IANID = ps;
energy.TS = time(now);
energy.cost= initial_cost;
energy.EA= U (p_s) ;
energy.pathID = p_s;
forall v_i ∈ Nbr(p_s) do
    energy.EA= NW_{si}×energy.EA;
    Send energy to node v_i;
end
}
```

reflection energy that propagates back to them, as well as total energy for all those nodes from which it receives energy. Then the node sums all energy it has received. High energy reflected by the node itself ensures that it is the core of a dense region. The pseudo-code for procedure of recursive activation spreading is presented in algorithm 3.

In the phase of *propagationMax*, each node broadcasts the value of reflection energy, then elects node with maximum reflection energy in a range as clusterhead. In this phase, messages sent by nodes have following fields:

1. Cost: the mean of this field is similar to the same field of energy.
2. nodeID: the identifier of node where message is originated.
3. Ref_energy: this field indicates reflection energy originated from the node nodeID and propagates back to itself.

Algorithm 3. Spreading activation

```
Procedure SA (energy, v_i ∈ V){
ref_energy(v_i, energy.originator,energy.TS)=energy.EA+
ref_energy(v_i, energy.originator,energy.TS);
if energy.EA > T&&energy.cost > 0 then
    forall v_j ∈ Nbr(v_i) do
        Create new energy;
        newenergy.EA=NW_ij×energy.EA;
        newenergy.cost=energy.cost - 1/W_ij;
        newenergy.pathID = energy.pathID + v_i;
        Send newenergy to v_j;
    end
end
}
```

Each node first elects itself to be clusterhead unless reflection energy carried by messages from others is greater than that of the node itself. The pseudo-code for this procedure is shown in algorithm 4.

Algorithm 4. propagation maximum reflection energy

```
Procedure propagationMax(v_i ∈ V, electionMSG) {
if electionMSG. ref_energy < ref_energy(v_i) then
    v_i gives up to be clusterhead;
end
if electionMSG.cost > 0 then
    forall v_j ∈ Nbr(v_i) do
        electionMSG.cost = electionMSG.cost - 1/W_ij;
        Send electionMSG to v_j;
    end
end
}
```

In this section, we have described how to choose clusterheads. In the next section, we will expatiate how a node to join one cluster.

3.3 Formation of Clusters

The set of prime nodes which are clusterheads can be represented by $P = \{p_1, p_2, \ldots, p_k\}$. As spreading begins, prime node ps initialize the five properties value of energy: $energy.EA = U(p_s)$. The initial energy of prime node p_s is determined by characteristic of the node itself. For instance, in sensor networks, $U(p_s)$ may be equal to power of the sensor. But in this paper, we will assume that all nodes in the network are uniform: $U(p_s) = 1$.

Each node v_i computes input energy from different prime nodes ps. The input energy, represented as $total\_energy(v_i, p_s)$, is the sum of the energy that initially activated from prime node ps and reaches node v_i. After energy arrives at node v_i, the value of corresponding $total\_energy(v_i, p_s)$ is updated. Termination condition is verified: $energy.EA < T$, if so, spreading will end at node v_i. Otherwise, $energy.EA$ is divided according to node v_i's local normalized weight. The property of cost should also be updated by: $energy.cost = energy.cost - 1/W(v_i, v_j)$ before energy is sent to node v_i's neighboring node v_j. If $energy.cost$ is less than zero, spreading will end at node v_j.

Each node maintains a set of values for energy from different prime nodes. It calculates the value of $total\_energy$ for these prime nodes from which it receives energy. Then the node will join the cluster led by the prime node from which it receives maximum $total\_energy$. The spreading process is shown in algorithm 3.

3.4 Dynamic Cluster

A node may join one cluster as well as its leaving. Nodes' leaving in our model is like the breaking of memory, which should not result in the reconstruction of overall network. When a node leaves its cluster, all its neighbors will decide to join the clusters which have most association to them. If one node does not receive enough energy from the clusterhead, it will elect itself to be head. As soon as one node elects itself to be clusterhead, all later changes resulted by leaving node will be effected while former changes are maintained. Joining process for a node is relatively simple. When a node joins the network, it sends joining request messages for all its neighbors' clusterhead and joins the cluster from which it receives maximum energy which should exceeds threshold, or the new node will elect itself to be clusterhead.

4 Evaluation

This section presents the simulation results of our SAMCC scheme to show its accuracy in connectivity based clustering. Metrics for measuring connectivity based graph clustering are not discussed very much in the past because of its complexity. In this paper, we will use performance measurement proposed by S. van Dongen [3], termed scaled coverage measure. The basic idea of this measurement can be found in [4]. We conduct simulations on graph obtained by the INET3.0 [11] which is a power law topology generator. We will compare our SAMCC scheme with centralized MCL scheme.

Figure 3(a) shows the effectiveness of the SAMCC scheme in clustering accuracy. We can see from figure 3(a) that the accuracy of the SAMCC scheme is very closer to that of MCL scheme. In this experiment, the value of energy cost is changed from 2 to 6. We compute the average value to compare with MCL. Node number is ranged from 3500 to 6000 for the least number of nodes required by INET3.0 is 3037.

Figure 3(b) indicates number of clusters discovered by SAMCC and MCL scheme with increasing number of nodes. From figure 3(b), we get that number of clusters discovered by our SAMCC scheme is a little higher than that of MCL scheme.

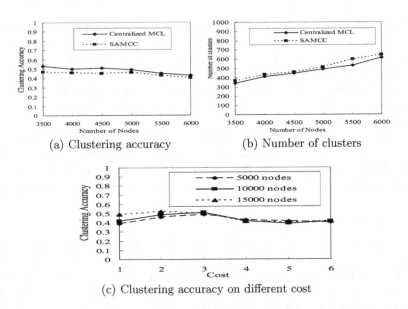

(a) Clustering accuracy   (b) Number of clusters

(c) Clustering accuracy on different cost

Fig. 3. Simulation results

Figure 3(c) indicates the effect of energy cost on clustering accuracy. It can be observed that the SAMCC algorithm yields good results when energy cost is set in 2 and 3. Clustering accuracy decreases when energy cost is above 4. This is mainly because of that an optimal clustering of a given graph according to scaled coverage measure minimizes both the number of intercluster edges and the number of nonneighbor vertices in each cluster [4]. This is not very suitable for large scale clustering.

5   Conclusion

Connectivity based clustering has very wide application in many aspects such as data classification, natural language processing, distributed computing. But most of the work in the past is based on graph theoretic techniques which need knowledge of the entire network. In this paper, we have proposed a clustering scheme based on spreading activation model which is an organization structure for human long-term memory. Our scheme can partition the whole network into clusters in a distributed and natural manner and can be scaled very well to different application scenarios. Our future work will focus on its application in the building of trust groups according to trust relations among members.

Acknowledgement

This work was supported by the National Science Foundation of China under grant No.90604006, the National Research Foundation for the Doctoral Program of Higher Education of China under grant No.20049998027, and the National Science Foundation of China under grant No.90104001.

References

1. D.W. Matula: Graph theoretic techniques for cluster analysis algorithms. In: Classification and clustering. (1977) 95–129
2. Z. Wu, R. Leahy : An optimal graph theoretic approach to data clustering: Theory and its application to image segmentation. IEEE Transactions on Pattern Analysis and Machine Intelligence **15**(11) (1993) 1101–1113
3. S. Dongen: A new cluster algorithm for graphs. Technical report, Amsterdam, The Netherlands, The Netherlands (1998)
4. L. Ramaswamy, B. Gedik, L. Liu: A distributed approach to node clustering in decentralized peer-to-peer networks. IEEE Trans. Parallel Distrib. Syst. **16**(9) (2005) 814–829
5. E. Hartuv, R. Shamir: A clustering algorithm based on graph connectivity. Inf. Process. Lett. **76**(4-6) (2000) 175–181
6. M.R. Quillian: Semantic memory. In Collins, A., Smith, E.E., eds.: Readings in Cognitive Science: A Perspective from Psychology and Artificial Intelligence. Kaufmann, San Mateo, CA (1988) 80–101
7. F. Crestani: Retrieving documents by constrained spreading activation on automatically constructed hypertexts. In: Fifth European Congress on Intelligent Techniques and Soft Computing, Aachen, Germany (1997) 1210–1214
8. R.L. Atkinson, E.E. Smith, S. Nolen-Hoeksema: Introduction to Psychology. Wadsworth Publishing Company, Boston, MA, USA (2002)
9. C.N. Ziegler,G . Lausen: Spreading activation models for trust propagation. In: EEE '04: Proceedings of the 2004 IEEE International Conference on e-Technology, e-Commerce and e-Service (EEE'04), Washington, DC, USA, IEEE Computer Society (2004) 83–97
10. M. Ceglowski, A. Coburn, J. Cuadrado: Semantic search of unstructured data using contextual network graphs. Technical report, Vermont,USA (2003)
11. J. Winick, S. Jamin: Inet-3.0: Internet topology generator. Technical report, University of Michigan,USA (2002)

Personalized Fair Reputation Based Resource Allocation in Grid

QingYuan Huang, YongJun Wang, JinShu Su, and YingZhi Zeng

School of Computer, National University of Defense Technology,
410073 ChangSha Hunan, China
walker_hqy@yahoo.com.cn

Abstract. Efficient resource allocation for submitted task is one of the main challenges in grid computing. Much work in this aspect has focused on resource discovery and usage. Resource allocation, which is an interface between resource discovery and usage, is always unvalued in the past while some resource owners may provide resources with poor quality. A personalized fair reputation scheme is proposed in this paper to overcome these limitations and to encourage collaboration in grid community. We present minimum and maximum threshold for reputation from other entities to decrease malicious competition. A rewarding mechanism is also proposed in our reputation scheme to encourage collaboration. Then we present how to integrate our reputation scheme into grid resource allocation approach. Experimental results show that our approach can work in the environment with high ratio of malicious nodes in grid.

1 Introduction

Grid computing [1] makes it possible of global virtual computing machine that associates a large number of heterogeneous resources working together like single computer. This large system includes three kinds of entities: resource provider, resource consumer and broker. Resource consumer will submit jobs that must be mapped to physical resources belonging to different providers with different intentions for execution through resource allocation mechanism.

The main responsibility of a grid resource allocation mechanism is selecting resources for tasks [2]. Finding a willing resource provider does not guarantee the resource consumer will be satisfied with its job. Some resource providers may provide resources with poor quality [3]. Selfish resource providers may offer resources to maintain the impression of cooperation, but not put in the necessary effort to provide the resources [4]. Worse in a environment lack of punishment, certain entities may join the network, not to submit jobs or to provide resources, but to propagate false resources or information for their own interest. So it is important to recognize resources with poor quality and to isolate malicious entities in grid. Reputation, which is computed through a mutual feedback mechanism, is suitable for such distributed environment. Malicious entities and resources with poor quality can be recognized through giving them low reputation.

T. Yakhno and E. Neuhold (Eds.): ADVIS 2006, LNCS 4243, pp. 408–417, 2006.

Much work has been done on integrating reputation of resources into grid resource allocation. [5] presents a hierarchical scheme to integrate eigentrust [6] into grid resource allocation, which needs to collect global reputation information in sub-domains. Efforts in [2] mainly focus on how to apply trust information to grid resource management while trust evaluation is less detailed. Whether reputation information is trusted is not considered very much in all these schemes.

Our contributions in this paper are fourfold. First, parameters in our proposed reputation scheme are personalized. Min and max threshold for indirect reputation which is obtained from others, are proposed to tackle with bad mouthing [7] attack launched by entities which provide dishonest indirection reputation information. A parameter for over punishment of bad behavior is also proposed in our reputation scheme to discourage entities which behave well and badly alternatively. Second, the concept of gain points, which is an indication of ones dedication to others, is proposed to ensure fairness and to encourage collaboration in grid. gain points can be gained from others through providing services to them. Those with little gain points will not be fully serviced. Third, our reputation scheme only collect limited indirect reputation information. Fourth, a scheme integrating our reputation scheme into grid resource allocation, which is under the assumption that there are some pre-trusted entities in grid, is proposed. The assumption is suitable for there are always some super-computing centers in grid.

This paper is organized as follows: Section 2, presents a personalized fair reputation (PFR) scheme. PFR based resource allocation algorithms are proposed in section 3. The performance and security analysis for proposed algorithms are presented in section 4. Section 5 gives some conclusions about our work.

2 Personalized Fair Reputation Scheme

Reputation schemes record transaction history of interacting entities, aggregate mutual feedback of them into a reputation metric for each participant. Resource consumers will use this metric for the purpose of evaluation and subsequent selection of potential resource providers [8]. There are three concerns in reputation based trust systems: personal reputation computing after each transaction, reputation storage mechanism to be trusted for reference of other entities and global reputation model. In our personalized fair reputation (PFR) system, we differentiate two kinds of reputation: direct reputation according to the entitys own experiences and indirect reputation from other entities opinion. Of course, direct reputation is prior to indirect reputation in grid resource selection. If there is conflict between them, direct reputation will get the priority.

2.1 Reputation Storage Mechanism

Reputation storage mechanism is important for the efficiency of reputation scheme. If all entities in grid tell truth and entities where indirect reputation information is stored are trusted, then entities that provide resources with poor quality can be quickly recognized. But thats not true in practical environment. So what we can do is just to decrease the risk of getting false indirect reputation as low as possible.

In distributed grid environment, our reputation storage mechanism is built on the assumption that there are some highly pre-trusted entities in grid. We will use these highly pre-trusted entities to store indirect reputation. Each entity can choose one or many these pre-trusted entities to get and put reputation information.

2.2 Local Reputation Computing

In grid environment with reputation, entities will rate each other after each transaction. For example, let x and y denote two entities. After entity y provides service for entity x according to the negotiation between them, entity x will mark the transaction as $m \in [0, 100]$ which is obtained through entity x's policy and the agreement between entity x and y. m is an indication of the degree that entity x is satisfied. Entity x may define a threshold for the degree of satisfaction. In this paper, two counters are used to count transactions, which are successful transactions, expressed as s_{xy}, and failure transactions, expressed as l_{xy}. The initial value of s_{xy} and l_{xy} are zero. For simplicity, if $m \geq threshold$,we rate the transaction as positive ($s_{xy}+1$), or if $m < threshold$, we rate the transaction as negative ($l_{xy}+1$). The personal local reputation after transaction i can be computed:

$$R_d(x, y, t_i) = (1 - \alpha)R_d(x, y, t_{i-1}) + \alpha \frac{s_{xy}}{s_{xy} + l_{xy}^{\beta}} \qquad (1)$$

where $\beta \geq 1, 0 < \alpha \leq 1, R_d(x, y, 0) = 0$. The parameter β is used to avoid the case in which direct reputation value $R_d(x, y, t_i)$ is not changed or even increased as failure transactions increase with successful transactions. The value of β is determined by entity x's preference. Entity y will records the transaction after completion of transaction i.

2.3 Global Reputation Model

The global reputation is determined by both direct reputation $R_d(x, y, t_i)$ from entity x's own experiences and indirect reputation from other's experiences. If entity x has experiences with entity y, it will apply its personal reputation as global reputation about entity y to grid resource selection. If entity x has no experience with entity y completely, it will query pre-trusted entity z which has associations with entity x to compute indirect reputation $R_r(x, y, t_i)$. If entity x has no transaction with entity y in the past and it can not get any reputation information from pre-trusted entities either, entity x will give a constant value to global reputation for following grid resource selection. So global reputation can be defined as:

$$R_g(x, y, t_i) = \begin{cases} R_d(x, y, t_i) & \text{If there are transactions between them} \\ R_r(x, y, t_i) & \text{If indirection reputation exists} \\ \lambda & \text{If no direct or indirect reputation} \end{cases} \qquad (2)$$

2.4   Practical Issues

There are four practical issues in reputation based trust systems [9]. **First is malicious competition.** Whether to trust entity k is one of the problems, as well as the indirect reputation from other entities. So we give two thresholds: maximum indirect reputation threshold max_{ir} and minimum indirect reputation threshold min_{ir}, to restrain malicious collective. Indirect reputation should be in $[min_{ir}, max_{ir}]$, or the threshold will be applied. **The second issue is multi-level trust.** In fact, reputation is already a multi-level fuzzy evaluation. In our reputation scheme, we will distinguish different entities, not different service. If one entity is not good at some services, it should promise them carefully, or the integral reputation will be compromised. So in the rest of this paper we will not distinguish the reputation of an entity and its resources. **Another practical issue is rewarding.** The concept of 'gain points' is proposed as rewarding mechanism. Each entity can gain 'gain points' from others through providing services to them. But different tasks have different importance. So how many 'gain points' service requestor paid for service provider should be negotiated. Let $GP(x, y, t_i)$ represents gain points entity x paid for entity y in ith transaction between them. Then total gain points entity y gained from entity x can be defined as:

$$GP(x, y) = \sum_{i=1}^{n} GP(x, y, t_i) \qquad (3)$$

n is total transaction times between entity x and entity y. Gain points satisfy the following formula:

$$GP(x, y) + GP(y, x) = 0 \qquad (4)$$

That's to say, if entity y provide service for entity x, then entity y will gain positive gain points, while entity x gains negative gain points. Gain points can be sold, bought and delegated from and to other entities. The final issue is **trust decay.** Trust decay with time is not proper in the environment lack of effective rewarding mechanism. For example, entity x has very high reputation while entity y has very low reputation. But if they both leave for a long time, the reputation of them will both become very low, even to zero. That's unfair for entity x. So in our opinion, trust should be consumed instead of decay with time. For example, entity y provides resources for entity x while entity x also provides resources for entity y. Let $GP(x, y)$ denote gain points entity y paid for entity x in jth resource request for x's resources. Then after trust consumption, reputation is:

$$R_d(x, y, t_n) = (1 - \frac{GP(x, y, t_j)}{GP(x, y)})R_d(x, y, t_n) \qquad (5)$$

Total gain points entity x gained from entity y will be changed as:

$$GP(y, x) = GP(y, x) + GP(y, x, t_j) \qquad (6)$$

We have developed a reputation scheme based on the concept stated above. In the rest of the paper, we'll explain how to integrate this reputation scheme into grid resource allocation.

3   Integrating PFR into Grid Resource Allocation

Grid is composed of a large number of dynamic, distributed entities in network [10,11]. When an entity submits a job, it queries all or a subset of entities in grid, collects responses from available resource providers, and chooses a subset of resources from the providers to execute its job [12]. The reputation based grid resource selection presented here is based under the assumption that there are some pre-trusted entities in grid.

In our model, we divide overall grid system into some logical covering domains of pre-trusted entities as illustrated in Figure 1. The edges between V_i and P_j

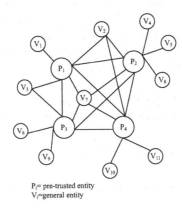

P_i= pre-trusted entity
V_i=general entity

Fig. 1. Pre-trusted entities covering domains

indicate that V_i belongs to P_j 's covering domain. When entity V_i interacts with entity V_k, V_i will get or put its reputation evaluation about entity V_k from or to pre-trusted entity P_j. Each entity may belong to one or many covering domains of different pre-trusted entities. This is determined by entity's own preferences.

Pre-trusted entities are not central administrative authority in our model. They are used to store indirect reputation information about entities that have transactions with entities in their domain. For example, when entity V_3 interacts with entity V_{11} for the first time, it will query pre-trusted entities P_1 and P_3 reputation information about entity V_{11}, P_1 and P_3 return reputation information about entity V_{11}. If P_1 and P_3 do not have any information about entity V_{11}, V_3 will give an initial reputation value of V_{11} according to its settings that are managed by V_3's reputation agent. In the following, three reputation-aware resource selection algorithms are presented to show how to integrate our reputation scheme into grid resource selection.

Let $task(x, t_i)$ denote the task originated at time t_i and entity x is the originator. In practice, resource requirement of $task(x, t_i)$ is diverse, such as memory, CPU time, storage, service, data, instrument and so on, and a task can be divided into many atomic subtasks and distributed over multiple machines. In this paper, for simplicity, it is proper to assume that all kinds of resource requirement are CPU time and tasks are indivisible. Under these assumptions, the resource requirement of $task(x, t_i)$ can be expressed as expected CPU execution time $EET(task(x, t_i))$. Entity x or its broker will be responsible for resource collection to execute $task(x, t_i)$. Our scheme does work after the available resources have been collected. Let $S_r(task(x, t_i))$ denote the available resources set. Then $S_r(task(x, t_i))$ can be defined as:

$$S_r(task(x, t_i)) = \{r_{e_1}, r_{e_2}, ..., r_{e_n}\} \tag{7}$$

The resource r_{e_j} represents available resource of entity e_j for $task(x, t_i)$. Entity x will choose a subset of the responses to execute its task. The resource r_{e_j} has four attributes including: (a)queuing delay, expressed as $D_q(task(x, t_i), r_{e_j})$, indicates time between task submission and starting on entity e_j. When resource request of $task(x, t_i)$ arrives, entity e_j may negotiate with entity x about how many available resources it can provide for entity x. However, entity e_j may not process the task immediately after the task is submitted for there are already many queuing tasks on entity e_j; (b)process delay, expressed as $D_p(task(x, t_i), r_{e_j})$ indicates time between task starting and completion. Total completion delay $D_c(task(x, t_i), r_{e_j})$ is:

$$D_c(task(x, t_i), r_{e_j}) = D_q(task(x, t_i), r_{e_j}) + D_p(task(x, t_i), r_{e_j}) \tag{8}$$

(c) Process cost, expressed as $C_p(task(x, t_i), r_{e_j})$, indicates gain points that entity x should pay for entity e_j. So the following equation is used to calculate process cost:

$$C_p(task(x, t_i), r_{e_j}) = GP(x, e_j, t_i) \tag{9}$$

Gain points are determined by the negotiation between them; (d) global reputation $R_g(x, e_j, t_i)$ of entity e_j, is obtained through the reputation mechanism stated above.

Minimum security risk algorithm: Not all entities will complete the submitted task according to the agreement between resource consumers and resource providers. Some entities may give up processing the task for unexpected reasons. Some are malicious. Isolating malicious entities will decrease the security risk of submitted task. Reputation is an indicator of what probability resource providers will complete the task successfully. So after all available resources for submitted task have been collected, we can sort the available resources in $S_r(task(x, t_i))$ by their corresponding owner's reputation. The first is the resource with highest reputation. Assuming that all resources in $S_r(task(x, t_i))$ satisfy the profile of the resource request for $task(x, t_i)$. Then we choose the resource whose owner's reputation is highest in $S_r(task(x, t_i))$ to execute $task(x, t_i)$.

Minimum practical completion delay algorithm: The resource with minimum completion delay attribute in $S_r(task(x, t_i))$ does not mean that it would complete $task(x, t_i)$ firstly. For example, r_{e_j}'s completion delay attribute is the minimum, but its reputation $R_g(x, e_j, t_i)$ is very low, only 20%, which means that it would give up processing $task(x, t_i)$ with the probability of (1-20%). The total practical completion delay of r_{e_j} should be:

$$D_{pc}(task(x, t_i), r_{e_j}) = D_c(task(x, t_i), r_{e_j}) \times (1 + 1 - R_g(x, e_j, t_i)) \tag{10}$$

Then the resources in $S_r(task(x, t_i))$ will be sorted by the value of $R_g(x, e_j, t_i)$. The resource with minimum practical completion delay will be selected to do $task(x, t_i)$.

Maximum performance/cost ratio algorithm: Resource consumers may pay for resource providers after they've been satisfied with their tasks. But how many gain points that resource consumers pay for resource providers should be negotiated before tasks execution begins. In our model, gain points rewarding mechanism is a two-party protocol. Developing a perfect rewarding mechanism is the future of our work. In this paper, we will present the basic idea of gain points rewarding mechanism. Basically, gain points that resource consumers pay for resource providers only represent the price of providers' resources. Of course, resource consumers will select the resources with good quality and low price. The resource collection phase is similar to the ones in minimum security risk algorithm. The difference is that the resources in $S_r(task(x, t_i))$ are sorted by performance/cost ratio, expressed as $PCR(task(x, t_i), r_{e_j})$. It is defined as:

$$PCR(task(x, t_i), r_{e_j}) = \frac{1}{GP(x, e_j, t_i) \times D_{pc}(task(x, t_i), r_{e_j})} \tag{11}$$

We use the reciprocal of practical completion delay stated in Minimum practical completion delay algorithm as performance value. The resource with Maximum performance/cost ratio will be selected to do the task.

4   Performance and Security Evaluation

This section presents the result of some simulations that show the effectiveness of our reputation scheme in grid resource allocation on performance and recognizing resource providers with poor quality. We conducted a simulation in 100Mbps network with 100 nodes. The resource selection with reputation process was simulated using a discrete event simulator. Tasks' generation is a random process and their expected CPU execution time (EET) is distributed in [1800s, 3600s]. We assume that about 20% of overall network nodes are malicious in performance analysis while 80% of overall network nodes are malicious in security analysis.

4.1   Performance Analysis

Our reputation scheme does work before tasks execution begins and after tasks finish. Resource consumers may get indirect reputation information of entities about which they have no knowledge from pre-trusted entities, and send their personal local reputation evaluation to pre-trusted entities after tasks finish. Average tasks completion delay, which is an average value of all tasks' completion delay, will be rated as performance measurement of overall grid resource selection that we present above. Table 1, 2 and 3 show the Average tasks completion delay of minimum security risk (MSR) algorithm, minimum practical completion delay (MPCD) algorithm, and maximum performance/cost ratio (MPCR) algorithm.

Table 1. Comparison of average completion delay using minimum security risk

# of tasks	EET	Not using reputation	MSR	Improvement
50	2312	2897	2369	18%
150	2846	3576	2996	16%
500	2719	3607	3689	-2%

Table 2. Comparison of average completion delay using minimum practical completion delay

# of tasks	EET	Not using reputation	MPCD	Improvement
50	2578	3231	2610	19%
150	2219	2801	2278	18.7%
500	2906	3645	3389	18.2%

Table 3. Comparison of average completion delay using maximum performance/cost ratio

# of tasks	EET	Not using reputation	MPCR	Improvement
50	2190	2871	2450	15%
150	3012	3790	3230	14%
500	2451	3248	2950	9%

Table 1 shows tasks' average completion delay using minimum security risk algorithm and its improvement comparing with not using reputation. From table 1, improvement of MSR algorithm decreased with the increasing of overload for some entities with low reputation may starve to death in MSR algorithm. And entities with high reputation become hot spots. That is why there are -2% improvement when number of tasks is 500.

Table 2 shows tasks' average completion delay using minimum practical completion delay algorithm and its improvement comparing with that of not using reputation. In table 2, average completion time reduced about 18% even in the environment with high overload for MPCD algorithm has taken both reputation and completion delay into account.

Table 3 shows the experiment results of maximum performance/cost ratio algorithm and its improvement comparing with that of not using reputation.

4.2   Security Evaluation

Security evaluation should include both resource providers' view and consumers' view. From providers' view, resource providers should have complete control of their resources. Providers may first serve for the entity who dedicates most for them. This can favor collaboration in grid. From consumers' view, they hope that their job should always be satisfied with good quality, and malicious entities which provide bad resources or spread bad information can be quickly recognized and isolated. Successful transaction ratio will be rated as security measurement of our reputation scheme in grid resource selection.

Table 4 shows the experiment result using minimum security risk algorithm. Successful transaction ratio of MSR algorithm is the highest among all the three algorithms we propose. But its queuing delay may also be the maximum.

Table 5 shows successful transaction ratio of minimum practical completion delay and its improvement comparing with that of not using reputation.

Table 4. Comparison of successful transaction ratio using minimum security risk

# of tasks	Not using reputation	MSR
50	20%	75%
150	22%	72%
500	18%	78%

Table 5. Comparison of successful transaction ratio using minimum practical completion delay

# of tasks	Not using reputation	MPCD
50	20%	71%
150	19%	72%
500	17%	68%

Table 6. Comparison of successful transaction ratio using maximum performance/cost ratio

# of tasks	Not using reputation	MPCR
50	23%	68%
150	17%	62%
500	22%	59%

Successful transaction ratio of MPCD algorithm is a little lower than that of minimum security risk algorithm. Table 6 shows successful transaction ratio of maximum performance/cost ratio and its improvement comparing with that of not using reputation.

In summary, experimental results show that integrating our PFR scheme into grid resource selection process can improve overall quality in performance and security.

5   Conclusion

Reputation management has become more and more important in large scale distributed system such as grid. Much work about reputation based trust management has been done in PGrid [13]. They collect reputation information in overall system, or just use local reputation. The first scheme goes against scalability, while the second ignores malicious activities that malicious entities do on others. In this paper, we present a personalized fair reputation scheme which collects limited reputation information. A rewarding mechanism is also proposed in our reputation scheme. Then we show how to integrate our scheme into grid resource selection. Our future work will focus on practical rewarding mechanism that can encourage collaboration in grid community.

Acknowledgement

This work was supported by the National Science Foundation of China under grant No.90604006, the National Research Foundation for the Doctoral Program of Higher Education of China under grant No.20049998027, and the National Science Foundation of China under grant No.90104001.

References

1. I. Foster, C. Kesselmann: The Grid:Blueprint for a New Computing Infrastructure. Morgan Kaufmann Publishers (1999)
2. F. Azzedin, M. Maheswaran: Integrating Trust into Grid Resource Management Systems. In: 2002 International Conference on Parallel Processing, Vancouver, B.C., Canada, The International Association for Computers and Communications, IEEE Computer Society Press (2002) 47–54
3. M. Maheswaran: Quality of service driven resource management algorithms for network computing. In: 1999 International Conference on Parallel and Distributed Processing Technologies and Applications (PDPTA '99). (1999) 1090–1096
4. N. Andrade, F. Brasileiro, W. Cirne, M. Mowbray: Discouraging free-riding in a peer-to-peer grid. In: HPDC13, the Thirteenth IEEE International Symposium on High-Performance Distributed Computing. (2004)
5. B. Alunkal, I. Veljkovic, G. von Laszewski, K. Amin: Reputation-based Grid Resource Selection. Technical report, New Orleans, Louisiana (2003)
6. S. D. Kamvar,M. T. Schlosser, H. Garcia-Molina: The EigenTrust Algorithm for Reputation Management in P2P Networks. In: Twelfth International World Wide Web Conference, 2003, Budapest, Hungary, ACM Press (2003)
7. C. Dellarocas: Mechanisms for coping with unfair ratings and discriminatory behavior in online reputation reporting systems. In: ICIS '00: Proceedings of the twenty first international conference on Information systems, Atlanta, GA, USA, Association for Information Systems (2000) 520–525
8. P. A. Bonatti, C. Duma, D. Olmedilla, N. Shahmehri: An integration of reputation-based and policy-based trust management. In: Semantic Web Policy Workshop in conjunction with 4th International Semantic Web Conference, Galway, Ireland (2005)
9. R. Sion: Ensuring fair trust in reputation based systems. In: USENIX Security Symposium 2004, San Diego, CA (2004)
10. I. Foster, C. Kesselman, S. Tuecke: The Anatomy of the Grid: Enabling Scalable Virtual Organizations. International Journal of Supercomputing Applications 15(3) (2002)
11. I. Foster, C. Kesselman, J. Nick, S. Tuecke: The Physiology of the Grid: An Open Grid Services Architecture for Distributed Systems Integration (2002)
12. V. Dignum, J. J. Meyer, F. Dignum, H. Weigand: Formal specification of interaction in agent societies. In: Proceedings of the Second Goddard Workshop on Formal Approaches to Agent-Based Systems (FAABS), Maryland. (2002)
13. K. Aberer, P. C. Mauroux, A. Datta, Z. Despotovic, M. Hauswirth, M. Punceva, R. Schmidt: P-grid: a self-organizing structured p2p system. SIGMOD Rec. 32(3) (2003) 29–33

Author Index

Lecture Notes in Computer Science

For information about Vols. 1–4143

please contact your bookseller or Springer

Vol. 4190: R. Larsen, M. Nielsen, J. Sporring (Eds.), Medical Image Computing and Computer-Assisted Intervention – MICCAI 2006, Part I. XXXVVVIII, 949 pages. 2006.

Vol. 4189: D. Gollmann, J. Meier, A. Sabelfeld (Eds.), Computer Security – ESORICS 2006. XI, 548 pages. 2006.

Vol. 4188: P. Sojka, I. Kopeček, K. Pala (Eds.), Text, Speech and Dialogue. XIV, 721 pages. 2006. (Sublibrary LNAI).

Vol. 4187: J.J. Alferes, J. Bailey, W. May, U. Schwertel (Eds.), Principles and Practice of Semantic Web Reasoning. XI, 277 pages. 2006.

Vol. 4186: C. Jesshope, C. Egan (Eds.), Advances in Computer Systems Architecture. XIV, 605 pages. 2006.

Vol. 4185: R. Mizoguchi, Z. Shi, F. Giunchiglia (Eds.), The Semantic Web – ASWC 2006. XX, 778 pages. 2006.

Vol. 4184: M. Bravetti, M. Núñez, G. Zavattaro (Eds.), Web Services and Formal Methods. X, 289 pages. 2006.

Vol. 4183: J. Euzenat, J. Domingue (Eds.), Artificial Intelligence: Methodology, Systems, and Applications. XIII, 291 pages. 2006. (Sublibrary LNAI).

Vol. 4182: H.T. Ng, M.-K. Leong, M.-Y. Kan, D. Ji (Eds.), Information Retrieval Technology. XVI, 684 pages. 2006.

Vol. 4180: M. Kohlhase, OMDoc – An Open Markup Format for Mathematical Documents [version 1.2]. XIX, 428 pages. 2006. (Sublibrary LNAI).

Vol. 4179: J. Blanc-Talon, W. Philips, D. Popescu, P. Scheunders (Eds.), Advanced Concepts for Intelligent Vision Systems. XXIV, 1224 pages. 2006.

Vol. 4178: A. Corradini, H. Ehrig, U. Montanari, L. Ribeiro, G. Rozenberg (Eds.), Graph Transformations. XII, 473 pages. 2006.

Vol. 4177: R. Marín, E. Onaindía, A. Bugarín, J. Santos (Eds.), Current Topics in Aritficial Intelligence. XIII, 621 pages. 2006. (Sublibrary LNAI).

Vol. 4176: S.K. Katsikas, J. Lopez, M. Backes, S. Gritzalis, B. Preneel (Eds.), Information Security. XIV, 548 pages. 2006.

Vol. 4175: P. Bücher, B.M.E. Moret (Eds.), Algorithms in Bioinformatics. XII, 402 pages. 2006. (Sublibrary LNBI).

Vol. 4174: K. Franke, K.-R. Müller, B. Nickolay, R. Schäfer (Eds.), Pattern Recognition. XX, 773 pages. 2006.

Vol. 4173: S. El Yacoubi, B. Chopard, S. Bandini (Eds.), Cellular Automata. XV, 734 pages. 2006.

Vol. 4172: J. Gonzalo, C. Thanos, M. F. Verdejo, R.C. Carrasco (Eds.), Research and Advanced Technology for Digital Libraries. XVII, 569 pages. 2006.

Vol. 4169: H.L. Bodlaender, M.A. Langston (Eds.), Parameterized and Exact Computation. XI, 279 pages. 2006.

Vol. 4168: Y. Azar, T. Erlebach (Eds.), Algorithms – ESA 2006. XVIII, 843 pages. 2006.

Vol. 4167: S. Dolev (Ed.), Distributed Computing. XV, 576 pages. 2006.

Vol. 4166: J. Górski (Ed.), Computer Safety, Reliability, and Security. XIV, 440 pages. 2006.

Vol. 4165: W. Jonker, M. Petković (Eds.), Secure, Data Management. X, 185 pages. 2006.

Vol. 4163: H. Bersini, J. Carneiro (Eds.), Artificial Immune Systems. XII, 460 pages. 2006.

Vol. 4162: R. Královič, P. Urzyczyn (Eds.), Mathematical Foundations of Computer Science 2006. XV, 814 pages. 2006.

Vol. 4161: R. Harper, M. Rauterberg, M. Combetto (Eds.), Entertainment Computing - ICEC 2006. XXVII, 417 pages. 2006.

Vol. 4160: M. Fisher, W.v.d. Hoek, B. Konev, A. Lisitsa (Eds.), Logics in Artificial Intelligence. XII, 516 pages. 2006. (Sublibrary LNAI).

Vol. 4159: J. Ma, H. Jin, L.T. Yang, J.J.-P. Tsai (Eds.), Ubiquitous Intelligence and Computing. XXII, 1190 pages. 2006.

Vol. 4158: L.T. Yang, H. Jin, J. Ma, T. Ungerer (Eds.), Autonomic and Trusted Computing. XIV, 613 pages. 2006.

Vol. 4156: S. Amer-Yahia, Z. Bellahsène, E. Hunt, R. Unland, J.X. Yu (Eds.), Database and XML Technologies. IX, 123 pages. 2006.

Vol. 4155: O. Stock, M. Schaerf (Eds.), Reasoning, Action and Interaction in AI Theories and Systems. XVIII, 343 pages. 2006. (Sublibrary LNAI).

Vol. 4154: Y.A. Dimitriadis, I. Zigurs, E. Gómez-Sánchez (Eds.), Groupware: Design, Implementation, and Use. XIV, 438 pages. 2006.

Vol. 4153: N. Zheng, X. Jiang, X. Lan (Eds.), Advances in Machine Vision, Image Processing, and Pattern Analysis. XIII, 506 pages. 2006.

Vol. 4152: Y. Manolopoulos, J. Pokorný, T. Sellis (Eds.), Advances in Databases and Information Systems. XV, 448 pages. 2006.

Vol. 4151: A. Iglesias, N. Takayama (Eds.), Mathematical Software - ICMS 2006. XVII, 452 pages. 2006.

Vol. 4150: M. Dorigo, L.M. Gambardella, M. Birattari, A. Martinoli, R. Poli, T. Stützle (Eds.), Ant Colony Optimization and Swarm Intelligence. XVI, 526 pages. 2006.

Vol. 4149: M. Klusch, M. Rovatsos, T.R. Payne (Eds.), Cooperative Information Agents X. XII, 477 pages. 2006. (Sublibrary LNAI).

Vol. 4148: J. Vounckx, N. Azemard, P. Maurine (Eds.), Integrated Circuit and System Design. XVI, 677 pages. 2006.

Vol. 4147: M. Broy, I.H. Krüger, M. Meisinger (Eds.), Automotive Software – Connected Services in Mobile Networks. XIV, 155 pages. 2006.

Vol. 4146: J.C. Rajapakse, L. Wong, R. Acharya (Eds.), Pattern Recognition in Bioinformatics. XIV, 186 pages. 2006. (Sublibrary LNBI).

Vol. 4145: L. Moreau, I. Foster (Eds.), Provenance and Annotation of Data and Processes. XI, 288 pages. 2006.

Vol. 4144: T. Ball, R.B. Jones (Eds.), Computer Aided Verification. XV, 564 pages. 2006.